MW00785843

WEST ACADEMIC PUBLISHING'S EMERITUS ADVISORY BOARD

WEST ACADEMIC PUBLISHING'S LAW SCHOOL ADVISORY BOARD

PROBLEMS AND MATERIALS ON
SECURED TRANSACTIONS
Sixth Edition

■ ■ ■

Stephen L. Sepinuck
Adjunct Professor
Vanderbilt Law School

Kara J. Bruce
Professor of Law
University of Oklahoma College of Law

AMERICAN CASEBOOK SERIES®

860 Blue Gentian Road, Suite 350
Eagan, MN 55121
1-877-888-1330

Printed in the United States of America

ISBN: 978-1-68561-540-6

To dad, whose love of learning I continue to admire.

SLS

To Michael, for his patience, encouragement, and support.

KJB

PREFACE

This book is designed for three-credit courses on secured transactions. In creating and revising the book through the first five editions, we have drawn on our decades of collective experience in teaching this course, our experience teaching other commercial law and statutory courses, our work in private practice, and our participation in various commercial law reform projects. The revisions to the book for this edition have been guided and informed by our continuing efforts – both successful and otherwise – to teach this subject and by recent developments in the law and in practice.

Our general approach to teaching code-based subjects is to focus on problems, rather than on cases. In that sense, this book is about teaching the skill of statutory analysis as much as it is the law relating to secured transactions. Accordingly, this book contains 186 problems but major excerpts from only seven cases. We have endeavored to provide before each problem a textual explanation of the relevant rules and the policies underlying them. Included in these explanations are a variety of charts and diagrams to help appeal to visual learners. None of this does or can substitute for a close reading of the statute and its comments, but it is designed to provide those who are new to the subject of secured transactions with enough context to make sense of the statutory scheme.

The subject of secured transactions is difficult for many students, probably because the terminology, transactions, and rules are new to them. Although it is often not possible to simplify the complex – at least not without risking oversimplification and imprecision – we have not tried to make the subject more difficult than it is. In fact, the problems in Chapters Two through Five – the core of this book – tend to start at a fairly simple level and then get progressively more intricate only after students have had the opportunity to grasp the applicable issues and master the applicable rules.

We encourage all who use this book – teachers and students alike – to send us their comments about it. Only with those comments can we improve the book in subsequent editions.

Finally, welcome you to the study of secured transactions. We love this area of law: its brilliant innovations, its foibles, and even its occasional bizarre choices.

We hope that affection is evident, at least occasionally, in the pages that follow and that some of that affection might even be infectious as you read them.

ELECTRONIC EXERCISES

This book is accompanied by 26 electronic exercises. Each exercise is referenced at a particular place in the book (somewhere in Chapters 2–5) and is designed to take 5-15 minutes to complete. Each exercise covers a discrete topic and is designed both to help students learn that topic and to give them a tool to test their understanding of it. The exercises are accessible both on CasebookPlus and the companion web site for the book:

http://www.sepinucksecured.com

TEST YOUR KNOWLEDGE

This book is also accompanied by eight electronic, multiple-choice exams. Each exam covers a main concept explored in this book, is referenced at the end of the chapter or chapter section that covers the concept (somewhere in Chapters 2–6), and is designed to assist students in assessing how well they have mastered that concept. Plan to spend 30-60 minutes on each exam. The exams are accessible on CasebookPlus.

WEB SITE FOR UPDATES & TEACHER RESOURCES

Periodic updates and supplements to this book will be posted in electronic form on both CasebookPlus and the companion web site for the book.

The teacher's manual and other resources for instructors are available on a teachers-only portion of both CasebookPlus and the companion web site.

http://www.sepinucksecured.com

ACKNOWLEDGMENTS

Thanks to the numerous colleagues who provided valuable feedback on the first five editions, thereby allowing us to remove ambiguities and correct errors. Thanks also to the many students who offered comments on the original manuscript or a previous edition. Profound thanks, admiration, and gratitude are due to Linda Rusch, who co-authored the first three editions. This book would not exist without her.

SUMMARY OF CONTENTS

TABLE OF CONTENTS

TABLE OF CASES

TABLE OF STATUTES

Article 12

Federal Constitution

Federal Statutes

Perishable Agricultural Commodities Act (7 U.S.C.)

Packers and Stockyards Act (7 U.S.C.)

Food Security Act (7 U.S.C.)

Bankruptcy Code (11 U.S.C.)

Connecticut Statutes

Delaware Statutes

District of Columbia Statutes

Florida Constitution

Florida Statutes

Georgia Statutes

Idaho Statutes

Illinois Statutes

Indiana Statutes

Iowa Statutes

Kansas Statutes

New Jersey Statutes

New Mexico Statutes

New York Statutes

North Carolina Statutes

North Dakota Statutes

Oklahoma Statutes

Ohio Statutes

Rhode Island Statutes

South Dakota Statutes

Tennessee Statutes

Texas Statutes

Utah Statutes

Vermont Statutes

Virginia Statutes

Washington Statutes

Other Uniform Laws

Restatements

PROBLEMS AND MATERIALS ON

SECURED TRANSACTIONS

Sixth Edition

CHAPTER ONE
COLLECTING DEBTS GENERALLY

SECTION 1. CREATING DEBT

Almost everyone in this country – with the possible exception of young children – is indebted to someone else. Businesses typically owe suppliers for goods and services acquired on credit and owe employees for their labors. Individuals typically owe their landlords or mortgage lenders as well as numerous stores, banks, and oil companies for goods and services acquired through use of credit cards. They might also owe for spousal or child support, medical services, or student loans. Both businesses and individuals also usually owe for utilities (electricity, water, phone service, *etc*.). Even governments are debtors. Like businesses, they have suppliers and employees. Most have also issued bonds to finance major construction projects, and thus remain obligated to repay those debts.

These examples demonstrate debt created in a consensual manner, through contract. However, debts may also be created without agreement, that is, in a nonconsensual manner. For example, a negligent driver might injure another person or damage a vehicle, thereby incurring liability in tort. A corporation that dumps pollutants into the environment might have liability under environmental laws to the government or to the victims of that pollution. A business or individual might owe the government money for income or property taxes, and most are likely to have such liability at some point during any given year.

A debt, whether created in a consensual manner or otherwise, is often referred to as an "*in personam*" obligation. This phrase means that the obligation to pay the debt is the personal obligation of the obligor (the debtor) to the obligee (the creditor).

The existence of all this debt is not necessarily unhealthy or unmanageable. The relationship between debtor and creditor is the engine of commerce. It is also one of the threads in the social fabric of a capitalistic society, binding us together. Moreover, the vast majority of debtors pay their obligations in full and on time. Perhaps they do so to preserve their ability to participate in commercial transactions: to acquire goods and services on credit. Perhaps it is because they fear the repercussions if they do not pay. Perhaps it is simply because they believe that paying their obligations is the moral thing to do.

However, not all debtors pay voluntarily. Some lack the liquid assets necessary to make a payment when due or lack sufficient assets of any kind to ever fully satisfy their obligations. Others might challenge the amount claimed to be due, dispute liability in full, or simply dislike a particular creditor (ex-spouses come to mind). Still others might never have intended to pay, and might be engaged in fraudulent or criminal conduct. In a general sense, this book is about how creditors can enforce payment of the debts owed to them.

Regulation of contracts that create debt. Although not the focus of this book, it is worth noting that a variety of legal rules govern the creation of contractual debts. The foundation of these rules is the substantive law of contract, which determines whether an obligation is created and, if an obligation is not fulfilled, the amount of the damages for that breach. On top of that foundation is a patchwork of state and federal laws and regulations. These rules do not provide a unitary, comprehensive scheme premised on a single philosophy or rationale. Instead, they have varying scopes (*e.g.*, some apply only to consumer transactions, others apply more broadly) and serve different purposes. They do, however, typically operate in one or more of three different ways: (1) by prohibiting or regulating certain contractual terms; (2) by requiring disclosure of information regarding a debt obligation; or (3) by limiting the permissible considerations in deciding whether to make a loan or to grant or deny credit.

Three examples of law regulating the contractual terms applicable to a debt are the Uniform Consumer Credit Code, usury laws, and the Federal Trade Commission (FTC) regulations. The Uniform Consumer Credit Code, adopted in part by several states, limits the amount of finance charges that a creditor may charge and prohibits some types of collection practices in consumer transactions.[1] Usury laws, which have been around for centuries and can be found at both the state and federal level, limit the interest rate that creditors may charge in certain types of transactions or for certain types of borrowers.[2] The FTC regulations prohibit creditors in consumer transactions from using a variety of contractual devices that the FTC has concluded are unfair. These include confessions of judgment, waivers of exemptions, wage assignments, and non-purchase-money, nonpossessory security interests in some household goods.[3] The FTC regulations also require that buyers be given three days

---

[1] *See* U.C.C.C. §§ 2.201, 2.202, 2.401, 3.305-3.307.

[2] *See, e.g.*, Minn. Stat. § 334.01.

[3] 16 C.F.R. Part 444. *See also* 12 C.F.R. Part 227.

to rescind purchase contracts made in certain door-to-door transactions (*i.e.*, at the buyer's residence).[4] These examples are just the tip of the iceberg. In preparing and reviewing loan documentation, it is essential to be familiar with all of the state and federal statutes and regulations that prohibit or limit particular terms in the contract between the parties.

Several laws regulate the creation of debt by requiring disclosure of the cost of the credit. The Truth in Lending Act[5] is a good example. Congress passed the Act to increase the information that prospective borrowers receive about the cost of credit they are seeking. Such disclosures address the interest rates, costs and fees, payment schedules, and prepayment rights. The theory underlying this legislation is that borrowers will be able to make intelligent decisions regarding credit transactions if they have the right information. The Consumer Leasing Act[6] requires similar disclosures in consumer leasing transactions. While these federal acts and the regulations promulgated under them require specified disclosures in some types of consumer transactions, other federal or state laws might mandate disclosure of additional information in a consumer transaction or mandate disclosure of similar information in other types of transactions in which debt is created.[7] Again, in preparing and reviewing contract documentation, it is necessary to have a thorough knowledge of all the applicable statutes and regulations.

Finally, some laws limit the permissible grounds for granting or denying credit. An example of this type of restriction is the Equal Credit Opportunity Act.[8] It prohibits a creditor from discriminating against potential debtors based upon their race, color, religion, national origin, sex or marital status. Congress passed the Equal Credit Opportunity Act in an attempt to control the factors lenders may use to determine a loan applicant's credit worthiness. Before the Act was passed, Congress found that lenders discriminated against applicants by denying credit on account of marital status, gender, and race even when those factors did not affect the applicant's ability or willingness to repay the loan.

The remedies for violation of these laws and regulations vary considerably. The typical remedy for charging a usurious rate of interest is forfeiture of the right to all

---

4 16 C.F.R. Part 429.

5 15 U.S.C. §§ 1601–1666j.

6 15 U.S.C. §§ 1667–1667f.

7 *See, e.g.*, U.C.C.C. §§ 3.201-3.209.

8 15 U.S.C. §§ 1691–1691f.

interest.[9] The remedy for violations of other laws might be denial of the right to collect the debt or statutory damages. Such statutory damages might be fairly minimal or, particularly if recoverable in a class action, quite extensive.

Because most (but not all) of the law governing the creation of debt is designed to protect consumer debtors, these laws are usually studied in detail in courses on Consumer Protection or Consumer Law.

SECTION 2. COLLECTING DEBTS NONJUDICIALLY

A. Some Basic Limits on Collection

Imagine that you are a creditor. Your debtor has not paid and is in default. In other words, a debt obligation has been validly created and is currently enforceable. How do you collect? What are your options?

Although creditors might have a legal right to be repaid, that legal right does not give them immunity from tort law. Despite what you might see on TV, creditors are not permitted to assault their debtors to induce them to pay the debts they owe. Such conduct, while perhaps effective in producing payment, would be both a tort and a criminal act. A creditor's legal right to be paid also does not generally give the creditor a right to take the debtor's property.

Illustration

Several months ago, Donna purchased a $900 gas grill on credit from SuperStore, a major department store. Although Donna has received several bills for the purchase price, she has paid nothing yet. The grill is located on the patio in her back yard. May Superstore send one of its employees to quietly retrieve the grill while Donna is at work? No. Although Donna had not paid for the grill, she nevertheless became the owner of it when she took delivery. *See* U.C.C. § 2-401. SuperStore would be committing theft (larceny, and possibly also trespass) by taking the grill back. That could give rise to both criminal sanctions and tort liability. It is worth noting that while Donna remains liable to SuperStore in contract for the unpaid portion of the purchase price, SuperStore's tort liability to

---

[9] In some states, however, the remedy is more severe. In Alaska, for example, the penalty is forfeiture of the right to all interest and disgorgement of double the amount of interest collected. *See* Alaska Stat. §§ 45.45.030, 45.45.040. Moreover, in some states, charging usurious interest is a criminal offense. *See, e.g.*, N.Y. Penal Law §§ 190.42, 190.40.

Donna for taking the grill back might be significantly higher. It may, for example, include punitive damages.

The result would likely be different if the creditor owned the goods.

Illustration

Several weeks ago, Homer borrowed Ned's $900 gas grill to host a barbecue party at his home. The party was a great success but Homer has not returned the grill, which remains in Homer's back yard. May Ned simply take the grill back while Homer is not around? Probably. Ned's actions would not constitute larceny or conversion of the grill because Ned has the right to possession. While taking the grill might involve a trespass (entering Homer's yard without permission) and therefore be actionable, Ned might have a license to enter Homer's yard for this limited purpose.[10]

B. Collecting Debt Through Informal Methods

The most common and least expensive way creditors attempt to collect is simply to request payment. The creditor may do this in person, by phone, through e-mail, or by sending a bill via the postal service. As requests become more persistent, the process is called "dunning."

Sending a bill works well when the debtor is able and willing to pay. Sometimes, however, debtors need to be "persuaded" to part with some of their cash. In such cases, collecting can be time consuming, expensive, and frustrating. Creditors often respond by seeking to exploit whatever leverage they have. Sometimes they threaten to report the debtor's failure to pay to a credit reporting agency. This might encourage the debtor to work out a payment schedule to avoid a bad credit rating and preserve the ability to obtain credit elsewhere. Sometimes they threaten to sue. This might work if the debtor fears the expense of legal action or the publicity associated with it.

If the debtor and creditor have an ongoing relationship, the creditor may threaten to sever it. For example, if the creditor supplies needed goods or services to the debtor, the creditor may threaten to cut the debtor off unless the debtor pays. If the debtor has no other source for what the creditor provides, this can be a very effective debt collection mechanism. Consider, for example, a provider of

---

[10] *See* RESTATEMENT (SECOND) OF TORTS § 198.

information technology. If the customer does not pay, the provider may refuse to provide updates, fix bugs, or otherwise maintain the system. Similarly, a pharmacist may refuse to sell any more medication until the customer pays for previous purchases. A manufacturer or wholesaler may refuse to supply needed inventory to a retail store until the store pays for the inventory it already received. If this refusal occurred shortly before the holiday season, the retail store's business could be devastated.

Even if the relationship will not continue, if the creditor has something the debtor desperately wants or needs, the creditor can threaten to withhold it. Along these lines, a few years back a law student damaged a golf cart during a student bar association outing. When the student refused to pay for the damage, the dean stepped in and threatened to withhold certification of the student's moral fitness, a requirement for admission to the state bar. The student paid.

Setoff. Another informal debt collection tool is setoff.[11] It is available when two people owe money to the other, and allows either of them to apply the receivable due against the amount owing, to "avoid the absurdity of making A pay B when B owes A."[12] For example, a right to setoff arises when two business each sells goods or services to the other, with payment to be made at a later date. Thus, if A sold to B on credit goods priced at $4,000 and B provided to A on credit services priced at $5,000, then either of them could exercise the right to net the two obligations off against each other:

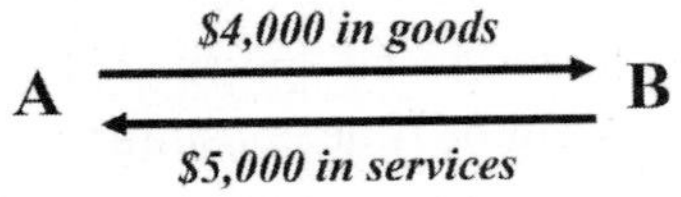

$4,000 in goods

A → **B**

A ← **B**

$5,000 in services

As a result, A would owe B $1,000.

Perhaps more commonly, the right to exercise a setoff arises when a person borrows money from a bank and also maintains a deposit account at the same institution. For example, assume Customer has $2,000 on deposit at Bank and owes Bank $10,000 to repay a loan Customer received from Bank. Customer is both a debtor of Bank (for the $10,000 loan) and a creditor of Bank (for the $2,000

---

[11] For an exploration of various issues relating to the right of setoff, *see* Stephen L. Sepinuck, *The Problems with Setoff: A Proposed Legislative Solution*, 30 WM. & MARY L. REV. 51 (1988).

[12] In re Strumpf, 37 F.3d 155, 157 (4th Cir. 1994), *rev'd on other grounds*, 516 U.S. 16 (1995).

deposit; a deposit account is mere a loan to the bank). Similarly, Bank is both a creditor of Customer (for the $10,000 loan) and a debtor of Customer (for the $2,000 deposit). If Customer fails to pay the loan when due, Bank may simply debit the deposit account. In other words, the $2,000 deposited with Bank could be offset from the $10,000 debt to reduce Customer's obligation to Bank to $8,000. In order to exercise the right of setoff, the debts must be both mature and mutual. Mature means due and owing; mutual means owed in the same capacity. In the example above, Customer's debt on the loan would not be mature if the loan were for a set term and that term had not expired.[13] Continuing with the above example, the debts would not be mutual if the bank deposits were held in Customer's individual name but the loan was made to a corporation of which Customer was the sole shareholder. The requirement that the debts be mature and mutual derives from the common law. In some situations, additional statutory rules limit the availability of setoff.[14]

C. Fair Debt Collection

Some creditors employ a debt collection agency to assist in or handle the collection of debts. Unfortunately, many debt collectors have engaged in abusive and harassing behavior. Consider the following testimony presented to the Subcommittee on Consumer Affairs of the Senate Committee on Banking, Housing and Urban Affairs in 1977.

Statement of Patricia M. Miller

I was told that the pride of a good agency collector is the effective use of scare tactics. This directly relates to taking advantage of a person's ignorance. Probably the best example is the implication of legal action. Although the agency brought suit against very few accounts, as permission to do so had to come through the client, the majority of debtors were informed that such action would be taken if the bill was not paid in full immediately. If a debtor asked if he would be imprisoned,

---

13 Similarly, Bank's liability on the deposit account might not be mature if the deposit were a timed deposit, such as occurs when a customer purchases a six-month or one-year certificate of deposit.

14 *See* 12 C.F.R. § 226.12(d) (now 12 C.F.R. § 1026.12(d)), *discussed in* Stephen L. Sepinuck, *Reg Z Requires Extra Effort to Obtain Security Interest in Deposit Account*, 26 CLARK'S SECURED TRANSACTIONS MONTHLY 5 (Jan. 2010); In re Okigbo, 2009 WL 5227844 (Bankr. D. Md. 2009).

the collector would reply either that he did not know or that the debtor should let his imagination run wild. It was not unusual to hear a collector inform the debtor that unless the bill was paid, they would be unable to receive medical services at any hospital, or that they had better nail their possessions to the floor before the law came and removed everything they owned.

Despite any laws regulating the number of calls allowed to a debtor over a period of time, many of these people were called as often as five, six times each day until a payment was received. These calls were not by any means congenial. For instance, my supervisor would make three consecutive calls; the first he would dun the debtor: The standard line being if the bill was not paid in full within 48 hours, he would suffer the consequences and then the phone would be hung up. The second call would be to inform the debtor that he would be sued and he had better find an attorney. The final call, the collector would raise his voice and ask the debtor if he had gotten an attorney. Many times, these calls would be placed at the debtor's place of employment.

If a debtor's home was called, many times a dunning message would be left with anyone who would answer the phone. This practice did not exclude children.

As you probably know, skiptracing a debtor is a large part of a collector's job. This involves obtaining information in whatever way possible to locate what is known as a "deadbeat." I had an account in my unit that was a skip from a real estate company. The only contact I had not used was the debtor's personal reference on the lease application. My supervisor told me to call the reference and suggest I was the debtor's girlfriend and I needed to get in touch with him. Reluctantly, I called and followed my supervisor's instructions. As it turned out, I located the debtor through this call, but only after his friend displayed his amazement that the debtor was not a devoted father and husband. I used my dunning name, as strongly suggested by the agency, as a means to protect myself.

Some collectors had more than one assumed name. This was to allow greater flexibility and leverage when skiptracing. For instance, if a debtor's place of employment was called, and the collector was unable to make contact, he would call again and tell anyone who answered that he was a special processor and was calling for service instruction for the debtor resulting from nonpayment of a debt. If the person refused to give any information, the collector would insist that he or she was obstructing justice and they would suffer the consequences. These false names were also used when a collector was trying to discuss the outstanding bill with the debtor's supervisor.

In response to the reported abuses, Congress enacted the Fair Debt Collection Practices Act.[15] Read the definitions of "debt" and "debt collector" in 15 U.S.C. § 1692a. The Act applies only if both the obligation being collected is a "debt" and the person attempting to collect it is a "debt collector."

As to the meaning of "debt," notice that it is defined in reference to an obligation owed by a "consumer." Thus, the Act applies only to consumer obligations – that is, to obligations incurred primarily for personal, family, or household purposes. *See* 15 U.S.C. § 1692a(5).

Illustration

You have been assigned to collect a past due loan owed by Duckpin Bowling Lanes, Inc. The loan is guaranteed by Joanna Duck, the sole shareholder of Duckpin Bowling Lanes, Inc. Do you have to worry about compliance with the Fair Debt Collection Practices Act when collecting from the corporation or from Ms. Duck? No. The corporation is not a "consumer" and hence its obligation to repay the loan is not a "debt" as defined in that Act. Although one could argue that Ms. Duck's guaranty was incurred for personal reasons, to protect her personal investment in the corporation, even though the loan to the corporation was not, courts have perfunctorily rejected this argument and concluded that such obligations are also not "debts" within the meaning of the Act.[16]

As to who qualifies as a "debt collector," it is important to note that neither the creditor to which a debt is owed nor the employees of that creditor are "debt collectors" under the Act. *See* 15 U.S.C. § 1692a(6)(A) (defining a "debt collector" to be someone who seeks to collect "debts owed or due . . . another"). This may seem counter-intuitive, but is based on the legislative conclusion that most of the abusive collection activities that the Act targets were performed by collection agencies, rather than by creditors. Accordingly, an entity that purchases a debt – even after default – and subsequently attempts to collect that debt for its own account does not qualify as a "debt collector" because that collection activity does not involve a debt owed to someone else.[17]

---

[15] 15 U.S.C. §§ 1692–1692o.

[16] *See* First Gibraltar Bank v. Smith, 62 F.3d 133 (5th Cir. 1995).

[17] Henson v. Santander Consumer USA Inc., 582 U.S. 79 (2017). Note, the Court in

That said, the term "debt collector" encompasses more than traditional debt collection agencies. In fact, the Supreme Court has ruled that an attorney, even one involved in litigation, can qualify as a "debt collector."[18] The issue is whether the attorney regularly collects or attempts to collect debts on behalf of another, a factual question that requires a careful review of the attorney's business.[19]

When the Fair Debt Collection Practices Act applies, it governs how the debt collector communicates with the debtor and with other persons about the debt. The Act also prohibits harassing and abusive behavior, false or misleading representations, and unfair or unconscionable means to collect debt. The following chart lists examples of some of the prohibited conduct.

Activity Prohibited	Provision (15 U.S.C.)
Calling before 8:00 am or after 9:00 pm.	§ 1692c(a)(1)
Using obscene or profane language.	§ 1692d(2)

Henson did not foreclose the possibility that debt buyer might qualify as a "debt collector" if the buyer operates a business "the principal purpose of which is the collection of any debts . . . owed or due another." 15 U.S.C. § 1692a(6). In other words, the Fair Debt Collection Practices Act *might* apply to an entity that qualifies as a debt collector even when the entity is collecting on a debt owed to itself.

18 *See* Heintz v. Jenkins, 514 U.S. 291 (1995). However, a law firm is not a "debt collector" within the meaning of the Fair Debt Collection Practices Act – except with respect to § 1692f(6) – merely because the firm regularly conducts non-judicial foreclosures of real property on behalf of mortgagee clients. *See* Obduskey v. McCarthy & Holthus LLP, 139 S. Ct. 1029 (2019). A law firm that conducts *judicial* foreclosures, however, might be a "debt collector," at least if the actions can lead to a money judgment against the property owner. *Compare* Bronstein v. Bayview Loan Servicing, LLC, 2020 WL 703652 (E.D. Pa. 2020) (law firm engaging in judicial foreclosure in Pennsylvania, where a deficiency judgment is available, is a "debt collector"), *with* Barnes v. Routh Crabtree Olsen PC, 963 F.3d 993 (9th Cir. 2020) (a judicial foreclosure of a deed of trust in Oregon is not debt collection because no deficiency judgment is available). *See also* Jordan v. Tucker Albin and Assocs., Inc., 2019 WL 4647339 (E.D.N.Y. 2019) (a law firm hired to *file* but not to enforce a mechanic's lien does not thereby become a "debt collector").

19 *See* Hester v. Graham, Bright & Smith, P.C., 289 F. App'x 35 (5th Cir. 2008) (evidence established attorneys attempted to collect consumer debts for four clients and on 450 occasions over 2 years; court concluded that sufficed to make the attorneys debt collectors).

Activity Prohibited	Provision (15 U.S.C.)
Contacting third parties, other than the consumer's attorney, spouse, or (if the consumer is a minor) parents.	§ 1692c(b), (d)
Making a false representation about the character or amount of the debt.	§ 1692e(2)
Making a false representation about the consequences of nonpayment.	§ 1692e(4)-(7)
Using any false or deceptive method to collect a debt or to obtain information.	§ 1692e(10)
Trying to collect any unauthorized amount.	§ 1692f(1)

While these prohibitions might seem reasonable, it is quite easy to run afoul of them. For example, sending a demand letter for an incorrect amount can violate the Act.[20] Threatening to take legal action when none is intended also violates the Act.[21] Consequently, attorneys and others acting as debt collectors must be very careful in what they do.[22] Civil liability for violations of the Act include actual damages, statutory punitive damages, costs, and attorney's fees.[23]

---

20 *See* Scott v. Riddle, 2000 WL 33980013 (D. Utah 2000) (attorney who sent a demand letter to writers of bad checks and included in that demand an $89 penalty for violating Washington's shoplifting statute was not entitled to the bona fide error defense in 15 U.S.C. § 1692k(c) because that deals with factual errors, not legal errors). *See also* Jerman v. Carlisle, McNellie, Rini, Kramer & Ulrich LPA, 559 U.S. 573 (2010) (bona fide error defense does not apply to an incorrect legal interpretation of the Act).

21 *See* Irwin v. Mascott, 112 F. Supp. 2d 937 (N.D. Cal. 2000).

22 *See* Gonzalez v. Kay, 577 F.3d 600 (5th Cir. 2009) (lawyer who allowed creditor to send collection letter on lawyer's letterhead may be engaged in misleading conduct by indicating that an attorney is involved in collection even if the letter contains a disclaimer to the contrary). Some courts have even held that the Act regulates communications from the creditor's lawyer to the debtor's attorney, if the creditor's lawyer is a debt collector. *See, e.g.*, Evory v. RJM Acquisitions Funding LLC, 505 F.3d 769, 773-74 (7th Cir. 2007); Misleh v. Timothy E. Baxter & Assocs., 786 F. Supp. 2d 1330 (E.D. Mich. 2011). *Contra* Guerrero v. RJM Acquisitions LLC, 499 F.3d 926, 934 (9th Cir. 2007) (communications directed solely to a debtor's attorney are not actionable under the FDCPA).

23 15 U.S.C. § 1692k.

Even when the Act does not apply, such as when the debtor is a business rather than a consumer, similar state legislation might. Several states have enacted laws regulating debt collection.[24] Moreover, a court might regard the federal Act as setting the standard of behavior for debt collection generally, so that conduct contrary to its prohibitions, even when those prohibitions are not directly applicable, might be tortious.

D. Fair Credit Reporting

In a credit-driven economy, some sort of system for reporting credit experience is necessary so that lenders can make intelligent, informed decisions about granting credit. That system needs accurate and complete information to serve its function. Credit reporting agencies gather information about debtors and provide reports to inquiring creditors. Creditors also often use the threat of a negative report to a credit reporting agency to convince a debtor to pay the debt to avoid that bad report. The level of abuse, the prevalence of reports with incomplete and inaccurate information, and concerns about privacy led Congress to enact the Fair Credit Reporting Act.[25]

The Act regulates consumer credit reports in several different ways. It gives consumers access to their reports, including their credit scores.[26] It limits the information that may be included in credit reports, prohibiting disclosure in most cases of bankruptcy filings that are more than ten years old and judgments or delinquent accounts that are more than seven years old.[27] It provides consumers

---

[24] *See, e.g.*, Minn. Stat. §§ 332.31-332.45.

Other federal laws can also apply. For example, the Telephone Consumer Protection Act, codified at 47 U.S.C. § 227, prohibits the use of automatic dialing systems to initiate a call to a residential telephone line, absent the prior consent of the called party or a regulatory exemption. This prohibition can apply to debt-collection activity. *Cf.* Schwartz-Earp v. Advanced Call Center Techs., LLC, 2016 WL 899149 (N.D. Cal. 2016) (by providing her cell phone number in the application for a store credit card, the applicant consented to being contacted on her cell phone about matters related to her credit card, including by third-party debtor collectors; therefore, the debt collector who called her on her cell phone using an automated dialing system did not violate the Telephone Consumer Protection Act).

[25] 15 U.S.C. §§ 1681–1681x.

[26] 15 U.S.C. § 1681g.

[27] 15 U.S.C. § 1681c(a).

with a process to dispute and correct information in their credit reports.[28] It requires those who provide information to credit reporting agencies to take some responsibility for the accuracy of the information provided.[29] And it limits the dissemination of reports, mostly to current and prospective creditors and employers of the consumer.[30] Violations can subject the reporting agency to compensatory, statutory, and punitive damages.[31] People who obtain consumer credit reports under false pretenses are even subject to criminal liability.[32]

It is important to understand the myriad ways in which credit reports are used. Obviously, one main use occurs in debt creation. Often when a consumer applies for credit, the potential creditor will obtain a credit report to assist in deciding whether or under what terms to extend credit. A second way credit reports are used is in deciding whether to establish a commercial relationship other than a lending one. For example, some employers and landlords routinely review the credit reports of those applying for a job or seeking to rent an apartment. Similarly, many bar examiners, when investigating applicants for the bar, pull a credit report on each applicant. Finally, credit reports also play a role in the debt collection process. Creditors seeking to collect a debt not only sometimes threaten to report nonpayment in an effort to cajole payment, they also sometimes access the debtor's credit report to gather information that might assist in collection. Such information may include the debtor's address and contact information, an indication of the debtor's assets and their location, or information bearing on the debtor's ability to pay. The Fair Credit Reporting Act applies to all such activities.

The Act does not govern all credit reports, however. It governs only consumer credit reports. As to business credit reports, there is no overriding federal law but there is a thriving market. Dunn and Bradstreet, for example, provides several types of business credit reports for large and small businesses. You can find examples of its credit reports at https://docs.dnb.com/mydnb/en-US/sample/COMPR. Of course, persons that request credit reports pay the reporting agency for the report, whether the reporting agency is reporting on businesses or consumers.

---

[28] 15 U.S.C. §§ 1681c(f), 1681i.

[29] 15 U.S.C. § 1681s-2.

[30] 15 U.S.C. § 1681b.

[31] 15 U.S.C. §§ 1681n, 1681o. *Cf.* 15 U.S.C. § 1681s-2(c) (limiting the liability of those who provide information to credit reporting agencies).

[32] 15 U.S.C. § 1681q.

E. Tort

In addition to federal or state regulation of the informal debt collection process, a creditor must also be careful not to incur tort liability to the debtor. A creditor will incur such liability if it or its agent engages in behavior that is negligent or constitutes defamation, abuse of process, malicious prosecution, or any of several other intentional torts. For example, some jurisdictions recognize causes of action for invasion of privacy and for infliction of emotional distress.[33]

Illustration

After Sarah made several purchases at the local convenience store with personal checks that were subsequently dishonored, the owner of the store posted a notice to employees instructing them not to accept any more checks from Sarah. The notice included Sarah's name and a photo of her taken by one of the store's video surveillance cameras. Although the notice was intended for employees, it was readily visible to customers. Sarah is deeply embarrassed by the notice. Is the store liable for damages?

In evaluating such a claim, a court might look to Section 652D of the Restatement (Second) of Torts. It provides:

> Section 652D Publicity Given to Private Life
>
> One who gives publicity to a matter concerning the private life of another is subject to liability to the other for invasion of his privacy, if the matter publicized is of a kind that
>
> (a) would be highly offensive to a reasonable person, and
>
> (b) is not of legitimate concern to the public.
>
> *Comment (a)* * * * [I]t is not an invasion of the right of privacy, within the rule stated in this Section, to communicate a fact concerning the plaintiff's private life to a single person or even to a small group of persons. * * *
>
> Illustrations:
>
> 1. A, a creditor, writes a letter to the employer of B, his debtor, informing him that B owes the debt and will not pay it. This is not an invasion of B's privacy under this Section.

---

33 *See* Annotation, *Public Disclosure of Person's Indebtedness as Invasion of Privacy*, 33 ALR 3d 154 (1970); Annotation, *Recovery by Debtor, under Tort of Intentional or Reckless Infliction of Emotional Distress, for Damages Resulting from Collection Methods*, 87 ALR 3d 201(1978).

2. A, a creditor, posts in the window of his shop, where it is read by those passing by on the street, a statement that B owes a debt to him and has not paid it. This is an invasion of B's privacy.[34]

Applying this rule, the court in *Mason v. Williams Discount Center, Inc.*, 639 S.W.2d 836 (Mo. Ct. App. 1982), imposed liability for posting a "no checks" list visible to customers in the checkout line. Accordingly, the store owner in the illustration is probably liable for damages for violation of Sarah's right to privacy if the jurisdiction whose law applies recognizes the right. Not all states do so.

SECTION 3. COLLECTING DEBTS JUDICIALLY

A. Obtaining and Enforcing Judgments

If informal collection efforts fail to prompt the debtor to pay, the creditor may seek recourse through the courts. This involves filing and winning a lawsuit against the debtor. The end result of winning a lawsuit is a judgment, which is merely a piece of paper stating that the debtor owes a specified amount of money to the creditor.

In many cases, the creditor can obtain a judgment fairly quickly and easily. The creditor files the suit, serves the complaint and summons, and the debtor never responds. The creditor then obtains a default judgment after a brief waiting period, often 20 or 30 days. In other cases, the process can be long and expensive. The debtor might be difficult to locate or serve with process. Alternatively, the debtor may raise defenses to the obligation (such as that the goods sold by the creditor were defective or that the accident that injured the creditor was not the debtor's fault), thereby precipitating discovery and requiring litigation. You learned all about the process for obtaining civil judgments in your course on Civil Procedure.

Confessions of judgment. A contractual creditor may attempt to shortcut the process of obtaining a judgment by including in the contract with the debtor a clause called a "confession of judgment." In a confession of judgment the "debtor consents in advance to the [creditor's] obtaining a judgment without notice or hearing, and possibly even with the appearance, on the debtor's behalf, of an

---

[34] RESTATEMENT (SECOND) OF TORTS § 652D.

attorney designated by the [creditor]."[35] Some consumer protection laws prohibit creditors from enforcing such a term.[36] Even if a confession of judgment is allowed in a particular transaction, states may regulate the process by which a confession of judgment is given validity because of due process or fairness concerns.[37]

Process after entry of judgment. In many of the courses taught in the first year of law school – Contracts, Torts, Property – entry of a judgment is the end of the process. It defines who wins and who loses. In the real world, however, entry of the judgment is often just one small step in the middle or even at the beginning of the process of collecting the obligation owed. The goal, after all, is not to be declared the winner, the goal is to be paid. Except in rare situations, the judgment itself does not constitute an order subjecting the judgment debtor to contempt for failure to comply. Although some creditors might rue its demise, ever since the novels of Charles Dickens graphically portrayed its abuses, we no longer have debtors' prison. We do not incarcerate people simply because they do not pay their debts, even if those debts are the subject of a judgment. Consequently, it is the rare debtor who, immediately after the judgment is entered, whips out a checkbook and asks "to whom should I make out the check?"

Judgment creditors therefore often need to engage in an additional process in order to collect. This additional process is called executing on the judgment. The process for executing on judgments varies from state to state. What follows is a very summary description of the process. Of course, a lawyer must always consult the relevant state statutes and cases to determine exactly how to execute on a judgment in that state.

Finding the debtor's assets. The first step in executing on a judgment is to identify and locate one or more assets of the debtor. Such assets may be real property, tangible personal property (such as cars, boats, furniture, or jewelry), or intangible rights (such as a bank account, brokerage account, or right to payment from an employer). Finding such assets is often not easy. If the debtor is resisting execution on the judgment, the debtor will not likely volunteer information about what the debtor owns and where it is. For that reason, a judgment creditor in most states is entitled to engage in post-judgment discovery, such as by taking depositions or serving interrogatories.

---

35 D.H. Overmyer Co., Inc. of Ohio v. Frick Co., 405 U.S. 174, 176 (1972).

36 *See* U.C.C.C. § 3.306; 12 C.F.R. § 227.13; 16 C.F.R. § 444.2.

37 *E.g.*, Minn. Stat. §§ 548.22, 548.23.

Illustration

You recently obtained a judgment against David for $15,000 on behalf of your client Joanne. You believe David has sufficient assets to pay this debt but that he is likely to be uncooperative and might even attempt to conceal his assets or put them in forms that would make them difficult to discover. You are preparing to take David's deposition. What questions will you ask to make sure you uncover everything of value?

In general, you want to identify all of David's assets. Some obvious questions are:

- Do you have an interest in any bank account, investment account, credit union account, or the like, in your own name or in any other name?
- Do you have an interest in any real estate in your own name or in any other name?
- In what jewelry, collectibles, and artwork, if any, do you have an interest?
- How much money do you have on you now? (Some debtors actually come to the deposition expecting to pay all or a portion of the debt.)
- Do you have a car?

This last question can be followed with "where did you park?" Although you likely have no right or ready ability to take the car while the debtor is sitting at the deposition, the debtor might not know that. This can therefore be a sly way to apply some pressure in the hope of eliciting the debtor's cooperation.

Many significant assets will be in a less obvious form, often as some sort of obligation owed to David. To identify these, a whole series of additional questions will be necessary:

- Have you loaned money to anyone who has not yet repaid in full?
- Have you sold property for which you have not yet received full payment?
- Have you performed services for which you have not yet received full payment?
- Does anyone owe you wages, salaries, commissions, licensing fees, royalties, or rental payments?
- Have you suffered any injuries to yourself or your property for which anyone might be liable to you?
- Are you a party to any pending litigation? Have you considered filing suit against anyone? If so, for what?

- Have you paid medical bills or other kinds of bills for which you expect to be reimbursed by insurance?
- Have you pawned any property which you still have the right to redeem?

In connection with this, note that a particularly tricky debtor might even try to "park" assets in places that might escape routine questioning, such as by overpaying or "pre-paying" a utility bill with all available liquid assets. Thus, you might need questions designed to uncover such activity:

- Do you have a security deposit with a lessor, landlord, utility company, or anyone else? Have you paid rent in advance?
- Have you prepaid – in whole or in part – or overpaid for any goods or services?
- Have you asked anyone to hold any funds or property for you? If so, who are they and what funds or property did you ask them to hold?

Another series of questions might attempt to locate information or documents that can, in turn, be useful in tracking down assets. For example:

- Do you own, rent, or use a safe or safe deposit box?
- Where do you keep your tax records and bank statements?

A final series of questions will be designed to uncover assets that David recently moved or transferred. As discussed below, such transfers might be avoidable, enabling you to recover the assets or their value for Joanne. Thus, you will want to ask questions such as:

- What gifts, if any, have you made in the last two years? To whom?
- What property, if any, have you sold in the last two years? What were the terms of the sale and who was the buyer?
- Are you currently leasing any property to anyone?
- Are you licensing any software or other intellectual property to someone else?[38]

No matter how careful and comprehensive your questions are, though, this method of locating assets is not very effective because between the time the debtor responds and the time you can obtain a writ of execution and get the sheriff to levy

[38] For additional questions commonly asked in aid of execution, see Byron Originals, Inc. v. Iron Bay Model Co., 2006 WL 1004827 (N.D. W. Va. 2006).

on the property, the debtor often will have moved the assets. Some debtors will even quit their job to avoid a garnishment of their wages. For this reason, the creditor might prefer to use other methods for obtaining information about the debtor's assets, such as hiring a private investigator.

Judicial liens and the execution process. Once the judgment creditor locates one or more assets of the debtor, the creditor will likely seek to obtain a lien on those assets. A lien is a type of property right, one that makes the property liable for a debt. In other words, the lien adds the "*in rem*" liability of the property to the *in personam* liability of the debtor. A judgment lien makes the debtor's real property liable for the judgment debt. An execution lien does the same with respect to the debtor's personal property. Armed with a judgment or execution lien, the creditor may then foreclose – typically by selling the property – to extract value from the property and thereby pay the debt. Judgment liens and execution liens are occasionally referred to as "judicial liens" because both arise from judicial process.

In most states, entry of the judgment itself or recordation of the judgment in the county records gives the judgment creditor a judgment lien on all of the judgment debtor's real property in that county. To obtain a lien on the judgment debtor's real property in another county, the judgment creditor typically needs merely to record the judgment there. To obtain a lien on the judgment debtor's real property in another state, the judgment creditor typically needs to have the judgment "domesticated" in that state,[39] and then record that judgment in the county where the real property is located.

The process to obtain a lien on tangible personal property is different. In most states, once the judgment creditor has located the tangible assets of the judgment debtor, the judgment creditor must then procure a "writ of execution" from the court clerk. This writ is then delivered to the appropriate law enforcement officer, most often the county sheriff or, if the judgment was issued by a federal court, to the U.S. Marshal for that district. The writ of execution directs the sheriff to "levy" on (*i.e.*, to seize or otherwise take possession or control of) the debtor's property. The act of levying creates an execution lien on the property seized in favor of the judgment creditor. In some states, the priority of the lien might relate back to when the writ is delivered to the sheriff instead of from when the levy takes place. Even in such states, however, the levy is necessary to create the lien.

---

[39] In 48 states (all but California and Vermont), the process of domesticating a foreign judgment is governed by the Uniform Enforcement of Foreign Judgments Act.

Because intangible personal property has no physical existence, and therefore cannot be seized by anyone, getting a judicial lien on intangible property requires yet another process. If the judgment debtor has a right to receive payment – for example, a right to wages or salary from an employer or a right to funds deposited with bank – then instead of obtaining a writ of execution directing the sheriff to levy on the judgment debtor's property, the judgment creditor can obtain from the court a writ of garnishment directing the person owing payment to remit to the judgment creditor whatever that person owes to the debtor.[40] Service of writ on the obligor typically creates a lien on whatever the garnishee owes to the judgment debtor.

If the judgment debtor owns an interest in a corporation, then UCC § 8-112 provides rules for how to obtain a lien on that interest.[41] Subject to an exception if the judgment debtor's property is subject to a security interest, the method varies depending on whether the interest is represented by a certificated security, an uncertificated security, or a security entitlement (*i.e.*, is credited to a securities account with a broker):

	Method for Obtaining a Judgment Lien
Certificated Security	only by actual seizure of the security certificate by the officer making the attachment or levy.
Uncertificated Security	only by legal process upon the issuer at its chief executive office in the United States.
Security Entitlement	only by legal process upon the securities intermediary with whom the debtor's securities account is maintained.

If the debtor owns an interest in a partnership or limited liability company, then the way to execute on that interest is through a charging order. Such an order, issued by a court, typically requires the entity to pay to the judgment creditor any distributions otherwise due to the judgment debtor, and it creates a judicial lien on the judgment debtor's transferable interest in the entity.[42] However, if distributions

---

[40] Garnishment can also be used to recover tangible personal property owned by the judgment debtor but in the possession of someone else.

[41] These rules also apply to an interest in a partnership or limited liability company if the partnership agreement or operating agreement for that entity choose to have the interests in the entity governed by Article 8 of the UCC.

[42] *See, e.g.*, Rice v. Downs, 288 Cal. Rptr. 3d 185, 194 (Ct. App. 2021).

will not be sufficient to satisfy the judgment in a reasonable amount of time, a court can order a sale of the judgment debtor's transferable interest.[43]

In a few states, most notably California, a judgment creditor may obtain a lien on some types of personal property (*e.g.*, a business's inventory, equipment, and accounts receivable) by filing a notice of the judgment with the Secretary of State.[44] One advantage of this process is that the judgment lien attaches not only to whatever property of those types that the judgment debtor owns at the time the notice is filed, but also to such property that the judgment debtor acquires afterwards.[45] In contrast, an execution lien – arising from levy on tangible personal property – almost never reaches property that the debtor judgment debtor later acquires but on which the sheriff has not levied. In some states, a garnishment lien will attach to future obligations owed by the garnishee to the judgment debtor, but that is not the norm.

Returning to real property and tangible property, after the judgment lien or execution lien is created, the sheriff (at the behest of the judgment creditor) will conduct an execution sale. This requires advertising the sale in a local newspaper and posting a notice of the sale in the courthouse (or perhaps on the court's website). The sale itself is then conducted as a public auction. The costs of the levy, if any, the advertising, and the auction are deducted from the sales price prior to using any of the proceeds to pay the judgment. If the remaining proceeds are not sufficient to fully satisfy the judgment debt, the creditor may obtain additional writs of execution and repeat the process against other property of the debtor until the judgment is satisfied.

Execution sales often result in very low sale prices for the assets sold, well below their true market value (usually defined as the price that would be arrived at through negotiation between a willing buyer and a willing seller, neither of whom is under a compulsion to buy or sell). Because of the minimal advertising, there are usually few bidders present at an execution sale and the buyer is often the creditor whose judgment is being collected. That creditor may make a credit bid, rather than

---

43 *See* Uniform LLC Act § 503(c); Uniform Limited Partnership Act § 703(b); Uniform Partnership Act § 504(b).

44 Cal. Civ. Proc. Code §§ 697.510, 697.530. *See also* Nev. Rev. Stat. § 353C.170(2) ("From the time of its recordation, the judgment becomes a lien upon all real and personal property situated in the county that is owned by the judgment debtor, or which the debtor may afterward acquire, until the lien expires").

45 *See* Cal. Civ. Proc. Code § 697.530(b).

a cash bid, in essence crediting the bid against the amount owed on the judgment. This allows the creditor to bid up to the amount of the debt without actually having to shell out any cash (other than to pay the sheriff's fees and costs of sale). That is why the judgment creditor often does not bid above the amount of the judgment, plus costs. It is the bid at the execution sale that determines how much is credited against the amount of the judgment. In fact, in the absence of competitive bidding, the judgment creditor's motivation is to bid as low as possible, well below the market value of the asset. If the creditor is the successful bidder at that price, it may then resell the asset at a higher price in a more usual setting, capturing the profit for itself. Meanwhile if there is a deficiency still owed on the judgment because the winning bid at the execution sale was less than the judgment amount, the creditor may continue to have the sheriff seize and sell the debtor's assets until the judgment is satisfied.

Courts do have some oversight over execution sales and can void a sale conducted in an improper manner. However, the general rule is that inadequacy of price alone is not sufficient to set aside a regularly conducted execution sale. Only if there is some irregularity in the sale process in addition to a very low price is a court likely to set the sale aside.

Time limits on execution. At common law, the time to execute on a judgment was limited to a year and a day. After that time period, the judgment became "dormant." That is, if a writ of execution was not issued within that time period, the creditor could not execute on the judgment without first bringing an action to "revive" the judgment. Many states now regulate by statute the time period during which writs of execution can be issued, such as by providing that writs of execution may be issued only within the first three years after entry of the judgment.[46]

In addition to limits on writs of execution, judgments themselves are subject to statutes of limitation that restrict the time period during which they may be enforced.[47] Unless an action to renew the judgment is commenced prior to the expiration of that statute of limitations period, the judgment becomes unenforceable. However, by renewing the judgment – in essence, getting a judgment on the judgment – the creditor is able to extend the life of the judgment to the term of another statute of limitations period.

---

[46] *See, e.g.*, Minn. Stat. § 550.01; Wash. Rev. Code § 6.17.020(1).

[47] *See, e.g.*, Minn. Stat. § 541.04; Wash. Rev. Code § 6.17.020(7).

To illustrate these two concepts consider the following example. Assume a judgment is entered on February 1, 2015. The relevant state statute provides that writs of execution may be issued within three years after the judgment is entered. The statute of limitations for judgments is 10 years. Thus on February 1, 2018, the judgment would be "dormant" and an action to revive the judgment must be brought to have writs of execution issued after that date. In order to extend the life of the judgment beyond February 1, 2025, the creditor must bring an action on the judgment before February 1, 2025. If the creditor obtains a judgment on the first judgment, the second judgment has a new life of 10 years. A creditor may continue this renewal process indefinitely or until the judgment is satisfied.

Post-sale redemption. Up until the moment an execution sale is completed, the debtor has a common-law right to "redeem" the property, that is to stop the sale and get the property back from the sheriff. To do this, the debtor must pay to the judgment creditor *the full amount of the debt* (including post-judgment interest and possibly also the sheriff's fees for levying and the creditor's expenses in conducting the sale). Some states have supplemented this common-law *pre-sale* redemption right with a statutory, *post-sale* right. In a state with such a statute, the debtor may redeem the property sold at the execution sale – particularly if it is real estate – by paying the *sale price* to the sheriff or the judgment creditor within a certain time period after the sale. Often during this period of statutory redemption, the debtor is entitled to remain in possession of the property. The risk of post-sale redemption and the fact that the debtor typically remains in possession during this period are additional factors that lead to the generally low prices at execution sales. Ironically, however, statutory redemption rights were created to give the debtor a remedy for the fact that execution sales yield low prices for other reasons. The type of property for which post-sale redemption is allowed (usually for real property and not personal property), who is entitled to redeem, and the process for redemption varies from state to state.

Enforcement of judgments across state lines. Sometimes the debtor will have property in a state other than the state in which a judgment has been entered. There are two methods for "transferring" a judgment from one state to another. The first method is to start in the second state an action on the judgment from the first state. Under the full faith and credit clause of the United States Constitution,[48] the second state must give full faith and credit to a valid judgment from the first state. The

---

[48] U.S. Const. art. IV, § 1, cl. 1.

ability to challenge the entry of judgment in the second state is severely limited. As one court explained:[49]

> It has been settled by the United States Supreme Court and courts of other states that the power of a state to reopen or vacate a foreign judgment is more limited than under the rules of civil procedure and that a foreign judgment cannot be collaterally attacked on the merits. After a foreign judgment has been duly filed, the grounds for reopening or vacating it are limited to lack of personal or subject matter jurisdiction of the rendering court, fraud in procurement (extrinsic), satisfaction, lack of due process, or other grounds that make a judgment invalid or unenforceable. The nature and amount or other aspects of the merits (*i.e.*, defenses) of a foreign judgment cannot be relitigated in the state in which enforcement is sought.
>
> It is also established that the existence of an error or irregularity in the law or facts of the foreign judgment, in the absence of one of the above grounds for reopening or vacating a foreign judgment, does not constitute grounds on which a court of the enforcing state may reopen and modify the foreign judgment. Assuming the necessary procedures are complied with, a foreign judgment must be enforced to its full extent, including any errors or irregularities contained therein.

By obtaining a judgment in the second state, the creditor will then be able to use the statutory processes in the second state for executing on that judgment.

The second method for transferring a judgment from one state to another for purposes of enforcement is to use the Uniform Enforcement of Foreign Judgments Act, now enacted by 47 states, the District of Columbia, and the U.S. Virgin Islands. The act provides a summary process for registering a judgment from one state with the court clerk in another state. The court clerk in the second state sends notice of the registration to the debtor and after a short waiting period, the creditor may then use state process in the second state to execute on that judgment.

"Fraudulent transfers." Some debtors who do not voluntarily pay their debts go beyond passive resistence. They actively try to keep their property out of the reach of their creditors. Some transfer their property to friends or family, either as gifts or for safekeeping. Some move their assets outside the jurisdiction where they are located. Clever debtors can find myriad ways to make collection difficult for their creditors.

---

[49] Matson v. Matson, 333 N.W.2d 862, 867-68 (Minn. 1983) (citations omitted).

The common law dealt with this problem by developing the concept of a fraudulent conveyance. The core principle underlying a fraudulent conveyance is quite simple. If a debtor transfers property to another person in order to delay or hinder creditors or to avoid paying a justly due debt, the transfer can be "voided" – that is, rescinded – thereby allowing the creditor to seize and sell the property. This concept is now codified in the Uniform Voidable Transactions Act.[50] At present 45 states, the District of Columbia, and the U.S. Virgin Islands have adopted the UVTA or its predecessor, the Uniform Fraudulent Transfer Act.

In addition to dealing with transfers made with intent to hinder, delay, or defraud, the UVTA also makes voidable some transfers for which the debtor did not receive reasonably equivalent value in exchange.[51] This type of voidable transfer is grounded in the oft-quoted maxim of the law: "a debtor must be just before being generous." The idea behind this maxim is that before an insolvent debtor gives property away, the debtor should provide for payment to the debtor's creditors. Because insolvent debtors by definition cannot pay all creditors, they should not be permitted to make gifts of their assets while leaving their creditors without recourse. This type of transfer is sometimes referred to as "constructive fraud" because voidance of the transfer does not depend upon the intent of the transferor.[52]

Consider the potential significance of this. Have you ever made a voidable transfer? In contemplating that question, ask yourself if you have given birthday or holiday presents recently. If you did, were you insolvent at the time? *See* UVTA § 2. Most students who borrow money for college or graduate school are insolvent.

B. Pre-judgment Remedies

Given the process described above for obtaining and executing on judgments, creditors are often justifiably worried about money running faster than due process. Creditors fear that when a lawsuit is filed to start the process of collecting a debt, the debtor will use the time before judgment and execution to become judgment-proof. That is, by the time the judgment is entered and the creditor is

---

[50] UVTA § 4(a)(1).

[51] UVTA §§ 4(a)(2), 5(a).

[52] When the UFTA was revised in 2014, the title was changed to the UVTA to remove any suggestion that fraudulent intent was necessary to void a transfer by an insolvent person for less than reasonably equivalent value, or to imply that a person who had made a transfer voided for that reason had any fraudulent intent.

ready to collect on it, the debtor will have no property for the creditor to seize and sell. Pre-judgment remedies speak to that concern. Most states have a process whereby a creditor can get an order – prior to trial of the liability issues and entry of a judgment against the debtor – that allows the sheriff to seize property and hold it for eventual satisfaction of the judgment, if one is obtained.

Two of the usual processes for a pre-judgment remedy are called attachment and garnishment. Attachment is a process typically used on tangible property in which the debtor has an interest. It operates in much the same manner as execution: the court clerk issues a writ of attachment – usually at the direction of a judge – directing a sheriff or marshal to levy upon certain personal property. The key difference between pre-judgment attachment and post-judgment execution is that the property levied upon in a pre-judgment attachment will not be immediately sold. Instead, the property will be held by the court for the eventual satisfaction of the creditor's judgment, if, in fact, the creditor obtains a judgment. If the creditor does not obtain a judgment, the property will be released to the debtor. Pre-judgment garnishment is much the same as post-judgment garnishment; it applies to property in the hands of third parties or obligations that a third party owes to the debtor. The main difference is that the writ directs the third party to deposit that property with or pay that obligation to the court, rather than turn it over to the creditor.

Needless to say, defendants in civil actions are not pleased to have their property tied up during the pendency of the lawsuit, particularly one the defendant hopes to win. Because these remedies significantly interfere with the debtor's property rights, and do so before the debtor's liability to the creditor is even adjudicated, not every creditor is entitled to use them. In most states the creditor must demonstrate some sort of exigency to obtain a pre-judgment remedy. A typical example is evidence that the debtor is hiding property outside the court's jurisdiction in an effort to avoid creditors. Moreover, many states require that there be some sort of notice to the debtor and a hearing prior to issuance of the order. States customarily also require that the creditor post a bond to protect the debtor from any harm that occurs if judgment in favor of the creditor is not forthcoming. In situations involving extreme urgency, a court may order that the debtor's property be seized without prior notice or a hearing, but only if provision is made for a hearing promptly after the seizure.

C. Exemptions

Not all of a debtor's assets may be subject to levy pursuant to a writ of execution, attachment, or garnishment. Most states exempt certain specified property of individual debtors (that is, human beings) from seizure or judicial sale. The types of property that the debtor may exempt from pre- and post-judgment remedies and the limits on the value of the property that may be exempted vary greatly from state to state. Each state's decision about what and how much property to exempt is usually based upon a mixture of history and modern needs. Nevertheless, almost all exemptions are grounded in one or more of three basic social policies.

First, debtors cannot go to their workplace without clothes, nor can they perform their jobs without tools of their trades. Exempting such property preserves people's ability to earn a living. Protecting future wages ensures that individuals retain their incentive to continue working and to be productive members of society. This policy is so important, there is a federal statute protecting some proportion of wages from garnishment.[53] Protecting retirement funds and disability payments helps prevent people from becoming public charges when their ability to maintain employment ceases. In short, one main purpose of exemptions is to make sure that people are able to be and have the incentive to be contributing members of society. If the law permitted creditors to make their debtors completely destitute, and thereby a drain on the public purse, the law would effectively be creating a system that indirectly used public funds to pay private debts.

Second, some property exemptions protect items of nominal value that the debtor might need but would do little to satisfy obligations to creditors. For example, used clothes, household goods, and family photographs typically have little or no resale value for the creditors that levy on and sell them. However, they can be costly or impossible to replace, and a creditor's threat to seize this property can lead a family to liquidate other assets, borrow from other people, or use other means to protect these items from creditors. To curb this leverage, most jurisdictions protect such personal property from the execution process.

Finally, and for similar reasons, the law protects some property that might have some value to creditors but to which the debtor has significant sentimental attachment. Using pre- or post-judgment remedies to seize wedding bands, engagement rings, and family heirlooms is generally regarded as excessive and prohibited through exemption laws, unless of course such property is unusually valuable.

---

[53] 15 U.S.C. §§ 1671-1677.

One of the most common exemptions is a homestead exemption. But the ubiquity of homestead exemptions is belied by the variation among them.[54] Six states – Florida, Iowa, Kansas, Oklahoma, South Dakota, and Texas – protect a debtor's home from execution, regardless of its value, although each state limits the area of land that is exempt.[55] In contrast, Kentucky's homestead exemption is limited to $5,000,[56] and three other states – Delaware,[57] New Jersey, and Pennsylvania – have no homestead exemption.

Personal property exemptions vary even more widely. Some states exempt certain types of property without regard to its value; others provide exemptions with value limitations. Some statutes exempt very specific types of property, such as a television or church pew. Others refer to a class of items, such as "household goods," and thus are more readily available. Find and examine the statute in the state where you are attending law school. Now try the following problem.

Problem 1-1

A. You have obtained a judgment for your client against Diaper Buddies, Inc., a day care center, for $40,000. During discovery, you learn that the business owns the following property, free and clear of any liens:
   (i) a van worth $15,000 used to shuttle kids between home and the day care center;
   (ii) child-sized furniture and play structures, collectively worth $4,000; and
   (iii) a bank account with a current balance of $847.23.

   Which property can you cause the sheriff to levy upon and sell? If only some of the property is subject to levy and sale, how is that portion to be determined? In answering these questions:

   1. If your last name begins with a letter from A to M, assume that the debtor is incorporated in Michigan;

---

54 For tables showing the differences in the state homestead exemptions, see http://www.sepinuckruschbankruptcy.com.

55 Fla. Const. Art. X, § 4; Fla. Stat. § 222.01; Iowa Code §§ 561.1, 561.2; Kan. Stat. § 60-2301; Okla. Stat. Ann. tit. 31, § 2; S.D. Codified Laws § 43-31-2; Tex. Prop. Code §§ 41.001, 41.002.

56 Ky. Rev. Stat. § 427.060.

57 Delaware allows a homestead exemption only if the debtor has filed a federal bankruptcy case. Del. Code Ann. tit. 10, §§ 4901, 4914.

2. If your last name begins with a letter from N to Z, assume that the debtor is incorporated in Nevada;

Note, the Michigan, and Nevada exemption statutes are available on the companion web page for this book: www.sepinucksecured.com.

B. Same facts and applicable law as in Part A, except that the business is a sole proprietorship and your judgment is against its owner, Buddy Friend. The property listed above belongs to Buddy. In addition, Buddy owns the following:

(i) household furniture and goods worth $2,000;
(ii) a washer and dryer worth $500;
(iii) a television worth $100;
(iv) a computer worth $1,300; and
(v) a collection of CDs and DVDs worth $1,100.

C. Same facts and applicable law as in Part B, but in addition:

1. Buddy draws $1,500 a week from the business for personal use. Can you reach that stream of income?
2. Buddy closed his business and went to work for a corporate day care provider for a weekly salary of $1,500. Can you garnish his wages? *See* 15 U.S.C. §§ 1671–1677.

D. Constitutional Considerations

Pre-judgment remedies – such as attachment and garnishment – raise constitutional issues. Pre-judgment remedies allow a creditor to use state process to interfere with the debtor's interest in property without the benefit of a judicial determination that the debtor in fact owes the creditor a legal obligation. Because state actors, such as sheriffs and judges, are involved in the pre-judgment remedial process, the Due Process Clause of the Fourteenth Amendment is implicated. It prohibits states from depriving people of a protected right, such as property rights, without due process of law.[58]

The Supreme Court's jurisprudence in this area has not been wholly consistent. In a 1969 decision arising out of a challenge to a Wisconsin statute, the Court ruled that a creditor could not freeze the debtor's wages merely upon application to the clerk of a state court without first giving the debtor notice and a hearing.[59]

---

[58] U.S. Const. 14th Amend.

[59] Sniadach v. Family Fin. Corp. of Bay View, 395 U.S. 337 (1969).

Three years later, the Court invalidated Florida and Pennsylvania statutes that authorized creditors to obtain a pre-judgment writ of replevin through an *ex parte* application to a court clerk and posting a bond for double the value of the property to be seized. Although the Florida statute guaranteed an opportunity for a hearing after seizure of goods and the Pennsylvania process allowed for a post-seizure hearing if the aggrieved party initiated one, neither provided for notice or an opportunity to be heard before the seizure. The Court concluded that such protections were inadequate.[60]

Two years after that, the Court retreated somewhat. In *Mitchell v. W.T. Grant Co.*,[61] the Court reviewed provisions of Louisiana law that permitted a creditor with a lien on property of the debtor to obtain a writ of sequestration on an *ex parte* application, and thus precipitate a pre-judgment seizure of the property without notice or opportunity for a hearing. Because the law required the creditor to provide a detailed affidavit in addition to a bond, and the writ could be issued only by a judge, the Court upheld the law. It concluded that these procedures reduced the likelihood of an erroneous pre-hearing deprivation and this, coupled with the debtor's right to an immediate post-seizure hearing, satisfied due process.

The following year, the Court came out the other way, albeit in a fairly easy case. The Court invalidated an *ex parte* garnishment statute that not only failed to provide for notice and prior hearing but also failed to require a bond, a detailed affidavit setting out the claim, the determination of a neutral magistrate, or a prompt post-deprivation hearing.[62]

The latest word from the Supreme Court on the Fourteenth Amendment Due Process Clause and pre-judgment remedies came in *Connecticut v. Doehr*.[63] In *Doehr*, the Court invalidated a state statute that authorized pre-judgment attachment of real estate without prior notice or a hearing, without a showing of extraordinary circumstances, and without a requirement that the person seeking the attachment post a bond. Moreover, unlike in *Mitchell*, where the attaching creditor already had an interest in the property and the action involved "ordinarily uncomplicated matters that lend themselves to documentary proof,"[64] the facts of *Doehr* involved

---

[60] Fuentes v. Shevin, 407 U.S. 67 (1972).

[61] 416 U.S. 600 (1974).

[62] North Georgia Finishing, Inc. v. Di-Chem, Inc., 419 U.S. 601 (1975).

[63] 501 U.S. 1 (1991).

[64] *Mitchell*, 416 U.S. at 609.

a claim for assault and battery that in no way involved the property. The Court reasoned that no matter how detailed the plaintiff's affidavit was, it would still contain only his version of the facts.[65] Accordingly, the risk of erroneous deprivation was too great for the procedure to satisfy the requirements of due process.

In addition to procedural due process concerns, engaging in legal processes that allow for a state officer to seize property or to enter dwellings or other buildings in order to do so raises concerns about the Fourth Amendment protection against unreasonable searches and seizures.[66] In *Soldal v. Cook County, Illinois*,[67] the Supreme Court ruled that an eviction proceeding in which the debtor's mobile home was seized prior to entry of the judgment of eviction raised issues under the Fourth Amendment. It stated:

> As a result of the state action in this case, the Soldals' domicile was not only seized, it literally was carried away, giving new meaning to the term "mobile home." We fail to see how being unceremoniously dispossessed of one's home in the manner alleged to have occurred here can be viewed as anything but a seizure invoking the protection of the Fourth Amendment. Whether the Amendment was in fact violated is, of course, a different question that requires determining if the seizure was reasonable. That inquiry entails the weighing of various factors and is not before us.[68]

What does all this mean for creditors? Well, when private actors act in concert with state actors, such as sheriffs and judges, those private actors may be civilly liable for a violation of a debtor's civil rights under 42 U.S.C. § 1983. What is more, such private actors are not entitled to qualified immunity based upon their good faith compliance with state law.[69] Creditors must therefore be cautious in their resort to pre-judgment remedies.

---

[65] 501 U.S. at 14.

[66] U.S. Const. 4th Amend. ("The right of the people to be secure in their persons, houses, papers, and effects, against unreasonable searches and seizures, shall not be violated . . . .").

[67] 506 U.S. 56 (1992).

[68] *Id.* 61-62.

[69] Wyatt v. Cole, 504 U.S. 158 (1992). *But cf.* Wyatt v. Cole, 994 F.2d 1113, 1120 (5th Cir. 1993) (the same case on remand; ruling that the private actors had an affirmative defense to liability "absent a showing of malice and evidence that they either knew or should have known of the statute's constitutional infirmity").

Moreover, while having a valid judgment will normally abate any procedural due process problems, post-judgment collection efforts might still suffer from severe search and seizure problems. First, a writ of execution may or may not authorize the sheriff to enter buildings. In some states, such authorization is implied.[70] In some, it is not.[71] And in others, the sheriff's authority apparently depends on what the writ says.[72] Second, even if the writ does authorize entry, the resulting search and seizure may not be constitutional if the writ was issued by a court clerk or justice of the peace, instead of a judge.[73]

E. Bankruptcy

Often when creditors are pursuing a debtor to collect debts, the debtor will seek the protection of the federal bankruptcy process.[74] As we work through the materials that follow in this book, we will often explore how the debtor's filing of a bankruptcy petition would affect the creditor's ability to collect the debt owed. Given that most law schools devote an entire course to bankruptcy, detailed exploration of the bankruptcy process must await that course. For now, consider this very general description.

Technically, a debtor need not be in financial distress to file bankruptcy; there is no requirement of insolvency or inability to pay debts. All that is required is that the debtor file a petition with the bankruptcy court.[75] Two things occur immediately upon such a filing. First, something called the "bankruptcy estate" is created. Into

---

[70] *See, e.g.*, Okla. Stat. tit. 12 § 1582 (authorizing sheriff to break open any building or enclosure to execute writ).

[71] *See, e.g.*,Wis. Stat. § 810.09 (requiring sheriff to get a warrant).

[72] *Compare* Wash. Rev. Code § 7.64.035(2) (indicating that a replevin order signed by a judge may direct a sheriff to break and enter a building or enclosure to obtain possession of the described property) *with* Wash. Rev. Code § 7.64.047(1) ("If the property or any part of it is concealed in a building or enclosure, the sheriff shall publicly demand delivery of the property. If the property is not delivered and if the order awarding possession so directs, the sheriff shall cause the building or enclosure to be broken open and take possession of the property.").

[73] Dorwart v. Caraway, 966 P.2d 1121 (Mont. 1997), *overruled on other grounds*, Trustees of Indiana Univ. v. Buxbaum, 69 P.3d 663 (Mont. 2003).

[74] The Bankruptcy Code is codified at 11 U.S.C. §§ 101-1532.

[75] 11 U.S.C. § 301.

that estate go all of the debtor's interests in property, that is, the debtor's assets.[76] An analogy might be useful. When an individual dies, their assets are immediately transferred into a testamentary estate. Well, bankruptcy is analogous to a person's financial demise. The bankruptcy petition operates as the attending physician's pronouncement of financial death, with the result that the debtor's property rights are immediately transferred into the bankruptcy estate. Second, virtually all efforts to collect a pre-petition debt of the debtor or to acquire possession or control of the debtor's property or the estate's property are enjoined by something called "the automatic stay."[77] This automatic stay operates without notice. Persons who violate the automatic stay, even if they take action without any notice of the bankruptcy filing, may be liable for damages to the debtor and for contempt of court.

When filing for bankruptcy protection, the debtor must choose whether to file the petition under Chapter 7, 11, or 13 of the Bankruptcy Code.[78] Chapter 7 is designed as a liquidation process. Chapters 11 and 13 are designed as reorganization processes. Whether a debtor is eligible to file under any of the chapters is determined under 11 U.S.C. § 109. In general, an individual debtor (a human being) may file under any of the three chapters. A non-individual debtor (such as a corporation or limited liability company) is ineligible to file under Chapter 13 and must therefore choose between a Chapter 7 or a Chapter 11 process.

In a Chapter 7 proceeding, a trustee is appointed to take charge of the bankruptcy estate and that trustee proceeds to sell the debtor's nonexempt assets, if there are any. Individual debtors (that is, human beings) are allowed to exempt from the estate and thus sale by the trustee, certain property of limited value.[79] To the extent property is exempted from the bankruptcy estate, the value available to pay creditors decreases. Creditors will file claims with the court and the court will

---

[76] 11 U.S.C. § 541.

[77] 11 U.S.C. § 362.

[78] For purposes of this discussion, cases under Chapter 12 are ignored. The Chapter 12 process bears a close resemblance to the Chapter 13 process but is restricted to family farmers with regular income. Chapter 12 was enacted with a sunset provision which Congress extended, let lapse, and then reinstated several times since its original enactment. In April 2005, Congress permanently enacted Chapter 12. Bankruptcy Abuse Prevention and Consumer Protection Act of 2005, Pub. L. No. 109-8, § 1001, 119 Stat. 23, 185 (2005) [hereinafter "2005 Bankruptcy Act"].

[79] 11 U.S.C. § 522.

determine whether the claims are allowed.[80] If allowed, the claims will be paid from the proceeds of the debtor's nonexempt assets according to a statutory distribution scheme.[81] The expenses of administering the estate are paid first, along with other claims given statutory priority, such as certain tax obligations and claims for spousal or child support.[82] If there is any value left after those creditors are paid, the remaining claims are paid on a pro rata basis.

In a Chapter 11 or 13 case, no trustee is appointed to take charge of the estate.[83] Rather the debtor remains in control of the property of the estate as the "debtor in possession."[84] The debtor proposes a plan to pay creditor claims over time – in full or in part – out of future income that the debtor expects to receive, whether through earnings, from the use of property of the estate, or otherwise. In most Chapter 11 proceedings, the creditors vote on the plan. If they approve the plan pursuant to specified formulae,[85] the court will confirm the plan as long as it meets certain other requirements.[86] If the creditors vote against the plan, the debtor has a limited ability to "cramdown" the plan on dissenting creditors.[87] If no plan is confirmed, the case will either be converted to a Chapter 7 case or dismissed.

In 2019, Congress created a new Subchapter 5 of Chapter 11 of the Bankruptcy Code, which became effective in February 2020.[88] Subchapter 5 is intended to provide small businesses and individuals with primarily business debts a faster and less expensive process for reorganizing under Chapter 11.[89] Under Subchapter 5,

---

[80] 11 U.S.C. §§ 501, 502.

[81] 11 U.S.C. § 726.

[82] 11 U.S.C. § 507.

[83] In Chapter 13, a trustee receives and disburses payments but does not generally manage the assets of the estate. *See* 11 U.S.C. § 1302. In the new Subchapter V of Chapter 11, discussed below, a trustee has limited duties. *See* 11 U.S.C. § 1183.

[84] 11 U.S.C. §§ 1107, 1303.

[85] 11 U.S.C. § 1126.

[86] 11 U.S.C. § 1129(a).

[87] 11 U.S.C. § 1129(b).

[88] 11 U.S.C. §§ 1181–1195.

[89] As originally enacted, Subchapter 5 was limited to persons with noncontingent, liquidated debts of no more than $2,725,625. As part of the Coronavirus Aid, Relief and Economic Security Act, Congress increased the debt limit to $7.5 million. *See* Pub. L. 116-136,

creditors do not vote on the plan or reorganization. Instead, the bankruptcy court will confirm the debtor's plan if the plan meets specified requirements, including that all of the debtor's projected disposable income for at least three years (or property with equivalent value) will be used to pay prepetition creditors.

In a Chapter 13 case, the creditors similarly do not vote on the plan but the plan must meet specified requirements.[90] Notably, if an unsecured creditor objects, the creditor must be paid in full or the debtor must devote all disposable income to payments under the plan for at least three years.[91]

Under both Chapter 11 and Chapter 13, creditors who object to a proposed plan get additional protections. First, each creditor must get as much as it would in a Chapter 7 liquidation case.[92] In addition, in a Chapter 11 case, the absolute priority rule applies. The absolute priority rule means that the entities with an ownership interest in the debtor (*e.g.*, shareholders of a corporate debtor) cannot retain any ownership interest in the *reorganized* debtor unless all creditors of the debtor are paid in full.[93] Finally, in both Chapter 11 and Chapter 13 cases, the court evaluates whether the plan the debtor has proposed is feasible.[94]

No matter under which chapter an individual debtor files, the debtor might receive a discharge of personal – *in personam* – liability on all pre-petition debts, to the extent those debts are not paid by the trustee or provided for in a confirmed plan of reorganization. The effect of the discharge is to prohibit the creditor from attempting to collect the discharged obligation from the debtor in the future.[95] A creditor may object to the debtor's discharge in general or to the dischargeability

---

§ 1113(a)(5) (codified at 11 U.S.C. 1182(1)).

90 11 U.S.C. § 1325.

91 11 U.S.C. § 1325(b)(1). A similar disposable income test applies in Chapter 11 cases filed by individual debtors. *See* 11 U.S.C. § 1129(a)(15).

92 11 U.S.C. §§ 1129(a)(7), 1325(a)(4).

93 11 U.S.C. § 1129(b)(2). This rule does not apply to cases under Subchapter 5. *See* 11 U.S.C. § 1181(a).

94 *See* 11 U.S.C. § 1129(a)(11), 1325(a)(6). In a case under Subchapter 5 of Chapter 11, confirmation requires that the court determine either that the debtor will be able to make all plan payments or that there is a reasonable likelihood that the debtor will be able to make all plan payments and the plan provides appropriate remedies if the debtor does not. 11 U.S.C. § 1191(c).

95 11 U.S.C. § 524(a).

of only the debt owed to it.[96] A business entity cannot get a discharge in Chapter 7 but can get one in Chapter 11.

SECTION 4. COLLECTING DEBTS SECURED BY CONSENSUAL AND STATUTORY LIENS

Not all creditors must resort to a judicial process to acquire a lien on some of the debtor's assets. In addition to judicial liens (those created by judicial process), such as judgment liens, execution liens and attachment liens, there are consensual liens (those created by contract) and statutory liens (those arising by operation of law). The chart at the end of this Chapter depicts some of the similarities and differences of the most common types of liens.

Consensual liens come in two flavors: those on real estate (commonly referred to as mortgages or deeds of trust) and those on personal property (referred to as security interests). The latter are the principal focus of this book. Of course, by their nature, consensual liens are available only to creditors who have a contract with their debtor. Involuntary creditors, such as tort victims, are rarely able to acquire a consensual lien. Moreover, not all voluntary creditors have the ability or need to obtain a lien. Some lack the bargaining power to negotiate for one, some lend to debtors who do not have any assets available to offer as collateral, some rely on other types of credit enhancement devices to ensure payment (*e.g.*, guaranties, letters of credit, or insurance),[97] and some extend credit to entities that are so creditworthy that the risk of nonpayment does not justify the time and expense of

---

[96] *See* 11 U.S.C. § 523 (objections to discharge of certain types of debts), § 727 (objections to discharge of all debts in a Chapter 7 case), § 1141 (objections to discharge in a Chapter 11 case), § 1328 (objections to discharge in a Chapter 13 case).

[97] Taking a consensual lien on property is ultimately about reducing the risk of nonpayment of the debt obligation, but is only one of several ways in which this risk of nonpayment may be reduced. While not the subject of the rest of this book, another common method of reducing the risk of nonpayment is to obtain the promise of another entity to be liable on the debt. For example, a lender may require as a condition of making or renewing a loan that an entity, other then the debtor to whom the loan is made, guarantee payment. The guarantor may incur that liability by signing a separate guarantee agreement or by merely co-signing the promissory note that evidences the obligation to pay. To further enhance the prospect of repayment, a lender may require that the guarantee itself be secured by personal property or real estate. Whenever more than one person is obligated on a debt to a creditor, the relationship among the obligors is governed, in part, by the principles of suretyship law. *See* RESTATEMENT (THIRD) OF SURETYSHIP AND GUARANTY (1996).

getting a lien. Whether these limitations on the availability of consensual liens makes their use by some creditors unfair to those who cannot obtain them is something you should consider periodically throughout this course.

Statutory liens are created by numerous state and federal statutes and are so varied and idiosyncratic that it is difficult to make general statements about them. There are, however, several common examples. Most states permit landlords and innkeepers to obtain a lien on personal property left in the premises and to sell such property in order to pay the tenant's overdue rent or a guest's outstanding bill. Many provide attorneys with a lien on any monetary recovery the attorney has obtained for a client to secure payment of attorney's professional fees. Many also award health care providers a lien for their services on any insurance or tort recovery of the patient that they have treated. Most taxing authorities – in particular, the Internal Revenue Service – are entitled to very powerful liens to secure payment of unpaid taxes. But perhaps the most common form of statutory liens are mechanic's liens. These protect repairmen, artisans, craftsmen, and mechanics who perform work on a specific piece of real or personal property. For example, a person who repairs an automobile is frequently entitled to a lien on the car, if it is still in the mechanic's possession, to cover the cost of the repair. Similarly, a contractor, subcontractor, or supplier involved in a construction project is normally entitled to a lien on the real property improved by the project. The process for collecting on the property that is subject to a statutory lien is normally prescribed by the statute creating the lien.

As is no doubt apparent, statutory liens are available only to certain, statutorily preferred types of creditors. Tort victims do not get them. Nor do lenders or most sellers who sell on credit.

The collection advantage. One advantage of having a statutory or consensual lien is that it is far easier and usually less expensive for the creditor to obtain possession of the collateral and sell it than it is to go through the entire judgment and execution process.

If the assistance of a sheriff is needed to gain possession of the property, the creditor with a lien can normally obtain a writ of replevin fairly quickly and on an *ex parte* basis. Replevin is a judicial process (sometimes called "claim and delivery") in which a creditor asserts that, as against the debtor, the creditor has a superior right to possession of the property. As with other prejudgment remedies, there is usually a process that allows for seizure after giving the debtor notice and an opportunity to be heard, as well as a process that allows for seizure of the property without the opportunity for a pre-seizure hearing but with the right to a hearing promptly afterward.[98] A creditor may be required to post a bond as well to protect the debtor against harm caused by a wrongful seizure.

The procedural due process concerns are unlikely to present a major problem because to demonstrate the right to possession the creditor need merely prove the existence of the lien and evidence of default, things which are "ordinarily uncomplicated matters that lend themselves to documentary proof."[99]

A creditor with a lien on property may also request a court to appoint a receiver. The appointment of a receiver happens more often in the context of a creditor with a mortgage on real estate than it does in relationship to a creditor with a security interest in personal property. Appointment of a receiver is within the sound discretion of the court and is most often granted when the creditor can show that the debtor is engaging in some sort of activity that is wasteful and harmful to the value of the asset. If appointed, a receiver takes over management and possession of the property pending the final disposition of the property in the debt collection process.

The priority advantage. Another considerable benefit of obtaining a lien on property to secure a debt is that the lien fixes the priority of the lienholder's claim to that asset as against other creditors who may claim an interest in that asset. Priority is most important if the debtor's assets do not have enough value to pay all of the debtor's debts. This concept can be illustrated by imagining a situation where the debtor's asset has a value of $10,000, Lienor 1 has an interest in that asset to secure a debt of $7,000, and Lienor 2 has an interest in that asset to secure a debt of $5,000:

Property Value	$10,000
Debt to Lienor 1	$7,000
Debt to Lienor 2	$5,000

As should be apparent, the property does not have enough value to satisfy the debts to both Lienor 1 and Lienor 2.

Now assume that the debtor defaults in its obligations to both lienors and Lienor 1 sells the property for $10,000 to Buyer. Assume Buyer takes the property free of

---

98 This process may permit seizure of the collateral even before the debtor has been served with the complaint. *See, e.g.*, T & C Leasing, Inc. v. BBMC, LLC, 2009 WL 1657362 (M.D. Pa. 2009).

99 Mitchell v. W.T. Grant Co., 416 U.S. at 609.

both of the creditors' interests.[100] If Lienor 1 has priority over Lienor 2, Lienor 1 takes the first $7,000 of the sale proceeds, leaving only $3,000 for Lienor 2:

Sale Price	$10,000
Distribution to Lienor 1	– $7,000
Residual Sale Proceeds (paid to Lienor 2)	$3,000

As a result, the debt to Lienor 1 is satisfied in full. The debt to Lienor 2 is partially satisfied: $3,000 of it is paid but $2,000 of it remains. If Lienor 2 wants to collect the remainder, Lienor 2 will have to pursue collection efforts against other assets of the debtor, if the debtor has any assets that Lienor 2 can find and that have unencumbered value that the debtor cannot exempt.

Of course, the result would be substantially different if Lienor 2 had priority and had sold the property for $10,000. Then Lienor 2 would take the first $5,000 of the sale proceeds, leaving $5,000 for Lienor 1:

Sale Price	$10,000
Distribution to Lienor 2	– $5,000
Residual Sale Proceeds (paid to Lienor 1)	$5,000

If Lienor 1 wants to collect the remaining $2,000 of the obligation that the debtor owes, Lienor 1 will have to find other assets of the debtor.

Of course, the creditor with the prior lien need not be the one who forecloses. Even junior lienors may foreclose their interests. Returning to the first scenario (in which Lienor 1 has priority over Lienor 2), if Lienor 2 forecloses on its lien that secures a $5,000 obligation, Buyer will take the property subject to the lien in favor of Lienor 1 (presently securing a $7,000 obligation). If Buyer is aware of Lienor 1's lien, Buyer will not offer more than $3,000 for the property and in fact may offer substantially less.

Property Value	$10,000
Debt to Lienor 1	– $7,000
Value of Property Sold	$3,000

---

[100] In Chapter Three, we will consider the state of the title in the property that a buyer purchases at a foreclosure sale. For present purposes, the usual rule is that the buyer takes title to the property purchased at the foreclosure sale free of the lien foreclosed and all liens subsequent in priority to the lien foreclosed and subject to all liens superior in priority to the lien foreclosed.

Consider this additional advantage to having a contractually granted interest in property. Assume the debtor's only valuable asset is worth $10,000. Creditor A who is owed $8,000 has taken a contractual interest in that asset and taken the steps necessary to fix its priority in that asset. Creditor B has not taken such an interest and is owed $5,000. Creditor C then enters into a contract with the debtor lending the debtor $2,000 and taking a contractual interest in the asset to secure the claim. Under applicable law, Creditor A has first priority and Creditor C has second priority in the asset:

Asset Value	$10,000
Debt to Creditor A	– $8,000
Residual Property Value	$2,000
Debt to Creditor C	– $2,000
Residual Property Value	$0

If Creditor B then gets a judgment against debtor for $5,000, Creditor B may enforce its judgment against the debtor's asset by having the sheriff levy on the asset and sell it at public auction. However, Creditor B will not get any money out of that action. A buyer purchasing the asset at the execution sale to enforce Creditor B's judgment will take the asset subject to Creditor A's and Creditor C's interests in that asset. In other words, a buyer would be acquiring an asset worth $10,000 but still subject to liens securing a total of $10,000 in debts. No buyer is likely to pay anything for that. Put another way, the value of the asset is "fully encumbered" due to the size of the obligations already owed to Creditor A and Creditor C that are secured by that asset.

There are other advantages to having a lien. Consider the next problem.

Problem 1-2

A. Revisit the illustration beginning on page 4. What would the result be if SuperStore had retained a consensual lien (*i.e.*, had retained a "security interest," *see* U.C.C. § 1-201(b)(35)) in the grill to secure payment of the purchase price? *See* U.C.C. § 9-609.

B. Revisit Problem 1-1(B). If your client had a security interest in each item of property listed and the same exemption statute were applicable, which items could Buddy exempt from that security interest and to what extent?

Bankruptcy. Creditors with liens (secured creditors) fare much better than unsecured creditors in the debtor's bankruptcy proceeding. First, as a general rule, a bankruptcy discharge operates on the debtor's "*in personam*" personal liability for debts, not the debt itself. Thus, even if the debtor receives a discharge and no longer remains liable for pre-bankruptcy debts, the debts themselves survive and the guarantors of the debtor's pre-bankruptcy obligations remain liable on their guarantees. Similarly, encumbered property retains its "*in rem*" liability. In other words, liens generally survive the bankruptcy process and the debtor's bankruptcy discharge.[101]

The main consequence of this is that secured creditors actually get paid in a debtor's bankruptcy, at least up to the value of their lien interest in the property. An illustration may be useful. Assume a debtor in a Chapter 7 case has ten creditors, each of whom is owed $10,000. The debtor also has nonexempt assets collectively worth $40,000. If all the assets were unencumbered (*i.e.*, not subject to any liens) and none of the creditors' claims was entitled to priority under the Bankruptcy Code distribution scheme,[102] the trustee would sell the assets and use the sale proceeds first to pay the costs of the sale and the trustee's own fees. If the costs of sale and the trustee's fees were $5,000,[103] that would leave $35,000 to be divided equally among the ten creditors ($3,500 each).

However, if one of the creditors had a lien on assets of the debtor worth $10,000 or more (*i.e.*, was fully secured), that creditor would be paid in full (either through a distribution by the trustee or by retaining the lien and then extracting value from the collateral using whatever collection rights the creditor has outside of bankruptcy). The remaining nine creditors would share in an estate now worth only $25,000 ($40,000 – $10,000 to lien creditor – $5,000 to trustee), receiving only about $2,775 each. In short, secured creditors feast first on the estate's buffet of assets, leaving the unsecured creditors to nibble on whatever crumbs remain afterwards.

In reorganization cases under Chapters 11 and 13, the result is pretty much the same. To confirm a reorganization plan, each creditor with a valid lien must receive at least the value of its lien unless it agrees otherwise.[104]

---

[101] *See* 11 U.S.C. § 524(a).

[102] 11 U.S.C. § 507.

[103] *See* 11 U.S.C. § 326(a).

[104] 11 U.S.C. §§ 1129(a)(7), (b)(2)(A), 1325(a)(5).

Another way in which secured creditors are preferred in bankruptcy is that they may be able to circumvent the automatic stay, and thereby get paid sooner. A party with an interest in property of the estate or of the debtor may move for relief from the automatic stay by making a motion in the bankruptcy court and proving either that its interest in property is not adequately protected or that the debtor has no equity in the property and the property is not necessary for an effective reorganization.[105] If relief from the stay is granted, that party may then use whatever collection rights it otherwise has against the property concerned.

Creditors with liens, however, have to be wary about the ability of the trustee to avoid the lien, effectively moving the creditor from the favored position of a secured creditor to the lesser position of an unsecured creditor. Lien avoidance can be based upon the failure of the secured creditor to take the appropriate steps to perfect its lien,[106] creating a lien in a manner that gives the creditor an avoidable preference,[107] or creating a lien that results in a fraudulent transfer to the creditor.[108]

Constitutional considerations. Just as debtors are endowed with some constitutional protections against creditors using the judicial debt-collection process, creditors with liens are also entitled to some constitutional protections of their own. Such protections are found in the clause prohibiting states from impairing the obligation of contract[109] and in the prohibition on government taking of property without just compensation.[110]

During the Great Depression of the 1930s, states enacted debtor-relief legislation in the form of moratoria on foreclosure, cancellations of contracts for deed, extensions of the statutory periods of redemption, and prohibitions on deficiency judgments.[111] Some of this legislation applied to contracts already in existence at the time of enactment as well as to contracts entered into afterward. The retroactive nature of the statutes' application to contracts entered into prior to

---

105 11 U.S.C. § 362(d).

106 11 U.S.C. § 544.

107 11 U.S.C. § 547.

108 11 U.S.C. § 548.

109 U.S. Const. art. I, § 10, cl. 1.

110 U.S. Const. 5th Amend.

111 For a description of such statutes, *see* J. Douglass Poteat, *State Legislative Relief for the Mortgage Debtor During the Depression*, 5 LAW & CONTEM. PROB. 517 (1938).

enactment raised significant concerns under the U.S. Constitution's prohibition of the impairment of the obligation of contract.

In evaluating whether a state statute impairs the obligation of contract, the analysis is three-fold. First, does the state law operate as a substantial impairment of the contract obligation? Second, if so, is the state law designed to promote a significant and legitimate public purpose? Third, is the law narrowly tailored to accomplish that purpose? If so, then the statute might be found to be a permissible change to the obligation of contract.[112] An example of this analysis appears in *Home Building & Loan Assoc. v. Blaisdell,*[113] upholding the extension of the statutory redemption period following a mortgage foreclosure sale.

If a state or federal statute enacted after the creditor has obtained its lien rights in the debtor's property eliminates or severely compromises those lien rights, the prohibition on taking of property without just compensation under the Fifth Amendment to the U.S. Constitution may also be implicated.[114]

SECTION 5. THE CREDITOR AND DEBTOR STRUGGLE

As you consider the material that you have read thus far and the material in the chapters that follow, think about the following. Essential to the functioning of a credit-based economy is the idea that obligations to pay can be enforced in some manner. The enforcement mechanisms should balance the need of the creditor to collect lawful obligations with the need of the debtor to remain a productive member of society. They should include restrictions on collection to ensure that creditors do not extract from the debtor or the debtor's property more than they are entitled to collect. They should also deal with the problem of debtors who incur more obligations than they have the ability to pay. This includes not only how to treat such debtors, but how to allocate available assets among a debtor's creditors. All of this requires careful consideration of a whole host of competing social policies and equitable principles, lest the balance of power between debtors and

---

[112] 2 RONALD D. ROTUNDA & JOHN E. NOWAK, TREATISE ON CONSTITUTIONAL LAW § 15.8 (3d ed. 1999 & Supp. 2005).

[113] 290 U.S. 398 (1934).

[114] *See* United States v. Security Indus. Bank, 459 U.S. 70 (1982). For much the same reason, the state and federal statutes that provide for a criminal to forfeit the instrumentalities of the crime typically have a defense for an innocent owner and permit a lienor to qualify as an owner. *See, e.g.*, 18 U.S.C. § 983(d).

their creditors or among creditors of the same debtor tip too far in one direction. Currently, this balancing act is performed by a hodgepodge of laws at both the state and federal levels. That may not make the most sense but it does make systematic change nearly impossible.

Problem 1-3

Any legal mechanism for collecting debts needs to balance several competing policies. That is probably all the more true with respect to the use of consensual liens, which can be created without judicial involvement and potentially enforced with minimal or no judicial or oversight. What policies should the law governing security interests – *i.e.*, the law governing consensual liens on personal property – seek to promote?

Comparison of Various Liens

		Type of Property	Governing Law	Possessor of Property
Consensual Liens	**Security Interest**	tangible & intangible personal property	U.C.C. 9 (mostly)	typically the debtor, but could be anyone
	Mortgage or Deed of Trust	real property	state real estate law	typically the debtor, but could be a lessee
Judicial Liens	**Judgment Lien**	real property	state statutes or the common law	typically the debtor, but could be a lessee
	Execution Lien	tangible personal and real property	state statutes or the common law	the sheriff or marshal
	Attachment Lien	tangible personal and real property	state statutes or the common law	the sheriff or marshal
	Garnishment	personal property	federal and state statutes	a third party
Statutory Liens	**Tax Lien**	all property	federal or state statute	anyone (for income tax); owner (for property tax)
	Mechanic's Lien	property improved by the mechanic	state statutes or the common law	the mechanic (unless real property is involved)
	Landlord's Lien	tangible personal property on premises	state statute or the common law	the landlord
	Attorney's Lien	monetary recovery	state statute or the common law	the lawyer

Chapter Two
Attachment of a Security Interest

SECTION 1. INTRODUCTION TO THE UNIFORM COMMERCIAL CODE

The Illinois Commercial Code, as enacted by the Illinois state legislature, is law. The Washington and Minnesota Commercial Codes are also law. The Uniform Commercial Code (UCC), however, is not law. The UCC is merely a model for states to enact or not as they please. It is the joint product of the Uniform Law Commission (ULC), a quasi-public organization comprised of representatives from each state and territory chosen by elected officials, and the American Law Institute (ALI), a private organization of lawyers, judges, and law professors to which one must be invited to become a member. Once those organizations finalize some portion of the UCC, each state must decide for itself whether to enact it, with or without any variation from the proposed text. In fact, the enacted version of the UCC in any many states contain numerous variations from the uniform text.

The UCC's origins date back to the 1940s. At that time, the existing uniform laws had become outdated in two ways. First, changes had occurred in the ways in which commercial activity was conducted and some of the new practices gave rise to new and different legal needs. Second, even for the most widely enacted of the uniform acts, uniformity was lacking because state legislatures and courts had added their own distinctive amendments and glosses.

It took the sponsoring organizations many years to complete their work and many more to obtain widespread enactment. However, by 1968 every state except Louisiana had enacted the UCC (by 1988, Louisiana adopted all of the UCC except Articles 2, 2A, and 6). To keep the law working smoothly, the sponsors established a Permanent Editorial Board (PEB) to periodically study and propose minor amendments to the UCC and to clarify the law on discrete issues. To date, the PEB has issued about 30 commentaries and reports that purport to answer particular interpretive problems about the UCC.

In addition to the minor clarifications made and changes proposed by the PEB, the sponsoring organizations have, over the years, significantly revised each of the original Articles of the UCC and drafted several new Articles. What follows is a short description of each article and the most recent revisions to it.

As that description shows, each article governs one aspect of commercial law or one component of a commercial transaction. While some transactions fall under only one article of the UCC, other transactions are governed simultaneously by two or more articles. Accordingly, the UCC contains provisions to deal with the possibility that a rule in one article might conflict with a rule in another article. *See, e.g.*, §§ 2-102, 3-102, 4-102, 8-103, 9-109, 9-110, 9-203, 9-331.[1]

Each section of the UCC is followed by official comments prepared by the chair and reporters of the drafting committee that wrote or revised that article. Even though the comments are not enacted into law, to fully understand any section, one must thoroughly read the official comments.

Article 1: General Provisions. Article 1 is a repository of general rules and definitions applicable to a transaction governed by one or more of the other articles. Article 1 was revised in 2001. All fifty states, the District of Columbia, and the U.S. Virgin Islands have enacted revised Article 1. In 2003, a few amendments were made to Article 1 as part of a revision of Article 7. Further amendments were made in 2022 in connection with a project to update the UCC to address emerging technologies.

Article 2: Sales. Article 2 applies to "transactions in goods" but is largely limited to *sales* of goods. Its major innovations were the de-emphasis of title in resolving controversies and several novel provisions on the formation of sales contracts. Article 2 has been a major force in the modernization of the common law of contract, in particular the shift from a subjective to objective theory of contract, as now reflected in the Restatement (Second) of Contracts. Amendments to Article 2 were proposed in 2003 but withdrawn in 2011. In 2003, a few amendments were made to Article 2 as part of the revision of Article 7. Some additional amendments, including to the scope of Article 2, were made in 2022. Every state other than Louisiana has enacted Article 2.

Article 2A: Leases. Article 2A was promulgated in 1987 to deal with leases of goods, a type of business transaction that had existed for a long time but which was increasing substantially, both in numbers and in dollar amounts. Many of Article 2A's rules were derived from and are similar to provisions of Article 2, but others, specifically the rules on damages, are tailored to the differences between a lease and a sale. Article 2A was amended slightly in 1990. In 2003, a few

---

1 From this point forward, citations to provisions of the Uniform Commercial Code will not be preceded by "U.C.C." unless necessary to prevent confusion.

amendments were made to Article 2A as part of the revision of Article 7. In 2010, a conforming amendment was made to Article 2A in connection with a revision of Article 9. Some additional amendments, including to the scope of Article 2A, were made in 2022. Every state other than Louisiana has enacted Article 2A.

Article 3: Negotiable Instruments. Article 3 deals with negotiable instruments, such as checks and promissory notes, by detailing the rights and liabilities of the parties who draft, acquire, or transfer them. Article 3 was revised in 1990 and that revision has been enacted in every state but New York. A few amendments were made in 2002 and those amendments have so far been adopted by eleven states and the District of Columbia. Further amendments were made in 2022.

Article 4: Bank Deposits and Collections. Article 4 governs bank deposits and collections. It provides rules on how items, such as checks, clear through the banking system. Article 4 was revised in 1990 and every state except New York has enacted Article 4 as revised (New York has the pre-revision version). A few additional amendments were made in 2002 and those amendments have been adopted by eleven states and the District of Columbia. A limited number of amendments were made to Article 4 in 2003, as part of the revision of Article 7, and in 2022.

Article 4A: Funds Transfers. Article 4A was added in 1989 and covers electronic funds transfers, a mechanism for making payment through the banking system that did not exist when Articles 3 and 4 were originally drafted. The volume of payments transferred in this manner exceeds $1 trillion per day, and Article 4A provides the procedural rules, along with rules allocating risks and liability, to ensure that such transfers can continue with a high degree of certainty of risk allocation at a relatively low cost. Article 4A has been adopted in all states. In 2012 a limited amendment was made to Article 4A to deal with the interface with federal consumer law regarding electronic funds transfer. That amendment has been adopted in 41 states and the District of Columbia. Article 4A was also amended slightly in 2022.

Article 5: Letters of Credit. Article 5 governs letters of credit, a commercial device that in most states had been governed almost entirely by common law. In a typical letter of credit transaction, a bank, at the request of an applicant (such as a buyer of goods or a tenant), issues to a beneficiary (such as a seller of goods or a landlord) a "letter" promising that the bank will, under certain conditions, honor drafts drawn by the beneficiary. Letters of credit are often issued in connection with a sale of goods – particularly an international sale of goods – to facilitate payment of the purchase price to the seller. A letter of credit might also be used in other transactions as an assurance of payment, in which case the letter is often referred to as a "standby" letter of credit. A letter of credit is similar to a guaranty but the issuing bank is primarily liable on a letter of credit, not secondarily liable. Article 5 was revised in 1995 and every state, the District of Columbia, and the U.S. Virgin Islands have enacted those revisions. In 2003, a few amendments were made to Article 5 as part of the revision of Article 7. The 2022 UCC Amendments also made some slight changes to Article 5.

Article 6: Bulk Transfers. Article 6 deals with bulk transfers. It is designed to protect the creditors of a business which sells all or virtually all of its inventory in a single transaction, something a business might do shortly before ceasing operations. In 1989, the ULC and ALI recommended that Article 6 be either repealed or revised. To date, 48 states have repealed Article 6. California and the District of Columbia have enacted the alternative, revised version. Maryland has retained the pre-1989 version.

Article 7: Documents of Title. Article 7 deals with documents of title, such as warehouse receipts and bills of lading, issued by a bailee of goods. It provides rules on the transfer of the documents of title, the rights arising out of documents of title, and the liabilities of a bailee of goods. Article 7 was revised in 2003 and 49 states (all but Vermont) and the District of Columbia have enacted the revision. Some additional changes were made to Article 7 in 2022 in connection with the project to update the UCC to address emerging technologies.

Article 8: Investment Securities. Article 8 defines the rights and liabilities of issuers, transferors, and transferees of investment securities (*e.g.*, stocks and bonds), as well as the rights and obligations of intermediaries, such as stock brokers. Article 8 does not address the disclosure requirements and other regulatory rules contained in federal and state laws governing the issuance and public offering of securities. It is instead concerned with the contractual relationship between and among those who buy, sell, and hold securities. Article 8 was revised in 1978 and again in 1994. The 1994 revision has been enacted in all states, the District of Columbia, and the U.S. Virgin Islands. In 2003, a small amendment was made to Article 8 as part of the revision of Article 7. In 2010, a conforming amendment was made to Article 8 in connection with a revision of Article 9. Additional amendments were made in 2022.

Article 9: Secured Transactions. Article 9, which deals principally with the use of personal property as collateral for an obligation, was the most novel component of the UCC when the UCC was first developed. Article 9 provided a single, unified, and inexpensive structure within which the immense variety of secured financing transactions involving personal property could occur. Article 9 was revised in 1972, in 1977, and again in 1999. The 1999 revision has been enacted in all states, the District of Columbia, Puerto Rico, and the U.S. Virgin Islands. In 2003, a few amendments were made to Article 9 as part of the revision of Article 7. In 2010, some modest amendments to Article 9 were promulgated. All 50 states, the District of Columbia, and Puerto Rico enacted those amendments. In 2018, a new subsection was added to each of two sections of Article 9.[2] Then, in 2022, substantial amendments were made to Article 9 in connection with the project to update the UCC to address emerging technologies.

Article 12: Controllable Electronic Records. The 2022 UCC Amendments to the UCC created a new Article 12 to address the rights in and transfer of "controllable electronic records," a term that encompasses cryptocurrencies and non-fungible tokens.[3]

The UCC is far from comprehensive. As we already saw in Chapter One, many federal laws – such as the Fair Debt Collection Practices Act, the Fair Credit Reporting Act, and the Bankruptcy Code – govern aspects of commercial activity. Even with respect to state law, the UCC is only one piece in a much larger legal puzzle. Much of the common law survives enactment of the UCC and supplements its provisions.[4] In other words, the UCC is built upon an edifice of common law, in particular the common law of contracts and property, and one must be careful not to overlook that underlying structure.

---

[2] Prior to the 2022 UCC Amendments, only Florida had enacted these provisions but several states had previously enacted similar rules as a non-uniform variation on the official text of Article 9. Additional states are adopting these two subsections when enacting the amendments. *See infra* p. 122.

[3] Articles 10 and 11 contained transition rules for earlier amendments. They are no longer relevant and have been removed from the official text of the UCC. The transition rules for the 2022 UCC Amendments were put in a new Article A, so as to avoid additional skips in the numbering of substantive Articles.

[4] *See* § 1-103(b) (referencing such doctrines as mistake, fraud, and estoppel).

Beyond this, there is a whole host of federal and state statutes that either supplement or supersede UCC provisions.[5] Most of these are fairly common rules, such as usury laws, so-called "lemon laws," and other consumer protection statutes.[6] A few deal with specific types of transactions that, although otherwise seemingly within the scope of the UCC, are expressly exempted from it.[7] Others are less common rules that might exist in only one or two jurisdictions, and for which careful lawyers must always be on the lookout.[8]

---

5 *See, e.g.*, §§ 2-102, 9-201 (referring to possible examples).

6 *E.g.*, Kan. Stat. §§ 16a-5-109 – 16a-5-112 (providing consumers with a right to cure certain defaults and restricting the repossession of goods from a dwelling; derived from the Uniform Consumer Credit Code); Va. Code § 59.1-21.3 (giving consumers a brief time to rescind certain transactions involving an in-home sales visit); *see also* 16 C.F.R. § 429.1 (providing a similar rule for door-to-door sales of consumer goods and services).

7 *See infra* note 122.

8 *See, e.g.*, Cal. Civ. Code § 1812.600 *et seq.* (requiring all auctioneers – apparently even secured parties selling their collateral at a public sale – to have a license and post a bond or be guilty of a misdemeanor); N.Y. Gen. Oblig. Law § 5-327 (providing that if a consumer contract provides that the creditor, seller, or lessor may recover attorney's fees if the consumer breaches any contractual obligation, then the consumer must be entitled to attorney's fees incurred as the result of a breach by the creditor, seller or lessor); Cal. Civ. Code § 1717(a) (doing the same but not limited to consumer transactions); Idaho Code § 12-120(3) (entitling prevailing party in action to collect on a negotiable instrument or relating to a sale of goods to reasonable attorney's fees); Ga. Code § 10-1-10 (providing that the secured party in a retail installment contract must give the defaulting buyer notice of its intention to pursue a deficiency and the option to elect a public sale); Ga. Code § 10-1-36 (doing the same for foreclosures of some security interests in a motor vehicle); Ga. Code § 10-1-8(a) (prohibiting security interests in a consumer's "clothing, softwares and other nondurable items"); Consolidated Aluminum Corp. v. Krieger, 710 S.W.2d 869 (Ky. Ct. App. 1986) (applying to a transaction, otherwise governed by UCC Article 2, a statute that invalidates contract clauses printed below the signature line unless referenced above the signature line); Mass. Gen. Laws ch. 255 § 13*I*(a) (prohibiting repossession of the collateral in a consumer credit transaction if the default consists of anything other than a material failure to make one or more required payments); Mass. Gen. Laws ch. 255 § 13J(d) (prohibiting a deficiency judgment in a consumer credit transaction if the unpaid balance is $2,000 or less).

SECTION 2. CREATING A SECURITY INTEREST: THE BASICS

A. The Big Picture

As should be evident from Chapter One, it is far better to be a creditor with a lien than a creditor without one. For several reasons, it is also often better to have a consensual lien than a nonconsensual lien, such as a judgment lien, an execution lien, or a statutory lien. First, consensual liens are generally not subject to a debtor's claim that the property is exempt from execution. Second, as we will see in Chapter Three, collecting on a consensual lien is often easier than the process for obtaining and executing on a judgment that we reviewed in Chapter One. Third, as we will see in this Chapter and in Chapter Five, a consensual lien is more likely to follow the collateral as it transmutes from one form to another, and often allows the lienholder to maintain its priority in the collateral even with respect to future extensions of credit.

So, what then is a consensual lien and how does a creditor acquire one? First, a note of limitation. Consensual liens on real property – usually called "mortgages" – are governed by real property law, which is not the subject of much uniform legislation and varies significantly from state to state. Mortgages are not governed by Article 9. *See* § 9-109(d)(11). Mortgages and the law governing them are typically covered in other law school courses, such as Property and Real Estate Transactions. Consequently, they are not discussed in this book, except occasionally to provide comparison and counterpoint to the discussion of consensual liens on personal property. In short, this book is about the creation, enforcement, and priority of consensual liens on *personal property*, not real property. Such a lien is called a "security interest," a term defined in § 1-201(b)(35) to mean, in part, "an interest in personal property or fixtures which secures payment or performance of an obligation."

Article 9 provides the dominant rules on how to create a security interest. However, it is not totally comprehensive. There are some types of transactions that create a security interest in personal property but which are not governed by Article 9. *See* § 9-109(d)(3), (8), (9), (12), (13).[9] This does not mean that the property

---

[9] The exclusion of security interests in an employee's right to wages, salary, or other compensation can be problematic when the employee is a professional athlete, celebrity, or other highly paid individual who wants to borrow against future earnings. The law outside Article 9 might make it extremely difficult to encumber such rights to payment. *See* In re Johnson, 554 B.R. 448 (Bankr. S.D. Ohio 2016), *aff'd*, 2017 WL 2399453 (6th Cir. BAP 2017); 16 C.F.R. § 444.2(a)(3).

involved in such transactions cannot be used as security for an obligation; it means merely that the law governing such liens is found elsewhere.

In addition, state laws outside Article 9 might prohibit the creation of a security interest in particular situations. For example:

- Kansas prohibits the creation of more than one security interest in a motor vehicle weighing 26,000 pounds or less.[10] Any attempt to create a second security interest in such a vehicle is void.
- New York apparently prohibits an art merchant to whom an artist consigns a work of art from obtaining a security interest in the art.[11]
- North Carolina prohibits a creditor from taking a security interest to secure certain extensions of credit if the interest rate exceeds 1.25% per month.[12]
- Washington prohibits the creation of a security interest in a "live dog or cat."[13]

Article 9, as enacted by the individual states, is part of the domestic law in the United States. When security interests are created in the international arena, Article 9 will apply only if applicable choice of law principles result in its application to the transaction. For certain types of collateral, there have been conventions promulgated through the United Nations process which might apply to the transaction. Some examples are the United Nations Convention on the Assignment of Receivables in International Trade and the UNIDROIT Convention on International Interests in Mobile Equipment. To determine what international conventions apply to a transaction and which countries are bound by a convention, consult www.unidroit.org or www.uncitral.org.

[10] Kan. Stat. § 8-135(6).

[11] *See* N.Y. Arts and Cultural Affairs Law § 12.01(a)(v) (McKinney's); Khaldei v. Kaspiev, 135 F. Supp. 3d 70 (S.D.N.Y. 2015).

[12] N.C. Gen. Stat. § 24-11(c). *See also* In re Worley, 2008 WL 2433195 (Bankr. D.N.C. 2008) (concluding that a creditor's efforts to take a security interest in violation of this statute constitutes an unfair and deceptive trade practice, entitling the debtor to recovery of attorney's fees incurred in seeking to avoid the lien).

[13] *See* Wash. Rev. Code §§ 31.04.430; 63.14.127; 63.10.070; 62A.9A-109(d)(15).

Several other states also restrict or prohibit transactions involving the financing of animals customarily used as pets. *See* Cal. Civ. Code § 1670.10 (declaring void as against public policy: (i) transactions in which the transfer of ownership of a dog or cat is contingent upon making payment after possession is transferred, and (ii) leases of a dog or cat); Conn. Stat. § 22-354a (substantially the same); N.J. Stat. § 56:8-211 (making unlawful a contract for a cat or dog in which the transfer of ownership is contingent on making payment after the transfer of possession); N.Y. Gen. Bus. Law § 753-e (banning contracts for the purchase of

- Minnesota treats a security interest in otherwise exempt household goods as void unless the security interest is created in connection with the transaction in which the debtor acquired the goods.[14]
- Maryland prohibits a lender from taking a security interest in personal property for any loan under $1,400, and any attempt to do so is void.[15]
- California requires that a specified notification be provided to an individual who co-signs a consumer credit contract for someone other than a spouse.[16] If the required notification is not provided, neither the obligation nor any security interest securing the obligation can be enforced against the co-signer.[17]

As this list suggests, statutes such as these tend to be highly idiosyncratic and lawyers must be on a constant lookout for them. There are, however, some more widespread restrictions. In most states, for example, the rules of professional responsibility require a lawyer who desires to obtain a security interest in personal property of a client (other than a claim that the lawyer is handling for the client or the proceeds of that claim) to disclose the transaction in understandable terms and advise the client in writing of the desirability of seeking independent legal counsel. A lawyer that fails to comply with these rules risks disciplinary action.[18] The Military Lending Act invalidates certain high-interest transactions with a member of the armed forces or a dependent of such a member.[19]

---

a dog or cat that "authorize the use of a dog or a cat as security where such dog or cat may be repossessed" upon nonpayment). *See also* Ind. Stat. § 24-4.5-2-407.5 (banning the leasing of live domestic animals); Mass. Stat. ch. 272 § 801(b) (banning the leasing of dogs); Nev. Rev. Stat. § 597.997(1) (prohibiting the leasing of any living animal intended for personal, family or household use if the animal is expected to have no more than a de minimis value at the end of the lease term).

[14] *See* Minn. Stat. § 550.37(4).

[15] *See* Md. Code, Com. Law § 12-311(c).

[16] Cal. Civil Code § 1799.91(a).

[17] Cal. Civil Code § 1799.95. Although this rule is phrased as a limitation on enforcement, it also constitutes a limitation on attachment.

[18] *See, e.g.*, In re Malone, 518 P.3d 406 (Kan. 2022); The Florida Bar v. Parrish, 241 So. 3d 66 (Fla. 2018).

[19] *See* 10 U.S.C. § 987; Cox v. Community Loans of Am., Inc., 2012 WL 773496 (M.D. Ga. 2012) (car title pawn transactions with members of the armed services were not sales with an option to repurchase but secured loan transactions that are void under the Military

Assuming that UCC Article 9 applies to the transaction and that no other law imposes additional requirements,[20] § 9-203 tells how to create the security interest so that it is enforceable against the debtor. This process is called "attachment" of the security interest. It might be helpful to think of it as a giant, invisible hand (the lien) grabbing (attaching to) particular pieces of the debtor's property (the collateral) to secure obligations owed to the creditor. The rules governing attachment of a security interest to personal property are in Article 9, Part 2. We will study the rules on attachment and on the scope of Article 9 in this Chapter.

Lending Act).

[20] The federal Truth in Lending Act and the regulations promulgated thereunder prohibit the issuer of a credit card from offsetting a cardholder's indebtedness arising from a consumer credit transaction against funds of the cardholder held on deposit with the issuer. 12 C.F.R. § 226.12(d)(1). This does not prohibit the issuer from obtaining or enforcing a consensual security interest in the deposits, 12 C.F.R. § 226.12(d)(2), but the Official Staff Interpretation to this rule states that, for a security interest to qualify for this exception:

> The consumer must be aware that granting a security interest is a condition for the credit card account (or for more favorable account terms) and must specifically intend to grant a security interest in a deposit account. Indicia of the consumer's awareness and intent include at least one of the following (or a substantially similar procedure that evidences the consumer's awareness and intent):
>
> A. Separate signature or initials on the agreement indicating that a security interest is being given.
>
> B. Placement of the security agreement on a separate page, or otherwise separating the security interest provisions from other contract and disclosure provisions.
>
> C. Reference to a specific amount of deposited funds or to a specific deposit account number.

Official Staff Commentary on Regulation Z, F.R.R.S. 6-1170.7. In a thoughtful opinion applying this interpretation, one court ruled that a credit union's setoff of a customer's deposit account was not authorized because the language in the credit card agreement purporting to grant the credit union a security interest was not separately signed and did not reference a specific amount of deposited funds or a specific deposit account number. Although the court concluded that placement of relevant language of the agreement in a box with bolded text was "minimally sufficient" to separate it from the other text of the agreement, despite its location among 26 numbered paragraphs of similar size, the court ruled that compliance with one of the three indicia "is necessary but not sufficient to establish that the security interest was affirmatively agreed to." Martino v. American Airlines Credit Union, 121 F. Supp. 3d 277, 287 (D. Mass. 2015). It then held that the agreement's language and the cardholder's subsequent use of the credit card were insufficient to create a consensual security interest under both TILA and a similar Massachusetts statute.

Once a security interest attaches to collateral, the creditor may enforce the security interest against that collateral. Of course, a secured creditor would prefer that the debtor just repay the obligation owed, but if the debtor defaults, the creditor may use one or more of the Article 9 enforcement processes to collect. All of those processes involve ways to extract value out of the collateral and are governed by the rules in Part 6 of Article 9. In contrast to the judgment execution process studied in Chapter One, the Article 9 enforcement process does not require court involvement. We will study the rules on enforcement of security interests in Chapter Three.

If the debtor and creditor were the only two people who ever had an interest in the collateral, the rest of Article 9 would be unnecessary. Unfortunately, that circumstance is often not the case; frequently one or more additional persons claims an interest in the collateral. The rest of Article 9 contains the rules governing perfection and priority of a security interest; that is, how the secured party's rights in the collateral stack up against the rights of persons, other than the debtor, claiming an interest in the collateral. Perfection refers to the step a creditor must take to give public notice of its security interest.

Why is public notice generally needed to perfect a security interest? The answer is a bit complicated and requires a slight digression. Imagine that a classmate granted you a security interest in something the classmate owns – a painting – to secure a loan you made to the classmate. Who's the owner of the painting? Well, "owner" is a term more for laypeople than lawyers. You might have heard the metaphor that ownership is a bundle of sticks, with each stick representing a different right. So, when we ask who the owner is, we really are asking who has ownership rights. Now, as between you and your classmate, who has ownership rights? The answer, of course, is that you both do. In short, whenever a security interest exists, there are at least two "owners" of rights in the collateral.

Of course, ownership rights are themselves invisible. To the extent someone else (an interested buyer perhaps) needs to determine who is the owner of a particular item of personal property, that determination is often based on possession. Yet when multiple parties have ownership rights, only one of them will have possession at any given time, and thus appear to the world to be the full owner. In short, whenever personal property is used as collateral, there is something of an ostensible ownership problem: one party appears to have full rights when in reality some other entity has some of them.

This creates a potential problem. If the debtor – your classmate in our example – remains in possession of the collateral, what is to stop the classmate from selling it

– or granting another lien on it – to an innocent third party? How is that third party to know of your lien? One possible solution is to say that the third party need not worry; that a subsequent buyer or lienor will take free of your rights. However, that would mean that your rights as the first lienholder are effectively subject to forfeiture for reasons beyond your control and the assurance of repayment that the collateral was meant to provide would be lost.

A second possible solution is to say *caveat emptor*: buyer beware. First in time is first in right. Your classmate cannot sell or pledge the property free of your lien. That indeed would be consistent with much of property law generally. However, there would still be a problem with certainty: instead of you, as the first lienor, having to worry about losing your lien, or at least losing its priority, the second lienor would have to worry that either: (i) its lien was never created, because your classmate who agreed to grant the lien did not have all the rights in the property and you did not join in the conveyance; or (ii) if the second lienor did acquire a lien, the second lienor's rights do not have priority over your rights. In other words, the second lienor would bear the risk of its inability to determine, before giving value in reliance on the collateral, that there might be a preexisting lien with superior rights in the property.[21]

So why not simply base priority on possession? If a lienor wants to ensure that no subsequent buyer or lienor will take free of its ownership rights, make the lienor take possession. The problem with that solution is that people often want to separate ownership from possession for perfectly legitimate commercial or personal reasons. Specifically, when creditors want to acquire rights in property to ensure repayment of the debt due them, they generally do not want possession of the property. They might have no expertise about what to do with it. They certainly do not want the responsibility for or the expense of caring for it. And if the debtor needs to use the property to generate income to pay off the debt (as might be the case with respect to manufacturing equipment), possession by the secured party would undermine the debtor's business and the prospect for repayment. Finally, some types of personal property are wholly intangible. For such property, a solution to the ostensible ownership problem cannot be based on possession because no one has possession.

Much of Article 9 is designed to deal with this problem: the apparently "secret" ownership rights of a secured party and the resulting need to provide notice of that

---

[21] You, as the first lienor, would also have this risk. In other words, there might be a "zeroth" lienor: someone who acquired a consensual lien before you did.

lien to persons interested in buying or taking another security interest in the property. Article 9's principal response to this problem is through the creation of recording systems for personal property. These recording systems provide a supplement to the information that possession alone provides. The dominant recording system under Article 9 involves filing in the appropriate state office something called a "financing statement," a short document that identifies the debtor, the creditor, and the collateral. This discussion of recording systems might strike a familiar chord; it might remind you of the system used to document ownership interests in real estate. Unfortunately, the methods used to provide the notice of a security interest in personal property – *i.e.*, the way to perfect – is necessarily much more complicated than that used for real property. This is because real property differs from personal property in at least two important respects:

First, real property never moves. You can remove underground ore or oil. You can even remove soil or timber. But the land stays where it is. In contrast, many other kinds of personal property move or, worse, are entirely intangible. Consequently, a recording system organized by property location will not work for many types of personal property.

Second, real property never stops being real property. In contrast, many kinds of personal property are in a constant state of transmutation. For example, inventory might be sold, the proceeds deposited in a bank account, and the funds later withdrawn to buy equipment. If the security interest is to follow the property through such transformations – and you should readily see why the secured party would want that – a recording system based solely on the type of property will not work.

There are other reasons why Article 9's filing systems will be more varied and more complicated than any of the real estate recording systems used in this country. For now, though, it is enough to understand two basic points. First, that attachment is the time when the security interest becomes enforceable against the debtor; perfection is the time when it becomes enforceable against most of the rest of the world, and it requires attachment plus, in most cases, some form of notice of the secured party's interest.[22] *See* § 9-308. Second, Part 3 of Article 9 prescribes at least one method of perfecting a security interest in each of the different types of

---

[22] *Cf.* Jonathan C. Lipson, *Secrets and Liens: The End of Notice in Commercial Finance Law*, 21 EMORY BANKR. DEV. J. 421, 517 (2005) (arguing that revised Article 9 violates this concept of public notice in numerous contexts).

personal property to which Article 9 applies.[23] We will study the details of the perfection process in Chapter Four.

As you might now suspect from this discussion of perfection, whether the security interest is perfected and the method of its perfection will have significant impact on the priority of the security interest as against other claims to the collateral. Recall that priority is the hierarchy of competing claims – other than the debtor's – to the collateral. Priority might also depend on a variety of other things, such as the type of property involved, who the competing party is (*e.g.*, a buyer, judicial lien creditor, or another secured party), and which interest arose first. The priority rules are also found in Part 3 of Article 9. We will study the priority rules in Chapter Five.

Because Article 9 is part of the UCC, it was drafted to work harmoniously with the principles and rules of the other UCC articles. Sometimes those non-Article 9 rules must be consulted in analyzing the attachment, perfection, or priority of a security interest in collateral. This book will not provide an in-depth study of those other UCC articles but it is important to be aware of the general subject matter covered in the other UCC articles and to consider whether provisions from the other articles are relevant to the issues raised.

B. The Three Requirements for Attachment of a Security Interest

We now begin our in-depth study of UCC Article 9. We start with the requirements for creating an enforceable consensual lien on personal property to secure performance of an obligation. In other words, we start with the process for attachment of a security interest. Read § 9-203(a) and (b),[24] together with the official comments to the section.[25]

---

[23] Note that filing a financing statement is not the only way to perfect a security interest in personal property. *See* § 9-310.

[24] If Article 9 does not govern the type of transaction, § 9-203 does not prescribe the rule for attachment of the security interest. Subsections (c) and (d) of § 9-109 describe several types of transactions that are excluded from the scope of Article 9. If the transaction is excluded from Article 9, then other law determines whether and how a consensual lien might attach to property to secure a debt. We will consider those exclusions from Article 9 in Section 8, Part C of this Chapter.

[25] Remember to read the comments to all the noted statutory provisions. Sometimes the answer to the questions posed will be found in the comments.

What is a security interest? The first sentence of the definition in § 1-201(b)(35) defines it as an interest in personal property to secure payment or performance of an obligation. Now read § 9-109(a)(1). Article 9 applies to "a transaction . . . that creates a security interest in personal property or fixtures by contract," that is, a consensual lien on that type of property. Thus, a security interest is a property interest in personal property created through an agreement of the parties. Article 9 is based upon a basic principle of property, the right to alienate interests in property, and upon a basic principle of contract, the ability to enforce a bargain.[26]

Reread § 9-203(a) and (b). Section 9-203(a) provides that a security interest attaches "when it becomes enforceable against the debtor with respect to the collateral." Subsection (b) contains the three requirements for enforceability, commonly known as attachment of a security interest:

(1) There must be a security agreement that meets specified criteria;
(2) Value must be given; and
(3) The debtor must have rights in the collateral or the power to transfer rights in the collateral to the secured party.

These three requirements may be satisfied in any order, but attachment – and thus "enforceability" – will not occur until *all three* are met. Upon attachment, the consensual lien in the property (that is, the *in rem* liability of the collateral) arises.

The next three sections of this Chapter explore, in detail and in order, these requirements for attachment.

SECTION 3. THE SECURITY AGREEMENT REQUIREMENT

Reread § 9-203(b)(3). It provides four alternative methods for satisfying the requirement of a security agreement. The predominant method is contained in subparagraph (A). It has two principal requirements: (i) the debtor has signed a security agreement (prior to the 2022 UCC Amendments, Article 9 used the word "authenticate" rather than "sign;" the change was made to harmonize terminology throughout the UCC and there is no difference in meaning); and (ii) the security agreement provides a description of the collateral.

---

[26] Steven L. Harris and Charles W. Mooney, Jr., *A Property-Based Theory of Security Interests: Taking Debtors' Choices Seriously*, 80 VA. L. REV. 2021, 2047-52 (1994). *Cf.* Thomas W. Merrill and Henry E. Smith, *The Property/Contract Interface*, 101 COLUM. L. REV. 773 (2001).

STOP. Notice what we just did. We took the language of a statutory provision and broke it down into its component parts. Now break it down further. Who is the debtor? What does "signed" mean? What is a "security agreement"? How specific must a description of collateral be? This process of breaking down the statutory text is something you should do every time you approach a new section of the UCC or any other statute. Such parsing of the statutory text will allow you to form a checklist of the questions that need to be answered in determining whether or to what the text applies. We now explore the elements of § 9-203(b)(3)(A) in depth.

A. The Signature Requirement

"Sign," like many terms in Article 9, is defined, albeit in Article 1 rather than in Article 9. It means, with the present intent to authenticate or adopt a record, to execute or attach a tangible symbol or to attach or logically associate with a electronic symbol. *See* § 1-202(b)(37). The term "record" is also defined. It means information inscribed on a tangible medium or stored in an electronic format but nevertheless retrievable in a perceivable form. *See* § 1-201(b)(31). Collectively, this means that, for a security agreement to be signed, the agreement must either be in writing or stored in an electronic medium that is retrievable in a perceivable form. An purely oral agreement (*i.e.*, one that is not recorded) cannot be "signed."

This conclusion is supported by comment 3 to § 9-203, which likens paragraph (b)(3) to a statute of frauds. The principal function of a statute of frauds is to require that the essential terms of the parties' agreement be reflected in a signed writing or record; it does this by making the existence of such a writing a prerequisite to the enforceability of the agreement. Like most statutes of frauds, however, § 9-203 has exceptions to the signature requirement, and hence to the requirement of a writing or record: an oral security agreement will be effective if the secured party has possession or control of the collateral and the collateral consists of one or more specified types of property. *See* § 9-203(b)(3)(B), (C), (D). In each of these circumstances, the secured party's possession or control of the collateral provides objective evidence of the debtor's grant of a security interest in the collateral to the secured party. Evidencing a security agreement through the secured party's possession or control of the collateral is discussed further in Section 3, Part E of this Chapter.

Who is the "debtor" for the purposes of the signature requirement in § 9-203(b)(3)(A)? Read § 9-102(a)(28). How does the definition of debtor relate to the property rights basis of Article 9? Consider the following problem.

Problem 2-1

Barbara has worked out a deal to borrow $1,000 from Chris. Before agreeing to take on the role of creditor, Chris insisted on two assurances of repayment: (i) that George guaranty the obligation; and (ii) that a valuable painting owned by Olivia serve as collateral for the loan. If all the parties agree, what will be the appropriate Article 9 label or labels for each party in the transaction? Who must sign the security agreement? *See* § 9-102(a)(28), (59), (72), (73).

In the usual case, the creditor or the creditor's lawyer drafts the document containing the terms of the security agreement. Regardless of who does the drafting, however, a security agreement is subject to the general rules of contract law regarding validity and enforceability.[27] Those contract doctrines operate in addition to the requirements discussed above for creating an enforceable security interest. Thus, if a security agreement is executed under circumstances that would render an agreement avoidable due to fraud, duress, incapacity or other invalidating cause, those doctrines would be available to invalidate the security agreement. Similarly, a security agreement is subject to traditional principles of contract regarding the interpretation of agreements.[28] Therefore, each party to a security agreement should consider carefully what a draft agreement says and how a court might interpret it.

B. The Description of the Collateral

1. Collateral Classifications

To be effective to create a security interest, a signed security agreement must contain a description of the collateral. *See* § 9-203(b)(3)(A).[29] What makes a description of collateral sufficient? In answering this question, it is important to consider the functions that the collateral description serves. First and foremost, the description identifies the property that serves as security for the obligation owed to

---

[27] *See* § 1-103(b).

[28] In re Invenux, Inc., 298 B.R. 442 (Bankr. D. Colo. 2003).

[29] If § 9-203(b)(3)(B), (C), or (D) applies to the creation of the security interest, the requirement of a collateral description does not apply.

the secured party. In light of the function of a security agreement – to transfer rights to property – it makes sense that the agreement must identify the property involved. Second, the description of the collateral serves an evidentiary function, not only to allow the secured party to enforce the security interest against the debtor, but also to make the secured party's property interest generally enforceable against a third party that has or later acquires an interest in the collateral. *See* § 9-201(a). Indeed, much of Article 9 is about ensuring that a security interest granted to a secured party is effective, not merely against the debtor, but also against others who claim or acquire a lien on or other interest in the collateral. Without a collateral description in the security agreement, the debtor and secured party could collude to stymie other parties who might later seek to assert or enforce rights in the debtor's property.

The UCC itself provides some guidance on the sufficiency of a collateral description. Section 9-108(a) provides that a description is sufficient "whether or not it is specific, if it reasonably identifies what is described." Presumably this means that, at least in some situations, collateral may be described by genre or type, rather than through a detailed itemization or lengthy description. For example, "my 2020 Toyota RAV4" should be sufficient even without including the vehicle identification number (at least assuming the debtor did not own more than one 2020 RAV4, thereby giving the description a latent ambiguity). It might even be an adequate collateral description, despite the error, for a 2021 Toyota RAV4, again provided there was no real possibility for confusion because the debtor owned only one RAV4 at all relevant times.[30] Similarly, "all my office furniture" would seem to be sufficient, making it unnecessary to include a catalogue of each item.[31]

Still, the standard in § 9-108(a) is not particularly helpful. Fortunately, subsection (b) provides more guidance. It indicates a variety of descriptive methods that, as a matter of law, are reasonable, and therefore sufficient. Chief among these is paragraph (3), which provides that the description may be by a type of collateral defined in the UCC.

---

[30] *See* In re Snelson, 330 B.R. 643 (Bankr. E.D. Tenn. 2005) (a security agreement that accurately described the size, make, model, and VIN of a mobile home, but misstated the model year, was sufficient).

[31] *See* Baldwin v. Castro County Feeders I, Ltd., 678 N.W.2d 796 (S.D. 2004) (description of collateral as "livestock" sufficient for security interest to attach even though the agreement form contained an unfilled space for designating the feedlot number).

This is the first, but by no means the last, time that we will encounter Article 9's classifications of property. In fact, you might have already noticed that the rules in § 9-203(b)(3) include several references to various types of collateral. *See* § 9-203(b)(3)(B), (C), (D) (referring to "certificated securit[ies]," "controllable accounts," "controllable electronic records," "controllable payment intangibles," "deposit accounts," "electronic documents," "electronic money," "investment property," and "letter-of-credit rights"). Throughout Article 9 we will find rules dependent on the type of collateral: attachment rules, enforcement rules, perfection rules, priority rules, and even some choice-of-law rules.

The main reason why Article 9 has so many rules dependent on the type of collateral involved is that, for different collateral types, different industry practices have developed. These practices have created varying expectations concerning how to approach different issues, chiefly priority contests, but also methods of giving notice of the existence of a security interest and rules relating to the enforcement of a security interest. To accommodate these industry practices while still having a unitary system of law relating to security interests in personal property, different rules are necessary for different collateral types. Regardless of the reasons, however, the classifications appear so pervasively throughout Article 9 that mastery of them is one of the unavoidable challenges of learning Article 9 and contributes greatly to its complexity.

What are the collateral types identified and used in Article 9? Perhaps the best way to answer that question is to first organize the different Article 9 classifications into two broad categories: (i) tangible personal property; and (ii) intangible personal property.

Tangible personal property is property that has mass, and thus constitutes "goods." *See* § 9-102(a)(44). All goods must be one of the following, mutually exclusive sub-classifications:

Tangible Property (Goods)

consumer goods	§ 9-102(a)(23)
equipment	§ 9-102(a)(33)
farm products	§ 9-102(a)(34) or
inventory	§ 9-102(a)(48).

Regardless of which one of the above sub-classifications of goods applies, goods might also fall under one or more of the following defined terms:

accessions	§ 9-102(a)(1)
as-extracted collateral	§ 9-102(a)(6)
fixtures	§ 9-102(a)(41) or
manufactured homes	§ 9-102(a)(53).

In addition, goods might also constitute "crops," "livestock," or "timber," terms that are not defined but which nevertheless appear in Article 9.

The other broad category – intangible property – is not itself a term used in Article 9. It is merely a list of all non-goods: property that has no physical existence, except in some cases a writing. Intangible property includes the following eleven, mutually exclusive classifications of property used in Article 9:[32]

Intangible Property	
accounts	§ 9-102(a)(2)
chattel paper	§ 9-102(a)(11)
commercial tort claims	§ 9-102(a)(13)
deposit accounts	§ 9-102(a)(29)
documents (of title)	§§ 9-102(a)(30), 1-201(b)(16)
instruments	§ 9-102(a)(47)
investment property	§ 9-102(a)(49)
general intangibles	§ 9-102(a)(42)
letter-of-credit rights	§ 9-102(a)(51) and
letters of credit	§§ 5-102(a)(10), 9-102(b)
money	§ 1-201(b)(24)

Many of these classifications have subclassifications.

Accounts include controllable accounts, health-care-insurance receivables, and some as-extracted collateral, § 9-102(a)(6), (27A), (46).

Documents of title can be either electronic or tangible. § 1-201(b)(16). Each of those can in turn be negotiable or nonnegotiable, § 7-104.

General intangibles include three subcategories: controllable electronic records, payment intangibles, and software, §§ 9-102(a)(42), (61), (76), (b), 12-102(a)(1). It also includes some supporting obligations. Payment intangibles include controllable payment intangibles. § 9-102(a)(27B).

Instruments, like documents of title, can be either negotiable or nonnegotiable, § 3-104. The classification also includes checks and promissory notes. *See* §§ 3-104(f), 9-102(a)(65), (b).

---

32 Another classification of personal property used in Article 9 is "financial asset." *See* § 9-102(b) (adopting the definition in § 8-102(a)(9)). Because it is rare for anything other than investment property to constitute a "financial asset," and because the term can include any type of property, the term is not listed here as a separate classification.

Investment property consists of several sub-classifications: commodity accounts; commodity contracts; security accounts; securities; and security entitlements, §§ 9-102(a)(14), (15), (b), 8-102(a)(15), (17), 8-501(a).[33]

Money can be either electronic or tangible, § 9-102(a)(31A), (79A), although electronic money has not yet been created.

The following Diagram depicts the relationship of the various classifications and subclassifications of property, except for some subclassifications of goods.

Classifications of Property

Accounts: Controllable Accounts; Health Care Insurance Receivables; As-extracted Collateral	**Chattel Paper**	**Commercial Tort Claims**	**Deposit Accounts**
Goods: Inventory; Equipment; Farm Products; Consumer Goods	**General Intangibles**: Payment Intangibles; Controllable Payment Intangibles; Software; Controllable Electronic Records; Supporting Obligations	**Documents**: Negotiable Electronic Documents; Negotiable Tangible Documents; Non-negotiable Electronic Documents; Non-negotiable Tangible Documents	**Instruments**: Checks; Negotiable Instruments; Promissory Notes; Non-negotiable Instruments
Investment Property: Certificated Securities; Securities Accounts; Commodity Accounts; Uncertificated Securities; Security Entitlements; Commodity Contracts	**Letter of Credit Rights**	**Letters of Credit**	**Money**: Electronic Money; Tangible Money

There is no substitute for a thorough understanding of what each classification of collateral is. Some of the classifications – such as inventory – are likely to ring familiar yet be defined in a surprisingly broad way. For example, "inventory" includes things that are not and never will be held for sale or lease. *See* § 9-102(a)(48)(D). Accordingly, to understand the scope of each term, you must

[33] Those unfamiliar with these types of financial assets should read the Prefatory Note to UCC Article 8, particularly Parts I, II, and III.A.

carefully read the statutory definitions and the accompanying comments. In doing so, bear in mind that, because Article 9's rules are premised on how prevailing commercial practices vary for the different classifications of property, the terms and their definitions are, at heart, designed to be functional and to draw distinctions based upon realities of commercial finance.

Problem 2-2

Below is a Venn diagram showing the relationship of the terms Goods, Consumer Goods, Equipment, Farm Products, and Inventory.

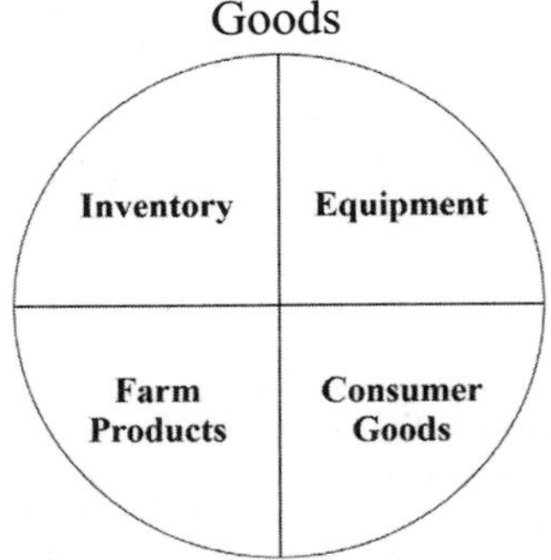

Add to the diagram the following additional subclassifications: (i) Crops; (ii) Fixtures; and (iii) Timber to Be Cut.

Three notes of caution are in order with respect to the UCC's classifications of collateral. First, in applying the statutory provisions of Article 9 itself, an item of property must be classified using the definitions in the UCC. That means that the parties' agreement to label a particular item of property differently does not control the collateral's true classification For example, if the issue is whether an asset is an "instrument" for the purposes of some Article 9 rule applicable to instruments, the asset must have the characteristics called for by the definition of instrument in § 9-102(a)(47) regardless of the label the parties have attached to the asset. Put simply, the parties to a secured transaction might refer to a horse as an "instrument," but the horse will not be one.

Second, although the UCC authorizes parties to describe collateral – in their private agreements and in certain public notices – by its classification, it does not require that they do so. Moreover, technically the statutory definitions apply wherever the defined term is used in Article 9, not to the use of that term in a private contract, such as a security agreement. Parties are free to express their agreements in whatever language they wish and to imbue terms, even terms used and defined in the UCC, with whatever meaning they desire. Thus, it is arguably inappropriate to assume that a term in a written security agreement carries with it the meaning ascribed to that term by the UCC.[34] On the other hand, Article 9 has been in force in every state in this country for well over a generation. Few of the commercial lawyers still practicing did so under prior law. As a result, it has created a sort of usage of trade for secured transactions, even those documented by nonlawyers.[35] Consequently, the UCC's definitions are highly probative in interpreting private security agreements and courts routinely apply those statutory definitions without even considering whether the parties meant something different.[36]

Third, for one type of collateral – commercial tort claims – and for various types of collateral in a consumer transaction, a description of collateral solely by its Article 9 classification is not sufficient. *See* § 9-108(e). In such cases, greater specificity is required.[37]

---

[34] *See, e.g.*, In re Eaddy, 2016 WL 745277 at *5-6 (Bankr. S.D. Ind. 2016) (suggesting that the term "accessions" in a security agreement need not have the meaning ascribed to it in § 9-335 because that definition is relevant only "to determine the priority of competing lienholders"). Using a statutory definition to interpret a private agreement is even more questionable when the applicable state's definition varies from the uniform text. For example, Kentucky has a non-uniform definition of "farm products" that includes "interests in horses" even if the debtor is not engaged in a farming operation. *See* Ky. Rev. Stat. § 355.9-102(1)(ah).

[35] Because financing statements are intended to provide public notice – that is, they speak to the world, not between contracting parties – their use of a term defined in Article 9 will, unless expressly indicated otherwise, carry the meaning that Article 9 ascribes to it.

[36] *See, e.g.*, In re 3P4PL, LLC, 2020 WL 4436354, at *7 (Bankr. D. Colo. 2020) (treating each of the terms "investment property, goods, documents, inventory, equipment, general intangibles, accounts, chattel paper [and] instruments" in a security agreement's description of collateral as meaning what Article 9 defines those terms to mean); Figueroa Tower I, LP v. U.S. Bank, 2019 WL 1467953, at *11-12 (Cal. Ct. App. 2019) (treating the Article 9 definition of "general intangibles" as applicable to a Deed of Trust that used but did not define the term); Porter Cap. Corp. v. Horne, 2016 WL 4197328 (N.J. Super. Ct. 2016) (looking to the Article 9 definitions of collateral types to determine the meaning of terms undefined in a security agreement); In re Wiersma, 324 B.R. 92 (9th Cir. BAP 2005) (security interest attached to debtor's contract claim because it was a "general intangible" and thus fell within the description of the collateral), *rev'd in part*, 483 F.3d 933 (9th Cir. 2007).

[37] At least one state also requires greater specificity in the description of a deposit account.

Stop. It is now time for you to carefully study the Article 9 classifications of collateral. Mastery of these terms is critical because almost everything in Article 9, and therefore much of the remainder of this book, depends on how the collateral is classified. If you do not acquire that mastery now, you will soon become very confused. The problems that follow are designed to help you start on that process.

Problem 2-3

Identify the proper classification for each item of collateral listed below.

A. A mobile home. *See* § 9-102(a)(23), (33), (44), (48). *See also* § 9-109(d)(11). A laptop computer used by a college professor.
B. Cattle fattened by a farmer for sale. Milk from the farmer's dairy herd. The farmer's tractor.
C. A refrigerator manufacturer's supply of sheet metal, toner cartridges for printers used in its sales office, and saw blades for cutting metal. *See* § 9-102 cmt. 4a.

Problem 2-4

A. Provide an example of some *valuable* goods that are "materials used or consumed in a business," and therefore constitute inventory pursuant to § 9-102(a)(48)(D).
B. Provide an example of goods that "are furnished by a person under a contract for service," and therefore constitute inventory pursuant to § 9-102(a)(48)(C).
C. Why does § 9-102(a)(48)(C) include in the definition of "inventory" goods that "are furnished by a person under a contract for service"?

e-Exercise 2-A
Classifying Receivables

See Colo. Rev. Stat. § 4-9-108(e)(3).

Problem 2-5

Identify the proper classification for each item of collateral listed below.

A. (i) A farm implement dealer's right to payment for a lawn mower that Farmer A purchased with an oral agreement to pay the purchase price in 60 days.
(ii) The same dealer's right to payment from Farmer B for a plow purchased on credit and for which Farmer B signed a piece of paper promising to pay the purchase price in 60 days.
(iii) The same dealer's right to payment from Farmer C for a tractor purchased on credit and for which Farmer C signed a writing promising to pay the purchase price over 12 months and granting the dealership a security interest in the tractor to secure the obligation to pay the purchase price.
See § 9-102(a)(2), (11), (47).

B. (i) A law firm's right to payment from clients for work to be performed.
(ii) a web page designer's right to payment in Bitcoin from a customer for services performed. *See* § 9-102 cmt. 12A.
(iii) A computer supplier's right to payment of monthly rent under a written lease of a network server to a law firm.
(iv) a retailer's right to payment from its bank in connection transactions in which customers effected payment using a credit card or debit card. *See* § 9-102 cmt. 5d.

C. (i) The right to have a loan repaid.
(ii) The right to receive a tax refund.
(iii) A cause of action for breach of contract.

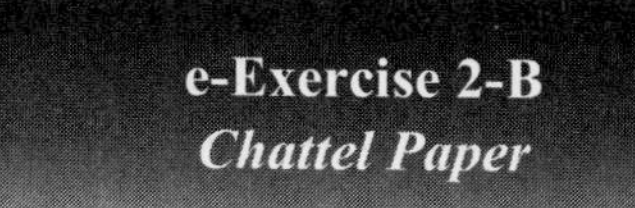

Problem 2-6

Identify the proper classification for each item of collateral listed below.

A. A liquor license. *See In re Chris-Don, Inc.*, 308 B.R. 214, 221 (Bankr. D.N.J. 2004), *rev'd on other grounds*, 367 F. Supp. 2d 696 (D.N.J. 2005).

B. A software developer's copyright to a computer program.

C. The receipt given to a farmer by a silo operator when the farmer stored grain there. *See* § 9-201(a)(30).

D. 100 shares of AT&T stock held in certificated form. A $10,000 U.S. government bond credited to Customer in Broker's records. *See* §§ 8-102(a)(9), (14)–(18), 8-501.

E. A non-fungible token representing ownership of an image of a cat eating a piece of pizza.[38]

e-Exercise 2-C
Changing Classification

2. Using Collateral Classifications in the Collateral Description

As simple as it might be to properly describe the collateral properly in a security agreement, secured parties nevertheless encounter difficulties with the descriptions they draft. Consider the following problem. In doing so, remember that one function of a security agreement is to transfer property rights in the intended collateral.

Problem 2-7

A. Which, if any, of the following descriptions of collateral would be adequate in a security agreement? *See* § 9-108.
   1. "All goods."
   2. "Equipment."
   3. "Some equipment."
   4. "All personal property."

B. Debtor is in the business of selling agricultural chemicals, fertilizers, and related products. Most of its financing comes from Bank. However, some of its suppliers also extend credit. One of them, Supply Co., has a security agreement covering:

   all inventory, including but not limited to agricultural chemicals, fertilizers, and fertilizer materials sold to Debtor by Supply Co.

---

38 If you question whether such an item would have value, see Erin Griffith, *Why an Animated Flying Cat with a Pop-Tart Body Sold for Almost $600,000*, N.Y. Times (May 27, 2021), https://www.nytimes.com/2021/02/22/business/nft-nba-top-shot-crypto.html.

Does Supply Co.'s security interest cover the portion of Debtor's inventory not acquired from Supply Co.? *See Shelby County State Bank v. Van Diest Supply Co.*, 303 F.3d 832 (7th Cir. 2002). Even if the security interest does not cover inventory acquired from other sources, what problems might Debtor nevertheless encounter in trying to use that other inventory as collateral? How would you re-draft the collateral description above to avoid the interpretive problem it presents?

Test Your Knowledge
Exam One – Classification

Paragraphs (4) and (5) of § 9-108(b) also validate a description of collateral by "quantity" or by a "computational or allocational formula or procedure." Unfortunately, it is not entirely clear what, if anything, these paragraphs do. Consider the following three descriptions:

1. "Debtor's three most recently purchased computers."
2. "600 bushels of wheat stored in the silo on Debtor's farm."
3. "30% of Debtor's equipment."

The first of these descriptions should be sufficient. After all, extrinsic evidence can be used to determine which three of Debtor's computers were purchased most recently.[39]

The second description might be sufficient, assuming there is only one silo on Debtor's farm. However, the second description does not actually indicate which bushels are encumbered. That might be a problem if, for example, the silo initially contained more than 600 bushels of wheat and Debtor removed some bushels from the silo. Were the bushels that were removed part of the collateral or were they unencumbered bushels? A court might use some tracing principle to resolve this problem,[40] but in the absence of such a principle, the second description does not

---

[39] This ignores the possibility that Debtor might have purchased multiple computers when purchasing the third most recent, thereby rendering the language ambiguous as to which computers fall under the description.

[40] *See infra* pages 93–95, discussing the "lowest-intermediate-balance" rule for dealing with cash proceeds in a deposit account.

make the collateral objectively determinable, and hence is problematic. As a result, it is not clear whether § 9-108(b)(4) or (5) makes the description effective.

The third description is even less likely to be effective. It provides no way for the parties or a court to determine which items of Debtor's equipment are part of the collateral and which items are not. As such, the third description fails to satisfy a principal purpose of the requirement that the security agreement contain a description of the collateral: to identify the property in which the secured party is acquiring rights.[41]

C. Drafting the Security Agreement

1. In General

So far, the discussion of § 9-203(b)(3)(A) has focused on the provision's two express and distinct requirements: (ii) the debtor's signature; and (ii) a description of the collateral. But the provision's reference to a "security agreement" suggests two more requirements.

Section 9-102(a)(74) defines a "security agreement" as an agreement that "creates or provides a security interest" and § 1-201(b)(35) defines "security interest," in part, as an interest in personal property "which secures payment or performance of an obligation." Combining these rules, we can see that § 9-203(b)(3)(A) requires that the debtor sign an agreement that "create[s] or provide[s] for" an interest in personal property that "secures . . . an obligation." This raises two questions. First, what words or language must the agreement use to "create or provide" for a security interest? Second, what words or language must the agreement use to identify the secured obligation?

Fortunately, the definition of "security agreement" is informed by its use of the word "agreement," which is itself defined. "Agreement" means "the bargain of the parties in fact, as found in their language or inferred from other circumstances." § 1-201(b)(3). This suggests some flexibility is appropriate. Moreover, the UCC is designed to simplify the law governing commercial transactions, *see* § 1-103(a)(1), and requiring specific language would be antithetical to that goal. Accordingly, courts have eschewed a formalistic requirement of specific language. As one court put it, no "magic language" is required to create or provide for a

---

[41] For further discussion of these descriptions and § 9-108(b)(4) and (5), see Stephen L. Sepinuck, *Describing Collateral by Quantity, Formula, or Procedure*, 10 THE TRANSACTIONAL LAW. 4 (Aug. 2020).

security agreement.[42] The court then ruled that an agreement providing that certain property would "become property of the Seller" if the buyer failed to pay the purchase price qualified as a security agreement. Similarly, although the security agreement must in some way indicate what obligation is secured,[43] it need not specify the precise amount of the obligation and a minor error in identifying the secured obligation might not prevent the security agreement from being effective.[44] Nevertheless, that does not mean that any language will suffice.

Problem 2-8

A. Which one of the following contains the best language to "create or provide for" a security interest? Which, if any, are insufficient?
   (i) Borrower hereby conveys Lender a security interest in . . . .
   (ii) Borrower agrees that Lender has a security interest in . . . .
   (iii) Borrower shall grant Lender a security interest in . . . .
   (iv) If Borrower fails to pay, Lender may take possession of . . . .

B. Which one of the following is the best language to identify the secured obligation (assume in each case that "Loan" is adequately defined in the document)? Which, if any, are insufficient?
   (i) In consideration for the Loan . . . .

---

42 In re Thompson, 315 B.R. 94, 103 (Bankr. W.D. Mo.), *modified*, 316 B.R. 326 (Bankr. W.D. Mo. 2004). For an example of another case dealing with this issue, see In re Outboard Marine Corp., 300 B.R. 308 (Bankr. N.D. Ill. 2003), in which the court surveyed the approaches to this issue and decided that the key inquiry was whether the document evidenced an intent to create a security interest.

43 *See, e.g.*, Allouf v. Allouf, 2015 WL 4880207, n.5 (Conn. Super. Ct. 2015) (noting ambiguity about whether the security agreement between a law firm and a client covered the client's obligation from a prior proceeding; the agreement recited the existing balance owed as part of the situation warranting the creation of a security interest but did not expressly identify what the collateral secured); In re Modafferi, 45 B.R. 370, 374 (S.D.N.Y. 1985) (a signed financing statement did not satisfy the requirements of § 9-203(b) in part because it did not identify the secured obligation); Needle v. Lasco Indus., Inc, 89 Cal. Rptr. 593 (Cal. Ct. App. 1970) (same).

44 *See, e.g.*, New W. Fruit Corp. v. Coastal Berry Corp., 1 Cal. Rptr. 2d 664 (Cal. Ct. App. 1991) (a security agreement describing the secured obligation as "all of Grower's obligations" was sufficient); In re Duckworth, 776 F.3d 453 (7th Cir. 2014) (a security agreement that mis-described the secured obligation could be reformed as between the debtor and the secured party).

(ii) In exchange for the Loan . . . .
(iii) . . . until the Loan is repaid in full.
(iv) . . . to secure repayment of the Loan.

Problem 2-9

You have agreed to loan $2,000 to Friend, who will sign a negotiable promissory note to evidence the debt. To secure the debt, Friend will grant you a security interest in the *Blue-Green Abelard*, a limited edition, reproduction Dr. Seuss sculpture that Friend owns and hangs in Friend's home (a picture of such a sculpture appears on the companion web site for this book). Draft the security agreement, using only one sentence.

2. The Composite Document Rule

What if none of the transaction documents, by itself, satisfies all the requirements discussed above? For example, if only some of the documents are signed by the debtor and only others describe the collateral, has § 9-203(b)(3)(A) been satisfied?

Article 9 does not answer this directly, but recall that the main requirement is that the debtor sign a "security agreement" and "agreement" itself is defined very broadly as the parties' bargain in fact. Perhaps as a result, courts have been fairly lenient; they have created something called the "composite document rule," which allows a creditor to use multiple documents to satisfy the requirements of § 9-203(b)(3)(A) when no single document, by itself, suffices. This has been a boon to putative secured parties who, judging from the amount of litigation, apparently have a penchant for making mistakes. The standard under the composite document rule has been laid out as follows:

> What must guide this examination is a determination of whether the parties intended to create a security interest. That is, there must be evidence within the transaction documents themselves indicating the parties' intent to create a security interest. . . .
>
> Determining whether the parties intended to create a security interest is a two-step process. The first step requires the court to decide whether there is a written document or documents containing language that objectively indicates that the parties intended to create a security interest. If such a document or documents exist, then the fact finder must determine whether

the parties actually intended to create a security interest. The first inquiry is a question of law; the second is a question of fact.[45]

IN RE SABOL
337 B.R. 195 (Bankr. C.D. Ill. 2006)

Perkins, Chief Judge.

This adversary proceeding is before the Court, after trial, on the complaint by Charles E. Covey, as Trustee of the Chapter 7 estate ("Trustee"), to determine the validity of a security interest held by Morton Community Bank ("Bank") in several items of sound equipment owned by Michael S. Sabol, one of the Debtors ("Debtor"). * * * The main issue is whether the Composite Document Rule can rescue the Bank from the absence of a security agreement.

The following facts are not in dispute. On May 25, 2002, the Debtor, doing business in the recording industry as Sound Farm Productions, completed an application for a Small Business Administration (SBA) guaranteed loan to expand his business, requesting approval of a loan from the Bank, as Lender, in the principal amount of $58,000. The Bank's application for the SBA guarantee, comprised of a separate page completed and signed by its loan officers dated June 3, 2002, contains a section entitled "Loan Terms," which includes a subsection for collateral, requesting information as to description, market value and existing liens. Among the assets listed on the application were assets the Debtor presently owned and pledged to BankPlus, in addition to two items he intended to acquire using a portion of the proceeds of the loan.

On July 5, 2002, the Debtor executed an SBA form promissory note in the principal amount of $58,000 payable to the Bank. In addition to the note, the Debtor signed another document, in letter format, which provided:

> In consideration for Morton Community Bank granting a loan to Michael S. Sabol DBA Sound Farm Productions, the undersigned does hereby authorize Morton Community Bank to execute, file and record all financing statements, amendments, termination statements and all other statements authorized by Article 9 of the Illinois Uniform Commercial Code, as to any security interest in the loan or refinancing presently sought by the undersigned, as well as all

[45] In re Outboard Marine Corp., 300 B.R. 308, 324 (Bankr. N.D. Ill. 2003) (citations omitted).

loans, refinancing or workouts hereafter granted by Morton Community Bank to Michael S. Sabol DBA Sound Farm Productions.

On July 18, 2002, the Bank filed a standard form Uniform Commercial Code (UCC) financing statement, covering inventory, accounts receivable and equipment. The financing statement was not signed by the Debtor. No separate document entitled "Security Agreement" was signed by the Debtor.

Although he initially dealt with loan officer Will Thomas, the Debtor testified that when he went to the Bank to sign the loan documents, a different loan officer handled the closing. He did not recall any discussion about a security agreement or a security interest. The Debtor testified that he signed the documents in order to comply with the Bank's requirements to obtain the loan. The proceeds of the loan were used for operating capital and to purchase additional equipment. The Debtor spent less than $20,000 for equipment, which he began to purchase shortly after he received the loan.

The Debtor and his wife, Rhonda K. Sabol, filed a joint petition for bankruptcy under Chapter 7 on February 14, 2005. They listed Morton Community Bank as a secured creditor, holding a security interest in "tools" valued at $12,410, with a total claim of $35,792.91. * * *

The Trustee contends that the Bank does not have a valid purchase money security interest under Article 9 of the UCC, because there is no separate document captioned "Security Agreement" or any language in any other document explicitly granting a security interest. The Bank, relying on the "Composite Document Rule," contends that the loan application, the promissory note, the authorization and the financing statement, taken together, establish an agreement to create a security agreement.

ANALYSIS

* * * Under Illinois law, which governs the issue of whether the parties have entered into a valid security agreement, a nonpossessory security interest does not attach and is not enforceable unless the debtor has [signed] a security agreement that contains a description of the collateral, value has been given, and the debtor has rights in the collateral. [§ 9-203(b)(3)(A)]. A "security agreement" is defined as "an agreement that creates or provides for a security interest." [§ 9-102(a)(73)]. A "security interest" is an interest in personal property or fixtures which secures payment or performance of an obligation. [§ 1-201(37)]. The requirement of a written security agreement is said to serve two purposes: the first being evidentiary in that it eliminates disputes as to what items are secured and the second in the

nature of a statute of frauds, by precluding the enforcement of claims based only on an oral representation. *In re Outboard Marine Corp.*, 300 B.R. 308 (Bankr. N.D. Ill. 2003). No particular words of grant or "magic words" are required to be included in a security agreement to create a security interest. Notwithstanding the lenity of the Composite Document Rule, there must be some language reflecting the debtor's intent to grant a security interest. Accordingly, a financing statement which does not contain any grant language by the debtor creating a security interest in the described collateral, but merely identifies the collateral, cannot substitute for a security agreement.

Notwithstanding the statutory requirement of a signed * * * security agreement that describes the collateral, some courts have adopted a liberal view of what suffices to meet that requirement. Under the "Composite Document Rule," two or more documents in combination may qualify as a security agreement. * * *

The pre-UCC era of chattel mortgages, and the technical and sometimes complex requirements associated therewith, fostered common law exceptions in the name of equity and pragmatism. Beginning in 1962, however, the UCC ushered in a new, simplified regime for documenting and perfecting secured transactions. Because the UCC reduces to an absolute minimum the formal requirements for the creation of a security interest, the need for those equitable exceptions no longer exists. In the interests of certainty and maintaining some identifiable standard, it is important to enforce the minimal formal requirements set forth in Article 9 of the UCC. Thus, an argument can be made that strict rather than liberal interpretation of the UCC documentation requirements is more consistent with the overall purpose of the UCC to create certainty and reliability in commercial transactions. Other courts have applied the Composite Document Rule narrowly.

The Bank relies upon the Debtor's testimony that he understood that by signing the loan documents that he was granting the Bank a security interest in the equipment that he was going to purchase, as reflected in his treatment of the Bank as a secured creditor in his bankruptcy schedules. The Bank also relies on the itemization of collateral on the loan application, the provision in the note regarding the Bank's rights in "collateral" and its rights upon default, the debtor's authorization and the description of the collateral in the financing statement. The Bank's reliance on the listing of collateral under the description of loan terms on its application for the SBA guarantee reveals nothing about the Debtor's intent to grant a security interest. The application consists of two separate portions: one completed by the Debtor and one completed by the Bank. The listing of the collateral appears on the Bank's portion of the document. That page was completed by officers of the Bank and is dated one week after the Debtor's signature on his application for the loan.

The Bank points to the provisions of the note which describe, generically, the Bank's rights in collateral and upon default. The note defines "Collateral" as "any property taken as security for payment of this Note." Upon default, the note authorizes the Bank to "take possession of any Collateral" and to "sell, lease, or otherwise dispose of any Collateral." The note also provides that the Bank may: "[b]id on or buy the Collateral at its sale;" "preserve or dispose of the Collateral;" "[c]ompromise, release, renew, extend or substitute any of the Collateral;" and "[t]ake any action necessary to protect the Collateral." The note does not identify the collateral. In fact, the note itself contemplates a separate security agreement. Under the heading of general provisions, the note provides that "Borrower must sign all documents necessary at any time to comply with the Loan Documents and to enable Lender to acquire, perfect, or maintain Lender's liens on Collateral."

The Debtor's authorization for the Bank to file a financing statement is equally inefficacious. It authorizes that filing "as to any security interest in the loan . . . presently sought by the [Debtor]." *In re Numeric Corp.*, 485 F.2d 1328 (1st Cir. 1973), relied on by the Bank, is distinguishable. In *Numeric*, although the parties had not signed a formal security agreement, the board of directors of the debtor authorized the preparation of a UCC financing statement to cover the creditor's security interest in certain equipment described in a bill of sale. Finding that the directors' resolution established "an agreement in fact" by the parties to create a security interest, the court held that the resolution, taken with the financing statement's itemization of the collateral, constituted a security agreement.

The Bank also relies on its UCC-1 financing statement. The financing statement, as permitted by the Revised UCC, was not signed by the Debtor. The financing statement was not filed by the Bank until July 18, 2001, almost two weeks after the loan was closed. No one from the Bank testified that the financing statement was presented to the Debtor at the time that he signed the document authorizing its filing. The Debtor's testimony that a security interest was not discussed contradicts any suggestion that the financing statement was presented to the Debtor at or prior to the loan closing. This Court will not presume that a financing statement, not shown to be contemporaneous, has any part to play in the Composite Document Rule.

In re Data Entry Service Corp.,81 B.R. 467 (Bankr. N.D. Ill. 1988), a case involving an SBA loan, relied on by the Bank, is factually distinguishable. In that case, in addition to the note, the debtor signed a Loan Agreement which listed as collateral, first liens on machinery, equipment, furniture and fixtures, inventory, accounts and general intangibles. Directly above the debtor's signature, at the end of the document, the Agreement provided that the debtor agreed to the conditions imposed. In addition, two financing statements describing the collateral were filed with the Secretary of State, each signed by the debtor. The court determined that the Loan Agreement, by itself or in conjunction with the signed financing statements, was sufficient to create a security interest in favor of the SBA. * * *

Whether considered alone or in combination, this Court finds that there is not sufficient evidence of the Debtor's intent to create a security interest in the documents relied on by the Bank. No language conveying a security interest to the Bank is found in any of the documents. There is no evidence that the Debtor read or reviewed, much less agreed to, the "loan terms" contained in the Bank's application to the SBA. The financing statement, containing the only description of collateral, is not signed by the Debtor and, in all likelihood, was never seen by him. What is left? Only boilerplate references in the note to the Bank's rights in "any collateral" and in the authorization to "any security interest."

Had the Bank's application for SBA guarantee, which listed the collateral, been signed by the Debtor, the minimal requirements of § 9-203 may well have been satisfied. But without a description of the collateral in a signed * * * document or in a separate document incorporated by reference into a signed * * * document, no security interest can be recognized. This Court is of the view that the Composite Document Rule is most appropriately used, if at all, to allow the debtor's intent to grant a security interest to be demonstrated by reference to the various loan documents where the debtor has signed * * * a document containing a description of the collateral that does not contain words of grant. The Rule should not be applied, however, to bypass the necessity of a signed * * * writing that describes the collateral, as that is the clearly stated minimum requirement of § 9-203.

Even though the Bank may have intended that there was to be a security interest, the Court does not view the result reached as unduly harsh. The primary purpose of Article 9 of the UCC was to create uniformity and certainty in commercial transactions. The steps required to be taken by secured parties to establish and protect their interests, having been reduced to a minimum, are simple and clearly laid out. It is not unreasonable to require that they be complied with.

NOTES

1. For a case focusing on the necessity of some granting language – that is, language purporting to transfer an interest in the collateral – see *In re Buttke*, 2012 WL 529241 (Bankr. D.S.D. 2012) (application for a certificate of title and certificate itself, each of which identified a security interest, did not *create or provide for* a security interest, and thus did not constitute a security agreement).

2. As the court in *Sabol* noted, the 1999 revisions to Article 9 removed a requirement that the debtor sign the financing statement. Consequently, debtors now rarely do. In reviewing older cases applying the composite document rule, be aware of this change. A signed financing statement is perhaps more probative regarding the intent to create a security interest than one that the debtor has not signed and perhaps not even seen.

Problem 2-10

You are counsel for the local bank. In looking over the documentation of a recent loan you find the following documents:

(i) a loan application, signed by the borrower two weeks before the loan was made, that indicates that the borrower's equipment is to serve as collateral;

(ii) a promissory note signed by the borrower and dated the day the loan was made; and

(iii) a financing statement identifying the borrower's name and address, describing the collateral as "equipment," and filed with other UCC records in the Secretary of State's office. See § 9-521(a) for an illustration of a financing statement.

A. If these are the only relevant documents, have the requirements of § 9-203(b)(3)(A) been satisfied?

B. In thinking about the composite document rule more generally, what facts and factors will be most relevant to whether separate documents collectively satisfy the requirements of § 9-203(b)(3)(A)?[46]

---

[46] Recent cases concluding that a security agreement did exist after applying the composite document rule include Crozier v. Wint, 736 F.3d 1134 (8th Cir. 2013) (promissory note signed by married couple that stated it was "secured by a filed UCC Financing Statement," together with a filed financing statement initialed by the husband could be sufficient to create

The composite document rule can be viewed as a bit of judicial grace for the lenders who fail at the relatively simple task of obtaining the minimal written evidence of a security agreement that § 9-203(b)(3) requires. For those lenders not saved from their documentation failure by the composite document rule, there might be yet another possible source of help: the common law of mistake. Its principles survive and supplement the UCC. *See* § 1-103(b). Accordingly, at least one court has indicated that a written security agreement could be judicially reformed under the contract-law doctrine of mistake to add an item of collateral inadvertently omitted.[47] However, taking advantage of the doctrine of mistake to expand the description of the collateral should be viewed as a long shot. Under normal circumstances, the parol evidence rule would prevent an effort to supplement or contradict a signed security agreement that a court finds the parties intended to be a fully integrated agreement (that is, the writing is the exclusive statement of the agreed terms). In other words, while multiple documents may be considered together when dealing with the *absence* of a signed security agreement, the parol evidence rule might prevent a court from considering other documents when there is a signed security agreement that purports to be the exclusive statement of all the agreed terms.[48]

---

a security interest if the husband was the sole owner of the collateral described in the financing statement or acted as an agent of the wife when he initialed the financing statement); Lopes v. Fafama Auto Sales, 2011 WL 6258818 (Mass. Ct. App. 2011) (combination of two documents signed by the car buyer – a bill of sale stating that the car dealer had a right to repossess the car for nonpayment and a certificate of title application listing the dealer as the sole lienor – constituted an authenticated security agreement); In re Weir-Penn, Inc., 344 B.R. 791 (Bankr. N.D.W. Va. 2006) (financing statement signed by the debtor and describing the collateral as equipment, inventory, and accounts, together with signed promissory note which provided that "[t]his Loan is secured by . . . the following previously executed, security instruments or agreements: UCC Financing Statement on all business assets bearing file # 048209 recorded 11/16/1997 with the WV Secretary of State" were sufficient to demonstrate an intent to secure the debt and to satisfy the requirements of § 9-203(b)(3)).

47 *See* In re Invenux, Inc., 298 B.R. 442 (Bankr. D. Colo. 2003) (evidence did not clearly demonstrate mutual mistake so as to warrant reformation). *See also* In re Schutz, 241 B.R. 646 (Bankr. W.D. Mo. 1999) (allowing reformation due to mistake of a retail installment contract and security agreement which misdescribed the make and model of the mobile home actually delivered to the buyer, so that seller's assignee held a valid security interest in it).

48 *See, e.g.*, In re Doctors Hospital of Hyde Park, Inc., 474 B.R. 576 (Bankr. N.D. Ill. 2012); In re Emergency Monitoring Techs., Inc., 366 B.R. 476 (Bankr. W.D. Pa. 2007). *See*

D. Additional Collateral Description Issues

1. After-acquired Property

One of the goals of the UCC is to facilitate commercial transactions. *See* § 1-103(a)(2). Imagine that you wish to open a new boutique. You need financing to acquire inventory, so you approach a local bank for a loan. After reviewing your credit application, credit report, and business plan, the loan officer decides to make the loan, provided you give the bank a security interest in all the inventory. The trouble is, you do not own any inventory yet. You will not – and, indeed, cannot – acquire the inventory until you get the loan. Thus, what the bank needs is not a security interest in whatever inventory you own at the time you sign the security agreement; it needs a security interest in the inventory you will acquire later. Even if your boutique were already in business and had a lot of inventory, what the bank would want is not merely a security interest in the inventory on hand now, but a security interest in whatever inventory you might happen to own at the time you go into default and the bank decides to foreclose. After all, you might not default for several months or years and by then whatever inventory you owned at the inception of the deal is likely to be long gone.

Article 9 deals with this by expressly authorizing a security agreement to cover "after-acquired property," that is property acquired by the debtor after the debtor signs the security agreement. § 9-204(a). As a result, both property owned by the

---

also In re Equipment Acquisition Res. Inc., 692 F.3d 558 (7th Cir. 2012) (even though parol evidence is not admissible to alter an unambiguous security agreement, it might be possible to reform a security agreement that erroneously purports to have the debtor grant the secured party a security interest in the secured party's own assets because such a transfer is impossible, does not make sense, and is ambiguous).

The doctrine of mistake might also be used to reform a security agreement that incorrectly describes the secured obligation. This should be easier than using the law of reformation to expand the security agreement's description of the collateral because § 9-203 does not expressly require that the signed security agreement describe the secured obligation. *But see* In re Duckworth, 776 F.3d 453 (7th Cir. 2014) (although a security agreement that mis-described the secured obligation as a note executed on December 13, 2008 – when the note was actually executed and dated December 15, 2008 – could be reformed as between the debtor and the secured party, reformation was not permitted to affect the rights of the debtor's bankruptcy trustee, who had the status of a judicial lien creditor and against whom parol evidence is inadmissible). *Contra* Restatement (Third) of Restitution and Unjust Enrichment §§ 12 cmt. f, 60(1) & cmt. b, 66 (while a purchaser for value takes free of a reformation claim, a lien creditor does not). *See also* Restatement (Second) of Contracts § 155 cmt. f.

debtor at the outset of a secured transaction and property acquired by the debtor later might secure the secured obligation:

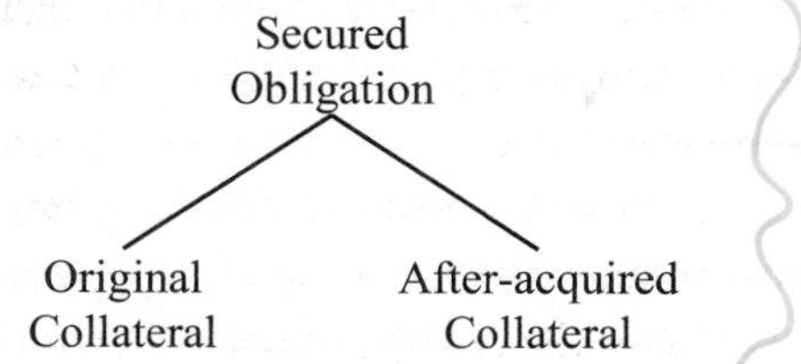

Absent this flexibility, it might be impossible to structure secured transactions in which the collateral will be purchased with loaned funds that make up all or part of the secured obligation. It would also be extremely cumbersome to maintain a security interest in collateral, such as inventory, which the debtor is constantly buying and selling. In essence, the debtor would have to sign a new security agreement every time the debtor purchased new inventory, which might well occur on a daily basis.

The authorization to encumber after-acquired property can raise interpretive issues, however, if the security agreement omits a clear reference to such property. Consider the following scenario:

> Construction Company agrees to grant Bank a security interest in all its earth-moving equipment to secure a $100,000 loan. At the time, Construction Company owns five bulldozers. Construction Company signs a security agreement that describes the collateral as "all of the debtor's bulldozers." A week after the security agreement was signed, Construction Company acquires another bulldozer. Does the security agreement cover the new bulldozer?

On these facts, the new bulldozer is "after-acquired" property. Whether the agreement in fact covers the new bulldozer is a matter of contract interpretation. Had the agreement described the collateral as "all of the debtor's existing and after-acquired bulldozers," or more broadly as "all of the debtor's existing and after-acquired equipment," there would be no problem; the new bulldozer would be covered. But what is the proper result given the actual phrasing of the description?

Many courts insist that the written agreement include some express reference to property that the debtor might acquire in the future before concluding that after-acquired property is in fact covered. They often support this approach with the classic mantra that an agreement should be interpreted against its drafter,[49] which in the case of a security agreement is almost always the secured party.

Other courts are a bit more lenient. They note that some types of collateral – in particular, inventory and accounts – constantly turn over. If the debtor's business is functioning properly, or even at all, existing inventory is sold and then replaced with new inventory. Existing accounts are paid off and new accounts are generated. By the time the debtor defaults and the secured party wishes to enforce its security interest, whatever inventory or accounts the debtor had when the debtor signed the security agreement may be long gone. For this reason, it is often unrealistic to think that the secured party wanted – or that the debtor expected – only the inventory or accounts on hand on the date the debtor signed the security agreement to serve as the collateral. Indeed, there might well be a sort of usage of trade that, when inventory or accounts are the collateral, after-acquired inventory or after-acquired accounts will be within the scope of the security agreement. Some courts go so far as to presume this. *See In re Filtercorp, Inc.*, 163 F.3d 570 (9th Cir. 1998).

Of course, no competent transactional attorney would, in reliance on a case such as *Filtercorp*, fail to include an express after-acquired property clause in a security agreement's description of the collateral. *Filtercorp* might save the attorney who omits such a clause from malpractice liability, but not from the burden, expense, and embarrassment of having to litigate the issue.

Beyond that, it is vital to remember that the presumption is grounded on the "unique nature of inventory and accounts receivable as 'cyclically depleted and replenished assets.' "[50] For that reason, the presumption applies, if at all, only to types of collateral that constantly turn over.[51] A security agreement covering other types of collateral – a construction company's bulldozers (*i.e.*, equipment), for example – would not benefit from that presumption and would not encumber after-acquired property unless the security agreement so states.

Even when inventory or accounts are involved, the presumption that the *Filtercorp* court was willing to entertain might be overcome. The issue is, after all,

---

[49] *See* RESTATEMENT (SECOND) OF CONTRACTS § 206 (1981).

[50] *Filtercorp*, 163 F.3d at 579.

[51] *Compare* Van Hattem v. Dublin Nat'l Bank, 2002 WL 245981 at *3 (N.D. Tex. 2002) ("a security agreement covering livestock does not reach after-acquired livestock unless the security agreement expressly so provides"), *with* Peoples Bank v. Bryan Bros. Cattle Co., 504 F.3d 549 (5th Cir. 2007) (a security interest in a cattle dealer's livestock presumptively includes after-acquired property).

according to both the *Filtercorp* court and the comments to Article 9, *see* § 9-108 cmt. 3, one of contract interpretation. For example, in *Stoumbos v. Kilimnik*,[52] the secured party had sold inventory and other property on credit to the debtor. In such a situation, it might well be that the parties intended the lien to cover only the property sold, not other assets of the buyer.

Also bear in mind that even in a transaction to which the *Filtercorp* presumption would apply, the parol evidence rule might exclude extrinsic evidence of the parties' intent or the meaning they ascribed to the written collateral description. Therefore, to be sure that the security interest will extend to after-acquired property, the signed security agreement should contain an express after-acquired property clause.

Problem 2-11

A. Developer is one of the premier software development companies in the country. To ensure that its employees always have the tools necessary to do their work, Developer replaces one-third of its desktop computers every year with a newer and faster model. Two years ago, Developer borrowed $15 million from Bank and to secure the loan gave Bank a security interest in "all equipment and all parts, accessories, and additions thereto." Does that security interest encumber the desktop computers purchased by Developer after it signed the security agreement?

B. If your jurisdiction presumes that a security interest in inventory or accounts encompasses after-acquired collateral, what aspects of a transaction might lead a court to conclude that after-acquired collateral is in fact not covered?

Article 9 restricts the effectiveness of an after-acquired property clause in a very minimal way. An after-acquired property clause is not effective to attach the security interest to after-acquired consumer goods, except in a limited circumstance, or an after-acquired commercial tort claim. Read § 9-204(b).[53] Federal law also

---

[52] 988 F.2d 949 (9th Cir. 1993) (discussed in *Filtercorp*).

[53] *See* § 9-108 cmt. 5. *See also* Helms v. Certified Packing Corp., 551 F.3d 675 (7th Cir. 2008) (lender's security interest did not attach to commercial tort claims pursuant to the terms of the security agreement because even though the filed financing statement expressly covered commercial tort claims and the security agreement gave the lender permission to amend the schedule of collateral to include commercial tort claims upon receiving

limits the effectiveness of an after-acquired property clause in certain types of transactions, such as non-purchase-money security interests in certain types of household goods.[54] Moreover, because a security agreement is a contract, common-law contract doctrines such as unconscionability and fraud might also be used to attack the validity of such a clause. However, because such clauses are so commonplace, particularly in commercial transactions, it is not often that an attack based upon those contract doctrines is successful.

2. Proceeds

One type of property that the secured party need not worry about describing in the security agreement is proceeds. That is because a security interest automatically attaches to identifiable proceeds of collateral. *See* §§ 9-203(f), 9-315(a)(2).

"Proceeds" is a broadly defined term, *see* § 9-102(a)(64), but is at its core a value-tracing concept. It includes whatever is received upon the sale, lease, license, exchange, or collection of the collateral. Thus, as the collateral is transmuted from one thing to another – for example, as inventory is sold so as to create accounts, which are then paid by check, which checks are in turn deposited into a bank account – each change generates proceeds. The term "proceeds" also includes claims for liability arising from, and insurance payable by reason of any damage to, the collateral. Distributions on account of collateral are also proceeds. For example, assume the collateral is shares of stock in a corporation and a dividend is declared and becomes payable to shareholders. The dividend is proceeds of the securities. Note, in all of these examples, the original collateral is gone or has been diminished in some way. The inventory was sold to a new owner; the debtor no longer owns it. The accounts, once collected, no longer exist. The insurance obviously takes the place of the lost value of the original collateral. Even the dividends are replacement value. When a corporation pays dividends to its

---

notification of the claim from the debtor, the secured party failed to make such an amendment); Waltrip v. Kimberlin, 79 Cal. Rptr. 3d 460 (Cal. Ct. App. 2008) (an after-acquired property clause is ineffective to cover later-arising commercial tort claims); The Epicentre Strategic Corp.– Michigan v. Perrysburg Exempted Village Sch. Dist., 2005 WL 3060104 (N.D. Ohio 2005) (the § 9-204(b) prohibition on assignment of after-acquired commercial tort claims means the claim must exist when the security agreement is signed).

[54] *See, e.g.*, FTC Credit Practice Rule, 16 C.F.R. § 444.2. *See also* 12 C.F.R. § 227.13.

shareholders, the money paid out diminishes the assets of the corporation and hence reduces the liquidation value of the shares of stock in the corporation.

Article 9 provides that a security interest automatically extends to whatever proceeds of the original collateral are identifiable, and to each successive generation thereafter. The reason for this rule is not difficult to discern. One of the main goals of a secured transaction is to provide the creditor with certainty that the debt will be repaid. That goal would be undermined if, after granting the security interest, the debtor could unilaterally do something to the collateral to render the secured party effectively unsecured. However, most debtors remain in possession and control of the collateral. Businesses need their equipment and inventory to remain in operation. Individuals need their cars to get to and from work. Without possession and control of this property, even when it is serving as collateral, the debtor might not be able to earn the money to pay off the loan. Consequently, Article 9 expressly contemplates that the debtor might retain possession and use of the collateral. § 9-205. Yet armed with possession, the debtor might sell the collateral. Alternatively, the collateral might be stolen, vandalized, or destroyed in a casualty (which is covered by insurance).

We have already seen that lenders can protect themselves somewhat from this by taking a security interest in after-acquired property. However, that is effective only when the new property fits within the security agreement's description of the collateral. A debtor about to go out of business might sell inventory but not buy any new inventory. Other debtors might collect accounts and use the money to buy new equipment. The wonderful thing about proceeds is that it almost does not matter into what the value of the original collateral is transferred. The security interest follows the transmutation and encumbers the new asset. Moreover, it does so without regard to whether the security agreement references "proceeds"[55] or whether its description of the collateral is broad enough to cover the property constituting proceeds.

Thus, assume a creditor has a security interest in a piece of the debtor's equipment, the debtor then sells the equipment for cash, uses the cash to buy inventory, and then trades the inventory for a consumer good. If the factual connection can be made at each exchange, that is, if the proceeds can be "identified" as stemming from the original collateral, the security interest attaches to the consumer good. The security agreement need not contain an after-acquired property clause and need not mention the words "proceeds," "cash," "inventory,"

---

[55] *But cf. infra* note 153.

or "consumer goods."[56] As a result of this, you cannot determine what property a security interest encumbers merely by looking at the description of the collateral in the security agreement. You must also look at what happened to any property after it became encumbered by the security interest.

As important as the concept of proceeds is, it is not limitless. After studying the definition in § 9-102(a)(64), tackle the following problem.

Problem 2-12

A. State Bank has a security interest in the Degas Museum's paintings. In which of the following, if any, will State Bank also have a security interest?
   1. A charcoal sketch by Rembrandt that the Degas Museum receives from trading one of its paintings to the Louvre.
   2. Funds the Degas Museum receives from leasing one of its paintings to the Prado.
   3. Funds the Degas Museum receives from allowing Poster Company to produce and sell reproductions of several of the museum's paintings.
   4. Funds the Degas Museum receives from exhibiting its paintings to the public.
   5. Funds the Degas Museum receives from selling annual memberships to the museum.

   How should the security agreement describe the collateral to ensure that all of the items mention above will be encumbered by the security interest?
B. Digger is a farmer who grows vegetables and raises pigs. State Bank has a security interest in Digger's "livestock."
   1. Does the security interest cover any piglets born after Digger signed the security agreement? If not, how could State Bank have drafted the collateral description in the security agreement to ensure that the newborn pigs were covered?
   2. Does the security interest cover pork from pigs Digger owned when Digger signed the security agreement?

---

[56] Note, even though § 9-204(b) prohibits a security interest from attaching to after-acquired consumer goods pursuant to an after-acquired property clause, it does not prevent a security interest from attaching to whatever proceeds of the original collateral are identifiable, even if those proceeds happen to be consumer goods.

C. State Bank has a security interest in all of Drought's "existing and after-acquired crops" to secure a multi-year loan. This year, Drought is participating in a federal soil conservation program under which Drought will receive money for taking acreage out of cultivation, that is, not planting any crops. Does State Bank have a security interest in the payment to be received under this federal program? *See In re Kingsley*, 865 F.2d 975 (8th Cir. 1989).

D. Lender has a security interest in a Manet painting owned by Collector. Collector contracts to sell the painting to Buyer for $10 million. Buyer repudiates and Collector sells the painting to Substitute for $8 million, after sending reasonable notification of the sale to Buyer. Collector then brings a breach-of-contract claim against Buyer for $2 million. *See* § 2-706(1). Is Collector's claim against Buyer proceeds of the painting? Why or why not?

Sometimes, when a debtor sells inventory or other collateral, the payment (or right to payment) that the debtor receives in return consists of different components. In such a situation, only some of the components might be proceeds of the collateral.

Illustration

Distributor sells sprockets and cogs to customers throughout the country. State Bank has a security interest in all of Distributor's existing and after-acquired inventory. Most of Distributors customers purchase on open account, and Distributor bills them at the end of each month. The bills include itemized amounts for: (i) packaging and handling; and (ii) the shipping charges of the carrier service. Are the amounts charged for packaging, handling, and shipping proceeds of Distributor's inventory?

What little authority exists on the issue indicates that amounts due for packaging and handling are proceeds of the inventory,[57] but that result is at least somewhat questionable.[58] The right to payment for such services are acquired "upon" the sale

---

[57] *See* Western Farm Service, Inc. v. Olsen, 90 P.3d 1053 (Wash. 2004); Johanson Transp. Serv. v. Rich Pik'd Rite, Inc., 164 Cal. App. 3d 583, 210 Cal. Rptr. 433 (Cal. Ct. App. 1985).

[58] *Cf.* Tompson v. Danner, 507 N.W.2d 550 (N.D. 1993) (payment for storage of crops in

of the inventory, which is all that § 9-102(a)(64)(A) purports to require, but they are not acquired not *for* the inventory. Does that matter? To the extent that proceeds is a value-tracing concept, amounts due for services rendered in connection with the sale do not appear to be a replacement for the value of the property sold.

On the other hand, a seller of goods that charges for the services that the seller provides in packing and handling the goods can, somewhat arbitrarily, allocate the purchase price between the goods and those charges. Indeed, some sellers advertise extremely low purchases prices as a lure to customers and make their real money through the associated charges. Because of that, it makes some sense to treat the amounts due or received for those charges as proceeds of the property sold.

The right to payment for shipping would likely be treated the same as the packaging and handling fees. However, it *might* be different if the amount due for shipping is a reimbursement for the same amount paid to a third-party carrier. In other words, if the amount due from the buyer for shipping is the amount billed by a third-party carrier, the concern about arbitrariness in how the various components of the total bill are calculated does not apply. For this reason, the shipping charges are arguably less "for" the inventory than the handling and packaging charges are. Nevertheless, even the right to payment for shipping is acquired "upon" the sale of the collateral.

The following problem explores this issue further.

Problem 2-13

A. Delicious Dining operates an upscale restaurant. State Bank has a security interest in Delicious Dining's existing and after-acquired inventory. Are all the funds received and due from providing meals to Delicious Dining's customers proceeds of that inventory? If not, what portions are not proceeds and why not?

B. Dragster is a retailer of motor vehicles. State Bank has a security interest in all of Dragster's existing and after-acquired inventory. In connection with its sale of cars, Dragster frequently receives for one or more of the following: (i) payment from customers for extended warranty protection; (ii) incentive payments from the car manufacturer; and (iii) a fee from the buyer's lender for originating a loan to the buyer. To which of these amounts, if any, will Bank's security interest attach? *See In re Greg James Ventures LLC*, 2008 WL 4829952 (Bankr. N.D. Cal. 2008).

---

connection with their sale were not proceeds of the crops).

In addition to whatever limits are implicit in the definition of proceeds itself, there are two restrictions on the extent to which a security interest will automatically attach to proceeds. First, if the proceeds are property outside the scope of Article 9, it is doubtful that the rule of § 9-315(a)(2) would be applicable.[59] Thus, for example, if the debtor used encumbered personal property to buy real estate, the security interest might not flow through into the real estate purchased. Whether it does or does not would likely be determined by the language of the parties' agreement and the real estate law of the relevant jurisdiction.

Second, it is important to remember that a security interest extends only to *identifiable* proceeds of the collateral. *See* § 9-315(a)(2). Thus, if the creditor cannot trace what happened when collateral was converted from one thing to another, the security interest might be lost. The UCC does not tell us when proceeds are or are not identifiable. It does, however, authorize the application of common-law rules and equitable principles to trace property that gets commingled. § 9-315(b)(2). Such commingling occurs most commonly when proceeds such as cash and checks are deposited into a bank account that already or subsequently contains credits that are not proceeds.

Comment 3 to § 9-315 identifies one of those tracing rules that could be applied in that situation: the "lowest intermediate balance rule." There are other tracing rules that could be used, such as FIFO (first in first out) and LIFO (last in first out), but the lowest intermediate balance rule is the one courts use most often.[60]

There are several ways to describe the lowest intermediate balance rule. The simplest description is the lesser of: (1) the amount of the proceeds; or (2) the lowest daily balance in the account between the time the proceeds were deposited and the time the creditor seeks to enforce its interest. A more complex but nevertheless more revealing way to describe the rule is as a process. You start with the day on which the proceeds are deposited. For each day thereafter, you look at what deposits are added and then at what withdrawals are made. To the extent possible, you treat each withdrawal as consisting of nonproceeds.[61] Thus, for

---

[59] *See* NCC Fin., LLC v. Shilen, 2019 WL 1458606 (Conn. Super. Ct. 2019) (ruling without much discussion or analysis that a secured party was not entitled to the proceeds of a life insurance policy that was purchased with the liquidated proceeds of the collateral).

[60] *See* Metropolitan Nat'l Bank v. La Sher Oil Co., 101 S.W.3d 252, 255-56 (Ark. Ct. App. 2003); General Electric Cap. Corp. v. Union Planters Bank, 409 F.3d 1049 (8th Cir. 2005) (reversing lower court's use of a "pro-rata" tracing principle, requiring use of the lowest intermediate balance rule, and providing an illustration of how the rule should be applied).

[61] In this sense, the lowest intermediate balance rule could be replaced with the acronym

example, consider the following account ledger for a debtor with a beginning balance of $6,000 of nonproceeds, who thereafter deposited $5,000 of proceeds:

	Deposits	Withdrawals	Balance
Day 0			$ 6,000
Day 1 (proceeds)	$5,000		$11,000
Day 2	$1,000		$12,000
Day 3		($8,000)	$ 4,000
Day 4	$6,000		$10,000

The lowest intermediate balance rule treats the current balance as containing $4,000 of proceeds (the lesser of the $5,000 initial deposit of proceeds and the lowest daily balance after that). In contrast, FIFO would treat the deposit account as containing $3,000 of proceeds and LIFO would treat it as containing no proceeds.

Now assume the third deposit occurred on the same day as the withdrawal. The ledger would look like this:

	Deposits	Withdrawals	Balance
Day 0			$ 6,000
Day 1 (proceeds)	$5,000		$11,000
Day 2	$1,000		$12,000
Day 3	$6,000	($8,000)	$10,000

The result of applying the lowest intermediate balance rule is that the deposit account would now be deemed to contain $5,000 of proceeds. The lowest intermediate balance rule is a great rule for the secured party because it treats the proceeds as remaining in the deposit account for as long as possible. This benefits the secured party because the funds withdrawn are often dissipated (*e.g.*, used to pay the debtor's current obligations) and are generally not recoverable from the recipient. *See* § 9-332.

This last point is illustrated by the following graphic. If you think of the deposit account as a vat containing two liquids – proceeds and nonproceeds (deposits are, after all, liquid assets) – the proceeds rise like oil to the top and, because the drain is at the bottom, the proceeds are the last assets to drain out of the deposit account.[62]

NPFO (non-proceeds first out).

[62] Do not overuse this metaphor. A deposit account is not a safe deposit box or other storage unit, and a deposit of funds with in bank account is not a bailment. Instead, a deposit

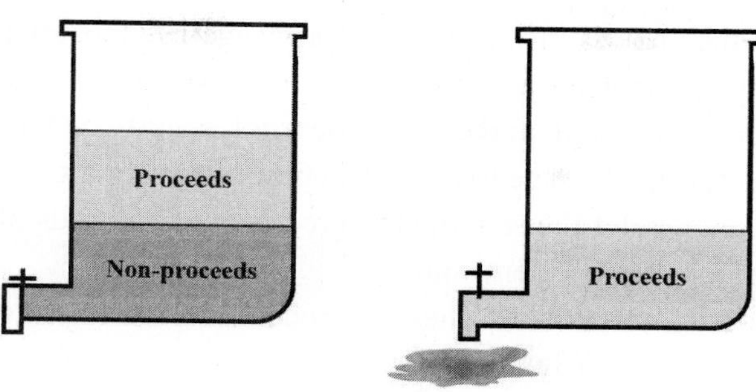

Problem 2-14

Dependable Delivery Service delivers appliances to the residences of people who purchase them at various local retail stores and home improvement centers. Sure Thing Auto has a security interest in Dependable's delivery van. Dependable's driver got into an accident and the van was totaled. The insurance company sent Dependable an $18,000 check to cover the loss and Dependable deposited that check into its deposit account at Bank.

A. Immediately after that deposit, the account balance was $24,875. At that point, what, if anything, serves as collateral for Sure Thing Auto?
B. The next day, Dependable withdrew $325 to pay several utility bills. Assuming that the jurisdiction follows the lowest intermediate balance rule, now what, if anything, serves as collateral for Sure Thing Auto?
C. A week later, Dependable deposited $3,450 it had received in payment from its clients. Now what, if anything, serves as collateral for Sure Thing Auto?
D. A few days later, Dependable used $21,000 from the deposit account to buy a new van. Now what, if anything, serves as collateral for Sure Thing Auto? What if, instead of buying a new van, Dependable used $21,000 from the deposit account to buy 21,000 $1 lottery tickets?

But tracing principles can do only so much. Consider a situation in which the collateral is destroyed in a casualty that also caused personal injury or damage to other property (*i.e.*, non-collateral). The casualty was caused by a tortfeasor's

---

is really an unsecured loan to a bank, and a deposit account is really nothing more than the bank's internal ledger documenting the depositor's loan to the depositary bank. *See, e.g.*, In re 3P4PL, LLC, 2020 WL 4436354, at *8 (Bankr. D. Colo. 2020).

negligence, and the debtor brings a tort claim against the tortfeasor, seeking $1 million in damages. The debtor and the tortfeasor then settle the claim for $400,000, but the settlement agreement does not specify what portion of the amount, if any, is for the damage to or destruction of the collateral. Some portion of the debtor's rights under the settlement agreement is proceeds of the collateral, but that portion might not be identifiable.[63]

Even if a security interest attaches to proceeds of collateral – for example because the debtor sold the original collateral, the proceeds are identifiable, and the proceeds are a type of property to which Article 9 applies – that does not mean that the security interest in the original collateral disappears. The security interest stays attached to the collateral disposed of unless some provision in Article 9 strips that security interest off of the collateral.

Read § 9-315(a)(1). Under that provision, unless the secured party authorizes the collateral transferred free of the security interest, or some other provision of Article 9 provides otherwise, the security interest continues in the collateral in the hands of the transferee. The secured party's authorization might be express or might be implied from the circumstances. For example, the secured party might explicitly authorize a debtor to sell inventory in ordinary course of business free of the security interest. Alternatively, the secured party might have impliedly authorized the transfer of the collateral free of the security interest through a course of conduct, such as if it knew of several previous transfers but never treated such transfers as a default or asserted its rights in the collateral transferred.

---

[63] *See* In re Montreal, Maine & Atlantic Ry., Ltd., 956 F.3d 1 (1st Cir. 2020) (a secured party that might have had a security interest in the debtor's contract claims arising from a catastrophic accident, but not the debtor's tort claims arising from the accident, failed to identify what portion, if any, of a global settlement of the claims were its collateral; consequently, the secured party had no right to any of the settlement proceeds); In re JMF Cab, Inc., 614 B.R. 648 (Bankr. D. Mass. 2020) (a bank with a security interest in the debtor's taxicab medallion did not have a security interest in the settlement of the debtor's lawsuit against Uber because that settlement was not identifiable proceeds of the medallion; although the complaint included a claim for the lost value of the medallion, nothing in the complaint or the settlement either apportioned the damages among the various harms or causes of action or provided a methodology to make such an apportionment); In re Aerogroup Int'l, Inc., 2019 WL 2120735 (Bankr. D. Del. 2019) (a secured party with a senior security interest in the debtor's intellectual property was not entitled to any portion of the proceeds of a settlement agreement that resolved a claim for diminution in value of the debtor's trademarks because nothing in the agreement allocated a portion of it to the trademarks; hence even if some portion of the settlement were for loss to the value of the collateral, that portion was not *identifiable* proceeds of the collateral).

Part 3 of Article 9 has several other rules – priority rules – that specify situations in which a transferee of collateral takes it free of the security interest. Some of those rules are mentioned in comment 2 to § 9-315. We will spend a fair amount of time in Chapter Five discussing these priority rules.

Because the security interest might follow and remain attached to the collateral transferred while also attaching to the proceeds received on disposition, the value of collateral available to satisfy the secured obligation might increase when the debtor sells collateral. However, the secured party is entitled to only one satisfaction of the debt owed.

Problem 2-15

Bank has a security interest in all of Developer's bulldozers to secure a loan. Developer wishes to sell a bulldozer to Buyer for $150,000 and use the funds to purchase a dump truck.

A. To facilitate the sale, Developer asks Bank to authorize the sale of the bulldozer free and clear of Bank's security interest, which Bank does. The sale is consummated and Developer uses the funds received to buy a dump truck. Does Bank's security interest attach to the dump truck? *See* § 9-315(a)(1), (2).
B. If Bank does not authorize the sale but Developer sells the bulldozer anyway and uses the funds received to buy a dump truck, in what property will Bank have a security interest?

3. Commingled Goods and Accessions

Another type of property that need not be described in the security agreement is commingled goods. These are defined in § 9-336(a) as "goods that are physically united with other goods in such a manner that their identity is lost in a product or mass." The concept can be depicted almost as an equation:

Commingled Good + Commingled Good = Product or Mass

The example used repeatedly in the comments involves combining flour and eggs to make cakes (although the commingling no doubt occurs before baking, as soon as the ingredients are combined to make cake batter). That is an example of a commingling that results in a product. An example of commingling that results in a mass would be when fungible property is combined with more of the same, such as when heating oil is poured into a tank that already contains some heating oil.

Article 9 provides that there can be no security interest in the original goods after they are commingled. § 9-336(b). Thus, one cannot have a security interest in the flour after it is used to make cake batter. However, any security interest attached to goods before they are commingled with other goods automatically attaches to the product or mass that results from the commingling. § 9-336(c). This occurs regardless of whether the security agreement mentions "commingled goods" or describes the product or mass.

In contrast to commingled goods, an accession is defined as a good affixed to another good in such a way that the identity of both goods is not lost. § 9-102(a)(1). Consider, for example, a bulldozer into which a new engine is installed. Because both the bulldozer and the new engine survive and remain separately identifiable after the installation process, each is now an accession to the other. The engine is an accession to the bulldozer and the bulldozer is an accession to the engine. The engine and the bulldozer taken together are referred to as the "whole."

There is no automatic attachment of a security interest to accessions. Continuing with the bulldozer and new engine example, assume that prior to installation SP-E had an attached security interest in the engine and SP-B had an attached security interest in the bulldozer. Whether SP-E's security interest extends to the bulldozer or SP-B's security interest extends to the engine is a matter of interpretation of the collateral description in the respective security agreements. The mere fact that the engine became an accession to the bulldozer does not affect the prior attachment of SP-E's security interest in the engine. Similarly, the mere fact that the bulldozer became an accession to the engine does not affect the prior attachment of SP-B's security interest in the bulldozer. § 9-335(a).

Problem 2-16

Designer makes expensive custom jewelry for the super rich, and is well known for using a proprietary alloy of two-thirds platinum and one-third gold, which Designer calls "elysium." Buyer commissioned Designer to make and sell a large emerald-elysium necklace. To make the necklace, Designer purchased on credit: (i) fifty carats of emeralds from Emerald Supplier; (ii) five troy ounces of gold from Gold Supplier; and (iii) ten troy ounces of platinum from Platinum Supplier. Each supplier retained a security interest in the goods it sold to Designer to secure payment of the purchase price. Designer then made the necklace using the goods acquired from the three suppliers.

A. Prior to Designer's sale of the necklace to Buyer, in what property does each supplier have a security interest?
B. How, if at all, would the analysis of Part A change, if Designer's security agreement with Gold Supplier described the collateral as "all gold sold to Designer by Gold Supplier and all proceeds thereof"?
C. How, if at all, would the analysis of Part A change, if Designer's security agreement with Platinum Supplier described the collateral as "all platinum sold to Designer by Platinum Supplier and all jewelry made therefrom"?
D. If Designer sells the necklace for $1 million, do the security interests of the suppliers attach to the funds received?

Problem 2-17

A. Bank has a security interest in Delivery Company's fleet of vans. Delivery Company uses the vans in two ways. Some are operated by Delivery Company's employees and used to deliver goods for customers in return for a fee. Others are leased on a yearly basis to Subsidiary, which is wholly owned by Delivery Company. Subsidiary, in turn, subleases the vans to customers for short-term periods, usually 2-15 days. Provide at least one example of each of the following:
   (i) proceeds;
   (ii) after-acquired property;
   (iii) accessions;
   (iv) a product or mass resulting from commingling the collateral with other goods.

   To which, if any, of these will the security interest have attached under the description of the collateral as "vans"? What significant assets of Delivery Company's business might not be covered by any of these terms? Redraft the collateral description to cover everything you identified that was omitted.
B. Review the Venn diagram provided in Problem 2-2. Add to the diagram the following additional terms: (i) accessions; and (ii) commingled goods. Give an example of each term for every place it appears in the diagram.

Problem 2-18

Two years ago, Sensational Press sold the principal assets of its publishing business to Basic Books. Basic Books paid part of the purchase price in cash and agreed to pay the balance over the next four years. To secure that obligation, Basic Books granted Sensational Press a security interest in all the equipment, inventory, and general intangibles sold as well as any "renewals, substitutions, replacements, accessions, proceeds, and products thereof." One of the items included in the sale was the copyright to a textbook on paleontology. Last year, Basic Books came out with a new edition of the textbook. Which of the following, if any, does the security interest of Sensational Press encumber?

1. The copyright to the new edition of the paleontology textbook.
2. The copies of the old edition of the paleontology textbook in Basic Book's warehouse.
3. The copies of the new edition of the paleontology textbook in Basic Books' warehouse.
4. A printing press that Basic Books purchased six months ago.

See 17 U.S.C. § 106(2); *FSL Acquisition Corp. v. Freeland Systems, LLC*, 686 F. Supp. 2d 921 (D. Minn. 2010). If you were drafting the security agreement for Sensational Press, how would you revise the collateral description?

e-Exercise 2-D
Proceeds, etc.

E. Possession or Control of Collateral Pursuant to an Unsigned Security Agreement

Read § 9-203(b)(3)(B) through (E). These subparagraphs provide that the secured party may satisfy the security agreement requirement for attachment by taking possession, control, or both of certain types of collateral pursuant to an oral or unsigned security agreement.[64] The types of collateral for which possession

---

[64] The provisions do not actually use the word "unsigned," but they do require a security agreement and if the debtor had signed that agreement, § 9-203(b)(3)(A) would be satisfied, and (b)(3)(B) through (D) would be left without relevance.

pursuant to an unsigned security agreement is effective are specified in § 9-313(a). Those collateral types are goods, instruments, tangible money, certificated securities, and negotiable tangible documents.

The types of collateral for which control pursuant to an unsigned security agreement is effective are:

Type of Collateral	Definition of "Control"
electronic documents	§ 7-106
investment property	§§ 9-106 & 8-106
deposit accounts	§ 9-104
electronic money	§ 9-105A
letter-of-credit rights	§ 9-107
controllable accounts,	
controllable electronic records	§ 12-105
controllable payment intangibles	

A combination of possession and control pursuant to an unsigned security agreement is effect for attachment of a security interest in chattel paper. *See* § 9-105 (defining control of chattel paper).

A quick review of the listed sections on control reveals that even though the same term is used for each of those types of collateral, what counts as "control" differs for each. Despite the differences, there is a common premise underlying the exceptions to the signature requirement for collateral in the possession or control of the secured party. The theory is that the secured party's dominion over the collateral provides the necessary objective indicia of a security agreement to satisfy the requirements of a statute of frauds, and the signature requirement is, in essence, a type of statute of frauds.[65]

It is important to understand, however, that possession or control of the collateral (or, in the case of chattel paper, possession and control) is not by itself sufficient to satisfy the requirements of § 9-203(b)(3). Consider the following illustration.

---

[65] You should question whether this theory really makes sense for each of the types of collateral concerned. It might be that the real motivation for the decision to create these exceptions to the signature requirement was a concern that revised Article 9 not upset prevailing practices in the relevant financial markets.

Illustration

On June 1, Caroline borrows Diane's diamond necklace and promised to return it by the end of the month. On June 5, Diane borrows $500 from Caroline and promises to repay the debt the following week. On June 12, Diane telephones Caroline and says that she does not yet have the money to repay the loan. She then says that Caroline should hold on to the necklace as collateral until Diane pays the debt. Caroline agrees. On June 13, Caroline sends a e-mail message to Diane restating what they agreed to on the phone and asking Diane to confirm by a reply message. On June 14, Diane replies with an e-mail of her own confirming that Caroline may hold onto the necklace as collateral until Diane repays the debt.

The § 9-203(b)(3) requirement was first satisfied on June 12. Prior to that, Caroline had possession of Diane's necklace but there was no security agreement, either written or oral. After the phone call on June 12, however, Caroline had possession of Diane's necklace pursuant to the parties' oral agreement that the necklace serve as collateral for the loan. Thus, § 9-203(b)(3)(B) was satisfied at that time.

When, if ever, was § 9-203(b)(3)(A) satisfied? On June 14. On June 13 there was arguably a written security agreement – Caroline's e-mail message to Diane – but it was not signed by the debtor (Diane). When, however, Diane responded with a confirmatory message, either her message or the two messages together would likely satisfy the requirement of a signed security agreement. As long as Diane's message was signed and the exchange contained an adequate description of the collateral, § 9-203(b)(3)(A) was satisfied.

If the secured party has possession or control of collateral pursuant to the debtor's security agreement, the secured party has some obligations in regard to that collateral. Read §§ 9-207 and 9-208.

We will return to the concepts of possession and control in more depth when we discuss possession and control as methods of perfection of the security interest in Chapter Four.

SECTION 4. THE VALUE REQUIREMENT

In addition to having a security agreement, attachment requires that "value has been given." § 9-203(b)(1). "Value" is a defined term. It includes any extension of credit, a commitment to lend, and any consideration sufficient to support a simple contract. § 1-204. In other words, it is the consideration provided in exchange for the grant of the security interest. While the definition of "value" is not so limited, it is generally useful to think of it as the loan or other extension of credit that gave rise to the secured obligation. A security interest by definition secures an obligation. § 1-201(b)(35). If there is no obligation, there is nothing for the collateral to secure and hence no security interest.

Although § 9-203(b)(1) is clear that value must be given, its use of the passive voice raises a question: given by who to whom? While value is normally provided *by the secured party* (in consideration for the transfer of property rights in the collateral), there is no requirement that the value go *to the debtor*. And in some transactions, perhaps many, the person who grants an interest in personal property to secure an obligation is not the person who receives the value. Review the definitions of "debtor" and "obligor" in § 9-102 and your answer to Problem 2-1. Now consider a situation in which a guarantor of a loan provides collateral to secure the debt. The value given by the secured party – the loan – of course goes to the borrower, not to the guarantor. Because the "debtor" on these facts is the guarantor (as the owner of the collateral), not the borrower, the debtor did not receive the value. Nevertheless, value "has been given" and the security interest can attach.

It is even possible to construct a scenario in which the debtor did not receive the value and has not promised to be responsible for the secured obligation. For example, when a student borrows money to pay college tuition, the lender might insist that the student's parent grant the lender a security interest in the parent's car to secure the student's obligation to repay the loan. On these facts, the parent is the debtor and the student is the obligor. Even though the parent is not an obligor (because the parent has not, on the facts provided, guaranteed or otherwise promised to repay the loan) and has not receive the value provided by the lender (the tuition loan), the security interest in the parent's car would attach and be enforceable (assuming the other requirements of § 9-203(b) are met).

Future advances. Assume that a debtor has signed a security agreement giving a security interest in all of the debtor's equipment to secure a loan of $100,000. A month later, the same lender makes an additional loan to the debtor of $20,000. Is that new loan of $20,000 secured by the security interest in the debtor's equipment? It certainly can be. Any new loan or other extension of credit after the debtor signs the security agreement is called a future advance. Article 9 expressly authorizes a security agreement to have the security interest it creates secure future advances. *See* § 9-204(c). Without such authorization any creditor who expected to make a series of additional advances to its borrower would need a new security agreement for each advance. Given that some financing arrangements call for extensions of credit on a very frequent – sometimes intra-day – basis, this would be unduly cumbersome.

Whether a security interest does or does not secure future advances is an issue of contract interpretation. Courts have made it very clear that, in order for future advances to be secured, the security agreement must have a future-advances clause. A typical future-advances clause might therefore provide that the security interest in the described collateral secures "all obligations now owed or hereafter owed by the debtor to the lender." The effect of such a clause is that the collateral can secure both indebtedness that exists at the time the security agreement is signed and future indebtedness (compare the diagram below to the diagram on page 85 depicting after-acquired collateral):

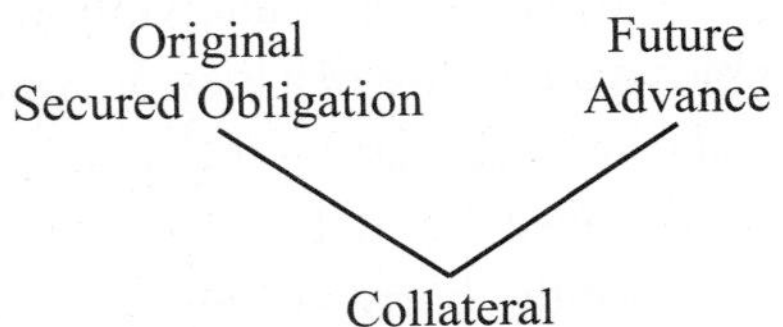

Even if a security agreement lacks a future-advances clause, and thus the collateral will not secure new loans made after the debtor signs the security agreement, the collateral might nevertheless secure subsequently accruing interest on the secured obligation and subsequently incurred collection costs. These obligations, sometimes referred to as "non-advances,"[66] are normally part of the secured obligation. Of course, whether they are or are not is a matter of contract interpretation and good drafting of the security agreement should leave no doubt about whether such obligations are in fact secured.

Before Article 9 was revised in 1999, there was a line of cases in which courts interpreted future advances clauses, despite their broad phrasing, to cover only advances of the same character as the original advance. Some courts also applied this "relatedness" rule to antecedent debt: that is, to debt incurred before the secured loan was made and the security agreement signed, but which the broadly drafted agreement purported to secure. The case of *In re Wollin*[67] was typical. In it, the debtors had purchased two automobiles with financing from a credit union.

---

66 We will see the concept of non-advances again in Chapter Five.

67 249 B.R. 555 (Bankr. D. Or. 2000).

Both security agreements included a "dragnet" clause (*i.e.*, a clause securing future advances) providing that "[t]he security interest secures . . . any other amount you owe the credit union for any reason now or in the future." Nevertheless, the court refused to treat a credit union's security interest in two automobiles as also securing either previously unsecured loans from the credit union or subsequent credit extended through a credit card issued by the credit union.

In a consumer case, such as *Wollin*, the relatedness requirement for antecedent debt and future advances might seem innocuous or even beneficial.[68] Nevertheless, creditors objected to this requirement on a number of grounds. Many argued, as the credit union did in that case, that it is inconsistent with the text of the UCC itself. *See* §§ 9-201, 9-204(c). Because of that, some complained that it is a judicial invention that implicitly treats secured transactions as if they were governed by the common law, rather than a fairly detailed legislative code. The relatedness rule also seems inconsistent with its own underlying rationale. In an effort to ensure that the debtor has truly assented to have the collateral secure antecedent debt and future advances, courts refuse to enforce the parties' agreement as written – which is normally the best evidence of their intent. Moreover, in the process, they relegate the unquestioned intent of the secured party to an irrelevancy. Most significantly, there is really no way to draft around the relatedness rule to ensure that all future advances will be covered, even if that is the true intent of both parties and even though that rule is ostensibly designed to give effect to their (or at least the debtor's) intent.

Revised Article 9 left the text of the relevant UCC provisions largely intact. A new comment 5 to § 9-204, however, expressly rejects judicial limits on the efficacy of a future advances clause. Although trying to change the law with a comment, rather than by a change to the statutory text, is potentially problematic, the approach appears to be have been successful. For example, in *Pride Hyundai, Inc. v. Chrysler Financial Co., LLC*,[69] the court enforced a dragnet clause in a commercial transaction without regard to whether the obligations were of the same kind as the original debt. In so doing, the court noted that refusing to treat a broadly drafted future advances clause to cover debts of a different type or class than the original advance would frustrate the intent of the parties, particularly in a commercial setting where the parties are presumed to have a certain level of sophistication

---

[68] For another case discussing the relatedness requirement for future advances, *see* In re James, 221 B.R. 760 (Bankr. W.D. Wis. 1998).

[69] 369 F.3d 603 (1st Cir. 2004).

regarding the transaction. The court also referred to the heightened standard of good faith in Revised Article 9 as a control on potential abuse by secured parties of a broad future-advances clause.[70] For the most part, courts have ruled similarly in consumer cases.[71] And, in an odd twist, in one state it is actually easier to for the security agreement to properly describe future advances than to describe existing indebtedness because the courts in that state require that antecedent debts be referred to with specificity.[72]

Now consider how lenders can simultaneously make use of two different concepts: after-acquired property and future advances.

---

[70] *Id.* at 615. *See also* In re Dumlao, 2011 WL 4501402 (9th Cir. BAP 2011) (language in consumer's car loan agreement with credit union providing that the vehicle secured "any other amounts or loans, including any credit card loan, you owe us for any reason now or in the future" was effective under § 9-204 to cover credit-card obligation, but case remanded to determine if clause violated the duty of good faith or was unconscionable given the adhesive nature of the agreement and the small font used). It is appropriate to consider the good faith duty of fair dealing in *interpreting* the parties' agreement. However, the duty of good faith cannot *override* terms to which the parties have agreed. *See* P.E.B. Commentary No. 10 (Feb. 10, 1994). To the extent either the *Pride Hyundai* or *Dumlao* court suggested the latter, that is a misapplication of the duty of good faith.

[71] *See* In re Zaochney, 2011 WL 6148727 (Bankr. D. Alaska 2011); In re Renshaw, 447 B.R. 453 (Bankr. W.D. Pa. 2011); In re Hobart, 452 B.R. 789 (Bankr. D. Id. 2011) (concluding that *Wollin* was no longer consistent with Oregon law); In re Brannan, 2011 WL 2076378 (Bankr. D. Mont. 2011); Educators Credit Union v. Guyton, 805 N.W.2d 736 (Wis. Ct. App. 2011); In re Massey, 2010 WL 99266 (Bankr. E.D. Okla. 2010). *But cf.* In re Keeton, 2008 WL 686938 (Bankr. M.D. Ala. 2008) (dragnet clause in security agreement in connection with car loan to joint debtors did not clearly encompass obligations later incurred by only one of them, and thus the collateral did not secure one debtor's individual credit card obligations); In re Howard, 312 B.R. 840 (Bankr. W.D. Ky. 2004) (enforcing a future advances clause in a promissory note executed in connection with the first of two car loans in part because the loans were similar).

[72] *See* Equity Bank v. Southside Baptist Church of Lead Hill, 599 S.W.3d 133 (Ark. Ct. App. 2020) (although the cross-collateralization clause in a security agreement referred to "all obligations, debts and liabilities" of the debtor to the secured party, "whether now existing or hereafter arising," it was insufficiently specific to cover an existing mortgage loan). For a criticism of several such "rules of explicitness, see Stephen L. Sepinuck, *Gotcha!: Caught in the Explicitness Trap*, 8 THE TRANSACTIONAL LAW. 1 (June 2018).

Illustration

Doubletime, Inc., which operates a shipping business, signed a security agreement granting State Bank a security interest in "all of Doubletime's existing and after-acquired equipment to secure all obligations owing now or in the future to State Bank." At the same time, State Bank loaned Doubletime $200,000. When all this took place, Doubletime owned a fleet of ten trucks (which constitute "equipment" within the meaning of the security agreement). One month later, Doubletime purchased a new truck (also constituting "equipment" under the security agreement). Two months after that, State Bank loaned Doubletime an additional $40,000. As a result of the after-acquired property clause, the collateral includes all eleven trucks: the original ten plus the newly purchased truck. As a result of the future-advances clause, all the collateral secures the entire $240,000 debt.

The combination of both a future-advances clause and an after-acquired property clause is called "cross-collateralization." As the diagram below shows, it allows original debt to be secured by both property that the debtor has rights in when the security agreement is signed and property that the debtor acquires rights in sometime later. It also allows future loans to be secured by both sets of collateral.

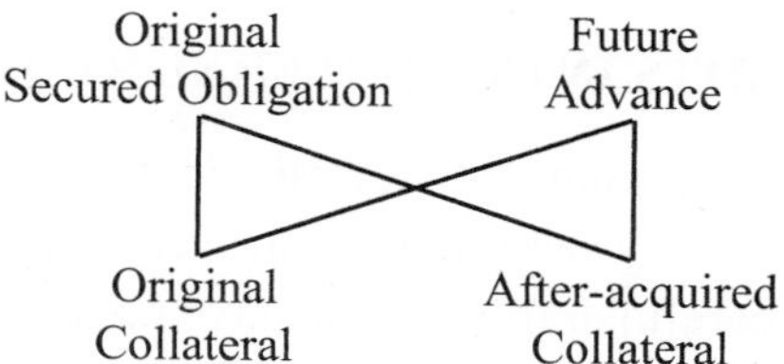

Now try the following problem, which involves cross-collateralization but also reviews the requirements for attachment that we have previously studied.

Problem 2-19

Seller is a retailer of home appliances. Many of its customers purchase items on credit using a credit card that Seller has issued. The credit card agreement with its customers contains the following language:

> Customer grants a security interest to Seller in all goods purchased with this credit card to secure all amounts owed on the credit card.

At a time when Daphne owed $2,000 on the credit card balance, Daphne purchased a new grill for $500 from Seller, using her credit card. Two weeks later (with the balance owed now at $2,500), Daphne purchased a new stove from Seller for $700. At the time of each purchase, Daphne signed a credit card receipt that listed the item ("grill" and "stove") and the amount of the purchase.

A. Assume that Daphne runs a catering business and uses all the items purchased with the credit card solely for business purposes. Does Seller have a security interest in the grill or the stove to secure any of the debt owed to Seller on the credit card? In considering this question, review §§ 9-108, 9-203. *Compare In re Cunningham*, 489 B.R. 602 (Bankr. D. Kan. 2013), *with In re Murphy*, 2013 WL 1856337 (Bankr. D. Kan. 2013). What are all of the issues that this practice raises?

B. How, if at all, would the analysis change if Daphne used all the items purchased with the credit card solely for personal, family, or household purposes? *See* § 9-204(b). *See also* FTC Credit Practice Rule, 16 C.F.R. § 444.2.

C. Identify two reasons why § 9-204(b) contains the limiting phrase "under a term constituting an after-acquired property clause."

SECTION 5. THE RIGHTS IN COLLATERAL REQUIREMENT

The last requirement for attachment, that the debtor either have rights in the collateral or the power to convey such rights to the secured party, § 9-203(b)(2), is perhaps so basic that less careful drafters might have neglected to include it. After all, a friend could offer you a security interest in the Mona Lisa in exchange for a sizeable loan, but you would be unwise to rely on that collateral when deciding whether to accept the deal. Although it might come as a shock, it is extremely unlikely that your friend has any property rights in da Vinci's masterpiece. Consequently, even if your friend signed an agreement purporting to grant you a security interest in the painting, you would not receive one.

Perhaps because the concept is so basic, rarely do issues arise about this requirement for attachment. When they do come up, they usually require reference to a source of law outside of Article 9. In other words, Article 9 will normally not tell us whether the debtor in fact has the rights or powers necessary to convey a security interest. Traditional property law might. Article 2 and the law of contracts might. The relevant law will often depend on the method by which the debtor claims to have acquired the rights or the powers involved.

One issue lurking in this simple concept is whether the purported collateral is indeed "property." For example, is a state-issued liquor license "property" to which a security interest can attach?[73] What about an airline's exclusive right to use specified gates at an airport, taxicab medallions, gaming licenses, and FCC broadcast licenses? The statute governing a government issued right or license might provide that the right or license is not "property" or is not transferrable, leading to an argument that an Article 9 security interest cannot attach to such a right or license.[74] For example, *In re Braniff Airways, Inc.*,[75] the Fifth Circuit held that exclusive access to airport gates was not property of the airline to which the gates had been assigned. Three years later, the FAA amended its regulations to allow airlines to sell such rights. As a result, courts have held that such rights are now property.[76]

Occasionally, there is also doubt about whether privately created rights qualify as property.[77] For example, some but not all courts have ruled that a season ticket

---

[73] *Compare* In re Ciprian Ltd., 473 B.R. 669 (Bankr. W.D. Pa. 2012) (a liquor license is personal property under Pennsylvania law and security interest did attach to it) *with* In re Circle 10 Restaurant, LLC, 519 B.R. 95 (Bankr. D.N.J. 2014) (a New Jersey liquor license is not property and therefore no security interest can attach to it); In re Jojo's 10 Restaurant, LLC, 455 B.R. 321 (Bankr. D. Mass. 2011) (Massachusetts law gives limited property rights in a liquor license only if the pledge is approved by the licensing authority; because no approval was granted, the debtor had no property rights in the license and no security interest attached to it); Concorde Equity II, LLC v. Bretz, 2011 WL 5056295 (Cal. Ct. App. 2011) (although California law prohibits the granting of a security interest in a liquor license, lender's security interest could and did attach to the proceeds of the a liquor license sold by a court-appointed receiver); Banc of Am. Strategic Solutions, Inc. v. Cooker Restaurant Corp., 2006 WL 2535734 (Ohio Ct. App. 2006), *appeal denied*, 861 N.E.2d 144 (Ohio 2007) (a liquor license is not property under Ohio law and thus no security interest may attach to it).

[74] *See infra* n.155 (discussing FCC broadcast licenses). *Compare* N.H. Rev. Stat. 270:63(I) ("A mooring permit shall not be construed as ownership of any real or personal property and shall not be transferred to any other person or location by gift, sale, lease, or rent except as provided in RSA 270:67"); 4 Pa. Cons. Stat. § 1327 (a gaming license does not create "an entitlement" and no licensee may sell, transfer, assign, or grant a security interest in a license).

[75] 700 F.2d 935 (5th Cir. 1983).

[76] In re Gull Air, Inc., 890 F.2d 1255, 1260 (1st Cir. 1989).

[77] *See* Bonem v. Golf Club of Georgia, Inc., 591 S.E.2d 462 (Ga. Ct. App. 2003) (golf club

holder's renewal option is really just the expectation of receiving an offer, and thus is not a property right. As is often the case, though, the split in authorities might be less indicative of disagreement and more attributable to differences in the underlying facts or the relevant law. It is worth noting that this issue usually arises in the context of a dispute about whether the rights come into the debtor's bankruptcy estate, not whether a security interest may attach.[78] It is not wholly clear that resolution of those two issues would or should be the same. What is clear, though, is that law outside Article 9 determines whether the debtor has rights that constitute an interest in property. *See* § 9-408 cmt. 3.

Even if the proffered collateral is property, the debtor might have only limited rights in it. May a debtor with limited rights in property grant a security interest in the property? The answer is a qualified yes. Article 9 does tell us that "title" to property is not particularly relevant. *See* § 9-202. Thus, a debtor that lacks title but owns all the other rights to an item of property often can grant a security interest in the property. Moreover, it is clear that even if a debtor contractually promises to Secured Party 1 not to grant a security interest in the collateral to anyone else, the debtor does have sufficient rights to grant a security interest to Secured Party 2 (and to Secured Parties 3, 4, and 5 . . .). *See* § 9-401(b).[79] Were this not true, there would be little need for many of the priority rules in Article 9.

On the other hand, as a general rule, if the debtor has only limited rights in the collateral, then the security interest will attach only to those limited rights. *See* § 9-203 cmt. 6. This concept is often referred to as "the derivation principle" and is the subject of the Latin phrase *nemo dat qui non habet* (one cannot give what one

---

membership not "property" but merely a license to use club's facilities). *See also* In re Personal Computer Network, Inc., 97 B.R. 909 (N.D. Ill. 1989) (business's right to keep a telephone number is property even though the telephone tariffs state that there is no vested right to keep a certain number); In re Kedrowski, 284 B.R. 439 (Bankr. W.D. Wis. 2002) (the right of an enrolled member of the Ho-Chunk Nation – a Native American nation – to a per capita distribution from the nation's gaming operations was property).

[78] *See* In re Walsh, 28 F.3d 1212 (4th Cir. 1994) (right to buy season tickets to Charlotte Hornets is property of the estate because the debtor had paid a $10,000 deposit for the right to buy up to 100 tickets each year). *Compare* In re Harrell, 73 F.3d 218 (9th Cir. 1996) (interest in Phoenix Suns season tickets not property of the estate) and In re Liebman, 208 B.R. 38 (Bankr. N.D. Ill. 1997) (option to renew Chicago Bulls season tickets was not an interest in property) *with* In re I.D. Craig Servs. Corp., 138 B.R. 490 (Bankr. W.D. Pa. 1992) (renewal right to Pittsburgh Steelers season tickets is property of the estate).

[79] *See also* Clapp v. Orix Credit Alliance, Inc., 84 P.3d 833 (Or. Ct. App. 2004).

does not have). Thus, for example, if the debtor has merely a leasehold in some equipment, the debtor can grant a security interest only in that time-limited right; the debtor cannot grant a security interest in the lessor's interest in the equipment.

Problem 2-20

Driscoll decided to go into business and borrowed $35,000 from Bank to open a shop called Driscoll's Fine Porcelain. On March 6, Bank made the loan and Driscoll signed a security agreement purporting to grant Bank a security interest in all "existing and after-acquired inventory" to secure all obligations owed to Bank. On that date, Driscoll's inventory consisted of several dozen figurines. Driscoll also had a contract with Wessex Co. to sell Driscoll samples of all its formal dinnerware for which Driscoll had partially paid in advance. The contract required Wessex to deliver the dinnerware by March 30. On March 15, Wessex packaged the dinnerware and marked it "For Shipment to Driscoll's Fine Porcelain." On March 25, Wessex delivered the dinnerware to a carrier service, which delivered the items to Driscoll's store on March 30. On what day or days did Bank's security interest attach to the figurines and dinnerware? Read §§ 2-401, 2-501, 9-203, 9-204(a). How should the security agreement have described the collateral to ensure that the security interest attached to Driscoll's rights in the dinnerware at the earliest possible time?

When a debtor has only limited rights to an item of personal property to be used as collateral, it can be a challenge to classify the collateral. In such a case, is the collateral the property or only the debtor's limited rights in it? Consider the following problem.

Problem 2-21

Architect contracts with Builder to provide whatever architectural services Builder needs, if any, for the next two years. At the time of contracting, Builder pays Architect a $100,000 retainer, to be used to cover Architect's services and expenses under the contract. Architect promptly deposits the retainer in a deposit account that contains, and will contain, no funds other than Builder's retainer. Applicable law treats Builder as the owner of the retainer until such time as Architect renders services or incurs expenses under the contract, but also treats Architect as having a security interest in the retainer.

A. May Builder grant a security interest in the retainer to someone other than Architect? If so, how would the collateral be classified?
B. May Architect grant a security interest in the retainer? If so, how would the collateral be classified?
C. How would Architect's contingent right to payment under the contract be classified?

The principle that a security interest normally attaches only to the debtor's limited rights in property is particularly important when a statute outside Article 9 imposes a trust on some of the debtor's property in favor of the government or a private entity. Such statutes, in essence, declare that some property in the possession or control of the debtor does not really belong to the debtor, with the result that the debtor might lack the ability to grant a security interest in those assets. This is particularly likely for a retailer, which might be in receipt of:

- sales taxes or cigarette taxes;[80]
- proceeds of sales of lottery tickets;[81] or
- proceeds of sales of stored value cards.[82]

Similarly, the assets of a buyer of produce – not merely the produce purchased, but virtually all the buyer's assets – might by federal law be impressed with a statutory trust for the benefit of the buyer's unpaid sellers.[83]

---

[80] *See, e.g.*, Insurance Co. of the State of Penn. v. HSBC Bank of USA, 829 N.Y.S.2d 511 (N.Y. App. Div. 2007), *rev'd on other grounds*, 882 N.E.2d 381 (N.Y. 2008).

[81] Ga. Code § 50-27-21(a); Tenn. Code § 4-51-120. *See also* In re Cooper, 2010 WL 2265658 (Bankr. E.D. Tenn. 2010). *But cf.* In re M.W. Sewall & Co., 431 B.R. 526 (Bankr. D. Me. 2010) (proceeds of instant lottery tickets were not held in trust for the state).

[82] In re Alco Stores, Inc., 536 B.R. 383 (Bankr. N.D. Tex. 2015).

[83] *See* Perishable Agricultural Commodities Act, 7 U.S.C. §§ 499a–499s. Similarly, under the Packers & Stockyards Act of 1921, 7 U.S.C. §§ 181-229, all of the livestock purchased by a packer, along with the meat or proceeds derived therefrom, might be held in trust for the benefit of all unpaid sellers of the livestock. 7 U.S.C. § 196(b). All poultry obtained by a live poultry dealer, along with the products and proceeds thereof, might be held in trust for the poultry dealer's unpaid suppliers. 7 U.S.C. § 197(b).

In some circumstances, however, the debtor has the *power* to transfer more rights than the debtor actually owns. Recall that § 9-203(a)(2) requires for attachment that the debtor have either rights in the collateral or the power to transfer rights in it. Such a power occasionally comes from the actual owner. For example, if the owner of personal property gives a relative permission to do so, the relative would have the power to transfer rights in the property to a creditor to secure the relative's debt to the creditor. Similarly, a subsidiary might allow its parent company to grant a security interest in property of the subsidiary.[84] When questions arise about whether such permission exists, they are often resolved pursuant to principles of agency law, which is among the many components of the common law that, in general, supplement the UCC. *See* § 1-103(b).

More commonly, a debtor's power to transfer greater rights than the debtor owns arises not from the rightful owner's permission, but from a legal rule. One example of such a rule is the second sentence of § 2-403(1). That sentence provides that a person with voidable title to goods can transfer good title to a good faith purchaser for value. The next sentence then identifies four situations in which a person has voidable title. In each of these situations, a buyer of goods can transfer more rights in the goods than the buyer actually acquired from the seller.

To illustrate how this can apply to the grant of a security interest, assume Buyer purchased and took delivery of goods. At the time of delivery, Buyer gave Seller a check for the goods. When Seller attempted to collect the check, the check was dishonored for insufficient funds. Meanwhile, Buyer purported to grant a security interest in those goods to Lender in return for a loan. The facts can be diagramed as follows:

---

[84] *See, e.g.*, In re WL Homes, LLC, 534 F. App'x 165 (3d Cir. 2013) (although a parent corporation might not have had sufficient rights in the deposit account of its wholly owned subsidiary to grant a security interest in the deposit account, the subsidiary consented to the use of the deposit account as collateral); In re Terrabon, Inc., 2013 WL 6157980 (Bankr. S.D. Tex. 2013) (a subsidiary, in whose name a certificate of deposit was issued after the subsidiary's parent company deposited the funds for that purpose, and which then executed a security agreement purporting the pledge the CD, did grant a security interest because, even if the parent company owned the CD, it consented to the subsidiary's use of the CD as collateral); American Bank & Trust v. Shaull, 678 N.W.2d 779 (S.D. 2004) (owner of collateral estopped from contesting debtor's rights in collateral as owner let debtor control the collateral, therefore debtor had power to transfer security interest in the collateral to secured party).

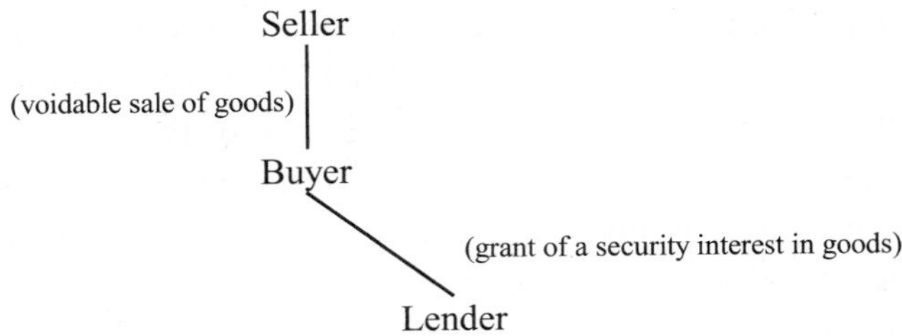

In the transaction with Seller, Buyer obtained voidable title to the goods. *See* § 2-403(1)(b). As between the two of them, Seller would have the right to reclaim the goods from Buyer. *See* § 2-507. In spite of that, Buyer has the right to transfer good title to a good faith purchaser for value, § 2-403(1), and Seller's reclamation right is subordinate to the rights of the good faith purchaser for value.[85] Lender, even though not a buyer, qualifies as a "purchaser" for value.[86] Thus, as long as Lender acted in good faith,[87] Lender will have obtained a security interest in the goods. Thus, by virtue of the operation of the rule in § 2-403(1), Buyer had the "power to transfer" to Lender – a secured party – greater rights than Buyer had as against Seller.

Now consider another provision in § 2-403(2). That rule allows a merchant in the business of selling a particular kind of good to transfer to a buyer the rights of a person who entrusted that kind of good to the merchant. The principal limitation on this power is that the buyer must qualify as a buyer in ordinary course of business. Read the definition of "entrustment" in § 2-403(3) and the definition of "buyer in ordinary course" of business in § 1-201(b)(9). Notice that the definition of buyer in ordinary course of business is much narrower than the definition of good faith purchaser for value. As a result, while a buyer in ordinary course of business almost always qualifies as a good faith purchaser for value, the reverse is not nearly as likely. A good faith purchaser for value might or might not qualify as a buyer in ordinary course of business. More relevant to our purposes, a secured party does not normally qualify as a buyer in ordinary course of business. Consequently, a secured party of the merchant cannot, for the purposes of § 9-203(b)(2), normally

---

85 *See* § 2-507 cmt. 3. A seller's reclamation rights under § 2-702 are also subject to the rights of a good faith purchaser for value. *See* § 2-702(3).

86 *See* §§ 1-201(b)(29), (30) (defining "purchase," and "purchaser"); 1-204 (defining "value").

87 *See* § 1-201(b)(20) (defining "good faith").

acquire the rights of the entruster from the merchant under § 2-403(2). *See* § 9-203 cmt. 6.

Problem 2-22

Determine who has rights to the property involved in each of the scenarios described below.

A. Thief steals a diamond necklace belonging to Owner, and then sells it to a Friend who has no knowledge of the theft.

B. Thief steals a diamond necklace belonging to Owner, and then uses it as collateral for a loan from Lender, who has no knowledge of the theft.

C. Buyer purchases goods from Seller after fraudulently representing that Buyer will resell them only in Poland. Buyer then resells them to Customer in the United States. Customer has no knowledge of the fraud.

D. Buyer purchases goods from Seller after fraudulently representing that Buyer will resell them only in Poland. For Buyer, the goods qualify as inventory and Creditor has a security interest in all Buyer's existing and after-acquired inventory.

E. Owner delivers a diamond necklace to Merchant to have its clasp fixed. Merchant is in the business of repairing and selling jewelry. Merchant, with intent to defraud, removes the stone and sells it to unsuspecting Customer.

F. Owner delivers a diamond necklace to Merchant to have its clasp fixed. Merchant is in the business of repairing and selling jewelry. Merchant, with intent to defraud, removes the stone and uses it as collateral for a loan from Bank.

G. Thief steals a diamond necklace belonging to Owner and brings it to Merchant for cleaning and minor repairs. Merchant is in the business of repairing and selling jewelry. Merchant sells the necklace to Customer, who has no knowledge of the theft.

Later in this Chapter and in Chapter Six, we will encounter additional rules that empower a debtor to transfer greater rights to property than the debtor has. For now, however, let us focus on the reverse: restrictions on the debtor's right to transfer property rights, and hence to grant a security interest.

Restrictions on Assignment. Just as there are agreements and rules that occasionally permit a debtor to transfer rights that the debtor does not own, there are also agreements and rules that purport to prevent a debtor from assigning rights that the debtor in fact does have. Such restrictions on assignment, if effective, can prevent a security interest from attaching to property the debtor owns. However, not all such restrictions are effective. Moreover, the rules relating to the effectiveness of such restrictions are numerous and incredibly complex. What follows is a somewhat brief discussion of these rules; enough to alert you to their existence, and perhaps whet your appetite for more, without making you give up, pull out your hair, or burn your book in frustration.

We begin with *contractual restrictions* on assignment. For example, consider a contract between a debtor and the counter-party to the contract – typically an "account debtor"[88] – that purports to either prohibit the debtor from assigning its rights under the contract or require the account debtor's consent to an assignment by the debtor. Such a contractual restriction on assignment involves a clash of two fundamental values in American law: (i) freedom of contract; and (ii) the free alienability of property (contract rights are now generally regarded as a type of property). The former suggests that the account debtor and the debtor should have the right to structure their affairs so to prevent an assignment from being effective. The latter suggests the opposite.

The common law includes some limitations on the ability of contracting parties to prohibit either or both of them from assigning contractual rights. For example, the Restatement (Second) of Contracts indicates that a contractual right can be assigned unless, among other things, assignment is "validly precluded by contract."[89] However, § 322 provides some principles for interpreting contractual terms that purport to restrict assignment:

> (1) Unless the circumstances indicate the contrary, a contract term prohibiting assignment of "the contract" bars only the delegation to an assignee of the performance by the assignor of a duty or condition.
>
> (2) A contract term prohibiting assignment of rights under the contract, unless a different intention is manifested,
>
> (a) does not forbid assignment of a right to damages for breach of the whole contract or a right arising out of the assignor's due performance of his entire obligation;
>
> (b) gives the obligor a right to damages for breach of the terms forbidding assignment but does not render the assignment ineffective;

---

[88] *See* § 9-102(a)(3) (defining "account debtor").

[89] RESTATEMENT (SECOND) OF CONTRACTS § 317(2)(c).

(c) is for the benefit of the obligor, and does not prevent the assignee from acquiring rights against the assignor or the obligor from discharging his duty as if there were no such prohibition.

The principle in subsection (1) – interpreting a restriction to apply only to the delegation of duties, not to assignment of rights – is codified in U.C.C. § 2-210(4). The principle in subsection (2)(b) is even more noteworthy. Pursuant to it, a contractual term stating merely that "neither party may assign its rights under this agreement" would not in fact prevent a party from making an effective assignment of rights. For an agreement to validly preclude assignment, it normally must include additional language, such as the phrase "and any attempted assignment is void."

Far more important than these interpretive principles are the statutory rules that override contractual restrictions on assignment. Article 9, in several extremely complex sections, prefers free alienability of property over freedom of contract. They do this by providing that many restrictions on assignment in a contract between an account debtor and the debtor do not prevent either the efficacy of an assignment to a secured party or the secured party's ability to enforce the assigned obligation. *See* § 9-406(d), (e), 9-407(a). The rules also provide that an assignment to a secured party does not and cannot constitute a default under the contract between the account debtor and the debtor. *See* §§ 9-406(d)(2), 9-407(a)(2), 9-408(a)(2), 9-409(a)(2). However, for some types of contracts, even though a security interest will attach to the obligation owed by the account debtor, the secured party might not be able to enforce the obligation against the account debtor. *See* §§ 9-408(a)–(d), 9-409. The extent of the secured party's rights against the account debtor is explored in Chapter Three.

Article 9 contains similar rules for dealing with *legal restrictions* on assignment, whether those restrictions are found in the common law or in a statute. *See* § 9-406(f), 9-408(c)(2), 9-409(a).[90] However, whether Article 9 will in fact override another statute that restricts assignment is somewhat questionable. This is illustrated by two cases regarding assignment of lottery winnings. In the first,[91] the

---

[90] Some states have not enacted the uniform text of § 9-406 and § 9-408. For example, New York has enacted only those rules that trump *contractual* restrictions on assignment, not the rules that trump *legal* restrictions on assignment. *See* N.Y. U.C.C. §§ 9-406, 9-408 (McKinney) (omitting uniform § 9-406(f) and § 9-408(c)).

[91] Texas Lottery Comm'n v. First State Bank of DeQueen, 254 S.W.3d 677 (Tex. Ct. App. 2008), *aff'd*, 325 S.W.3d 628 (Tex. 2010).

Texas Court of Appeals ruled that § 9-406(f) takes precedence over a Texas statute prohibiting assignment of state lottery winnings, even though the lottery statute was more recent and more specific, because § 9-406(f) makes clear that it controls over other law. A few weeks later, the California Court of Appeals ruled that the California Lottery Act, which also restricts the assignment of lottery winnings, trumped § 9-406(f) because the specific rules in the Lottery Act controlled over the more general rules in Article 9, even though Article 9 was enacted more recently.[92] Whatever the merits of these two decisions might be, collectively they provide a moral. While one might be able to comfortably rely on the rules in Article 9 to override contractual restrictions on assignment (and perhaps common-law restrictions as well), one cannot blithely assume those rules will override state statutory restrictions.[93] Indeed, many statutory restrictions on assignment – such as those discussed on pages 54-55 – appear in consumer-protection statutes and deal with goods, yet nothing in § 9-406 or § 9-408 purports to apply to restrictions on assignment of goods. Moreover, Article 9's rules will undoubtedly not override legal restrictions on assignment arising under federal or international law.[94]

This point about Article 9's rules not overriding federal restrictions on assignment is important in a variety of contexts. For example, a registered

---

[92] Stone Street Capital, LLC v. California State Lottery Comm'n, 80 Cal. Rptr. 3d 326 (Cal. Ct. App. 2008). *See also* Clark v. Missouri Lottery Comm'n, 463 S.W.3d 843 (Mo. Ct. App. 2015) (a bank obtained a security interest in a lottery winner's right to future distributions despite a state statute prohibiting the assignment of lottery proceeds because § 9-406 provides otherwise, expressly purports to prevail in the event of conflict with other law, and thus overrides that other state statute).

[93] *See also* Fenway Fin., LLC v. Greater Columbus Realty, LLC, 995 N.E.2d 1225 (Ohio Ct. App. 2013) (§ 9-406 did not override Ohio statute that prohibits a brokerage from paying real estate commission to a creditor of a broker).

[94] For this reason, there is some question whether a security interest can attach to a licensee's rights under an *exclusive* license to a copyright. There is language in a Ninth Circuit decision suggesting that the Copyright Act "does not allow a copyright licensee to transfer its rights under an exclusive license, without the consent of the original licensor." Gardner v. Nike, Inc., 279 F.3d 774, 780 (9th Cir. 2002). If that is indeed a correct statement of federal law, then § 9-408 would not override that rule. Moreover, it appears that the court was suggesting not that a restriction on assignment in the license agreement would be effective, but that active affirmative consent by the licensor is needed. In other words, silence prevents assignment. However, the Ninth Circuit's analysis has been heavily criticized. *See, e.g.*, Traicoff v. Digital Media, Inc., 439 F. Supp. 2d 872, 877-79 (S.D. Ind. 2006) (citing authorities).

trademark symbolizes the goodwill of the business to which it relates. Because of this, the owner is permitted to transfer a registered trademark only if there is an accompanying a transfer of the associated goodwill.[95] This rule applies to transfers for security, regardless of whether they purport to be absolute in form[96] or structured as a security interest.[97] Moreover, an attempted assignment in gross – that is, without the associated goodwill – is not only void, but might also invalidate the mark.[98] Hence, pursuant to federal law, a security interest will not attach to a registered trademark unless the security agreement also purports to encumber the associated goodwill.

Potentially more significant are the federal rules relating to the assignment of rights to payment under the Medicare and Medicaid programs. Those rules require states participating in the programs to prohibit payment under the plan to anyone other than the service provider.[99] Although there is authority ruling that this does not prohibit a service provider from using its right to payment under the plans as security for a loan,[100] they might prevent a factoring arrangement in which the rights to payment are sold outright,[101] which would otherwise be an Article 9 transaction.[102]

Another context in which federal law *might* restrict assignment is when the federal government is an account debtor that owes money to a contractual counter-party. The federal Assignment of Claims Act generally prohibits a federal

---

95 15 U.S.C. § 1060.

96 *See* Clorox Co. v. Chem. Bank, 40 U.S.P.Q.2d 1098 (T.T.A.B. 1996).

97 *See* Haymaker Sports, Inc. v. Turian, 581 F.2d 257 (C.C.P.A. 1978).

98 *See* Clorox Co. v. Chem. Bank, 40 U.S.P.Q.2d 1098 (assignment in gross of an intent-to-use application was not only invalid but the resulting registration for such mark was also rendered void).

99 *See* 42 U.S.C. § 1396a.

100 *See, e.g.*, In re Missionary Baptist Found. of Am., Inc., 796 F.2d 752, 756-59 (5th Cir. 1986); Lock Realty Corp. IX v. U.S. Health, LP, 2007 WL 724750, at *1 (N.D. Ind. 2007); Credit Recovery Sys., LLC v. Hieke, 158 F. Supp. 2d 689, 693 (E.D. Va. 2001); In re Parkview Adventist Med. Ctr., 2015 WL 4692538, at * 3 (Bankr. D. Me. 2015); In re East Boston Neighborhood Health Ctr. Corp., 242 B.R. 562, 573 (Bankr. D. Mass. 1999).

101 *See* In re Assist-Med., Inc., 2017 WL 5900538, at *5-6 (Bankr. S.D. Tex. 2017).

102 *See infra* pp. 142-35.

contractor from transferring "the contract . . . or any interest in the contract."[103] There is a limited exception, however, that permits contractors to assign to a bank or other financing institution "amounts due" from the federal government, but not "if the contract forbids the assignment."[104] How this language, and similar language in the regulations,[105] interacts with § 9-406(d) is unclear. The language could override § 9-406(d). After all, § 9-406 is state law, and to the extent that federal conflicts with it, the federal law governs. Alternatively, the reference to what "the contract" forbids might refer not only to what the agreement states, but to the legal obligations of the parties arising from the agreement. In other words, the language does not refer to whether the "agreement" prohibits assignment, it refers to whether the "contract" prohibits assignment.[106] Consequently, the language might be deemed to incorporate state law that limits restrictions on assignment, whether that law is in Article 9 or part of the common law of contract.

Problem 2-23

Sam owns a hay baler that he has contracted to sell to Barbara for $10,000. Their written agreement provides that neither Sam nor Barbara may assign his or her respective rights under the agreement to any other person and that any attempted assignment of such rights is void.

A. If Sam were to grant a security interest in his rights under the agreement with Barbara, what would be the collateral classification? *See* § 2-301.
B. If Barbara were to grant a security interest in her rights under the agreement with Sam, what would be the collateral classification? *See* § 2-301.
C. If, in return for a loan, Sam signed a security agreement purporting to grant State Bank a security interest in his rights under the agreement with Barbara, would the grant be effective to create a security interest? *See* §§ 2-210, 9-406, 9-408.

---

[103] 41 U.S.C. § 6305(a).

[104] 41 U.S.C. § 6305(b)(1), (3).

[105] *See* 48 C.F.R. § 32.802(c).

[106] *Cf.* § 1-201(b)(3), (12) (defining "agreement" as the bargain of the parties and defining "contract" as the legal obligation that results from an agreement).

D. If, in return for a loan, Barbara signed a security agreement purporting to grant State Bank a security interest in her rights under the agreement with Sam, would the grant be effective to create a security interest?

E. How, if at all, would the analysis change if the agreement did not contain a clause barring assignment, but applicable contract law prohibited assignment in connection with contracts of this type?

One arguable benefit of Article 9's anti-assignment rules is that they seemingly allow a security interest to attach to the debtor's interest in a general partnership, limited partnership, or limited liability company even if the entity formation documents prohibit partners or members from assigning their interests or require the consent of the other partners or members to an assignment.[107] *See* § 9-408(a). However, overriding a contractual restriction on the assignment of an ownership interest in a business entity involves a third fundamental value of American law: freedom of association (or, as more colloquially phrased, the "pick-your-partner principle"). As a result, the principle of free alienability of property butts up against two competing values: freedom of contract and freedom of association. To deal with this, several states adopted non-uniform language to Article 9 or enacted statutes outside Article 9 to exempt interests in one or more of such entities from Article 9's anti-assignment rules.[108] In addition, the Permanent Editorial Board drafted a commentary that, although never issued in final form, rejected the conclusion that § 9-408 overrides restrictions on assignment in entity formation documents. The draft commentary was based on the observation that § 9-408 operates on an agreement between the debtor and an account debtor but the entity itself, which is likely to be an "account debtor" under § 9-102(a)(3), is usually not a party to its own formation documents, and the other partners or members, for whose benefit the restriction operates, are not account debtors.[109]

---

[107] The anti-assignment rules do not apply to collateral constituting investment property.

[108] *See* Ala. Code § 10A-5A-1.06(e); Colo. Rev. Stat. § 7-90-104; Del. Code Ann. tit. 6, §§ 9-408(e)(4) 15-104(c), 15-503(f), 17-1101(g), 18-1101(g); Ky. Rev. Stat. Ann. §§ 275.255(4), 362.1-503(7), 362.2-702(8); Tex. Bus. & Com. Code §§ 9.406(j), 9.408(e); Va. Code §§ 8.9A-406(k); 8.9A-408(g), 13.1-1001.1(B), 50-73.84(C).

[109] If the entity is a party to the agreement restricting assignment, then § 9-408 might apply and override the restriction. Landress v. Sparkman, 2020 WL 561893 (E.D.N.C.). The ruling in *Landress* is questionable for other reasons, however. *See* Stephen L. Sepinuck, *What Choice Do I Have? – Choice-of-Law Clauses Governing Attachment of a Security*

Despite the comfort provided by the draft commentary, some business lawyers remained concerned that there is insufficient protection for the "pick your partner" policy. Accordingly, in 2018 the UCC's sponsoring organizations promulgated a new § 9-406(k) and a new § 9-408(f) to make it more clear that neither section overrides a restriction on the transfer of an ownership interest in a general partnership, limited partnership, or limited liability company. Only Florida enacted these provisions prior to finalization of the 2022 UCC Amendments.[110] However, as noted above, several states already had nonuniform rules addressing the issue and several more have, pursuant to a legislative note included in the 2022 UCC Amendments, adopted these provisions when enacting the amendments.

When seeking to obtain a security interest in the rights associated with a membership in a limited partnership or limited liability company, one must consider not only the efficacy of any restriction on assignment in the entity's organizational documents but also how the statute that governs formation of the entity affects the efficacy and scope of the security interest.

For example, the Delaware Limited Liability Company Act does not refer to a member's "membership interest,"[111] and instead carefully distinguishes among a member's economic rights, control rights, and membership status. In connection with this, the Act establishes two default rules relating to assignment: (i) members may assign their economic rights; and (ii) members cannot assign their control rights or membership status.[112] The company's operating agreement can alter either or both of these rules, but if the agreement is silent a member cannot transfer voting rights associated with membership or membership status.[113] Thus, unless the

---

Interest, 10 THE TRANSACTIONAL LAW. 9 (June 2020); Carl S. Bjerre & Stephen L. Sepinuck, *Spotlight*, COMMERCIAL LAW NEWSLETTER 11 (March 2020).

[110] *See* 2022 Fla. Sess. Law Serv. Ch. 2022-119 (enacting Fla. Stat. §§ 679.4061(12), 679.4081(8)).

[111] The Delaware Act does, however, refer to "[a] limited liability company interest" see Del. Code, tit. 6, § 18-702(a), (b), and to "a member's interest," *id.* § 18-702(c).

[112] Del. Code, tit. 6, § 18-702(a), (b).

[113] In New York, the rules are similar. Unless the operating agreement provides otherwise, an assignee of a membership interest acquires the member's rights to receive distributions and an allocation of profits and losses, but not the right to participate in the management of the company or to exercise the member's other rights or powers of a member. N.Y. Ltd. Liab. Co. Law § 603(a)(2), (3). The provisions of the Uniform LLC Act are also similar. *See* Uniform LLC Act §§ 102(24), 502(a), (b), (f).

company's operating agreement expressly provides otherwise, a secured party acquires no security interest in voting or management rights associated with a membership interest in a Delaware limited liability company.

Problem 2-24

A. Diaz and Jimenez each owns a 50% of Dribble, LLC, a Delaware limited liability company. The operating agreement for Dribble has no term relating to the assignment of a membership interest. In return for a loan to Dribble, Dribble granted Lender a security interest in substantially all of its assets, Diaz and Jimenez each guaranteed the debt, and Diaz and Jimenez each signed a security agreement purporting to grant Lender a security interest in "Debtor's entire membership interest in Dribble LLC."
   1. To what rights, if any, of Diaz and Jimenez did Lender's security interest attach?
   2. How, if at all, would the analysis of Part A(1) change if the operating agreement stated that "no member may assign or grant a security interest in any of such member's rights as a member without the prior written consent of all other members"?
   3. How, if at all, would the analysis of Part A(1) change if Diaz was the sole owner of Dribble, LLC and only Dribble and Diaz had signed security agreements?

B. To induce Hedge Fund to make a secured loan to Doublecross, LLC, a California limited liability company, the members of Doublecross duly amended the company's operating agreement to require Hedge Fund's prior written consent to: (i) any grant of a security interest in personal property of the company; or (ii) any future amendment to the operating agreement. The amended operating agreement also expressly states that any attempt to grant a security interest in the company's personal property without the requisite prior written consent is void. Are these restrictions effective or can Doublecross grant a security interest in its personal property without Hedge Fund's prior written consent? *See* §§ 9-406(d), 9-408(a); Cal. Corp. Code § 17701.12(a).

Article 9's anti-assignment rules apply principally to rights to payment and other contract rights – accounts, chattel paper, general intangibles, and promissory notes – because it is primarily in that context that the principle of freedom of contract butts up against the principle that property should be freely alienable. But what about contractual restrictions on the assignability of other types of property, for example goods? Nothing in § 9-406 of § 9-408 purports to override a contractual restriction on a person's ability to grant a security interest in goods. Does that mean such a restriction is effective? Consider the following illustration.

Illustration

Sports League owns trademarks to the Sports League's own logo and to the logos of the teams in the league. Sport League regularly licenses the trademarks to manufacturers, so that they may make and sell clothing and other merchandise bearing these logos. The standard License Agreement that Sports League uses limits how each licensee may sell merchandise bearing a trademarked logo and states that "Licensee shall not, without Licensor's prior written consent, grant a security interest in any of Licensee's rights under this Agreement or any Trademarked Merchandise, and any attempt to grant a security interest without such consent is ineffective."

Manufacturer entered into such a License Agreement, giving Manufacturer license to manufacture and sell sweatshirts bearing the logos of the teams in the league. May Manufacturer grant a security interest in the license? May it grant a security interest in the sweatshirts bearing a trademarked logo and manufactured pursuant to that license? *See* §§ 2-403, 9-401, 9-408.

The answer to the first question is rather straightforward. Section 9-408(a) undoubtedly allows Manufacturer to grant a security interest in the license. As will be explored more fully in Chapter Three, the secured party might have no ability to sell, sub-license, or enforce that license, however.

The answer to the second question is much more complicated. Neither § 9-406 nor § 9-408 applies to the goods. Instead, the ability of Manufacturer to grant a security interest in the goods – or, to put it another way, the enforceability of the License Agreement's restriction on Manufacturer's ability to grant a security interest in the goods – is left to other law. *See* § 9-401(a). There is no clear answer to what other law provides, but some things are known.

First, Sports League does not have, by the mere license itself, any rights to the goods manufactured pursuant to the license, although Sports league could obtain an injunction against a breach of the license if, for example, Manufacturer were to start selling the goods in a manner or location that violates the terms of the license. As result, it is far from clear that either contract law or property law would enforce a restriction on a person's rights to transfer its own goods.

Second, § 2-403 protects purchasers of goods (the term "purchaser" includes a secured party). A purchaser acquires all title which his transferor had or had power to transfer. Arguably, this rule overrides a contractual restriction on the grant of a security interest in goods.

Third, if Sports League had obtained a security interest in the goods (to secure its rights to payment and other rights under the License Agreement), then § 9-401(b) would apply. It provides that an agreement between the debtor and secured party which prohibits a transfer of the debtor's rights in collateral or makes the transfer a default does not prevent the transfer from taking effect. It would be anomalous indeed if a licensor that actually had rights in the goods (a security interest) could not restrict the debtor from granting a security interest in the goods but a licensor who had no rights in the goods could so restrict the debtor.

However, even if the restriction in the license is ineffective to prevent a security interest from attaching to the goods, the grant of the security interest would no doubt be a breach of the license agreement. On this point, note that when § 9-406 and 9-408 override a contractual restriction on assignment, they also declare that the assignment is not a breach. *See* §§ 9-406(d)(2), 9-408(a)(2). Section 9-401(b) does not do that. When § 9-401(b) applies, it merely allows for the security interest to attach. Moreover, breach of the license agreement would almost assuredly give Sports League the right to terminate the license. If Sports League does so, it could probably get an injunction against any sale of the goods.[114] So, while it seems likely that Manufacturer could grant a security interest in the goods without the consent of Sports League, it is possible that Sports league could prevent the secured party from conducting a disposition or otherwise transferring the goods.[115]

---

[114] The "first sale" doctrine, which prevents a trademark owner from asserting rights after the goods have entered the stream of commerce, would not apply because the goods have not yet been sold. Even if Manufacturer had subcontracted the manufacturing process to another entity, which then made and sold the goods to Manufacturer, the first sale doctrine would be unlikely to apply. That doctrine kicks in following a sale that puts the goods into the stream of commerce. A sale by the manufacturer to the trademark licensee is not such a transaction.

[115] It is possible that § 9-201(a) would subordinate Sports League's rights to the rights of the secured party. However, it is not clear that § 9-201(a) operates in that manner and, to the extent that Sport's League's trademark rights are a matter of federal law, § 9-201(a) could not affect them. Section 9-201(a) is explored more fully in Chapter 5.

SECTION 6. SPECIAL ATTACHMENT RULES: AUTOMATIC ATTACHMENT

For some types of collateral, no explicit statement in the security agreement is necessary for the security interest to attach to it. We have already seen two examples of this: (i) the automatic attachment of a security interest to proceeds of the collateral; and (ii) the automatic attachment of a security interest to the product or mass that results from commingling collateral with other goods. Review §§ 9-203(f), 9-315(a)(2), 9-336(c). Article 9 includes several additional automatic attachment rules, situations when there need be no explicit description of the collateral type in the security agreement for the security interest to attach to the undescribed property. Frequently, this is because the undescribed property is so intricately associated with some other, expressly covered property such that a security interest should naturally extend to the undescribed property. The relevant rules are contained in subsections (f) through (i) of § 9-203.

Certain investment property. Read § 9-203(h) and (i). If the security agreement describes the collateral to include a securities account, it necessarily covers all securities entitlements in that account. Similarly, if the described collateral includes a commodities account, all commodity contracts within that account are also covered. In less formal language, if the collateral is an account at a brokerage house, the security interest automatically extends to the securities and commodity contracts credited to that account.

This rule is particularly important in consumer transactions. Recall the special rule of § 9-108(e)(2), which provides that description of securities accounts or security entitlements by type is not adequate in a consumer transaction. Thus a collateral description of just "securities account" or "securities entitlement" is not a sufficient description of the collateral in a consumer transaction. Among other things, this makes covering after-acquired security entitlements very difficult. However, if a collateral description in a security agreement in a consumer transaction stated "all securities accounts at Brokerage House," that description would not be a description *merely* by type under § 9-108(e)(2) and would be sufficient under § 9-108. The rule of § 9-203(h) would then come into play. The security interest would attach to all securities entitlements held in that securities account whether there currently or acquired in the future. *See* § 9-108 cmt. 5.

Rights in a secured obligation. Read § 9-203(g). This provision is easiest to understand by considering the following situation. Assume Landowner borrows money from Lender, giving Lender a promissory note in return and granting Lender a mortgage in described real estate. As we learned in Chapter One, there are two obligations, the *in personam* obligation to pay the loan owed by Landowner to Lender and the *in rem* obligation of the real estate as security for the debt. The *in personam* obligation is represented by the promissory note and the *in rem* obligation is granted in the mortgage. Now assume Lender in turn needs to borrow money from Bank. In the transaction between them, Lender grants a security interest to Bank in the promissory note Lender received from Landowner to secure the loan that Bank makes to Lender. Thus we have two transactions: the first which is not governed by Article 9, and the second which is:

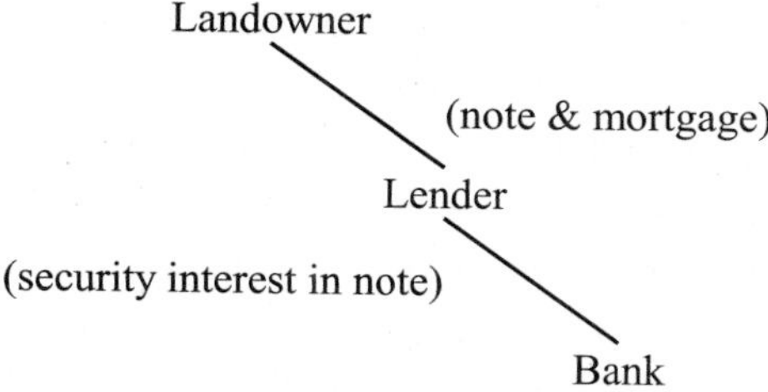

Subsection (g) provides that when Bank's security interest attaches to the promissory note, it also attaches to Lender's rights under the mortgage, and it does so automatically, without any need for the security agreement to reference the mortgage. The same analysis applies if the transaction between Landowner and Lender had been a security interest in personal property to secure a debt. In short, when a right to payment is offered as collateral, the security interest extends to any lien securing that payment. There is one caveat with respect to mortgages. If Bank wants to be able to foreclose the mortgage in the event both Lender and Landowner default on their obligations to pay, Bank will probably want to file an assignment of the mortgagee's (Lender's) rights under the mortgage in the real estate records given the usual rules found in real estate law regarding who has the ability to conduct a valid foreclosure of the mortgage. *Cf.* §§ 9-109(d)(11), 9-607(b).

Supporting obligations. Subsection (f) does for guarantees what subsection (g) does for liens. Again an example is useful. Debtor sells goods on credit to Purchaser. The obligation of Purchaser to pay for the goods is an "account." Debtor has required Purchaser to obtain a guarantor for the obligation to pay in order to reduce the risk of nonpayment. Purchaser did so by getting another person to sign an agreement with Debtor guaranteeing to pay the obligation in the event Purchaser does not. The guarantee agreement is a "supporting obligation" in relationship to the "account." *See* § 9-102(a)(78).[116] If Debtor later borrows money from Bank and grants Bank a security interest in Debtor's accounts, Bank's security interest attaches not only to the account but also to the supporting obligation: the obligation of the guarantor on the guaranty. The security agreement need not mention the guaranty or use the phrase "supporting obligation" for this to occur.[117]

Problem 2-25

Distributor sells construction and earth-moving equipment to builders and developers. Several years ago, Distributor granted State Bank a security interest in all of Distributor's existing and after-acquired inventory, accounts, and chattel paper to secure a $50 million loan. Last week, Distributor reached a tentative agreement for Buyer to purchase all of Distributor's earth-moving equipment (Distributor decided to focus its business on construction equipment) for $20 million.

A. If, in connection with the transaction, Buyer provides Distributor with each of the following, to which will State Bank's security interest attach?
    1. A security interest in the earth-moving equipment purchased by Buyer to secure payment of the purchase price due to Distributor.
    2. A mortgage on real property that Buyer owns to secure payment of the purchase price.
    3. A guaranty agreement pursuant to which Owner promises to pay up to $10 million if Buyer fails to make payment to Distributor when due.
    4. A standby letter of credit from National Bank on which Distributor may draw if Buyer fails to make payment when due.

B. With respect to anything in Part A as to which State Bank's security interest will not or might not attach, what should State Bank do to ensure that it acquires an enforceable interest?

Test Your Knowledge
Exam Two – Attachment

---

[116] A letter-of-credit right can also be a supporting obligation. Such rights are discussed in Chapter Six.

[117] The guarantor's obligation on the guarantee is probably a general intangible, if it were necessary to describe it as a specific type of collateral.

SECTION 7. CREATING AN ENFORCEABLE SECURITY INTEREST: THE SCOPE OF ARTICLE 9

A. Form of a Transaction

1. Leases

So far we have been concentrating on creating an enforceable security interest by contract when the parties intended to create a security interest. Read § 9-109(a)(1). It provides that Article 9 applies to any transaction, "regardless of its form," that creates a security interest in personal property or fixtures by contract. In short, neither form nor intent matters, substance does.[118] Consequently, the parties need not label their arrangement as a security agreement or refer to the interest created as a security interest. All that they need do is give expression to a deal that, in economic terms, is a security device.

Consider a seller of furniture that allows customers to purchase on credit. You might have seen ads that say "no money down, no interest until next year." Now assume that the written sales agreement, which the customer signs, provides that the seller retains title to the goods until the customer makes all the required payments. This is known as a "conditional sales contract." The passing of title to the goods is conditioned on full payment by the customer. The purpose of that clause is to allow the seller to reclaim the goods should the customer not fully pay. Accordingly, it is a security device and the agreement creates a security interest governed by Article 9, even though the written agreement never uses the phrases

---

[118] The old version of Article 9 applied to "any transaction (regardless of its form) which *is intended to* create a security interest in personal property." U.C.C. § 9-102(1)(a) (superseded) (emphasis added). The drafters of revised Article 9 in 1999 purposefully omitted the reference to intent in an effort to signal that the economic substance of the transaction is what matters. A sentence added to § 9-109 comment 2 in 2010 makes this even more clear: "the subjective intention of the parties with respect to the legal characterization of their transaction is irrelevant to whether this Article applies, as it was to the application of former Article 9 under the proper interpretation of former Section 9-102." As one court explained:

> The intent to put the transaction in a particular legal pigeonhole . . . is irrelevant. . . . "The question for the court to decide is whether the true nature of the transaction is such that the legal rights and economic consequences of the agreement bear a greater similarity to a financing transaction or to a sale."

In re Hawaii Island Air, Inc., 2019 WL 2041705, at *4 (Bankr. D. Haw. 2019) (*quoting* In re Evergreen Valley Resort, Inc., 23 B.R. 659, 661 (Bankr. D. Me. 1982)).

"security interest" or "lien." In short, retention of title by a seller of goods creates a security interest (assuming the other requirements of § 9-203(b) are satisfied),[119] and does not in fact prevent title from passing to the buyer. *See* § 2-401. This point is made expressly in the penultimate sentence of § 1-201(b)(35).[120] The seller is therefore also a secured party and the buyer is a debtor.

Now consider a transaction that is denominated a lease of goods. In such a transaction, the lessor – who by definition retains title to the property – transfers possession and use of the goods to the lessee for a period of time in exchange for the lessee's periodic payment of rent. *See* § 2A-103(1) (definition of lease). If the lessee fails to pay, the lessor may reclaim the goods. Notice, this can look a lot like a conditional sale. In both, one party pays for possession and use of the property over time, while the other party has a right to take the goods back if payment is not made. This raises the interesting problem of when a transaction labeled as a "lease" is truly a sale in which the seller, by calling itself a "lessor," has retained title as a security device.

The UCC deals with this problem through a sort of economic reality test.[121] In a true sale, the seller does not expect to get the property back if the buyer pays. In a true lease, the lessor does expect to get the property back after the lessee pays and the lease term expires. Accordingly, the UCC bases the determination on whether there is a reasonable likelihood that the party denominated as "lessor" truly retains a valuable, residual economic interest in the goods. This usually revolves around whether the lease term equals or exceeds the entire economic life of the goods or whether some provision of the lease agreement is likely to trigger an event that prevents the goods from ever reverting back to the lessor while they still have

---

[119] The agreement pursuant to which the seller retains title must describe the goods, *see* § 9-203(b)(3)(A), and according to at least one court must be signed by the debtor. *See* Stamey Cattle Co. v. Wright, 2019 WL 722597 (S.D. Ga. 2019) (invoices of a credit seller of cattle, which provided that "[t]itle will transfer when full payment is received" could function as a security agreement but only if the invoices were signed by the buyer).

[120] *See also* § 2-401; Usinor Industeel v. Leeco Steel Products, Inc., 209 F. Supp. 2d 880 (N.D. Ill. 2002).

[121] Real property law in most states does the same. *See, e.g.*, Vic's Antiques and Uniques, Inc. v. J. Elra Holdingz, LLC, 143 N.E.3d 300 (Ind. Ct. App. 2020) (treating a 20-year lease of real property with an option to purchase for $1 at the end of the lease term as a sale with a retained mortgage, rather than as a lease).

economic life. If either of these is true, the UCC treats the transaction as a sale with a retained security interest. If not, the UCC treats the transaction as true lease.[122]

The consequences of this determination are varied and important, as the chart beginning on the next page illustrates.[123] First, there are significant tax and accounting consequences. For example, if the transaction is a true lease, then the rent is income to the lessor and probably a deductible expense to the lessee. Moreover, the lessor may be entitled to a depreciation deduction for the goods. On the other hand, if the transaction is a credit sale, the rental payments are not deductible by the lessee. Instead, the lessee – who is really a buyer – may claim the depreciation allowance, and the lessor – as a seller – might have recognizable gain or loss on the sale. Accounting rules permit a lessee to treat the rental payments as periodic expenses but, in contrast, require a credit buyer's balance sheet to show a debt for the unpaid purchase price.

---

[122] *See* In re Pillowtex, Inc., 349 F.3d 711 (3d Cir. 2003); In re Schultz, 2022 WL 16752855 (Bankr. E.D. Mich. 2022) (if the lessor has "a meaningful reversionary interest . . . the parties have signed a lease, not a security agreement. If there is no reversionary interest, the parties have signed a security agreement, not a lease") (*quoting* In re QDS Components, Inc., 292 B.R. 313, 332-33 (Bankr. S.D. Ohio 2002)).

More than a dozen states have statutes that expressly exempt "rental-purchase agreements" from Article 9. These agreements involve the lease of consumer goods to a consumer for an initial period of four months or less. *See, e.g.*, Utah Code Ann. §§ 15-8-3, 15-8-4 (defining a "rental-purchase agreement" and providing that it shall not be deemed a security interest under former § 1-201(37)). Some limit their scope to agreements in which the debtor has no obligation beyond four months, *see* Ariz. Rev. Stat. § 44-6801; Ark. Code § 4-92-102; Fla. Stat. § 559.9232(1)(e), (2)(f); Idaho Code § 28-36-102; La. Rev. Stat. § 9:3352; Me. Rev. Stat. tit. 9-A, § 11-105; Wash. Rev. Code § 63.19.010(5); In re Minton, 271 B.R. 335 (Bankr. W.D. Ark. 2001) (interpreting the Arkansas statute), and thus would probably not be thought to create security interests anyway. *See* U.C.C. § 1-203. Others are not expressly limited to situations in which the debtor has no obligation beyond four months as long as the "initial period" is four months or less. *See, e.g.*, Ala. Code § 8-25-1; Cal. Civ. Code § 1812.622; Colo. Rev. Stat. § 5-10-301; 815 Ill. Comp. Stat. 655/1; Ind. Code § 24-7-2-9; Iowa Code § 537.3604; Ky. Rev. Stat. § 367.976; Md. Code, Com. Law § 12-1101; Tenn. Code § 47-18-603(7). *See also* In re Knowles, 253 B.R. 412 (Bankr. E.D. Ky. 2000) (interpreting the Kentucky statute as exempting such agreements from Article 9).

[123] When real property is involved, there can be other consequences. For example, the summary proceedings available to evict a tenant might not apply if the putative lease is really a sale with a mortgage, and the court with subject matter jurisdiction to hear the putative landlord's claim to recover the property might be different. *See, e.g.*, Vic's Antiques and Uniques, Inc., 2020 WL 769638.

Second, if the transaction is a lease, Article 2A governs. If it is a credit sale with title retained as a security device, Articles 2 and 9 apply. Depending on whether some aspects of Article 9 are complied with, this can undermine the right of the lessor/seller to get the goods back by giving a superior claim to the goods to other creditors of the lessee/buyer.

Third, if the "lessee" fails to fulfill its obligations under the lease, the lessee's bankruptcy might not be far behind. If the lessee in fact ends up in bankruptcy, characterization of the transaction as a lease or credit sale will greatly affect the ability of the debtor or trustee to retain the property. If the transaction is a lease, the goods may be retained only if the lease contract is performed according to its terms. If the transaction is a sale, it might be possible to keep the goods while paying the lessor/seller over time either the amounts due under the lease or the value of the goods, whichever is less.[124]

THE SIGNIFICANCE OF THE SALE/LEASE DISTINCTION

	Credit Sale (no security interest)	**Sale & Security Interest (disguised as a lease)**	**True Lease**
Governing Law	Article 2	Articles 2 & 9	Article 2A
Can Seller/Lessor get goods back for nonpayment?	No	Yes	Yes
Tax/Accounting Realization Event	Yes	Yes	No
Tax/Accounting Depreciation Allowance	Buyer	Buyer/Lessee	Lessor
Tax/Accounting Payments	No Effect	No Effect	Income to Lessor & deduction to Lessee.

[124] *See, e.g.*, In re Paz, 179 B.R. 743 (Bankr. S.D. Ga. 1995).

	Credit Sale (no security interest)	Sale & Security Interest (disguised as a lease)	True Lease
Rights of Creditors of Buyer/Lessee	Can potentially get goods.	Can potentially get goods if Lessor/Seller did not perfect a security interest.	Cannot get goods, might be able to attach rights to lessee's leasehold interest.
Effect of Buyer/Lessee Bankruptcy	Seller's rights will likely be significantly modified. Seller might recover nothing.	If Lessor/Seller perfected its security interest, its property rights are protected but can be modified. Lessor/Seller entitled to lesser of debt or value of goods.	Lessor entitled to have all lease obligations performed or the goods returned.

Given the significance of the lease/credit sale distinction, it is perhaps not surprising that the UCC provides some rather complicated rules for making the determination. Read § 1-203. Subsection (a) provides minimal help; it merely states that whether a transaction structured as a lease is really a lease or is instead a sale and retained security interest depends upon the facts of the case. More guidance is found in subsection (b), which lays out four circumstances in which the transaction definitively creates a security interest. If the circumstances in subsection (b) are not present, that does not mean that the transaction is a lease; it merely means that the analysis falls back to the general, fact-specific standard of subsection (a). In such a case, subsection (c) contains a list of contractual terms that are not to be regarded as determinative, although they might still be relevant. Subsections (d) and (e) contain some guidance on the meaning of phrases found in subsection (b).[125]

---

[125] It is important to understand that subsections (d) and (e) are *not* definitions. Look at subsection (d). Its first sentence indicates that consideration is nominal in a specified situation and its second sentence indicates that consideration is not nominal in two specified situations. Even collectively, these sentences are not a definition. When neither sentence applies, the subsection simply provides no guidance on whether consideration is or is not nominal. This point is analogous to a tenet of basic logic. Each sentence is phrased, in essence, as "if X, then Y." Such a statement provides no guidance about what the happens if the stated condition is not true. In other words, if not X, then nothing certain follows. For much the same reason, subsection (e) does not define anything either.

This issue of whether the transaction creates a true lease or a security interest is an often litigated matter. After reviewing § 1-203, attempt the problem that follows.

Problem 2-26

Consider the following transactions in which Car Dealer "leases" a new $16,400 car to Driver. Driver is responsible for all maintenance and insurance on the car. Driver is obligated to pay the rent for the entire "lease" term even if Driver returns the car to Car Dealer before the end of the "lease" term. In each case, the present value of all the rental payments to become due under the agreement is $16,400. In which of these scenarios, if any, is the transaction really a sale with title retained by the "lessor," and thus in reality a security arrangement?

A. A 20-year lease at $140 per month. Car Dealer gets the car at end of "lease" term.

B. A 4-year lease at $400 per month.
   1. Car Dealer gets car at end of "lease" term.
   2. Driver has option to buy for $5 at end of "lease" term.
   3. Driver has option to buy for $1,000 at end of "lease" term.

C. How does your analysis change in any of the scenarios if Driver can return the car to Car Dealer before the end of the lease term without further obligation to make any remaining monthly payments?

In making the sale/lease distinction for bankruptcy purposes, courts tend to apply the UCC rules. For tax and accounting purposes, the rules distinguishing a lease from a sale are a bit different.[126] Although the analysis will often produce the same conclusion for these different purposes, in some cases it might be possible to structure a transaction as a sale for some purposes and as a lease for others.

This point is important because it also underlies how subsection (b) operates. As already noted, if subsection (b) does not apply – *i.e.*, if it fails to indicate that the transaction as a sale – then the inverse (the transaction is not a sale) is not necessarily true. Instead, the analysis reverts to the basic standard of subsection (a).

[126] *See, e.g.*, Rev. Proc. 2001-28, 2001-1 C.B. 1156; Rev. Proc. 2001-29, 2001-1 C.B. 1160; Financial Accounting Standards Board, Financial Accounting Statement 140 (2000).

2. Consignments and Sales or Return

We now consider how Article 9 deals with consignments. Before doing so, however, it useful to distinguish among bailments, entrustments, and consignments.

A bailment is any situation in which one person agrees to hold goods of another for that person's benefit. Leaving your pet dog or cat with a friend or kennel while you travel out of town is a bailment. In that example, there is a transfer of possession but no transfer of property rights.

An entrustment is a bailment in which the bailee is a merchant who deals in goods of that kind. Bringing a diamond necklace to jeweler to have the clasp fixed is an entrustment. In such an entrustment, there is also no transfer of property rights. However, as explored in connection with Problem 2-22 the merchant acquires the *power* to transfer the entruster's rights to a buyer in ordinary course of business. *See* § 2-403(2).

A consignment is an entrustment for the purpose of sale. The consignor delivers goods to a merchant for the merchant to sell. Some merchants, particularly those who sell used goods or locally produced art and crafts, do not own the goods they offer for sale. Instead, the owner (the "consignor") has merely delivered possession of the goods to the merchant (the "consignee") for sale, with the understanding that, upon sale, the merchant will remit the proceeds to the owner after deducting a specified amount or percentage (a commission) for itself. In effect, the consignee is functioning as the consignor's selling agent. The consignor retains ownership of the goods and the consignee must return the goods to the consignor if they are not sold by an agreed upon date or upon the consignor's demand.

As might be apparent from the foregoing discussion, entrustment is a subset of bailment and consignment is a subset of entrustment:

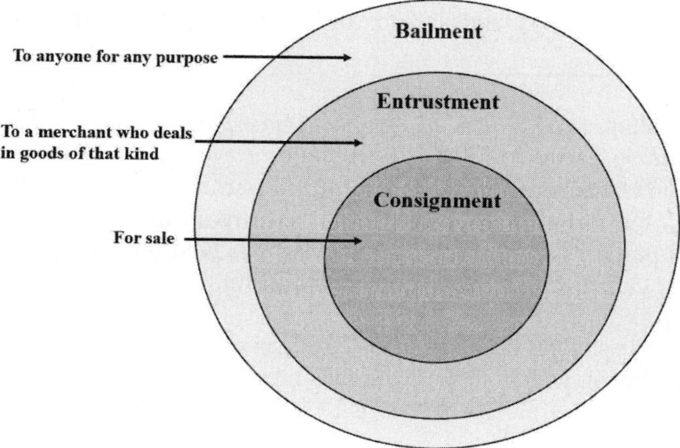

Although a consignment – like an entrustment – also does not transfer property rights from the consignor to the consignee (at least as between the two of them), the law treats a consignment differently from an entrustment in two important respects: (i) the consignment transaction is itself an Article 9 transaction (subject to some exceptions); and (ii) the consignee is empowered to transfer a security interest in the consigned goods to one or more third parties (again, subject to some exceptions). There are two principal reasons for this.

First, just as a credit sale of goods can often be documented as a lease, with the retention of title by the seller operating as a security device, it can alternatively be documented as a consignment (the economics are similar and the documents are easily manipulable). Consider, for example, a transaction labeled and structured as a consignment but pursuant to which the consignor has no right to demand the goods back and the consignee is obligated to buy the goods if the consignee fails to sell them by a specified date. In such a transaction, there is no meaningful distinction between the consignor's retention of title and a security interest.

Second, in consignment transactions, the arrangement between the consignor and the consignee is generally invisible to everyone other than the consignor and the consignee. The consignee has possession of goods and those goods appear to be the consignee's inventory; none of the consignee's customers or creditors might be aware that the goods are in fact owned by the consignor.

Article 9 deals with this problem by bringing many consignment transactions within its scope. *See* § 9-109(a)(4). By doing this, the law obviates the need to distinguish between a true consignment and a secured transaction disguised as a consignment, something that has long been troublesome in commercial law.[127] Moreover, consignors are impelled to provide public notice of their retained interests in consigned goods. However, Article 9's definition of "consignment" is a limited. It excludes: (i) transactions unlikely to confuse other creditors of the

---

[127] *See* Peter Winship, *The "True" Consignment Under the Uniform Commercial Code, and Related Peccadillos*, 29 Sw. L.J. 825 (1975).

The distinction between a true consignment and a security device might still matter for some purposes. For example, the consignee's property insurance might not cover goods owned by third parties, and thus might exclude goods held on consignment. *Cf.* Italian Designer Import Outlet, Inc. v. New York Central Mut. Fire Ins. Co., 891 N.Y.S.2d 260 (N.Y. Sup. Ct. 2009).

Some states have statutes that exempt the consignment of fine art from Article 9 and treat it instead as a bailment, with both the consigned property and its proceeds held in trust for the consignor. *See, e.g.*, Cal. Civ. Code §§ 1738.5 – 1738.9; Mont. Code §§ 22-2-501 – 22-2-505.

consignee; and (ii) transactions for which the burden of complying with Article 9 would outweigh the benefits. *See* § 9-102(a)(20).

This legal regime in effect creates three categories:

(1) False consignments: security transactions disguised as consignments, which are within the scope of Article 9 under § 9-109(a)(1);
(2) True consignments that fall within the definition of "consignment" under § 9-102(a)(20), and thus are brought within the scope of Article 9 by § 9-109(a)(4); and
(3) True consignments that fall outside the § 9-102(a)(20) definition of "consignment" (perhaps because they involve property worth less than $1,000 or property that was consumer goods in the hands of the consignor), and thus are outside the scope of Article 9.[128]

If a true consignment is governed by Article 9 (the second category above), the consignor's interest in the consigned goods is called a "security interest,"[129] the consignor constitutes an Article 9 "secured party,"[130] and the consignee is an Article 9 "debtor."[131] Such a consignor must then comply with the requirements of Article 9 – such as by providing public notice of its interest in the consigned goods – or risk losing the goods to some other creditor of the consignee.[132] In other words, the

---

[128] If a transaction is a true consignment but not within the definition of consignment in § 9-102(a)(20), the transaction is a bailment. The bailee's ability to transfer rights in the goods will be determined under the law of bailments. *See* § 9-102 cmt. 14. Typically, the bailee will only be able to transfer its own rights, not the rights of the bailor, to another person. *See* In re Haley & Steele, Inc., 2005 WL 3489869 (Mass. Super. Ct. 2005) (delivery of consumer goods to merchant buyer that is excluded from the definition of "consignment" by § 9-102(a)(20)(C) should not be regarded as a sale or return under Article 2, and therefore subject to all the merchant's creditors – which would be worse than treating the transaction as a consignment and subjecting the goods to the merchant's secured creditors – and is instead simply a bailment).

[129] *See* § 1-201(b)(35).

[130] *See* § 9-102(a)(21), (73)(C).

[131] *See* § 9-102(a)(19), (28)(C).

[132] Article 9 governs certain consignment transactions solely for the purpose of determining the consignor's rights against creditors of the consignee or buyers of the goods; the relationship of the consignor to the consignee is governed by other law.. Thus, the consignor need not comply with Article 9's rules on enforcement. *See* §§ 9-109 cmt. 6, 9-601(g). *See also* In re Fine Diamonds, LLC, 501 B.R. 159 (Bankr. S.D.N.Y. 2013).

rights of a true consignor in a transaction governed by Article 9 are subject to the ability of the consignee to grant a security interest in the goods unless the true consignor perfects its "security interest" in the goods. *See* § 9-319.[133]

Unfortunately, just in case this was not complex enough, there is yet another possibility: a "sale or return" transaction. A sale or return is not an Article 9 transaction, instead it is governed by § 2-326. Read § 2-326 and comment 1. In a sale or return transaction, the goods are sold to a merchant for resale – and hence the merchant acquires title to the goods – but the merchant has the option to return the goods for credit against the obligation to pay the price. This transaction might look a lot like a true consignment. The key differences are that in a true consignment, the goods are not sold to the consignee, the consignor retains title, and the consignee has an *obligation* to return them if they are not sold; in a sale or return, the goods are sold, the buyer acquires title, and the buyer has merely an *option* to return them if they are not sold.[134]

It is often very difficult to determine which of the four categories any particular transaction falls under, although the following chart might help.

	Description / Attributes of Transaction	**Governing Law**	**Rights of Third Parties**
False Consignment	Consignment structure is a security device. No realistic chance that "consignor" will ever get the goods back, perhaps because the "consignee" will use them in a manufacturing process or has an obligation to buy them. The contractual obligation to pay upon resale might be about *when* payment is due, not *whether* it is due.	Article 9	Goods and their proceeds are subject to creditors of the consignee.

[133] Section 9-319 is another rule – like § 2-403, discussed earlier in this Chapter – that gives a debtor the power to transfer greater rights than the debtor has. As between a "true consignor" and a "true consignee," the consignee would normally have the obligation to return unsold goods to the consignor because such goods are, in fact, still the consignor's property. However, § 9-319 gives the consignee the power to transfer greater rights than the consignee has – specifically, the power to transfer the *consignor's* rights. Consequently, the consignee can grant an effective security interest in the goods to a secured party. *See* § 9-203(b)(2).

[134] *See* In re Morgansen's Ltd., 302 B.R. 784 (Bankr. E.D. N.Y. 2003); In re Haley & Steele, Inc., 2005 WL 3489869 (Mass. Sup. Ct. 2005).

	Description / Attributes of Transaction	Governing Law	Rights of Third Parties
True Consignment	Consignor retains title and has a right to get the goods back and no exception applies.	Article 9	Goods and their proceeds are subject to creditors of the consignee (unless, in some cases, the consignor perfects).
	Consignor retains title and has a right to get the goods back and one or more of the following is true: (i) the consignee is known by its creditors to be substantially engaged in selling the goods of others; (ii) the aggregate value of the goods is less than $1,000; (iii) the goods were consumer goods in the hands of the consignor.	Law of Bailments	Goods are *not* subject to creditors of the consignee. Proceeds of the goods might be held by the consignee in trust for the consignor.
Sale or Return	Title to the goods is transferred to the buyer, but the buyer has the option to return the goods.	Article 2	Goods and their proceeds are subject to creditors of the buyer.

Of course, in a sale or return transaction, the seller might "retain title" or otherwise obtain by agreement a security interest in the goods to secure payment of the purchase price after the goods are delivered to the buyer. Article 9 would govern that retention of title or security interest. *See* §§ 2-401, 9-109(a)(5).

Problem 2-27

Music Emporium, Inc. sells used and new musical instruments. Sometimes Music Emporium buys the used instruments for resale and sometimes it agrees to sell them for the owner "on consignment."

A. Charlie, the headmaster of a private school, agreed to let Music Emporium sell several used musical instruments owned by the school "on consignment." Charlie and Music Emporium agreed upon the sale price for each item and Charlie agreed that Music would be able to keep 5% of the sale price received when it remitted the proceeds to the school. The total sales price of the instruments was $1,200. Is this transaction covered by Article 9? If so, who is the debtor and who is the secured party? How should the secured party make sure that the requirements of § 9-203 are fulfilled? Can Music Emporium grant an enforceable security interest in those musical instruments to its lender, State Bank?

B. After Connie decided that she no longer wanted to be a drummer, she brought her drum set to Music Emporium and agreed to let Music Emporium sell the drum set. Connie and Music Emporium agreed that the sale price would be $1,100 and that Music would keep 5% of the sale price and remit the rest of the price to Connie upon the sale. Is this transaction covered by Article 9? If so, who is the debtor and who is the secured party? How should the secured party make sure that the requirements of § 9-203 are fulfilled? Can Music Emporium grant an enforceable security interest in the drum set to its lender, State Bank? Would your answer change if Connie were a professional drummer?

C. Would your answer to A above change if Music Emporium had a sign in its window that stated it held goods on consignment for sale as part of its inventory? *See In re Valley Media, Inc.*, 279 B.R. 105 (Bankr. D. Del. 2002).

3. Options and Other Structures

Because form does not matter, it is possible to create a security interest using other devices. Indeed, there might be an infinite number of ways to create a security interest. For one more example, imagine that Connoisseur sells a treasured painting to Friend for $10,000 and the sales agreement requires Connoisseur to buy the painting back in one year for $11,000. In a normal sales transaction, the buyer keeps the property and the seller keeps the money. That is not true in this transaction. What is really going on? The purchase price is actually a one-year loan from the buyer, Friend, to the seller, Connoisseur, at 10% interest. The painting is serving as collateral. If Connoisseur defaults on the obligation to "buy the painting back," Friend will simply retain the painting. The form of the transaction might be a sale with an obligation to repurchase, but the reality is that it is a loan with personal property as collateral.[135] Similarly, it is possible that a sale

---

[135] *See* Stillwater Nat'l Bank & Trust Co. v. CIT Group/Equip. Fin., Inc., 383 F.3d 1148 (10th Cir. 2004) (repurchase obligation made ostensible sales transaction really a security arrangement). *Cf.* In re Palmdale Hills Prop., LLC, 457 B.R. 29 (9th Cir. BAP 2011)

with an *option* to repurchase – rather than an *obligation* to repurchase – might qualify as a secured transaction.

Problem 2-28

Historian sells an antique desk to Relative for $10,000, retaining an option to buy it back one year later for $11,000. Under what circumstances should this transaction be regarded as creating a security interest? In other words, what additional facts would lead you to conclude that the form of the transaction as a sale with an option to repurchase should be disregarded in favor of treating it as a secured loan? As you consider this question, identify which party would be the debtor if the transaction does create a security interest.

Because the form of a transaction does not control, contracting parties cannot avoid the applicability of Article 9 merely by including language in their agreement or employing a structure designed to obscure the economic reality of their relationship.[136] That said, it is worth noting that some transactions in personal property always create a security interest. These include conditional sales and sales with an obligation to repurchase. Others, such as leases and sales with an option to repurchase, might or might not, depending on the specifics of the deal. Finally, some transactions that seem very similar to secured transactions, such as pawning arrangements, are typically statutorily excluded from Article 9's coverage. When that is not the case, however, Article 9 might well apply.[137]

Despite the uncertainty in some cases, the implications for the transactional attorney are clear. If there is any doubt about whether a transaction falls within or outside Article 9, the prudent lawyer will document the transaction in the manner required by Article 9 and the manner required by whatever other law might be applicable.

(repurchase agreements relating to mortgage loans were true sales, not secured transactions, even though the putative buyer had an obligation to resell identical loans and the loans were unique, because the transaction documents unambiguously indicated the parties' intent was that the transaction be a true sale).

[136] *See* In re Hawaii Motorsports, LLC, 2020 WL 7233187 (Bankr. D. Mont. 2020) (language in the parties' agreement providing that the debtor holds the financed property and its proceeds "in trust" for the financier did not create a true trust, merely a security interest).

[137] *See* In re Schwalb, 347 B.R. 726 (Bankr. D. Nev. 2006).

Problem 2-29

Software Developer created a popular game for use on computers and tablets. On June 1, Software Developer entered into an agreement with Buyer for Buyer to purchase all of Software Developer's rights to the game. The agreement contains the following terms:

(i) Buyer shall pay Software Developer $20,000 on June 1 and $480,000 on December 1.

(ii) On June 1, Software Developer shall transfer a master copy of the game software to Buyer.

(iii) Software Developer "hereby" transfers to Buyer all existing licenses of the game software by Software Developer to its customers. Buyer accepts the transfer and agrees to perform all of Software Developer's remaining duties under the licenses.

(iv) If Buyer makes the required $480,000 payment by December 1, Buyer will automatically become the owner of Software Developer's rights to the game software.

The agreement is silent about Buyer's right to use or to license the software during the period between June 1 and December 1. Does the agreement create a security interest?

B. Sales of Accounts, Chattel Paper, Promissory Notes, and Payment Intangibles

Article 9 also applies to a few transactions that are true sales, rather than collateralized loans. Read § 9-109(a)(3). These include sales of accounts, sales of chattel paper, sales of promissory notes, and sales of payment intangibles. To facilitate this, the term "security interest" is defined to include these types of sales and the terms "debtor," and "secured party" expressly include the parties to these types of sales. *See* §§ 1-201(b)(35), 9-102(a)(28)(B), (73)(D). One reason such sales are included within the scope of Article 9 is similar to the reason that consignments are included within the scope of Article 9. It is often very difficult to determine whether the transaction is a sale or a granting of a security interest and thus it makes sense to include both transactions within the scope of Article 9. Consider the following three scenarios:

1. Company A is in the business of selling furniture. Sometimes it sells the furniture on credit to its customers creating an account (*i.e.*, Customers'

agreement to pay Company A constitutes an "account" under § 9-102(a)(2)). Company A sells its accounts outright to Bank:

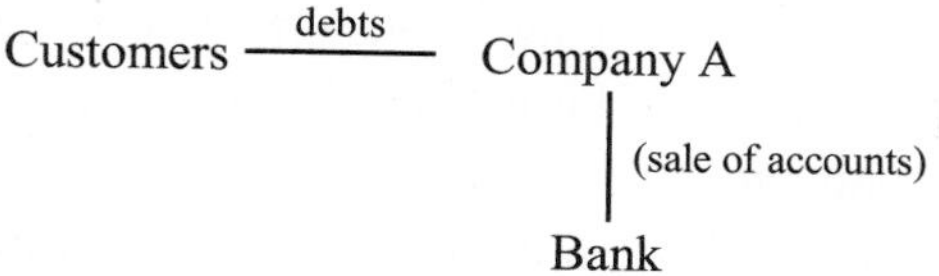

As a result, Bank has the risk of loss and the opportunity to gain from the transaction. If it collects more from the account debtors than it paid Company A, Bank will not have a duty to remit the excess back to Company A, and therefore will profit. If it collects less, Bank will have no right to collect the deficiency from Company A, and will accordingly suffer a loss. *See* § 9-608(b).

2. Company B is also in the business of selling furniture, often on credit in transactions that create an account. Company B borrows money from Bank and grants Bank a security interest in its accounts to secure the loan:

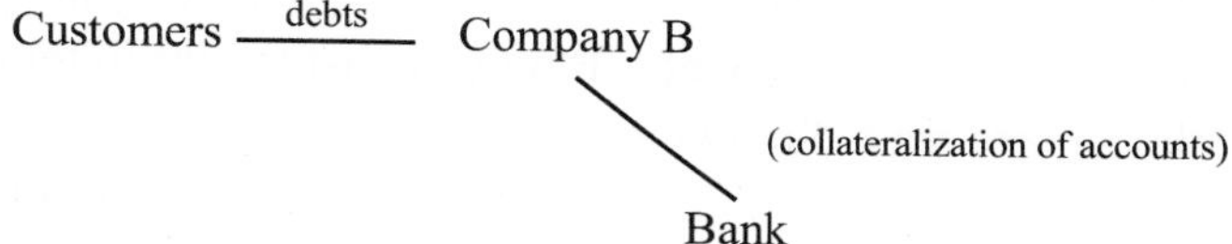

In this transaction, unless otherwise agreed, Company B is the one who has the risk of loss from poor collections and the opportunity to gain from excessive ones. If Company B defaults on the loan and Bank collects the accounts, Bank will have a duty to remit any collections in excess of the loan balance (and collection costs) back to Company B. Conversely, if Bank is unable to collect enough from the account debtors to satisfy Company B's obligation to it, Company B remains liable for the deficiency. *See* § 9-608(a)(4).

3. Company C also sells furniture on credit in transactions that create an account. When Company C approaches Bank for money in exchange for an interest in Company C's accounts, they work out an arrangement whereby Company C will bear the risk of loss from poor collections but Bank will retain the opportunity to gain from excessive ones. From the Bank's perspective, this is a sort of "heads I win, tails you lose" proposition. In short, if Bank collects more on the accounts than it advanced to Company C, Bank will not have a duty to remit the surplus collections back to Company

C. However, if Bank collects less from the account debtors than it paid to Company C, Company C remains liable for the deficiency.

Scenario 1 is a pure sale transaction. Scenario 2 is a pure borrowing transaction. Scenario 3 is a hybrid, with attributes of both. Should it be regarded as a sale or a borrowing? As comments 4 and 5 to § 9-109 make clear, Article 9 provides no help in determining whether this is a sale or a loan transaction. However, Article 9 addresses this problem by covering all three transactions. In each, Bank is a "secured party." Companies A, B, and C each qualify as a "debtor." The customers in each scenario are "account debtors." § 9-102(a)(3).

The implications of this are fairly staggering, at least in Scenario 1 and perhaps also in Scenario 3. A true sale is an absolute transfer of ownership of the asset involved. Consequently, a seller of accounts – such as Company A – retains no property interest in the accounts sold. Read § 9-318(a). Nonetheless, Article 9 expressly provides that such a seller can, after the sale, grant an enforceable security interest (either through sale or a transfer for security) in the accounts to another person (such as Finance Company) as long as the first transferee (Bank) has not perfected its interest. Read § 9-318(b). For now, do not worry about what it takes to perfect an interest in an account. Rather, consider the interaction between § 9-318 and the requirements for attachment of a security interest. Do you see how the rule of subsection (b) gives the debtor (Company A) the ability to transfer to another (Finance Company) greater rights than the debtor actually has? § 9-203(b)(2). It does not matter whether Finance Company buys the account or merely takes an interest in the account to secure an obligation.

A second reason Article 9 governs sales of accounts relates to the filing system that Article 9 creates for perfection. Recall that Article 9 creates a recording system for interests in personal property to deal with the ostensible ownership problem resulting from the creation of liens: multiple owners of the property not all of whose interests are readily apparent to others who might wish to acquire an interest in such property. When accounts are truly sold there are not multiple owners, but there is often still an ostensible ownership problem. Normally we think a business is the rightful owner of the accounts it generates. Returning to Example 1, where Company A has sold its accounts to Bank, consider what would happen if Company A later tries to sell its accounts to Second Bank. How is Second Bank to know if Company A still owns them? It could contact the customers (the account debtors), but that would be impractical if there were many of them and they might not know of the sale to Bank anyway, at least not if the sale were recent or if Bank arranged for Company A to collect the accounts on Bank's behalf. To deal with this problem, sales of accounts are governed by Article 9 and the buyer (who is deemed to be a "secured party") must normally record its interest in the accounts in order to perfect that interest and thereby ensure priority over those who later purport to acquire rights in the accounts.

A third reason that sales of accounts, chattel paper, promissory notes, and payment intangibles are included within the scope of Article 9 is to facilitate a transaction called a securitization. While this type of transaction might be very complex in reality, the basic idea is relatively simple and can be illustrated with the following example:

> 4. Company D is in the business of selling furniture, often on credit in transactions that generate accounts. Company D sells its accounts to SPE (Special Purpose Entity), a corporate entity that is created solely for the purpose of buying the accounts. SPE issues equity securities *(i.e.*, stock) in itself in the public market for securities. The money raised from the sale of these securities is used to purchase the accounts from Company D. The amounts collected from the account debtors are then used by SPE to pay dividends or other returns to the equity security purchasers.

Transactions such as these serve very important functions in the financial markets. From Company D's perspective, it is able to realize value from its accounts (or other rights to payment) without having to wait for the account debtors to pay. It can then reinvest that money or otherwise use that money to run its business. While it might be able to do the same thing by selling the accounts to a single entity, the accounts might be so voluminous that no single purchaser could be found to buy them all or any that could be found might insist on buying at a steep discount. This process allows the accounts to be sold in a much more competitive market. From the perspective of SPE and the equity securities purchasers, the rules of Article 9 help give them assurance that SPE will have a first priority interest in the accounts. They also help insulate SPE and the equity security holders from the effects of any bankruptcy of Company D. As a result, Article 9 facilitates this method of financing for Company D.

Even though sales and securitizations of accounts, chattel paper, promissory notes, and payment intangibles are generally governed by Article 9, some specific types of such transactions are excluded from the scope of Article 9. Read § 9-109(d)(4) through (8).

Problem 2-30

A. What is the reason for the exclusions in § 9-109(d)(4) and (5)?

B. For the last 17 years, Degas has operated a picture framing business under the name "Picture This" out of a small storefront in the local mall. Degas wishes to sell the business to Botticelli and retire. As part of the purchase and sale agreement, Botticelli will be buying all of Degas' equipment, inventory, and accounts. Does Article 9 apply to any aspect of this transaction?

C. Retailer assigns its receivables to Purchaser. Does Article 9 apply to this transaction if:

   1. Purchaser pays Retailer 70% of what Purchaser collects, minus the costs of collecting?
   2. Purchaser pays Retailer 70% of the face amount of the receivables, regardless of the amount actually collected, but if Purchaser is unable to collect at least 25% of the face amount of any receivable, Purchaser can require Retailer to buy that receivable back?

   If Article 9 does apply to either or both of these transactions, who is the debtor and who is the secured party? How should the secured party make sure that the requirements of § 9-203 are satisfied?

D. When structuring a transaction such as any of those described in Part B or C, should you ever rely on your own conclusion that the transaction is excluded from Article 9 by one of these exceptions?

C. Interests Created Under Law Other Than Article 9

Other articles of the UCC provide that a security interest arises upon the happening of particular events. Paragraphs (5) and (6) of § 9-109(a) bring those types of security interests within the scope of Article 9 and § 9-203(c) makes clear the general rule on how to attach a security interest is subject to the provisions of those other articles.

Retention of title. You might recall from the brief discussion of conditional sales contracts on page 129 that, in such a transaction, the seller retains title to the goods sold so that the seller will be able to get the goods back in the event the buyer does not pay. The UCC treats the retention of title in such a situation as a security device. Thus, a seller of goods who delivers the goods to the buyer but who "retains title" to the goods until the buyer pays in full has in effect created a security interest. §§ 2-401, 1-201(b)(35). Despite the phrase "retain title" in the sales agreement, title passes to the buyer upon delivery of the goods; the UCC treats this phrase as merely creating a security interest and not as a term that prevents or delays title from passing. Section 9-109(a)(5) makes it clear that Article 9 applies to a security interest created in this manner.

Shipment under reservation. Similarly, sometimes the seller ships goods to the buyer using a carrier. When the seller does so, it might ship the goods "under reservation." The seller does so by obtaining from the carrier a document of title that covers the goods being shipped. The document of title must comply with § 2-505 to effect a shipment "under reservation." If the seller does so, the seller has a security interest in the goods and the carrier should not release the goods to the buyer until the buyer has paid in full. Review the definition of security interest in § 1-201(b)(35), which recognizes this manner of creating a security interest. In some respects, this can be a nonconsensual security interest. That is because the buyer need not agree to the seller's actions in creating a shipment under reservation. A security interest is created by shipment under reservation even if the buyer has not agreed to the process and even if the seller's actions in shipping in this manner is a breach of the sales contract with the buyer. § 2-505(2).

Buyer's security interest for the price pre-paid and some damages upon rightful and effective rejection or justifiable and effective revocation of acceptance. Finally, the buyer in an Article 2 transaction might also acquire a security interest in the goods. Assume the buyer has received delivery of the goods and those goods do not conform to the requirements under the contract. In exercise of its Article 2 remedies, the buyer rightfully and effectively rejects the goods or justifiably and effectively revokes acceptance of the goods. §§ 2-601, 2-602, 2-608. The buyer in possession of the goods has a security interest in those goods to cover any part of the price the buyer has paid and certain incidental damages incurred in taking care of the goods. § 2-711(3).[138] The buyer's security interest does not depend upon the consent of the seller.

Agricultural and other statutory liens. Article 9 brings agricultural liens within its scope. Read § 9-109(a)(2) and the definition of "agricultural lien" in § 9-102(a)(5). *Cf.* § 9-109(d)(1), (2). Agricultural liens are nonconsensual liens

---

[138] A lessee of goods has a security interest in the same situation. § 2A-508(5). The lessee's security interest does not depend upon the consent of the lessor.

that arise pursuant to a state statute outside Article 9. That statute determines how, when, and to what the lien attaches. An agricultural lien is not a "security interest," as that term is defined in § 1-201(b)(35), but the lienholder is a "secured party," § 9-102(a)(73)(B), the property subject to the lien is "collateral," § 9-102(a)(12), and the person whose property is subject to the lien is a "debtor," § 9-102(a)(28). Consequently, many of Article 9's rules relating to security interests also apply to agricultural liens. For simplicity, Chapters Two through Five omit further discussion of agricultural liens. Instead, they are covered in Chapter Six.

Other nonconsensual liens that arise by statute, such as mechanic's liens, are not included within the scope of Article 9, § 9-109(d)(1) and (2), except to the extent Article 9 has a rule governing the priority between a security interest and the lien. *See* § 9-333.

Deference to other law. Article 9 also contains exclusions for situations where other law provides the method of creating an interest to secure payment or performance of an obligation. Read § 9-109(c) and (d).

Section 9-109(c)(1) reflects the fact that federal law might preempt the application of Article 9 because Article 9 is state law. This principle would obviously be true even if not reflected in § 9-109(c)(1) because of the supremacy clause of the U.S. Constitution.[139]

Paragraphs (2) and (3) of § 9-109(c) reflect the policy that when the state or a governmental unit of the state is a debtor, another state statute might provide the manner for attaching, perfecting, and enforcing an interest in state assets to secure state obligations. Article 9 defers to that other state law.[140]

---

[139] U.S. Const. art. VI, cl. 2. For examples of application of this principle in the context of security interests in personal property, see In re AvCentral, Inc., 289 B.R. 170 (Bankr. D. Kan. 2003) (Federal Aviation Act preempts Article 9 regarding security interests in aircraft); Surgicore, Inc. v. Principal Life Ins. Co., 2002 WL 1052034 (N.D. Ill. 2002) (Article 9 does not govern a claim by health care provider against an ERISA-governed employee benefit plan; if the plan were not an ERISA plan, the assignment by the patient to the health care provider would be within the scope of Article 9, § 9-109(d)(8)).

[140] Old Article 9 excluded any "transfer by a government or governmental subdivision." § 9-104(e) (repealed). This exclusion applied regardless of whether another statute governed. *Cf.* § 9-109(c)(2). Several states preserved that rule when enacting revised Article 9, so that revised Article 9 does not apply when one of those states or a governmental agency of one of those states is the debtor. *See, e.g.*, Fla. Stat. § 679.1091(4)(n); 810 Ill. Comp. Stat. 5/9-109(d)(13); Ind. Code § 26-1-9.1-109(d)(14); Ky. Rev. Stat. § 355.9-109(q); Ohio Rev. Code § 1309.109(d)(14).

Other exclusions. Several other transactions are excluded from the scope of Article 9 by the various paragraphs of § 9-109(d). These exclusions are based on a potpourri of policy reasons, some of which are explained in comments 10-16 to the section.

Consider § 9-109(d)(3). Why should wage assignments be excluded from Article 9? Does this mean that a person cannot validly assign his or her right to wages?[141]

Section 9-109(d)(9) excludes assignments of judgments as original collateral from the scope of Article 9. However, assignments of judgments are common and governed by non-Article 9 law.[142]

Now read § 9-109(d)(11). This provision and the basic scope provision in § 9-109(a)(1) draw the line between transferring interests in "real" property and transferring interests in "personal" property. For example, if real property is used as collateral to provide security for repayment of a loan, the debtor will grant a mortgage to the lender. That mortgage will be governed by real property law, not Article 9. Similarly, when a lessor leases real estate to a lessee, that transaction is governed by real property law and not Article 9. Those are the easy examples.

Now consider a seller or lessor of real property who wants to use its right to payment under the sales contract or lease as security for a loan. Use of the seller's right to payment as collateral is an Article 9 transaction, even though the right to payment arose out of a real estate transaction.[143] In contrast, use of the lessor's right to payment is, apparently, not governed by Article 9, *see* § 9-109(d)(11) (referring to a transfer of rents), although it is difficult to discern why these two situations should be treated so differently.[144]

Finally, assume instead that a *lessee* under a real property lease wants to use its rights under the lease as collateral for a loan from a lender. When the lessee assigns its rights under the lease to the lender to secure the loan, is that transaction an

---

The exclusion in § 9-109(c)(4) is discussed in Chapter Six.

[141] *See* 12 C.F.R. § 227.13; 16 C.F.R. § 444.2.

[142] *See, e.g.*, Minn. Stat. § 548.13.

[143] *See* In re The IT Group, Inc., 307 B.R. 762 (D. Del. 2004) (assignment of right to proceeds of real estate sales contract was an Article 9 transaction).

[144] For a discussion of the historical background, see Julia Patterson Forrester, *Still Crazy After All These Years: The Absolute Assignment of Rents in Mortgage Loan Transactions*, 59 FLA. L. REV. 487 (2007).

assignment of rights in personal property and thus subject to Article 9 or an assignment of an interest in real property and not subject to Article 9? The lessee's rights under the lease have two aspects. The real property aspect is that the lessee has a right to possession and use of the real estate in accordance with the terms of the lease. The contract right aspect is that the rights and obligations as between the lessee and the lessor are set forth in the agreement of the parties. Should it matter whether the lender in the hypothetical is interested in obtaining possession of the real estate in the event the lessee defaults on its obligation to the lender?[145]

Read the remaining exclusions in § 9-109(d). What are the policy reasons for excluding those transactions from the scope of Article 9? Excluding a transaction from Article 9 does not mean that the asset involved cannot be used to secure an obligation. Rather, the diligent lawyer involved in such a transaction must search out the other law and determine how to effectuate the parties' intent in the transaction.

A diligent lawyer must also be on the lookout for non-uniform versions of § 9-109(d), which might add to, eliminate, or alter the exclusions in the uniform text. For example, California's version of § 9-109(d)(8), which excludes a security interest in an insurance claim or policy, applies only to loans made by the insurance company.[146] As a result, California's exclusion does not apply – and the state's Article 9 does apply – when anyone other than the insurer provides financing for and takes a security interest in an insurance policy.[147] In contrast, the New York version of § 9-109(d)(8) expressly extends the exclusion to cover a security interest in an annuity contract,[148] a issue on which courts in other states are divided.[149]

---

[145] *See* In re Tops Appliance City, Inc., 372 F.3d 510 (3d Cir. 2004) (grant of a security interest in "general intangibles . . . including leasehold interests in . . . real estate" was governed by Article 9 when the creditor sought the proceeds from the sale of the lessee's interest in the leases to a third party).

[146] *See* Cal. Com. Code § 9109(d)(8).

[147] *See* John Hancock Ins. Co. (U.S.A.) v. Goss, 2015 WL 5569150 (N.D. Cal. 2015), *subsequent ruling in*, 2015 WL 9303987 (N.D. Cal. 2015) (insurance premium financier failed to comply with § 9-620).

[148] N.Y. U.C.C. § 9-109(d)(8).

[149] *Compare* Espinosa v. United of Omaha Life Ins. Co., 137 P.3d 631 (N.M. Ct. App. 2006) (a security interest in a right to payment under a structured settlement of a tort claim, funded by an annuity, was excluded from the scope of former Article 9 both as arising out of a tort claim and as an interest in an insurance policy); In re Nitz, 739 N.E.2d 93 (Ill. App. Ct. 2000)

e-Exercise 2-F
Interests under Other Law

Problem 2-31

Developer recently completed a commercial real estate project that includes several properties designed for retail use. Developer has located two businesses that want to acquire the immediate ownership or use of a retail property but to pay over time. Specifically, Tenant wants to rent Building A for 25 years, with rent of $15,000 due on the first of each month. Buyer wants to buy Building B for $2.5 million, but use a promissory note secured by a mortgage for the entire the purchase price.[150] The note will require payment of $15,000 per month for 25 years.

Developer wants to use the resulting rights to payment from Tenant and Buyer as collateral for a loan from Bank. Will Article 9 apply to Bank's security interest in Developer's right to payment due from Tenant? Will Article 9 apply to Bank's security interest in Developer's right to payment from Buyer?

Problem 2-32

National Bank is lending money to Duane for operation of Duane's business, a craft shop that Duane runs as a sole proprietor. National Bank wants a security interest in: (i) Duane's personal savings account at State Bank; (ii) a cause of action Duane has against an employee for conversion of property from the store; and (iii) a judgment that Duane obtained against a supplier for breach of contract. To what extent will Article 9 apply to a security interest in those assets? *See* § 9-109.

(similarly treating a security interest in a right to payment under a structured settlement funded by an annuity as an interest in an insurance policy excluded from former Article 9), *with* United States v. Poling, 73 F. Supp. 2d 882 (S.D. Ohio 1999); In re Vinzant, 108 B.R. 752 (Bankr. D. Kan. 1989) (both ruling that life annuity contracts were not insurance policies for the purposes of the exclusion under former Article 9).

[150] This works out to an interest rate of 5.26%.

Problem 2-33

Same facts as in Problem 2-25 In addition, the sales agreement between Distributor and Buyer requires Buyer to: (i) acquire an insurance policy covering destruction of or loss or damage to the earth-moving equipment Distributor is selling to Buyer, and naming Distributor as the loss payee; and (ii) pay for an insurance policy, to be issued to Distributor, that insures against Buyer's default on its payment obligation to Distributor.

A. To which of those insurance policies, if any, will State Bank's security interest attach? *See* §§ 9-102(a)(78), 9-109(d)(8), 9-203(f).

B. To the extent State Bank's security interest will not or might not attach to the insurance policies, what should State Bank do to ensure that it acquires an enforceable interest in them?

Problem 2-34

As in-house counsel for National Bank, you are preparing a form security agreement for the Bank to use when it makes a commercial loan and expects to obtain a security interest in all of the borrower's assets. Critique the draft description of collateral below. In so doing, assume another clause of the agreement states that "any term defined in the UCC has the meaning assigned to it in the UCC." In particular, is there reason to include the bracketed language? *See* §§ 9-108(c), 9-109. What other language should be added or deleted, and why?

All existing and after-acquired [personal property, including]:

(i) accounts; (ii) chattel paper;
(iii) commercial tort claims; (iv) controllable electronic records
(v) deposit accounts; (vi) documents;
(vii) general intangibles; (viii) goods;
(ix) instruments; (x) investment property;
(xi) letter of credit rights; (xii) letters of credit;
(xiii) money; (xiv) securities accounts;
(xv) supporting obligations; and
(xvi) proceeds, products, and profits of, and accessions to, any of the foregoing.

Test Your Knowledge
Exam Three – Scope of Article 9

SECTION 8: THE EFFECT OF DEBTOR'S BANKRUPTCY ON ATTACHMENT OF A SECURITY INTEREST

After-acquired property clauses. When a debtor files bankruptcy, the automatic stay prevents any act to create a security interest in the debtor's property.[151] This does not affect a lien created prior to the filing of the bankruptcy petition but does prevent any postpetition act to create a lien. Of course, a security agreement with an after-acquired property clause operates somewhat automatically; the security interest will automatically attach to new property as soon as the debtor acquires rights in it. Just in case such automatic attachment is not an "act" within the meaning of the automatic stay, the Bankruptcy Code contains another provision that makes an after-acquired property clause ineffective after the bankruptcy petition is filed, thus preventing the security interest from encumbering property that the debtor's estate or the debtor acquires rights in after the debtor files bankruptcy.[152]

Proceeds. This restriction on the reach of an after-acquired property clause does not apply to proceeds, however. The secured party's security interest can attach to any proceeds of the original collateral the debtor or the estate acquires postpetition, as long as the debtor acquired rights in the original collateral pre-petition.[153] Thus, any new property constituting identifiable proceeds will be covered by the security agreement. The key will be doing whatever tracing is necessary to identify the newly acquired property as proceeds. Note, many courts have ruled that, for this purpose, the term "proceeds" in the Bankruptcy Code means the same thing as it does in Article 9. However, those rulings predate the 1999 revisions to Article 9, which expanded the definition of proceeds. The equivalence of meaning might not continue.[154]

---

[151] 11 U.S.C. § 362(a)(4).

[152] 11 U.S.C. § 552(a).

[153] 11 U.S.C. § 552(b). It is perhaps worth noting that a security interest will attach to proceeds acquired post-petition only "to the extent provided by [the] security agreement and by applicable nonbankruptcy law." *Id.* This language suggests that the security agreement must expressly reference proceeds for the security interest to reach post-petition proceeds, even though Article 9 does not require such an express reference for a security interest to attach to proceeds generally. *Cf. supra* note 55 and accompanying text.

[154] *But cf.* In re Las Vegas Monorail Co., 429 B.R. 317, 343 (Bankr. D. Nev. 2010) (ruling that the expended definition of "proceeds" in revised Article 9 applies in determining the

Let us pause for a moment to consider the implications of these bankruptcy rules for how secured transactions should be structured and security agreements drafted. If all or a significant part of the collateral will consist of after-acquired property – such as a future stream of revenue – then the secured party will lose rights to the postpetition flow of that stream unless the revenue is identifiable proceeds of other collateral. Thus, for example, a secured party will have a security interest in postpetition accounts if those accounts are identifiable proceeds of inventory in which the secured party has a security interest. However, if the accounts arise from the provision of services, the accounts will likely not be proceeds of other collateral and the Bankruptcy Code will prevent attachment to the accounts generated postpetition.

Illustration

Two years ago, Detail Auto, Inc. granted an enforceable security interest in "existing and after-acquired inventory, accounts, and general intangibles" to Bank to secure a $100,000 loan from Bank. Detail Auto repairs and paints cars. Most of its customers pay by credit card. Three months ago, Detail Auto filed a Chapter 11 bankruptcy petition. At that time, its inventory was worth $20,000 and it had $25,000 in credit card receivables. Auto Detail has continued to operate its business postpetition and during that time has purchased $10,000 in inventory and generated $15,000 in additional credit card receivables.

Pre-petition Inventory & Credit Card Receivables. Auto Detail's inventory on hand when the bankruptcy petition was filed is encumbered by Bank's security interest. Because the security agreement expressly covers after-acquired inventory, it does not matter whether Detail Auto acquired the pre-petition inventory before or after it signed the security agreement. Section 552(b) of the Bankruptcy Code has no bearing on this collateral. The credit card receivables that Auto Detail had when the bankruptcy petition was filed are also encumbered. They are payment intangibles, and hence also general intangibles, *see* § 9-102 cmt. 5d, and thus are covered by the security agreement.

Postpetition Inventory. The inventory acquired by Auto Detail postpetition might or might not be subject to Bank's security interest.

---

scope of 11 U.S.C. § 552(b), even though the parties entered into the security agreement before revised Article 9 became effective).

Section 552(b) prevents the after-acquired property clause in the security agreement from encumbering that inventory. So, the only way that some or all of that inventory is subject to Bank's security interest is if it is identifiable proceeds of pre-petition collateral. For example, if Auto Detail – either pre-petition or postpetition – sold pre-petition inventory or collected pre-petition credit card receivables, and used the funds received thereby to purchase the postpetition inventory, then the inventory so purchased will be subject to Bank's security interest because it is identifiable proceeds of pre-petition collateral.

Postpetition Credit Card Receivables. To the extent the postpetition credit card receivables arose from the sale of collateralized inventory – that is, either inventory acquired pre-petition or inventory acquired postpetition but which is identifiable proceeds of pre-petition collateral – then it is identifiable proceeds of collateral and covered by Bank's security interest. To the extent that the postpetition credit card receivables arose from the provision of services or from the sale of unencumbered inventory, they are not covered by Bank's security interest.

Because of how § 552(b) operates, secured creditors should, to the extent possible, draft their security agreements to ensure that any expected future revenue on which they are relying to be collateral will be proceeds of other collateral. In other words, in describing the collateral, the security agreement should list not merely the anticipated revenue stream, but whatever property of the debtor will generate that revenue stream.[155]

---

[155] For cases in which the secured party failed, to its detriment, to do this, see *id.* (collateral described as "net revenue" from the operation of a monorail); In re Gateway Access Solutions, Inc., 368 B.R. 428 (Bankr. M.D. Pa. 2007) (collateral described as "lease conversion payments").

One important context in which the issue arises is in the financing of broadcasters. The most valuable asset of many broadcasters is their broadcast license. Federal law prohibits license holders from assigning their license without the FCC's prior consent, 47 U.S.C. § 310(d), and the FCC has long interpreted this rule as prohibiting the creation of a security interest in an FCC license. However, the FCC has indicated that a creditor may take a security interest in the proceeds of a broadcast license. In re Cheskey, 9 FCC Rcd. 986, 987 (1994). Relying on this ruling, some lenders have taken a security interest in the future proceeds of the borrower's FCC licenses, rather than in the licenses themselves. The problem with this approach is that § 552 of the Bankruptcy Code prevents an after-acquired property clause from operating post-petition unless the post-petition property is proceeds of

Future advances. The Bankruptcy Code also affects the status of future advances. If the secured party makes an advance to the debtor after the filing of the bankruptcy petition, that advance will be unsecured even though the security agreement might have an otherwise valid future-advances clause. For post-petition advances to be secured, the secured party must get court approval.[156]

Bankruptcy estate. If the property is already subject to the security interest at the time of filing, the property is nonetheless part of the debtor's bankruptcy estate.[157] Upon filing the petition, the automatic stay prevents the secured party from taking any action against the property subject to the security interest or against the debtor to enforce the debt owed even if bankruptcy is a default in the debtor's obligation to the secured party.[158] We will consider grounds for lifting the stay in the next Chapter as we study the secured party's remedies on the debtor's default.

Secured claims. We have already seen that the bankruptcy process favors secured claims because it operates on only the debtor's *in personam* liability, not the *in rem* liability of the collateral. But having an interest (such as a security interest) in the debtor's property might or might not give the creditor a secured claim in the debtor's bankruptcy case. Whether the creditor has a secured claim and the extent to which its claim qualifies as a secured claim are determined by 11 U.S.C. § 506(a). This section provides that "[a]n allowed claim of a creditor secured by a lien on property in which the estate has an interest . . . is a secured claim to the extent of the value of such creditor's interest in the estate's interest in such property." This rather cryptic language is really fairly simple to understand: the amount of a secured claim is limited by the value of the collateral. For example,

---

pre-petition collateral. Thus, the argument goes, because the license itself is not and cannot be collateral, any receivable generated by a post-petition contract to sell cannot be proceeds of pre-petition collateral. It is at best after-acquired property, to which no pre-petition security interest can attach. Nevertheless, courts in several recent decisions have ruled that a security interest can, if properly drafted, attach pre-petition to the "economic value" of a license and that any post-petition sale of the license will then generate proceeds of that economic value, which the security interest will encumber. *See* In re Tracy Broad. Corp., 696 F.3d 1051 (10th Cir. 2012); In re TerreStar Networks, Inc., 457 B.R. 254 (Bankr. S.D.N.Y. 2011).

[156] 11 U.S.C. § 364.

[157] *See* 11 U.S.C. § 541(a); United States v. Whiting Pools, Inc., 462 U.S. 198 (1983).

[158] 11 U.S.C. § 362(a).

a creditor owed $1,000 that has the only lien on property worth $1,000 or more has a $1,000 claim that is fully secured. However, if the collateral were worth only $800, then the secured claim would be limited to $800, and the creditor would have an unsecured claim for the $200 balance due. In short, creditors with undersecured claims have both a secured claim and an unsecured claim.

The arithmetic gets a bit more complicated – but not much more – if there are multiple liens on the same property. Now, in addition to knowing the amount due to each lienor and the value of the collateral, we also need to know the relative priorities of the liens. Consider the following:

Property Value	$1,000
Debt to Lienor A	$800
Debt to Lienor B	$3,000

If Lien A has priority over Lien B, then Lienor A has an $800 secured claim. That leaves only $200 of value in the collateral left for Lienor B, who therefore has a $200 secured claim and a $2,800 unsecured claim:

Property Value	$1,000
Debt to Lienor A	– $800
Residual Property Value	$200
Debt to Lienor B	$3,000

If Lien B had priority, the result would be substantially different: Lienor B would have a $1,000 secured claim and a $2,000 unsecured claim; Lienor A would have an $800 wholly unsecured claim.

Property Value	$1,000
Debt to Lienor B	– $1,000
Residual Property Value	$0
Remaining Debt to Lienor B	$2,000
Debt to Lienor A	$800

Post-petition interest. A secured creditor is entitled to post-petition interest on its secured claim only out of excess equity.[159] Thus, an undersecured creditor is not entitled to accrue interest on either the secured or unsecured portion of its claim during the pendency of the bankruptcy case. That means the secured party is not compensated for the time value of money for the time it takes the bankruptcy case

---

[159] *See* 11 U.S.C. § 506(b).

to be resolved. Only oversecured creditors are allowed to accrue interest on the claim during the bankruptcy case, and even then only to the extent the collateral can cover it. Bankruptcy Code § 506(b) also provides that oversecured creditors are entitled to any "reasonable fees, costs, or charges provided for under the agreement . . . under which such claim arose," that is, the security agreement.

Adequate protection. During the bankruptcy proceeding, the secured party is entitled to adequate protection of its security interest in the collateral.[160] Thus, for example, if the collateral is likely to depreciate through usage or lack of care or is not adequately insured against loss, and such depreciation or loss threatens the value of the secured party's interest in the collateral, the secured party is entitled to be insulated from this risk. Similarly, if the collateral consists of money or deposit accounts, the secured party is entitled to be protected against the risk that the collateral will be dissipated, as it might be if used to pay for goods, services, or other expenses. Adequate protection can be provided through a replacement lien on other collateral, periodic payments to the secured party, or the existence of a sufficient equity cushion so that the secured party is not hurt by the decrease in the collateral valuation.[161] The type of adequate protection provided will depend upon the risk that exists. However, it is important to note that adequate protection is not a guaranty that the secured party will suffer no loss during the bankruptcy proceeding. If the value of the secured party's interest in the collateral declines during the course of the bankruptcy process, the secured party has very few options for recapturing that value. If the court awarded an adequate protection measure and that measure ends up being inadequate, the secured party might have a super priority administrative expense claim.[162] In other words, it might be entitled to a claim that is higher on the distribution list than all other *unsecured* claims. However, that might not be much protection for the creditor if all of the debtor's assets are encumbered and there are no assets available to pay any of the unsecured claims.

Debtor use of collateral. After a bankruptcy petition is filed, the debtor is entitled to use property subject to a security interest without court approval if such use is in the ordinary course of business and the property subject to the security

---

[160] *See* 11 U.S.C. §§ 362(d)(1), 363(e); 364(d)(1)(B).

[161] *See* 11 U.S.C. § 361.

[162] 11 U.S.C. § 507(b).

interest is not "cash collateral."[163] If the use of the property is not in the ordinary course of business or is of cash collateral, the usage must first be approved by the court. For this reason, when a business debtor files for bankruptcy protection, one of the first things that happens is a hearing to condition the use of the "cash collateral" to enable the debtor to run its business.

For example, assume the debtor owns and operates a clothing store. In order to finance the operation of the store, the debtor obtained a loan from State Bank secured by all of the debtor's inventory, then owned or thereafter acquired in order to secure any and all obligations owed to State Bank at the time or in the future. Sales of inventory generated proceeds in the form of cash and checks. The debtor deposited the cash and checks to its checking account held at State Bank. Prior to the bankruptcy filing, the debtor used funds from the checking account to purchase more inventory, pay down the debt to State Bank, and pay other bills such as utilities, rent and employee's wages. When the debtor filed bankruptcy, it had $30,000 in the checking account at State Bank. Assuming that the entire $30,000 could be traced as proceeds of the inventory sold, the amount in the checking account is "cash collateral."

After the bankruptcy petition is filed, the debtor may continue to operate its store by selling inventory in the same manner the debtor did before the bankruptcy proceeding commenced. This is true even though the inventory is part of State Bank's collateral. However, the debtor's authorization to use the cash collateral is much more limited. Moreover, to the extent inventory is sold after the bankruptcy petition is filed, the proceeds from that inventory might also be "cash collateral" of State Bank.[164] On top of that, neither State Bank nor any other is lender likely to loan any more money to the debtor without substantial restrictions on what the debtor may do with the funds and substantial assurances of repayment. As a result, all of the debtor's liquid assets are likely to be cash collateral that the debtor cannot use without court approval.

If the debtor is not able to use the cash collateral to pay wages, utilities and other critical expenses, the debtor will soon go out of business. Accordingly, the cash collateral hearing is where the court must balance the interest of the debtor in using the cash collateral to operate its business and the interest of the secured party in

---

[163] 11 U.S.C. § 363(c).

[164] 11 U.S.C. § 363(a). Remember, a secured party may assert its security interest in proceeds that arise after the filing of the bankruptcy petition, but not in other after-acquired property. 11 U.S.C. § 552(b).

protecting the value of its collateral. The secured party is likely to insist on adequate protection not only of its interest in the existing inventory but also of its interest in proceeds generated through sale of the inventory. A likely resolution of the situation is for the bankruptcy judge to grant to the secured party a new security interest on inventory acquired after the bankruptcy filing so that the overall value of the secured creditor's collateral does not diminish.

Value of collateral. As you can see, the question of collateral valuation is critical to the ability of the secured party to protect itself in the event the debtor files bankruptcy. The Bankruptcy Code provides a general standard for determining valuation.[165] Based upon that standard, courts use any of several different valuation measures depending upon the context in which the valuation question arises. Some of the most commonly used valuation measures are "going concern value" (the value of the asset to an ongoing business), "liquidation value" (the amount that the asset would yield in a forced sale), and "replacement value" (the cost of replacing the asset).[166]

Summary. As you can see from this short summary, the debtor's filing of a bankruptcy petition means that the relationship between the secured party and the debtor changes dramatically. The debtor gets the benefit of the automatic stay, the ability to deal with the collateral, a restriction on the scope of the collateral to property in which the debtor had an interest at the time of the bankruptcy filing (and its proceeds), and relief from accruing interest or other charges if the secured party is undersecured. The secured party gets the benefit of adequate protection of its secured claim, the ability to follow proceeds of original collateral, and the ability to accrue interest and other charges against the property if the secured party is oversecured.

---

[165] 11 U.S.C. § 506(a).

[166] The 2005 amendments to the Bankruptcy Code amended 11 U.S.C. § 506 to direct the court to use "replacement value" to value personal property of an individual debtor in a Chapter 7 or 13 case in determining the secured claim of the creditor. 2005 Bankruptcy Act, Pub. L. No. 109-8, § 327, 119 Stat. at 99-100.

CHAPTER THREE
ENFORCEMENT OF SECURITY INTERESTS

SECTION 1. INTRODUCTION

Imagine that you have been laid off or have suffered an illness, and have been unable to work for a while. Your bills have mounted while your savings have dwindled. You now have the debts listed below (the first two are just this month's obligation; the others are the total balance). You have not yet defaulted on either the car loan or your apartment lease (which is why the amount listed for these debts is merely the required payment for one month). You manage to find new employment, but you are not earning as much as before and have little hope of being able to pay off all your obligations. As your paychecks come in, which debts do you pay? In other words, how do you prioritize your obligations?

Creditor	Amount Due
Landlord	$1,200
Car Lender	$400
Physician	$1,500
Credit Cards	$5,400
Utilities (all 3 months behind):	
Electricity & Gas	$150
Telephone	$180
Cable TV	$170
Total:	**$9,000**

Most people will pay their rent and car loans first, perhaps the electricity and gas bill next, and then deal with the remainder to the extent assets are available. The rationale for this is not difficult to discern. The electricity and gas company gets paid before many other creditors because it has something the debtor wants: more service. Debtors fear loss of that service and thus will choose to make at least some payment. For the same reason, if the physician's care were still needed and the physician threatened to discontinue care without some payment, chances are the physician's bill would move up the debtor's list.

The landlord and car lender get paid even before the electric company because they can take away something the debtor wants to keep: the apartment and the car. With respect to the car lender, this is the true benefit of having the car as collateral. It makes voluntary payment more likely. In short, having collateral often moves a creditor up on the debtor's payment list.[1] Indeed, the purpose in becoming a secured creditor is not to take the collateral; it is to get paid. No matter how inexpensive and expeditious it might be, going after the collateral is a distasteful endeavor.

Still, some secured creditors need to – and in fact do – enforce their liens on the collateral. This Chapter is about what secured creditors may and must do in that process. The upcoming chapters discuss perfection (Chapter Four) and priority (Chapter Five) of security interests. But those topics deal with the secured party's rights in the collateral vis-à-vis the rights of some third party; neither perfection nor priority is needed for a secured party to have the right to enforce its security interest in the collateral. For the secured party to have that right, the only legal prerequisite is that the security interest must have attached. *See* §§ 9-203, 9-201(a).

The general concept underlying enforcement of the security interest is simple, even though the details of how enforcement occurs can become complex. The concept is merely to obtain the value of the collateral securing the obligation and apply that value toward all or part of the obligation owed. For example, consider a debtor who has granted a security interest in a car to secure a loan for all or part of the price of the car. A secured party that chooses to enforce its security interest will typically begin by repossessing the car. The secured party will then usually sell the car and apply the sale proceeds to pay the costs of repossession and sale, and then, to the extent possible, to the remaining amount due on the loan. Alternatively, consider a business debtor that has granted a security interest in accounts to secure a loan. To enforce its security interest in those accounts, the secured party normally will collect the obligations owed by the account debtors and apply the amounts collected against the outstanding loan balance.

---

1 While having collateral might make voluntary payment more likely, it is worth noting that debtors use numerous strategies in prioritizing their payments. For example, there is an incentive to pay debts bearing a higher rate of interest before debts that bear a lower rate of interest, and thus many debtors employ this approach. However, there is evidence that paying the smallest debts first is the most successful strategy in terms of reducing the total amount of debt because of the psychological reward associated with having fewer creditors. *See* David Gal, Blakeley B. McShane, *Can Small Victories Help Win the War? Evidence from Consumer Debt Management*, 49 J. Marketing Research No. 4, 487-501 (2012).

Most security agreements condition the secured party's ability to enforce the security interest on the debtor's "default": that is, on the debtor's failure to satisfy one of its contractual obligations to the secured party. The secured party and debtor can agree that the debtor need not be in default for the secured party to be permitted to enforce its rights in the collateral. Nevertheless, the fact remains that in most transactions in which the collateral secures a payment obligation of the debtor, the expectation of both parties is that, if the debtor pays in a timely manner and otherwise complies with the terms of the security agreement, the secured party will not seek recourse against the collateral.

To continue the examples above, if the debtor who has granted a security interest in a car continues to pay the required monthly installment payments on the loan, the secured party will not take and sell the car. Instead, the secured party will apply the monthly payments to the loan obligation. If the debtor who has granted a security interest in accounts to secure a loan continues to make payment on the loan in compliance with the parties' agreement, the secured party will usually not attempt to collect from the account debtors the amounts they owe on the accounts. The secured party will typically leave that task to the debtor.

Because default is, in the vast majority of secured transactions, a prerequisite (*i.e.*, a condition) to the secured party's right to enforce the security interest, we begin our discussion of enforcement with default.

SECTION 2. DEFAULT

A. Default Clauses

Although Article 9 conditions many of the secured party's enforcement rights upon the existence of a "default," Article 9 does not define "default." *Compare* §§ 9-601(a), 9-607(a), 9-609(a). Instead, what constitutes a default is governed by the parties' security agreement or loan agreement.[2] Accordingly, drafting a default clause is very important. Part of a drafter's job in defining default is to imagine all the things that could go wrong as the transaction or the parties' relationship continues into the future.[3]

---

[2] *Cf.* Chesapeake Inv. Servs., Inc. v. Olive Group Corp., 2003 WL 369682 (Mass. Super. Ct. Jan. 30, 2003) (subordinated creditor lacked grounds for declaring a default and accelerating the debt under the terms of the loan agreement because such action would interfere with the subordination agreement with another creditor).

[3] Notice that this sentence is written from the perspective of the creditor, that is, from the

Most obviously, the debtor could fail to make one or more payments when due. Thus, failure to pay in accord with the agreement is almost invariably included in the definition of default. But many other events could increase the risk of future nonpayment, even though the debtor has made all payments to date on time. For example, the collateral might depreciate in value or the debtor might dispose of collateral so that, if the debtor later fails to pay, the value of the collateral will be insufficient to satisfy the secured obligation. Similarly, the collateral might become encumbered with a lien that "primes" the security interest, that is, have a higher priority than the secured party's security interest in the collateral. If the debtor is operating a business, a change in management or an economic recession might affect the debtor's ability or willingness to pay. The point is, the secured party wants to be able to declare a default and use its enforcement rights whenever it perceives the need to do so due to some increase in risk. This is not to say that the secured party will actually exercise its enforcement rights at the first sign of a problem, merely that it wants the contractual authority to do so.

Once you, as the secured party's lawyer, have identified the circumstances that should constitute a default and trigger enforcement rights, but before you have drafted the clause defining default, you should review the non-UCC law in the relevant state (*i.e.* the state whose law will govern the transaction) to determine whether each contemplated circumstance is a permissible basis for default. Some states have statutes or administrative regulations that limit the permissible grounds for default in specified types of transactions, particularly consumer transactions. For example, Massachusetts law provides that:

> In any consumer credit transaction involving a loan that is secured by a non-possessory security interest in consumer goods a provision relating to default is enforceable only to the extent that the default is material and consists of the debtor's failure to make one or more payments as required by the agreement, or the occurrence of an event which substantially impairs the value of the collateral.[4]

---

view of the secured party. This is partly because the secured party is generally the one who drafts the security agreement. It is also because the debtor is typically not nearly as concerned as the creditor with what might undermine the parties' relationship after the debtor receives the loan.

4 Mass. Gen. Laws. ch. 255 § 13*I*(a). *See also* Idaho Code § 28-45-107; Kan. Stat. § 16a-5-109; Mo. Stat. § 408.552; R.I. Gen. Laws § 6-51-3(a) (providing similarly with respect to automobile loans); Nev. Rev. Stat. § 97.304 (in automobile retail installment contracts, default is limited to a failure to pay as required by the agreement and situations when "[t]he prospect of payment, performance or realization of collateral is significantly

Problem 3-1

Douglass, Clay and Webster, P.C. is a law firm with 27 lawyers that specializes in transactional work. Because the firm's expenses are fairly constant but its income is irregular, the firm needs financing to make payroll and pay other recurring expenses. First Bank has agreed to loan the firm $800,000, secured by the firm's accounts.

A. Identify every event that might increase First Bank's risk in connection with the transaction and which, therefore, should qualify as an event of default. Your list should include events relating to the law firm's finances, events relating to the law firm's personnel or operations, and events relating to the collateral.
B. Draft the default clause for the Loan and Security Agreement.

So far we have been concentrating on default in the context of a loan agreement, which is common component of a secured transaction. It is important to remember, however, that a security interest can arise in a transaction that does not involve a loan or even a debt. For example, as we saw in Chapter Two, Article 9 applies to a sale of accounts, chattel paper, payment intangibles, or promissory notes. *See* § 9-109(a)(3). Default is a concept that has minimal relevance to such a transaction. Consequently, the secured party/buyer in such a transaction may collect on the collateral irrespective of whether any default has occurred. That is because, given the nature of the transaction as a sale, the seller/debtor no longer has any rights in the collateral. Similarly, if a security interest arises by operation of law under another Article of the UCC, *see* § 9-109(a)(5), (6), there might be no security agreement and hence no contractual definition of default.

---

impaired"); In re Henderson, 492 B.R. 537 (Bankr. D. Nev. 2013) (default-on-bankruptcy clause in retail installment contract for automobile is unenforceable under Nevada law); U.C.C.C. § 5.109.

In contrast, at least one state has a statute that can create a default in circumstances as to which the parties' agreement is silent. Louisiana Civil Code Article 1783 provides:

> When the obligation is subject to a term and the obligor fails to furnish the promised security, or the security furnished becomes insufficient, the obligee may require that the obligor, at his option, either perform the obligation immediately or furnish sufficient security. The obligee may take all lawful measures to preserve his right.

This allows the secured party to demand additional collateral and, if none is provided, to accelerate the debt.

B. Acceleration and Cure

Imagine a lending arrangement in which the debtor is obligated to make periodic payments of principal and interest on the loan pursuant to a set schedule. In fact, the vast majority of lending transactions require payment in installments, typically on a weekly, monthly, quarterly, or yearly basis. Now assume that the debtor failed to make a periodic payment when due under the loan agreement and that such failure constitutes a default. What amount may the creditor seek to collect from the debtor: the missed payment amount or the entire balance of the loan? Unless the loan agreement has an acceleration clause that permits the creditor to demand payment of the entire debt, the creditor may seek to collect only the missed payment because the rest is simply not yet due. If the debt is secured, the secured party may similarly seek to extract value from the collateral only to the extent of the missed payment.

Obviously, this rule creates a very burdensome situation for creditors. If they want to sue the debtor, they must wait for a default on each installment before seeking judicial assistance in collecting it.[5] For secured creditors, the rule is even worse. If they foreclosed on the collateral, such as by selling it, they would be entitled to keep the amount of the missed installments but would have to return any amount in excess of that (*i.e.*, a "surplus") to the debtor. This could seriously undermine their secured status for the remainder of the debt.

For these reasons, virtually every installment loan agreement includes an "acceleration clause." Such a clause provides that, in the event of any default, the entire loan balance becomes due either automatically or at the option of the lender. There are few limits on the lender's ability to accelerate a debt after default other than the general obligation of good faith that applies to the enforcement of every contractual right. *See* § 1-304. *See also* Restatement (Second) of Contracts § 205. However, sometimes a loan agreement will provide that the lender may accelerate the entire loan balance at will or any time it deems itself insecure. Such

---

[5] They need not sue separately on each installment. For example, they could bring a single action to collect several missed payments. The point is, though, that they could not seek to collect any particular installment prior to its due date and for a loan with a lengthy payment period, this would require either the expense of many separate lawsuits or waiting a long time before seeking recourse in the courts. Waiting a long time to file a lawsuit could render the action barred by the applicable statute of limitations, which generally sets a period of time in which to bring suit after the cause of action accrued. A cause of action typically accrues when the breach occurs, and in an installment loan, a breach occurs each time an installment is not paid when due.

"insecurity" clauses are subject to some limitations in § 1-309. Read that section and the definition of "good faith" in § 1-201(b)(20).[6]

Problem 3-2

A. Three years ago, First Bank made a $750,000 secured, working capital loan to Digital Enterprises, secured by a security interest in Digital's accounts. The terms of the loan agreement provide that Digital must give First Bank 30 days' advance notification of any change in its place of business and, within 45 days of the end of its fiscal year, a copy of its audited financial statement. The loan agreement also provides that First Bank may accelerate the debt for violation of any term of the loan agreement. Last year, Digital moved its business headquarters from Silicon Valley to Seattle, without first notifying First Bank. Digital's fiscal year ended three months ago, but First Bank has not received a copy of Digital's audited financial statement. If Digital has made all loan installment payments on time, may First Bank nevertheless call in – *i.e.*, accelerate – the loan? Why or why not? Does it matter if First Bank has learned that last week Digital lost its two largest customers, who collectively account for 60% of Digital's sales? What if the real reason that First Bank wanted to accelerate was that, because of some bad investments and regulatory pressures, it needs the money? *See* §§ 1-304, 1-201(b)(20). Is § 1-309 relevant to this question? In answering these questions, ignore any non-statutory defense, such as waiver or estoppel, Digital might have. Such defenses will be explored in Problem 3-20.

B. How, if at all, would the analysis of Part A be affected if the state whose law governs defines "good faith" merely as "honesty in fact"?

Article 9 does not require a creditor to notify the debtor that a default has occurred or that the right to accelerate has been or is about to be exercised. Law outside Article 9 might require such notification.[7] So too might the parties'

---

[6] Former § 1-201(19) provided that good faith "means honesty in fact in the conduct or transaction concerned." Several states retained this definition of good faith when enacting revised Article 1.

[7] *See, e.g.*, Me. Rev. Stat. Ann. tit. 9-A, § 5-111; Mo. Rev. Stat. § 408.555. Additionally, if a creditor has repeatedly accepted late payments, notification might be needed before a creditor can insist that future payments on time be basing a default on another late payment.

agreement. However, because loan agreements are written primarily by the creditor, they rarely impose upon the creditor a duty to notify the debtor of default or acceleration. Creditors often worry that they might innocently neglect to provide such notification, especially if the personnel involved in originating a transaction are unlikely to be the individuals tasked with monitoring or enforcing it.[8] They also fear what the debtor, once notified, might do with or to collateral. A nefarious debtor might damage or conceal it. But even honest debtors might act in ways that are not in the secured creditor's interest. For example, if the collateral is inventory, perhaps the debtor will conduct a liquidation sale that unloads the inventory at far below its value. Or perhaps the debtor will take the proceeds and, instead of turning them over to the secured creditor as the security agreement requires, use the funds to pay suppliers, employees, or taxes. Few debtors will spend time or money to insure or maintain collateralized equipment that a creditor is likely to seize soon.

Debtors sometimes ask for notification because, at least in theory, they might be able to locate another lender to provide replacement financing. But the reality is that few debtors will be able to obtain alternative financing in a short time period after they have already defaulted. That is particularly so given that most debtors have no right to simply cure the default – and thereby "de-accelerate" the debt – such as by tendering the past due amounts Once acceleration has occurred, the debtor normally has only one way to avoid collection efforts: to pay the entire amount due. Nothing in UCC Articles 3 or 9 requires a creditor to accept a tendered cure of a default (*i.e.*, payment of just the past-due installments). *See* § 9-623.[9]

See, e.g., Buzzell v. Citizens Auto. Finance, Inc., 802 F. Supp. 2d 1014 (D. Minn. 2011)

[8] In this respect, note that the personnel who were involved in making the loan and obtaining the security interest might no longer be employed by the creditor or might have changed duties by the time the debtor defaults. Similarly, the secured party might outsource administration of the loan to another company.

[9] Mississippi has a non-uniform version of § 9-623(b) that allows a debtor to redeem the collateral by tendering "[f]ullfillment of all obligations secured by the collateral then due or past due (excluding any sums that would not be due except for an acceleration provision)." Miss. Stat. 75-9-623(b)(1). Read literally, this allows the debtor to discharge the security interest by paying current and past-due charges. Such a literal interpretation would permit every debtor in an Article 9 transaction, immediately after the transaction was entered into when no amount was yet due, to redeem the collateral and thereby avoid the security interest. More likely, the provision was intended allow the debtor *cure* – not *redeem* – by paying current and past-due amounts. *See* Stephen L. Sepinuck, *Non-Uniform UCC Text Jeopardizes All Secured Transactions Governed by Mississippi Law*, 9 THE TRANSACTIONAL

However, for some types of loans, law outside the UCC might require the creditor to accept payment of the arrearage and to reinstate the original due dates of all future installments. The most common type of statute giving the debtor a right to cure a default applies to a home mortgage loan.[10] A few states also give debtors a limited right to cure a default in a consumer credit transaction[11] or when the collateral is a motor vehicle,[12] and such states typically prohibit the creditor from taking action against collateral during the cure period.[13] However, even in states that have such statutes, there might be some defaults – such as the failure to insure the collateral – for which the statute provides no right to cure,[14] and other defaults that simply cannot be cured.[15] Finally, in a Chapter 11 or Chapter 13 bankruptcy case, the debtor might have a right to cure the default through confirmation of a reorganization plan.[16]

LAW. 8 (Aug. 2019). There is also some authority for the proposition that the debtor must also cure non-monetary defaults. *See* Bombardier Cap., Inc. v. Royer Homes of Miss., Inc., 2005 WL 8170128 (S.D. Miss. 2005).

10 *See, e.g.*, N.J. Stat. § 2A:50-57; N.M. Stat. Ann. § 58-21A-6.

11 *See, e.g.*, Mass. Gen. Laws ch. 255, § 13*I*(b), (c), (e); Wis. Stat. § 425.105; W. Va. Code § 46A-2-106. *See also* U.C.C.C. § 5.111 (enacted in some form in Colorado, Iowa, Kansas, Maine, and South Carolina).

12 *See, e.g.*, 625 Ill. Comp. Stat. 5/3-114(f-7) (providing a right to cure if the owner has paid 30% of the total payments for the car); Walczak v. Onyx Acceptance Corp., 850 N.E.2d 357 (Ill. Ct. App. 2006) (affirming class certification in action against secured party for disposing of collateral without first providing notification of the right to cure).

13 *See, e.g.*, Soberanis v. City Title Loan, LLC, 2017 WL 1232437 (D.S.C. 2017) (a debtor stated a cause of action against a secured party for conversion by alleging that the secured party repossessed the debtor's car without first sending a required notification of the debtor's right to cure).

14 *See* W. Va. Code § 46A-2-106.

15 *See* In re Jones, 591 F.3d 308 (4th Cir. 2010) (filing for bankruptcy protection is a default that the debtor cannot cure, and therefore the state statute requiring pre-enforcement notification of the right to cure does not apply).

16 *See* 11 U.S.C. §§ 1124, 1129, 1322, 1325.

C. Rights upon Default

Upon default, a secured party has several options: (i) it may follow the processes provided in Part 6 of Article 9; (ii) it may avail itself of the remedies provided for in the security agreement; or (iii) it may utilize the processes for collecting a debt that are available under other law. *See* §§ 9-601, 9-604. These rights are cumulative, so that a secured party may combine some of Article 9's enforcement rules with the judicial processes for debt collection generally. For example, a secured party may use judicial process to acquire possession of the collateral and then follow the rules in Article 9 for selling it.[17] Alternatively, a secured party might use Article 9 to acquire possession of the collateral and then employ judicial process to sell it. The secured party's choice of what enforcement path to follow is often affected by the level of the debtor's cooperation or resistance or the degree of risk that any desired action not expressly authorized by a court might later be deemed to be improper.

During the enforcement process, the secured party will also have duties to the debtor and obligors. These duties might be imposed by the terms of the security agreement or by the provisions of Article 9.[18] Duties might also arise from other sources of law. For example, a secured party enforcing its security interest against a consumer debtor must also comply with whatever consumer-protection laws apply.[19] In most situations the duties imposed by different laws will be cumulative:

---

[17] Although Article 9 itself rejects any election of remedies, state laws outside Article 9 might occasionally require the secured party to choose one path to enforcement. For example, California law requires the creditor under a retail installment contract to choose between obtaining a judgment on the debt and enforcing its security interest in the goods. Cal. Civ. Code § 1812.2. *See also* In re Harris, 120 B.R. 142 (Bankr. S.D. Cal. 1990) (secured party in retail installment contract made binding election to forego its security interest by obtaining a money judgment).

[18] In rare circumstances, the secured party might not know who the debtor is. For example, if the original debtor sells the collateral after granting a security interest in it, the secured party might have no knowledge or notice of the sale, and thus no reason to know that the buyer is now the debtor. *See* § 9-102(a)(28). In such circumstances, the secured party owes no duty to the unknown debtor. §§ 9-605, 9-628. This exculpatory rule apparently encompasses not only Article 9 duties, but those arising under other law as well. *See* § 9-605 cmt. 2. *But see* § 9-201(b), (c).

[19] *See* § 9-201(b), (c); Mass. Gen. Laws ch. 255 § 13J. *See also* Johnson Cty. Auto Credit, Inc. v. Green, 83 P.3d 152 (Kan. 2004) (creditor liable for failure to comply with Kansas consumer protection statute when enforcing its security interest in debtor's motor vehicle).

the secured party will need to comply with all of them. In the rare instance when the rules on enforcement in Article 9 conflict with some other applicable rule of law (such that compliance with both laws is not possible), the creditor might need to file a declaratory action to seek a court determination of which set of requirements is paramount.

Remember, a secured party includes some consignors of goods[20] and a buyer of accounts, chattel paper, payment intangibles, and promissory notes. § 9-102(a)(73). In those transactions, the secured party is usually not required to comply with the duties imposed in Part 6 of Article 9. § 9-601(g).

Problem 3-3

First Bank has a security interest in Doctor's Lexus to secure a loan used to finance Doctor's practice. The security agreement provides that any loss or suspension of the Doctor's license to practice medicine is an event of default. The loan officer at First Bank just read in the local newspaper that Doctor settled a medical malpractice claim brought by a former patient, by agreeing to pay an undisclosed amount of damages and by agreeing not to practice medicine for six months. The loan officer, who wants to call in the loan and repossess the Lexus, has consulted with you for advice. How do you advise the loan officer to proceed? *See Turner v. Firstar Bank*, 845 N.E.2d 816 (Ill. Ct. App. 2006); *Robertson v. Horton Brothers Recovery, Inc.*, 2005 WL 736681 (D. Del. 2005).

SECTION 3. ENFORCEMENT AGAINST TANGIBLE COLLATERAL

A. Taking Possession

When the debtor defaults, the secured party's first step in realizing on the value of tangible collateral is usually to acquire possession or control of the collateral (unless the secured party already had possession pursuant to the security agreement). Read § 9-609. In connection with this effort, the secured party may require the debtor to assemble the collateral and make it available to the secured party. § 9-609(c). If the debtor fails to comply, the secured party may either use a judicial process to obtain possession or may proceed privately and simply take whatever items of the collateral it is able to find. § 9-609(a), (b).

---

[20] Those whose transaction qualifies as a consignment under § 9-102(a)(20).

The reference to "judicial process" in § 9-609 means state-law procedures, such as replevin, in which the secured party obtains a court writ instructing the sheriff to seize specified property (the collateral) and deliver it to the plaintiff (the secured party). Such judicial process might require notification to the debtor and a hearing to establish whether the judge should issue the writ. In the hearing, the only issue is usually whether the debtor is in default on its obligations, thereby entitling the secured party to possession. In many cases, however, the secured party proceeds *ex parte* (remember the discussion of due process in Chapter One) and obtains the writ without notifying the debtor of the hearing. In either case, the judge might require the secured party to post a bond to compensate the debtor for losses caused if it is later determined that seizure of the collateral should not have been ordered.

It is often less expensive and might be easier for the secured party to take possession of the collateral without using judicial process. Article 9 expressly authorizes the secured party to take the property without judicial process so long as it can do so without causing a "breach of the peace." § 9-609(b)(2). That phrase is not defined in Article 9.[21] The cases construing it are legion, and not particularly consistent.[22] Still, some things are fairly clear. Actual violence need not occur for

---

[21] A few states have statutory rules on what constitutes breach of the peace during a repossession. *See, e.g.*, Colo. Rev. Stat. § 4-9-601(h) ("For purposes of this part 6, in taking possession of collateral by self-help, 'breach of the peace' includes, but is not limited to, engaging in the following actions without the contemporaneous permission of the debtor: (1) Entering a locked or unlocked residence or residential garage; (2) Breaking, opening, or moving any lock, gate, or other barrier to enter enclosed real property; or (3) Using or threatening to use violent means."). Louisiana, which generally does not authorize repossession unless the debtor has abandoned the collateral or consented to the repossession after or in contemplation of default, *see infra* note 35, does allow specified secured parties a limited right to repossess motor vehicles, provided that can be done without a breach of the peace. La. Rev. Stat. § 6:966(B). For this purpose, "breach of the peace" includes: (i) unauthorized entry into a closed dwelling, whether locked or unlocked; and (ii) seizing control of the collateral following an oral protest by a debtor. La. Rev. Stat. § 6:955(C).

Other states have defined "breach of the peace" for the purposes of criminal law, *see, e.g.*, Wyo. Stat. Ann. § 6-6-102(a) ("A person commits breach of the peace if he disturbs the peace of a community or its inhabitants by unreasonably loud noise or music or by using threatening, abusive or obscene language or violent actions with knowledge or probable cause to believe he will disturb the peace."). Presumably, any action that violates the applicable criminal law will also constitute a breach of the peace for the purposes of § 9-609. However, breach of the peace under § 9-609 is likely to encompass things that do not rise to the level of a criminal act.

[22] *See* Timothy R. Zinnecker, *The Default Provisions of Revised Article 9 of the Uniform*

a breach of the peace to take place; the mere threat of violence or a substantial risk of injury to the debtor, the secured party, or bystanders will make a repossession effort improper.[23] Similarly, use of a uniformed police officer is not allowed, unless the officer is acting pursuant to a court order or writ. *See* § 9-609 cmt. 3. The reason for this is that while the secured party might have a *contractual* right to possession, the debtor has a *legal* right to make the creditor go to court to enforce it. Therefore, the presence of a police officer to facilitate repossession is a false display of authority. Indeed, a police officer who assists in a repossession might well be liable for violating the debtor's civil rights.[24]

One fact that is often relevant in breach of the peace litigation is the degree of any trespass involved. Courts treat a trespass as serious, but not determinative, of whether a breach of the peace has occurred.[25] While it is difficult to draw firm conclusions about what creditors may and may not do, it does appear that commercial premises are a better target than residential premises. Accessing open or unlocked property is better than breaking open locked structures. And entering a detached garage is better than entering a home.[26] In fact, creditors should never enter the home without consent. Of course, that consent can be provided by anyone with apparent authority; permission from the landlord or even a babysitter will normally be all that is needed as long as there is no objection from anyone else who is present.

Commercial Code: Part 1, 54 BUS. LAW. 1113, 1140-46 (1999).

[23] *See* Callaway v. Whittenton, 892 So. 2d 852 (Ala. 2003).

[24] *See* Hyman v. Capital One Auto Fin., 826 F. App'x 244 (3d Cir. 2020) (rejecting a police officer's qualified immunity defense but reducing the jury's punitive damages award from $500,000 to $30,000); Vassal v. Palisades Funding Corp., 2020 WL 2797274 (E.D.N.Y. 2020) (a debtor stated a cause of action under § 1983 against the police officers who allegedly assisted a repossession by ordering the debtor out of the vehicle, arresting him, and giving the keys to the vehicle to the repossession agents).

[25] *See* Westbrook v. NASA Federal Credit Union, 2019 WL 1056356, at *4 n.4 (N.D. Ala. 2019) ("Trespass alone is insufficient to create a breach of the peace, and the parties here do not dispute that the automobile was located in an open carport.").

[26] *See* Madden v. Deere Credit Servs., Inc., 598 So. 2d 860, 867 (Ala. 1992) ("the potential for breaches of the public peace and tranquility as a result of unauthorized intrusions on property escalates in direct proportion to the presence of fences, gates, signs, and other indicia of nonassent to entry."). *Cf.* Salisbury Livestock Co. v. Colorado Central Credit Union, 793 P.2d 470 (Wyo. 1990) (allowing jury to decide whether trespass on secluded ranch was reasonable).

The security agreement might – and if it is well drafted, will – expressly authorize entry onto the debtor's property. That should insulate a repossession effort from being an actionable trespass, at least if the debtor does not revoke that authorization before or during the repossession attempt, but will not necessarily satisfy the prohibition on breach of the peace.

Of course, no matter what the security agreement provides, the secured party has no express authorization to trespass on a third party's property. However, the secured party might nonetheless be privileged to do so. Consider Restatement (Second) of Torts § 198, which some courts expressly look to in this context:[27]

> § 198. Entry To Reclaim Goods On Land Without Wrong Of Actor
>
> (1) One is privileged to enter land in the possession of another, at a reasonable time and in a reasonable manner, for the purpose of removing a chattel to the immediate possession of which the actor is entitled, and which has come upon the land otherwise than with the actor's consent or by his tortious conduct or contributory negligence.
>
> (2) The actor is subject to liability for any harm done in the exercise of the privilege stated in Subsection (1) to any legally protected interest of the possessor in the land or connected with it, except where the chattel is on the land through the tortious conduct or contributory negligence of the possessor.
>
> Comment on subsection (1)
>
> * * *
>
> *d. Necessity of demand by actor.* The entry must be made for the purpose of removing the actor's chattel, and at a reasonable time and in a reasonable manner. Ordinarily a demand on the possessor, either to deliver the chattel at the border of the land or to permit the actor to go on the land and get it, is required before an entry can reasonably be made. If, however, it appears that such a demand would be futile, or that the delay which it would necessitate would subject the chattel to a danger of serious harm, entry without demand may be reasonable.[28]

---

[27] *E.g.*, Droge v. AAAA Two Star Towing, Inc., 468 P.3d 862 (Nev. Ct. App. 2020); Salisbury Livestock Co. v. Colorado Central Credit Union, 793 P.2d 470 (Wyo. 1990).

[28] RESTATEMENT (SECOND) OF TORTS § 198. Copyright 1965 by the American Law Institute. Reproduced with permission. All rights reserved. *See also* Brooks v. Leon's Quality Adjusters, Inc., 2016 WL 4539967 (E.D. Cal. 2016) (a repossession agent did not breach the peace by removing the debtor's car from the parking lot where the debtor was employed, even though the employer had posted signs stating "No Repo Vehicles," "No Trespassing," "Private Property," and "Check With Guard Before Entering Plant," because California law provides that the owner of chattels does not commit trespass by going on the land of another to take them without breaching the peace).

The following two cases illustrate the analysis courts use in deciding whether a repossession breached the peace. In reviewing them, catalogue the factors that the courts deemed relevant to the "breach of the peace" inquiry.[29]

RUSSELL V. SANTANDER CONSUMER USA, INC.
2020 WL 3077944 (E.D. Wis. 2020)

NANCY JOSEPH, United States Magistrate Judge

Steven and Nancy Russell bought a 2013 Dodge Journey from a dealership in Illinois. Santander Consumer USA, Inc. purchased the Russells' retail installment contract for the vehicle. After the Russells fell behind on their payments, Santander obtained a judgment of replevin and enlisted AssetsBiz-Wisconsin, LLC, and its repossession agent, Michael Sancinati, to repossess the Russells' vehicle. The Russells now sue AssetsBiz and Sancinati for violations of the Fair Debt Collection Practices Act ("FDCPA"), 15 U.S.C. § 1692 and sue all three defendants for violations of the Wisconsin Consumer Act ("WCA"), Wis. Stat. 421 *et seq.*, stemming from the repossession.

AssetsBiz and Sancinati move for summary judgment as to the FDCPA and WCA claims against them. The Russells also move for summary judgment as to their claims against AssetsBiz, Sancinati, and Santander. For the reasons discussed below, the defendants' motion is denied and the Russells' motion is granted.

FACTS

On March 14, 2017, Santander commenced a lawsuit against the Russells in the Racine County Circuit Court to recover possession of their 2013 Dodge Journey. The Racine County Circuit Court entered a judgment of replevin on April 20, 2017.

At approximately 10:45 a.m. on October 14, 2018, Steven Russell was inside his home in Racine when he heard his vehicle's security alarm go off. Russell's friend, Eric Peckman, told Russell that someone was taking his vehicle. Russell testified that he looked out of his window and saw that the hood of his Dodge Journey was up. Because he did not know who was by his vehicle or what he was getting into, Russell testified that he took his gun out of his safe for his own protection. Russell went out of the door of his house and stood to the back of the vehicle for nine

---

[29] Secured parties must be very careful in conducting repossessions on Native American reservations. Such action might not be legal or might be subject to any number of restrictions (advance notification, tribal council approval, *etc.*). To deal with this – and with the commercial development that many Native American tribes wish to foster on tribal property – the ULC has developed a Model Tribal Secured Transactions Act based on Article 9.

minutes while Sancinati attempted to disconnect the Journey's battery. Russell did not make any moves towards the vehicle, he simply sat and waited for Sancinati to come to the back of the vehicle.

Once Sancinati came to the back of the vehicle, Russell testified that he asked Sancinati what he was doing. Sancinati responded that he was there to repossess the vehicle and attempted to show Russell some documents. Russell testified that he told Sancinati that he did not care what documents Sancinati allegedly had, Sancinati was to "put the vehicle down and get the hell off [his] property." Russell testified that while he told Sancinati that he had a loaded gun, he never removed the firearm from his pocket. After Russell told Sancinati that he had a gun and that Sancinati needed to leave, Sancinati ceased his efforts to repossess the vehicle and drove away, leaving the vehicle in place.

Sancinati, in contrast, testified that after Russell exited his residence, he told Sancinati that he had a loaded .45 in his hand and pointed the gun, point blank, at Sancinati's chest. Sancinati testified that while the gun was pointed at him, he attempted to show Russell his paperwork, but Russell "wouldn't have it." Sancinati testified that Russell told Sancinati to leave his property, and Sancinati complied.

Sancinati testified that he parked down at the end of the street and called the Racine Police Department because he feared for his safety. Sancinati testified that he told the police that he was doing a repossession and the vehicle owner came out and threatened him with a gun. Russell testified that approximately thirty minutes after Sancinati left, officers from the Racine Police Department arrived at his door. The officers asked Russell to step outside, which he did. Russell was searched and asked about his firearm. Russell informed the officers that his gun was back in the safe in his bedroom and that he was unarmed. Russell testified that the officers placed him in handcuffs and walked him to the back of the squad car. Russell testified that he was in the squad car for twenty-two minutes. By the time he was released, the Dodge Journey was gone. Sancinati testified that while Russell was handcuffed and in the back of the squad car, the officers told him that "if [he] wanted to go get the vehicle, [he] could go get it."

* * *

ANALYSIS

The Russells sue AssetsBiz and Sancinati under both the FDCPA and the WCA, and sue all three defendants under the WCA. The Russells allege that AssetsBiz and Sancinati violated the FDCPA by repossessing the vehicle in violation of Wisconsin law, specifically, that Sancinati "breached the peace" when he repossessed the vehicle. The Russells' two claims under the WCA similarly stem from Sancinati's alleged breach of the peace. The Russells further argue that Santander is liable under the WCA for AssetsBiz and Sancinati's wrongful actions.

1. Breach of the Peace (FDCPA and WCA Claims Against AssetsBiz and Sancinati)

The Russells contend that AssetsBiz and Sancinati breached the peace, as a matter of law, when Sancinati repossessed the Russells' Dodge Journey, thus violating the FDCPA, The FDCPA expressly prohibits a "debt collector" from using "unfair or unconscionable means to collect or attempt to collect any debt." 15 U.S.C. § 1692f. The term "debt collector" generally is defined as excluding repossessors and other enforcers of security interests. 15 U.S.C. § 1692a(6). However, a repossessor may not take or threaten to take nonjudicial action to dispossess a person of property if there is no present right to possession of the property claimed as collateral through an enforceable security interest. Wisconsin law allows that upon an entry of a judgment for replevin in favor of the creditor, the creditor shall have the right to either: (1) have execution issued to require the sheriff of the county where the collateral or leased goods may be to take the same from the debtor and deliver it to the creditor (i.e., a "judicial repossession") or (2) immediately exercise the right to nonjudicial recovery of the collateral or leased goods, * * * (i.e., a "nonjudicial repossession"). If the creditor chooses to exercise the right to nonjudicial recovery of the collateral, he may not commit a "breach of the peace" while doing so. Thus, if the creditor breaches the peace, there is no right of possession and the FDCPA is violated.

The issue of whether a repossessor "breached the peace," however, only comes into play if the creditor chooses to exercise the right to nonjudicial recovery of the collateral. I have already determined that AssetsBiz and Sancinati engaged in a nonjudicial recovery of the collateral. Thus, the issue before me is whether the defendants breached the peace when repossessing the Russells' vehicle.

Under Wisconsin law, if a creditor repossesses in disregard of the debtor's unequivocal oral protest, the creditor commits a breach of the peace. The rationale behind this is that repossessions are "emotional matters" and a "verbal objection to a repossession is the precursor to violence, and [ ] it should not be necessary for a debtor to resort to violence to provide the breach of the peace necessary to defeat a self-help repossession." *Hollibush v. Ford Motor Credit Co.*, 508 N.W.2d 449, 455 (Ct. App. 1993). A creditor cannot avoid a "breach of the peace," however, by simply calling law enforcement for help when the debtor unequivocally objects to the repossession. In other words, the creditor cannot side-step the requirement of first obtaining the "execution" before involving law enforcement in the repossession.

The Russells' situation is unique. The parties do not dispute that Sancinati attempted to repossess the Dodge Journey, that Steven Russell unequivocally objected to the repossession and told Sancinati that he had a firearm (although the parties dispute whether Russell actually pointed the firearm at Sancinati's chest), and that Sancinati left. AssetsBiz and Sancinati argue that this was one repossession attempt – and clearly no breach of the peace occurred under Wisconsin law because Sancinati left when Russell objected. The situation did not end there, however. Sancinati then called the police, who arrived within minutes (according to the Russells) or within thirty minutes (according to the defendants). Either way, AssetsBiz and Sancinati argue that this commenced a second, independent, repossession attempt – this time ending with Steven Russell's step-daughter, Morgan Spring (who frequently drove the Dodge Journey), allowing the repossession to take place while Steven Russell was detained in the back of a squad car for questioning regarding allegedly pointing a gun at Sancinati's chest.

AssetsBiz and Sancinati argue that even though Russell may have unequivocally objected to the first repossession attempt, this does not mean that Sancinati breached the peace during his "second and successful" repossession attempt. AssetsBiz and Sancinati argue that if a debtor unequivocally objects to one repossession attempt, this does not mean that the creditor cannot keep attempting self-help repossession. They argue that Wisconsin law does not require a creditor to pursue judicial remedies after a debtor's objection.

While Wisconsin law does not specifically address this issue, what *Hollibush* does teach, however, is that "no means no" and self-help repossession in the face of a debtor's contemporaneous objection constitutes a breach of the peace. In other words, if the debtor says "no," the self-help repossession must cease. Wisconsin law is not crystal clear on what must take place after the debtor's objection. But I do not agree with AssetsBiz and Sancinati that repossession efforts can recommence, as occurred in this case, as soon as thirty minutes after the debtor objects to the repossession. While *Hollibush* does not specifically address what must occur after a debtor objects to a self-help repossession, the court does favorably cite both case law and legal commentary that states if a debtor protests the repossession, the secured party should pursue its remedies in court.

The defendants cite a case from the Kansas Court of Appeals, *Wade v. Ford Motor Credit Co.*, 668 P.2d 183 (1983) in support of the proposition that a debtor's refusal to consent after demand for possession does not, in and of itself, require resort to legal channels for recovery. But in *Wade*, the secured party waited one month between two separate repossession attempts. The court noted that "the potential for violence was substantially reduced by the passage of this time." *Id.* at 189. Even assuming AssetsBiz and Sancinati are correct that Wisconsin law does not require a secured party to pursue judicial remedies after the debtor objects to a self-help repossession, it is entirely unclear how the passage of (at most) thirty minutes is long enough to calm emotions and reduce the threat of violence.

* * * I find that the undisputed material facts demonstrate that the Russells are entitled to judgment as a matter of law as to their claim that AssetsBiz and Sancinati violated 15 U.S.C. § 1692f(6) when they repossessed the Dodge Journey.

* * *

2. Santander's Liability Under the WCA

The Russells also sue their creditor, Santander, under Wis. Stat. § 425.206(2)(a) and Wis. Stat. §§ 427.104(1)(h) and (1)(j) for the illegal repossession. The Russells move for summary judgment on their WCA claims against Santander and as to Santander's affirmative defenses. The Russells argue that Santander cannot avoid liability under the WCA by acting through its repossession agents. It is undisputed that Santander hired a non-party, P.K. Willis, to repossess the Russells' vehicle. P.K. Willis in turn hired AssetsBiz to conduct the physical repossession of the Russells' vehicle. Thus, Santander argues that it is not liable for the actions of AssetsBiz and Sancinati because there was no contractual relationship between Santander and AssetsBiz and because there is no case law to support that a creditor is vicariously liable for the actions of a third-party repossession company.

The court in *Gable v. Universal Acceptance Corp. (WI)*, 338 F. Supp. 3d 943 (E.D. Wis. 2018) addressed a similar issue. In *Gable*, the creditor, UAC, had a contract with a repossession company, RPI. The parties' contract expressly classified RPI as an independent contractor and not an agent of UAC. RPI's agent, Chase, physically repossessed the plaintiffs' vehicle. The plaintiffs sued UAC, RPI, and Chase under Wis. Stat. § 425.206(2)(a) and §§ 427.104(1)(g) and (j). UAC argued that it could not be held liable under the WCA because RPI was an independent contractor under its contract with UAC and not its agent, and because Chase was also not UAC's agent but RPI's agent. Santander is in a similar position as UAC – both were two parties removed from the act of repossession. In *Gable*, the creditor (UAC) hired RPI to repossess Gable's vehicle, and RPI hired Chase to do the actual repossession. Similarly, in this case, Santander hired P.K. Willis to repossess the vehicle, who in turn hired AssetsBiz to conduct the actual repossession. Santander presumably does have a contract with P.K. Willis and P.K.

Willis presumably has a contract with AssetsBiz. But having an actual contract does not matter. The *Gable* court cited Wis. Stat. § 425.206(2)(a), which states that "[i]n taking possession of collateral or leased goods, no merchant may . . . [c]ommit a breach of the peace." * * * The court found that "[r]egardless of the language UAC included in its contract with RPI, it was UAC that directed RPI to repossess Gable's car, and it is UAC that falls within the definition of merchant contained in the WCA." The court continued: "It was UAC's authority to repossess Gable's car that RPI was exercising. That UAC chose to authorize RPI to exercise its right under Wisconsin law to take possession of its collateral extra-judicially does not mean it can avoid liability for actions taken on its behalf and at its request." *Id.* at 955.

The only difference between *Gable* and this case is that the Russells did not also sue P.K. Willis. It is irrelevant that Santander did not contract with AssetsBiz. As in *Gable*, P.K. Willis repossessed the Russells' vehicle on Santander's authority, and P.K. Willis utilized AssetsBiz to do so. Thus, Santander cannot insulate itself from liability under Wisconsin law by utilizing third-parties to exercise its right to repossession. P.K. Willis and AssetsBiz were taking action at Santander's request. Like *Gable*, the repossession agent (RPI/P.K. Willis) used its agent (Chase/AssetsBiz) to repossess the plaintiff's vehicle. The court found that *despite* the creditor's (UAC) contractual relationship with RPI expressly stating that RPI was an independent contractor and *not* an agent of UAC, and despite the fact that the repossession agent (RPI) used its own agent (Chase) to repossess the vehicle, the court still found that UAC could be liable to the plaintiff under the WCA. I agree with the *Gable* court's reasoning. The "merchant" has an independent duty under the WCA to not breach the peace while taking possession of collateral. It would defeat the purpose of the statute if a "merchant" could escape liability under the WCA by using a third-party to take possession of the collateral. Thus, Santander is liable for the breach of the peace under the WCA.

CONCLUSION

I find that AssetsBiz, Sancinati, and Santander are liable to the Russells for damages. The Russells reserved the issue of damages for trial. The clerk's office will contact the parties to set a telephonic status conference to schedule a trial on damages.

GILES V. FIRST VIRGINIA CREDIT SERVICES, INC.
560 S.E.2d 557 (N.C. Ct. App. 2002)

McGee, Judge

Richard Giles and Joann Giles (plaintiffs) appeal the trial court's order granting First Virginia Credit Services, Inc.'s (First Virginia) motion for summary judgment in part.

Plaintiffs filed a complaint against defendants First Virginia and Professional Auto Recovery, Inc. (Professional Auto Recovery) for wrongful repossession of an automobile. Plaintiffs alleged in an amended complaint that First Virginia . . . and Professional Auto Recovery wrongfully converted and/or repossessed the automobile and plaintiff's personal property located with the automobile * * * and that * * * removal of the automobile constituted breach of the peace in violation of [§ 9-503] * * *.

In an affidavit filed by plaintiffs in opposition to First Virginia's motion for summary judgment, plaintiffs' neighbor, Glenn A. Mosteller (Mr. Mosteller), stated that he was awakened around 4:00 a.m.

> by the running of a loud diesel truck engine on the road outside my house. Evidentially [sic] the truck was stopped because I lay in bed for a while and did not get up. I then became concerned and went to the window to see what was going on. At this time I saw a large rollback diesel truck with a little pickup truck on the truck bed behind it. The truck only had its parking lights on. The truck . . . started going toward the Giles' yard. It still only had its parking lights on. About that time, a man jumped out of the truck and ran up the Giles' driveway. Their car was parked up at their house. Then the car came flying out back down the driveway making a loud noise and started screeching off. . . . At about the same time, the rollback also pulled off real fast making a real loud diesel noise and went down [the road]. . . . I got to the phone, called the Giles and told them someone was stealing their car. . . . My lights were on . . . and the Giles' lights were on and that portion of our neighborhood had woken up. Richard Giles came out in his yard and we hollared a few words back and forth and I jumped in my truck ... to try to get the police. About 5 minutes later a police car came up and pulled into the Giles' yard. Then another police car came then a Sheriff's Deputy car came. Then another police car came. . . . There was a great commotion going on out in the street and in our yard all to the disturbance of the quietness and tranquility of our neighborhood. . . . It scared me and it scared the Giles.

Joann Giles stated in a deposition that she was awakened by Mr. Mosteller's telephone call in which he told her that someone was stealing her car. She stated she ran to see if the automobile was parked outside and confirmed that it was gone. Joann Giles testified she woke up her husband and gave him the telephone; he ran outside into the yard and heard Mr. Mosteller "hollering" at him from across the street. Plaintiffs testified in their depositions that neither of them saw the car being repossessed but were only awakened by their neighbor after the automobile was gone. During the actual repossession, no contact was made between Professional Auto Recovery and plaintiffs, nor between Professional Auto Recovery and Mr. Mosteller.

* * * In an order dated 15 June 2000, the trial court: * * * granted First Virginia's motion for summary judgment in part, stating that there was no genuine issue as to any material fact as to the conversion or repossession of the motor vehicle * * *. Plaintiffs appeal.

* * *

Our Courts have long recognized the right of secured parties to repossess collateral from a defaulting debtor without resort to judicial process, so long as the repossession is effected peaceably. * * * Our General Assembly codified procedures for self-help repossessions, including this common law restriction, in the North Carolina Uniform Commercial Code (UCC). [Section 9-503], in effect at the time of the repossession in this case, reads in part,

> Unless otherwise agreed a secured party has on default the right to take possession of the collateral. In taking possession a secured party may proceed without judicial process if this can be done without breach of the peace or may proceed by action.

The General Assembly did not define breach of the peace but instead left this task to our Courts, and although a number of our appellate decisions have considered this self-help right of secured parties, none have clarified what actions constitute a breach of the peace.

[Section 9-503], at issue in this appeal, has been replaced by [revised § 9-609], which states that a secured party, after default, may take possession of the collateral without judicial process, if the secured party proceeds without breach of the peace. In [comment 3] to the new statutory provision, our General Assembly continued to state that, "[l]ike former Section 9-503, this section does not define or explain the conduct that will constitute a breach of the peace, leaving that matter for continuing development by the courts." * * *

The courts in many states have examined whether a breach of the peace in the context of the UCC has occurred. Courts have found a breach of the peace when actions by a creditor incite violence or are likely to incite violence.

Other courts have expanded the phrase breach of the peace beyond the criminal law context to include occurrences where a debtor or his family protest the repossession. Some courts, however, have determined that a mere oral protest is not sufficient to constitute a breach of the peace.

If a creditor removes collateral by an unauthorized breaking and entering of a debtor's dwelling, courts generally hold this conduct to be a breach of the peace. Removal of collateral from a private driveway, without more however, has been found not to constitute a breach of the peace. Additionally, noise alone has been determined to not rise to the level of a breach of the peace.

Many courts have used a balancing test to determine if a repossession was undertaken at a reasonable time and in a reasonable manner, and to balance the interests of debtors and creditors. Five relevant factors considered in this balancing test are: "(1) where the repossession took place, (2) the debtor's express or constructive consent, (3) the reactions of third parties, (4) the type of premises entered, and (5) the creditor's use of deception." *Davenport*, 818 S.W.2d at 29 (citing 2 J. White & R. Summers, *Uniform Commercial Code* § 27-6, at 575-76 (3d ed. 1988)).

* * *

In applying these factors to the undisputed evidence in the case before us, we affirm the trial court's determination that there was no breach of the peace, as a matter of law. Professional Auto Recovery went onto plaintiffs' driveway in the early morning hours, when presumably no one would be outside, thus decreasing the possibility of confrontation. Professional Auto Recovery did not enter into plaintiffs' home or any enclosed area. Consent to repossession was expressly given in the contract with First Virginia signed by Joann Giles. Although a third party, Mr. Mosteller, was awakened by the noise of Professional Auto Recovery's truck, Mr. Mosteller did not speak with anyone from Professional Auto Recovery, nor did he go outside until Professional Auto Recovery had departed with the Giles' automobile. Further, neither of the plaintiffs were awakened by the noise of the truck, and there was no confrontation between either of them with any representative of Professional Auto Recovery. By the time Mr. Mosteller and plaintiffs went outside, the automobile was gone. Finally, there is no evidence, nor did plaintiffs allege, that First Virginia or Professional Auto Recovery employed any type of deception when repossessing the automobile.

There is no factual dispute as to what happened during the repossession in this case, and the trial court did not err in granting summary judgment to First Virginia on this issue. * * *

The trial court's order granting partial summary judgment for First Virginia is affirmed.

A secured party that breaches the peace in a repossession effort is generally liable for conversion, trespass to chattels, or some similar common-law tort.[30] Moreover, as the *Russell* case shows, use of independent contractors, such as a repossession agent or company, to conduct the repossession will not insulate the secured party from liability. The obligation to avoid a breach of the peace is a nondelegable duty. § 9-609 cmt. 3.[31]

In addition to complaining about the repossession itself, the plaintiffs in *Giles* alleged that the defendant wrongfully converted some of plaintiffs' personal property that had been in their car. The trial court denied the defendants' motion for summary judgment on that claim, concluding that there were genuine issues of

---

[30] Because breaching the peace renders the repossession unlawful, meaning that there is no longer a present right to take the collateral, most courts ruling on the issue have concluded that a repossession agent that breaches the peace during a repossession in connection with a consumer transaction can be liable under the federal Fair Debt Collection Practices Act. *See, e.g.*, Richards v. PAR, Inc., 954 F.3d 965 (7th Cir. 2020); Gerbasi v. Nu Era Towing and Serv., Inc., 443 F. Supp. 3d 411 (W.D.N.Y. 2020); Vassal v. Palisades Funding Corp., 2020 WL 2797274 (E.D.N.Y. 2020); Goodwin v. His Choice Towing & Recovery, LLC, 2019 WL 7944075 (N.D. Ga. 2019); Oliver v. ARS Ohio LLC, 2019 WL 343249 (N.D. Ohio 2019); Wright v. Santander Consumer USA, Inc., 2018 WL 2095171 (M.D. Fla. 2018); Soberanis v. City Title Loan, LLC, 2017 WL 1232437 (D.S.C. 2017); Mkhitaryan v. U.S. Bancorp, 2012 WL 6204840 (D. Nev. 2012); Williams v. Republic Recovery Servs., Inc., 2010 WL 2195519 (N.D. Ill. 2010); Alexander v. Blackhawk Recovery and Investigation, LLC, 731 F. Supp. 2d 674 (E.D. Mich. 2010).

In contrast, because the secured party is not a "debt collector" under the FDCPA, the secured party cannot be liable under that act if a repossession agent breaches the peace. *See* Beal v. Public Service Credit Union, 2018 WL 3913992 (E.D. Mich. 2018). *See also* Gill v. Board of Nat'l Credit Union Admin. for Sikh Fed. Credit Union, 2018 WL 5045755, at *12 (E.D.N.Y. 2018) (even if a breach of the peace occurred, because the debtor was clearly in default and was not legally entitled to possession of his car, the debtor's damages would be limited to amount of damage to the car).

[31] *See* Williamson v. Fowler Toyota, Inc., 956 P.2d 858 (Okla. 1998).

material fact as to the reasonableness of the creditor's action in taking that property. The defendant did not appeal that ruling.

This dichotomy – the reasonableness of the repossession of the car but the uncertain reasonableness of the secured party's possession of the items within it – serves as yet another reminder of how careful repossessing secured parties must be with respect to such property.[32]

As if that were not enough to keep creditors and repossession agents on their guard, there is something creditors need to be far more worried about inadvertently taking than other *property*. Repossessing a car when there are people inside is a criminal act – kidnaping – and happens more commonly than you might think.

Problem 3-4

A. You represent First Bank. First Bank has asked you to prepare a manual for its repossession agents about how to conduct a repossession without a breach of the peace. What advice will you put in the manual with respect to the following questions?

1. How should repossession of the debtor's inventory and equipment occur? For example, if the debtor operates a hardware store, how may

---

[32] *See also* Gable v. Universal Acceptance Corp. (WI), 338 F. Supp. 3d 943 (E.D. Wis. 2018) (a secured party that had not authorized the repossession agent to charge a fee to return personal property in the debtor's repossessed vehicle was not be liable under the Fair Debt Collection Practices Act for the agent's attempt to collect the fee, but the secured party might be liable in conversion for the property not returned); In re House, 2017 WL 2579026 (Bankr. S.D. Miss. 2017) (secured party liable for $500 for not returning items allegedly in the debtors' car at the time of repossession despite testimony of that the secured party's business practice was to inventory and store items of value); Duncan v. Asset Recovery Specialists, Inc. 2017 WL 2870520 (W.D. Wis. 2017) (although the debtor did not have a claim under the Fair Debt Collection Practices Act based on her mistaken belief that the repossession agent sought to charge her $100 to return property within the repossessed car, the debtor might have a conversion claim); Reed v. Les Schwab Tire Centers, Inc., 2011 WL 692904 (Wash. Ct. App. 2011) (tire seller that had a security interest in customer's tires did not commit conversion by removing tires and wheels from the customer's car, bringing them to the seller's place of business to there separate the tires from the wheels, and returning the wheels the following day; the seller's actions were justified and the customer suffered no damages for the temporary loss of the wheels).

Some states have statutes that specify what a secured party may do or must do with personal property inside a repossessed vehicle. *See, e.g.*, La. Rev. Stat. § 6:966(F).

the repossession agent secure control over the inventory and equipment?

2. What time of day should repossession of a consumer debtor's automobile take place or not take place?
3. If a debtor or third person objects to a repossession attempt, and the repossession agent withdraws without taking the collateral, how long should the agent wait before making another attempt to repossess the collateral?
4. To what extent may the repossession agent lie to or deceive the debtor or other person in possession of the collateral?

B. Your friend Driver has a car loan from First Bank. The loan is in default and Driver anticipates that First Bank will seek to repossess the car. What may Driver do to thwart attempts to repossess? What advice will you give to Driver with respect to thwarting repossession? *See, e.g.*, Ariz. Rev. Stat. § 13-2204; Kan. Stat. § 21-5830; Tex. Penal Code § 32.33(b); Wash. Rev. Code § 9.45.060; Wis. Stat. § 943.84; 11 U.S.C. § 727(a)(2).

C. What, if anything, would you advise First Bank to put in its lending documents to facilitate its ability to repossess collateral without breach of the peace? *See* §§ 1-103, 1-302, 9-601(a), 9-602, 9-603, 9-624.

Problem 3-5

You represent Speedy Motors, a retailer of new and used cars, primarily to consumers. Speedy Motors frequently sells car on credit. When it does so, Speedy Motors retains a security interest in the car sold to secure payment of the purchase price, applicable sales taxes, and all related amounts that the customer owes.

When a customer defaults and Speedy Motors repossesses the car, the car will often contain various items of personal property, such as loose change, sporting goods, CDs, books, clothing, or an after-market sound system. But the car might contain almost anything, including pets, alcoholic beverages, health aids, prescription medications, private medical records, or things belonging to the debtor's friend, relative, or employer. Typically, Speedy Motors holds any such property for the debtor to retrieve. However, the storage costs occasionally start to run up when the debtor does not promptly retrieve the items and Speedy wants to be able to recoup those costs.

What would you advise Speedy Motors to include in its form security agreement to ensure that, no matter what happens to be in the car, Speedy

Motors will not be incurring liability by repossessing the car and its contents? Draft appropriate language. What problems do you foresee? *See* §§ 9-108, 9-204(b).

In addition to complying with § 9-609 by avoiding a breach of the peace, the secured party must be careful to comply with whatever non-uniform amendments to Article 9 that the applicable state has enacted. For example:

- Rhode Island requires a secured party repossessing a motor vehicle without the debtor's knowledge to notify the local police department within one hour after the repossession.[33]
- Connecticut requires 15 days advance notification of any electronic self-help, prohibits electronic self-help entirely if the secured party has reason to know it will result in grave harm to the public interest, and provides for nonwaivable consequential damages for its wrongful use.[34]
- Louisiana has a non-uniform version of Article 9 that generally does not permit the secured party to repossess collateral unless the debtor has abandoned the collateral or consented to the repossession after or in contemplation of default.[35]

---

33 R.I. Gen. Laws § 6A-9-609(b)(2). Indiana has a similar requirement. *See* Ind. Stat. § 26-2-10-6 (requiring a repossession agent that intends to repossess a vehicle or watercraft to provide the county sheriff's office, before or within two hours after a repossession, with the name of the agent's company, a description of the property, the name of the person believed to be in possession or who was in possession, and the address where the property is believed to be located or was located).

34 Conn. Gen. Stat. § 42a-9-609(d). *See also* Conn. Gen Stat. § 42-419 (subjecting consumer leases to similar rules); Colo. Rev. Stat. § 4-9-609 (prohibiting a secured party from rendering equipment unusable by disabling a computer program "if immediate injury to any person or property is a reasonably foreseeable consequence of such action"); Cal. Civ. Code § 2983.37 (prohibiting some car dealers from using electronic tracking technology to locate a vehicle or using starter interruption technology to disable a vehicle unless specific disclosures are made at the time of contract formation and warnings are issued prior to disablement).

35 *See* La. Rev. Stat. § 10:9-609. However, other Louisiana statutes give specified secured parties a limited right to repossess motor vehicles. *See* La. Rev. Stat. §§ 6:965, 6:966, 6:966.1.

Similarly, the secured party must comply with any applicable law outside Article 9 that deals with repossession of collateral. For example:

- The District of Columbia has fairly extensive regulations with respect to the repossession of an automobile purchased on credit.[36]
- Wisconsin prohibits repossession of a motor vehicle until fifteen days after the secured party notifies the debtor of the debtor's right to cure and prohibits repossession from the debtor's dwelling except at the debtor's voluntary request[37]
- Iowa requires mediation before a secured party may enforce a debt against farm products or farming equipment.[38]
- Massachusetts permits repossession in connection with a consumer credit transaction only after a payment default; a creditor may proceed against the collateral following any other default only after a prior hearing.[39]

Occasionally, secured parties effect a constructive repossession, rather than an actual one. They do this by exercising control over the collateral in a manner that renders it unusable. This can deprive the debtor of the benefit of the collateral and can forestall further depreciation that might come with the debtor's continued use. A notable example of this involved Mel Farr, a former Detroit Lions football player.

---

[36] If the debtor's only default is nonpayment of one or more installments and payment is no more than 15 days late, the secured party must provide the debtor with 10 days' advance notification of the intent to repossess. D.C. Mun. Regs. tit. 16, § 341.3. The secured party must, within one hour after repossession, notify the police department of the repossession. D.C. Mun. Regs. tit. 16, § 340.4. The debtor has 15 days after repossession to redeem the vehicle and the secured party must notify the debtor of that right within five days after repossession. D.C. Mun. Regs. tit. 16, § 341.4, 5. The secured party must provide at least 10 days' notification of a sale of the vehicle and must conduct a public sale if the debtor has paid at least 50% of the cash price. D.C. Mun. Regs. tit. 16, § 344.2, 5, 6. If conducting a private sale, the secured party must credit the debtor with the higher of the actual sale proceeds or the fair market value of the vehicle. D.C. Mun. Regs. tit. 16, § 345.1. A failure to comply with any of these regulations prevents the debtor from being liable for a deficiency and constitutes an unfair trade practice. D.C. Mun. Regs. tit. 16, §§ 340.5, 6, 346.1, 2.

[37] *See* Wis. Stat. § 425.206; Duncan v. Asset Recovery Specialists, Inc., 968 N.W.2d 661 (Wis. 2022) (the garage in the debtor's multi-story apartment building was part of her "dwelling," and thus a repossession from the garage was actionable).

[38] Iowa Code § 654.6.

[39] Mass. Gen. Laws ch. 255 § 13J(a), (b).

Mr. Farr owned several automobile dealerships[40] and specialized in selling and leasing cars to people with no credit history or a bad credit history. To compensate for the high risk of nonpayment, Mr. Farr charged his customers high interest rates and required payment weekly, rather than monthly. Perhaps most important, the cars his companies sold and leased were equipped with an ignition lock, attached to the dashboard. If a customer paid on time, the customer was provided with a code to enter into the device to unlock the ignition. If the customer failed to pay, the code was withheld and the customer would be unable to start the car.[41]

Problem 3-6

A. Does § 9-609 authorize the use of an ignition lock to prevent debtors from starting their cars after failing to make a weekly payment? If not, what does? Does the prohibition on breaching the peace apply to the use of an ignition lock?
B. How might technology be used in the future to aid secured parties in quickly gaining access to or control over their collateral? What policy issues might such uses of technology raise?

When the secured party takes possession of collateral in which it has a security interest, the secured party has an obligation to take reasonable care of the collateral. *See* § 9-207. This is because the repossession in and of itself does not effect a transfer of the debtor's rights in the collateral to the secured party or to anyone else. The secured party must complete either the process described in Article 9 or some

---

40 In fact, by 1998 the Mel Farr Auto Group was the top African American-owned business in the country and the thirty-third-largest auto dealership in the United States, grossing almost $600 million annually. *See* DEREK T. DINGLE, BLACK ENTERPRISE TITANS OF THE B.E. 100S: BLACK CEOS WHO REDEFINED AND CONQUERED AMERICAN BUSINESS (John Wiley & Sons 1999).

41 In June 2000, Mr. Farr settled an action brought by customers who complained that the ignition lock turned off their cars when the cars were in motion. Each of the 1,500 customers received coupons worth $200. By 2002, Mr. Farr had sold all of his new car dealerships.

At least one state prohibits the use of ignition locks and other devices for remotely disabling a vehicle. *See* N.Y. Gen. Bus. Law § 601(10); N.Y. U.C.C. § 9-102(a)(60-a). For additional discussion of ignition locks, see Michael Corkery & Jessica Silver-Greenberg, *Miss a Payment? Good Luck Moving That Car*, DealBook, New York Times (Sept. 24, 2014).

state-law judicial process to foreclose the debtor's interest in the collateral.[42] To put it simply, repossession and foreclosure are not synonyms. Repossession operates, as the word itself implies, merely on possession or control of the collateral; foreclosure operates on the debtor's rights in the collateral.

Redemption. Once the secured party has repossessed the collateral, the debtor has very limited options to get the property back from the secured party without the secured party's consent. Some law outside Article 9 might provide the debtor with a right to cure the default and reinstate the original payment terms (review the material in Section 2(B) of this Chapter), but that right is not likely to be widely available. Article 9 provides only one option for the debtor to regain the property from the secured party. Up until foreclosure, the debtor, a secondary obligor, or a lienholder may redeem the collateral. That is, any one of them may tender to the secured party full payment of the secured obligation plus the secured party's reasonable expenses in enforcing the security interest, and thereby free the collateral of the security interest and compel the secured party to return the property. *See* § 9-623.[43] This right cannot be waived in the security agreement. *See* §§ 9-602(11), 9-603, 9-624. Nevertheless, few debtors avail themselves of the right to redeem. Why do you think that is? In contemplating that question, consider what you learned about acceleration in Section 2(B) of this Chapter.

Foreclosure is the process of terminating the debtor's right of redemption and the debtor's property rights in the collateral. That is, upon foreclosure, the debtor no longer has the right to redeem and no longer has any property rights in the collateral. Foreclosure may be effected in any one of three ways: (i) disposition of collateral; (ii) acceptance of collateral in partial or full satisfaction of the obligation; or (iii) collection on the collateral. The first two can be used for any type of collateral. The last applies only to collateral that is itself a debt or other obligation owed *to* the debtor (*e.g.*, to accounts, chattel paper, deposit accounts, instruments, or payment intangibles). The remainder of this section and all of the next section of this Chapter discuss each of these processes in turn.

---

42 *See* Motors Acceptance Corp. v. Rozier, 597 S.E.2d 367 (Ga. 2004).

43 Automotive Fin. Corp. v. Smart Auto Ctr., Inc., 334 F.3d 685 (7th Cir. 2003).

B. Disposition of Collateral

The most common way for a secured party to access the value of the collateral is to dispose of the collateral: in other words, to sell, lease, or license it. Read § 9-610. A disposition may be effected through a public transaction (*i.e.*, an auction) or through a private transaction (anything other than an auction, such as an advertised sale with a firm price or an individually negotiated sale). In either case, the two main requirements under Article 9 are that the secured party provide advance notification of the disposition and that the disposition be commercially reasonable.[44]

Just as we saw with respect to default, cure, and repossession, non-uniform amendments to Article 9 – or state or federal laws outside Article 9[45] – might impose additional duties or restrictions with respect to how a disposition is to be

---

[44] These requirements of notification and commercial reasonableness apply to dispositions by the secured party. If the debtor conducts the disposition, the secured party might be able to circumvent these duties, at least if the secured party is not controlling the debtor's actions. *Compare* Border State Bank v. AgCountry Farm Credit Servs., 535 F.3d 779 (8th Cir. 2008) (lenders were not required to give junior secured party notification of a sale of the collateral, although held at their insistence, because the debtor itself conducted the sale and remitted the proceeds to the lenders); Bremer Bank v. Matejcek, 916 N.W.2d 688 (Minn. Ct. App. 2018) (a secured party had no duty to notify a joint debtor of the sale of the collateral or to conduct the sale in a commercially reasonable manner because the secured party merely consented to the other debtor's sale, it did not conduct the sale), *with* Regions Bank v. Trailer Source, 2010 WL 2074590 (Tenn. Ct. App. 2010) (senior secured creditor's control over and approval of debtor's sale of collateralized trailers after default was sufficient to trigger the requirement, with respect to junior secured creditor, that the sale be conducted in a commercially reasonable manner). *See also* Stephen L. Sepinuck, *Debtor's Negotiation of Foreclosure Sale Might Ease Secured Creditor's Burden in Complying with Article 9*, 26 CLARKS' SECURED TRANSACTIONS MONTHLY 7 (June 2010).

Similarly, these requirements do not apply if the sale is conducted by the trustee in the debtor's bankruptcy proceeding, even if the secured party receives most of the sale proceeds. In re Reno Snax Sales, LLC, 2013 WL 3942974 (9th Cir. BAP 2013).

[45] Although national banks have argued that the federal law chartering the bank preempts the application to them of state statutes governing enforcement of liens, those arguments have not fared well. Epps v. JP Morgan Chase Bank, 675 F.3d 315 (4th Cir. 2012); Aguayo v. U.S. Bank, 653 F.3d 912 (9th Cir. 2011). On the other hand, cases such as Crespo v. WFS Fin. Inc., 580 F. Supp. 2d 614 (N.D. Ohio 2008), cast doubt on the effectiveness of state laws on enforcement to the extent that a particular federal statute preempts the operation of those state laws. *See* Watters v. Wachovia Bank, 550 U.S. 1 (2007); Cuomo v. The Clearing House Assoc., L.L.C., 557 U.S. 519 (2009).

conducted or how notification of the disposition is to be provided. *See* § 9-611 cmt.10.

For example, Ohio law provides that a secured party whose interest was created through a retail installment sale must use a public sale to dispose of the collateral.[46] North Dakota enacted a non-uniform version of § 9-611(c)(3), expanding the persons entitled to notification when the collateral is consumer goods.[47] In Massachusetts, because a deficiency in a consumer credit transaction is calculated by subtracting the collateral's fair market value – not the disposition proceeds – from the unpaid balance of the secured obligation,[48] a notification of disposition in connection with such a transaction must describe the deficiency as the difference between the amount owed on the loan and the fair market value of the collateral.[49]

Other states have imposed a variety of requirements to protect particular types of debtors or particular types of collateral.[50] And federal law prohibits a disposition

---

[46] *See* Ohio Rev. Code § 1317.16; Daimler/Chrysler Truck Fin. v. Kimball, 2007 WL 4358476 (Ohio Ct. App. 2007).

[47] N.D. Cent. Code. § 41-09-108(3)(c).

[48] *See* Mass. Gen. Laws ch 255, § 20B(e)(1).

[49] *See* Williams v. American Honda Fin. Corp., 98 N.E.3d 169 (Mass.), *disposition following answer to certified questions*, 907 F.3d 83 (2d Cir. 2018). *See also* Randall v. Ally Fin. Inc., 491 F. Supp. 3d 1 (D. Mass. 2020) (ruling that the *Williams* decision applied not merely prospectively, but also to notifications sent before the decision was made).

[50] Georgia requires the seller/secured party in a retail installment contract, within ten days after a repossession, to give the buyer/debtor written notice – sent by registered or certified mail or by statutory overnight delivery – of its intent to seek a deficiency. Failure to do so bars the creditor from obtaining a deficiency judgment. Ga. Code § 10-1-10; Parham v. Peterson, Goldman & Villani, 675 S.E.2d 275 (Ga. Ct. App. 2009).

Nevada imposes additional notification requirements on secured creditors who seek to dispose of a motor vehicle or construction equipment, and failure to comply prevents the creditor from seeking a deficiency. *See* Nev. Rev. Stat. §§ 482.516, 482.5161; In re Dinan, 425 B.R. 583 (Bankr. D. Nev. 2010).

California law also imposes enhanced notification requirements on a secured party planning to dispose of a motor vehicle. *See* Cal. Civil Code § 2983.2. Courts apply these rules rather strictly. *See, e.g.*, Mora v. Harley-Davidson Credit Corp., 2010 WL 4321602 (E.D. Cal. 2010); Juarez v. Arcadia Fin., Ltd., 61 Cal. Rptr. 3d 382 (Cal. Ct. App. 2007).

New York imposes additional and detailed notification requirements for the sale of shares in a residential cooperative apartment. *See* N.Y. U.C.C. § 9-611(f) (McKinney's); Stern-Obstfeld v. Bank of Am., 915 N.Y.S.2d 456 (N.Y. Sup. Ct. 2011). Compliance with these notification rules is apparently a condition to having an effective sale. *See* Newman v.

without a court order if the collateral is owned by a member of the military while the service member is on active duty or within various specified times thereafter.[51] The bottom line is that Article 9 is the place to start – but not the place to end – when searching for the rules that you or your client must follow when enforcing a security interest in personal property.

1. Notification of the Disposition

Article 9's notification rules are contained in §§ 9-611 through 9-614. They detail under what circumstances notification is required, to whom it must be sent, what information it must contain, and, for transactions other than consumer transactions, provide guidance on how long before the disposition to send the notification. These rules cannot be waived in the security agreement. *See* § 9-602(7); *but see* §§ 9-603, 9-624(a).

The purpose of the notification requirement is to give the debtor information that the debtor might use to protect the debtor's interest in the collateral and ensure that

---

Federal Nat'l Mortg. Ass'n, 2014 WL 7334192 (N.Y. Sup. Ct. 2014).

Florida law prescribes the manner in which a security interest in an alcoholic beverage license may be enforced. *See* Fla. Stat. § 561.65(5), (6); VMI Ent., LLC v. Westwood Plaza, LLC, 152 So. 3d 617 (Fla. Ct. App. 2014).

Maryland requires: (i) 10 days' notification to a consumer borrower prior to repossession, (ii) a post-repossession notification to a consumer borrower of the right and amount to redeem, (iii) a pre-sale notification to a consumer borrower of the time and place of the sale; and (iv) following a private sale, an accounting to any borrower that includes, among other things, the purchaser's name and address and the number of bids sought and received. Md. Code, Com. Law § 12-1021(c), (e), (j). *See also* Gardner v. Ally Fin. Inc., 61 A.3d 817 (Md. 2013) (for the purposes of this law, vehicles were sold at a private sale, not a public sale, because, even though the public was invited through weekly advertisements in the *Baltimore Sun*, non-dealers had to provide a refundable $1,000 deposit to attend, which obscured the transparency that is the hallmark of an open, public sale); Smith v. Toyota Motor Credit Corp., 2013 WL 1325460 (D. Md. 2013) (this law requires a secured party to give advance notification of the time and place of a sale, regardless of whether the sale is conducted as a private or public sale).

[51] 50 U.S.C. § 3953(c). *See also* United States v. B.C. Enters., Inc., 667 F. Supp. 2d 650 (E.D. Va. 2009) (creditor is strictly liable for damages resulting from unauthorized sale regardless of whether the creditor knew of the debtor's military status). The act does not apply, however, if the collateral is owned indirectly by the service member, such as by a corporation owned and controlled by the service member. Newton v. Bank of McKenney, 2012 WL 1752407 (E.D. Va. 2012).

the collateral is not disposed of for significantly less than its fair market value. In particular, the debtor might use the information in the notification to:

(1) Exercise the right of redemption;
(2) Bid at the sale, if the disposition is by public sale;
(3) Challenge any aspect of the disposition before it is made; and
(4) Locate potential purchasers.

Whether the notification is really useful in these respects is questionable.

For example, the notification is unlikely to provide much information that assists the debtor in redeeming the collateral. The notification need not specify the amount the debtor must pay to redeem and, because that amount is likely to change on a daily basis (as interest accrues on the secured obligation), it is unlikely that the amount required to redeem will be included in the notification. The notification is also unlikely to indicate the real deadline for redeeming the collateral. That is because the notification need state only the date after which a private sale might be held, or the time and date of a planned public sale – not the date the sale will actually be conducted – but redemption rights do not end until the disposition occurs or a contract for a disposition is made. *Compare* § 9-613(1)(E) *with* § 9-623(c).

Similarly, even though courts often say that notification gives the debtor an opportunity to monitor the disposition to ensure it is commercially reasonable,[52] the notification is unlikely to identify the buyer, indicate the sale price, or specify what efforts the secured party made to find a buyer. Thus, the notification is unlikely to contain information that would provide the debtor with a basis for obtaining a preliminary injunction against the sale.

What is clear, however, is that the purpose of the notification requirement is *not* to advertise the sale. While the amount and nature of advertising for a sale might be important, these factors relate to the commercial reasonableness of the disposition, which is a requirement separate and distinct from the duty to send notification of the disposition.

Read the notification rules and then answer the problems that follow.

e-Exercise 3-A
The Parties' Roles

---

[52] *See, e.g.*, Meuelo v. East West Bank, 2019 WL 1567561, at *5 (Cal. Ct. App. 2020).

Problem 3-7

Two years ago, Mr. & Mrs. Derailleur borrowed $40,000 from First Bank to open a bicycle repair shop. They gave First Bank a security interest in the equipment of the shop. They also got Mrs. Derailleur's father, Mr. Grant, to guarantee the loan, and Mr. Derailleur's grandmother, Ms. Olsen, to pledge $20,000 of her Microsoft stock to secure the loan. The stock certificate was reissued in First Bank's name so that it could easily be sold in the event of default.

The business never prospered and its financial difficulties contributed to a growing rift between the Derailleurs. In October, the Derailleurs – who are now in the midst of a divorce and are living apart – defaulted on the loan from First Bank. On November 1, First Bank peaceably repossessed the equipment. On November 5, Part Supply, Inc. sent a letter to First Bank requesting notification of any disposition of the equipment. The Derailleurs owe Part Supply several thousand dollars for spare parts it sold to them on credit.

A. If First Bank wishes to sell the stock on the open market (the NASDAQ stock exchange) and the equipment through an auction at its offices, to whom must it send notification of each proposed sale? *See iFlex Inc. v. Electroply, Inc.*, 2004 WL 502179 (D. Minn. 2004).

B. On November 12, First Bank sent a letter to the Derailleurs' home notifying them that the stock would be sold on the open market sometime after November 28th and that the equipment would be sold at a public auction at 3:00pm on December 1st at First Bank's offices. The content of the letter complied with § 9-613. Mrs. Derailleur, who was no longer residing at the house, never saw the letter. Also on November 12, First Bank called Mr. Grant and verbally related to him all the information in the letter. Has Bank complied with the rules of Article 9 regarding the method and content of the notification of disposition?

Problem 3-8

First Bank, which has a security interest in Driver's car to secure Driver's obligation to pay a loan for the purchase price, peaceably repossessed Driver's car after Driver failed to make two consecutive monthly payments. The next day, First Bank mailed to Driver the following letter:

> First Bank
> 123 1st Avenue
> Spokane, WA 99201
>
> June 1, 2023
>
> Driver:
>
> Due to your default, we recently repossessed your Mazda Miata automobile and intend to sell said property at a private sale sometime after June 15, 2023.
>
> We will use the sale proceeds to first pay our costs associated with the sale and then reduce the amount you owe. If we receive less money than you owe, you will owe us difference. If we receive more money than you owe, we will refund the difference to you (unless instructed to pay it to someone else).
>
> You may get your automobile back by paying us the full amount you owe (not just the past due payments) before June 15, 2023. To learn the exact amount you must pay, or if you desire additional information about the sale, call us at (509) 456-7890.

Fifteen days after sending the letter, First Bank sold the car at a dealers-only auction.

A. Did the letter comply with the notification requirements of Article 9? *Compare* § 9-613(1), (2) *with* § 9-614(1). What is the effect of the difference in wording between § 9-613(1) and § 9-614(1)? *See In re Downing*, 286 B.R. 900 (Bankr. W.D. Mo. 2002). *See also* § 9-612.

B. What if First Bank had sent the letter by certified mail, return receipt requested, and seven days later the letter was returned "Moved – Left No Forwarding Address"? *See Jones v. Flowers*, 547 U.S. 220 (2006).

C. What, if anything, should the secured party include in the security agreement to deal with the possibility that the debtor might not receive a notification of disposition? *See* §§ 9-602, 9-603, 9-624. Draft appropriate language.

e-Exercise 3-B
Notification of Disposition

2. Commercial Reasonableness

Every aspect of a disposition by a secured party must be commercially reasonable. § 9-610(b). *See also* § 9-627. This is a factual question and no list of the relevant factors could possibly be exhaustive. The comments and cases tell us, however, that any or all of the following might be important:

- Whether the disposition should have been conducted by public or private sale;[53]
- The time and place of the disposition, *see* § 9-610(b), and in particular the delay, if any, before the disposition, *see* § 9-610 cmt. 3;
- Whether the collateral should have been disposed of in bulk or in separate parcels, *see* § 9-610 cmt. 3;
- Whether and how the collateral should have been prepared prior to disposition (such as by cleaning or repairing it), *see* § 9-610 cmt. 4;
- The method and amount of advertising or other efforts to locate potential buyers; and
- The terms of the disposition (such as the warranties made by the secured party), *see* § 9-610(b).

Because the price received for the collateral will be used to determine the amount of any surplus to which the debtor is entitled or, more likely, the amount of the deficiency for which the obligor is liable, the price is one of the most critical terms. Nevertheless, a low price alone is not sufficient to conclude that the disposition was commercially unreasonable, although it is grounds for closely scrutinizing the other aspects of the transaction. *See* § 9-627(a) & cmt. 2. *See also* § 9-610 cmt. 10. Indeed, when the price is low, courts often have no trouble finding some basis for concluding that the secured party acted unreasonably.[54] Moreover, because the secured party has the burden of proof on commercial reasonableness, it can be difficult for the secured party to obtain summary judgment once the debtor or a secondary obligor raises the issue.

---

[53] *See* Automotive Fin. Corp. v. Smart Auto Ctr., Inc., 334 F.3d 685 (7th Cir. 2003) (sale of cars at a dealer-only auto auction is a commercially reasonable disposition).

[54] Will v. Mill Condominium Owners' Ass'n, 848 A.2d 336 (Vt. 2004) (holding that a condo association's foreclosure sale of the debtor's condominium interest, though public, was not commercially reasonable because: (1) only one person bid; (2) the lone bidder purchased the debtor's interest for precisely the amount of the debtor's delinquent dues, attorneys' fees, and costs of foreclosure; (3) the seller told the lone bidder the minimum acceptable bid, and the bidder bid precisely that amount; and (4) the sales price was less than 5% of the fair market value of the condominium and, indeed, less than 5% of the debtor's equity in it had it been subject to the mortgage that the seller and bidder erroneously believed it to be).

For example, in *VFS Leasing v. Bric Constructors, LLC*,[55] the secured party, VFS, brought action against debtors and guarantors to recover the deficiency remaining after a sale of collateral. The secured party presented by affidavit the following description of the process it used to sell the collateral:

> Before the sale date, VFS sends e-mails advertising the sale of the equipment to all Volvo Rents (VRI) and Volvo Construction Equipment Services (VCES). The equipment is then placed for sale through VFS's exclusive Preferred Offering website accessed through IronPlanet.com ("the Preferred Offering site"). The remarketing department establishes three prices based on its assessment of current market conditions: a starting price, a reserve price, and a "win it now" price. The starting price is the lowest price at which dealers can bid and is designed to entice bidding. The reserve price is the lowest price that VFS will accept and it is hidden from all dealers. The "win it now" price is the price at which dealers may purchase the equipment immediately without waiting for the auction results. If, at the auction's conclusion, the high bid equals or exceeds the reserve price, the equipment is sold. If the reserve price has not been met at the auction's conclusion but a dealer has placed a bid, the equipment may be sold to that dealer. In exchange for maintaining the Preferred Offering site, Iron Planet charges a service fee in the amount of 3% of the equipment's final selling price.
>
> If the equipment is not sold via the Preferred Offering site, it is offered for sale through Iron Planet's public auction site accessed via IronPlanet.com ("the auction site"). Iron Planet has approximately 450,000 registered users in connection with its auctions and has conducted internet auctions for more than ten years. Iron Planet advertises its auctions on its website, as well as in trade journals and publications. Potential buyers can view equipment offered for sale through the auction site via an internet preview offered before the auction's start. An auction for each item of equipment begins at a predetermined advertised start time. Iron Planet sets a starting price to entice bidding, and the equipment is sold for the highest bid above this starting price. Each item is allotted six minutes, and any successful bid placed in the last three minutes of an auction will extend the auction by three minutes. In exchange for maintaining the auction site, Iron Planet charges a service fee in the amount of 7% of the equipment's final selling price.

---

[55] 2012 WL 2499518 (Tenn. Ct. App. 2012).

> Here, each leased hauler was repossessed on September 10, 2008, inspected on September 18, 2008, and determined to have a certain number of hours of use. Beginning on October 10, 2008, each repossessed hauler was offered for a certain price on the Volvo Preferred Offering site, but no offers were received. On October 22, 2008, each hauler was assigned a minimum bid and was listed on Iron Planet's auction site. On October 30, 2008, each hauler was advertised for sale and auctioned on Iron Planet's worldwide internet sale via the auction site. The auction results for the four haulers were as follows: 1 bid, sale price of $194,000; 39 bids, sale price of $192,000; 33 bids, sale price of $170,000; and 18 bids, sale price of $142,000. The October 30, 2008 Iron Planet auction site sale during which the four haulers were sold involved the sale of 10.98 million dollars of equipment. At the time of the sale, Iron Planet had 415,000 registered users who had access to the sale. The sale had over 1,000 different bidders, and 52% of the items received international bids. The auction had 12,588 viewers/prospective buyers.

In response, the guarantor submitted her own affidavit, which included the following:

> 1. I am the principal member of Bric Constructors LLC and a Defendant in this case. I am familiar with industry standards for the sale of construction equipment. * * *
>
> 4. This equipment was not auctioned in a commercially reasonable manner.
>
> 5. On [one specified item], there was only one bidder. This is because there was a button on the web-site that said buy it now. Pressing this button allowed a bidder to by-pass the auction and simply purchase the equipment for $194,000. The purchaser of the equipment then listed it for $279,500 on EquipmentTrader.com. * * *
>
> 6. [Another specified item] was sold for $192,000. The tailgate was not installed, in the picture, even though it was available. It was resold for $239,000 on MachineTrader.com. * * *
>
> 7. [A third item] sold on IronPlanet.com for $170,000. It was resold on Rock & Dirt.com for $249,000. * * *
>
> 9. All of this equipment sold on 10/30/08. Industry standards require that the purchaser inspect the equipment. No prospective purchaser was

permitted to view any of the equipment in person, or test the equipment in any way. The auction wrote a paragraph about the equipment, however, the narratives were not complete because the equipment was located in a yard that was not large enough to test the equipment.

10. The photos of all the equipment are of the equipment with dirt in the bed of the trucks. It is important to remove everything from the bed of a dump truck, prior to a sale, so that the prospective purchaser can inspect the bed for rust. The trucks were not cleaned. They were sold in the same condition as they were removed from our job site. Dirt was caked on many places on the trucks.

11. The industry standard for sale of dump trucks requires that the dirt be removed from the truck bed, and that the truck be cleaned. Sometimes, the trucks should be painted, and minor repairs effected. These trucks did not require any repairs, because we kept our equipment in excellent condition, and had major repairs done through Volvo. If these trucks had been cleaned, and the service records produced, they would have sold for a higher price.

The appellate court, in a single paragraph, concluded that the conflicting affidavits presented genuine issues of material fact as to whether VFS disposed of the collateral in a commercially reasonable manner. It therefore reversed the trial court's summary judgment in favor of VFS.

Given that many debtors and secondary obligors pursued for a deficiency will claim that a disposition was commercially unreasonable, and given that commercial reasonableness is such a fact-driven issue that it is difficult for the secured party to be certain that its conduct will later be deemed to have been appropriate, what may the secured party do to lessen its exposure on this issue? *See* §§ 1-103, 1-302, 9-602, 9-603, 9-624.

Problem 3-9

A. Seed Company has a security interest in DeWitt's wheat crop to secure payment of the price of the seed that Seed Company sold to DeWitt. Shortly after harvest, Seed Company peaceably repossessed DeWitt's wheat crop, took it to the local grain elevator, and sold it at the current market price. DeWitt argues that Seed Company did not act in a commercially reasonable manner because the market price at harvest time is always lower than at other times. DeWitt argues that Seed Company should have waited for the market to rise in order for Seed Company to have acted in a commercially reasonable manner. Is DeWitt correct? §§ 9-610, 9-627.

B. First Bank has retained you to write a standard form security agreement for its use in documenting commercial loans. What do you want in the security agreement to address the issues raised by the commercial reasonableness standard in § 9-610? *See* §§ 1-103, 1-302, 9-602, 9-603, 9-624. For what kinds of collateral is it most important that the security agreement provide for disposition in a specified manner?

3. Other Restrictions on Conducting a Disposition

In some cases, other law might come into play and restrict the secured party from conducting a disposition. For example, if the debtor manufactures goods without complying with the Fair Labor Standards Act,[56] sale of the goods can be enjoined.[57] Similarly the secured party might have a problem if the goods violate the patent or trademark rights of a third party[58] or the packaging violates the copyright or trademark rights of a third party.

4. Distribution of Proceeds and Other Effects of a Disposition

Article 9 provides precise rules on how cash proceeds of a disposition are to be disbursed. The proceeds go first to cover the costs of repossessing the collateral and the expenses incurred in preparing for and conducting the disposition. *See*

---

[56] *See* 29 U.S.C. § 215.

[57] *See* Henry Bregstein, Note, *Secured Creditors and Section 15(a)(1) of the Fair Labor Standards Act: The Supreme Court Created a New Property Interest*, 14 CARDOZO L. REV. 1965 (1993); Karen L. Able, Note, *Hot Goods" Liability: Secured Creditors and the Fair Labor Standards Act*, 87 COLUM. L. REV. 644 (1987).

[58] If the debtor has *bought* goods from the patent owner (or from a licensee of the patent owner), that sale will exhaust the patent rights in the goods. *See* Impression Products, Inc. v. Lexmark Int'l, Inc., 581 U.S. 360 (2017). Accordingly, even if the debtor acquired the goods subject to a contractual restriction on use or resale, the patentee would not have an infringement claim against the secured party based on the secured party's disposition of the goods. However, if the debtor *manufactured* goods pursuant to a license from the patentee, the patentee might still have patent rights in the goods and might, therefore, have an infringement claim against a secured party that disposes of the goods in a manner that violates the license.

§ 9-615(a)(1). Then they are used to pay off the obligation owed to the foreclosing secured party. *See* § 9-615(a)(2). If there are proceeds left over, they are distributed to junior lienors and consignors who demand a share. *See* § 9-615(a)(3), (4). Finally, if proceeds remain after all this, the debtor is normally entitled to them as a surplus. *See* § 9-615(d).

Article 9 also has rules on how to deal with *noncash* proceeds. *See* §§ 9-102(a)(9), (58), 9-615(c) & cmt. 3. These rules apply if, for example, the disposition buyer paid in kind or purchased on credit (*i.e.*, on open account or with a promissory note). For the most part, the rules allow the secured party to choose between: (i) presently crediting the secured obligation with the value of whatever the buyer provided; or (ii) treating whatever the buyer provided as replacement collateral and waiting to credit the secured obligation until such noncash proceeds are converted into cash proceeds.

To the extent that proceeds of a disposition – whether cash or noncash – are credited to the secured obligation, that obligation is reduced. If the proceeds so credited are insufficient to fully satisfy the secured obligations – so that a deficiency remains – the obligor normally remains liable for that deficiency. *See* § 9-615(d). In a consumer-goods transaction, the secured party has an obligation to explain how the surplus or deficiency was calculated. *See* § 9-616.

The rules relating to surpluses and deficiencies are different if the secured transaction was a sale of accounts, chattel paper, payment intangibles, or promissory notes. In such a transaction, there really is no secured obligation (*i.e.*, the collateral does not secure a debt) and the debtor retains no residual interest in the collateral (*i.e.*, the property sold). Accordingly, in such a case, the debtor is not entitled to any surplus and the obligor has no liability for any deficiency. § 9-615(e).

Beyond its indirect effect on the secured obligation, the principal consequences of a disposition are that it: (i) transfers to the foreclosure sale buyer or other transferee all of the debtor's rights in the collateral; and (ii) discharges the security interest of the foreclosing secured party – and all junior liens – in the collateral disposed of. § 9-617(a). This is true regardless of whether the disposition yields a surplus or deficiency. It is also true even if the disposition failed to comply with Article 9's requirements, say perhaps because it was commercially unreasonable or the secured party failed to send reasonable notification, provided the transferee acted in good faith. § 9-617(b).

A secured party may purchase the collateral at the disposition if the disposition is by public sale (*i.e.*, auction) or if the collateral is of a type customarily sold on a recognized market or the subject of widely distributed standard price quotations. § 9-610(c). In those circumstances, the secured party may also use what is commonly referred to as a "credit bid." Instead of paying the purchase price with actual cash, only to then disburse the sale proceeds to itself as the foreclosing creditor, the secured party is essentially permitted to set off the secured obligation against the purchase price. In this way, the secured party will not have to pay anything to buy the collateral unless it is willing to pay more than the secured obligation (and the costs of the sale). In fact, the secured party will rarely pay more than the amount the debtor owes and, in the context of a public sale, will typically bid as little as it can get away with. As long as it is the highest bidder, it can capture the full value of the property (by later reselling later it at a higher price, presumably something closer to its true fair market value) while maximizing the deficiency for which the debtor remains liable.

To illustrate how this works, consider the following example:

> Secured Party has a security interest in an item of collateral worth \$20,000. The secured obligation is \$25,000. At this point it appears that the debtor will be on the hook for about a \$5,000 deficiency, but let's see what happens. After the debtor defaults, Secured Party repossesses the collateral and prepares to conduct a disposition by public sale. Despite a reasonable amount of advertising, few bidders come to the sale and Secured Party is the high bidder for \$12,000. The costs of sale are \$1,000. Because Secured Party is permitted to credit bid, it does not actually pay any money. Instead, its bid amount is credited first to the costs of the sale, with the remainder (\$11,000) credited against the secured obligation (\$25,000). That leaves the debtor liable for a \$14,000 deficiency (\$25,000-\$11,000). If the secured party later resells the collateral for \$18,000, the secured party is permitted to retain the resulting profit while still pursuing the debtor for the full \$14,000 deficiency.

If all this seems rather unfair to the debtor, and potentially lucrative for Secured Party, remember that the mere fact that the debtor is liable for the deficiency does not mean that Secured Party will actually collect any of it. Moreover, Article 9 provides some protection against low price dispositions in which the secured party or persons related to the secured party are transferees of the collateral at the disposition. *See* § 9-615(f).[59]

---

[59] State consumer-protection laws may, on occasion, bar an action for a deficiency. *See,*

e-Exercise 3-C
The Effect of Disposition

Problem 3-10

Diamond Jim ("DJ") is the proud owner of the Faith Diamond, the less valuable but equally cursed sister of the Hope Diamond. Since acquiring the diamond several years ago for $60,000, DJ has suffered several financial setbacks. After each, DJ used the diamond as collateral for a loan. The first of these was to First Bank, the second was to Second Bank, and the last was to Third Bank. Assume the priority of the lenders' security interests in the Faith Diamond is in the order of the security interests' creation.

Several weeks ago DJ defaulted on the loan from Second Bank and Second Bank peaceably repossessed the diamond. Second Bank gave proper notification of its intent to sell the diamond by public sale and has advertised the sale extensively. Bidding is expected to be competitive, with the result that the high bidder will probably have to pay fair value for whatever rights to the diamond that the high bidder will receive. Assume that if the diamond were unencumbered it would still be worth $60,000. Assume further that DJ owes $25,000 to First Bank, $10,000 to Second Bank, and $15,000 to Third Bank. Answer the following questions:

---

e.g., U.C.C.C. § 5.103 (prohibiting an action for a deficiency in certain low-price transactions). Alternatively, they might require that a deficiency be calculated based on some specified procedure for calculating the value of the collateral, rather than on the price obtained at the disposition. *See, e.g.*, Conn. Gen. Stat. § 36a-785(g) (applicable to low-priced motor vehicles and low-priced vessels); Mass. Gen. Laws ch. 255, § 20B(d), (e) (barring a deficiency in a consumer credit transaction involving a motor vehicle if the debt was $2,000 or less at the time of default and the secured party had a non-possessory security interest in the vehicle; if the debt exceeds that amount, providing that a deficiency is to be computed using the fair market value of the vehicle, not the sale price); *cf.* Williams v. American Honda Fin. Corp., 98 N.E.3d 169 (Mass. 2018) (a secured party complied with Massachusetts law – which requires that a deficiency on a car loan be calculated based on the car's fair market value rather than the foreclosure sale price – by using the price received at a dealer's only auction, rather than retail value).

A. Assume the high bidder is not one of the Banks and pays $30,000. The costs of the sale are $3,000.
   1. How should the proceeds of the disposition be disbursed? *See* § 9-615(a).
   2. What happens to each of the three security interests and why? *See* § 9-617(a).
   3. What liability, if any, does DJ still have to each Bank? In answering this, do not confuse the *in rem* liability of the collateral with the *in personam* liability of the obligor.

B. Assume the high bidder (again, not one of the Banks) pays only $11,000 and the costs of the sale are $3,000.
   1. How should the proceeds of the disposition be disbursed?
   2. What happens to each of the three security interests?
   3. What liability, if any, does DJ still have to each Bank?

C. Given the analysis and answers to Parts A and B, up to what amount should a bidder be willing to spend? What should the bidder think about in making this determination?

D. What difference, if any, would it make to the analysis of Part A(1) if DJ has not defaulted on the obligations to First Bank or Third Bank? *See* *Compass Bank v. Kone*, 134 P.3d 500 (Colo. Ct. App. 2006).

E. What difference, if any, would it make to the analysis of Parts A and B if Second Bank were the purchaser of the diamond at the foreclosure sale? *See* § 9-615(f).

Let us pause for a moment to consider further the rule of § 9-615(a)(3)(A), which allows a junior secured party to share in excess proceeds of a disposition if the senior secured party receives a demand therefor from the junior secured party. While this rule might make sense in isolation, it is probably useful to consider it as part of a sequence of actions and notifications between secured parties. Typically, the sequence looks something like this:

SP-1 perfects	SP-2 perfects (or notifies SP-1 of its security interest)	SP-1 sends SP-2 notification of a disposition	SP-2 sends SP-1 a demand to share in excess proceeds

SP-1's act to perfect its security interest – typically by filing a financing statement – generally provides public notice of SP-1's security interest in the collateral.[60] That enables SP-2, when it later acquires its security interest, if it wishes, to notify SP-1 of its security interest. Regardless of whether SP-2 does that, if SP-1 later plans to dispose of the collateral, SP-1 will usually be required to notify SP-2 of the disposition, under either § 9-611(c)(3)(A) or (B). Upon receipt of that notification, SP-2 will then have the information it needs to send a demand to share in excess sale proceeds under § 9-615(a)(3)(A).

Of course, a number of things might interfere with this sequence. For example, if the collateral were consumer goods, SP-1 would have no duty to notify SP-2 of the disposition. *See* § 9-611(c)(3). Now consider the following problem.

Problem 3-11

Several years ago, Director borrowed $3.2 million from First Bank and in return granted First Bank a security interest in all Director's investment property, which consisted of publically traded securities, to secure the loan. First Bank promptly perfected its security interest. Subsequently, Director approached Second Bank for a loan, offering to grant a security interest in some publically traded securities. Because the securities are customarily traded on a recognized market, First Bank will have no duty under Article 9 to notify either Director or Second Bank of any disposition of the securities. Because Second Bank would typically respond to such a notification by demanding a share of any excess proceeds of the disposition, how can Second Bank ensure that First Bank does not remit excess proceeds to Director?

A secured party conducting a disposition of the collateral makes to the transferee a warranty of title, possession, and quiet enjoyment with respect to the collateral if such a warranty would arise in a voluntary disposition of that type of property.[61] The secured party may disclaim that warranty but must do so expressly. § 9-610(d)–(f).

---

[60] As we will see in Chapter Four, there might be several reasons why perfection does not provide much notice of SP-1's security interest.

[61] For an example of such a warranty that arises in a sale of goods, *see* § 2-312.

Occasionally, particularly when the collateral consists of property covered by a certificate of title or is governed by a recording system of registered ownership (*e.g.*, motor vehicles, aircraft, copyrights), the transferee at a disposition needs a title-clearing document in order to record title in the transferee's name. This can be a problem if the secured party is not the record owner and the law governing such property requires the record owner's authorization or signature to transfer title. Article 9 addresses this problem by expressly authorizing the secured party to issue a transfer statement, which entitles the transferee to have the title certificate or ownership registry reflect the transferee's ownership. *See* § 9-619.

5. Rights of Secondary Obligors

Many loan transactions are supported by a guaranty. Such a guaranty can be created by co-signing a promissory note or by executing a separate document denominated as a guaranty agreement. In the terminology of Article 9, guarantors are "secondary obligors." *See* § 9-102(a)(59), (72). A secondary obligor is a surety for the debt and has various rights at common law against the principal obligor.[62]

One of those rights is "reimbursement" from the primary obligor of any amounts that the secondary obligor pays to the creditor on the debt for which the primary obligor is liable. Alternatively, a secondary obligor might have only a partial right to collect from the primary obligor, in which case, the right to collect is called a right to "contribution." The difference between reimbursement and contribution can be illustrated as follows. Assume A and B both sign a promissory note for $10,000 payable to a creditor. A and B agree between themselves that A is to be the primary obligor and B is the secondary obligor (perhaps because A receives all of the loan proceeds). At some later point, B pays the creditor $10,000 to satisfy the debt. B has a right as against A to be reimbursed for the entire amount, $10,000. Now assume that the deal between A and B was that each would be responsible for half of the debt (perhaps because they shared equally the loan proceeds), even though the creditor remained free to collect the entire $10,000 from either one. B later pays the creditor $10,000. B has a right to contribution of $5,000 from A because B has paid more than B's share of the debt.

---

[62] The law of suretyship is an essential part of financing transactions. More detail concerning the general principles of suretyship can be found in the RESTATEMENT (THIRD) OF SURETYSHIP AND GUARANTY (1996).

Another right of a secondary obligor is the right of "subrogation." To be subrogated is to step into the shoes of another and to assert whatever rights that other party would have. This is most relevant when the principal obligation is secured because it gives the secondary obligor the benefit of the collateral. Continuing the example above, assume that in the loan transaction, A granted the creditor a security interest in A's equipment to secure the $10,000 debt. A and B have agreed that A is primarily liable for the entire debt. A defaulted and B paid the creditor $10,000. B would now be subrogated to the creditor's right to enforce its security interest against A's equipment.

A third right of a secondary obligor is the right of "exoneration," which allows the secondary obligor to ask a court to compel the primary obligor to perform its obligation to the creditor. Continuing with the example above, if A refuses to pay the creditor, B may seek a judicial order compelling A to pay the creditor.

With that background, now consider how Article 9 deals with the rights of a secondary obligor as against a secured party disposing of the debtor's collateral. For the most part, a secondary obligor has the same rights that the debtor has, other than the right to any surplus resulting from a disposition. No obligor, primary or secondary, may waive the rights listed in § 9-602 prior to default.[63] *Cf.* § 9-603 (allowing agreements to set the standards by which some of the secured party's duties will be measured); § 9-624 (allowing certain rights to be waived after default). A secondary obligor is entitled to the same notification of an intended disposition that the debtor is. § 9-611(c). *But see* §§ 9-605, 9-628 (relieving the secured party of this duty if the secured party does not know who the secondary obligor is or how to contact the secondary obligor). Similarly, a consumer obligor, whether primary or secondary, is entitled to an explanation of how the creditor calculated the surplus or deficiency if the transaction was a consumer-goods transaction. *See* § 9-616. Finally, a secondary obligor has the same redemption rights that a debtor has. § 9-623.

In at least one way, however, Article 9 treats a secondary obligor substantially different from the debtor. This occurs whenever a secondary obligor acquires the collateral. If a secondary obligor buys the collateral at a disposition, the provisions of § 9-615(f) control how the surplus or deficiency is calculated. Alternatively, if a secondary obligor takes over the collateral from the secured party, that "take over" might not be a disposition of the collateral and the secondary obligor will then have

---

[63] At least one state has modified this rule to allow secondary obligors to waive the rights listed in § 9-602. *See* Wash. Rev. Code § 62A.9A-602.

the rights and obligations of a secured party in disposing of the collateral. *See* § 9-618. Distinguishing between situations when a secondary obligor acquires the collateral pursuant to a § 9-610 disposition and when a secondary obligor "takes over" the collateral under § 9-618 can be very difficult.

Problem 3-12

First Bank calls you for advice regarding its recent repossession, from a debtor that has now gone out of business, of several items of equipment. The equipment, which secures a $1.2 million debt to First Bank, is in serious disrepair and in its current state will not sell for nearly enough to pay that debt. At best, the equipment will bring only about $280,000. The cost of repairing the equipment is about $300,000 but there is no assurance that, once repaired, the equipment will sell for enough to justify the repair effort. The loan is guaranteed and First Bank wants to avoid doing anything that might impair the liability of the guarantor for any deficiency. How should First Bank proceed? Devise at least two ways for First Bank to protect its interests without the guarantor's cooperation. § 9-601.

C. Acceptance of the Collateral in Full or Partial Satisfaction of the Debt

When seeking to enforce a security interest, most secured parties are not interested in acquiring the collateral. Instead, they merely want whatever value they can extract from it. In some situations, however, the secured party might be the one most interested in acquiring the collateral or even the only person interested in acquiring it. This can occur when the collateral is a family heirloom and the secured party is another member of the family. It can also occur when the collateral is an interest in a closely-held business and the secured party is the holder of the only other interest in that business.

One way Article 9 accommodates such situations is by allowing the secured party to acquire the collateral at a disposition. However, the secured party is permitted to do this only if the disposition is by public sale or the collateral is either customarily sold on a recognized market or otherwise subject to widely distributed standard price quotations. § 9-610(c).[64] Efforts to circumvent these rules – such as

---

[64] Although § 9-610(c) authorizes a secured party to buy at a private sale in only very limited circumstances, the subsection is not among the provisions identified in § 9-602 as one that the parties cannot waive or vary. Nevertheless, the security agreement cannot vary the

by creating a new entity and selling the collateral at a private sale to that new entity – are unlikely to work.[65]

Another method for allowing the secured party to acquire the collateral – a method which constitutes an enforcement mechanism entirely different from disposition – is to simply accept the collateral in partial or full satisfaction of the secured obligation. Read § 9-620. In order to use this method, often referred to as "strict foreclosure," the secured party must send a proposal to the debtor and the debtor must consent to it. § 9-620(a)(1). If the proposal is to accept the collateral in full satisfaction of the debt, that consent may be manifested simply by the debtor's failure to object in a timely manner. § 9-620(c)(2). If the proposal is to accept the collateral in partial satisfaction of the debt, the debtor's consent must be manifested in a signed record. *See* § 9-620(c)(1). Any attempt to have the debtor consent to acceptance in advance of default, such as in the security agreement, is ineffective. *See* §§ 9-602(10), 9-620(c)(1).

In a consumer transaction, the secured party is prohibited from accepting the collateral in partial satisfaction of the debt; only full strict foreclosure is permitted. §§ 9-620(g), 9-624(b). In addition, if the collateral is consumer goods and the debtor has paid 60% of the purchase price (in the case of a purchase-money security interest) or 60% of the secured loan (for nonpurchase-money security interests), the secured party is prohibited from conducting a strict foreclosure. In such situations, the secured party must conduct a disposition pursuant to § 9-610. § 9-620(e), (f). The reason for this is that, when the debtor has paid that much, there is a reasonable likelihood that the debtor has built up equity in the collateral and a consumer debtor

---

rule – that is, the agreement cannot authorize a secured party to buy at any private sale – because a purchase by the secured party at a private sale is essentially a strict foreclosure governed by §§ 9-620, 9-621, and 9-622, and such rules cannot be modified prior to default. *See* §§ 9-602(10) & cmt. 3, 9-624(b). *Cf.* Bruce v. Cauthen, 515 S.W.3d 495 (Tex. Ct. App. 2017) (secured party violated § 9-610(c) by purchasing the collateral at a private sale; although the security agreement expressly acknowledged that a public sale might be impossible due to securities laws, and that a private sale would be commercially reasonable even if it produced less than what a public sale would, it did not expressly modify the prohibition in § 9-610(c)).

[65] *See* Edgewater Growth Cap. Partners LP v. H.I.G. Cap., Inc., 68 A.3d 197, 211 n.70 (Del. Ch. 2013). *Cf.* Marine Elec. Sys., Inc. v. MES Fin., LLC, 2022 WL 17450059, at *7 (D.N.J. 2022) (because a portion of secured obligation would, after the disposition, transfer from the secured party conducting disposition to the original lender, a proposed private sale of the collateral to the original lender would violate § 9-610(c)).

might not fully appreciate the significance of failing to object to the creditor's proposal.

Under Article 9 prior to the 1999 revision, secured parties who waited for months or years after repossessing the collateral before conducting a disposition were occasionally deemed to have accepted the collateral in satisfaction of the debt. As a result, they were barred from collecting any deficiency based on the price received at the eventual sale. Revised Article 9 rejects the notion of such a "constructive strict foreclosure" by requiring the secured party's consent in a signed record to any acceptance of the collateral. § 9-620(b) & cmt. 5.

Just as the secured party must normally notify secondary obligors and other lienors of an intended disposition, the secured party must also normally send them a proposal to accept the collateral. § 9-621. If any of the persons to whom the proposal must be sent objects in a timely manner, the acceptance does not become effective. § 9-620(a), (d). In that situation, the secured party is then relegated to its other remedies after default, such a conducting a disposition pursuant to the process described in § 9-610. However, because an acceptance in full satisfaction of the debt would necessarily discharge any secondary obligor's liability, a proposal to retain the collateral in full satisfaction of the secured obligation need not be sent to secondary obligors. *See* § 9-621(b).

If a secured party accepts collateral in full or partial satisfaction of the obligation secured, § 9-622 specifies the effect of that acceptance. As with a disposition, acceptance transfers to the secured party all of the debtor's rights in the collateral and discharges subordinate interests. Acceptance does not affect interests superior in priority to the security interest being foreclosed.

Problem 3-13

State Bank has a security interest in three diamond bracelets owned by Olivia, a consumer, to secure a loan to her brother Bill to finance his go-cart business. Bill has defaulted on the loan and State Bank has taken possession of the bracelets. The original loan amount was $75,000 and the current balance is $50,000. Credit Union also has a security interest in the bracelets to secure a loan to Olivia. That loan has a current balance of $10,000 and Credit Union has a proper financing statement on file.

A. The value of the three bracelets is estimated at $200,000 and State Bank is considering proposing to accept the bracelets in full satisfaction of the secured obligation.

1. Is this allowed? *Compare* § 9-620(a) *with* § 9-610(b). *See also* § 9-620 cmt. 11. *Cf. Eddy v. Glen Devore Personal Trust*, 131 Wash. App. 1015 (2006). Is it a good idea from the perspective of State Bank?
2. To whom must State Bank send its proposal? *See* § 9-621. Is this different from the persons to whom State Bank would have to send notification of a disposition under § 9-610? When should State Bank send its proposal to retain the collateral in satisfaction of the debt? What should the proposal state?
3. Who should object to the proposal?
4. Assume State Bank sent the proposal to all the parties specified in § 9-620 and § 9-621, all of those parties received it, and no one objected. Approximately three months later, State Bank sold the three bracelets to a jeweler for $220,000. Olivia consulted you when she found out and wants to know if she can recover from State Bank the $170,000 difference between the $50,000 loan balance and the $220,000 State Bank received from the jeweler.
5. Assume State Bank sent the proposal to all the parties specified in § 9-620 and § 9-621 but some or all were not received and, as a result, no one objected. Would the proposal be effective? *See* § 1-201(b)(36).
6. If State Bank sent the proposal to some, but not all, of the parties specified in § 9-620 and § 9-621, and no one objected, would the proposal be effective? *See* § 9-620(a), (c).
7. If State Bank sent the proposal to all the parties specified in § 9-620 and § 9-621 and someone sent an objection but State Bank never received it, would the proposal be effective?
8. If the proposal is effective, what happens to Credit Union's security interest?

B. The projected value of the three bracelets is only $20,000 and State Bank wishes to propose accepting the bracelets in satisfaction of $20,000 of the $50,000 obligation.
   1. Is that allowed? If not, is there another way to structure the transaction to the same effect?
   2. To whom must State Bank send its proposal? Would it make any difference if Bill owned the bracelets and Olivia had guaranteed the debt?

C. What provisions should State Bank included in its security agreement and guarantees to help in the event that State Bank later wishes to retain collateral in full or partial satisfaction of the secured obligation? §§ 9-602, 9-603, 9-624.

e-Exercise 3-D
Timeline for Acceptance

e-Exercise 3-E
Limits on Waiving Rights

Article 9 requires no particular language in a proposal to accept collateral, and contains no safe-harbor form for such a proposal (as it does for a notification of disposition). A bit of guidance on what should be included is provided in comment 4 to § 9-620, which states that a proposal "should specify the amount . . . of the secured obligations to be satisfied, state the conditions (if any) under which the proposal may be revoked, and describe any other applicable conditions." Still, this leaves a lot for the secured party decide. So what should be included in a proposal to accept collateral?

One thing that a proposal definitely should include is an indication of the collateral the secured party is proposing to accept, particularly if the proposal relates to only some of the collateral. In addition, if the security agreement encumbers after-acquired property, it would be wise to indicate (i) the date (and time) that the proposal will be effective (if the secured party receives no timely objection)[66] and (ii) state that the proposal includes all collateral acquired by the debtor before the effective date (and time). Even if the collateral does not include after-acquired property, the proposal should probably make it clear that it covers proceeds generated before the effective date (and time). This might be very important if, for example, the collateral includes an interest in a subsidiary. The debtor could, after receiving the proposal, cause the subsidiary to make a distribution of a substantial portion of its assets and then surrender ownership of the

---

[66] The effective date is also important if the proposal is to accept the collateral in partial satisfaction of the secured obligation. Knowing when a portion of the debt is discharged will be necessary to calculate how much interest accrues thereafter.

now-depleted subsidiary to the secured party pursuant to the acceptance. If the proposal did not cover the distributions – which would be proceeds under § 9-102(a)(64)(B) – the secured party might find that all or a substantial portion of the secured obligation has been satisfied in return for an interest in a valueless entity.

SECTION 4. ENFORCEMENT AGAINST OBLIGATIONS OWED TO THE DEBTOR

When the collateral consists of accounts, chattel paper, instruments, or payment intangibles, there are necessarily two debts: a debt owed *to* the debtor (the collateral) and a debt owed *by* the debtor (the secured obligation).[67]

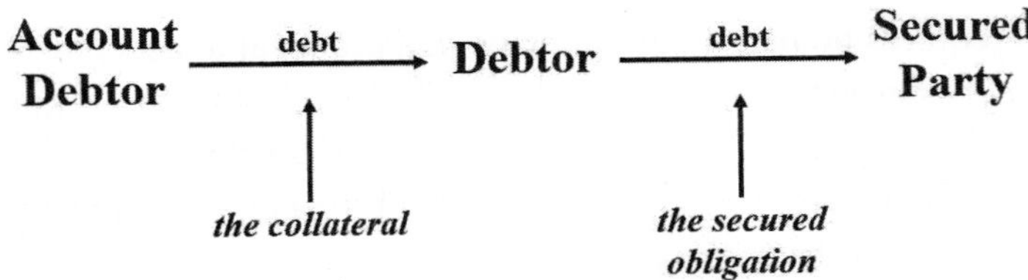

In such situations, in an effort to enforce the secured obligation, the secured party is free to foreclose on the collateral – the right to payment from the account debtor – by disposition under § 9-610 or by acceptance under § 9-620. However, there might not be much of a market for such property. Therefore, those enforcement mechanisms might not help the secured party realize the value of the collateral. Fortunately, Article 9 provides a third alternative: collection of the obligation owed to the debtor.

A. Instruction to Pay

To collect against obligations owed to the debtor, the secured party need merely provide the person obligated to the debtor – typically called an "account debtor"[68]

---

[67] Actually, the secured obligation is owed by the *obligor*, which as you might recall need not be the *debtor* (the owner of the collateral). § 9-102(a)(28), (59). In most situations, however, the debtor and obligor are the same entity, and the diagram is based on that assumption.

[68] An "account debtor" is a person obligated on an account, chattel paper, or a general

– with a notification instructing that person to make payment directly to the secured party. *See* § 9-607. The secured party may send such notification any time after default, and even before default if the security agreement authorizes the secured party to do so. § 9-607(a). Why might the debtor and secured party want to collect on collateral before default, and why might the debtor agree to permit it? There are several reasons.

First, from the secured party's perspective, collecting on collateral requires that the secured party be informed about who the account debtors are, how to contact them, and what they owe. Having this information throughout the life of the secured transaction allows the secured party to monitor the collectability and genuineness of the receivables. In contrast, acquiring that information after default can be problematic. Debtors who have defaulted and are facing enforcement action by the secured party might not be particularly cooperative or forthcoming with information.

Collecting on the collateral prior to default also enables the secured party to control how the debtor uses the funds. In essence, as funds are collected, the secured party might retain some to pay down the secured obligation according to the parties' agreement, and then give the debtor access to the remainder (*i.e.*, loan a portion of the collections back to the debtor) only if the debtor is not in default and has agreed to use the funds in a manner authorized by the secured party.

The debtor might agree to allow the secured party to collect before default for any of several reasons. The secured party might be more experienced in collecting and able to do it less expensively than the debtor can. The secured party might require this right as a condition to making the loan, and have the bargaining power to back that up. Finally, the debtor might be concerned that a change in the collection process after default might signal to the debtor's customers (the account debtors) that the debtor is experiencing financial distress, which might prompt the customers to take their business elsewhere. By allowing the secured party to collect at the outset – and by setting up a collection process that is invisible to the debtor's customers, one where the customers remit payment to an address or deposit account in the name of the debtor but controlled by the secured party – the debtor can avoid a situation that might alarm its customers.

---

intangible. *See* § 9-102(a)(3). It does not include the obligor on a negotiable instrument (even if the instrument is part of chattel paper) or the person obligated on a commercial tort claim, deposit account, or letter-of-credit rights, all of which also involve obligations owed to the debtor.

Collecting on collateral in the absence of default is also important when the secured transaction is an outright sale of accounts, chattel paper, promissory notes, or payment intangibles. *See* § 9-109(a)(3). In such a transaction, the very nature of the deal is that the buyer (the secured party) is entitled to proceeds of the receivables and hence should be entitled to collect them. In other words, "default" is a somewhat meaningless concept to a sale of receivables.

Regardless of whether the secured party's collection efforts begin before or after default, no prior notification to the debtor or to any other lienor is necessary. Consequently, if the debtor did not authorize collection pre-default, the first the debtor might learn of the secured party's action is when the debtor starts contacting the account debtors to inquire why they have, apparently, not paid their obligations.

Before an account debtor receives a signed instruction to pay the secured party, the account debtor may discharge its obligation by paying the debtor. Once an account debtor receives an instruction to pay the secured party, however, the account debtor may no longer discharge its obligation by paying the debtor; it may discharge its obligation only by paying the secured party. § 9-406(a). From the account debtor's perspective, this rule is a bit scary. If the account debtor pays the debtor after receiving an instruction to pay the secured party, the account debtor will have to pay a second time (presumably it may seek restitution from the debtor of the first payment, but the likelihood of collecting might be slim if the debtor is already in default to its lenders). Yet the account debtor might have no prior contact with the secured party or even knowledge of the secured party's interest in the account debtor's obligation. Because of that, the secured party's notification to pay must comply with § 9-406(b). In addition, the account debtor may request proof from the secured party that the debtor has really made an assignment of the obligation (*i.e.*, granted a security interest in the obligation) to the secured party. Until the secured party furnishes that requested proof, the account debtor may continue making payments to the debtor. § 9-406(c).

If, after an account debtor has received an instruction to pay the secured party, the debtor ceases to owe the secured obligation (perhaps because the debtor has fully paid it), the debtor can require the secured party to release the account debtor from any further obligation to the secured party. *See* § 9-209.[69] The debtor also has the right to redeem the collateral prior to collection. § 9-623.

---

[69] Note, § 9-209 does not apply to accounts, chattel paper, or payment intangibles that were sold. § 9-209(c).

Note that the rules in § 9-406(a) through (c) apply only to account debtors.[70] What if the person obligated to the debtor does not fall within the definition of account debtor, as would be the case if the obligation owed to the debtor was memorialized in an instrument or qualified as a deposit account? If the collateral were a negotiable instrument, the secured party's right to collect would be determined under Article 3. If the collateral were a non-negotiable instrument, the secured party would qualify as an assignee of a contract and the common law governing assignments of contract rights would determine the rights and duties of the parties. If the collateral were a deposit account, the secured party would likely have to seek judicial help unless it already has an agreement with the depositary institution. *See* § 9-607(a)(4), (5) & cmt. 7.

B. Defenses to the Obligation to Pay

The secured party qualifies as an "assignee" of the contractual right to payment that the assignor (the debtor) has against the account debtor.[71] As an assignee, the secured party is subject to all of the terms in the contract between the account debtor and the assignor.[72] Thus, the account debtor may assert against the secured party any defense to payment or claim in recoupment[73] that the account debtor could assert against the debtor and which arose out of the same transaction that gave rise to the account debtor's obligation. § 9-404(a)(1). The account debtor may also set off against its obligation to the secured party any other claim or defense the account

---

[70] Even though the definition of "account debtor" includes a person obligated on a general intangible, the rules of § 9-406(a) through (c) do not apply to all obligors on a general intangible, only those obligors on payment intangibles, a subset of the general intangible category.

[71] *See* § 9-102(a)(6A), (6B); Worthy Lending LLC v. New Style Contractors, Inc., 201 N.E.3d 783 (N.Y. 2022); First State Bank Nebraska v. MP Nexlevel, LLC, 48 N.W.2d 708 (Neb. 2020).

[72] *See* Systran Fin. Servs. Corp. v. Giant Cement Holding, Inc., 252 F. Supp. 2d 500 (N.D. Ohio 2003) (a buyer of accounts that is seeking to collect from the account debtor is subject to the arbitration clause in the contract between the debtor and the account debtor).

[73] A claim in recoupment is a claim to reduce the amount owing on an obligation based on rights arising out of the same transaction. *Cf.* U.C.C. § 3-305, cmt. 3 (distinguishing defenses from claims in recoupment).

debtor has against the debtor, which arose prior to the account debtor's receipt of notification of the assignment to the secured party. § 9-404(a)(2).

For example, if the debtor sold a tractor on credit to a buyer (the account debtor), and the debtor's secured party seeks to enforce that obligation, the buyer could assert any defense to payment or claim in recoupment arising from the tractor sale (such as if the tractor were defective, giving rise to a right to reject the tractor or a claim for breach of warranty), regardless of whether that defense or claim arose before or after the time the buyer learned of the assignment. The buyer could also use as a defense to payment any claim it has against the debtor arising out of a completely unrelated transaction, but only if that claim arose before the buyer received notification of the secured party's interest in the debtor's right to payment for the tractor.[74]

Note, the distinction between defenses to payment arising from the same transaction and claims arising out of separate transactions is much like the difference between compulsory and permissive counterclaims. Note also that the rules in § 9-404(a) about what defenses and claims an account debtor may assert against the secured party are wholly consistent with rights of contract assignees generally.[75] This latter point might be particularly relevant if the person obligated to the debtor is not an account debtor and thus the rules of § 9-404(a) do not apply.

Bear in mind, though, that a notification of the assignment sufficient to affect the account debtor's right to assert unrelated claims against the secured party is different from the § 9-607(a) notification instructing the account debtor to pay the secured party. Notification of the assignment under § 9-404 need merely inform the account debtor of the secured party's interest in the account debtor's obligation; it need not instruct the account debtor to alter its normal payment practices. One consequence of the rules in § 9-404 (and the common law of contract assignment)

---

[74] Determining whether a defense arises out of the same or a different transaction can be tricky. *See* In re Communication Dynamics, Inc., 300 B.R. 220 (Bankr. D. Del. 2003) (holding that a contract in which there are multiple deliveries counts as one transaction for purpose of § 9-404). Determining whether a claim under a separate transaction arose before the account debtor received a notification of assignment can also be difficult. *See* Puritan Fin. Corp. v. Bechstein Constr. Corp., 980 N.E.2d 135 (Ill. Ct. App. 2012) (account debtor's rights against the debtor on unrelated cartage contracts that the account debtor had fully performed did not arise before notification of assignment because no cause of action yet existed, presumably because no invoice had yet been issued and payment was not yet due).

[75] *See* RESTATEMENT (SECOND) OF CONTRACTS § 336.

is that the secured party has an incentive to inform account debtors early on of the assignment, long before it seeks to enforce the account debtors' obligations.

Of course, if the account debtor does raise a defense or seek to set off an unrelated claim, the secured party might have little or no knowledge about the merits of such a defense or claim. Even with knowledge of all the underlying facts, it might be difficult to determine the validity of a defense or the amount of any claim. Article 9 deals with this by authorizing the secured party to settle claims and defenses, but requires the secured party so doing to act in a commercially reasonable manner (as long as it has recourse against the debtor or a secondary obligor for uncollectible obligations). *See* § 9-607(c) & cmt. 9.

Problem 3-14

Doug and Anne each own an antique store in the same town. Each has a steady clientele, so Doug and Anne occasionally buy and sell to each other items that they think one of their normal customers is likely to want. In all such transactions, payment is due within 30 days of delivery.

Two months ago, Doug granted to State Bank a security interest in his existing and after-acquired accounts receivable to secure a loan from State Bank. Three weeks ago, Doug sold a $2,000 desk and a $200 vase to Anne. Last week, Anne sold a $500 chair to Doug. Neither has yet paid the other for his or her purchase.

A. May State Bank now notify Anne to pay State Bank the debt that Anne owes Doug? *See* § 9-607(a).
B. Does State Bank have a right to collect from Anne before the end of the 30-day period? *See* § 9-404(a).
C. How much may State Bank collect from Anne?
D. Assume that the vase that Anne purchased from Doug proved not to be an antique, but a modern reproduction, and Anne insisted that Doug take it back. If State Bank notifies Anne to pay State Bank, how much, if anything, must Anne remit? *See* § 9-404(a).
E. How, if at all, would the answer to Part D change if State Bank had notified Anne of its security interest in Doug's accounts before she sold the chair to Doug? *See* § 9-404(a).
F. When State Bank sent a letter to Anne instructing Anne to pay her obligation to Doug directly to State Bank, Anne ignored the letter and paid Doug. Should Anne be worried that she will have to pay again? *See* § 9-406(a). What should Anne have done? *See* § 9-406(c) & cmt. 4.

G. In attempting to collect the funds from Anne, State Bank called Anne 10 times a day, often at home after 10 p.m. Has State Bank violated any requirement of Article 9 in its collection efforts? *See* § 9-607(c).

H. 1. Does State Bank have a duty to notify Doug that it is seeking to collect from Anne?

   2. Does State Bank have a duty to notify any other lienholders that have an interest in Anne's obligation to Doug that it is seeking to collect from Anne? *Cf.* §§ 9-611(c)(3), 9-621(a).

   3. Does State Bank have a duty to notify any secondary obligor on Doug's debt to State Bank that it is seeking to collect from Anne?

C. Agreements Not to Assert Defenses and Anti-Assignment Rules

In some situations, the debtor and account debtor might have agreed that the account debtor will not be able to assert defenses to the obligation against any assignee of the contract, such as a secured party. If so, that agreement is enforceable if the conditions of § 9-403(b) are met.[76] Alternatively, the account debtor might have entered into an agreement with the secured party, pursuant to which the account debtor promises not to assert against the secured party any defense or claim the account debtor has against the debtor. In either case, whether the parties' language exhibits such an agreement can become a matter of contract interpretation.[77] In some circumstances, the account debtor and debtor may agree to modify the account debtor's obligations. The situations in which that modification is effective against the secured party are described in § 9-405.

---

[76] Note that such an agreement between the account debtor and debtor not to assert defenses does not preclude all defenses of the account debtor, § 9-403(c), and in some transactions, such an agreement might not be enforceable. *See* § 9-403(d), (e).

[77] *See* Maple Trade Fin., Inc. v. Lansing Trade Group, LLC, 2011 WL 1060961 (D. Kan. 2011) (account debtor that signed debtor's invoices acknowledging receipt of the goods was not estopped from denying receipt in action brought by factor that had loaned against the invoices in reliance on the account debtor's acknowledgment; unless it agrees otherwise, an account debtor is entitled to raise defenses arising under the contract and estoppel is not an agreement to waive those rights); Compressors Plus, Inc. v. Service Tech De Mexico, S.A. de C.V., 2004 WL 1243183 (N.D. Tex. 2004), *report and recommendation adopted*, 2004 WL 1402566 (N.D. Tex. 2004) (language stated that buyer accepted goods and would pay according to invoices was not a waiver of defenses).

Problem 3-15

A. What terms should a secured party include in its security agreement with the debtor to facilitate collection against account debtors? *See* §§ 1-103, 1-302, 9-602, 9-603, 9-607(c), 9-624.

B. What terms should a secured party insist that the debtor include in its agreements with account debtors? *See* §§ 9-403, 9-404, 9-405, 9-406.

Review the discussion in Chapter Two of Article 9's anti-assignment rules. Those rules override many contractual and legal restrictions on assignment. Like so many things in Article 9, application of those rules depends on the classification of the collateral: different rules apply to different types of collateral. The other factors relevant to determining which rule applies include:

(i) whether the restriction on assignment is contractual or legal;
(ii) whether the transaction to which the restriction applies is a sale (remember, Article 9 applies to the sale of several types of property, *see* § 9-109(a)(3)) or the use of the collateral to secure an obligation; and
(iii) whether the restriction prohibits the assignment, requires a third party's consent to the assignment, or make an unauthorized assignment a breach or default of the debtor's contract with the account debtor.

The two charts on the following page categorize the anti-assignment rules in sections 9-406 and 9-408. In so doing, the charts indicate for each of various types of collateral whether the rules in those sections:

(i) completely override the restriction (rendering the restriction "ineffective" to limit or affect an assignment of the property);
(ii) do not apply (leaving the restriction "unaffected by Article 9");[78] or
(iii) do something in between: override the restriction but leave the secured party with little or no ability to enforce its rights to the property ("partly ineffective").

---

[78] If the restriction on assignment is unaffected by Article 9's anti-assignment rules, the restriction will usually be effective. On occasion, however, other law might invalidate a restriction. For example, a term in a partnership agreement that prohibited partners from assigning their partnership interests to anyone of a particular race or gender would likely be unenforceable.

Contractual Restrictions

	Regarding Sale		Regarding Lien	
	Prohibits or Requires Consent	**Makes a Default**	**Prohibits or Requires Consent**	**Makes a Default**
Accounts & Chattel Paper	Ineffective § 9-406(d)(1)	Ineffective § 9-406(d)(2)	Ineffective § 9-406(d)(1)	Ineffective § 9-406(d)(2)
Payment Intangibles &	Partly Ineffective § 9-408(a)(1), (d)	Ineffective § 9-408(a)(2)	Ineffective § 9-406(d)(1)	Ineffective § 9-406(d)(2)
General Intangibles	Unaffected by Article 9	Unaffected by Article 9	Partly Ineffective § 9-408(a)(1), (d)	Ineffective § 9-408(a)(2)
Health-Care-Insurance	Partly Ineffective § 9-408(a)(1), (d)	Ineffective § 9-408(a)(2)	Partly Ineffective § 9-408(a)(1), (d)	Ineffective § 9-408(a)(2)

Legal Restrictions

	Regarding Sale		Regarding Lien	
	Prohibits or Requires Consent	**Makes a Default**	**Prohibits or Requires Consent**	**Makes a Default**
Accounts & Chattel Paper	Ineffective § 9-406(f)(1)	Ineffective § 9-406(f)(2)	Ineffective § 9-406(f)(1)	Ineffective § 9-406(f)(2)
Payment Intangibles &	Partly Ineffective § 9-408(c)(1), (d)	Ineffective § 9-408(c)(2)	Partly Ineffective § 9-408(c)(1), (d)	Ineffective § 9-408(c)(2)
General Intangibles	Unaffected by Article 9	Unaffected by Article 9	Partly Ineffective § 9-408(c)(1), (d)	Ineffective § 9-408(c)(2)
Health-Care-Insurance	Partly Ineffective § 9-408(c)(1), (d)	Ineffective § 9-408(c)(2)	Partly Ineffective § 9-408(c)(1), (d)	Ineffective § 9-408(c)(2)

You might ask, what would be the benefit of having a security interest in an obligation owed to the debtor if the secured party was not able to enforce the security interest? Put another way, why would a creditor ever want a security interest in an obligation of an account debtor if the secured party cannot compel the account debtor to make payment or render performance to the secured party? There are two main reasons, and they are related to each other.

First, if the security interest attaches to the debtor's contractual right (despite the restriction on assignment), the security interest will automatically extend to proceeds of the right. So, for example, if the collateral is a franchise agreement or partnership interest, then if the debtor's rights are ever sold or if the partnership makes a distribution to partners, the security interest will automatically extend to such proceeds. § 9-315(a)(2). This is true even if the relevant contracts or applicable law will not enable the secured party to enforce the debtor's contract rights. Of course, the security agreement could be drafted to include such later-arising property as part of the original collateral (*i.e.*, describe the collateral to include after-acquired distributions on account of partnership interest), but that brings us to the second reason: bankruptcy.

As discussed in Chapter Two, beginning on page 153, if the security interest did not encumber the debtor's contract rights, merely whatever property the debtor later acquired pursuant to or in exchange for those rights, the Bankruptcy Code would cut off the security interest in any such property that the debtor acquired or became entitled to post-petition. *See* 11 U.S.C. § 552(a). In contrast, if such post-petition property were proceeds of collateral (*i.e.*, the security interest encumbered the debtor's contract rights), then the security interest would attach to such property regardless of whether the debtor acquired that property prepetition or post-petition. *See* 11 U.S.C. § 552(b).[79]

---

[79] A similar issue has come up with respect to broadcast licenses. The Federal Communications Act provides that "[n]o . . . station license, or any rights thereunder, shall be transferred, assigned, or disposed of in any manner," without the advance approval of the FCC. 47 U.S.C. § 310(d). The FCC has long interpreted this language as prohibiting an assignment for security purposes: that is, as prohibiting the creation of a security interest in an FCC license. However, the FCC issued a clarifying order in which it concluded that a creditor could take a security interest in the proceeds of a broadcast license. *See* In re Cheskey, 9 FCC Rcd. 986, 987 (1994). Unfortunately, this does not solve the problem created by § 552(a) of the Bankruptcy Code, which cuts off a security interest in property the debtor acquired post-petition if that property is not proceeds of other collateral. As a result, there is seemingly no way for a creditor to have a security interest in the proceeds of a broadcast license if those proceeds are generated post-petition. Moreover, the anti-assignment rules of Article 9 do not solve this problem because they, as state law, cannot override a federal restriction on assignment of the broadcast license.

e-Exercise 3-F
Anti-Assignment & Scope

D. Application of Proceeds of Collection

The proceeds of collection are dealt with in much the same manner as the proceeds of a disposition. Just as disposition proceeds go first to the costs of the disposition, proceeds of collections may be applied first to the costs of collection. §§ 9-607(d), 9-608(a)(1)(A). After those expenses are satisfied, the proceeds of the collection are applied to the obligation owed to the secured party engaged in the enforcement effort and then to any subordinate lienors who have demanded a share of the collections from the secured party. § 9-608(a).

The resulting rights and liabilities of the parties are also similar to those arising after a disposition. If the collection does not satisfy the obligation owed to the secured party, the obligor owes a deficiency. If the collection generates more than enough to satisfy the obligations owed to a collecting secured party and any subordinate lienors entitled to payment under § 9-608, the surplus belongs to the debtor. Of course, this liability for the deficiency and entitlement to the surplus rule does not apply if the transaction between the debtor and the secured party was a sale of accounts, chattel paper, payment intangibles or promissory notes. § 9-608(b).

The main difference in effect between a collection and a disposition deals with the rights of senior secured parties. As we have seen, a senior secured party has no right to the proceeds of a disposition. However, a senior secured party might be entitled to the proceeds of a collection. *See* §§ 9-607 cm. 5, 9-608 cmt. 5; *cf.* § 9-615(g). The rules governing which party will be entitled to the collection

---

Courts have responded to this with some creative jurisprudence. *See* In re Tracy Broad. Corp., 696 F.3d 1051 (10th Cir. 2012) (although federal law prohibits a security interest from attaching to an FCC license itself, a security interest can attach to the right to receive proceeds of a future sale of the license; this right attaches upon acquisition of the license and, because that occurred pre-petition, § 552 of the Bankruptcy Code does not apply even if on the petition date there was no agreement to sell the license); In re TerreStar Networks, Inc., 457 B.R. 254 (Bankr. S.D.N.Y. 2011) (although federal law prohibits a security interest from attaching to an FCC license itself, a security interest can attach to the "economic value" of the license; because this lien attached pre-petition, § 552 of the Bankruptcy Code does not apply even if, on the petition date, no proceeds of the license existed and there was no agreement to sell the license).

proceeds are part of Article 9's priority scheme, which we will study in Chapter Five.

Now try your hand at the following problem, which reviews everything we have covered about collecting on collateral.

Problem 3-16

First Finance Inc. loans money to consumers for purchase of new automobiles, taking a security interest in the consumer's new automobile to secure payment of the price.

A. First Finance sold one of these contracts to State Bank for $10,000. The principal amount the consumer owes on the car purchase contract is $15,000.
   1. May State Bank collect from the consumer obligated on the contract?
   2. When collecting payments from the consumer, must State Bank act in a commercially reasonable manner?
   3. When, if ever, will State Bank be able to go after the consumer's car?
   4. If State Bank seeks to dispose of the consumer's car, to whom must it give notification of the disposition?
   5. If State Bank collects $15,000 from the consumer, does State Bank owe $5,000 to First Finance?
   6. If State Bank collects $7,000 from the consumer, does First Finance owe State Bank $3,000?

B. How, if at all, would the analysis to Part A change if the agreement between First Finance and State Bank included a warranty by First Finance that State Bank would collect at least $10,000 of the principal obligation of the consumer on the car purchase contract (*i.e.*, that First Finance would reimburse State Bank for any uncollectible obligation of the consumer, up to the difference between $10,000 and the principal amount actually collected)?

C. How, if at all, would the analysis to the questions in Part A change if, instead of selling the car purchase contract to State Bank, First Finance had used the contract as collateral for a $10,000 loan from State Bank?

D. Assume that State Bank made a loan of $10,000 to First Finance, all of which is still owing, secured by a security interest in the car purchase contract First Finance has with its customer. That customer owes $15,000 on its obligation to pay for the car, and has defaulted in its obligation to pay. State Bank peaceably repossessed the car and received $7,000 by conducting a proper disposition of the car. What amount remains owing by the customer and what amount remains owing by First Finance if State Bank incurred the following costs in enforcing its rights? *See* §§ 9-607(d), 9-608(a)(1)(A), 9-615(a)(1).

1. $200 to employ a collection agency to collect payments from the customer.
2. $300 to employ a repossession company to repossess the car from the customer.
3. $400 in attorney's fees for litigating with First Finance over its liability for the deficiency after State Bank's enforcement efforts?

Problem 3-17

A. Why does Article 9 not indicate that junior liens are discharged when a senior secured party collects the collateral (as opposed to when the senior secured party disposes of or accepts the collateral)?

B. Why does Article 9 provide that a junior secured party who disposes of collateral takes cash proceeds of the disposition free of any claim of a senior secured party, *see* § 9-615(g), but does not provide a similar rule for when a junior secured party collects on the collateral?

SECTION 5. REMEDIES FOR THE SECURED PARTY'S VIOLATIONS OF ITS DUTIES

There are numerous ways in which a secured party could err in its efforts to enforce a security interest. For example, the secured party might mistakenly believe that debtor had defaulted and then collect on or repossess the collateral without the right to do so. The secured party could repossess collateral in a manner that breaches the peace. With respect to a required notification, the secured party could fail to give it at all, fail to provide it to all the appropriate parties, fail to include in it some essential information, or fail to send it at the appropriate time. The secured party could act in a commercially unreasonable manner when collecting on or disposing of the collateral. Or, the secured party could attempt to accept collateral in full or partial satisfaction of the debt when required to conduct a disposition.

Given the wide range of possible errors, it is perhaps not surprising that Article 9 provides a variety of different remedies for such errors. *See* §§ 9-625, 9-626, 9-628. The basic measure of recovery is the "[l]oss caused by a failure to comply" with Article 9. *See* § 9-625(b). Whether this includes consequential damages remains a bit unclear. Article 1 provides that consequential damages are not recoverable unless "specifically provided" for in the UCC or by other rule of law. *See* § 1-305. Section 9-625(b) does not expressly mention "consequential damages," and comment 3 suggests that the damages available under § 9-625 are merely the amount needed to put the claimant in the position it would have been if no violation had occurred, which § 1-305 indicates is the normal measure of damages. On the other hand, § 9-625(b) does expressly state that recoverable damages include "loss resulting from the debtor's inability to obtain, or increased costs of, alternative financing," and that would seem to be one type of consequential damage, and perhaps open the door to other types of consequential damages. At present, though, courts do not seem to have walked through that door.[80]

In addition, if the collateral is consumer goods, the secured party might be liable for some rather substantial statutory damages. *See* §§ 9-625(c)(2), 9-628(d), (e). Other, somewhat less onerous, statutory damages are available for noncompliance with some specified sections. *See* § 9-625(e), (f), (g). If the secured party's conduct qualifies as a tort, as would typically be the case if a breach of the peace occurs during a repossession attempt, all the applicable tort remedies, including punitive damages, would be available. *See* §§ 1-103, 9-625 cmt. 3. Finally, as explained in this case excerpt, a secured party who violates Part 6 of Article 9 might be barred from attempting to collect a deficiency. Do you agree with its conclusions, particularly those concerning aggregation of remedies?

COXALL V. CLOVER COMMERCIAL CORP.
781 N.Y.S.2d 567 (Kings Cty. Civ. Ct. 2004)

* * *

Deficiency

When the secured party has disposed of the collateral in a commercially reasonable manner after sending reasonable notification to the debtor, the debtor will be liable for any deficiency if the proceeds of the disposition are not sufficient

---

[80] *See* Forthill Constr. Corp. v. Blue Acquisition, LLC, 2020 WL 949256 (S.D.N.Y. 2020) (because consequential damages are not available under the UCC unless expressly provided for, a secured party was not liable for lost profits and lost salary allegedly attributable to the secured party's failure to comply with Article 9); Proactive Techs., Inc. v. Denver Place Assocs. Ltd. P'ship, 141 P.3d 959 (Colo. Ct. App. 2006) (ruling under former Article 9 that consequential damages in the form of lost profits are not available for conducting a commercially unreasonable disposition).

to satisfy the debt and allowed expenses. *See* § 9-615(d). Former Article 9 was silent, however, on whether the secured party that had failed to send reasonable notification or had not disposed of the collateral in a commercially reasonable manner or both, as here could obtain a deficiency judgment against the debtor.

> Three general approaches emerged. Some courts have held that a noncomplying secured party may not recover a deficiency (the "absolute bar" rule). A few courts held that the debtor can offset against a claim to a deficiency all damages recoverable under former Section 9-507 resulting from the secured party's noncompliance (the "offset" rule). A plurality of courts considering the issue held that the noncomplying secured party is barred from recovering a deficiency unless it overcomes a rebuttable presumption that compliance with former Part 5 would have yielded an amount sufficient to satisfy the secured debt.

§ 9-626 comment 4.

In New York, the departments of the Appellate Division were not in agreement as to which of the approaches to follow, with the Second Department alone adopting the "absolute bar" rule. The "absolute bar" rule appears to have been the approach required by pre-Code law.

Revised Article 9 resolves the conflict and uncertainty for transactions other than consumer transactions by adopted the "rebuttable presumption" rule. *See* § 9-626(a)(3). The limitation of the "rebuttable presumption" rule to non-consumer transactions "is intended to leave to the court the determination of the proper rules in consumer transactions," and the court "may continue to apply established approaches." § 9-626(b).

It is clear, therefore, that the "rebuttable presumption" rule is now the law in the Second Department for non-consumer transactions. The question remains, however, whether the "absolute bar" rule is to be applied in these actions, involving, as they do, a consumer transaction. A review of the legislative history provides no guidance. The Report of the New York State Law Revision Committee that accompanied Revised Article 9 through enactment states only that, "(w)ith respect to consumer defaults, Revised Article 9 makes no recommendation whatsoever, leaving the courts free to shape a remedy as is appropriate in each case." The New York State Law Revision Commission, 2001 Report on the Proposed Revised Article 9, at 158.

Up to now, New York courts have not distinguished between consumer and non-consumer transactions in fashioning rules where the enforcement provisions of

Article 9 were silent, suggesting that the "rebuttable presumption" rule will be adopted for all transactions. But at this time, for a court sitting in the Second Department, there is an "absolute bar" rule that has not been legislatively displaced by Revised Article 9.

Having found, therefore, that Clover Commercial failed to comply with both the reasonable notification and commercially reasonable disposition requirements of Article 9, the "absolute bar" rule precludes it from recovering a deficiency from the Coxalls.

* * *

Coxall's Claim Against Clover

* * * [D]oes Mr. Coxall have a remedy for Clover Commercial's failure to comply with Article 9, beyond being relieved of any liability for a deficiency?

* * * Under Article 9, "a person is liable for damages in the amount of any loss caused by a failure to comply" with the statute. § 9-625(b). "Damages for violation of the requirements of [the statute] . . . are those reasonably calculated to put an eligible claimant in the position that it would have occupied had no violation occurred." § 9-625 comment 3. There are, however, both supplements to and limitations on this general liability principle.

"[A] debtor . . . whose deficiency is eliminated or reduced under Section 9-626 may not otherwise recover . . . for noncompliance with the provisions . . . relating to enforcement." § 9-625(d). This provision "eliminates the possibility of double recovery or other over-compensation," but "[b]ecause Section 9-626 does not apply to consumer transactions, the statute is silent as to whether a double recovery or other over-compensation is possible in a consumer transaction." § 9-625 comment 3. Respected commentators "argue that double recoveries should be denied in consumer cases too." *See* White and Summer, Uniform Commercial Code, § 25-13, at 919 (5th ed. 2000).

The law in New York under Former Article 9 allowed a debtor to recover any loss resulting from the secured party's noncompliance, even though the secured party was deprived of recovery for a deficiency because of noncompliance. Here again, since Revised Article 9 does not displace existing law for consumer transactions, this Court must apply the pre-revision law. At the least, denial of a deficiency to the noncomplying secured party should not preclude the debtor's recovery of the statutorily-prescribed minimum damages.

Revised Article 9, like its predecessor, "provides a minimum, statutory, damage recovery for a debtor . . . in a consumer goods transaction" that "is designed to ensure that every noncompliance . . . in a consumer-goods transaction results in liability." *See* § 9-625(c) & comment 4. The debtor may recover "an amount not less than the credit service charge plus 10 percent of the principal amount of the obligation or the time-price differential plus 10 percent of the cash price." § 9-625(c). The statute "does not include a definition or explanation of the terms" used in the damage formula, but "leaves their construction and application to the court, taking into account the . . . purpose of providing a minimum recovery." § 9-625 comment 4.

Here, according to the Contract, the time-price differential is $1,036.24 and 10% of the cash price is $810.00, for a total statutory damage recovery of $1,846.24. Mr. Coxall is entitled to this recovery even if he sustained no actual loss from Clover Commercial's failure to comply with Article 9. But, although Clover Commercial failed to comply with both the requirement for reasonable notification and the requirement for a commercially reasonable disposition, it is obligated for only one statutory damage remedy.

Mr. Coxall would also be entitled to the value of the personal property that, he says, was contained in the vehicle when it was repossessed, but which has not been returned to him. But Mr. Coxall introduced no admissible evidence of that value.

* * *

At least one other court has ruled that the absolute bar rule applies in consumer transactions.[81] In contrast, about one-third of the states have made the rebuttable presumption rule applicable to consumer transactions through enactment of a non-uniform version of § 9-626(b).[82] Even if the right to a deficiency is lost, any

---

[81] *See* In re Downing, 286 B.R. 900 (Bankr. W.D. Mo. 2002) (discussing the insufficiency of the secured creditor's notification of sale to the debtor and, consequently, its inability to obtain a deficiency judgment, because the notification failed to inform the debtor (1) whether the sale would be public or private, (2) that the debtor would be liable for any deficiency remaining, (3) what the creditor claimed the indebtedness to be at the time of sale, and (4) that the debtor was entitled to an accounting of the exact amount of his indebtedness). *See also* Hamilton v. Muncy, 2017 WL 4712410 (Ky. Ct. App. 2017) (implicitly applying the absolute bar rule when ruling that a secured party, whose notification of disposition did not comply with § 9-614, was not entitled to a deficiency).

[82] *See* Fla. Stat. § 679.626; Idaho Code § 28-9-626; 810 Ill. Comp. Stat. 5/9-626; Ind. Code § 26-1-9.1-626; Kan. Stat. § 84-9-626; La. Rev. Stat. § 10:9-626; Md. Code, Com. Law § 9-626; Mich. Comp. Laws § 440.9626; Miss. Code § 75-9-626; Neb. Rev. Stat. U.C.C.

claim of the creditor against the debtor in tort, such as for fraud, probably survives. In other words, the absolute bar rule and the rebuttable presumption rule operate on contract liability, not tort liability.[83]

A secured party's liability for failure to comply with Article 9's rules on enforcing security interests runs to any person injured by that failure. Such persons can include the debtor, the obligor, or any other person with a lien on some or all of the collateral, but do not include a creditor with no interest in the collateral.[84]

A secured party has some defenses to liability. It has no liability to a debtor or an obligor unless it knows who that person is and how to communicate with that person. *See* § 9-628(a), (b). This can be important if, for example, the original debtor has sold the collateral without informing the secured party. If the buyer acquired the collateral subject to the security interest, a point we will explore in Chapter Five, the buyer will become the "debtor," *see* § 9-102(a)(28), and would normally have all the rights to notification that the original debtor had. A secured party is also insulated from liability if it acts under the reasonable belief that the transaction is not a consumer transaction or consumer-goods transaction or that the collateral is not consumer goods. *See* § 9-628(c).

Article 9's main rules regarding the secured party's liability for error in enforcing its security interest can be summarized by the following chart:

---

§ 9-626; N.J. Stat. 12A:9-626; N.D. Cent. Code § 41-09-121; Ohio Rev. Code § 1309.626; S.D. Codified Laws § 57A-9-626; Tenn. Code § 47-9-626; Va. Code § 8.9A-626; Wash. Rev. Code § 62A.9A-626 (making the rebuttable presumption rule applicable to both consumer and non-consumer transactions). *See also* Horizon Bank v. Huizar, 178 N.E.3d 326 (Ind. Ct. App. 2021) (a secured party's liability for statutory damages under § 9-625(c) was properly reduced by the amount of the deficiency owing after the vehicle was sold because the sale was commercially reasonable).

[83] *See* In re Lancaster, 252 B.R. 170 (Bankr. N.D. Cal. 2000) (creditor's fraud claim survives application of the absolute bar rule).

[84] iFlex Inc. v. Electroply, Inc., 2004 WL 502179 (D. Minn. 2004).

RESULT WHEN FORECLOSING CREDITOR FAILS TO COMPLY WITH PART 6 OF ARTICLE 9

	Creditor Seeks to Collect a Deficiency	Debtor Seeks Damages
Commercial Transaction	***Rebuttable Presumption Rule*** § 9-626(a)(3), (4). The deficiency is limited to difference between the amount of the secured obligation and what a proper foreclosure effort would have yielded. That difference is presumed to be zero. The creditor has the burden of how much, if anything, would have remained due after a proper foreclosure.	***Actual Damages*** Debtor is entitled to whatever damages it can prove resulted from the creditor's failure to comply with the UCC, as provided by § 9-625(b) and limited by § 9-625(d). ***Statutory Damages*** § 9-625(c)(2). If the collateral is consumer goods.
Consumer Transaction	***No Statutory Rule*** *See* § 9-626(b). Courts will, presumably, apply either the Rebuttable Presumption Rule or the Absolute Bar Rule.	***Actual Damages*** § 9-625(b). ***Statutory Damages*** If the collateral is consumer goods, § 9-625(c)(2); additional damages under § 9-625(e)(5), (6).

e-Exercise 3-G
Limits on Deficiencies

Problem 3-18

About nine months ago, First Bank loaned Driver $12,000 to purchase a car, taking a security interest in the car to secure the loan. The loan agreement called for payments of $500 per month for 30 months. Driver made the first nine payments and then defaulted by failing to make the next two. Shortly thereafter, First Bank peaceably repossessed Driver's car. Two weeks later, First Bank sold the car for $6,000. Assume that the retail value of the car was $8,000 and that Driver's outstanding obligation to First Bank, including expenses of the sale, was $9,000.

A. If First Bank fully complied with Part 6 of Article 9, what, if anything, does Driver owe as a deficiency?

B. Assume that First Bank Sold the car to one of its employees. Assume also that First Bank's transaction with Driver was not a consumer transaction.
   1. If First Bank fully complied with Part 6 of Article 9, what, if anything, does Driver owe as a deficiency? *See* §§ 9-610(c), 9-615(f).
   2. If First Bank failed to send to Driver any notification of the intended disposition, what, if anything, does Driver owe as a deficiency? What liability, if any, does First Bank have to Driver? *See* §§ 9-625, 9-626.

C. Assume that First Bank's transaction with Driver was a consumer transaction. If First Bank failed to send to Driver any notification of the intended disposition, what, if anything, does Driver owe as a deficiency?

Problem 3-19

Several years ago, Baker Street Finance Company provided the financing for Douglas to purchase three original paintings by a famous artist. At that time, Douglas gave Baker Street a security interest in the paintings to secure the loan. Two months ago, Douglas defaulted on the loan and Baker Street peaceably repossessed the paintings. At that time, the outstanding balance was $100,000. Last week, Baker Street sold the paintings to an art gallery for $300,000.

A. Douglas just learned of the sale and has consulted you to ascertain whether he can obtain the $200,000 surplus value. Does he have a right to it?

B. Assume that Second Finance had a second-priority security interest in the paintings to secure a $50,000 debt and that Baker Street did not notify Second Finance that Baker Street intended to sell the paintings. Does Second Finance have any recourse against Baker Street?

C. Would it make any difference if the security agreement provided that "in no event shall Secured Party be liable to any party to this agreement for more than $1,000 in the event Secured Party breaches any requirement of Article 9"? *See* § 9-602(13).

SECTION 6. EFFECT OF OTHER LAW ON THE SECURED PARTY'S ENFORCEMENT EFFORTS

A secured party seeking to enforce its security interest needs to think about a variety of court-developed doctrines and statutes outside of Article 9 that might or should affect its collection efforts. This section briefly discusses the common-law doctrines most likely to be relevant and the effect of a debtor's bankruptcy proceeding.

A. Waiver and Estoppel

In the course of its relationship with a debtor or obligor, the secured party might engage in conduct that either constitutes a waiver of rights the secured party has or estops the secured party from asserting its rights. For example, assume the secured party has made an installment loan secured by the debtor's inventory. The debtor is supposed to make periodic payments but is continually late. After about the tenth late payment, the secured party decides that it considers the loan to be in default and starts enforcement efforts. Some courts will hold that the secured party has either waived its right to insist on timely payments or is estopped from asserting its right to timely payments, particularly when the debtor can show that it relied on the secured party's failure to protest the late payments. In essence, a court will treat the course of performance – the debtor's late payment and the secured party's acceptance of late payment – as an indication that the parties have tacitly decided not to abide by the terms of their written agreement regarding what constitutes a default.

To avoid this result, many security agreements and lending agreements contain an "anti-waiver" clause which provides that the secured party's action or inaction does not waive any rights it might have under either the agreement or applicable law and that any single waiver not be deemed to constitute a continuing waiver of the same right. Some courts treat such an anti-waiver clause as precluding a finding of implied waiver from the secured party's conduct. Such an anti-waiver clause is not usually effective against an estoppel argument, however, because part of the estoppel argument is that the debtor was injured by its reasonable reliance on the secured party's failure to act differently. Whether the inclusion of an anti-waiver clause makes the debtor's reliance on the secured party's inaction unreasonable is a question of fact.

B. Lender Liability

The term "lender liability" refers to a variety of causes of action under which the lender incurs liability to the debtor or to third parties dealing with the debtor.[85]

---

[85] Descriptions of the various claims can be found in Bruce E.H. Johnson, *Lender Liability*

Some actions are based upon the secured party's breach of its contractual obligations to the debtor. Such obligations might be in a form of commitment to lend or a promise not to declare a default in the loan. Some are based upon the claim that, even though the secured party had the contractual right to engage in collection efforts, the secured party violated its obligation of good faith in doing so. § 1-304. Some actions rest upon tort concepts. For example, perhaps the secured party has committed fraud, defamed the debtor, or unjustly interfered with the debtor's business opportunities. Some claims are based upon principles of agency and unjust enrichment. These might arise if the secured party exercised control over the debtor's enterprise to the unjustified detriment of third parties dealing with the debtor. Finally they might involve a violation of any of a number of statutes that impose duties on the secured party, such as consumer protection laws or environmental protection legislation. *See* § 9-201.

Consider the following case, which discusses lender liability issues in connection with a secured party's enforcement of a security interest.

IN RE CLARK PIPE AND SUPPLY CO., INC.
893 F.2d 693 (5th Cir. 1990)

E. Grady Jolly, Circuit Judge

Treating the suggestion for rehearing en banc filed in this case by Associates Commercial Corporation ("Associates"), as a petition for panel rehearing, we hereby grant the petition for rehearing. After re-examining the evidence in this case and the applicable law, we conclude that our prior opinion was in error. We therefore withdraw our prior opinion and substitute the following:

Litigation Checklist: A Summary of Current Theories and Developments, 59 UMKC L. REV. 205 (1991). *See also* Helen Davis Chaitman, *The Ten Commandments for Avoiding Lender Liability*, 511 PLI/COMM 9 (Sept.-Oct. 1989). According to the article, the ten commandments are:

I. Thou Shalt Not Make a Sudden Move;
II. Thou Shalt Not Tell a Lie (Or Fudge the Truth);
III. Thou Shalt Honor Thy Commitments;
IV. Thou Shalt Not Run Thy Borrower's Business;
V. Thou Shalt Not Bail Thyself out on Thy Brother's Money;
VI. Thou Shalt Keep Thine Own Files Clean;
VII. Thou Shalt Transfer a Troubled Loan to a Workout Officer;
VIII. Thou Shalt Confer with Workout Counsel;
IX. Thou Shalt Think Carefully Before Suing on a Deficiency;
X. Thou Shalt Not Be Arrogant.

In this bankruptcy case we are presented with two issues arising out of the conduct of the bankrupt's lender during the ninety days prior to the bankrupt's filing for protection from creditors. The first is whether the lender improved its position vis-a-vis other creditors during the ninety-day period and thus received a voidable transfer. If so, the second question is whether the lender engaged in such inequitable conduct that would justify subordination of the lender's claims to the extent that the conduct harmed other creditors. Since we decide that equitable subordination is an inappropriate remedy in this case, we need not decide whether avoiding the transfer and equitable subordination are duplicative or complementary remedies.

I

Clark Pipe and Supply Company, Inc., ("Clark") was in the business of buying and selling steel pipe used in the fabrication of offshore drilling platforms. In September 1980, Associates and Clark executed various agreements under which Associates would make revolving loans secured by an assignment of accounts receivable and an inventory mortgage. Under the agreements, Clark was required to deposit all collections from the accounts receivable in a bank account belonging to Associates. The amount that Associates would lend was determined by a formula, i.e., a certain percentage of the amount of eligible accounts receivable plus a certain percentage of the cost of inventory. The agreements provided that Associates could reduce the percentage advance rates at any time at its discretion.

When bad times hit the oil fields in late 1981, Clark's business slumped. In February 1982 Associates began reducing the percentage advance rates so that Clark would have just enough cash to pay its direct operating expenses. Clark used the advances to keep its doors open and to sell inventory, the proceeds of which were used to pay off the past advances from Associates. Associates did not expressly dictate to Clark which bills to pay. Neither did it direct Clark not to pay vendors or threaten Clark with a cut-off of advances if it did pay vendors. But Clark had no funds left over from the advances to pay vendors or other creditors whose services were not essential to keeping its doors open.

One of Clark's vendors, going unpaid, initiated foreclosure proceedings in February and seized the pipe it had sold Clark. Another attempted to do so in March. The resulting priority dispute was resolved only in litigation. . . . When a third unpaid creditor initiated foreclosure proceedings in May, Clark sought protection from creditors by filing for reorganization under Chapter 11 of the Bankruptcy Code.

The case was converted to a Chapter 7 liquidation on August 31, 1982, and a trustee was appointed. In 1983, the trustee brought this adversary proceeding against Clark's lender, Associates. The trustee sought the recovery of alleged preferences and equitable subordination of Associates' claims. Following a one-day trial on August 28, 1986, the bankruptcy court entered judgment on April 10, 1987, and an amended judgment on June 9, 1987. The court required Associates to turn over $370,505 of payments found to be preferential and subordinated Associates' claims. The district court affirmed on May 24, 1988.

* * *

III

The second issue before us is whether the bankruptcy court was justified in equitably subordinating Associates' claims. This court has enunciated a three-pronged test to determine whether and to what extent a claim should be equitably subordinated: (1) the claimant must have engaged in some type of inequitable conduct, (2) the misconduct must have resulted in injury to the creditors of the bankrupt or conferred an unfair advantage on the claimant, and (3) equitable subordination of the claim must not be inconsistent with the provisions of the Bankruptcy Code. *In the Matter of Missionary Baptist Foundation of America, Inc.*, 712 F.2d 206, 212 (5th Cir. 1983) (*Missionary Baptists I*). Three general categories of conduct have been recognized as sufficient to satisfy the first prong of the three-part test: (1) fraud, illegality or breach of fiduciary duties; (2) undercapitalization; and (3) a claimant's use of the debtor as a mere instrumentality or alter ego. *Id.*

In essence, the bankruptcy court found that once Associates realized Clark's desperate financial condition, Associates asserted total control and used Clark as a mere instrumentality to liquidate Associates' unpaid loans. Moreover, it did so, the trustee argues, to the detriment of the rights of Clark's other creditors.

Associates contends that its control over Clark was far from total. Associates says that it did no more than determine the percentage of advances as expressly permitted in the loan agreement; it never made or dictated decisions as to which creditors were paid. Thus, argues Associates, it never had the "actual, participatory, total control of the debtor" required to make Clark its instrumentality under *Krivo Industrial Supply Co. v. National Distillers & Chemical Corp.*, 483 F.2d 1098, 1105 (5th Cir.1973), *modified factually*, 490 F.2d 916 (5th Cir.1974) (elaborated in *Valdes v. Leisure Resource Group*, 810 F.2d 1345, 1354 (5th Cir.1987)). If it did not use Clark as an instrumentality or engage in any other type of inequitable conduct under *Missionary Baptist I*, argues Associates, then it cannot be equitably subordinated.

A

We first consider whether Associates asserted such control over the activities of Clark that we should consider that it was using Clark as its mere instrumentality. In our prior opinion, we agreed with the district court and the bankruptcy court that, as a practical matter, Associates asserted total control over Clark's liquidation, and that it used its control in a manner detrimental to the unsecured creditors. Upon reconsideration, we have concluded that we cannot say that the sort of control Associates asserted over Clark's financial affairs rises to the level of unconscionable conduct necessary to justify the application of the doctrine of equitable subordination. We have reached our revised conclusion primarily because we cannot escape the salient fact that, pursuant to its loan agreement with Clark, Associates had the right to reduce funding, just as it did, as Clark's sales slowed. We now conclude that there is no evidence that Associates exceeded its authority under the loan agreement, or that Associates acted inequitably in exercising its rights under that agreement.

We think it is important to note at the outset that the loan and security agreements between Associates and Clark, which are at issue here, were executed in 1980, at the inception of their relationship. There is no evidence that Clark was insolvent at the time the agreements were entered into. Clark was represented by counsel during the negotiations, and there is no evidence that the loan documents were negotiated at anything other than arm's length or that they are atypical of loan documents used in similar asset-based financings.

The loan agreement between Associates and Clark established a line of credit varying from $2.2 million to approximately $2.7 million over the life of the loan. The amount that Associates would lend was determined by a formula: 85% of the amount of eligible accounts receivables plus 60% of the cost of inventory. Under the agreement, Clark was required to deposit all collections from the accounts receivable in a bank account belonging to Associates. Associates would, in turn, re-advance the agreed-upon portion of those funds to Clark on a revolving basis. The agreement provided that Associates could reduce the percentage advance rates at any time in its discretion.

When Clark's business began to decline, along with that of the oil patch generally, Associates advised Clark that it would reduce the advance ratio for the inventory loan by 5% per month beginning in January 1982. After that time, the company stopped buying new inventory and, according to the Trustee's expert witness, Clark's monthly sales revenues amounted to less than one-fifth of the company's outstanding accounts payable. Clark prepared a budget at Associates' request that indicated the disbursements necessary to keep the company operating. The budget did not include payment to vendors for previously shipped goods. Associates' former loan officer, Fred Slice, testified as to what he had in mind:

> If he [the comptroller of Clark] had had the availability [of funds to pay a vendor or other trade creditor] that particular day, I would have said, "Are you sure you've got that much availability, Jim," because he shouldn't have that much. The way I had structured it, he wouldn't have any money to pay his suppliers. . . .
>
> But you know, the possibility that–this is all hypothetical. I had it structured so that there was no–there was barely enough money–there was enough money, if I did it right, enough money to keep the doors open. Clark could continue to operate, sell the inventory, turn it into receivables, collect the cash, transfer that cash to me, and reduce my loans.
>
> And, if he had ever had availability for other things, that meant I had done something wrong, and I would have been surprised. To ask me what I would have done is purely hypothetical[;] I don't think it would happen. I think it's so unrealistic, I don't know.

Despite Associates' motive, which was, according to Slice, "to get in the best position I can prior to the bankruptcy, *i.e.*, I want to get the absolute amount of dollars as low as I can by hook or crook," the evidence shows that the amount of its advances continued to be based on the applicable funding formulas. Slice testified that the lender did not appreciably alter its original credit procedures when Clark fell into financial difficulty.

In our original opinion, we failed to focus sufficiently on the loan agreement, which gave Associates the right to conduct its affairs with Clark in the manner in which it did. In addition, we think that in our previous opinion we were overly influenced by the negative and inculpatory tone of Slice's testimony. Given the agreement he was working under, his testimony was hardly more than fanfaronading about the power that the agreement afforded him over the financial affairs of Clark. Although his talk was crass (e.g., "I want to get the absolute dollars as low as I can, by hook or crook"), our careful examination of the record does not reveal any conduct on his part that was inconsistent with the loan agreement, irrespective of what his personal motive may have been.

Through its loan agreement, every lender effectively exercises "control" over its borrower to some degree. A lender in Associates' position will usually possess "control" in the sense that it can foreclose or drastically reduce the debtor's financing. The purpose of equitable subordination is to distinguish between the unilateral remedies that a creditor may properly enforce pursuant to its agreements with the debtor and other inequitable conduct such as fraud, misrepresentation, or the exercise of such total control over the debtor as to have essentially replaced its decision-making capacity with that of the lender. The crucial distinction between what is inequitable and what a lender can reasonably and legitimately do to protect its interests is the distinction between the existence of "control" and the exercise of that "control" to direct the activities of the debtor. As the Supreme Court stated in *Comstock v. Group of Institutional Investors*, 335 U.S. 211, 229 (1948): "It is not mere existence of an opportunity to do wrong that brings the rule into play; it is the unconscionable use of the opportunity afforded by the domination to advantage itself at the injury of the subsidiary that deprives the wrongdoer of the fruits of his wrong."

In our prior opinion, we drew support from *In re American Lumber Co.*, 5 B.R. 470 (D. Minn. 1980), to reach our conclusion that Associates' claims should be equitably subordinated. Upon reconsideration, however, we find that the facts of that case are significantly more egregious than we have here. In that case, the court equitably subordinated the claims of a bank because the bank "controlled" the debtor through its right to a controlling interest in the debtor's stock. The bank forced the debtor to convey security interests in its remaining unencumbered assets to the bank after the borrower defaulted on an existing debt. Immediately thereafter, the bank foreclosed on the borrower's accounts receivable, terminated the borrower's employees, hired its own skeleton crew to conduct a liquidation, and selectively honored the debtor's payables to improve its own position. The bank began receiving and opening all incoming mail at the borrower's office, and it established a bank account into which all amounts received by the borrower were deposited and over which the bank had sole control. The bankruptcy court found that the bank exercised control over all aspects of the debtor's finances and operation including: payments of payables and wages, collection and use of accounts receivable and contract rights, purchase and use of supplies and materials, inventory sales, a lumber yard, the salaries of the principals, the employment of employees, and the receipt of payments for sales and accounts receivable.

Despite its decision to prohibit further advances to the debtor, its declaration that the debtor was in default of its loans, and its decisions to use all available funds of the company to offset the company's obligations to it, the bank in *American Lumber* made two specific representations to the American Lumbermen's Credit Association that the debtor was not in a bankruptcy situation and that current contracts would be fulfilled. Two days after this second reassurance, the bank gave notice of foreclosure of its security interests in the company's inventory and equipment. Approximately two weeks later the bank sold equipment and inventory of the debtor amounting to roughly $450,000, applying all of the proceeds to the debtor's indebtedness to the bank.

Associates exercised significantly less "control" over the activities of Clark than did the lender in *American Lumber.* Associates did not own any stock of Clark, much less a controlling block. Nor did Associates interfere with the operations of the borrower to an extent even roughly commensurate with the degree of interference exercised by the bank in *American Lumber.* Associates made no management decisions for Clark, such as deciding which creditors to prefer with the diminishing amount of funds available. At no time did Associates place any of its employees as either a director or officer of Clark. Associates never influenced the removal from office of any Clark personnel, nor did Associates ever request Clark to take any particular action at a shareholders meeting. Associates did not expressly dictate to Clark which bills to pay, nor did it direct Clark not to pay vendors or threaten a cut-off of advances if it did pay vendors. Clark handled its own daily operations. The same basic procedures with respect to the reporting of collateral, the calculation of availability of funds, and the procedures for the advancement of funds were followed throughout the relationship between Clark and Associates. Unlike the lender in *American Lumber*, Associates did not mislead creditors to continue supplying Clark. *Cf. American Lumber*, 5 B.R. at 474. Perhaps the most important fact that distinguishes this case from *American Lumber* is that Associates did not coerce Clark into executing the security agreements after Clark became insolvent. Instead, the loan and security agreements between Clark and Associates were entered into at arm's length prior to Clark's insolvency, and all of Associates' activities were conducted pursuant to those agreements.

Associates' control over Clark's finances, admittedly powerful and ultimately severe, was based solely on the exercise of powers found in the loan agreement. Associates' close watch over Clark's affairs does not, by itself, however, amount to such control as would justify equitable subordination. *In re W.T. Grant*, 699 F.2d 599, 610 (2d Cir. 1983). "There is nothing inherently wrong with a creditor carefully monitoring his debtor's financial situation or with suggesting what course of action the debtor ought to follow." *In re Teltronics Services, Inc.*, 29 B.R. 139,

172 (Bankr. E.D.N.Y. 1983) (citations omitted). Although the terms of the agreement did give Associates potent leverage over Clark, that agreement did not give Associates total control over Clark's activities. At all material times Clark had the power to act autonomously and, if it chose, to disregard the advice of Associates; for example, Clark was free to shut its doors at any time it chose to do so and to file for bankruptcy.

Finally, on reconsideration, we are persuaded that the rationale of *In re W.T. Grant Co.*, 699 F.2d 599 (2d Cir. 1983) should control the case before us. In that case, the Second Circuit recognized that

> a creditor is under no fiduciary obligation to its debtor or to other creditors of the debtor in the collection of its claim. [citations omitted] The permissible parameters of a creditor's efforts to seek collection from a debtor are generally those with respect to voidable preferences and fraudulent conveyances proscribed by the Bankruptcy Act; apart from these there is generally no objection to a creditor's using his bargaining position, including his ability to refuse to make further loans needed by the debtor, to improve the status of his existing claims.

699 F.2d at 609-10. Associates was not a fiduciary of Clark, it did not exert improper control over Clark's financial affairs, and it did not act inequitably in exercising its rights under its loan agreement with Clark.

B

Finally, we should note that in our earlier opinion, we found that, in exercising such control over Clark, Associates engaged in other inequitable conduct that justified equitable subordination. Our re-examination of the record indicates, however, that there is not really any evidence that Associates engaged in such conduct. Our earlier opinion assumed that Associates knew that Clark was selling pipe to which the suppliers had a first lien, but the issue of whether the vendors had a first lien on the pipe was not decided by our court until a significantly later time. In addition, although the trustee made much of the point on appeal, after our re-study of the record, we conclude that it does not support the finding that Associates encouraged Clark to remove decals from pipe in its inventory.

We also note that the record is devoid of any evidence that Associates misled other Clark creditors to their detriment. *See, e.g., Matter of CTS Truss, Inc.*, 868 F.2d 146, 149 (5th Cir. 1989) (lender did not represent to third parties that additional financing was in place or that debtor was solvent, when the opposite was true).

When the foregoing factors are considered, there is no basis for finding inequitable conduct upon which equitable subordination can be based. We therefore conclude that the district court erred in affirming the bankruptcy court's decision to subordinate Associates' claims.

* * *

NOTE

For a case in which the court concluded equitable subordination was appropriate, see *In re Winstar Communications, Inc.*, 554 F.3d 382 (3d Cir. 2009).

Problem 3-20

Now that you have read a bit about waiver, estoppel, and lender liability, revisit Problem 3-2. If you were First Bank's counsel, what advice would you give with respect to its desire to call in the loan? Is there anything you should have put into the security agreement that could have helped First Bank?

C. Marshaling

Marshaling is an equitable doctrine that junior lienors can occasionally use against senior lienors to force the senior to leave some or all of the collateral for the benefit of the junior. It applies when a senior secured party or other senior lienor has several different items of collateral that could be used to satisfy the debt. In such cases, the junior lienor may obtain a court order requiring the senior to first go after the items in which the junior lienor does *not* have an interest, so as to free up equity in the items of collateral in which the junior does have an interest.[86] This concept can be illustrated by the following example.

Assume First Bank has a first priority security interest in two assets, A and B, to secure $25,000 in debt. Asset A is worth $10,000 and Asset B is worth $20,000. Second Bank has a second priority security interest in Asset

---

[86] *See* In re King, 305 B.R. 152, 169-70 (Bankr. S.D. N.Y. 2004).

B to secure $5,000 in debt and no security interest in Asset A. The parties' relationship to the collateral could be diagramed as follows:

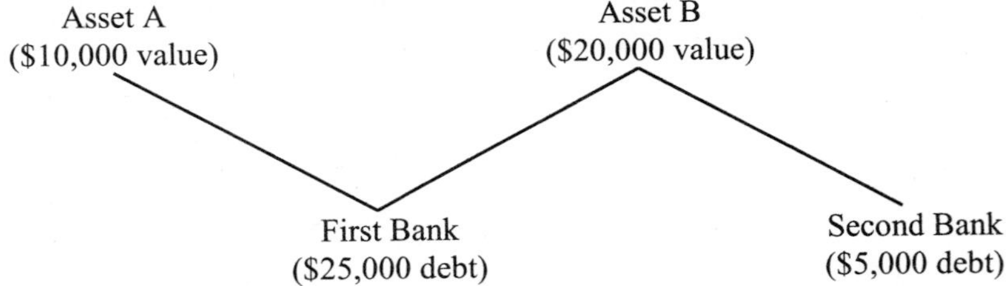

If First Bank began enforcing its security interest by selling Asset B for $20,000, First Bank's action would wipe out Second Bank's security interest in Asset B, § 9-617(a), without generating any proceeds for Second Bank, § 9-615(a). First Bank could then enforce its security interest in Asset A for the remaining $5,000 owed, but any resulting surplus would go to the debtor, not to Second Bank, because Second Bank has no security interest in Asset A. As a result, Second Bank would become an unsecured creditor relegated to the judgment and execution process described in Chapter One in order to collect. To avoid this, Second Bank could seek a judicial order compelling First Bank to marshal against Asset A: that is, to enforce its security interest by foreclosing against Asset A before proceeding against Asset B. If First Bank foreclosed in that order, it would realize $10,000 from the foreclosure of Asset A towards the obligation owed to it. When it then enforced its security interest against Asset B, only $15,000 would be remaining due to First Bank. If First Bank sold Asset B for $20,000, the resulting $5,000 surplus would be distributed to Second Bank, provided Second Bank made the appropriate demand for a share of the proceeds. § 9-615(a).

Marshaling is an equitable doctrine to which there are several equitable defenses and limitations. For example, it will not be applied to the detriment of the senior lienor, such as might result if marshaling would cause delay in proceeding against quickly depreciating collateral. It will also normally not be available to force a creditor to foreclose on the debtor's homestead. It will not be available if the different items of collateral were provided by different debtors.[87] Finally, it is unavailable if another junior lienor would be prejudiced. For example, continuing with the illustration above, if Third Bank had a subordinate security interest in

[87] *See* In re Global Serv. Group, LLC, 316 B.R. 451 (Bankr. S.D.N.Y. 2004).

Asset A for $4,000, no marshaling order would be available. After all, the same principle which would entitle Second Bank to force First Bank to go against Asset A (to free up equity in Asset B) would also entitle Third Bank to force First Bank to go against Asset B (to free up equity in Asset A). In essence, the competing equities and interests of Second Bank and Third Bank cancel each other out, with the result that courts will not get involved.

One thing courts are divided on is whether marshaling is available when the debtor is in bankruptcy. On the one hand, the Bankruptcy Code gives the bankruptcy trustee the rights of a creditor with a judicial lien on all of the debtor's assets.[88] This suggests that a junior lienor cannot force a senior to marshal against assets of the estate because that would prejudice a junior lienor: the trustee. On the other hand, the trustee's status as judicial lien creditor exists not to protect the trustee, but to facilitate the trustee's representation of the unsecured claimants. Unsecured claimants normally have no standing to either make or object to a marshaling request.

Two final points about marshaling are worth noting. First, bear in mind that marshaling is a judicial doctrine and the junior lienor must go to court to obtain this equitable remedy. If the junior lienor waits and the senior goes after the jointly held collateral first, then the junior lienor is simply out of luck. A senior creditor, such as First Bank, does not have a duty to "marshal" and the junior creditor has no claim against the senior for breach of a fiduciary obligation.[89]

Second, it is not uncommon for senior lienors, at the inception of their transaction with the debtor, to attempt to avoid any later obligation to marshal by including either a disclaimer of the duty to marshal in its contract with the debtor or a waiver of marshaling rights in an agreement with the junior lienor. Such a waiver in an intercreditor agreement would likely be given effect. Even if the waiver is not binding on a court in equity, such a court is unlikely to exercise its equitable powers to benefit a junior lienor that has expressly agreed to waive marshaling rights. In contrast, it is far from clear that a disclaimer in the senior lienor's contract with the debtor of the duty to marshal would affect the rights of a junior lienor. In general, a contract between two parties has no impact on the rights of third parties. *But cf.* § 9-201(a).

---

[88] *See* 11 U.S.C. § 544(a)(1).

[89] Simmons Foods, Inc. v. Capital City Bank, Inc., 270 B.R. 295 (D. Kan. 2001), *aff'd*, 58 F. App'x 450 (10th Cir. 2003).

Problem 3-21

National Bank has a first priority lien on Digger's home and farming equipment to secure a debt of $100,000. State Bank has a junior lien on the equipment to secure a debt of $60,000 and Savings & Loan has a junior lien on Digger's home to secure a debt of $75,000. The equipment is worth $50,000 and the home is worth $120,000. Is State Bank entitled to a marshaling order against National Bank? If not, what can State Bank do to protect its interests?

D. Bankruptcy

When a secured party begins enforcement efforts after the debtor defaults, the secured party typically seeks to repossess or collect on the collateral in which it has an interest. When the debtor is engaged in business, such an enforcement action often interferes with the debtor's business and sometimes makes continuation of that business impossible. Even if a court later determines that the secured party's efforts were wrongful (*i.e.*, that the debtor was not in default or that the secured party breached the peace in repossessing the collateral), that judgment will not resurrect a business as a going concern. Thus, a failing business debtor's typical response to the secured party's collection efforts is to file for bankruptcy protection.

If the debtor is an individual, the secured party is less likely to have a security interest on all of the debtor's personal property (often referred to as a "blanket lien," because it covers everything) and instead have a security interest in only some particular items. Nevertheless, a repossession effort might trigger a bankruptcy filing if the collection efforts are against critical items, such as a car or a manufactured home.

Most security agreements and loan agreements treat filing for bankruptcy protection as a default and provide that such a default accelerates the due date of all amounts owing. Even if the agreements do not so provide, the debt is in fact accelerated so as to be currently due because of the manner in which "claims" are defined and treated.[90]

What happens next and how the secured party extracts value from the collateral depends on many things. Chief among them are the type of bankruptcy proceeding and whether the debtor has any equity in the collateral.

---

[90] *See* 11 U.S.C. § 101(5) (definition of claim), § 501 (ability to file a claim), § 502 (allowance of claim).

In Chapter 7 cases, if the collateral is worth more than the total of the claims it secures and any exemption amount to which the debtor is entitled, then the collateral is of value to the estate and the trustee has an incentive to maximize the price at which it is sold. Accordingly the trustee will conduct the sale. Often the trustee will sell the collateral subject to the secured party's lien, in which case the secured party will have to deal with the buyer when seeking to enforce its rights. However, the trustee is also authorized to sell the collateral free and clear of liens provided the trustee adequately protects the interest of the secured party.[91] As a practical matter, this means the lienholder will be paid the amount of its claim from the proceeds of the sale.

If the property is worth less than the debt owed to the secured creditors and any exemption amount to which the debtor is entitled, the trustee will probably abandon the property or can be forced to abandon it.[92] This will remove the property from the bankruptcy estate and effectively return the estate's interest in the property to the debtor. The automatic stay still applies, because it protects property of the debtor as well as property of the estate.[93] At this point, one of four things will occur: reaffirmation, redemption, repossession, or – perhaps – retention.

Reaffirmation. In some cases, particularly when the debtor has built up a substantial amount of exempt equity in the collateral, the debtor might wish to reaffirm the debt. This allows the debtor to keep the collateral while making periodic payments to the secured creditor. In essence, the debt as reaffirmed will not be discharged in the bankruptcy proceeding.[94] If the debtor defaults after bankruptcy, the secured creditor may exercise all of its nonbankruptcy remedies with regard to the collateral, including repossession and foreclosure. More significantly, the creditor may attempt to collect any deficiency from the debtor, since the debtor will remain obligated on the underlying obligation.

Reaffirmation is often the only feasible means for a Chapter 7 debtor to retain possession of desired collateral. Yet it has its drawbacks. First, the creditor will almost certainly require the debtor to reaffirm the entire obligation. For example, if a debt for $8,000 were secured by a lien on a car worth only $6,000, the debtor

---

[91] 11 U.S.C. § 363(e), (f).

[92] 11 U.S.C. § 554.

[93] 11 U.S.C. § 362(a)(5).

[94] *See* 11 U.S.C. § 524(c).

would likely have to promise to pay the entire $8,000 debt, perhaps with interest, costs, and the creditor's attorney's fees added on. Thus, reaffirmation generally makes economic sense only with respect to property in which the debtor has equity. Second, reaffirmation requires the consent of the creditor. Some lenders prefer to cut their losses and terminate relationships with bankrupt borrowers. Reaffirmation cannot be imposed upon them. Third, reaffirmation requires an affidavit from the debtor's counsel that the reaffirmed obligation will not impose an undue hardship on the debtor, or if the debtor is not represented by counsel, approval of the court based on a finding of no undue hardship.

Redemption. The second option some debtors have in a Chapter 7 proceeding is to redeem the property.[95] To redeem, the debtor must pay the lienor the amount of the "allowed secured claim." That amount is limited by the value of the collateral. Thus, using the example above of an $8,000 debt secured by a lien on a $6,000 car, the debtor could redeem the car by paying the secured creditor $6,000 in cash. The debtor need not pay the $2,000 balance; that is treated as an unsecured claim in the bankruptcy case, and will usually be discharged following whatever distributions the trustee makes.

Redemption is far from a panacea for debtors, however. First, the debtor must come up with the necessary cash; the debtor is not permitted to redeem in installments.[96] Of course, most bankrupt debtors do not have a ready supply of cash. To get it, they must normally either borrow it or convert some of their exempt and unencumbered property into a liquid form. The first option might prove impossible, because bankruptcy debtors have great difficulty finding willing lenders, and the second might be undesirable.

Second, redemption is available only in limited circumstances. It applies only to individual debtors and covers only tangible personal property that is intended primarily for personal, family, or household purposes. It is unavailable to corporate debtors and cannot be used either for real property or for property used in a business. Moreover, the property must be either wholly exempt or have been abandoned by the trustee and the secured obligation must be for a consumer debt that is dischargeable in the bankruptcy process. For the most part, redemption is a paper right that is rarely exercised.

---

[95] 11 U.S.C. § 722.

[96] *See id.*

Repossession. By far the most common thing that happens to the collateral is repossession. Secured claimants do not relish the idea of waiting an extended period of time before they get paid, and thus are often eager to enforce their liens, using whatever nonbankruptcy rights they have. Most debtors in bankruptcy have already defaulted on their obligations and have no ability or desire to try to cure those defaults. A note of caution for the creditor is in order, however. Even though secured claimants in a Chapter 7 case are not paid by the trustee, or indeed out of the bankruptcy estate at all, they are subject to the automatic stay. The stay enjoins not only acts to collect from the debtor but also specifically prohibits acts against the collateral.[97]

Thus, a secured party intent on enforcing its rights against the collateral after the debtor has filed bankruptcy must get relief from the automatic stay. This is so even if the secured party has managed to repossess the collateral prior to the filing of the bankruptcy petition. Until the debtor's rights in the collateral have been foreclosed pursuant to the Article 9 process for disposition or acceptance, the debtor retains sufficient rights in the collateral for it to be part of the debtor's bankruptcy estate and thus subject to the automatic stay.[98] This is true even if the secured party obtained a certificate of title in the secured party's own name in anticipation of the need to convey a clean certificate of title in a subsequent disposition of the collateral. *See* § 9-619.[99] Not only is collateral that the secured party repossessed before the petition still subject to the stay, but one circuit court has ruled that a creditor violates the stay simply by refusing to return the property to the debtor post-petition.[100] Several other courts have followed this decision.[101] About the

---

[97] 11 U.S.C. § 362(a)(4), (5).

[98] *See* In re Moffett, 356 F.3d 518 (4th Cir. 2004).

[99] In re Estis, 311 B.R. 592 (Bankr. D. Kan. 2004); In re Robinson, 285 B.R. 732 (Bankr. W.D. Okla. 2002).

[100] *See* In re Knaus, 889 F.2d 773 (8th Cir. 1989).

[101] *E.g.*, In re Sharon, 234 B.R. 676 (6th Cir. BAP 1999) (rejecting assertion that the creditor's right to adequate protection allows it to retain possession until such protection is provided); In re Abrams, 127 B.R. 239, 241 (9th Cir. BAP 1991). *See also* In re Del Mission Ltd., 98 F.3d 1147, 1151 (9th Cir. 1996) (state violated stay by not paying to debtor taxes it was ordered to return); Commercial Credit Corp. v. Reed, 154 B.R. 471 (E.D. Tex. 1993) (because creditor returned property within 19½ hours, violation of the stay was not willful). *But cf.* In re Boggan, 251 B.R. 95 (9th Cir. BAP 2000) (§ 362(b)(3) might protect a creditor whose statutory lien is contingent on possession from having to relinquish possession).

same number have criticized it or otherwise ruled to the contrary.[102] The issue therefore remains sufficiently clouded that secured parties in possession of collateral should be very cautious, particularly given the damages potentially available to an aggrieved debtor.[103]

A secured party is entitled to relief from the stay either: (i) for cause, including the lack of adequate protection of the secured claimant's interest in the property; or (ii) if the debtor has no equity in the property and the property is not necessary to a successful reorganization.[104] In Chapter 7 cases, "cause" and lack of adequate protection are rarely an issue. Instead, secured creditors in Chapter 7 liquidations typically seek relief under the second prong because the property is by definition not needed for a successful reorganization. Relief for them therefore depends on whether the property is worth more than the debt. In most cases it is not, and the secured party obtains quick relief from the stay, repossesses the property using its nonbankruptcy rights, and then forecloses its lien by selling the property under whatever nonbankruptcy rules are applicable. Even if relief from the stay is not available, perhaps because the debtor has exempt equity in the property, as soon as the stay expires,[105] the secured party may take whatever steps are permissible under non-bankruptcy law to enforce its lien.

Retention. If a Chapter 7 debtor is not in default on the secured obligation, the debtor might be permitted to simply retain the collateral and continue to make

---

[102] *E.g.*, In re Kalter, 292 F.3d 1350 (11th Cir. 2002) (secured party had right to possession of and title to repossessed automobile; debtor's mere right to redemption did not make car property of the estate under Florida law); In re Lewis, 137 F.3d 1280 (11th Cir. 1998) (same based on Alabama law); In re Diaz, 416 B.R. 902 (Bankr. S.D. Fla. 2009) (despite the 2001 amendments to Article 9, *Kalter* remains good law); In re Bernstein, 252 B.R. 846 (Bankr. D.D.C. 2000) (passive retention of possession is not an "act" to exercise control); In re Massey, 210 B.R. 693 (Bankr. D. Md. 1997) (creditor entitled to retain possession pending court determination that adequate protection has been provided). *But see* In re Moffett, 356 F.3d 518 (4th Cir. 2004) (rejecting the Eleventh Circuit's analysis in *Lewis* and concluding that the debtor's redemption rights do make the collateral property of the estate). *See also* Thomas E. Plank, *The Creditor in Possession under the Bankruptcy Code: History, Text, and Policy*, 59 MD. L. REV. 253, 314 n.299 (2000) (referring to rulings that such conduct does violate the stay as "the most egregious examples of judicial misunderstanding of the stay and property of the estate").

[103] *See* 11 U.S.C. § 362(k).

[104] 11 U.S.C. § 362(d).

[105] 11 U.S.C. § 362(c).

payments as they become due. However, the issue rests on some language of the Bankruptcy Code that is rather difficult to interpret and courts are divided on whether this practice is permitted.[106]

Reorganization. Reorganization proceedings under Chapter 11 and 13 operate very differently from Chapter 7 liquidations. Both involve proposing and confirming a reorganization plan. Of course, even before a plan is proposed, a secured claimant may seek relief from the stay. In reorganization proceedings, both grounds for stay relief can be relevant. Relief from the stay is often available under the first prong, for cause, including lack of adequate protection. Whether it is available usually hinges on the degree of risk to the secured party's secured claim. Such risks include depreciation of the collateral through use of the collateral, failure to maintain adequate insurance on the collateral, and dissipation of the collateral. However, a court might find other ways to protect the secured party's interests in the collateral rather than simply by lifting the stay so as to permit repossession and foreclosure. For example, the court might require the debtor to procure and maintain insurance or to make periodic debt service payments to the secured party to compensate for the risk of depreciation.[107]

Relief from the stay under the second prong requires two things: that the debtor have no equity in the collateral *and* that the collateral not be necessary to an effective reorganization. The second prong is often very difficult for the secured party to meet and courts will usually accept – at least for a while – the debtor's representation about what property is needed. However, the court might grant relief if it concludes that the debtor cannot confirm a reorganization plan within a reasonable time.

If the secured party cannot obtain relief from the stay, the reorganization plan will dictate when and how the secured party will be paid and what happens to the collateral. In a Chapter 11 proceeding, the plan may call for de-acceleration of the debt, curing any default, and reinstating of the original payment schedule. If so, the secured party is deemed "unimpaired" and does not have the right to vote on the reorganization plan.[108] If, instead, the plan calls for a different payment schedule, perhaps with a lower interest rate or longer payment period, the secured party's claim is considered impaired and the secured party will be entitled to vote on the

---

[106] *See* In re Dumont, 581 F.3d 1104 (9th Cir. 2009).

[107] 11 U.S.C. § 361.

[108] 11 U.S.C. § 1124(2).

plan. This right to vote gives the creditor significant bargaining leverage; in most cases a plan can be confirmed only if all classes of creditors vote in favor of the plan.[109] Moreover, the secured creditor agrees otherwise, the creditor must receive over the life of the plan payments that have a present value at least equal to the amount of the secured claim and the creditor must retain a lien on the property for the amount of the secured claim.[110]

In a Chapter 13 proceeding, the debtor might similarly propose to cure a default and reinstate the original payment schedule.[111] The debtor might also propose a different schedule for paying off the secured debt during the plan period. Unlike in most Chapter 11 cases, however, a secured party in a Chapter 13 proceeding does not get to vote on the debtor's proposal. Nevertheless, the secured creditor receives substantial protection. The reorganization plan cannot be confirmed unless the secured party has agreed to the payment proposal, the debtor surrenders the collateral to the secured party, or the secured party retains its lien on the collateral for the amount of its secured claim and receives payments under the plan equal to the present value of the amount of the secured claim.[112] This last requirement occasionally poses a significant challenge for the debtor. Chapter 13 plans are not permitted to last longer than five years yet sometimes the debtor will not have enough cash flow to pay the present value of the amount of the secured claim over a five-year period. In such cases, the debtor is somewhat at the mercy of the

---

[109] There is a process – referred to as "cramdown" – for confirming a plan even if one or more classes of creditors votes against the plan. Because it is nearly impossible for the debtor's prepetition owners to retain their ownership in the reorganized debtor following a cramdown, the process is rarely used. However, in 2019, Congress created a new Subchapter 5 of Chapter 11 of the Bankruptcy Code, which became effective in February 2020. *See* §§ 1181–1195. Subchapter 5 is designed to provide small businesses and individuals with primarily business debts a faster and less expensive process for reorganizing. The process is restricted to debtors with noncontingent, liquidated debts of no more than $7.5 million. *See* 11 U.S.C. § 1182(1). Under Subchapter 5, creditors do not vote on the plan or reorganization. Instead, the court will confirm the debtor's plan if the plan meets specified requirements, including that all of the debtor's projected disposable income for at least three years (or property with equivalent value) will be used to pay prepetition creditors. *See* § 1191.

[110] 11 U.S.C. § 1129(b)(2)(A).

[111] 11 U.S.C. § 1322(b)(2), (3), (5).

[112] 11 U.S.C. § 1325(a)(5).

secured creditor. Without the creditor's consent, the debtor will have to surrender the collateral.

There are numerous requirements for confirming a reorganization plan in both a Chapter 11 case and a Chapter 13 case. A full exploration of these requirements must await a course on bankruptcy law. For now, the following chart gives some comparison of the effect of a bankruptcy proceeding on an Article 9 secured party.

COMPARISON OF DIFFERENT BANKRUPTCY PROCEEDINGS

	Chapter 7	Chapter 11	Chapter 13
Description	Liquidation	Reorganization	Individual Debt Adjustment
Process	Nonexempt assets are liquidated and proceeds distributed to unsecured creditors. Most remaining debts of individual debtors are discharged.	Debtor proposes for court and creditor approval a plan for generating income and paying at least the liquidation amount of debts over time. Most remaining debts are discharged.	Debtor proposes a plan to pay at least the liquidation amount of all debts out of future disposable income. Most remaining debts are discharged.
Who Controls	Trustee.	The debtor, as debtor in possession, but monitored by a committee of creditors.	Trustee collects and disburses funds, but debtor generally manages affairs pursuant to plan.
Duration	Usually less than six months.	Traditionally, one or more years, more recently faster.[113]	Usually three or five years.
Treatment of Secured Debts	Lien survives and generally dealt with outside the bankruptcy process.	Obligations often modified, but creditor's interest in collateral is protected.	Obligations often modified, but creditor's interest in collateral is protected.

---

[113] The shorter periods are attributable a variety of developments, including the growing use plans negotiated before the petition, the use of Chapter 11 to liquidate quickly, and the enactment of legislation to streamline reorganization of small businesses.

	Chapter 7	Chapter 11	Chapter 13
Benefits to Debtor	Quick and easy way to discharge debts.	Maintain control.	Keep nonexempt assets and can get expanded discharge.

Problem 3-22

Six months ago, First Bank loaned Driver $12,000 to purchase a new car and Driver granted First Bank a security interest in the car to secure the loan. Driver made the first two monthly payments on time but has remitted nothing since then. Efforts to repossess the car were unsuccessful, so last week First Bank obtained a writ of replevin from the local Superior Court directing the sheriff to seize the car and deliver it to First Bank. Yesterday, Driver filed for Chapter 7 bankruptcy protection. Which of the following would violate the automatic stay?

A. Delivering the writ of replevin to the sheriff and having the sheriff execute it. If the writ had been delivered to the sheriff last week and the sheriff were planning on enforcing it today, could First Bank simply stand by and allow that to occur?

B. Filing a proof of claim. 11 U.S.C. § 501.

C. Sending Driver a monthly statement indicating the amount outstanding on the loan.

D. Sending Driver a letter requesting reaffirmation of the debt.

E. Asking the district attorney to prosecute Driver for fraud in connection with the loan transaction. *See* 11 U.S.C. § 362(b)(1).

F. What difference, if any, does it make to each of the questions above if First Bank is unaware that Driver has filed a bankruptcy petition? *See* 11 U.S.C. § 362(a), (k).

SECTION 7. CONCLUSION

Now that we have covered the secured party's rights – and potential liability – in connection with enforcing a security interest, it is time to consider what if anything the security agreement should say about such matters.

Problem 3-23

A. You are general counsel for First Bank. What provisions should the bank include in its standard form security agreement that might protect it from liability arising from its enforcement of a security interest? *See* §§ 9-602, 9-603 and 9-624.

B. First Bank has asked its outside counsel to draft a manual for its loan officers to follow when enforcing security interests. The manual should describe the procedures to follow, discuss the issues that frequently arise in enforcement of security interests, and provide general advice that will help First Bank avoid liability to the debtor and others when enforcing its security interests. As the first step in drafting that manual, the law firm has turned to you – one of the new associates – to identify the ten things that loan officers should most be concerned about when enforcing a security interest and to describe what the loan officers should do or refrain from doing with respect to each. In making your selection, consider the frequency or likelihood that the issue or problem will arise as well as the potential and degree of First Bank's liability for error.

Another way – other than through express terms in the security agreement – to enhance the secured party's rights in commercial loan transactions is through the use of a dual-debtor structure. This structure requires that there be at least two entities, one of which is a subsidiary of the other, and the subsidiary be the entity with the principal assets to serve as collateral. In essence, one or more lenders makes a loan secured by both the subsidiary's assets and by the parent's ownership interest in the subsidiary. The following diagram illustrates the transaction, with Holding Company as the parent and Operating Company as the subsidiary:

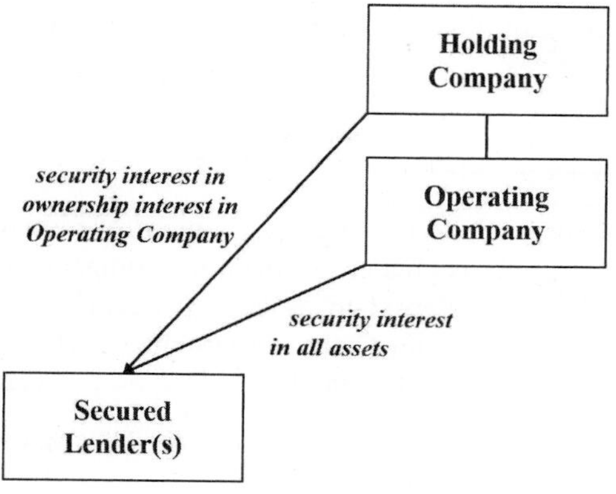

Note, the parent-subsidiary relationship might predate the secured loan or might be created in connection with the loan. In other words, the lender or lenders might, as a condition of making the loan, require the borrower to create a subsidiary and to contribute its assets to the subsidiary. Note also, at least for the purposes of this discussion, that it does not matter to which entity the loan is made. The loan could be made to Holding Company and guaranteed by Operating Company or it could be made to Operating Company and guaranteed by Holding Company.[114]

There at least three *potential* benefits to this dual-debtor structure. First, if some valuable assets of Operating Company have a restriction on transfer that Article 9 will not override – FCC broadcast licenses, for example – this structure can allow the secured party to get at least an indirect access to the value of those assets by encumbering Holding Company's ownership interest in Operating Company. That said, there might be, in addition to a restriction on the transfer of Operating Company's assets, a restriction on a change of control of Holding Company, which could be triggered by a foreclosure of Holding Company's ownership interest in Operating Company. So, the applicable law would need to be examined closely before this structure is used in an effort to bypass restrictions on transfer. Moreover, getting a security interest in Holding Company's ownership interest in Operating Company would not, by itself, prevent Operating Company from selling or otherwise dissipating its assets.

Second, if the security agreement so provides and neither Operating Company's organizational documents nor the law applicable to the those documents provides otherwise, the secured party can, upon default, exercise Holding Company's rights to vote its ownership interest in or to manage the operations of Operating Company.[115] The secured party right could, at least theoretically, use this power to prevent Operating Company from filing a bankruptcy petition or to compel Operating Company to consent to a proposed acceptance of collateral. However, there is a significant amount of case law refusing to permit a creditor from blocking

---

[114] The risk that a guarantee – and the guarantor's grant of a security interest – will be avoided as a fraudulent transfer is greater if Operating Company guarantees a loan to the Holding Company (commonly referred to as an "upstream" guaranty) and if Holding Company guarantees a loan to Operating Company (commonly referred to as a "downstream" guaranty). *See, e.g.*, In re Image Worldwide, Ltd., 139 F.3d 574 (7th Cir. 1998).

[115] *See* Stephen L. Sepinuck. *Giving Secured Parties the Right to Vote Pledged Equity*, 13 THE TRANSACTIONAL LAW. 1 (Feb. 2023).

a debtor's right to file a bankruptcy petition.[116] Similarly, it is far from clear that a court would allow a secured party, through its exercise of control over a debtor, to compel the debtor to consent to an acceptance of collateral. Allowing it would make the concept of "consent" meaningless and would presumably be subject to attack under applicable corporate law,[117] and possible as a breach of the duty of good faith.

Third, and perhaps most important, the structure can expedite and simplify the foreclosure process. For example, Operating Company's assets might include goods scattered across the country and in various states of disrepair. In such circumstances, it might be challenging to conduct a commercially reasonable disposition of the goods. At a minimum, there would be some uncertainty about whether a sale would be commercially reasonable if the secured party failed to make the goods available to prospective purchasers or failed to repair the goods prior to the sale. By using this structure, the secured party could foreclose on Holding Company's ownership interest in Operating Company, rather than on Operating Company's assets, and thereby avoid all that uncertainty. If, as is likely, the secured party acquired the ownership interest in Operating Company, it could then deal with Operating Company's assets as owner, rather than as a secured party. Alternatively or additionally, Operating Company's assets might include real property, for which the applicable foreclosure process is slow and expensive. The secured party could – in a matter of days – conduct an Article 9 disposition of Holding Company's ownership interest in Operating Company, *see* § 9-612(b), and thereby avoid the lengthy real property foreclosure process, including and any post-

---

[116] *See* In re Intervention Energy Holdings, LLC, 553 B.R. 258 (Bankr. D. Del. 2016) (an amendment to the debtor's LLC operating agreement which made the debtor's secured lender a member of the LLC, required the unanimous consent of all members to file a bankruptcy petition, and eliminated the lender's fiduciary duties as a member was tantamount to an absolute waiver of the LLC's right to seek bankruptcy protection and thus void as against federal public policy); In re Lexington Hospitality Group, LLC, 577 B.R. 676 (Bankr. E.D. Ky. 2017) (similar); In re Lake Mich. Beach Pottawattamie Resort LLC, 547 B.R. 899 (Bankr. N.D. Ill. 2016) (similar). *But cf.* In re DB Cap. Holdings, LLC, 463 B.R. 142 (10th Cir. BAP 2010) (dismissing a Chapter 11 case on the ground that the debtor's manager was not authorized to file the bankruptcy petition; the debtor's LLC agreement had been amended at the demand of the debtor's main lender to prohibit the debtor from filing for bankruptcy).

[117] *See* Kleeberg v. Eber, 2020 WL 4586904 (S.D.N.Y. 2020) (even though an acceptance of collateral was completed pursuant to Article 9, that was not a bar to unwinding the transaction if it resulted from a breach of fiduciary duty by the secured party that was both a trustee and a beneficiary of the trust that was the indirect owner of the debtor).

sale, statutory right of redemption Operating Company might have. In essence, the dual-debtor structure allows a secured party to bypass the real property foreclosure process and its numerous debtor protections. Wow![118]

Test Your Knowledge
Exam Four – Enforcement

[118] Although some have criticized the use of the dual-debtor structure to achieve these results, *see, e.g.*, Martin A. Schwartz, *Legal Magic: Turning Real Property Foreclosures into Uniform Commercial Code Sales*, 94 FLA. BAR J. 39 (May/June 2020), what little case law exists suggests that the process works. *See, e.g.*, Wickapogue 1 LLC v. Blue Castle (Cayman) Ltd., 2023 WL 2071291 (E.D.N.Y. 2023) (an individual who pledged, as security for a loan to an LLC, her 100% interest in the LLC was not entitled to a preliminary injunction against a public sale of her interest; the planned sale of her interest did not clog the equitable right of redemption for the real property that the LLC had mortgaged to secure the loan because the individual had a statutory right to redeem her interest in the LLC prior to the sale; and the balance of hardships did not weigh in the individual's favor even though the LLC allegedly had substantial equity in the real property); HH Cincinnati Textile L.P. v. Acres Cap. Servicing LLC, 2018 N.Y. Misc. LEXIS 2472 (N.Y. Sup. Ct. 2018).

CHAPTER FOUR
PERFECTION OF SECURITY INTERESTS

SECTION 1. OVERVIEW OF PERFECTION

In the previous Chapters we learned what it takes to attach and enforce a security interest. In this Chapter we consider what it takes to perfect such an interest. Perfection refers to the process the secured party uses to protect and preserve its priority in the collateral, particularly from those who might later acquire an interest in it. We have already seen in some of the enforcement rules the benefit of priority. *See, e.g.*, §§ 9-608(a), 9-615(a) (providing that the obligation to a foreclosing senior lienor is paid in full out of the proceeds of the collateral before the proceeds are used to pay junior lienors at all). As a general rule, a risk-averse creditor will want as high a priority as possible for its lien on the debtor's asset in order to decrease the risk of non-payment.

Establishing priority depends on several things. The two most important are: (i) the order in which the interests were created – that is, attached; and (ii) whether those interests are perfected. It is vital to remember, though, that perfection has no impact on the secured party's rights against the debtor. Failure to perfect a security interest does not prevent the secured party from determining that the debtor is in default or from disposing of or collecting on the collateral. Put simply, attachment is all a secured party needs to have a security interest that is enforceable against the debtor. Perfection is what the secured party needs to establish the priority of its security interest against the remainder of the world.[1]

In general, perfection of a security interest requires just two things: attachment plus satisfaction of one other applicable step. Read § 9-308(a), (b). That applicable step – known as a perfection method – is, in many instances, the provision of some form of notice to the commercial world of the secured party's interest in the collateral. It is the rough equivalent for personal property of what recording a mortgage is for real property.

---

1 Although § 9-201(a) states that a security agreement is effective against other creditors of the debtor and purchasers of the collateral, this general principle is subject to the many priority rules we will study in Chapter Five, most of which require the security interest to be perfected to have priority over the rights of such third parties.

Why is such notice needed? For the same reason mortgages must be recorded. Whenever a lien exists on property, there are at least two "owners" of the collateral: the debtor and the lienholder. Because only one of them (usually the debtor) will be in possession or control of the property, and thus appear to the world to be the full owner, there is something of an "ostensible ownership" problem: one party appears to have full rights in the property when in reality some of the rights are owned by another entity.

This creates a potential problem. If the debtor remains in possession of the property, what is to stop the debtor from selling it – or granting another lien on it – to an innocent third party? How is that third party to know of the existing lien? One possible solution is to say that the third party need not worry; that a subsequent buyer or lienor will take free of an existing lienor's rights. However, such a result would mean that the existing lienor's rights are effectively subject to forfeiture for reasons beyond its control and the goal of having collateral – greater certainty of repayment – is not satisfied.

A second possible solution is to say *caveat emptor*: buyer beware. First in time is first in right. The debtor cannot sell or pledge the property free of an existing lienor's rights. That indeed would be consistent with much of property law generally. But then there would still be a problem. Instead of the first lienor having to worry about losing its lien, or at least losing its priority, a buyer or second lienor would have to bear the risk that did not acquire all the rights in the property that it expected to acquire because the debtor did not have all the rights in the property and the remaining rights-holders did not join in the conveyance. Without some way to reliably determine if there is a valid preexisting lien with a superior rights in the collateral, a buyer or subsequent lienor would lack the ability to determine whether or how much value to give in exchange for rights in the property.

Article 9 is really about this whole problem: the apparently "secret" ownership rights of a secured party and the resulting need to provide notice of the secured party's lien to persons interested in acquiring a security interest in or buying the collateral. To provide this notice, Article 9 creates a type of recording system for personal property.

Do not take the analogy to a real property recording system too far, though. The rules on how to provide notice of a lien on personal property are, by necessity, much more complex than the rules governing real estate. To be sure, some types of personal property (*e.g.*, fixtures) are very similar or related to realty. Accordingly, we might expect or want the notice system for ownership interests in such property to be connected to the real estate recording system, which is based on the location of the property.

However, many other kinds of personal property move (*e.g.*, aircraft, ships, motor vehicles) – or worse, are entirely intangible (*e.g.*, accounts, copyrights) – and thus a recording system organized by property location will not work for them. Perhaps for these types of property we will need a system based on the location of the debtor. Beyond that, many kinds of personal property are in a constant state of transmutation. For example, inventory is sold to generate accounts, which are paid by check, which are then deposited into a bank account, the funds from which might be withdrawn to buy equipment. As we have seen, the security interest remains attached to the debtor's property throughout these transmutations through the rules relating to proceeds. *See* § 9-315(a)(2). Thus, a recording system organized by type of property will not work. Finally, recording systems are likely to be totally inconsistent with the basic concepts underlying the existing mechanisms for transferring rights in some types of property (*e.g.*, money or negotiable instruments). Perhaps notice for such property will have to be provided through possession.

To deal with all these complexities, Article 9 has five different perfection methods:

(1) Filing a financing statement in the appropriate government office;
(2) Taking possession of the collateral;
(3) Acquiring control of the collateral;
(4) Mere attachment of the security interest (that is, the security interest is automatically perfected upon attachment); and
(5) Complying with some other law that determines how to perfect.

The appropriate method of perfection depends on the type of collateral. For some collateral types, only one method of perfection is permitted. For others, there are two or more permissible methods of perfection. When that is the case, the different perfection methods might result in different priorities. Although lawyers and lenders would naturally begin their analysis and planning of a particular transaction by determining the proper (or most preferable) method to perfect, we will defer discussion of that issue until Section 3 of this Chapter. Instead, we will begin our exploration of perfection in Section 2 by studying the dominant method of perfecting a security interest: filing a financing statement. Section 3 then covers the other four perfection methods and the choice of which perfection method to use, with the understanding that use of one of these alternatives might accord the security interest a higher priority.

Section 4 of this Chapter covers Article 9's choice-of-law rules that govern the perfection step. Because Article 9 is enacted at the state level, it needs to and does contain choice-of-law rules for when a transaction or a dispute could implicate the law of two or more states. These rules provide an occasional wrinkle in determining how to perfect a security interest.

Finally, Section 5 of this Chapter addresses the question of how to maintain perfection of a security interest if something changes after the secured party initially perfects. Such changes might concern the debtor, the secured party, the collateral, or the amount secured. In short, a secured party should not "perfect it and forget it." The secured party needs to be vigilant to maintain perfection of its security interest, and thus protect its interest in collateral from any claims of third parties.

As you embark upon the study of the perfection methods required or allowed by Article 9, keep in mind the big picture. Taking the perfection step in relation to a security interest is not necessary for the secured party to enforce the security interest against the debtor. The perfection step is relevant to the priority of the security interest as against other parties' interests in the same piece of property. Thus, understanding the perfection rules explored in this Chapter sets the stage for study of the priority rules in Chapter Five.

Because perfection relates to priority, from here on the debtor is only a bit player in our story. Perfection and priority are about the secured party's rights to the collateral relative to the rights of other secured parties, lien creditors, buyers, donees, statutory lienors, and the bankruptcy trustee. When two or more of these parties start fighting over the collateral, the debtor rarely has much of an interest (beyond that of spectator) in who wins. One consequence of this is that all of the normal equitable principles that underlie the rules governing the creditor-debtor relationship have little or no bearing on perfection and priority issues. In short, in Chapters One through Three we made sure to examine most issues from the perspective of both the debtor and the creditor. From now on, the debtor's perspective is almost irrelevant. In Chapters Five and Six, we will examine the priority rules from the perspectives of the two or more competing claimants to which the rules apply, bearing in mind that each claimant wants to have first priority in a particular asset of the debtor. In this Chapter, we will examine perfection rules from the perspective of the secured party and from the perspective of whoever else might have an interest in – or, more likely, might later wish to acquire an interest in – the collateral. In connection with this, bear in mind that each wants not only priority, but also sufficient information to be assured that it has or will have priority.

SECTION 2. FILING A FINANCING STATEMENT AS A METHOD OF PERFECTION

Unless an exception applies, filing a financing statement is the appropriate method for perfecting a security interest. *See* § 9-310(a). That statement should immediately raise two questions. First, what is a financing statement? Second, what does it mean to "file" one?

A financing statement is a one-page document (or its electronic equivalent) in which the secured party identifies itself, the debtor, and the collateral. *See* §§ 9-102(a)(39), 9-502(a). A sample form – one that filing offices must accept – is contained in § 9-521(a). A financing statement's purpose is to provide notice of the secured party's interest in the collateral, so that people later wishing to acquire a security interest in the same property, or wishing to buy the property outright, have a way of learning that someone other than the debtor has rights in the property. To file a financing statement is to present it, with the appropriate filing fee, to the filing office (usually a governmental entity such as the applicable state's secretary of state's office, department of licensing, or a county recorder's office). *See* §§ 9-102(a)(37), 9-501, 9-516(a). If an analogy is helpful, think of a financing statement as a posting on a public message board.

Why not simply require the secured party to inform all interested parties directly of its interest in the collateral? Because, at the time the secured party acquires its security interest, it has no way of identifying who might later wish to acquire an interest in the collateral. A prospective buyer might not come onto the scene for months or years. Similarly, another lender might not even contemplate loaning money to the debtor and acquiring a security interest for a substantial period of time. Even the debtor might not be considering entering into such a transaction. So, we need a system for the secured party to communicate with interested – but unknown – future parties.

This raises the questions of who uses the filing system and how they use it. The main users are consensual secured parties and buyers, although potential lien creditors sometimes also use it before causing the sheriff to levy on property. There is no single answer to how they use it, but in the prototypical situation, a secured party uses the filing system in two distinct ways: to search for prior interests and to record its own interest, thereby leaving a message for those who search later. In essence, most secured parties are both filers and searchers. When acquiring an interest in the collateral they both search for prior interests and file to protect themselves against subsequent ones.

As we go through the remainder of the material on filing, keep these two different roles in mind. Our goal is to understand not only the rules about how to file, but also how those rules affect the search process.

A. The Essential Content of a Financing Statement

Despite their importance in secured transactions, financing statements are really quite simple. Section 9-502(a) requires that a financing statement contain only three pieces of information:[2]

(1) The name of the debtor;
(2) The name of the secured party; and
(3) An indication of the collateral.[3]

The theory underlying such a minimal approach is that financing statements provide inquiry notice. *See* § 9-502 cmt. 2. In other words, they provide just enough

---

2 In an attempt to deal with fraudulently filed financing statements, New Jersey amended its version of § 9-502 in 2015. Among other things, this amendment requires that a financing statement indicate that "the collateral is within the scope of [Article 9]." N.J. Stat. 12A:9-502(a)(3). There are at least three problems with this non-uniform rule.

First, Article 9's scope is expressed in reference to *transactions*, not to *collateral. See* § 9-109. Thus, for example, Article 9 covers a transaction creating a security interest in goods, but not a sale of goods. Consequently, read literally the rule is somewhat nonsensical.

Second, several of the exclusions from scope in § 9-109(d) are difficult to apply, with the result that the filer might not know for sure whether a transaction is within the scope of Article 9. The same uncertainty exists with respect to leases of goods, which might constitute an installment sale with a retained security interest. Article 9 authorizes the filing of a precautionary financing statement in connection with many such transactions, *see* § 9-505, but the filer often cannot – and often does not wish to – represent that the transaction is within the scope of Article 9.

Finally, Article 9 expressly permits the filing of a financing statement that indicates the collateral as "all assets" or "all personal property." *See* § 9-504(2). Such an indication frequently covers property – such as insurance policies and tort claims – that is not and cannot be covered by a transaction within the scope of Article 9.

For an article critical of the New Jersey legislation, see *An Effort to Combat Bogus Financing Statements, New Jersey Amendments to Article 9 Backfire Big-Time*, CLARKS' SECURED TRANSACTIONS MONTHLY 1 (Jan. 2016).

3 A financing statement that covers fixtures in a fixture filing, timber to be cut, or as-extracted collateral must also describe the real property to which the collateral is related, indicate the record owner of the real property (if different from the debtor), and indicate that the statement is to be filed in the real estate records. *See* § 9-502(b).

information to: (i) alert the searcher to inquire further; and (ii) direct the searcher to the source for more information. Indeed, because a financing statement may be filed before a security interest attaches, *see* § 9-502(d), financing statements necessarily do not indicate who *has* an interest in the collateral, merely who *might have* an interest in it. This inquiry notice perspective is a critical difference between the functioning of the Article 9 filing system and most other recording systems, such as those for real estate, aircraft, ships, and copyrights. Keep this inquiry notice function in mind as we further examine the requirements for an effective financing statement. In addition, try to identify what role each piece of essential information has.

1. The Debtor's Name

The debtor's name is the most critical information in a financing statement. That is because financing statements are indexed in the filing office according to the debtor's name. *See* § 9-519(c), (f). That index is what searchers use to find the financing statement. If the name used for the debtor on a financing statement is in error, it might be difficult if not impossible for a subsequent searcher to find the financing statement. For example, imagine that you are contemplating making a secured loan to "Digital Equipment, Inc." To begin your inquiry of whether there are existing security interests, you search the public records for filed financing statements against your prospective debtor. If a previously secured party intending to file against this corporation omitted the first word of the debtor's name, and thereby identified the debtor as "Equipment, Inc." in its financing statement, your search is not likely to uncover that earlier filing.

To deal with this, Article 9 has some detailed rules regarding the debtor's name. First, § 9-503(a) provides guidance on what the debtor's name is. For example, if the debtor is a registered organization, such as a corporation, limited partnership, or limited liability company,[4] its correct name is the name that appears in the public record of the debtor's jurisdiction of organization (in essence, the name on its state-issued "birth" certificate).[5] §§ 9-503(a)(1), 9-102(a)(68).

---

[4] A limited liability partnership is a type of general partnership and thus is not a registered organization. *See* § 9-102 cmt. 11 (as modified by PEB Commentary No. 17 (June 29, 2012)).

[5] In connection with this, note that in some states the name listed on the debtor's organizational documents – *e.g.*, its articles of incorporation – might not perfectly match the

Second, Article 9 has rules on the effect of an error in a financing statement. A financing statement is not rendered ineffective merely because it has a minor error that is not seriously misleading. § 9-506(a). The "seriously misleading" standard, which applies to an error affecting any of the three items of required information in a financing statement, is rather vague. However, subsections (b) and (c) provide greater clarity with respect to an error in the debtor's name. Under these provisions, if a search under the debtor's "correct" name yields a filing with an error in it, then the filing is not seriously misleading because of that error (and thus is effective unless some additional error renders it ineffective). If a search under the debtor's correct name does not produce a previously filed financing statement, that statement is seriously misleading and is not effective.

Because searches are conducted by computer, the filing office's standard search logic is therefore critically important to the efficacy of a filing with an error in the debtor's name. If that search logic will disclose in response to a search request only those filed financing statements that list a name for the debtor that exactly matches the name in the search request, then any filing with a slight error in the debtor's name will be ineffective. For example, in one case a filed financing statement listed the debtor as "Net work Solutions, Inc." but the debtor's correct corporate name was "Network Solutions, Inc." A search conducted pursuant to the filing office's search logic did not turn up the filed financing statement with a space between "Net" and "work." Therefore, the court held that the financing statement with the extra space was insufficient to perfect the secured party's security interest.[6] Similar results have been reached with respect to missing punctuation and typographical errors in the debtor's name.[7]

---

name entered in the state's electronic database of names of registered organizations. The differences might result from error during entry of the name or from a limitation on the size of the name field in the database. To deal with this, Article 9 defines the debtor's name in reference to that appearing in a "public organic record." *See* § 9-102(a)(68). As a result, the correct name is not the name in the electronic database, but the name stated to be the debtor's name on the document filed with or issued by the state to form the registered organization. *See* § 9-102(a)(71).

6 Receivables Purchasing Co. v. R & R Directional Drilling, LLC, 588 S.E.2d 831 (Ga. Ct. App. 2003).

7 *See* In re C.W. Mining Co., 488 B.R. 715 (D. Utah 2013) (financing statements identifying the debtor as "CW Mining Company," rather than as "C. W. Mining Company," its registered name, were ineffective to perfect because a search under the debtor's correct name would not have disclosed the filings that lacked the periods and space); In re PTM

In other states, however, the search logic is much more forgiving. In fact, many UCC filing offices follow the Model Administrative Rules promulgated by the International Association of Commercial Administrators ("IACA"), the professional organization for filing officers.[8] The Model Administrative Rules include rules on search logic. Pursuant to those rules, in the name of an organization:

- All punctuation marks and accents are disregarded;
- All spaces are disregarded;
- No distinction is made between lowercase and uppercase letters;
- The word "the" at the beginning of the debtor's name is disregarded; and
- The character "&" is replaced with the word "and."[9]

Accordingly, if the financing statement against Network Solutions, Inc. had been filed in a jurisdiction that followed these rules, the financing statement would have been effective despite the erroneous space.

The discussion above focused on organizational debtors. Unfortunately, dealing with the name of individual debtors has been more challenging. After all, what is the "correct name" of an individual and how do you ascertain it? Presumably lenders do not want to rely on what the debtor tells them because that undermines the certainty and integrity of the system and creates the potential for fraud. A passport might be a reliable source but many individuals do not have one. The debtor's birth certificate could be the definitive source but many individuals do not actually identify themselves by the name on their birth certificate, preferring instead to use a middle name or nickname for their given name or to use a spouse's surname for their original surname.

Prior to the 2010 amendments to Article 9, courts struggled with this problem. Several ruled that a filed financing statement identifying an individual debtor by a nickname or a shortened version of the debtor's given name was insufficient. Thus, "Mike" instead of "Michael" or "Chris" instead of "Christopher" or "Christine" was

---

Techs., Inc., 452 B.R. 165 (Bankr. M.D.N.C. 2011) (financing statements that omitted the "h" in the debtor's name and which were not disclosed in a "standard" web search but were disclosed in a "non-standard" web search were ineffective to perfect because the filing office's rules provide for an exact word match and the "standard" search is the one that follows these rules).

8 *See* IACA, Model Admin. Rules (2015) (available on the companion web page for the book).

9 *Id.* §§ 503.1.2, 503.1.3.

ineffective to perfect, unless a search under the full name produced the filing.[10] Several of these courts also indicated that the debtor's middle name was required. However, a few courts treated filings that used a nickname or shortened version of a personal name as effective if that was the name the debtor customarily used.[11]

It is fairly easy to see how these issues affect the filing process. If the secured party gets the debtor's name wrong on the financing statement – either because of a misspelling[12] or because the secured party fails to use the name that a court later determines is the debtor's "correct" name – the financing statement will be ineffective to perfect unless the financing statement happens to be disclosed in response to a search under the debtor's correct name. One possible solution to this is to disclose all filed financing statements with names that come close to matching the name searched. Consider, though, how that affects the search process.

Problem 4-1

You submitted a search request to your state's UCC filing office seeking all filings against "Jennifer Lowell Douglas." In response, you received a list of 97 financing statements, none of which exactly matches the name you

---

10 *See* In re Green, 2012 WL 5550767 (Bankr. D.N.M. 2012) (financing statements identifying the debtor as "Ron Green," the name on his driver's license, were ineffective because a search under the debtor's legal name, "Ronnie J. Green," did not reveal the filings); In re Larsen, 2010 WL 909138 (Bankr. S.D. Iowa 2010) ("Mike D. Larsen" instead of "Michael D. Larsen"); In re Jones, 2006 WL 3590097 (Bankr. B. Kan. 2006) ("Chris Jones" instead "Christopher Gary Jones"); In re Borden, 353 B.R. 886 (Bankr. D. Neb. 2006) ("Mike Borden" instead of "Michael R. Borden"), *aff'd*, 2007 WL 2407032 (D. Neb. 2007); In re Berry, 2006 WL 2795507 (Bankr. D. Kan.), *opinion supplemented*, 2006 WL 3499682 (2006) ("Mike" instead of "Michael"); In re Kinderknecht, 308 B.R. 71 (10th Cir. BAP 2004) ("Terry J. Kinderknecht" instead of "Terrance Joseph Kinderknecht").

11 In re Miller, 2012 WL 3589426 (C.D. Ill. 2012) (although the debtor's birth certificate identified him as "Ben Miller," a financing statement identifying him as "Bennie A. Miller" was sufficient because a financing statement must contain the debtor's "correct name," not "legal name" and for this purpose the name on the debtor's driver's license, social security card, and tax returns was the debtor's correct name); Peoples Bank v. Bryan Bros. Cattle Co., 504 F.3d 549 (5th Cir. 2007) ("Louie Dickerson" instead of Brooks L. Dickerson" was effective because the debtor held himself out to the community as Louie Dickerson and frequently used his nickname in business affairs).

12 *See* In re Fuell, 2007 WL 4404643 (Bankr. D. Idaho 2007) (spelling the debtor's last name "Fuel" instead of "Fuell"); Pankratz Implement Co. v Citizens Nat'l Bank, 130 P.3d 57 (Kan. 2006) (listing the debtor's first name as "Roger" instead of Rodger").

provided. Three list the debtor as Jennifer Douglas, one as Jennifer L. Douglas, two as Jenny Douglas, four as Jennifer Douglass and the remainder list the debtor with a middle initial other than L or a middle name that begins with a letter other than L. Which, if any, of these filings would be effective if the debtor it concerned was actually your Jennifer Lowell Douglas? Which of these, from your perspective, should the filing office have omitted in its response?

The 2010 amendments to Article 9 dealt with these issues by providing states with two options for dealing with an individual debtor's name. *See* § 9-503(a). Alternative A, known as the "only-if" rule, and by far the more widely adopted alternative, requires filers to use the name of the debtor's driver's license, if the license has not on its face expired and the license is issued by the state whose law governs perfection by filing.[13] If the debtor does not have such a driver's license, the filer must use either the "individual name of the debtor" or the "surname and first personal name of the debtor." Alternative B, known as the "safe harbor" rule, provides that a financing statement will sufficiently identify the debtor if it uses one of these three alternatives: (i) the debtor's "individual name"; (ii) the name on the debtor's driver's license (if the driver's license is issued by the state whose law governs perfection by filing); or (iii) the debtor's surname and first personal name.

Problem 4-2

Anna recently divorced her long-time husband. In the divorce settlement, she received the marital home, a vacation home in another state, and much of the couple's art collection. She is also entitled to receive substantial sums in support and additional cash once her former husband sells other assets. At the moment, however, Anna lacks the liquidity needed to maintain her lifestyle and has applied for a sizeable loan from State Bank. The loan is to be secured by Anna's art collection. In determining what name or names to file and search against, you review the following documents: (i) a birth certificate in the name of "Anastasia Beata Ceauşescu"; (ii) a current U.S. Passport in the name of "Anastasia Beata Davenport"; (iii) a driver's license, issued six months ago, in the name of "Anna C. Davenport"; (iv) tax returns

---

[13] For the most part, the state's law that governs perfection by filing against collateral owned by an individual debtor will be the state where the individual debtor resides. *See* §§ 9-301, 9-307.

in the name of "Anastasia C. Davenport"; (v) pleadings in the divorce proceeding in the name of "Anastasia Beata Ceauşescu Davenport; and (vi) a credit application in the name of "Anna Ceauşescu."

A. What name or names do you list on the financing statement and what name or names do you search against if Anna resides in the jurisdiction that issued the driver's license (and thus that jurisdiction's law governs perfection by filing) and that jurisdiction has enacted Alternative A to § 9-503?

B. How, if at all, would your answer to Part A be different if the jurisdiction that issued the driver's license has enacted Alternative B to § 9-503?

C. How, if at all, would your answer to Part A be different if Anna does not reside in the jurisdiction that issued her driver's license?

The rigidity of Alternative A's only-if rule is often ameliorated by the standard search logic used by the filing office. For example, IACA's Model Administrative Rules treat a personal name as equivalent to the first initial of that name and treat the absence of a personal name or initial as the equivalent of all personal names and initials.[14] As a result:

A Search Under Any of the Following	Will Yield Filing Against Any of the Following
Stephen Sepinuck Stephen L. Sepinuck Stephen Lewis Sepinuck S.L. Sepinuck S. Lewis Sepinuck	Stephen Sepinuck Stephen L. Sepinuck Stephen Lewis Sepinuck S.L. Sepinuck S. Lewis Sepinuck

Consequently, no matter which of these versions of the debtor's name is deemed "correct," a search under that correct name in a state that follows the IACA Model Rules will yield a filing using any of the other variations. As a result, a filing under any of those "incorrect" names will be effective.

Subsumed within the issue of the debtor's "correct name" for the purpose of a financing statement is, of course, identifying the correct debtor or debtors, an issue explored in Problem 2-1. Getting the debtor's name correct on the financing statement requires that the secured party identify and list all those entities and individuals who have property rights in the collateral. In other words, if a security

---

[14] *See* IACA, Model Admin. Rule § 503.1.4 (2015).

interest is to be perfected by filing a financing statement, then a financing statement must be filed against every entity or individual that has a property interest (other than a lien interest) in the collateral.

e-Exercise 4-A
The Debtor's Name

2. The Secured Party's Name

Section 9-502 also requires that, to be effective to perfect a security interest, a financing statement contain the name of either the secured party or the secured party's representative. However, whereas § 9-503 provides a great amount of detail about the debtor's name, it says little about the secured party's name; dealing with only one minor point in subsection (d). Presumably, an error in the name of the secured party on a financing statement is subject to the seriously misleading test of § 9-506(a). However, financing statements are not indexed under the secured party's name and searches are not normally conducted against the name of the secured party. Consequently, the rules of § 9-506(b) and (c) do not apply to an error in the secured party's name and little guidance is given about when such errors make a financing statement seriously misleading. Read the last paragraph of comment 2 to § 9-506. Does that help?

3. Indicating the Collateral

The third requirement in § 9-502 is that the financing statement indicate the collateral covered. In considering what this requires, it is vital to bear in mind an important distinction. Section 9-203(b)(3)(A), dealing with attachment, refers to a security agreement that "provides a description of the collateral." Section 9-502(a)(3), dealing with perfection by filing, refers to a financing statement that "indicates the collateral covered." This difference in language – describing vs. indicating – is intentional. It signals that the rules are different.

This difference should not be surprising. After all, security agreements and financing statements serve different purposes. A security agreement is a document that creates a security interest (*i.e.*, transfers property rights) in the collateral. Consequently, it needs to identify the property that *is or will be* the collateral, although it may do so in general terms. In contrast, a financing statement merely provides public notice of what property *might be* collateral. It is designed to create inquiry notice, alerting a reasonably diligent searcher to seek more information if circumstances justify doing so. Accordingly, § 9-504(2) provides that an indication of collateral in a financing statement as "all assets" or "all personal property" – phrases that would not be adequate as a description of collateral in a security agreement, § 9-108(c) – is sufficient.

But the rules on indicating and describing collateral are not completely unrelated. Section 9-504(1) also provides that an indication of collateral in a financing statement is sufficient if describes collateral pursuant to § 9-108. In other words, a financing statement that *indicates* the collateral covered in a way that satisfies the standard for *describing* the collateral in a security agreement is effective (provided the other information in the financing statement is correct), even though such level of detail is not required.

Despite the more relaxed standard for financing statements, a filed financing statement that contains an inaccuracy in the indication of collateral might not be effective to perfect a security interest in the mis-identified collateral. In one case,[15] for example, the financing statement identified the collateral as a "648G skidder, serial number DW648GX568154." The asset at issue was a model 548G skidder, serial number DW548GX568154. The court described the error as seriously misleading to creditors and held that the indication was insufficient to perfect the security interest. Courts in other cases have been more forgiving.[16]

---

[15] In re Pickle Logging, Inc., 286 B.R. 181 (Bankr. M.D. Ga. 2002).

[16] *See* Knoxville TVA Employees Credit Union v. Houghton, 2018 WL 3381506 (E.D. Tenn. 2018) (dicta indicating that an error of one digit in a filed financing statement's description of a boat's identification number did not render the financing statement ineffective to perfect); Bishop v. Alliance Banking Co., 412 S.W.3d 217 (Ky. Ct. App. 2013) (a filed financing statement that accurately identified the collateralized backhoe by make, model and year but that misstated the first three digits of the serial number – 1100249697 instead of JJG0249697 – was sufficient to perfect); Maxus Leasing Group, Inc. v. Kobelco Am., Inc., 2007 WL 655779 (N.D.N.Y. 2007) (secured party was perfected despite omission of digit in serial number used in financing statement's description of the collateral; error was minor and did not render filing seriously misleading); Stroud Nat'l Bank v. Owens, 134 P.3d 870 (Okla. Ct. Civ. App. 2006) (omission of first digit of vehicle identification number in description of bobcat and error in its model year did not render the description seriously misleading). *Compare* In re Snelson, 330 B.R. 643 (Bankr. E.D. Tenn. 2005) (ruling that an error in the last two digits of a vehicle identification number on the *certificate of title* for a mobile home was a minor error that was not seriously misleading and therefore did not undermine perfection).

Even if not inaccurate, an indication of collateral in a financing statement can be insufficient in other ways. For example, an indication of collateral that merely references the description in the security agreement – a so-called incorporation by reference – is insufficient unless the security agreement is filed with the financing statement.[17]

Problem 4-3

You are a judge. You are currently presiding over several cases in which the efficacy of a financing statement is in dispute. Determine in each of the following situations whether the secured party's authorized and filed financing statement is sufficient to perfect its security interest.

A. The debtor is a corporation. In the corporate articles of incorporation, filed in its state of incorporation, the name of the debtor is ABC, Inc. The financing statement has identified the debtor as "ABC Inc." (*i.e.*, omits the comma). What if the financing statement had "ABC Co." as the name of the debtor?

B. The debtor's registered name is Northwest Technology Associates, Inc. The financing statement lists the debtor by its trade name, "Technological Solutions." *See In re Asheboro Precision Plastics, Inc.*, 2005 WL 1287743 (Bankr. M.D.N.C. 2005).

C. The debtor is incorporated in Delaware under the name "Designated Interiors, Inc." The financing statement lists the debtor as "Designated Interiors, Inc., a Delaware corporation."

D. The secured party's name is Empire Finance Company. The financing statement lists the secured party by its trade name, "The Money Fountain."

E. The secured party's corporate name is National Bank of Nevada but the name listed for the secured party on the financing statement is simply "National Bank."

F. The signed security agreement describes the collateral as "existing and after-acquired inventory and equipment."

---

17 *See* § 9-504 cmt 2; PEB Commentary No. 26 (Aug. 12, 2022).

In contrast, a security agreement, which does not serve the same notice function, may describe the collateral by referring to another, unattached document, such as a bill of sale, because the items constituting collateral are "objectively determinable." *See, e.g.*, FSL Acquisition Corp. v. Freeland Sys., LLC, 686 F. Supp. 2d 921 (D. Minn. 2010).

1. The financing statement indicates the collateral as "all assets."
2. The financing statement indicates the collateral as "inventory and accounts."

G. The signed security agreement describes the collateral as a backhoe and correctly states the backhoe's model and serial number.
   1. The financing statement indicates the collateral as "personal property listed on Exhibit A" but Exhibit A is not filed.
   2. The financing statement indicates the collateral as "equipment listed on Exhibit A" but Exhibit A is not filed.

H. Chris Dashiell and Pat Dobbs run a detective agency called "Dashiell & Dobbs" and granted a security interest in their "office furnishings" to State Bank in a signed security agreement.
   1. What if the financing statement listed the name of the debtor as "Dashiell & Dobbs" and the collateral as "all equipment"?
   2. What if the financing statement listed as collateral "desks, chairs, computers located at 351 Main Street" and the detective agency was located at 153 Center Street? What if the agency had offices at both locations but the security interest covered only the property at Center Street?

Problem 4-4

Medical Partnership provides preventative and primary patient care to clients. Six months ago, it was discovered that Able, who at that time was one of the partners, had submitted fraudulent insurance claims seeking compensation for work not performed and had embezzled funds from the Partnership. Pursuant to the partnership agreement, the other partners promptly fired Able as an employee and expelled him from the partnership. Almost immediately afterwards, Able started providing patient care through another entity, in violation of a non-competition clause in Able's employment contract with Medical Partnership.

Medical Partnership plans to sue Able for the damages caused by Able's actions. To do this, it has obtained financing from Litigation Finance Company ("LFT"), and granted LFT a security interest in all of the partnership's claims against Able. Assume the security agreement sufficiently describes the collateral. If LFT files in the appropriate office an otherwise sufficient and authorized financing statement, which of the following indications of the collateral in the financing statement will be effective to perfect LFT's security interest?

A. "All claims of debtor against Able relating to Able's conduct while as a partner or employee of debtor."
B. "All assets."
C. "All commercial tort claims."

e-Exercise 4-B
Errors in Financing Statements

B. Other Required But Non-essential Content

Filing office duties. Presentation of a financing statement to the filing office with the appropriate fee constitutes filing. § 9-516(a).[18] What happens to the financing statement after that is largely immaterial, at least from the perspective of the creditor who filed it and provided the creditor has proof of filing. As we have already seen, the filing office is supposed to index a financing statement according to the debtor's name. § 9-519(c). However, if the filing office mis-indexes the financing statement, that mistake does not affect the effectiveness of the filing. § 9-517. Indeed, if the filing office inadvertently discarded the financing statement, it would remain effective (although the secured party might have difficulty proving that the financing statement was actually filed, if the issue ever arose). The filing office is also supposed to assign a unique number to each financing statement. § 9-519(a), (b). This facilitates the later filing of amendments to the financing statement. Amendments to a financing statement must reference that unique filing number, § 9-512(a)(1), and that reference enables the filing office to associate the financing statement and the amendment in its records. A financing statement and its amendments can be retrieved from the filing office by a search under either the debtor's name or the unique filing number. § 9-519(f).

---

[18] As with most other things we have studied, one must be on the lookout for different rules under the law of the applicable state. Louisiana enacted a non-uniform version of § 9-516(a) and omitted § 9-516(d). As a result, a filing is not made until the filing office accepts it. *See* La. Rev. Stat. § 10:9-516; Signature Credit Partners, LLC v. Casaic Offset & Silkscreen, Inc., 2012 WL 1999494 (W.D. La. 2012) (continuation statement submitted by secured party's agent and improperly rejected by the filing office was not effective).

Article 9 imposes deadlines on how long a filing office may take in fulfilling some of its duties. It is supposed to index a financing statement within two business days of receiving it, § 9-519(c), (h), and is supposed to respond to search requests within two business days, § 9-523(c), (e). However, a filing office's failure to comply with these performance standards has no effect on the rights of the filer or any user of the filing system. § 9-523 cmt. 8.

Although Article 9 assigns several other, technical duties to filing offices, the filing officers are emphatically not supposed to verify the accuracy of the information in a filing or judge the efficacy of a filing. In essence, Article 9 treats the offices as mere repositories of what secured parties provide to them (an admittedly unflattering description, but slightly better than describing them as receptacles). The drafters feared that if the filing officers substantively reviewed each filing, they would undoubtedly get it wrong on occasion, and then both filers and searchers would have to deal with the resulting chaos.

In spite of this, the drafters did give the filing officers the duty to check for missing – as opposed to inaccurate – information, and to reject financing statements that lack any of a fairly lengthy list of things. *See* §§ 9-516(b), 9-520(a), (b). Note, the list of information which, if missing, justifies rejection of a financing statement, goes beyond the three essential items listed in § 9-502(a). It includes a mailing address for both the debtor and the secured party and an indication of whether the debtor is an individual or an organization. *See* § 9-516(b)(4), (5).[19]

If the financing statement is rejected because it lacks any of the § 9-516(b) information, it is not considered filed and thus will not be sufficient to perfect a

[19] Some states have added to lists of required information either in their version of § 9-502 or in their § 9-516(b). For example the debtor's tax identification number is required in South Dakota for the financing statement to be sufficient to perfect: S.D. Codified Laws § 57A-9-502(a). North Dakota does not require that, to be effective, a financing statement include the debtor's social security number or taxpayer identification number, *see* N.D. Cent. Code § 41-09-73, but it does provide that a financing statement will be ineffective if the filing office rejects the financing statement because it lacks that number. *See* N.D. Cent. Code § 41-09-87(2)(h), as amended by 2013 North Dakota Laws Ch. 257 § 25. Michigan also used to required such numbers on financing statements, *see* In re C.J. Rogers, Inc., 39 F.3d 669 (6th Cir. 1994), but no longer does, *see* Mich. Comp. L. Ann. §§ 440.9502, 440.9516. Idaho requires that a financing statement covering farm products contain the address of both the debtor and the secured party, the debtor's social security number or a substitute created by the secretary of state, a description "by category" of the farm products and "the amount of such products, where applicable," and an indication of the county or counties in which the farm products are produced or located. Idaho Code § 28-9-502.

security interest. For this reason, even though § 9-516(b) information is not technically included in the requirements for an effective financing statement, a secured party must pay attention to § 9-516(b) and avoid a conspicuous omission.

It might make some sense to distinguish between the truly essential information required by § 9-502(a) and the other information semi-required by § 9-516(b). Unfortunately, as soon as the drafters decided to authorize filing officers to reject some filings, they had to deal with the inevitable reality that the officers will occasionally get even this fairly simple task wrong, either by accepting a financing statement that they should have rejected or by rejecting one they should have accepted. Accordingly, there are rules to deal with each of these eventualities.

If a financing statement is rejected for a reason not permitted under § 9-516(b), the financing statement is still effective as a filed financing statement as long as it meets the requirements of § 9-502. However, a purchaser who gives value in reasonable reliance on the absence of the financing statement from the filing system is protected; a financing statement that was wrongfully rejected is not effective against such a purchaser, even though it is effective as against other parties. § 9-516(d). Of course, because the original filer will know that its filing was rejected, *see* § 9-520(b), it can take whatever action is necessary to make sure that the filing office accepts its financing statement, and thereby minimize the risk that it will lose out to a searcher who cannot find the financing statement.

If the filing office accepts a financing statement that it should have refused because it lacks § 9-516(b) information, and that filing complies with § 9-502, the filing is effective as a filed financing statement. § 9-520(c). However, if a filed financing statement contains an error in § 9-516(b)(5) information – in other words, if the financing statement incorrectly lists the debtor's address or incorrectly identifies the debtor as an individual or organization – the financing statement will not be effective against other secured parties or purchasers who give value in reasonable reliance upon the incorrect information. *See* § 9-338. This rule, which is essentially a priority rule, is discussed in Chapter Five. Errors in other types of § 9-516(b) information – specifically, information described in a paragraph of subsection (b) other than paragraph (5), such as the address of the secured party listed in paragraph (4) – do not affect the effectiveness of the financing statement.

Problem 4-5

Complete the following chart. For each type of error listed, indicate in the left-most blank column whether the filing office is supposed to accept or reject a financing statement with the error indicated. In the next column, indicate whether a financing statement with such an error would be effective if it were filed. If the answer to that depends on facts you do not have, indicate the standard that would be used to evaluate the efficacy of the financing statement. In the next column, indicate what impact, if any, the error would have on the search process. In other words, how would a searcher trying to acquire information from the filing system be affected? Finally, in the far right-hand column, indicate what efficacy, if any, a financing statement with the error indicated would have if the filing office rejected it.

Error in Financing Statement	Should Filing Office Accept or Reject the Financing Statement?	Efficacy of Financing Statement if Accepted	Effect on Search Process of Such a Filed Financing Statement	Efficacy of Financing Statement if Rejected
Missing Address for Debtor				
Missing Address for Secured Party				
Incorrect Address for Debtor				
Incorrect Address for Secured Party				
Missing Name of Secured Party				
Incorrect Name of Debtor				
Incorrect Name of Secured Party				
Missing Collateral Indication				

C. The Mechanics of Filing

1. Authority to File

Former Article 9 required financing statements to be signed by the debtor. To facilitate electronic filing, revised Article 9 removed that requirement and substituted an authorization requirement. For a financing statement to be effective to perfect a security interest, the debtor must authorize its filing. *See* §§ 9-509, 9-510. Such authority is conclusively established by the debtor's signature on a security agreement. Upon signing of the security agreement, the secured party is authorized to file a financing statement that indicates collateral in the same way that the security agreement describes it. § 9-509(b). However, if the secured party wants to file the financing statement before the debtor signs the security agreement[20] or wants to have an indication of collateral that differs in some way from the description in the security agreement, the secured party must obtain the debtor's permission in a signed record. § 9-509(a)(1).[21]

What if a prospective lender files a financing statement without the debtor's authorization and the debtor later accepts a loan and signs a security agreement, thereby authorizing the filing? Apparently, the authorization is to be given retroactive effect. The common law of agency normally prohibits a retroactive ratification from impairing the rights of any third party that arose prior to the ratification,[22] and thus suggests that retroactive authorization could, at best, make the filer's priority date from the moment of authorization, not the earlier time of filing. However, the last sentence of § 9-509 comment 3 indicates that the priority issue is governed by Article 9, not by other things, such as the law of retroactive ratification. Thus, a financing statement that was unauthorized when filed but which is subsequently authorized is apparently as effective as if authorized when

---

[20] Recall that § 9-502(d) authorizes a prospective secured party to file a financing statement before a security interest attaches and even before the debtor and creditor have entered into a security agreement.

[21] If the transaction is structured as a lease of goods and the putative lessor wants to file a financing statement in case the transaction is later deemed to be a sale with a retained security interest, the lessor will have statutory authorization to file a financing statement if the signed lease agreement is deemed to create a security interest but not have such authorization if the transaction is a true lease. Accordingly, the lease agreement (or some other signed document) should expressly authorize the lessor to file a financing statement against the lessee.

[22] *See* RESTATEMENT (THIRD) OF THE LAW OF AGENCY § 4.02 (2006).

filed. Comment 4 to § 9-322 makes the point more clearly. Because the notice function of a financing statement is served regardless of whether the financing statement was authorized when filed (*i.e.*, authorization is invisible), subsequent authorization makes the financing statement fully effective from the date filed. Assuming courts will follow this comment and give retroactive effect to post-filing authorization, a secured party might have little incentive to obtain the requisite authorization prior to filing, perhaps rendering Article 9's authorization requirement virtually meaningless. About the only incentive to get authorization prior to filing would be the threat of a tort action for disparagement of title or other actual damages under § 9-625(b) for failure to comply with Article 9. The $500 penalty provided in § 9-625(e) might not be much of a disincentive.

Problem 4-6

Darrow & Douglas, LLP, a law firm, granted a security interest in the firm's "existing and after-acquired inventory and equipment" to State Bank in a signed security agreement. The financing statement listed the secured party's name, the correct name of the debtor, and the collateral as "all assets." Assuming the filing is made in the correct place, is the filing effective to perfect State Bank's security interest? *See* § 9-509.

2. Where to File

Section 9-501 tells the secured party where within a particular state to file a financing statement. Notice that two offices are designated: (i) the place for recording real estate mortgages if the collateral is of a type related to real estate; and, (ii) for everything else, another office, which in most states is the secretary of state's office.[23] Among transactional lawyers, the real estate recording office is often referred to as the "local" office and the secretary of state's office is often

---

[23] As with almost everything else in Article 9, lawyers have to be on the lookout for non-uniform filing rules. For example, Georgia requires local filing for security interests in "growing crops," Ga. Code § 11-9-501(a)(1)(A), and Arkansas requires local filing "if the debtor is engaged in farming operations and the collateral is a farm-stored commodity financed by a loan through the Commodity Credit Corporation of the United States Department of Agriculture," Ark. Code § 4-9-501(a)(2). Florida law requires filing with the Division of Alcoholic Beverages and Tobacco of the Department of Business and Professional Regulation to perfect a security interest in an alcoholic beverage license. *See* Fla. Stat. § 561.65(4); United States v. McGurn, 596 So. 2d 1038 (Fla. 1992).

referred to as the "central filing" office. This is because there are numerous real estate recording offices in each state, one located in each county for the real estate located in that county, but the secretary of state's office is located in one place, usually the state's capital or largest city. Later in this Chapter (Section 4), we will consider the rules that determine in which state a financing statement must be filed to perfect a security interest. For right now, however, we will assume we are in the correct state and our choice is between the local filing office and the central filing office in that state.

3. The Duration of a Filing's Effectiveness

A recorded mortgage on real property is effective indefinitely. That is, it remains effective unless and until a release of mortgage is recorded. In an era where information is stored electronically, and is therefore not difficult or costly to maintain, one might expect that a financing statement would also be effective indefinitely. That is, it would remain both in the filing office and effective to perfect until the creditor has it removed. However, unlike real property, the existence of which typically spans several geologic eras, personal property often has a short useful life. Moreover, most loans secured by personal property are for substantially shorter periods of time than most real estate loans, where 15-, 20-, and even 30-year mortgages are standard. Beyond this, there is some benefit to removing old records from the filing office's records. It removes a cloud on the debtor's title to the property identified in the financing statement and it lessens the possibility that a search request will yield financing statements that no longer relate to an active deal but which will nevertheless prompt a prudent searcher to conduct further investigation.

Of course, the filing office could be cleared of outdated records by simply requiring the secured party to remove its filing as soon as the secured debt is paid off. In fact, Article 9 does this to some extent. *See* § 9-513(a)–(c). However, the drafters also decided to make financing statements effective for only a limited duration (somewhat like the self-destructing instructions given to Jim Phelps and Ethan Hunt in the "Mission Impossible" television series and movies).

In general, a financing statement is effective for five years from the date of filing.[24] *See* § 9-515(a). At the end of the stated time period, the effectiveness of

---

[24] Certain financing statements are effective for longer than a five-year period. In a "public-finance transaction" (defined in § 9-102(a)(67)) or a "manufactured-home transaction" (defined in § 9-102(a)(54)), the period of effectiveness of a financing statement

the financing statement lapses. If the effectiveness of the financing statement lapses, a security interest perfected by the filed financing statement becomes unperfected and will be deemed to be retroactively unperfected as against purchasers for value. § 9-515(c). To avoid that lapse in effectiveness, a secured party must file a "continuation statement" before the end of the period of effectiveness. *See* § 9-102(a)(27). To prevent secured parties from simply filing their continuation statements at the same time they file their financing statements, a continuation statement must be filed no sooner than six months before the effectiveness of the financing statement would otherwise lapse. § 9-515(d). Thus, for example, if a financing statement were filed on September 14, 2012, an effective continuation statement would have to be filed somewhere between March 14, 2017 and September 14, 2017: the shaded area in the illustration below.

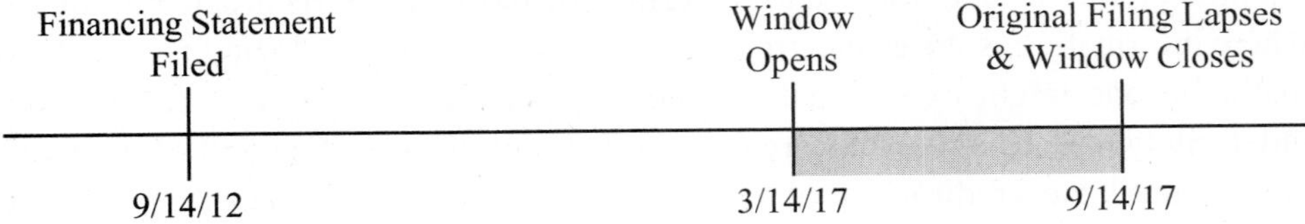

A continuation statement filed either before that six-month window opens or after it closes is ineffective. If a continuation statement is timely filed, the financing statement's effectiveness is extended for another five-year period from the date that the financing statement would have otherwise lapsed if not continued. § 9-515(e).

Continuing with the example above, assume that a continuation statement was timely filed on June 1, 2017.

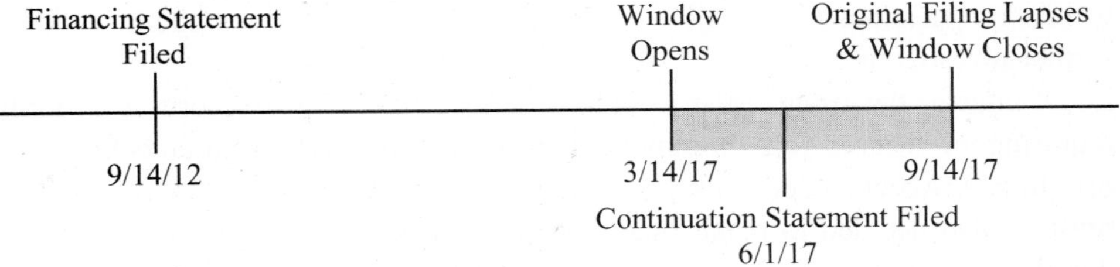

The financing statement would therefore remain effective until September 14, 2022. That is, it remains effective for an additional five full years (not for five years from when the continuation statement was filed). The secured party may extend a

---

is 30 years. § 9-515(b). If the debtor is a "transmitting utility" (defined in § 9-102(a)(81), the effectiveness of a financing statement does not lapse through the mere passage of time. § 9-515(f).

financing statement's effectiveness indefinitely by filing successive continuation statements every five years (in the six-month window).

As should probably not be surprising, the secured party does not need the debtor's authorization to file a continuation statement. *See* § 9-509(d). If it did, the debtor might withhold such authorization, thereby jeopardizing the secured party's continued perfection in the collateral, in an effort to extract some valuable concession from the secured party (such as a reduction in the secured obligation or a lowering of the applicable interest rate).

The filing office is not supposed to remove the debtor's name from the index or the financing statement from the filing system until one year after lapse of the financing statement. §§ 9-519(g), 9-522(a). Even if an authorized termination statement is filed, the financing statement to which it relates is supposed to remain in the filing system until one year after the financing statement would have lapsed of its own accord. *See* § 9-513 cmt. 5.

4. Other Types of Filings

A continuation statement is really just one type of amendment to a financing statement. *See* § 9-512(a). *See also* § 9-521(b) (showing an amendment form). When the secured obligation is paid off, the debtor or secured party might also wish – and the secured party can be required – to file another type of amendment, a "termination statement." *See* § 9-513. *See also* § 9-102(a)(80) (defining "termination statement"). Amendments may also be used to add or release collateral, change the debtor's name or address, change the secured party's name or address, or record an assignment of the security interest to a new creditor. § 9-514. The following chart might be useful.

Type of Filing		Code	When Needed
Financing Statement		§ 9-502	At conception of deal
Amendment	Continuation Statement	§ 9-515	To continue effectiveness beyond 5 years
	Termination Statement	§ 9-513	To remove cloud from title
	Other	§ 9-512, § 9-514	To change a name or address; to add or release collateral; to assign the filing

Problem 4-7

A. When would a secured party want to amend a financing statement to release collateral?
B. When must a termination statement be filed? *See* § 9-513.
C. For each type of amendment to a financing statement, whose authorization to file is needed? *See* §§ 9-509, 9-510, 9-511.

In the last few years, several cases have arisen in which a termination statement was filed with respect to collateral still encumbered by a secured obligation.[25] Some of these have been high-profile cases involving very large secured obligations, others have been more mundane. Regardless of the amount at issue, these cases raise some very interesting questions, such as those posed in the following problem.

Problem 4-8

Two years ago, State Bank loaned $2 million to Dunkirk Enterprises, Inc. and in returned received a security interest in Dunkirk's existing and after-acquired equipment, inventory, and accounts. At the time of the loan, State Bank perfected by filing a financing statement in the appropriate office.

A. Last month, National Bank attempted to terminate one of its own financing statements. In doing so, it mistakenly transposed the number of the financing statement to be terminated, with the result that the termination statement referenced State Bank's financing statement against Dunkirk. Is the termination statement effective?

---

25 *See, e.g.*, In re Motors Liquidation Co., 777 F.3d 100 (2d Cir. 2015); In re Wheeler, 580 B.R. 719 (Bankr. W.D. Ky. 2017); Fjellin ex rel. Leonard Van Liew Living Trust v. Penning, 41 F. Supp. 3d 775 (D. Neb. 2014); In re Residential Cap., LLC, 497 B.R. 403 (Bankr. S.D.N.Y. 2013); In re RAG East, LP, 2013 WL 796616 (Bankr. W.D. Pa. 2013); International Home Products, Inc. v. First Bank of Puerto Rico, 495 B.R. 152 (D.P.R. 2013); In re Hickory Printing Group, Inc., 479 B.R. 388 (Bankr. W.D.N.C. 2012); In re Negus-Sons, Inc., 460 B.R. 754 (8th Cir. BAP 2011); AEG Liquidation Trust v. Toobro N.Y. LLC, 932 N.Y.S.2d 759 (N.Y. Sup. Ct. 2011); Official Comm. of Unsecured Creditors v. City Nat'l Bank, 2011 WL 1832963 (N.D. Cal. 2011); Roswell Cap. Partners LLC v. Alternative Constr. Techs., 2010 WL 3452378 (S.D.N.Y. 2010), *aff'd*, 436 F. App'x 34 (2d Cir. 2011).

B. Last week, Employee, the State Bank loan officer in charge of the Dunkirk file, mistakenly filed a termination statement for the financing statement filed against Dunkirk. Is the termination statement effective?

C. What would a person find when searching the records of the filing office one month after the events in Part A or Part B? Given your answer to this question, what information does the public record really convey to those who conduct a search?

Section § 9-518 authorizes – but does not require – a debtor or secured party who believes a filed record is inaccurate or wrongfully filed to file an "information statement." A debtor might choose to do this to inform people that a filed financing statement was unauthorized.[26] A secured party might wish to inform people that an amendment or termination statement was unauthorized.

Problem 4-9

How, if at all, would the analysis of Problem 4-8(B) change if State Bank subsequently filed an information statement declaring that the termination statement was unauthorized?

5. Collateral Held in Trust

When the collateral consists of property held in trust, slightly different the rules apply for where to file a financing statement and what name to use for the debtor. Some trusts, such as Delaware statutory trusts, are legal entities separate and distinct from their settlors, trustees, and beneficiaries. Under applicable law, such a trust holds title to the trust estate.[27] Accordingly, when such a trust grants a security interest in personal property, the trust itself is the debtor for the purposes of Article 9. As a result, any financing statement to be filed in the jurisdiction where the debtor is located should be filed where the trust is located. *See* U.C.C. §§ 9-301, 9-307.

---

[26] Many states have provided for a process for removing unauthorized filings from the filing records. See the report by the National Association of Secretaries of State entitled "State Strategies to Subvert Fraudulent Uniform Commercial Code (UCC) Filings" dated April 2014, and available at http://www.nass.org/reports/surveys-a-reports/.

[27] *See* Del. Code tit. 12, §§ 3801(a), 3805(f).

Other trusts, including most common-law trusts, are not distinct legal entities. Instead, under applicable law, the trustee of such a trust holds legal title to the trust estate. In such cases, the trustee is the "debtor," and any financing statement to be filed in the debtor's location should be filed where the trustee is located.

But even though a financing statement might need to be filed where the trustee is located, that does not mean that the financing statement should use the name of the trustee as the name of the debtor. An individual or entity functioning as a trustee would not want a financing statement dealing with trust property to be filed under the trustee's name because such a filed financing statement would create a cloud on the title to the trustee's own property. Accordingly, when the collateral consists of property held in trust, the name to be used for the debtor on a financing statement should be either the trust's name, if it has one, or the name of the settlor or testator. The following chart depicts what name to use for the debtor, and what additional information is required, when the collateral is property held in trust.

<table>
<tr><th rowspan="2">Trust is a Registered Organization</th><th colspan="2">Trust is Not a Registered Organization</th></tr>
<tr><th>Organic Record of the Trust Specifies a Name for the Trust</th><th>Organic Record of the Trust Does Not Specify a Name for the Trust</th></tr>
<tr><td>The name for the trust stated in the public organic record most recently filed with or issue by the jurisdiction of organization. § 9-503(a)(1).</td><td>The name specified. § 9-503(a)(3)(A)(i).</td><td>The name of the settlor or testator. § 9-503(a)(3)(A)(ii).</td></tr>
<tr><td></td><td colspan="2">Indicate that the collateral is held in trust (by checking the first box on line 5). § 9-503(a)(3)(B).</td></tr>
<tr><td></td><td></td><td>Somewhere provide information sufficient to distinguish the trust from other trusts having one or more of the same settlors or testators. § 9-503(a)(3)(B)(ii).</td></tr>
</table>

SECTION 3. OTHER METHODS OF PERFECTION

As noted in the first section of this Chapter, there are other methods for perfecting a security interest in personal property. In some instances, these methods are optional alternatives, and filing remains an effective method to perfect. In other cases, these methods are substitutes for filing a financing statement, and filing is ineffective to perfect. *See* §§ 9-312(b) and 9-311(a). Determining which method or methods apply to any particular type of collateral requires a review of several different provisions of Article 9. The place to begin is § 9-310(a), which tells us filing a financing statement is necessary to perfect a security interest unless an exception applies. Section 9-310(b) then lists those exceptions, serving as a road map to §§ 9-308, 9-309, 9-311, 9-312, 9-313, and 9-314.[28] Unfortunately, instead of organizing the rules by collateral type, and telling us which perfection method is required or permitted for each, the rules are organized by perfection method. As a result, it is somewhat tedious to make sense of the whole. Although you should read thoroughly all the relevant provisions, the following chart might prove useful for organizing the perfection methods by the type of original collateral. The chart is based on Article 9 as updated by the 2022 UCC Amendments.[29]

---

[28] The last two paragraphs of § 9-310(b) refer to exceptions to the filing requirement in § 9-315 for proceeds and in § 9-316 for property perfected under the law of a different jurisdiction. These exceptions will be covered later in this Chapter.

[29] This chart does not deal with the perfection methods permitted for proceeds of original collateral, which are discussed later in this Chapter. Treat the chart as a starting point for your search for the appropriate rules, not the final answer.

PERFECTION BY COLLATERAL TYPE

	Filing	Possession	Control	Automatic
Goods				
Consumer Goods[30] [31]	✓	✓		✓ (PMSI[32] or security interest arising under Arts. 2 or 2A)[33]
Equipment[29] [30]	✓	✓		✓ (security interest arising under Arts. 2 or 2A)[32]
Farm Products	✓	✓		✓ (security interest arising under Arts. 2 or 2A)[32]
Inventory[29] [30]	✓	✓		✓ (security interest arising under Arts. 2 or 2A)[32]
Goods Held By Issuer of Nonnegotiable Document	✓	✓[34]		
Goods Held by Bailee	✓	✓[35]		

---

30 Except for motor vehicles covered by a certificate of title statute. Perfection in such goods is generally accomplished by having the security interest noted on the certificate. Although filing a financing statement is normally the method to perfect when titled collateral is inventory, if the debtor leases, but does not sell, the titled goods, compliance with the certificate of title statute is required to perfect the security interest. *See* § 9-311(d).

31 Except when a federal filing system preempts Article 9's filing system (*e.g.*, for a security interest in an aircraft, documented vessel, or rolling stock).

32 *See* § 9-309(1).

33 *See* 9-312(c), (d), (f).

34 Can be perfected by the bailee's receipt of notification of the secured party's interest. § 9-312(d).

35 Can be perfected by the bailee's authenticated acknowledgment that it holds for the secured party's benefit. § 9-313(c).

<table>
<tr><th></th><th>Filing</th><th>Possession</th><th>Control</th><th>Automatic</th></tr>
<tr><td colspan="5">Rights to Payment</td></tr>
<tr><td>Accounts (other than Health Care Insurance Receivables or Controllable Accounts)</td><td>✓</td><td></td><td></td><td>✓ (if not a significant portion of accounts or a sale of lottery winnings)[36]</td></tr>
<tr><td>Chattel Paper</td><td>✓</td><td colspan="2">✓</td><td></td></tr>
<tr><td>Commercial Tort Claims</td><td>✓[37]</td><td></td><td></td><td></td></tr>
<tr><td>Controllable Accounts</td><td>✓</td><td></td><td>✓</td><td></td></tr>
<tr><td>Controllable Payment Intangibles</td><td>✓</td><td></td><td>✓</td><td></td></tr>
<tr><td>Deposit Accounts</td><td></td><td></td><td>✓</td><td>✓ (if the secured party is the depositary bank)[38]</td></tr>
<tr><td>Health Care Insurance Receivables</td><td>✓</td><td></td><td></td><td>✓ (if granted to the healthcare provider)[39]</td></tr>
<tr><td>Instruments</td><td>✓</td><td>✓</td><td></td><td>✓ (temporary; permanent if a sale of promissory notes)[40]</td></tr>
<tr><td>Payment Intangibles</td><td>✓</td><td></td><td></td><td>✓ (if not a significant portion or if a sale)[41]</td></tr>
</table>

---

36 *See* § 9-309(2), (14).

37 An indication of collateral only by type of collateral *might be* insufficient in a financing statement. *See* § 9-108(e)(1); Stephen L. Sepinuck, *Perfecting a Security Interest in a Commercial Tort Claim*, 13 THE TRANSACTIONAL LAW. 6 (Feb. 2023).

38 *See* § 9-104(a)(1).

39 *See* § 9-309(5).

40 *See* §§ 9-309(4) (sales of promissory notes), 9-312(e), (g).

41 *See* § 9-309(2), (3).

	Filing	Possession	Control	Automatic
Other				
Certificated Securities	✓	✓	✓	✓ (temporary or if secured party is the broker or securities intermediary)[42]
Controllable Electronic Records	✓		✓	
Documents of Title	✓	✓ (if tangible)	✓ (if electronic)	✓ (temporary)[43]
General Intangibles (other than controllable electronic records, payment intangibles or software)[44]	✓			
Investment Property (other than Certificated Securities)	✓		✓	✓ (if the secured party is the broker or securities intermediary)[45]
Money		✓ (if tangible)	✓ (if electronic)	
Software[46]	✓	✓ (if embedded in goods)		
Supporting Obligations				✓

A. Alternative Filing Systems

In three circumstances, Article 9 defers to the perfection method specified in other law:

- When federal law preempts the Article 9 filing system with one of its own, *see* § 9-311(a)(1);
- When a state certificate of title statute applies, *see* § 9-311(a)(2), (3); and

---

[42] *See* § 9-312(e), (g).

[43] *See* § 9-312(e), (f), (g).

[44] Except when a federal filing system preempts Article 9's filing system (*e.g.*, for a security interest in a copyright registered with the Copyright Office).

[45] *See* §§ 9-308(f), (g), 9-309(10), (11).

[46] Except if the collateral is a copyright registered with the Copyright Office.

- When the state has enacted an alternative central filing system for a particular type of collateral, *see* § 9-311(a)(2).

In each of these situations, filing a financing statement is neither necessary nor sufficient to perfect a security interest. Instead, the secured party must record its interest in that alternative system.

Using those alternative systems is a way of providing notice to the world of the secured party's interest in the collateral. For that reason, each of these methods is a close analog to filing a financing statement and serves the same basic function. That said, these alternative systems function differently from the Article 9 filing system. The Article 9 system is debtor-based. Filings are indexed by the debtor's name and searches are conducted by the debtor's name. In contrast, the federal filing systems and the certificate of title statutes are property-based, and therefore more closely resemble a real estate recording system. The filer in each of these property-based systems uses the system to document ownership of each piece of property covered by the system, often by recording the actual transaction documents (*e.g.*, deed or mortgage, the assignment of a copyright, the agreement for the purchase and sale of an aircraft). Searches are typically conducted against each individual piece of property, rather than against the putative owner. The fact that many property-based systems require the filing of the transaction documents has several important implications, as illustrated in the following chart of the differences between property-based and debtor-based filing systems.

Property-Based Filing Systems (*e.g.*, for aircraft, copyrights & ships)	**Debtor-Based Filing Systems (*e.g.*, the UCC)**
In some, required to file the transaction documents.	May, but need not, file transaction documents.
Cannot pre-file (before the parties enter into the transaction).	May pre-file.
Filing generally shows who *has* rights.	Filing shows who *might have* rights.
Might have lengthy grace period for filing (and a long indexing period).	No grace period, generally (and a short indexing period).

Property-Based Filing Systems (*e.g.*, for aircraft, copyrights & ships)	Debtor-Based Filing Systems (*e.g.*, the UCC)
Filed documents are on record permanently.[47]	In general, filings are effective for five years.
Rely on title concept.	Title is generally immaterial (*cf.* §1-201(b)(35)).
In some, filing is necessary to document the existence of property rights.	Not necessary to document existence of property.

What property is subject to a federal filing system?[48] Comment 2 to § 9-311 refers to the federal filing system for civil aircraft as one which preempts Article 9's filing system.[49] No doubt security interests in ships must be recorded pursuant to

---

47 The permanence of filings in property-based systems can be problematic. Creditors occasionally neglect to clear up the records (*i.e.*, file a lien release) after a loan is repaid. In property-based systems, the filed records remain a cloud on the title of every owner thereafter. Fixing the problem can be very difficult. Individual creditors die. Banks and other lenders merge, fail, and assign loans. Tracking down who has the authority to file a lien release for an old loan can be very time consuming. The problem exists in the UCC system as well, but the limited time during which financing statements are effective makes it less likely the issue will come up and, when it does, makes tracking down the appropriate party less difficult.

48 This preemption of the Article 9 filing system as a method of perfection is a narrower preemption than the preemption by federal law we discussed in Chapter Two. If a federal law preempts the Article 9 filing system as a method of perfection under § 9-311, the rest of Article 9 continues to apply. If federal law preempts Article 9 under § 9-109(c)(1), then Article 9 might be preempted in its entirety. The scope of the preemption under § 9-109(c)(1) and the more limited preemption under § 9-311 is determined by interpretation of the federal law.

49 *See* 49 U.S.C. §§ 44107, 44108 (requiring that notice be filed with the FAA Aircraft Registry to perfect a security interest in aircraft). *See also* In re AvCentral, Inc., 289 B.R. 170 (Bankr. D. Kan. 2003) (holding that a federal filing is necessary even though the debtor and the secured creditor both understood at the time they created the security interest that the debtor would not be operating the aircraft, but instead disassembling them and converting their components to inventory for sale).

While filing with the FAA is normally required to perfect a security interest in an airframe and its engines, a UCC filing might be necessary to perfect a security interest in accessions to the aircraft. Moreover, for aircraft of a certain size, it might be advisable to record the security interest with the International Registry of Mobile Assets, which is an online registry based in Dublin, Ireland established pursuant to the Cape Town Convention, which the

the Ship Mortgage Act.[50] Apparently, federal law also preempts Article 9's filing system with respect to railroad cars, locomotives, and other rolling stock. For security interests in such property, filing with the Surface Transportation Board is required to perfect.[51] Whether federal law preempts Article 9 for recording interests in intellectual property is slightly less certain. Some of the laws governing such property predate the original version of Article 9 and therefore do not expressly reference security interests. It is therefore difficult to ascertain whether the systems they establish for recording ownership of intellectual property are intended to cover consensual liens. Nevertheless, a fair amount of judicial consensus has emerged. A federal filing is necessary to perfect a security interest in a registered copyright.[52] In contrast, federal filings are not needed to perfect a security interest in trademarks

---

United States has ratified.

[50] *See* 46 U.S.C. §§ 31321–31330 (detailing how to create, perfect, and enforce security interests in vessels).

[51] *See* 49 U.S.C. § 11301; In re California W. R.R. Inc., 303 B.R. 201 (Bankr. N.D. Cal. 2003).

Federal law also provides that compliance with regulations to be issued by the Secretary of the Interior is the exclusive means to perfect a security interest in certain Alaskan fishing rights. *See* 16 U.S.C. § 1855(h)(1)–(3). Such regulations will, apparently, provide for recordation of security interests with a central registry to be created by the National Marine Fisheries Service. However, no such registry currently exists and until the regulations are final, perfection is governed by other law. *See* Sustainable Fisheries Act, Pub. L. No. 104-297, § 110(e), 110 Stat. at 3592 (codified at 16 U.S.C. § 1855 note). *See also* Gowen, Inc. v. F/V Quality One, 244 F.3d 64, 70 (1st Cir. 2001) (security interests effective and perfected by otherwise applicable law "remain so at least until the establishment of the registry").

[52] *See* In re Peregrine Entm't, Ltd., 116 B.R. 194 (C.D. Cal. 1990); In re Avalon Software, Inc., 209 B.R. 517 (Bankr. D. Ariz. 1997); In re AEG Acquisition Corp., 127 B.R. 34 (Bankr. C.D. Cal. 1991), *aff'd*, 161 B.R. 50 (9th Cir. BAP 1993). *See also* In re Franchise Pictures LLC, 389 B.R. 131 (Bankr. C.D. Cal. 2008) (filing with the Copyright Office is necessary to perfect a judicial lien on a copyright). *But cf.* In re World Auxiliary Power Co., 303 F.3d 1120 (9th Cir. 2002) (UCC filing does perfect an interest in property that could be registered as a copyright but has not yet been, rejecting *Avalon Software* and *AEG Acquisition*).

or trade names.[53] They are similarly not needed to perfect a security interest in patents.[54]

Almost all states have a certificate of title statute for motor vehicles, most of which are modeled on the Uniform Motor Vehicle Certificate of Title and Anti-Theft Act. If, as is common, a state's act provides that a security interest must be noted on the certificate of title for the secured party's rights to have priority over those of a lien creditor, *see* UMVCTA §§ 21, 25, then the certificate of title act provisions generally displace Article 9's filing system. U.C.C. §§ 9-102(a)(10) (definition of certificate of title); 9-311(a)(2), (3). However, a certificate of title statute will not displace the Article 9 filing system when the collateral is inventory held by a person that sells goods of the kind and that person is the one who created the security interest. § 9-311(d). Thus, a lender that is financing the inventory of an automobile dealer and that acquires a security interest in the dealer's inventory of automobiles will not be able to perfect its security interest in the cars by having its interest noted on the certificates of title. Instead, to perfect its security interest the lender must comply with the Article 9 perfection methods, such as by filing a financing statement.

In general, complying with a federal law that preempts the Article 9 filing system, an applicable certificate of title statute, or an alternate central filing system for particular collateral types is treated as the equivalent of the filing of a financing statement under Article 9. § 9-311(b). Apparently this means that at least some of Article 9's references to filing a financing statement include by implication compliance with such other law. *See* § 9-311 cmt. 6. However, this is not true for all such references. For example, we have already seen that § 9-516(a) provides

---

53 *See, e.g.*, Trimarchi v. Together Dev. Corp., 255 B.R. 606 (D. Mass. 2000) (ruling UCC filing was needed and that federal filing was ineffective).

54 *See, e.g.*, In re Cybernetic Servs., Inc., 252 F.3d 1039 (9th Cir. 2001) (UCC filing effective); In re Tower Tech, Inc., 67 F. App'x 521 (10th Cir. 2003) (filing with Patent Office is ineffective); In re Coldwave Systems, LLC, 368 B.R. 91 (Bankr. D. Mass. 2007) (filing with the Patent Office did not perfect a security interest); In re Pasteurized Eggs Corp., 296 B.R. 283 (Bankr. D.N.H. 2003) (filing with the Patent Office ineffective).

Recording the secured party's interest with the Patent Office may, however, be necessary to have priority over subsequent purchasers. *See* 35 U.S.C. § 261. That said, recording the assignment federally might impair the ability of the debtor to bring an infringement action. Such an action must be brought by all joint owners to avoid the possibility of subjecting the defendant to duplicative actions. *See* McKesson Automation, Inc. v. Swisslog Italia S.P.A., 2008 WL 4820506 (D. Del. 2008) (staying infringement action until the plaintiff – who had apparently paid off a secured loan but recorded no reassignment back – could clear up title).

that communication of a record to a filing office and tender of the appropriate fee constitutes filing. This rule applies to Article 9 financing statements but apparently not to property governed by a certificate of title statute. For such property, perfection depends upon compliance with the certificate of title statute, which might or might not protect a person who delivers the appropriate documents and payment to the certificating office, if the certificating office fails to make the proper notation.[55] Similarly, when federal law governs perfection, one must look to the applicable federal law to determine if perfection occurs when the records are presented to the appropriate office, when the office properly records the interest of the secured party, or some other time.[56]

---

[55] For cases ruling or suggesting that perfection occurs when the necessary documents are submitted to the titling office, see In re Thompson, 2018 WL 2717044 (Bankr. W.D. Va. 2018); In re Thompson, 2014 WL 2919313 (Bankr. W.D. Mich. 2014); In re Conklin, 511 B.R. 688 (Bankr. D. Id. 2014); In re Rumble, 2011 WL 1740966 (Bankr. W.D. Mo. 2011); In re Hartline, 2009 WL 2971762 (Bankr. M.D. Tenn. 2009). *See also* Uniform Motor Vehicle Certificate of Title and Anti-Theft Act § 20(b) (a security interest is perfected by the delivery to the relevant Department of the existing certificate of title, if any, the application for a certificate containing the name and address of the lienholder, and the applicable fee).

For cases ruling or suggesting the opposite, see McCarthy v. BMW Bank of N. Am., 509 F.3d 528 (D.C. Cir. 2007); In re O'Neill, 370 B.R. 332 (10th Cir. BAP 2007); Johnson v. Branch Banking and Trust Co., 313 S.W.3d 557 (Ky. 2010); In re Shepard, 2010 WL 1257672 (Bankr. D.S.D. 2010); In re Anderson, 2007 WL 1839699 (D. Ariz. 2007); In re Anderson, 351 B.R. 752 (Bankr. D. Kan. 2006); In re Darrington, 251 B.R. 808 (Bankr. E.D. Va. 1999).

Some jurisdictions follow a relation-back rule: if the security interest is properly noted the certificate of title, perfection relates back to when the documents were presented to the titling office with the appropriate fee. *See, e.g.*, Hyden v. AmeriCredit Fin. Servs., Inc., 2015 WL 1949747 (Bankr. D. Ariz. 2015); In re Baker, 345 B.R. 261 (D. Colo. 2006). *But see* In re O'Neill, 370 B.R. 332 (disagreeing with *Baker*).

[56] The Ship Mortgage Act provides that an assignment "filed in substantial compliance with this section is valid against any person from the time it is filed with the Secretary," 46 U.S.C. § 31321(a)(2), suggesting that rule for perfecting interests in ships is the same as the rule in § 9-516(a). The Copyright Act states that recordation of a document in the Copyright Office gives all persons constructive notice of the facts stated in the recorded if, "after the document is indexed by the Register of Copyrights, it would be revealed by a reasonable search under the title or registration number of the work," 17 U.S.C. § 205(c). This language suggests, but comes a bit short of actually stating, that recording occurs before indexing. Subsection (d) adds a relation-back rule: as between two conflicting transfers, the one executed first prevails if it is recorded first or it is recorded within one month after its execution in the United States or within two months after its execution outside the United States.

Problem 4-10

Steven Duke, the famous and prolific horror novelist, gave First Bank a security interest in his rights to royalties on 37 different books to secure a $300,000 loan. What must First Bank do to perfect that interest? Does the answer to that question depend on whether Duke or his publisher owns the copyrights? How many filings will it need? *See* 17 U.S.C. §§ 201(d), 204, 205; *Broadcast Music, Inc. v. Hirsch*, 104 F.3d 1163, 1166 (9th Cir. 1997).

Problem 4-11

A. Why does § 9-311(d) contain an exception for inventory held for sale or lease by a person engaged in the business of selling goods of that kind? In other words, why is compliance with the certificate of title statute not the appropriate way to perfect if the collateral is inventory?

B. Derelict Motors has approached First Bank for a $400,000 loan to be secured by its fleet of used cars. Most of these cars are held for sale, but some are provided to the sales staff and the owner for personal transportation and two are loaned on a daily basis to customers whose own cars are being repaired by Derelict's mechanics. What must First Bank do to perfect its security interest in all the cars? What information does First Bank need to answer this question reliably and how should it get that information? *See* §§ 9-102(a)(10), 9-311(a)(2), (d).

C. Driver borrowed $4,000 from State Bank to buy an all-terrain vehicle (ATV) for use in a ranching business and granted a security interest in the ATV to State Bank to secure the loan. State Bank filed a financing statement properly indicating the collateral as an "all-terrain vehicle." Is State Bank's security interest perfected? What do you need to know to answer that question? *See* §§ 9-102(a)(10), 9-311(a)(2), (d). *See also In re Renaud*, 308 B.R. 347 (8th Cir. BAP 2004); *In re Gaylord Grain L.L.C.*, 306 B.R. 624 (8th Cir. BAP 2004).

D. Daytona borrowed $9,000 from City Bank to take a vacation. In return, Daytona granted City Bank a security interest in Daytona's station wagon. City Bank had Daytona endorse the back of the certificate of title for the car and took possession of the certificate. Is City Bank's security interest perfected? *See In re Global Environmental Services Group, LLC*, 2006 WL 980582 (Bankr. D. Haw. 2006).

B. Perfection by Possession

Possession is the only method to perfect a security interest in tangible money as original collateral. § 9-312(b)(3). It is also a permissible method for perfecting a security interest in goods, certificated securities, instruments, and tangible negotiable documents of title. § 9-313(a). For other types of collateral – those that, by their nature, have no physical existence and cannot be possessed by anyone (*e.g.*, accounts, controllable electronic records, electronic documents, electronic money, and general intangibles) – possession is not an effective method to perfect a security interest. For chattel paper, which might be evidenced by tangible records, intangible records, or both, perfection can be obtained by a combination of possession of each authoritative tangible record and control of each authoritative intangible record. *See* § 9-314A.[57]

Note that while filing may also be used to perfect a security interest in instruments, chattel paper, and negotiable documents of title, possession (or in the case of chattel paper, possession and control) can entitle the secured party to a better priority. *See* §§ 8-303, 9-330, 9-331. Chapter Five will explore in more detail the various priority rules and how they affect the decision about which perfection method to employ.

The theory underlying possession as a perfection method is that, like filing a financing statement, it gives notice to the commercial world of the secured party's interest in the collateral. It is premised on the assumptions that anyone considering acquiring an interest in the property would naturally wish to see it (and possibly also take possession of it), that such inspection would necessarily reveal the creditor's possession, and that such revelation would, or at least should, alert the person conducting the inspection to the possibility that the possessing creditor might claim some rights in the property.

---

[57] Prior to the 2022 UCC Amendments, Article 9 distinguished between tangible chattel paper, which was written, and electronic chattel paper, which was intangible. A security interest in tangible chattel could be perfected by filing or possession; a security interest in electronic chattel paper could be perfected by filing control. One problem with that approach was that the records comprising chattel paper could consist of some that were tangible and some that were electronic. Another problem was that, after a security interest was perfected by possession or control, electronic records could be printed or written records could be converted into an electronic file. The amendments eliminated the distinction between tangible and electronic chattel paper and created a unified perfection method of possession and control of all authoritative copies. Perfection by filing remains effective.

At its most basic level, this probably makes sense. For example, suppose that Debbie pledges a diamond ring to Chris as collateral for a loan and delivers possession of the ring to Chris. In all likelihood, it would be very difficult while Chris retained possession of the ring for Debbie either to sell it or use it as collateral for a loan from someone other than Chris. Any likely buyer would want to see the ring and would wonder why Debbie did not have it.

You should, however, question the possession-gives-notice theory. After all, continuing with the example above, Debbie might be able to sell the ring to someone who already knows what it looks like. In doing so, she could explain her lack of possession by simply saying that she loaned the ring to Chris. Beyond that, the possession-gives-notice theory is hampered by the fact that Article 9 does not define "possession." *See* § 9-313 cmt. 3. Presumably, this is one of the issues on which the common law – with all its uncertainty – supplements the Code. *See* § 1-103(b).[58]

At least two things about possession are clear. First, a secured party may possess the collateral through an agent. *See* § 9-313 cmt. 3.[59] Indeed, corporate entities, such as banks, necessarily must act through human agents, and a contrary rule would prevent them from ever being deemed to have possession. Second, the debtor may not serve as the secured party's agent for this purpose. *Id.* Beyond this, however, the boundaries of possession might be very difficult to discern.

Consider goods that are kept in a safe deposit box at a bank. Are they in the possession of the person who rented the box or in the possession of the bank? If the renter were using the goods as collateral for a loan from the bank, the issue would be critical. Does it matter that the debtor cannot get to the goods without the Bank's consent and cooperation? Or, is the Bank's similar lack of complete control the important fact. Put another way, what is critical to the secured party's possession, the secured party's control or the debtor's lack of it? Which is more in keeping with the possession-gives-notice theory? There are no easy or clear answers to these questions.

---

[58] Cissell v. First Nat'l Bank of Cincinnati, 476 F. Supp. 474, 491 (S.D. Ohio 1979).

[59] Delivery of a certificated security in registered form to a secured party perfects an interest in the certificated security. § 9-313(e). *See also* § 8-102(a)(15), (16) (definition of certificated security), (13) (definition of "registered form"). Such delivery can be accomplished by giving possession of the certificated security to an agent of the secured party. *See* § 8-301(a).

On occasion, a third person – not the debtor and not the secured party or an agent of the secured party – maintains possession of the collateral. Article 9 deals with such a bailee's possession in three different ways. First, if collateral is a type of property for which a security interest can be perfected by possession, *see* § 9-313(a), and the collateral is neither goods covered by a document of title issued by the bailee nor certificated securities, the secured party may perfect its security interest in the collateral by getting the bailee to acknowledge in a signed record that the bailee holds the collateral for the secured party's benefit. § 9-313(c). However, the bailee has no obligation to provide such an acknowledgment and, even if it does provide an acknowledgment, it acquires no duties to the secured party beyond those it agrees to have. *See* § 9-313(g). Second, if the bailee has issued a nonnegotiable document of title covering goods in its possession, the secured party may perfect its security interest in the goods by getting the bailee to issue the document of title in the name of the secured party or by merely notifying the bailee of the secured party's interest. *See* § 9-312(d). Note, the bailee need not respond to this notification or agree to hold the goods on the secured party's behalf. Filing as to the goods also works. Third, if a bailee has issued a negotiable document of title covering the goods in its possession, then ownership of the goods is effectively locked up in the document and to properly perfect a security interest in the goods, the secured party should perfect a security interest in the document of title. *See* § 9-312(c)(1) & cmt. 7. This may be accomplished either by filing against or taking possession of the document of title.[60] Consider how much notice is provided by each of these perfection methods for collateral in the possession of a bailee.

Possession as a method of perfection is generally effective only so long as possession is retained. § 9-313(d) and (e). However, to accommodate certain industry practices, *see* § 9-313 cmt. 9, perfection can continue after the secured party delivers collateral to a third party, provided certain instructions precede or accompany delivery. *See* § 9-313(h). Perfection can also continue for a brief period after the secured party returns the collateral to the debtor. *See* § 9-312(f), (g).

During the time a secured party has possession of collateral, the secured party has the rights and duties as to the collateral specified in § 9-207.

---

[60] Security interests in goods covered by a negotiable or nonnegotiable document of title are explored in more depth in Chapter Six.

Problem 4-12

To secure a $50,000 loan, First Bank has a security interest in a $250,000 negotiable promissory note owned by and payable to Deserving Enterprises, Inc. First Bank has possession of the note. Deserving wants to borrow an additional $100,000 to be secured by the note. First Bank is willing to advance that additional amount, but Second Bank is willing to do so at a much lower interest rate. If Second Bank makes the loan and gets a security interest in the note, which of the following will suffice to perfect that interest?

A. First Bank agrees to hold the note for itself and Second Bank. *See* §§ 9-312(a), 9-313(a), (c). Is First Bank likely to do this? If not, what alternative ways to perfect do you recommend?

B. The majority shareholder of Deserving Enterprises, who is not an employee of the company, agrees to hold the note for both First Bank and Second Bank.

C. How, if at all, would the analysis of Part A change if the debt owed to Deserving were not evidenced by a promissory note but were instead recorded on the company's ledgers as an account receivable and First Bank had possession of the ledgers?

Problem 4-13

Diversified Enterprises signed a security agreement granting National Bank a security interest in all of Diversified's "inventory and equipment now owned or hereafter acquired" to secure a $1,000,000 line of credit. Diversified stores part of its inventory with Storage Monster, a warehouser of goods. How may National Bank perfect by possession its security interest in the items stored with Storage Monster in each of the following situations?

A. Storage Monster issued to Diversified several tangible negotiable warehouse receipts covering Diversified's goods in Storage Monster's warehouse.

B. Storage Monster issued to Diversified several tangible non-negotiable warehouse receipts covering the items in Storage's warehouse.

C. Storage Monster did not issue any warehouse receipts to Diversified covering the items in Storage Monster's warehouse.

Problem 4-14

First Bank wishes to acquire a security interest in some manufacturing equipment purchased by Big Dipper Manufacturing, Inc., and currently operated by its subsidiary, Little Dipper Manufacturing, Inc. What should First Bank do in conducting its search for existing security interests to be sure that it has uncovered all that are perfected? In answering this question, first determine all the ways a creditor could perfect a security interest in the equipment and then devise a method for discovering any security interest actually perfected in each of those possible ways.

C. Perfection by Control

Control is a method of perfection for investment property, deposit accounts, controllable electronic records, controllable accounts, controllable payment intangibles, electronic documents, electronic money, and letter-of-credit rights. *See* §§ 9-310(b)(8), 9-314.[61] For deposit accounts, electronic money, and letter-of-credit rights as original collateral (*i.e.*, not constituting proceeds), control is the exclusive method of perfection. *See* § 9-312(b).

Despite use of the same word, the term "control" is defined differently for these various types of collateral:

Type of Collateral	Definition of "Control"
electronic documents	§ 7-106
investment property	§§ 9-106 & 8-106
deposit accounts	§ 9-104
electronic money	§ 9-105A
letter-of-credit rights	§ 9-107
controllable accounts,	§§ 9-107A & 12-105
controllable electronic records	
controllable payment intangibles	

[61] As noted above, a combination of control and possession is a permissible method to perfect a security interest in chattel paper. *See* § 9-314A.

Although the various definitions of "control" have similarities, and the drafters have endeavored to harmonize them as much as possible, each is specific to the particular type of collateral involved.

Control is a conceptual analog to possession for certain types of intangible collateral, property for which physical possession is impossible. Accordingly, many of the rules associated with perfection by control are the same as those for perfection by possession. For example, just as perfection by possession can occasionally provide a better priority than perfection by filing, we will see in Chapter Five that a secured party can sometimes obtain a better priority by perfecting through control than through some other permissible method. Similarly, just as perfection by possession will be lost when the secured party relinquishes possession, control is sufficient to perfect a security interest only as long as the secured party retains control. *See* §§ 9-314(b), (c), 9-314A(b). Finally, a secured party in control of the collateral has many of the same rights and duties as a secured party in possession. *See* §§ 9-207, 9-208. One notable difference from the possession-based rules, however, is that a secured party can still have control over these types of assets even if the debtor has access to them. *See* §§ 9-104(b), 8-106(f), 12-105(a)(1)(B), (b)(2), (c).

However, the control-gives-notice theory might be even weaker than the possession-gives-notice theory. For example, a depositary bank has no duty to tell anyone that it has granted control of a deposit account to a third party. § 9-342. In reviewing the various ways of acquiring control of collateral, consider which are likely to provide interested parties with reason to suspect that the secured party might have a security interest.

We now focus briefly on control of one type of property: deposit accounts.[62] Read § 9-104. Notice that the depositary bank with a security interest in the deposit account automatically has control of the deposit account. For a secured party that is not the depositary bank, there are four methods for obtaining control: (i) enter into a control agreement with the depositary bank and the debtor, § 9-104(a)(2); (ii) become the depositary bank's customer on the deposit account, § 9-104(a)(3); (iii) obtain the acknowledgment of someone with control that it has control on

---

[62] Chapter Six explores control of investment property and control of controllable accounts, controllable electronic records, and controllable payment intangibles.

behalf of the secured party, § 9-104(a)(4);[63] or (iv) obtain the agreement of the depositary bank to serve as an agent of the secured party, § 9-104 cmt. 3.

Nothing requires a depositary bank to become another party's agent or to enter into a control agreement, *see* § 9-342, and obtaining the assent of most banks has proven to be much more difficult than the drafters of revised Article 9 anticipated. Depositary banks want to ensure that their own rights are protected and that they will incur no liability to the secured party for their own errors or delays in complying with the secured party's instructions. Perhaps more important, they want to ensure that the agency agreement or control agreement does not interfere with their normal processes for posting credits and debits to a deposit account. To deal with this problem, an ABA Task Force produced a model deposit account control agreement, and commentary thereto, for use in commercial transactions involving a security interest in a deposit account.[64] This model is the product of much negotiation and is intended to be generally acceptable to both the lending community (specifically, their legal counsel) and the operational departments of depositary institutions.

Problem 4-15

Demolition Equipment, Inc., a manufacturer of industrial equipment, signed a security agreement granting Lender a security interest in all of Demolition's "inventory, equipment, accounts, deposit accounts, and general intangibles, now owned or hereafter acquired" to secure a $1,000,000 line of credit. Demolition has a checking account maintained at Bank that is used in the course of its business.

A. How, if at all, can Lender perfect the security interest in the checking account without Bank's cooperation? *See* §§ 9-104, 9-312(b).

B. How, if at all, can Lender determine if anyone else has a perfected security interest in the checking account?

C. Lender, Demolition Equipment, and Bank enter into an agreement under which Bank promises that, within three business days after receiving

---

[63] This method, added by the 2022 UCC Amendments, makes it easier for multiple secured parties to have control.

[64] *See* Joint Task Force on Deposit Account Control Agreements, *Initial Report of the Joint Task Force on Deposit Account Control Agreements*, 61 BUS. LAW. 745 (2006); Joint Task Force on Deposit Account Control Agreements, *Additional Report*, 64 BUS. LAW. 801 (2009).

Lender's instructions with regard to the funds credited to Demolition Equipment's checking account, Bank will honor those instructions.

1. Why does Bank want three days to comply to comply with Lender's instructions? *See Initial Report of the Joint Task Force on Deposit Account Control Agreements,* 61 BUS. LAW. 745 (2006).
2. What might happen during those three days?
3. Given this three-day period for Bank to comply with Lender's instructions, is Lender's security interest in the checking account perfected?

D. Automatic Perfection

The last method of perfection – automatic perfection – abandons any pretense of providing notice. In such circumstances, attachment of the security interest alone is sufficient for the security interest to be perfected. Automatic perfection exists because the drafters concluded that, in certain situations, the cost of requiring notice would greatly exceed any benefit it produced. But even accepting that conclusion, automatic perfection has a cost. While automatic perfection makes it very easy for the secured party to perfect, it can make it very difficult for a subsequent searcher – someone interested in acquiring rights in the collateral – to learn about the existing, perfected security interest. The discussion that follows highlights some of the more important automatic perfection rules. For each, consider what impact it has on a subsequent searcher. How would such a person discover that a security interest encumbers the collateral?

1. Purchase-money Security Interests in Consumer Goods

Consider the following scenario. Retailer sells a new wide-screen plasma TV on credit to Customer, for use in Customer's home. The signed credit agreement includes the grant of a security interest to Retailer. Retailer need not file a financing statement or possess the TV in order to perfect its security interest. *See* §§ 9-310(b)(2), 9-309(1). This is because Retailer has a "purchase-money security interest" ("PMSI"), *see* § 9-103, and the collateral constitutes of consumer goods, *see* § 9-102(a)(23). The rationale for this automatic perfection rule is fairly obvious. The consumer is unlikely to tolerate perfection by possession and requiring a filing to perfect would add costs to ordinary consumer transactions and inundate the filing offices with thousands of filings for which few people will ever search. After all, with the possible exception of cars and boats, used consumer goods are rarely used as collateral.[65]

This brings us to an exception to this automatic perfection rule. Assume that instead of selling home electronics, Retailer is a car dealer and the property Customer purchased on credit was a car for personal use. To perfect its security interest, Retailer will have to comply with the applicable certificate of title law even though the collateral is consumer goods and the security interest is a PMSI.

Bear in mind the two requirements of this automatic perfection rule: (1) the security interest must be a PMSI; *and* (2) the collateral must be consumer goods that are not subject to a certificate of title law as described in § 9-311. So, for example, if Customer had purchased the plasma TV for use in the waiting room at her auto repair shop, the collateral would be equipment, not consumer goods. Retailer would therefore have to file a financing statement or take possession of the TV in order to perfect its security interest. A similar result would occur if Customer, having purchased the TV several months ago for use in her home, borrowed money from Bank to take a vacation and gave Bank a security interest in the TV to secure the debt. Even though the collateral is consumer goods, the security interest would not be a PMSI. For Bank to perfect its interest in the TV, it must either take possession of it or file a financing statement.

Let us examine more closely the definition of a PMSI, a concept relevant not just to perfection, but also to priority. Read § 9-103(b)(1) and then read the definitions in subsection (a). Subsection (b)(1) and the definitions determine whether the security interest is a PMSI. To be a PMSI, the collateral must be "purchase-money collateral" and the secured obligation must be a "purchase-money obligation." To illustrate these requirements, consider the following examples.

1. Seller sold a piece of equipment to Buyer on credit and retained a security interest in the item sold to secure the unpaid portion of the purchase price. In this case, the collateral is purchase-money collateral and the obligation is a purchase-money obligation because it was incurred for "all or part of the price of the collateral." § 9-103(a)(2).

---

[65] Indeed, it is an unfair credit practice to take a nonpossessory, non-purchase-money security interest in some types of household goods. *See* 16 C.F.R. §§ 444.1(i), (j), 444.2(a)(4). *See also* 12 C.F.R. §§ 227.12(d), 227.13. Unfair credit practices are illegal, *see* 15 U.S.C. § 45(a)(1), but there is no private right of action for engaging in them. Instead, enforcement is left to the FTC (although there might be a private remedy for violating a state consumer-protection statute).

Now consider an alternative example.

2. Creditor made a loan to Borrower that Borrower used to purchase a new piece of equipment. Borrower granted Creditor a security interest in that equipment to secure the loan. Borrower's obligation to Creditor on the loan is also a purchase-money obligation, this time because it was "for value given to enable the debtor to acquire rights in or use of the collateral."

Thus, both a seller of goods and a lender can obtain a PMSI. Now change one fact in example 2.

3. Borrower did not use the loaned funds to purchase the new piece of equipment. Instead, Borrower used the loaned funds to pay some bills and used other funds to purchase the equipment. The obligation of Debtor on the loan is, apparently, not a purchase-money obligation because of the last eight words of subsection (a)(2): "if the value is in fact so used." For a lender to have a PMSI, it must be able to directly trace the loaned funds to the purchase of the collateral. If the loan is first commingled in the borrower's checking account, the resulting security interest might not be a PMSI.[66]

Now change a different fact.

4. Borrower did use the funds Creditor loaned to purchase the new piece of equipment but instead of granting a security interest in that piece of new equipment to secure the loan, Borrower granted Creditor a security interest in some other property Borrower already owned. Now the loan is not a purchase-money obligation because it did not enable Borrower to acquire the collateral. It enabled Borrower to acquire a piece of equipment but that equipment was not the collateral. Accordingly, Creditor's security interest in the already-owned property is not a PMSI.

---

[66] *Compare* In re Winchester, 2007 WL 420391 (Bankr. N.D. Iowa 2007) (bank's security interest in piano dolly was not a PMSI because debtor had purchased the dolly two weeks before the bank made the secured loan), *with* First Nat'l Bank in Munday v. Lubbock Feeders, L.P., 183 S.W.3d 875 (Tex. Ct. App. 2006) (to qualify as a PMSI, loan must be "closely allied" with debtor's purchase of the collateral but need not precede that purchase; advances made as much as 18 days after debtor's purchase were closely allied because they could be traced to the purchase (in some unspecified manner)); In re Murray, 352 B.R. 340 (Bankr. M.D. Ga. 2006) (debt incurred for documentary fee, certificate of title fee, and extended service contract, in connection with motor vehicle purchase, was all for the "price" of the vehicle, and thus creditor had a PMSI).

Notice that the examples above all involved equipment. If the goods are inventory, § 9-103(b)(2) provides greater leeway for what constitutes a PMSI. The easiest way to understand this rule is through another example.

5. Debtor signed a security agreement granting SP a security interest in all existing and after-acquired inventory to secure all existing debts and future advances. Debtor then acquired Item A as inventory, using a loan from SP (Loan A) to pay all or part of the purchase price. Some time later, SP made another loan (Loan B) to Debtor to enable Debtor to acquire Item B as inventory. Under the rule of § 9-103(b)(1), SP's security interest in Item A to secure Loan A is a PMSI and Lender's security interest in Item B to secure Loan B is also a PMSI. However, because of the after-acquired property clause in the security agreement, Loan A is also secured by Item B. Moreover, because of the future advances clause, Loan B is also secured by Item A. If § 9-103(b)(1) were the only rule, the security interest in Item A to secure Loan B and the security interest in Item B to secure Loan A would not be PMSIs. This is where the rule of § 9-103(b)(2) kicks in. Under it, both the security interest in Item A to secure Loan B and the security interest in Item B to secure Loan A are also PMSIs. As a result, Lender's interests in Items A and B are fully PMSIs.

Former Article 9 was silent about whether purchase-money status existed in the following situations:

(1) The purchase-money collateral secures a non-purchase-money obligation (*i.e.*, the collateral secures additional debt);
(2) The purchase-money obligation is secured by non-purchase-money collateral (*i.e.*, additional collateral secures the debt); or
(3) The debtor later refinances the purchase-money obligation.

Revised Article 9 now contains express rules to deal with such matters when the transaction is not a consumer-goods transaction. Read § 9-103(f), (g). Also, review the definition of "consumer-goods transaction" in § 9-102(a)(24). In essence, these rules allow a security interest to be a PMSI in part and a non-PMSI in part, and they provide that refinancing a purchase-money obligation does not destroy PMSI status. In addition, Article 9 now contains rules for how to allocate payments between the purchase-money and non-purchase-money portions of the secured obligation. *See* § 9-103(e). If a transaction is a consumer-goods transaction, the official text of Article 9 provides no guidance on how to deal with these issues. *See* § 9-103(h).

Several states have dealt with this textual vacuum by enacting a non-uniform version of § 9-103 to make these rules applicable to consumer-goods transactions.[67] In other states, courts must supply the applicable rule.[68]

Problem 4-16

A. In July, Dan purchased a refrigerator on credit from Appliance Heaven. To secure the price owed, Dan signed a security agreement granting a security interest in the refrigerator to Appliance Heaven.
   1. How should Appliance Heaven perfect its security interest in the refrigerator? Would it matter if Dan purchased the refrigerator for use in the employee break room at his manufacturing business?
   2. A week after Dan purchased the refrigerator, Dan purchased a new stove from Appliance Heaven. The security agreement Dan signed granted Appliance Heaven a security interest in the refrigerator and stove to secure the purchase price of both the stove and the refrigerator. How should Appliance Heaven perfect its security interest in both the stove and refrigerator?

B. Donna purchased a new car from Auto World, Inc. To finance the purchase, Donna borrowed part of the purchase price from State Bank and signed a security agreement granting State Bank a security interest in the car to secure the loan. How should State Bank perfect its security interest? *See* § 9-309(1).

C. Daniel has approached First Bank for a $7,000 personal loan. He has offered as collateral the 29-foot boat he keeps up at the lake. The state's

---

[67] *See, e.g.*, Fla. Stat. § 679.1031(6); Idaho Code § 28-9-103(f); Ind. Code § 26-1-9.1-103; Kan. Stat. § 84-9-103; La. Rev. Stat. § 10:9-103(f); Md. Code, Com. Law § 9-103(f); Neb. Rev. Stat. U.C.C. § 9-103(f); N.D. Cent. Code § 41-09-03(6); S.D. Codified Laws § 57A-9-103(f).

[68] *See* In re Jett, 563 B.R. 206 (Bankr. S.D. Miss. 2017) (because the transformation rule, not the dual-status rule, should be applied to PMSIs in consumer goods, a bank's PMSI in the debtors' vehicle lost purchase-money status when the debtors and bank refinanced the debt and included in it two previously unsecured loans).

certificate of title statute does not cover boats.[69] What should First Bank do, before making the loan, to check for perfected security interests in the boat? In answering this, be sure to contemplate all the possible ways a security interest in the boat could be perfected.

D. On October 1, Debra borrowed $25,000 to purchase a new grand piano for personal use. Credit Union made the check payable directly to the seller, which delivered the piano to Debra's home that same day. On October 2, Credit Union received an updated credit report on Debra and decided that Debra was not as good a credit risk as it had thought. A loan officer immediately called Debra and she agreed to grant the Credit Union a security interest in the piano to secure the debt. She went to the Credit Union's offices later that day and signed a security agreement. Is Credit Union's security interest perfected? *See* § 9-103(a)(2).

2. Associated Collateral

In some situations, perfection of an interest in one type of collateral automatically perfects a security interest in another type of collateral. *See* §§ 9-310(b)(1), 9-308(d), (e). The rationale for not requiring a filed financing statement, possession, or control for perfection in these situations is that there is such a close connection between the original collateral and the collateral for which the automatic perfection rule applies that taking the perfection step for the original collateral is sufficient notice of the secured party's interest in the associated collateral.

To illustrate § 9-308(d), assume a secured party perfects a security interest in an account. The account is supported with a guarantee from a third party. The guarantee is a "supporting obligation." *See* § 9-102(a)(78). You might remember from Chapter Two that if a security interest attaches to a right to payment, such as an account, it also attaches automatically to any supporting obligation. § 9-203(f). Section 9-308(d) then does for perfection what § 9-203(f) does for attachment: by perfecting a security interest in the account, the secured party automatically perfects its security interest in the supporting obligation.

A similar rule applies to perfection of a security interest in a right to payment that is itself supported by a lien, mortgage, or security interest. Recall from Chapter

---

[69] The boat is far too small to be covered by the Ship Mortgage Act, and thus perfection is not preempted by federal law. *See supra* pages 292-293.

Two that a security interest in a right to payment automatically extends to a lien securing that right. *See* § 9-203(g). Well, such automatic attachment is supplemented with automatic perfection. Perfecting a security interest in a right to payment automatically perfects the security interest in any supporting lien. *See* § 9-308(e). Thus, for example, if a right to payment is secured by a mortgage in real estate, and the security interest in the right to payment is perfected, the security interest in the mortgage will be automatically attached and perfected. This means that recording an assignment of the mortgage in the real estate records is not necessary to perfect a security interest in the mortgage. Recording an assignment of the mortgage might, however, be necessary as a matter of real estate law for the secured party to be able to foreclose on the mortgage. *Cf.* § 9-607(b) (authorizing such recording in order to permit nonjudicial foreclosure).

3. Other Automatic Perfection Rules

The remaining automatic perfection rules, *see* §§ 9-310(b)(2), 9-309(2)–(14). 9-312(e), are an eclectic array of provisions with no general unifying theme. Three deal with security interests that arise by operation of law under some other article of the UCC and for which the secured party might not think to file a financing statement. *See* § 9-309(6)–(8). Two relate to types of transactions that were not within the scope of former Article 9: sales of payment intangibles and promissory notes. *See* § 9-309(3), (4). They were brought within Article 9 in 1999 so that its priority and collection rules could apply, not to require public notice of the transaction. Accordingly, automatic perfection was deemed appropriate. One provides temporary perfection – lasting only 20 days from when attachment occurs – if the collateral consists of certificated securities, negotiable documents, or instruments and the secured party gave new value. *See* § 9-312(e). Most of the remainder involve highly specialized financing transactions, *see* § 9-309(5), (10), (11), (13), (14), or transactions that are really not financing transactions at all, *see* § 9-309(12).

Perhaps the most important of this remaining eclectic mix of rules is § 9-309(2), which provides for automatic perfection of an assignment of accounts or payment intangibles which does not, either by itself or in conjunction with other assignments to the same assignee, transfer a significant part of the debtor's accounts or payment intangibles. Note, use of the word "assignment" allows the provision to cover both a collateralized borrowing (*i.e.*, the use of accounts or payment intangibles to secure a debt) and an outright sale, each of which is an Article 9 transaction. *See* §§ 9-102(a)(7A), (7B), 9-109(a)(3). Compare this rule with § 9-109(d)(4) through

(7), which excepts from Article 9 altogether certain assignments of rights to payment.

In deciding whether an assignment of accounts or payment intangibles transfers a significant part of the debtor's outstanding receivables, courts look not only at the percentage of outstanding receivables that are transferred but also whether the assignee regularly receives assignments of receivables from others. The automatic perfection rule of § 9-309(2) is designed to protect casual and isolated transactions, in which no one would think of filing. *See* § 9-309 cmt. 4. Consequently, an assignee who is regularly engaged in commercial financing and routinely receives assignments of receivables is expected to perfect by filing. *Id.*[70]

Another provision of particular note is § 9-309(5). This provision reflects the inclusion within the scope of revised Article 9 of an assignment of rights under a health care insurance policy. While Article 9 does not apply to the assignment – either outright or as security for a debt – of claims under most types of insurance as original collateral,[71] Article 9 does apply to the assignment of a health-care-insurance receivable. § 9-109(d)(8).[72] A health-care-insurance receivable is a type

---

[70] *See also* Smith v. MCF Capital, LLC, 2019 WL 13217125 (S.D. Miss. 2019) (a security interest that lawyers had in a colleague's contingent right to attorney's fees in a single pending case was automatically perfected under § 9-309(2) because the one receivable was less than 15% of the colleague's total receivables and the lawyers, even though sophisticated, were not commercial lenders who regularly purchased receivables).

[71] Recall, however, that a claim under an insurance policy might be proceeds of other collateral, a fact that is recognized in § 9-109(d)(8). § 9-102(a)(64).

The fact that Article 9 does not apply to a security interest in insurance claims or policies as original collateral does not mean it is impossible to get a security interest in such things. It means merely that the common law governs the attachment, perfection, and priority of such a security interest. *See, e.g.*, In re Barbato, 2021 WL 5173354 (Bankr. W.D.N.Y. 2021) (a bank's security interest in two annuity contracts – structured as a conditional assignment – was perfected under New York common law when the issuer of each annuity received and acknowledged notification of the bank's interest; the bank's security interest in one of the annuities was also perfected by possession of the annuity contract).

[72] As a result, Article 9 does not govern how to either obtain or perfect a consensual lien on an insurance policy as original collateral. Such matters are left to the common law. *See, e.g.*, In re JII Liquidating, Inc., 344 B.R. 875 (Bankr. N.D. Ill. 2006) (Article 9 does not apply to a security interest in unearned insurance premiums, and thus the insured's premium financier did not need to file a UCC financing statement to perfect its security interest; it needed merely to obtain the right to cancel the policies). *See also* In re St. James Inc., 402 B.R. 209 (Bankr. E.D. Mich. 2009); In re Silver State Helicopters, LLC, 403 B.R. 849 (Bankr. D. Nev. 2009).

of account, § 9-102(a)(2), and is defined as a claim or right to payment under an insurance policy for health care goods or services provided to the insured. § 9-102(a)(46).

To understand this automatic perfection rule, consider the following scenario. You are ill or suffer an injury for which you require treatment from a physician or hospital. Fortunately, your health insurance will cover all or part of the cost of such treatment. When you arrive for the treatment, the health care provider requires that you assign to it your claim for reimbursement from your insurer. That assignment from you (the patient) to the health care provider of your right to payment under a health insurance policy is governed by Article 9. As a result, the health care provider needs to have a method of perfecting its interest in that claim under the policy of insurance but, as you can imagine, it would be very burdensome if the health care provider had to file a financing statement against each one of its patients. For that reason, § 9-309(5) allows for automatic perfection of the health care provider's security interest in the claim under the insurance policy. Note, however, if the health care provider then further assigns – either outright or as security for a debt – that right to payment to another entity, such as the lender financing the health care provider's business, that further assignment creates a security interest governed by Article 9 in favor of the lender. *See* § 9-109(d)(8). However, the lender would have to file a financing statement to perfect its security interest in the claim under the insurance policy. The automatic perfection of § 9-309(5) applies only to the first assignment of the claim under the health insurance policy, the one from the patient to the health care provider. The subsequent assignment from the health care provider to the lender is likely to cover many insurance claims, but because it involves only one debtor (the health care provider), it is not unusually burdensome for the lender to file a financing statement to perfect.

Some states have non-uniform automatic perfection rules. For example, in New York, which treats rights in a cooperative apartment as personal property, the cooperative association can have a security interest, called a "cooperative organization security interest," in a cooperative interest to secure obligations incident to ownership of that cooperative interest.[73] Such a cooperative organization security interest is automatically perfected.[74]

---

[73] *See* N.Y. U.C.C. (McKinney's) § 9-102(27-d).

[74] *See* N.Y. U.C.C. (McKinney's) § 9-308(h). *See also* In re McCoy, 496 B.R. 678 (Bankr. E.D.N.Y. 2011).

Problem 4-17

A. Diseased signed a document assigning to his physician any rights to collect under Diseased's health insurance policy for services rendered by his doctor. Does the physician need to do anything to perfect her interest in the rights under the insurance policy?

B. Doctor signed a security agreement granting State Bank a security interest in all "accounts now owned or hereafter acquired" to secure a loan from State Bank. Does State Bank need to do anything to perfect its security interest in the proceeds of health care insurance policies which Doctor's patients assign to Doctor?

C. Discounter, a payee on several negotiable promissory notes, transferred those notes to Financial Servicer in return for 80% of the face amount of the notes. The transfer agreement provides that if Financial Servicer does not collect at least 90% of the face amount of the notes from the obligors on the notes, Financial Servicer has a right of recourse against Discounter for the difference between its actual collections and 90% of the face amount of the notes. Does Financial Servicer need to take any action under Article 9 in order to perfect its interest in those notes?

SECTION 4. CHOICE OF LAW ISSUES

So far we have been assuming that getting the security interest perfected does not depend upon where the debtor is located, where the collateral is located, or the method used to perfect. Now that we have explored the various methods of perfection, we turn our attention to the question of what state's law governs perfection of the security interest. This question is necessary because Article 9 is enacted at the state level, not as a matter of federal law.

It is also necessary for a very practical reason. In general, parties are free to select any state's law to govern their commercial transaction, at least if that state bears a reasonable relationship to the transaction.[75] This freedom does not apply to the law governing perfection, however.[76] That is because of what perfection is all about. Whereas attachment and enforcement concern the relative rights and duties of the debtor and the secured party – in short, it is about their contractual

---

[75] *See* § 1-301(a).

[76] *See* § 1-301(c).

relationship – perfection is about the secured party's relationship to others who have acquired or wish to acquire rights in the collateral. In other words, it is about providing notice of the secured party's interest in the collateral to the remainder of the commercial world. Obviously, the terms of the debtor's agreement with the secured party cannot alter the way that notice is provided; if it did, the commercial world could not be expected to find it. Accordingly, the debtor and secured party cannot alter the way in which the secured party may perfect. They cannot alter the applicable perfection methods (*e.g.*, filing, control, possession) and, if perfection is to be accomplished by filing, they cannot alter the proper state in which to file. Searchers need to know where to search.

To help understand the issue further and appreciate the Article 9 solution to it, imagine that in State A parties are litigating whether a security interest is perfected. Assume the secured party is located in State A, the debtor is located in State B, and the tangible collateral is located in State C. The court in State A will first look to its choice-of-law principles to determine which state's law will apply to the litigation. That choice of law rule is in § 1-301. In all likelihood, unless the agreement of the parties specifies otherwise, the court in State A will determine that State A's law applies to the litigation. The court will then look to Article 9 as enacted in State A to determine which state's law governs perfection, the effect of perfection and non-perfection, and priority. *See* §§ 9-301 through 9-307. In other words, those provisions in Article 9 as enacted in State A will tell the court what state's law to look at to determine whether the secured party has taken the proper perfection step as to the collateral at issue. If the court in the first instance had determined that State B's law applied to the litigation, the court would have looked at State B's enactment of Article 9, including State B's version of § 9-301 through § 9-307, to determine which state's law to look at to determine if the secured party had taken the proper steps to perfect its interest.

The purpose of this two-step process – first determine which state's law applies generally, then look to that state's version of Article 9 to determine which state's law governs perfection – solves what would otherwise be a huge problem. Secured parties need to be able to reliably determine what state's law governs perfection at the inception of their transactions, when they make their loans and seek to perfect their security interests. In particular, if they plan to perfect by filing a financing statement, they need to know in which state to file. Because all 50 states have enacted the choice-of-law rules in § 9-301 through § 9-307 in their uniform version, it does not matter in which state the litigation is commenced or which state's law applies generally to a dispute, things a secured party could know only with the benefit of foresight. The law governing perfection, the effect of perfection and non-perfection, and priority will be largely independent of where the litigation occurs or what the agreement between the debtor and the secured party provides.[77] Thus we can ignore the initial choice-of-law question that the forum state must answer and focus instead on determining the state whose law governs perfection, something the secured party can determine at the inception of the transaction.

Before we study the details of the Article 9 choice-of-law rules, one more preliminary item should be addressed. The rules in § 9-301 through § 9-307 determine which state's law governs perfection, the effect of perfection and non-perfection, and priority issues. "Perfection" as used in these sections does not mean the same as "perfection" in § 9-308(a): attachment plus an applicable perfection step. Rather "perfection" as used in § 9-301 through § 9-307 means only the "perfection step." Thus, one must look outside Article 9 to determine which state's law governs attachment, as well as such other issues as the scope of Article 9 and the enforcement of a security interest. *See* § 9-301 cmt. 2.[78]

If all states had enacted the uniform version of Article 9, none had any other statutes pertaining to these issues, and the case law interpreting Article 9 was uniform throughout the country, this choice-of-law question would never matter. However, we have already seen that states have enacted non-uniform rules concerning the scope of Article 9,[79] attachment of a security interest,[80] and

---

77 We have to worry a little due to the enactment of non-uniform versions of § 9-109, the scope section. *See* PEB REPORT, EFFECT OF NON-UNIFORM SCOPE PROVISIONS IN REVISED ARTICLE 9 OF THE UNIFORM COMMERCIAL CODE (2004). If a transaction is outside the scope of Article 9 as enacted in a particular state, Article 9 as enacted in that state will not govern the applicable perfection step. Indeed, the whole concept of perfection might not apply. We also have to worry a little if a non-U.S. forum has jurisdiction over the litigation where perfection might be an issue. The non-U.S. forum might decide to look to the law of a country other than the United States. Whether that other law would then direct the court back to U.S. law for purposes of determining perfection of the security interest is an interesting issue. International choice of law issues are beyond the scope of these materials.

78 *See* Royce v. Michael R. Needle, P.C., 381 F. Supp. 3d 968 (N.D. Ill. 2019) (Article 9 contains no choice-of-law rule for issues involving the attachment of a security interest; accordingly, under general choice-of-law principles, attachment of a security interest was governed by the law of Illinois, where the secured party was located and the collateral was generated, not Pennsylvania where the debtor is located).

79 *See supra* Chapter Two, notes 122 & 127.

80 *See supra* Chapter Two, notes 10–13. *See also supra* Chapter Two, notes 90 & 108

enforcement of a security interest.[81] To determine which state's law governs these issues, a court will need to apply traditional conflict-of-law principles. A choice-of-law clause in the security agreement will often be helpful but it will not be determinative, particularly on such matters as whether the debtor has rights in the collateral or the power to convey rights in it.[82]

The basic choice-of-law rule for perfection is contained in § 9-301(1): absent an exception, the law of the debtor's location governs the perfection step. That rule is subject to the exceptions contained in § 9-303 through § 9-306, each of which is based on the type of collateral involved:

property covered by a certificate of title statute	§ 9-303
deposit accounts	§ 9-304
investment property	§ 9-305
letter-of-credit rights	§ 9-306

The basic rule is also subject to the exceptions in two other subsections of § 9-301. First, the law of the state where the collateral is located governs the perfection step for a security interest in three circumstances: when the secured party perfects its security interest through possession of collateral, § 9-301(2); when the collateral is fixtures and perfection is through a fixture filing, § 9-301(3)(A); and when the collateral is timber to be cut, § 9-301(3)(B). Second, the law of the state where the wellhead or minehead is located will govern perfection of a security interest in as-extracted collateral. § 9-301(4).

As you can see, however, the basic rule of the debtor's location applies to virtually all non-realty related collateral in which the secured party seeks to perfect by filing. Section 9-307 then provides guidance on where the debtor is located for purpose of this rule. This begins with an inquiry into what kind of entity the debtor is. The location of a registered organization is determined under § 9-307(e) and (g). Read § 9-102(a)(71) for the definition of registered organization. In general, this will be the location in which it is registered. Thus a corporation is deemed located

---

(dealing with non-uniform rules overriding restrictions on assignment).

[81] *See supra* Chapter Three, notes 9–15, 33–39, 46–50 & 82.

[82] *See* Stephen L. Sepinuck, *What Choice Do I Have? – Choice-of-Law Clauses Governing Attachment of a Security Interest*, 10 THE TRANSACTIONAL LAW. 9 (June 2020). *See also* RESTATEMENT (SECOND) OF CONFLICT OF LAWS § 187(2)(b) (a contractual choice of law will not be respected if the chosen law would violate a fundamental policy of the jurisdiction whose law would govern but for the parties' selection).

in its state of incorporation. The location of an individual or an organization other than a registered organization is determined under § 9-307(b), (c) and (d). In general, an individual debtor is located at his or her principal residence and non-registered organizations are located at their place of business if they have one or their chief executive office if they have more than one. Determining the debtor's principal residence or chief executive office can be difficult, but rarely are there more than two likely possibilities. *See* § 9-307 cmt. 2.

Problem 4-18

To secure a $1,000,000 line of credit, Digital Appliances signed a security agreement granting a security interest to National Bank in all its "existing and after-acquired goods, accounts, chattel paper, instruments, deposit accounts, general intangibles, documents of title, investment property, letter-of-credit rights, and money." Digital is in the business of manufacturing and selling wireless headphones. You have learned the following information. Digital is incorporated in Minnesota. Its corporate offices are located in St. Paul, Minnesota, its manufacturing facility is located in Mason City, Iowa, and it stores its manufactured headphones prior to sale in a warehouse in Minnesota. You have determined that Digital has the following items of collateral. As to each item of collateral, which state's law will govern perfection of National Bank's security interest?

A. Various component parts used in manufacturing headphones. The parts are located at the manufacturing facility in Iowa.

B. Completed headphones stored in the warehouse in Minnesota.

C. Completed headphones stored in a bonded warehouse in Wisconsin run by Storage Monster and for which Storage Monster has issued a negotiable warehouse receipt. Digital has possession of the warehouse receipt.

D. A checking account at State Bank. State Bank is incorporated in New York and the checking account is held by the branch located in Wisconsin.

E. Amounts due and owing from several retailers that have purchased headphones from Digital. The retailers are located in Iowa and Minnesota.

F. Negotiable promissory notes payable on demand, to the order of Digital, and issued by Music Heaven in payment for headphones. Music Heaven is incorporated in Iowa.

G. Contracts signed by several retailers promising to pay for headphones purchased and granting Digital a security interest in those headphones to secure the purchase price. The retailers are located in Iowa and Minnesota.
H. Cash on hand in the amount of $10,000. The cash is at Digital's corporate office.
I. Trucks for transporting headphones between the storage warehouse and the various retailers.

Problem 4-19

Dawn wants to borrow money from First Bank to finance her bookstore. First Bank proposes to take a security interest in all of the bookstore's inventory, equipment, and accounts. The bookstore will be located in Wisconsin in a small town near the border with Illinois. Dawn lives across the border in Illinois. What do you need to know to determine which state's law governs perfection of First Bank's security interest?

e-Exercise 4-D
Choice of Law

Test Your Knowledge
Exam Five – Obtaining Perfection

SECTION 5. POST-CLOSING CHANGES THAT MIGHT AFFECT PERFECTION

After a security interest is perfected, some events might cause the security interest to become unperfected in some or all of the collateral. We have already seen a few of those things in the preceding material in this Chapter.

For example, we know that if a security interest is perfected by possession or control of the collateral and the secured party loses possession or control, perfection of the security interest will end. §§ 9-313, 9-314. *But cf.* § 9-312(f), (g) (providing for temporary perfection upon release of possession of some types of collateral). We also know that the mere passage of time might cause perfection of a security interest to lapse due to the limited duration of the effectiveness of a financing statement. § 9-515. The secured party can prevent the expiration of the financing statement by filing an effective continuation statement within the last six months before the financing statement would otherwise expire. § 9-515(c). As the following case excerpt demonstrates, attorneys must be very careful to avoid malpractice liability resulting from such a loss of perfection.

BARNES V. TURNER
606 S.E.2d 849 (Ga. 2004)

Fletcher, Chief Justice

[In October, 1996, William Barnes, Jr. sold his auto-parts company to the Lipps, who paid $40,000 at the closing and executed a ten-year promissory note in favor of Barnes for the $180,000 balance. The note was secured by a blanket lien on the Lipps's assets. Barnes's attorney, David Turner, Jr., perfected Barnes's security interest by filing UCC financing statements but did not inform Barnes that under § 9-515, financing statements are effective for only five years, although their effectiveness may be continued for another five years by filing a continuation statement no earlier than six months before the end of the initial period. No renewal statements were filed and in October, 2001, the original financing statements lapsed. By that time, the Lipps had pledged the collateral to two other lenders. Both of those lenders properly perfected their security interests, which put them in a senior position to Barnes when his financing statements lapsed. Barnes is still owed more than $140,000 under the promissory note, and one of the Lipps is now in Chapter 7 bankruptcy.

Barnes sued Turner for malpractice in 2002. The trial court dismissed the action, finding that the only possible incident of malpractice was Turner's failure in 1996 to inform Barnes of the limited effectiveness of the filed financing statements, and thus the four-year statute of limitations had run. The court of appeals affirmed and Barnes appealed to the state supreme court.]

1. Barnes contends that the Court of Appeals erred in simply looking to Turner's actions in October 1996 as constituting the malpractice. If Turner had renewed the financing statements in 2001, Barnes argues, there would have been no lapse in his security interest and thus no malpractice. Barnes contends that Turner's duty was to safeguard his security interest, which Turner could have satisfied by *either* informing Barnes of the renewal requirement or renewing the financing statements in 2001. Under this view, Turner breached his duty in 2001, when he failed to do both, and thus the statute of limitations on Barnes's action has not expired. For the following reasons, we agree. * * *

Turner contends that he was not retained to file renewal statements. While Georgia's appellate courts have not previously addressed this issue, decisions from other states make clear that an attorney in Turner's position must at least file original UCC financing statements, even absent specific direction from the client. We agree. An attorney has the duty to act with ordinary care, skill, and diligence in representing his client. In sale of business transactions where the purchase price is to be paid over time and collateralized, it is paramount that the seller's attorney prepare and file UCC financing statements to perfect his client's security interest. We further hold, for the reasons given below, that if the financing statements require renewal before full payment is made to the seller, then the attorney has some duty regarding this renewal. Otherwise the unpaid portion of the purchase price becomes unsecured and the seller did not receive the protection he bargained for.

Safeguarding a security interest is not some unexpected duty imposed upon the unwitting lawyer; it goes to the very heart of why Turner was retained: to sell Barnes's business in exchange for payment. We do not, as the dissent contends, demand that the lawyer "ascertain the full extent of the client's 'objectives' "; only that the lawyer take reasonable, legal steps to fulfill the client's *main, known* objective – to be paid for the business he sold.

* * * When the dissent argues that Turner's duty was simply to "close" the transaction, it fails to recognize that closing this particular transaction meant taking the reasonable steps that competent attorneys would take to legally secure their clients' right to receive payment for the businesses they have sold. Where payment is to be made in less than five years, Georgia law does not require renewal of the initial financing statements and thus the lawyer's duty is only to file the initial statements. But where payment is to take longer than five years, the lawyer – being trusted by his client to know how to safeguard his security interest under Georgia law – has some duty regarding renewal of the financing statements. The question is the nature of that duty.

Under the dissent's view, a client has to specifically ask his lawyer to renew the financing statements for this to be among the lawyer's duties. But how can the client be expected to know of this legal requirement? He hires the lawyer because the lawyer knows the law. The client cannot be expected to explicitly ask the lawyer to engage in every task necessary to fulfill the client's objectives.

The Court of Appeals held that a failure to inform by Turner was the sole possible grounds for malpractice. But this is too narrow a definition of Turner's duty. The duty was not necessarily to inform Barnes of the renewal requirement; often transactional attorneys do no such thing and simply renew the financing statements themselves. These attorneys have not breached a duty. Turner's duty was to safeguard Barnes's security interest. There were two means of doing so: by informing Barnes of the renewal requirement, or by renewing the financing statements himself in 2001. Either one would have been sufficient to comply with Turner's duty, and any breach of that duty occurred only upon Turner's failure to do both.

Further, if Turner's only duty arose in 1996, then Barnes had to bring suit before the financing statements could even be renewed to comply with the four-year statute of limitations. Barnes contends that any such action would have been dismissed as unripe because he was still a secured party at the time. He is correct. The dissent's view deprives Barnes and any clients in his position of any remedy for malpractice. The dissent's view precludes Barnes from ever maintaining a malpractice suit against Turner, who failed to take a simple, necessary action that will likely leave Barnes without his business and without over 78% of the purchase price he is still owed for that business.

The dissent's hyperbole about the effect of this opinion mischaracterizes our holding, which is based on a unique set of facts: a collateralized, payment-over-time arrangement in exchange for a sale of business where the payment period exceeds the five-year life span afforded to initial financing statements under [§ 9-515]. The lawyer, being retained to protect his client's interests in connection with the sale of his business, is the only party who knows the legal requirements for maintaining the effectiveness of the security interest. He can either share this knowledge with his client – a very simple step – or renew the financing statements before they expire – an equally simple step. The dissent's concern over the expansion of attorney duties is unwarranted.

2. The dissent also argues that imposing a duty to renew on Turner is an adoption of the "continuous representation rule," which Georgia courts have rejected except in personal injury cases. * * * [However, t]he continuous representation rule is not implicated in this case. We are *not* holding that a failure to inform by Turner in 1996 was a continuing wrong that tolled the statute of limitations until 2001. To the contrary, we are holding that a failure to inform in 1996 means that Turner undertook a duty to renew in 2001, and the statute of limitations began running from the date of alleged breach of *that* duty.

In light of the foregoing considerations, we reverse the Court of Appeals's decision that affirmed the trial court's grant of Turner's motion to dismiss. Barnes's malpractice action was filed within four years of the failure to renew the financing statements in 2001, and thus may proceed.

Lapse of the effectiveness of the financing statement is a very obvious way in which perfection might be lost. Another way perfection might be lost arises from the temporary nature of some automatic perfection rules, so that if the secured party is relying on one of these rules for perfection, the period of perfection is short-lived. § 9-312. To deal with this, the secured party needs to perfect under an alternative method prior to the expiration of the temporary perfection period. If the secured party does so, the security interest remains continuously perfected. *See* § 9-308(c).

To illustrate, assume that a security interest in an instrument is automatically perfected under § 9-312(e). Before the end of the 20-day time period of automatic perfection, the secured party files an effective financing statement in the correct place covering the instrument. The security interest would be perfected continuously from the start of the time of automatic perfection until the financing statement is no longer effective to perfect. One of the things a secured party may do, therefore, to maintain continuous perfection of its security interest is to use another method of perfection to remain perfected continuously. As we will see when studying Article 9's priority rules in Chapter Five, continuity of perfection is often vital to maintaining priority.

In the remainder of this section, we consider other types of changes, in addition to those we already know about, that might occur after the security interest is initially perfected and which might affect the perfected status of that security interest. These changes greatly add to the complexity of Article 9.

If you think about it for a moment, such complexity should not be surprising. In a real estate recording system, which is indexed by property, it does not matter if the owner of some property changes his or her name. Similarly, a change in the debtor's location is immaterial because the system is organized by the location of the property, which never changes. Finally, real estate stays real estate. You can remove timber or coal or natural gas, but the land never stops being land and it remains fixed in location. Other property-based recording systems are similarly unconcerned about what happens after an interest is recorded. For example, the federal filing system for copyrights need not worry about the location of the copyright owner, the location of the copyright (which of course has no physical situs) or how the copyright is being used.

In contrast, virtually everything relevant to perfection of an Article 9 security interest can change after perfection is obtained:

- Debtors might change their names or location;
- The property might move to a new jurisdiction;

- The debtor might alter the use of the property, causing its classification to change; and, most important,
- The debtor might sell or trade the collateral, acquiring an interest in proceeds, which might be of a very different type than the original collateral, yet not terminating the creditor's interest in the original collateral now owned by someone new (who obviously has a different name, might be located in a different jurisdiction, and for whom the collateral has a different classification).

Article 9 needs to deal with all of these possibilities. One way to do so would be simply to provide that the changes are irrelevant; a perfected secured party remains perfected despite these changes. That would make it easy for the initial secured party to remain perfected but potentially very difficult for searchers who seek to discover if the debtor's property is encumbered. Another alternative would be to provide that any change which, had it occurred prior to perfection, would have required the secured party to do something different to perfect, immediately terminates perfection. This rule would be very burdensome for secured parties. They would have to continuously monitor their debtors and the collateral for changes and, even if they reacted quickly to changes, their priority could shift if they were not the first to react.

Article 9 takes a sort of middle approach. It requires the secured party to take action to remain perfected in some cases but not in others. It also gives the secured party various time periods within which to act. In doing this, it seeks to allocate the reciprocal burdens between the initial secured party and subsequent searchers in a manner that allows the system to function reasonably well for all. However, if you thought the rules governing perfection of a security interest were complex before, you'll now need to increase your tolerance for complexity.

The discussion below organizes the changes into four main categories:

(1) Changes in the collateral or method of perfection;
(2) Changes in the loan;
(3) Changes in the debtor; and
(4) Changes in the secured party.

For each type of change, we will consider how it affects the perfected status of the security interest. The last problem in this Chapter then asks you to consider how the various rules for maintaining perfection affect the task of the searcher seeking to determine if property is already encumbered.

One of the ways to stay organized is to ascertain whether the secured party's security interest was initially perfected, identify the change in circumstances, identify what effect, if any, the change has on the perfection (attachment plus the perfection step) the secured party had previously achieved, and then identify what the secured party should do to maintain continuous perfection of its security interest in spite of the change. This last step involves thinking about what the secured party could do before such a change to prevent the change from affecting the secured party's perfected status, how the secured party could monitor for the change, and how the secured party should react once the change occurs in order to maintain or regain perfection.

A. Changes in the Collateral or Perfection Method

1. Acquisition of Collateral

After the initial perfection of the security interest, the debtor might acquire additional items of property.[83] Does the security interest attach to those additional items? If the security agreement has an after-acquired property clause and the additional items fall within the collateral description in the security agreement, the security interest will attach to the newly acquired items, § 9-204(a), subject to the limitations in § 9-204(b). If the security agreement does not contain an after-acquired property clause or the new items do not fall within the security agreement's description of the collateral, then the secured party would not have a security interest in the new items.

Assuming that the security interest does attach to the new items of property, the next question is whether the security interest is perfected in those new items without the secured party having to take any additional perfection steps. In general, to answer this question you can ignore the security interest in the original collateral and simply inquire whether the secured party has complied with any of the applicable perfection methods for the type of property involved.

For example, if the secured party has filed an authorized, *see* §§ 9-509, 9-510, and otherwise sufficient financing statement in the appropriate office, then it will be perfected in the new property provided: (i) the new property is of a type which may be perfected by filing in the office where the financing statement has already been filed, *see* §§ 9-301–9-307, 9-501; and (ii) the indication of the collateral in the financing statement is broad enough to cover the new collateral. It is not necessary that the financing statement reference "after-acquired" property in its indication of

---

[83] For purposes of the discussion, assume the additional items of property are not proceeds of original collateral. Proceeds are discussed in the next part of this section.

the collateral. *See* § 9-204 cmt. 7; § 9-502 cmt. 2. So, a secured party with a proper filing against "inventory" will be automatically perfected in whatever new inventory the debtor acquires and to which its security interest attaches. This is one reason why secured parties often prefer to indicate the collateral in a financing statement by type, rather than by individual item.

If, perhaps because the original financing statement identified the collateral specifically by item, the indication of collateral in the filed financing statement is not broad enough to cover the new collateral, but the security interest nevertheless attaches to those new items, the secured party may file an amendment to the original financing statement to add the new collateral. § 9-509(a). As to that new collateral, the financing statement will be effective from the date of the amendment. § 9-512.

If the secured party has not filed a financing statement to perfect its security interest, but is instead relying on perfection by possession, control, automatic perfection, or perfection under other law pursuant to § 9-311, then to perfect its interest in the new items of collateral, the secured party will have to take the appropriate step for that type of collateral. For example, assume the secured party has a security interest in instruments perfected by possession. The debtor acquires a new instrument that is not proceeds of other collateral. Even though the secured party's security interest would attach to that instrument if the signed security agreement covers after-acquired instruments, the secured interest in the new instrument would not be perfected by filing or possession because the secured party will not have taken either of those perfection steps with respect to the new instrument (*i.e.*, the secured party has not taken possession of the new instrument and has not filed a financing statement as to any collateral). The only way the security interest in the new instrument would be perfected is if the automatic perfection rule in § 9-312(e) applies (which requires giving new value). Of course, if the secured party later files against or takes possession of the instrument, the security interest in the new instrument will be perfected as of that time.

Problem 4-20

On March 1, National Bank filed an authorized financing statement against Doublequick Cooking Corp. (the debtor's correct name) in the secretary of state's office in Minnesota, the state in which Doublequick is incorporated. The financing statement listed the collateral as "inventory." On March 10, Doublequick signed a security agreement granting National Bank a security interest in "all inventory now owned or hereafter acquired" to secure "all obligations now or hereafter owed to National Bank." On

March 11, National Bank loaned Doublequick $500,000 and Doublequick signed a promissory note promising to repay that amount on demand of National Bank. Doublequick manufactures and sells microwave ovens.

A. On what date was National Bank's security interest in Doublequick's inventory of ovens first perfected? *See* §§ 9-203(b), 9-308(a).
B. On March 15, Doublequick acquired a shipment of parts that will be used in assembling the microwave ovens. Does National Bank have to do anything to have a perfected security interest in those parts? If not, when will its security interest in the parts be perfected?

To aid you in your analysis, below is a time line of the facts. You should routinely make a time line or otherwise diagram the facts of any perfection problem; doing so makes it much easier to perform the necessary analysis.

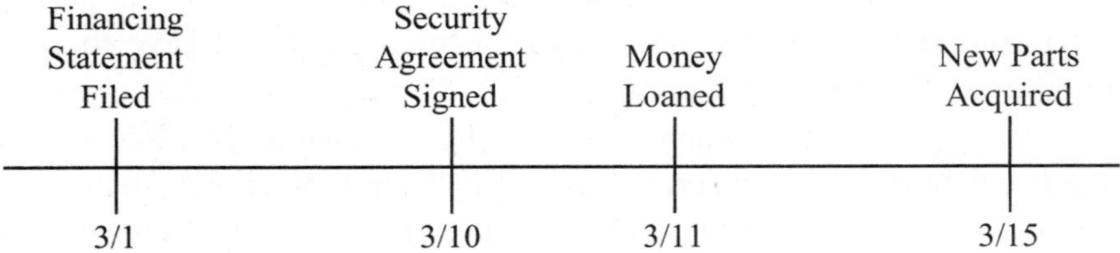

There is at least one scenario[84] in which the debtor's acquisition of new property might actually undermine the perfection of the security interest in the original collateral. Consider the following scenario:

Last year, David applied for and received a Stears credit card. The credit card contract grants Stears a security interest in each item of property purchased on credit from Stears with the card. It also provides that each item so purchased will serve as collateral for all the debts incurred with the card. Stears filed no financing statement. Last month, David used the credit for the first time. He purchased a washing machine for home use on credit from Stears using the Stears credit card. Because the washing machine is consumer goods and Stears has a purchase-money security interest, Stears' security interest is automatically perfected. *See* § 9-309(1).

---

[84] Another scenario can arise when an initial transfer of an account or payment intangible is automatically perfected under § 9-309(2) because it constitutes an "insignificant" portion of the debtor's receivables but the debtor then transfers additional accounts or payment intangibles to the secured party and, when aggregated, the transfers constitute a significant portion and thus are no longer eligible for automatic perfection.

Last week, David purchased a pool table for home use from Stears. That transaction too was on credit, using the Stears credit card. One would normally assume that Stears' security interest in the pool table to secure payment of the price of the table is an automatically perfected PMSI, just as its security interest in the washing machine was automatically perfected.

The uncertainty comes from the term in the credit card agreement that makes each item purchased with the card security for all debts owed on the card. This is a permissible term, *cf.* § 9-204(b), that results in cross-collateralization: the washing machine secures both the debt for the washing machine and the debt for the pool table; the pool table also secures both debts. The diagram below illustrates this point.

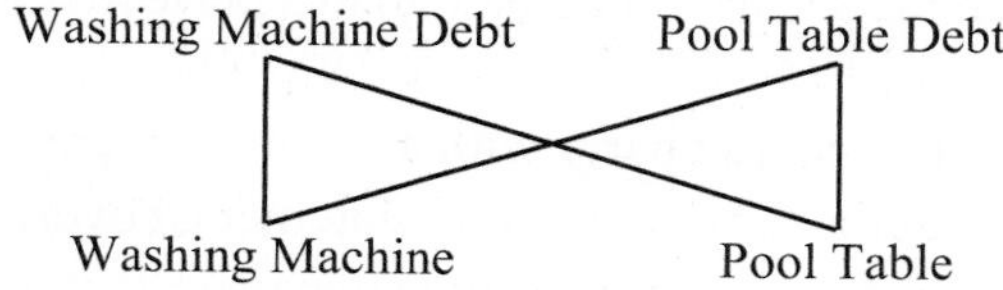

At a minimum, to the extent that the pool table secures the debt for the washing machine and to the extent the washing machine secures the debt for the pool table, no PMSI is involved. *See* § 9-103(b). Thus, under no theory are the security interests represented by the diagonal lines perfected. However, as discussed in connection with Problem 4-16(A)(2), cross-collateralization might undermine PMSI status entirely. In other words, the existence of the interests represented by the diagonal lines might destroy the purchase-money character of the interests represented by the vertical lines. *Cf.* § 9-103(f), (h). *See also* 9A WILLIAM D. HAWKLAND, UNIFORM COMMERCIAL CODE SERIES, Rev. § 9-103:5 (2000 & Supp. 2013-14). The issue is one that Article 9 itself does not answer in the context of a consumer-goods transaction but leaves to the courts in each state to resolve. If the cross-collateralization that arises with the second transaction destroys the purchase-money character of Stears' security interests, not only will Stears be unperfected in the pool table, but it will lose its perfection in the washing machine.

2. Proceeds of Original Collateral

When a debtor disposes of collateral, the security interest automatically attaches to the identifiable proceeds of the collateral. *See* § 9-203(f), 9-315(a)(2), (b). If the security interest in the original collateral was perfected in any manner, the security interest in the proceeds will also be perfected, at least for a limited time. § 9-315(c). However, the security interest in the proceeds becomes unperfected on the 21st day after the security interest attaches to them unless the secured party perfects its interest in the proceeds pursuant to § 9-315(d).

Section 9-315(d) provides for three methods for perfection of a security interest in proceeds to extend perfection beyond the 20-day period of temporary perfection. Taking them in reverse order from their presentation in the statute, the first method is relatively simple. If whatever the secured party has already done to perfect a security interest in the original collateral – or whatever it does in the 20-day period – is sufficient to perfect a security interest in the proceeds without respect to their status as proceeds, then the security interest remains perfected beyond the 20-day period. § 9-315(d)(3).

Thus, for example, if a secured party with a security interest in inventory (but not accounts) files an authorized financing statement covering inventory and accounts, and the debtor sells some inventory in a manner that generates accounts, then the security interest in the accounts as identifiable proceeds remains perfected for as long as the filing remains effective. In short, the authorized filing as to accounts is effective to perfect the security interest that attached to the accounts as identifiable proceeds of inventory. Recall, a financing statement may be filed before the security interest attaches. § 9-502(d). As you can see, the rule in § 9-315(d)(3) is not much of a boon to secured parties. It just means that if they either had the luck or foresight to get it right in advance, or they do whatever is otherwise necessary to perfect in the proceeds in the 20-day period, they remain perfected.

Second, if the proceeds are identifiable "cash proceeds," a secured party perfected in the original collateral remains perfected beyond the 20-day period. § 9-315(d)(2). As to what constitutes "cash proceeds," *see* § 9-102(a)(9).

Finally, the most complicated proceeds perfection rule is found in § 9-315(d)(1). It provides for automatic perfection beyond the initial 20-day period if all three of the following criteria are satisfied:

(1) The security interest in the original collateral is perfected by the filing of a financing statement;

(2) A security interest in the proceeds can be perfected by filing a financing statement in the same office in which the financing statement covering the original collateral was filed; and

(3) The proceeds are not acquired with cash proceeds.

Perfection under this rule will continue as long as the financing statement covering the original collateral is effective. § 9-315(e).

To illustrate the application of these rules, consider the following three scenarios, each based on the same initial transaction:

1. Bank obtained a security interest in all existing and after-acquired inventory of Debtor to secure a loan Bank made to Debtor. Bank perfected its security interest in the inventory by filing a financing statement against Debtor in the proper location. Thereafter, Debtor sold some inventory for money (as defined in § 1-201(b)(24)), and that money remains identifiable. Bank's security interest attached to the money as identifiable proceeds of the inventory, § 9-315(a)(2), and Bank's security interest in the money was automatically perfected upon attachment for at least 20 days, § 9-315(c). Because money is a type of "cash proceeds," *see* § 9-102(a)(9), Bank need not do anything for its security interest in the money to remain perfected beyond the 20-day period. § 9-315(d)(2).[85]

2. Debtor traded other inventory for a piece of equipment that is not subject to a certificate of title law. Bank's security interest attached to the equipment as identifiable proceeds of the inventory, § 9-315(a)(2), and Bank's security interest in the equipment was automatically perfected upon attachment for at least 20 days, § 9-315(c). Pursuant to § 9-315(d)(1), Bank's security interest in the equipment will remain perfected beyond the 20-day period. This is because:

(1) A filed financing statement covers the inventory (the original collateral), § 9-315(d)(1)(A);

(2) A security interest in the equipment may be perfected by filing a financing statement in the office where the financing statement was filed (*i.e.*, the place to file against equipment is the place to file against inventory), § 9-315(d)(1)(B); and

(3) The equipment was not acquired with cash proceeds, § 9-315(d)(1)(C).

Note that Bank's filed financing statement did not – and need not – include equipment in the indication of the collateral. It is sufficient that Bank's

---

[85] Although § 9-312(b)(3) provides that possession is the only method to perfect a security interest in tangible money, that rule is expressly subject to an exception for perfection pursuant to the proceeds rules of § 9-315(c) and (d).

financing statement covers the inventory and is filed in the office where Bank would file to perfect a security interest in equipment.

If, in contrast, the equipment were subject to a certificate of title statute, so that the proper method to perfect a security interest in it would be to have the security interest noted on the certificate of title, Bank's security interest in the equipment would not remain perfected under § 9-315(d)(1). Instead, Bank would need to comply with the certificate of title statute to maintain perfection of its security interest in the equipment beyond the 20-day period of temporary perfection for proceeds. § 9-315(d)(3).

3. Debtor sold other inventory and received payment by check. Debtor then used the check to purchase a piece of equipment that is not subject to a certificate of title law. Bank's security interest attached to the equipment as identifiable proceeds of the check, which in turn was identifiable proceeds of inventory. *See* §§ 9-102(a)(64), 9-315(a)(2). Bank's interest in the equipment is temporarily perfected for a period of 20 days but it will remain perfected beyond that period only if Bank perfects as to the equipment by taking an appropriate step to perfect its interest in the equipment (*i.e.*, amends its financing statement to cover the equipment or takes possession of the equipment). *See* § 9-315(d)(3). Section 9-315(d)(2) is not satisfied because the equipment is not cash proceeds. Section 9-315(d)(1) is not satisfied because the current proceeds (the equipment) were acquired with cash proceeds. *See* § 9-315(d)(1)(C).

If Bank acts to perfect within 20 days of when the security interest attached to the equipment, Bank's security interest will be continuously perfected. In this regard, § 9-509(b)(2) provides Bank with authorization to file a financing statement covering the equipment. If Bank acts to perfect after the 20-day period expires, Bank's security interest in the equipment will be perfected, but that perfection will date only to the moment of Bank's new act to perfect, it will not relate back to Bank's perfection in the original collateral, the inventory. As a result, Bank might have a lesser priority for its security interest in the equipment. *See* § 9-322.

As should be clear from the examples above, to apply the proceeds perfection rules in § 9-315(c) and (d), one must begin by analyzing whether the security interest was perfected in the initial collateral. The analysis must then proceed methodically, dealing with each subsequent event. In short, analyze the issue chronologically and skip nothing.[86]

Problem 4-21

On March 11, National Bank acquired a security interest in all of the existing and after-acquired inventory of Doublequick Cooking Corp. to secure "all obligations now or hereafter owed to National Bank." Ever since that date, Doublequick has been indebted to National Bank. National Bank perfected that security interest on March 11 by filing in the appropriate office a sufficient financing statement indicating the collateral as "inventory." Doublequick manufactures and sells microwave ovens.

A. On September 1, Doublequick delivered a truckload of microwave ovens to Inexpensive Appliances, Inc. and received a check in partial payment of the purchase price and a promissory note for the balance. Does National Bank have a perfected security interest in the check? Does it have a perfected security interest in the note? *See* §§ 9-102(a)(9), 9-315(c), (d).

B. If Doublequick then deposits the check into a checking account held at First Bank, does National Bank have a perfected security interest in the checking account?

C. Doublequick receives a cash payment from Inexpensive Appliances on the obligation owed on the promissory note.
   1. Doublequick then uses some of that cash to purchase a new computer for use in its corporate office. Does National Bank have a perfected security interest in the computer?
   2. Doublequick uses the remainder of the cash to purchase parts for the microwave ovens it will manufacture. Does National Bank have a perfected security interest in those new parts?

D. 1. How, if at all, would the analysis of Part C change if the financing statement indicated the collateral as "all assets"?
   2. How, if at all, would the analysis of Part C change if the financing statement indicated the collateral as "inventory and proceeds thereof"?

---

[86] For a good example of this methodical analysis, albeit with minor flaws, see In re 3P4PL, LLC, 2020 WL 4436354 (Bankr. D. Colo. 2020).

Problem 4-22

A. In May, Duncan purchased a refrigerator on credit from Appliance Heaven and granted a security interest in the refrigerator to secure the purchase price. Appliance Heaven did not file a financing statement to perfect its security interest in the refrigerator. Duncan purchased the refrigerator for use in his house. In November, Duncan sold the refrigerator to Sam for $400 in cash. Does Appliance Heaven have a perfected security interest in the $400?

B. In June, Desdemona purchased a freezer on credit from Appliance Heaven and granted a security interest in the freezer to secure the purchase price. Appliance Heaven did not file a financing statement to perfect its security interest in the freezer. Desdemona purchased the freezer for use in her house. In December, Desdemona traded the freezer to Sam for a set of golf clubs. Does Appliance Heaven have a perfected security interest in the golf clubs?

Problem 4-23

Deciduous operates a plant nursery that supplies trees and shrubs for landscapers. On May 1, to secure "all obligations then owed or thereafter owing" to First Bank, Deciduous granted First Bank a security interest in all of Deciduous' existing and after-acquired inventory and equipment. On the same day, First Bank filed in the appropriate office an otherwise sufficient financing statement indicating the collateral as "inventory and equipment." It is now December, and Deciduous owes First Bank $50,000. In which of the following will First Bank have a perfected security interest?

A. A computer Deciduous purchased in June to use for inventory management. Does it matter how Deciduous acquired the money used to buy the computer?

B. A truck Deciduous purchased in July to make deliveries. Does it matter how Deciduous acquired the money used to buy the truck?

C. Accounts created in August when Deciduous sold inventory on credit.

D. A horse Deciduous acquired in September for personal riding pleasure by trading inventory.

E. A horse Deciduous purchased in October for personal riding pleasure. Does it matter how Deciduous acquired the money used to buy the horse?

Problem 4-24

A. Why does § 9-315(d) distinguish between first-generation proceeds and second-generation proceeds acquired with cash proceeds? Is it more difficult for the secured party to monitor what is happening to its collateral in one instance than in the other? If the burden on the secured party does not explain the rule, what must?

B. How do the three different rules of § 9-315(d) affect searchers? In other words, for each of those three perfection rules, identify how, if at all, the rule makes the searcher's task more difficult.

Problem 4-25

Trucking Company owns a fleet of commercial trucks that it leases on a short-term basis to independent truck drivers. Lender has a security interest in all of the trucks. Lender has not filed a financing statement but did, with respect to each truck, comply with the applicable certificate of title statute and had its security interest noted on the certificate for each truck.

Yesterday, Trucking Company filed for bankruptcy protection. At that time, Trucking Company had a deposit account at Bank with a credit balance of $243,000. All of that balance is traceable to payments made to Trucking Company by independent truckers on truck leases. Lender does not have a control agreement with Bank.

What two facts do you need to know to be able to determine whether Lender has a perfected security interest in Trucking Company's deposit account at Bank, and why are those facts important?

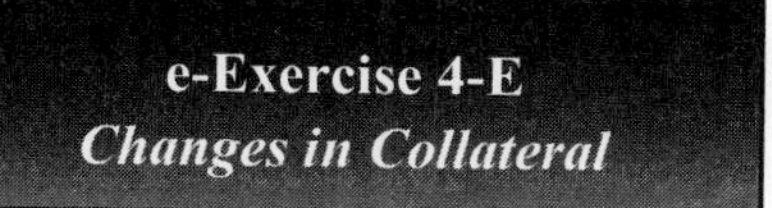

3. Change in the Location or Characterization of Collateral

In most circumstances, a change in the location or characterization of the collateral will not trigger a need to do anything to maintain perfection of the security interest. Consider the following three illustrations:

1. SP has a security interest in D's "existing and after-acquired cast iron sculptures," which D manufactures and sells. SP perfected its security interest by filing an effective financing statement covering "inventory" in the state in which D is located. Later, D started using one sculpture as equipment (*e.g.*, as a display item no longer held for sale). Under § 9-507(b), the change in the classification of that sculpture does not affect the validity of the financing statement as a perfection step as to that sculpture, with the result that the security interest in that sculpture remains perfected.

2. SP has a security interest in equipment perfected by a financing statement filed in the jurisdiction where D is located. Thereafter, D moves a piece of equipment to another state. Because the location of the debtor, not the location of the collateral, determines the state in which to file, *see* § 9-301(1), SP's filing remains fully effective with respect to the moved equipment.

3. SP has a security interest in collateral perfected through possession. SP moved the goods to another state while maintaining possession of the goods. When the goods moved from State A to State B, the governing law changed from State A's law to State B's law. *See* § 9-301(2). However, because SP's possession is effective to perfect in both State A and State B, SP's security interest remains perfected. *See* § 9-316(c).[87]

In some circumstances, however, a change in the use or location of the collateral will affect the perfection of the secured party's security interest. Typically this occurs when the change alters the appropriate method of perfection or the governing law. Consider the following three additional scenarios:

4. SP perfected its security interest in D's inventory of used automobiles by filing an effective financing statement in the state in which D is located. D is a person in the business of selling used automobiles. Later, D started using one of the automobiles as equipment (*i.e.*, no longer held the item for sale). Immediately upon the change in classification, filing ceased to be an appropriate perfection method. The proper way to perfect is now by having the security interest noted on the certificate of title. § 9-311(a)(2), (d). SP's

---

[87] This assumes that what counts for possession in State A and in State B encompasses what the secured party has done to possess the collateral. Because possession is not defined and is dependent on case law in the relevant state, it is possible that whatever the secured party was doing in State A to possess would not qualify as possession in State B.

security interest in the automobile used as equipment became unperfected. *See* § 9-311 cmt. 4.

5. SP perfected its security interest in D's automobile by getting its interest noted on the car's certificate of title, issued by the Department of Motor vehicle in State A. D thereafter obtained a new certificate of title for the car from State B. The moment D submitted the application for the new certificate of title, the law governing perfection changed from State A to State B. *See* § 9-303(b), (c). However, even if the new certificate of title fails to indicate SP's security interest, SP's security interest is not immediately unperfected. *See* § 9-316(d). Instead, SP has four months after issuance of the new certificate of title to get its security interest noted on the new certificate of title to avoid that interest from being deemed unperfected as against purchasers for value of the collateral. *See* § 9-316(e).[88]

6. SP properly perfected a security interest in timber to be cut by filing an effective financing statement in the real property records in the county where the timber is located. § 9-301(3), 9-501(a)(1)(A). The timber is then cut. According to the comments to § 9-501, SP's security interest became unperfected because the proper place to file the financing statement is now in the central filing office of the state in which the debtor is located. *See* §§ 9-301(1), 9-501(a)(2).

In a few situations, it remains unclear whether a change in the collateral's use or location affects the secured party's perfection. Consider the following illustration and the problem that follows it.

7. SP perfected a security interest in fixtures by filing an effective fixture financing statement in the real estate records in the county where the fixtures were located. *See* § 9-301(3)(A), 9-501(a)(1)(B). D removed the fixtures from the real estate and transported them to another county. Does SP need to do anything to have its security interest remain perfected in the goods that were previously fixtures? By analogy to the timber to be cut example, one could reason that once the goods ceased being a fixture, the proper place to

---

[88] Note, unlike in scenario 4, the loss of perfection in scenario 5 applies only with respect to purchasers for value. With respect to others who might assert a claim to the collateral – *e.g.*, donees and lien creditors – perfection does not lapse. The consequences of this, which we might refer to as "partial perfection," are explored in Chapter Five.

file was in the state of the debtor's location, § 9-301(1), and the central filing office within that state, § 9-501(a)(2). Unlike the timber to be cut example, the comments to these sections do not indicate an answer to this question.

Problem 4-26

On March 11, National Bank acquired a security interest in all of the "existing and after-acquired inventory" of Doublequick Cooking Corp. to secure all obligations now or hereafter owed to National Bank. National Bank perfected that security interest by filing in Minnesota (where Doublequick is located) a sufficient financing statement indicating the collateral as "inventory." Doublequick manufactures and sells microwave ovens.

A. On September 1, Doublequick took several microwave ovens out of its warehouse and installed them in employee break rooms. Does National Bank have a perfected security interest in those microwave ovens? *See* § 9-507(b).
B. On September 15, Doublequick shipped several truckloads of microwave ovens to its warehouse in Iowa. Does National Bank have a perfected security interest in the microwave ovens?
C. If National Bank's security interest in any oven became unperfected in Part A or B, how could National Bank have drafted the documents at the inception of the transaction, but without fundamentally changing the deal, to avoid the problem?

Problem 4-27

In the process of financing Dewey's acquisition of a riding lawnmower to be used at Dewey's home, Security Bank acquired a purchase-money security interest in the mower. That security interest was automatically perfected under § 9-309(1). Dewey then went into the business of mowing lawns and started using the mower in that business. This caused the mower to become "equipment." Must Security Bank now file a financing statement in the jurisdiction where Dewey is located to have a perfected security interest in the mower? What provision of Article 9, if any, answers this question? *See* §§ 9-102(a)(23), 9-507(b).

Problem 4-28

A. Deanna, who lives in Minnesota, granted a security interest in her car to State Bank to secure a loan for the purchase price. State Bank had its security interest noted on the certificate of title for the car. The certificate of title was issued by the Minnesota Department of Motor Vehicles.
   1. Deanna moved to Wisconsin. Deanna did not get a new certificate of title for her car. Is State Bank's security interest in the car perfected? *See* § 9-303(b), (c); *In re Baker*, 430 F.3d 858 (7th Cir. 2005).
   2. Deanna moved to Wisconsin and the Wisconsin Department of Motor Vehicles issued a new certificate of title for her car. Through a mistake in the Wisconsin DMV office, State Bank's security interest was not noted on the Wisconsin certificate of title. Is State Bank's security interest in the car perfected? *See* §§ 9-303(b), 9-316(d), (e).

B. Daryl granted a security interest in his boat to State Bank. Daryl lives in Iowa and Iowa does not issue certificates of title for boats. State Bank filed a sufficient financing statement covering the boat in the Iowa secretary of state's office. Although Daryl continued to reside in Iowa, he relocated the boat to a lake in northern Minnesota. In compliance with Minnesota law, Daryl obtained a certificate of title for the boat from the Minnesota Department of Natural Resources. Is State Bank's security interest in the boat perfected?

The chart that follows organizes several of the rules described above concerning how changes in the collateral affect perfection, if perfection was through filing a financing statement. Use it for assistance in organizing and comparing the rules it covers, not as a substitute for reading and understanding those rules.

CHANGES IN COLLATERAL AFFECTING THE VALIDITY OF A FINANCING STATEMENT

	Change of Location or Use of Collateral	**First Generation Non-cash Proceeds Acquired**	**Non-cash Proceeds Acquired with Cash Proceeds**
Financing statement still indicates the collateral; no change in perfection method	No new filing is needed.	No new filing is needed.	No new filing is needed.

	Change of Location or Use of Collateral	First Generation Non-cash Proceeds Acquired	Non-cash Proceeds Acquired with Cash Proceeds
Financing statement no longer indicates the collateral	No new filing is needed, § 9-507(b).	No new filing is needed, § 9-315(d).	New filing is needed within 20 days, § 9-315(d).
Change alters the perfection method	Action is needed immediately. *See* § 9-311.	New filing is needed within 20 days, § 9-315(d).	New filing is needed within 20 days, § 9-315(d).

In addition to the rules discussed above, there are two temporary automatic perfection rules that apply when possession of the collateral changes. *See* § 9-312(f), (g). Each is designed to accommodate a particular commercial practice that developed prior to the advent of former Article 9. For example, if a secured party has a security interest in an instrument perfected by possession, the secured party may relinquish possession for certain purposes and the security interest will remain perfected for 20 days. § 9-312(g). This rule allows the secured party to return the instrument to the debtor for, among other things, presentation to the maker or drawee for payment. Similarly, a secured party may permit a bailee of goods to make the goods available to the debtor for a legitimate business purpose, such as sale, exchange, shipping or processing, and the security interest in the goods will remain perfected for 20 days. § 9-312(f).

Of course, the secured party need not rely on automatic perfection in either of these situations. If it filed an effective financing statement covering the collateral before relinquishing possession, the secured party would remain continuously perfected. *See* § 9-308(c). However, as the comments point out, requiring such a filing to remain perfected would cause secured parties to clutter the files with records of exceedingly short-term transactions. § 9-312 cmt. 9.

Once the 20-day period of temporary perfection expires, the security interest will become unperfected unless the secured party has perfected by regaining possession of the collateral or in some other permitted manner before the expiration of that time period. § 9-312(h).

Problem 4-29

Diversified Enterprises signed a security agreement granting National Bank a security interest in all of Diversified's "inventory, documents of title, and instruments now owned or hereafter acquired" to secure a $1,000,000 line of credit. Diversified stores most of its inventory with Storage Monster, a warehouser of goods. National Bank took possession of all Diversified's instruments, most of which are promissory notes received from customers in exchange for goods that Diversified sold on credit.

A. Assume that Storage Monster has issued tangible negotiable warehouse receipts for the goods and that National Bank has taken possession of the warehouse receipts. Diversified now wants to get a truckload of microwave ovens out of the warehouse and deliver them to one of its vendors. To do so, Diversified needs to present the tangible negotiable warehouse receipts to Storage Monster. If National Bank relinquishes possession of the warehouse receipts to Diversified, will National Bank's security interest in the goods still be perfected? *See* § 9-312(f). What, if anything, would you advise National Bank to do before or after it relinquishes possession of the negotiable warehouse receipt to Diversified to ensure that its security interest in the goods will remain perfected?

B. Assume that Storage Monster has not issued a warehouse receipt for the goods it is holding for Diversified but that it has acknowledged in a signed record provided to National Bank that it was holding the items of inventory subject to National Bank's security interest. Diversified then removed from the warehouse several items of inventory. Does National Bank have a security interest in the removed items? If so, is that security interest perfected?

C. Diversified wants to present one of the notes to the maker, Microwave Heaven, for payment. If National Bank delivers the note to Diversified for that purpose, will National Bank's security interest still be perfected? *See* § 9-312(g). What, if anything, would you advise National Bank to do before or after it delivers the note to Diversified to ensure that its security interest in the note will remain perfected?

D. Several months after Diversified signed the security agreement with National Bank, Diversified acquired another negotiable note from Microwave Heaven. Diversified is the payee of the note and has possession of the note. Is National Bank's security interest perfected? What, if any, additional facts do you need to know to answer that question? *See* §§ 9-312(e), 9-102(a)(57).

B. Changes in the Loan

We already learned in Chapter Two, when we discussed attachment, that a security agreement may provide that the collateral secures obligations that the debtor incurs to the secured party in the future. *See* § 9-204(c). If the original security agreement provides that the collateral will secure future advances, the secured party need take no additional steps when it loans more money for those future advances to be secured. If the security agreement does not contain a future advances clause, the advance will not be secured by the collateral unless the creditor and debtor either amend their security agreement or enter into another security agreement to secure that advance.

If the security interest is perfected when the secured party loans more money pursuant to a future advances clause, the security interest will also be perfected with respect to that future advance. The future advances clause need not be contained in the financing statement. § 9-204 cmt. 7; § 9-502 cmt. 2. If you think about it, this makes perfect sense. Perfection is about the collateral, not the amount of the secured obligation. Even the amount of the initial secured obligation need not be described in the financing statement. *See* § 9-502(a). Indeed, there is no place to mention it on the standard paper form. *See* § 9-521(a).[89] Beyond that, the amount of the secured obligation changes on a daily basis, increasing as interest accrues and decreasing with every payment made. It would therefore be futile to require that financing statements describe the amount of the secured obligation.

There is one circumstance in which a change in the loan amount might change the perfected status of a security interest. Recall that a purchase-money security interest in consumer goods that are not subject to a certificate-of-title law is automatically perfected under § 9-309(1). Can changes in the loan amount "unperfect" the security interest if the security interest is no longer characterized as a "purchase-money security interest?" Consider the following example.

> SP was granted a purchase-money security interest in a consumer's home entertainment system. SP did not file a financing statement. Three months after the purchase, SP agreed to refinance the transaction by lending the consumer more money, with the entire new loan balance secured by the home entertainment system. Does SP have a purchase-money security interest in the home entertainment system?

---

[89] It would also not be apparent from the secured party's possession of the collateral.

If this were not a consumer-goods transaction, SP would still have a PMSI in the goods to the extent the loan debt was a purchase-money obligation. *See* § 9-103(f). In other words, SP would have a PMSI securing the portion of the debt incurred to purchase the collateral and a non-PMSI securing the new amounts loaned. However, the official text of Article 9 does not apply this rule to consumer-goods transactions, and instead leaves it to courts to determine whether refinancing the loan affects the purchase-money nature of the security interest. *See* § 9-103(h). Accordingly, in some states, refinancing the original secured obligation can transform a PMSI into a non-PMSI, with the result that the security interest will become unperfected if the secured party relied on the automatic perfection rule of § 9-309(1).[90]

Problem 4-30

On March 11, National Bank acquired a security interest in all of the existing and after-acquired inventory of Doublequick Cooking Corp. to secure "all obligations now or hereafter owed to National Bank." National Bank perfected that security interest the next day by filing in the appropriate office a sufficient financing statement indicating the collateral as "inventory." Doublequick manufactures and sells microwave ovens. On April 15, National Bank loaned Doublequick an additional $20,000 to enable Doublequick to pay its tax bill. Does National Bank have to do anything to make sure its additional loan is secured by a perfected security interest in Doublequick's inventory? *See* § 9-502 cmt. 2.

C. Changes in the Debtor

After a security interest is perfected, a debtor's name, location, or organizational structure might change. Perhaps more important, the collateral could be sold to a new person, who thereby becomes the debtor. In a system in which the dominant method of perfection is by filing a financing statement, which itself is keyed to the debtor's name and location, it should not be surprising that changes in the debtor's name, location, organizational structure, and identity will often affect whether the security interest remains perfected.

---

90 *See supra* notes 67–68 and accompanying text.

1. Change in the Debtor's Name

Name changes are of course not relevant to a security interest perfected by possession, control, notation on a certificate of title, or automatically. In none of those situations is the notice that such perfection provides, if any, indexed by the debtor's name. A name change is relevant, however, to a security interest perfected by filing a financing statement. *See* § 9-507(b), (c). That section provides that if a change in the debtor's name renders a filed financing statement seriously misleading under the test in § 9-506, the filed financing statement will be rendered ineffective to perfect a security interest in collateral acquired by the debtor more than four months after the name change. As to collateral that the debtor owned at the time of the name change or which the debtor acquired within four months after the name change, the financing statement with the old name remains effective. To maintain the effectiveness of the financing statement with respect to collateral acquired by the debtor more than four months after the name change, the secured party must amend the financing statement to provide the correct name of the debtor before the four-month period expires. Section 9-509 authorizes the secured party to file such an amendment. If the secured party amends the financing statement after the four-month period expires, the amended financing statement is effective to perfect, but not from the date of the original filing, only from the date of the amendment. *See* § 9-507 cmt. 4.

Problem 4-31

A. On March 11, National Bank acquired a security interest in all of the existing and after-acquired inventory of Doublequick Cooking Corp. to secure "all obligations now or hereafter owed to National Bank." Ever since that date, Doublequick has been indebted to National Bank. National Bank perfected that security interest the next day by filing in the appropriate office a sufficient financing statement indicating the collateral as "inventory." Doublequick manufactures and sells microwave ovens. On December 1, Doublequick changed its name under applicable law to Ovenlast, Inc. It is now May 1 of the following year. Does National Bank have a perfected security interest in the microwave ovens in which Ovenlast has an interest?

B. You represent First Bank, which is contemplating making a $25 million loan to Dirt Compactors, Inc., a company which specializes in preparing roadways for surfacing. The loan is to be secured by Dirt Compactor's equipment, which consists mostly of very large and expensive machinery.

In searching for existing, perfected security interests, how old of a name change could be relevant?

Problem 4-32

A. Review the facts and your analysis of Problem 4-2(A). How, if at all, does § 9-507(c) affect your search for financing statements filed against the debtor?

B. The state in which the debtor is located has enacted Alternative A of § 9-503(a) and (b). Explain whether and if so, how, each of the following events could result in a change of the debtor's name:
   1. Marriage or divorce.
   2. A court order changing the debtor's name.
   3. Issuance of a new driver's license.
   4. Expiration of the debtor's driver's license.

C. You are in-house counsel to Bank, which has made a sizeable loan to an individual. The loan is secured by existing and after-acquired collateral. What would you advise Bank to do – in other words, what monitoring should Bank perform – to protect itself from the possibly negative consequences of a future change in the debtor's name in a state that has enacted Alternative A of § 9-503(a) and (b)? *See* § 9-507 cmt. 4.

Problem 4-33

Three years ago, Deep Six Excavation, LLC granted Bank a security interest in all of its existing and after-acquired inventory and accounts to secure a sizeable loan. At that time, Bank filed in the appropriate office a financing statement identifying the debtor as "Deep Six Excavation, Inc." At that time, regulations promulgated by the filing office mandated that the words and abbreviations "Company, Corp., Corporation, Inc., Incorporated, L.L.C., Limited Liability Company, L.P., and Limited Partnership" be disregarded in official searches. As a result, when the financing statement was filed, an official search under the debtor's correct name – Deep Six Excavation, LLC – would have disclosed the filing. Nine months ago, the filing office changed its regulations so that none of these organizational words is disregarded in an official search. Thus, an official search conducted since that time against the debtor's correct name would not reveal Bank's filed financing statement. In what collateral, if any, is Bank's security interested perfected by its filed financing statement? *See* § 9-507(b), (c).

2. Adding or Subtracting Debtors on a Financing Statement

A secured party may file an amendment to add a debtor to or delete a debtor from a financing statement. § 9-512(d), (e). A financing statement is effective as to an added debtor from the time of the addition. The debtor to be added must authorize the amendment. § 9-509(a)–(c). The financing statement is effectively terminated as to a debtor deleted from the financing statement.

3. Change in the Debtor's Location

When the debtor's location determines which state's law governs perfection of the security interest, *see* §§ 9-301(1), 9-305(c), a change in the debtor's location can change the governing law.[91] When it does, § 9-316(a) and (b) govern whether the secured party must do anything to maintain perfection of the security interest. The basic rule is that the secured party has four months to re-perfect pursuant to the law of the new jurisdiction. If, however, the initial financing statement filed in the old jurisdiction will expire before the end of the four-month period, the secured party needs to perfect in the new state (or file a continuation statement in the old state) before the initial financing statement expires.[92] Subsection (h) provides a similar rule for collateral acquired by the debtor after the relocation.

If the debtor's relocation merely changes the debtor's address within a jurisdiction but does not change the applicable law for determining perfection, a financing statement containing the old address is still sufficient to perfect. A correct address for the debtor is not necessary for the financing statement to be sufficient to perfect, § 9-502, and thus cannot be seriously misleading under § 9-506.[93]

---

[91] This problem does not apply to a security interest perfected by possession because perfection of such a security interest is governed by the law of jurisdiction where the collateral is located. *See* § 9-301(2).

[92] In a few circumstances, the location of an entity other than the debtor will determine the jurisdiction's law that governs how to perfect a security interest. §§ 9-304, 9-305, 9-306. If the location of one of those entities changes, § 9-316(f) and (g) address what the secured party must do to maintain perfection of the security interest.

[93] *See* In re Hergert, 275 B.R. 58 (Bankr. D. Idaho 2002).

Problem 4-34

Detective, an individual and a resident of Coeur d'Alene, Idaho, owns and operates a small detective agency with offices in both Idaho and Spokane, Washington. Three years ago, Detective borrowed $75,000 from Security Bank and granted Security Bank a security interest in all of Detective's "existing and after-acquired equipment" to secure the loan. At that time, Security Bank filed a financing statement with the individual's correct name and listing the collateral as "equipment" in the secretary of state's office in Idaho. Security Bank also had its security interest noted on the certificate of title issued by Idaho and covering the car that Detective uses for her surveillance activity.

A. Did Security Bank file its financing statement in the proper place? *See* §§ 9-301(1), 9-307(b). Is Security Bank's security interest in the car perfected? §§ 9-303, 9-311.

B. Assume that Security Bank had properly perfected its security interest through its actions detailed above. Three weeks ago, Detective moved and became a resident of Washington.

   1. Does Security Bank have a perfected security interest in Detective's equipment, including the car, now? If so, what must it do to maintain perfection? *See* § 9-316.
   2. Last week, Detective purchased some new surveillance devices. Does Security Bank have a perfected security interest in those devices? *See* § 9-316(a), (h).
   3. If Security Bank had originally filed in Washington, would it have had a perfected security interest prior to Detective's move in the equipment, other than the car? Would it have a perfected security interest in the equipment, other than the car, now?
   4. A week after Detective moved to Washington, Detective applied for a new Washington certificate of title for the car. Is Security Bank's security interest in the car still perfected?
   5. One of the pieces of equipment that Detective moved from Idaho was an ATV for which Washington, but not Idaho, requires a certificate of title. Detective applied for a Washington certificate of title a week after she moved to Washington. Is Security Bank's security interest in the ATV perfected?

4. Disposition of Collateral

Assume that a security interest in collateral is perfected by an effective financing statement filed against the debtor in the correct location. The debtor sells or gives the collateral to another person. Does the security interest remain perfected in the collateral even though it is now in the hands of that transferee?

To answer this question we must begin by determining whether the security interest remains attached to the collateral. After all, attachment is a prerequisite for perfection. *See* § 9-308(a), (b). If the security interest does not remain attached to the collateral upon its disposition, the question of perfection becomes moot.

In general, a security interest does remain attached to the collateral despite transfer of the collateral to a new owner, unless the secured party authorized the transfer free of the security interest. *See* § 9-315(a)(1). There are many exceptions to this rule. These exceptions, which strip the security interest off of the collateral upon transfer of the collateral, will be discussed in Chapter Five. For now, let us assume that, due to the force of § 9-315(a)(1), the security interest remains attached to the collateral despite the transfer.

The second thing to determine is whether the financing statement filed against the original debtor remains effective to perfect, even though the transferee is now the "debtor" with respect to that collateral. *See* § 9-102(a)(28). In general, it does. *See* § 9-507(a). The financing statement that was filed and effective against the original debtor remains effective to perfect the security interest even though the debtor named in the financing statement (the transferor) is no longer the debtor that has an interest in the collateral. No new filing is required as against the transferee.

Consider the implications of this rule on a subsequent searcher. A potential secured creditor wishing to check whether there are any perfected security interests on the proffered collateral will have to search for filings not only against the current owner, but potentially against previous owners as well. *See* § 9-507 cmt. 3. Fortunately, much of the burden seemingly imposed by this rule is ameliorated by the priority rules that protect buyers of property. Again, we will study those in Chapter Five.

There is one major exception to this rule that the financing statement remains effective despite transfer of the collateral: if collateral is transferred to a person that is located in another jurisdiction. In such a situation, the secured party has one year to re-perfect in the new jurisdiction. To illustrate, consider the following example.

> SP has a non-possessory security interest in Debtor's goods. SP filed an effective financing statement covering the goods in State A, where Debtor is located. Thereafter, Debtor transferred the goods to Transferee and the

security interest remained attached to the goods. Transferee is located in State B. The law of the state in which Debtor is located (State A) ceased to apply immediately upon the transfer, at which time the law of the state in which Transferee is located (State B) became the law governing perfection. *See* § 9-301(1). Pursuant to § 9-316(a)(3), as enacted in State B, the filing in State A remains effective to perfect for up to one year but will not be effective to maintain perfection of the security interest more than one year after the transfer of the collateral to Transferee. To maintain perfection, SP must perfect its security interest against Transferee in State B within the one-year period. As to authority to file a financing statement against Transferee in State B, see § 9-509(c).

If SP takes the perfection step within the one-year period specified in § 9-316(a), the security interest will be continually perfected. If SP does not re-perfect within that period, the security interest becomes unperfected and is deemed retroactively unperfected as against purchasers for value. § 9-316(b).

These same rules usually apply when a corporate entity reincorporates in a new state. Imagine, for example, that a Washington corporation wishes to reincorporate in Florida for tax or licensing purposes. If the corporation had granted a security interest in some of its personal property, you might be tempted to analyze this as a relocation of the debtor, possibly with a change in name as well. In all probability, however, the Washington and Florida corporations are separate entities, with the result that the transaction is properly viewed not as a relocation of the debtor but as a transfer of the collateral to a transferee located in a different state. *See* § 9-316 cmt. 2, ex. 4. The same rule would normally apply if a partnership decided to incorporate in another state; that too would involve a transfer of the collateral to a new entity. The same principle applies to changes in entity form within a single state: such a change is generally regarded as a change in debtor (*i.e.*, a transfer of the collateral to a new debtor), rather than as a change in name. However, with respect to any such reincorporation or entity conversion, it is important to check applicable state law on whether it results in a new entity. For example, Delaware law allows a corporation to convert to a limited liability company and provides that, upon doing so, the new entity "shall, for all purposes of the laws of the State of Delaware, be deemed to be the same entity as the corporation."[94]

---

[94] Del. Code Ann. tit. 8, § 266(h). *See also* Del. Code Ann. tit. 6, § 18-214(g) (dealing with foreign entities converting into Delaware LLCs). Some state statutes are unclear on this

Finally, what if the security interest were perfected by a non-filing method and the debtor transfers its interest in the collateral to another person? If the secured party perfected its security interest by possession or control, the secured party remains perfected as long as it has possession or control of the collateral. §§ 9-313, 9-314. *See* § 9-205.[95] If the security interest is automatically perfected, the security interest will remain perfected even if the debtor transfers its interest in the collateral, unless the automatic perfection rule provides only for temporary automatic perfection and such automatic perfection expires. *See* §§ 9-312(e), (f), (g), 9-309(6). In either case, it is unlikely to matter if the transferee is located in a different jurisdiction. Think about it. For a security interest perfected by possession, the law governing perfection is where the collateral is located. If the collateral is in the secured party's possession, governing law is unlikely to change merely because the debtor transferred ownership. *See* §§ 9-301(2), 9-316(c). For a security interest perfected automatically or by control, the location of the debtor is the relevant question, §§ 9-301(1), 9-316(a), and thus the governing law could change. However, the secured party would have to worry about remaining perfected only if the law of the second jurisdiction were different from the law of the first jurisdiction, either through enactment of some non-uniform rule or through variation in judicial interpretation.

Problem 4-35

On March 11, National Bank acquired a security interest in all of the existing and after-acquired inventory of Doublequick Cooking Corp., a Minnesota corporation, to secure "all obligations now or hereafter owed to National Bank." National Bank perfected that security interest the next day by filing in the appropriate Minnesota office a sufficient financing statement indicating the collateral as "inventory." Doublequick manufactures and sells microwave ovens. On September 1, Doublequick delivered a shipment of finished microwave ovens to Best Retailers, Inc. in satisfaction of a

---

point. *See, e.g.*, Ohio Rev. Code. § 1705.391 (providing that "[t]he converting entity is continued in the converted entity" but also providing that [t]he converted entity exists, and the converting entity ceases to exist").

95 If the secured party released possession of the collateral, that might change the applicable law under § 9-301 because the security interest would no longer be a possessory security interest. There is no four-month grace period for obtaining perfection in that scenario. *See* § 9-316(a) (not applicable to perfection under § 9-301(2)).

pre-existing obligation that Doublequick owed to Best Retailers. Assuming that National Bank's security interest in the microwave ovens continues notwithstanding their transfer to Best Retailers, is that interest still perfected? If Best Retailers were incorporated in Iowa, how would that change your analysis? *See* §§ 9-507(a), 9-316(a).

Problem 4-36

A. Two years ago, Dragster purchased a new car for personal use with financing from Bank. At that time, Bank obtained a written security agreement and saw to it that its security interest was properly recorded on the vehicle's certificate of title, pursuant to the state's Motor Vehicle Certificate of Title Act. Two months ago, Dragster sold the car to Buyer. Buyer paid by check, which Dragster deposited into an account at Savings & Loan. Does Bank's security interest in the car remain perfected?

B. Three years ago, Dodge purchased a new car for personal use with financing from Lender. At that time, Lender obtained a written security agreement and saw to it that its security interest was properly recorded on the vehicle's certificate of title, pursuant to the state's Motor Vehicle Certificate of Title Act. Two months ago, Dodge traded the car in toward the purchase of a new car from Bankrupt Motors, a dealer in new and used cars. Bankrupt Motors is financed by Bank, which has a security interest in all of Bankrupt Motors' existing and after-acquired inventory. Bank has a proper financing statement on file to perfect that security interest. There is no question that Bank has a perfected security interest in the car that Dodge traded in. *See* § 9-311(a), (d). If Lender has no filing against Bankrupt Motors, is Lender's security interest in the trade-in still perfected? *See First National Bank of the North v. Automotive Finance Corp.*, 661 N.W.2d 668 (Minn. Ct. App. 2003). What provision of the Code most clearly answers this question? *See* §§ 9-507, 9-303(b), 9-311(a), (b), (c), (d) & cmt. 6.

Problem 4-37

A. Look back at Problem 4-14 and your answer to it. Now that we have learned more about acquiring and maintaining perfection, what additional things should First Bank do when conducting its search for existing security interests to make sure it has uncovered all security interests that could still be perfected?

B. Demolition Specialists, Inc., a Washington corporation, has come to Bank for a $700,000 loan to buy a large demolition crane from Raze Enterprises, a Nebraska business. What UCC searches does Bank need to conduct and why to be certain it will have the only perfected lien on the crane?

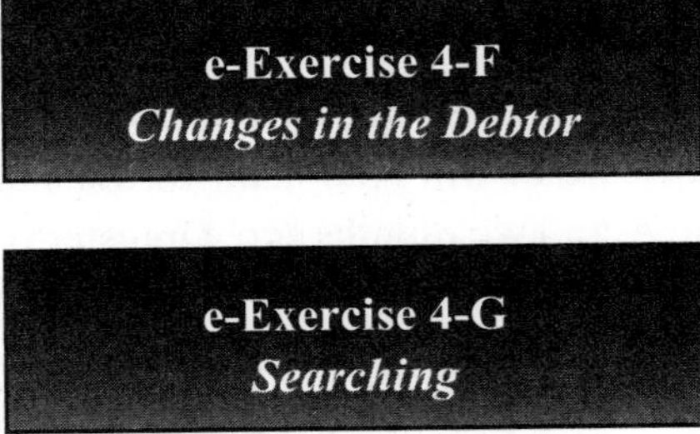

CHANGES IN THE DEBTOR AFFECTING THE VALIDITY OF A FINANCING STATEMENT

	Debtor Name or Location Changes	**Sales or Trades (collateral with new owner)**
Change does not render the filing seriously misleading or affect governing law	No new filing is needed.	No new filing is needed. § 9-507(a).
Change makes the filing seriously misleading but does not affect governing law	Filing is needed to remain perfected in collateral acquired more than four months after change, § 9-507(c).	No new filing is needed, § 9-507(a).
Change affects the governing law (makes a new jurisdiction the place to file against the collateral)	New filing is needed within four months, § 9-316(a)(2), (h).	New filing is needed within one year, § 9-316(a)(3).

5. Debtor Bankruptcy

As we have seen, if the debtor files for bankruptcy protection, the assets in which the secured party has a perfected security interest become property of the debtor's bankruptcy estate.[96] The secured party in possession or control of collateral is subject to an action by the trustee to turn over the collateral to the trustee.[97] The automatic stay prevents the secured party from taking any action to create, perfect or enforce its security interest in property of the estate or property of the debtor.[98]

However, an exception to the automatic stay allows the secured party to take whatever post-petition steps are necessary to maintain perfection of its security interest.[99] This allows the secured party to file a continuation statement despite the pending bankruptcy proceeding. It also allows the secured party to take whatever step is necessary to prevent a temporary automatic perfection period from expiring.[100]

We have also seen that the Bankruptcy Code prevents an after-acquired property clause in the security agreement from reaching property the debtor acquires after commencement of the bankruptcy case, but that it does not interfere with the security interest's automatic attachment to proceeds.[101] In relation to this, the Bankruptcy Code does nothing to alter the effectiveness of a previously filed financing statement. Such a financing statement will therefore remain effective to

---

[96] *See* 11 U.S.C. § 541.

[97] *See* 11 U.S.C. §§ 542, 543.

[98] 11 U.S.C. § 362(a).

[99] *See* 11 U.S.C. § 362(b)(3).

[100] *Cf.* In re Reliance Equities, Inc., 966 F.2d 1338 (10th Cir. 1992) (nothing in the Bankruptcy Code prevents a temporary automatic perfection period from expiring post-petition); In re Schwinn Cycling and Fitness, Inc., 313 B.R. 473 (D. Colo. 2004) (following *Reliance Equities*). *But cf.* In re Crowell, 304 B.R. 255 (W.D.N.C. 2004) (bankruptcy tolls four-month grace period in which to refile after the debtor moves to a new location). *See also* In re Stetson & Assocs., Inc., 330 B.R. 613 (Bankr. E.D. Tenn. 2005) (lapse of perfection after bankruptcy petition is filed does not make security interest avoidable because under § 9-515(c) lapse is not retroactive with respect to a lien creditor, such as the bankruptcy trustee).

[101] *See* 11 U.S.C. § 552.

perfect a security interest in proceeds to the same extent that it would have been had there been no bankruptcy proceeding.

D. Changes in the Secured Party

Virtually nothing that happens to the secured party after it perfects will affect perfection of a security interest. Although a valid financing statement must have the name of the secured party, a subsequent change in the secured party's name is not relevant to the effectiveness of the financing statement. § 9-507(b). A change in the location of the secured party cannot undermine perfection of its security interest because the jurisdiction in which the secured party is located does not govern perfection in the first instance. Finally, if a perfected security interest is assigned to another person, the security interest remains perfected without the need to file any notice of the assignment or otherwise indicate in the public record that the assignee is now the secured party. *See* § 9-310(c). The original secured party may file an amendment to a previously filed financing statement to make the assignee the secured party of record, *see* § 9-514, but perfection will continue even if no such amendment is filed. Note, the rule of § 9-310(c) – that a perfected security interest remains perfected despite assignment by the secured party – applies regardless of the method of perfection. Consequently, a security interest perfected by compliance with a certificate of title statute remains perfected if the secured party transfers the security interest (unless, perhaps, the certificate of title statute provides otherwise).[102]

Problem 4-38

On March 11, 2016, National Bank acquired a security interest in all of the existing and after-acquired inventory of Doublequick Cooking Corp. to secure "all obligations now or hereafter owed to National Bank." National Bank perfected that security interest the next day by filing in the appropriate office a sufficient financing statement indicating the collateral as "inventory." Doublequick manufactures and sells microwave ovens.

---

102 *See, e.g.*, In re Rice, 462 B.R. 651 (6th Cir. BAP 2011); In re McMullen, 441 B.R. 144 (Bankr. D. Kan. 2011); In re Clark Contracting Servs., Inc., 438 B.R. 913 (W.D. Tex. 2010); In re Scott, 427 B.R. 123 (Bankr. S.D. Ind. 2010); In re Wuerzberger, 284 B.R. 814 (Bankr. W.D. Va. 2002).

A. On December 15, 2016, National Bank changed its name to Nations Bank. Does Nations Bank have a perfected security interest in Doublequick's inventory?
B. On December 15, 2016, National Bank sold the loan to State Bank.
   1. Does State Bank have a perfected security interest in Doublequick's inventory?
   2. It is now March 15, 2021. Does State Bank have a perfected security interest in Doublequick's inventory?

Problem 4-39

The chart below lists a variety of perfection rules. They start with the easiest rules for the perfecting secured party and move down to the most burdensome rules for the secured party. For each rule, determine what impact, if any, it has on a person searching for perfected security interests. In other words, how does the perfection rule affect the search process?

Code Provision	**Filing Rule**
§ 9-309(1)	No filing needed for a PMSI in consumer goods.
§ 9-507(a)	No new filing needed on transfer of collateral to a buyer located in the same jurisdiction.
§ 9-507(b)	No new filing needed if classification of collateral changes in a way that does not alter the method of perfection.
§ 9-315(d)(2)	Continuously perfected in identifiable cash proceeds if perfected in the original collateral.
§ 9-315(d)(1)	Continuously perfected in identifiable first-generation proceeds if original filing is in right office as to the type of proceeds.
§ 9-507(c)	Refile within four months of a seriously misleading debtor name change, but only as to after-acquired collateral.
§ 9-316(a)(2)	Refile in new state within four months after debtor moves to a new state.

Code Provision	Filing Rule
§ 9-312(g)	Remain perfected for 20 days upon delivery of an instrument or certificated security to the debtor for a reason stated in that section.
§ 9-312(e)	Automatically perfected for 20 days in a certificated security, negotiable document or instrument acquired for new value.
§ 9-315(d)(1)	Re-perfect within 20 days against proceeds acquired with cash proceeds if the indication of collateral in the financing statement does not cover the proceeds.
§ 9-309(1)	Re-perfect immediately if refinancing destroys PMSI status.
§ 9-311	Re-perfect immediately if classification of collateral changes in a way that alters the method of perfection to a non-Article 9 method.

Test Your Knowledge

Exam Six – Maintaining Perfection

Chapter Five
Priority of Security Interests

SECTION 1. BASIC PRIORITY CONCEPTS

The first three Chapters of this book dealt with the rights of creditors against their debtors (and vice-versa). As we moved to the concept and rules of perfection in Chapter Four, we started dealing with the fact that there might be multiple claimants – other than the debtor – to the same property of the debtor. We learned that the perfection rules are designed, for the most part, so that these claimants can learn of each other in time to protect themselves. In other words, the perfection methods provide a mechanism for entities contemplating acquiring an interest in the collateral to ascertain who, other than the debtor, might already have an interest, and to adjust their behavior accordingly.

This Chapter, and a substantial portion of Article 9 litigation, concerns the rules that rank the rights of competing claimants to the same item or items of property. In essence, they deal with what happens when one or more parties fail to use the perfection rules properly, either by failing to perfect or by failing to ascertain or properly take into account the existence of prior perfected interests.[1] The priority rules are often not phrased in reference to such a failure in planning, but they are nevertheless best understood that way; the claimant who loses almost always could have done something differently to avoid the loss.[2] That something might have been a way to gain a better priority or it might simply have been refusing to give value in reliance on acquiring an interest in the collateral.

As should be apparent from the preceding two paragraphs, a secured party's priority depends largely on whether it is perfected and, if so, when and how it perfected. Often these facts will simply help determine a creditor's priority under the applicable priority rule. In other cases, they might affect which priority rule

---

[1] As we saw when we studied enforcement in Chapter Three, a creditor generally wants as high a priority as possible for its lien interest in order to reduce the risk of non-payment.

[2] *See* In re Samuels, 526 F.2d 1238, 1247-48 (5th Cir. 1976) (noting that there was no unfairness in ruling that a secured party with a perfected security interest in after-acquired cattle had priority over the unpaid sellers of recently sold cattle, even though the secured party had cut off the funding that would have allowed the debtor to pay for the cattle, because the sellers could have protected their interests in any of several ways).

applies. This is why the study of priority is somewhat complicated. Article 9 has dozens of different priority rules, most of which are located in Subpart 3 of Part 3, §§ 9-317–9-339. *See also* §§ 9-110(4), 9-312(c)(2), 9-316(b), (e), 9-340, 9-515(c), 9-516(d). Most of the rules are fairly easy to understand and apply.[3] The main "trick" to resolving a priority conflict is to ascertain which rule or rules apply (yes, more than one rule might govern a single dispute). For the most part, this in turn depends on six factors:

(1) The type of property involved (*e.g.*, equipment, chattel paper);
(2) Whether, when, and how the secured party perfected its security interest;
(3) What type of interest in the collateral the competing claimant has;
(4) Whether any interest is a PMSI;
(5) The extent to which the secured obligation includes future advances; and
(6) Whether property has been commingled or become an accession or fixture.[4]

Probably the two most important of these factors are the type of property involved (the collateral classification) and the type of interest the competing claimant has. The competing claimant could have a lien – either a judicial lien, consensual lien (*i.e.*, a security interest), or statutory lien – or it could be someone who has retained or acquired rights in the collateral further up or down the chain of title (*e.g.*, a buyer, lessee, or licensee).

These variations are depicted in the diagrams below. In order to enhance your understanding of the parties' transactions and relationships – which is key to ascertaining which rules apply – it is important to get into the habit of diagraming the claimants and their interests in the collateral. In the diagrams, diagonal lines represent liens and vertical lines represent other transfers of ownership rights (*e.g.*, sales, leases, and gifts). Throughout this Chapter, the priority disputes discussed will be accompanied by a diagram that uses this general format.

Each of the diagrams is accompanied by a list of the sections of Article 9 that govern the type of priority dispute the diagram depicts. As you can see, some of the

---

[3] For this reason, most priority litigation is not about what a particular priority rule means or how to interpret it. Instead, it is typically about whether a party perfected its interest properly, whether a perfected security interest remains perfected despite some subsequent event, or what Article 9 classification the collateral falls under (which in turn affects which priority rule applies).

[4] This last question is addressed in Chapter Six.

relationships are governed by a staggering number of different rules, a fact which can make the analysis complex. We will start with some of the simpler relationships. Specifically, this Chapter addresses the priority rules that are critical to a basic understanding of the Article 9 scheme. After you finish this Chapter, you should have a good understanding of the priority rules that govern most security interests in goods, accounts, deposit accounts, chattel paper, instruments, and general intangibles. Chapter Six then explores transactions and priority rules that are not integral to a basic understanding of Article 9. Specifically, Chapter Six covers accessions, commingled goods, fixtures, investment property, and letter-of-credit rights, along with the rules on new debtors, consignments, federal tax liens, and lien avoidance in bankruptcy.

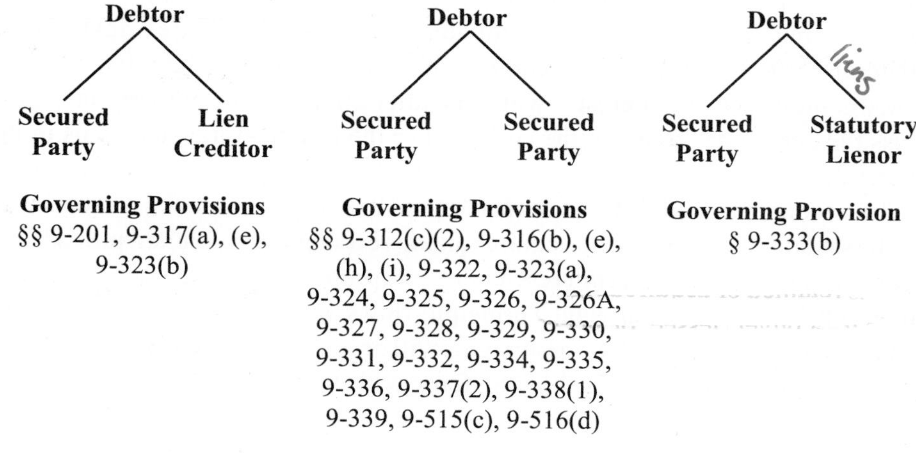

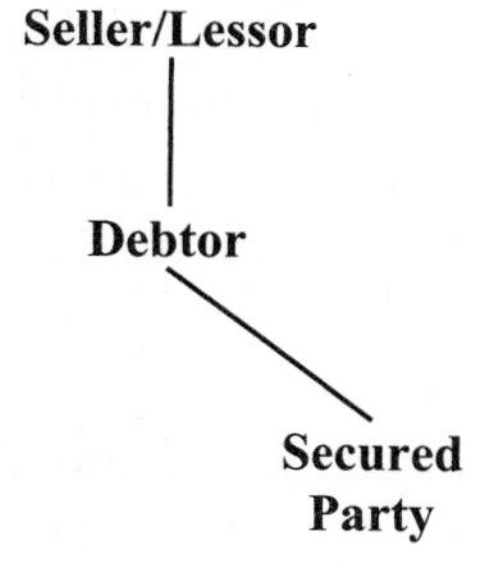

Governing Provisions
§§ 2-401, 2-403, 2-507, 2-702, 2A-305, 2A-307(1), 9-110(4)

Debtor

Secured Party **Buyer/Lessee**

Governing Provisions
§§ 2A-307(2), (3), 3-302, 8-303, 9-316(b), (e), (h), (i), 9-317(b), (c), (e), 9-320, 9-321, 9-323(a), (c)–(g), 9-330, 9-331, 9-332, 9-337(1), 9-338(2), 9-515(c), 9-516(d), 12-104

e-Exercise 5-A
Purchasers, Buyers & SPs

Fundamental property-law principles. The priority rules of Article 9, like the priority rules applicable to real estate and those included in other statutory or common-law schemes, are built upon two fundamental principles of property law. The first of these principles – sometimes referred to as the "derivation principle" – is that a person can transfer only those rights in property that the person has. In other words, a transferee's rights are derived from, and therefore limited to, the rights of the transferor. We encountered this principle when we learned about the requirements for attachment of a security interest. One of those requirements is that the debtor must have rights in the collateral or power to transfer rights in the collateral. § 9-203(b)(2). That requirement rests on the principle that a person cannot grant a security interest – which is, after all, a type of property interest – unless the person has rights in the collateral or the power to transfer rights in the collateral.

The second principle, based in part upon the first, is that the sequence of transfers matters: a person who acquires an interest in property should prevail over anyone who later acquires an interest in the same property from the same transferor. This "first in time, first in right" principle flows from the derivation principle because an initial transfer of property rights will necessarily deplete the transferor's rights in the property, leaving the transferor with few or no rights to transfer to anyone else.

As might already be apparent, the "first in time" principle is not absolute. Indeed, the whole concept of perfection is about when the law should deviate from that principle. In many situations, a party is not permitted to invoke the "first in time" principle unless and until that party has taken some step the law regards as providing notification to the public of its interest in the property. This is certainly true under Article 9; such public notification is the key attribute of perfection of most security interests.[5] Nevertheless, perfection should not be thought of entirely as an exception to the "first in time principle." Instead you should think of it as having been incorporated into the principle. Thus, as you might already have predicted, instead of basing priority of a security interest entirely on when it was created (attached), the law will base priority largely on when it was perfected (or when the applicable perfection step was taken).

---

5 Review the discussion in Chapter Four on the problem of "ostensible ownership."

The relevance of reliance. The various parties contesting for priority in the collateral are likely to have different reliance interests in it. In other words, some of them will have taken actions to their detriment in anticipation of being able to seek recourse from the collateral, others will not have done so at all or to the same extent. These differences in the parties' reliance on the collateral tend to affect the priority that Article 9 accords to them.

At one extreme is a judicial lien creditor. It was owed a debt – perhaps because it loaned the debtor money on an unsecured basis or was the victim of a tort for which the debtor is liable – long before it established any relationship to the collateral. Put simply, it did not rely on the collateral in deciding to become a creditor of the debtor and probably also did not rely much or at all when it acquired the judicial lien.

At the other extreme are buyers, lessees, and licensees. Each of them provided value to the debtor for the express purpose of acquiring rights in specified property. They are always reliance parties.

Somewhere in between are statutory lienors. Some, such as a mechanic who repaired the debtor's car or a jeweler who repaired the debtor's watch, and who has retained possession of the repaired item pending payment, might have relied on its control over that asset in agreeing to provide parts and services without prepayment. On the other had, a landlord with a lien on personal property that a defaulting tenant left behind has a more accidental relationship to the property. A taxing authority with a statutory lien on all of the debtor's property similarly did not specifically rely on any of it. After all, it is not really a voluntary creditor at all.

Secured parties too run the gamut. A seller who sells goods on credit and retains a security interest in the goods sold often relies heavily on the collateral and has a relationship to it that predates the debtor's. A purchase-money lender also has a strong expectation of being able to resort to the purchased item if the debtor does not pay. In contrast, a secured party with a blanket lien on all of the debtor's existing and after-acquired personal property and whose debt is supported by guarantees or other credit enhancement devices might have only a limited concern about any particular piece of the debtor's property.

Consider these varying reliance interests when evaluating Article 9's priority rules. In doing so, remember that rules covering "purchasers" apply to buyers, lessees, licensees, secured parties, and even donees. *See* § 1-201(b)(29), (30). Rules applicable to "purchasers for value" cover all such entities except donees. *See* § 1-204.

Priority analysis is asset specific. The study of priority is premised upon the idea that determining the hierarchy of lien claims in property is an asset-specific exercise. We have already seen that classification is asset-specific (one item of collateral might be inventory while another item is equipment), attachment is item-specific (a security interest might attach to one piece of collateral at one time and to another item at another time or not at all), and perfection too must be evaluated and analyzed item by item (a security interest might be perfected in one item of collateral and unperfected in another or it might be perfected by one method for some collateral and by another method for other collateral). Similarly, indeed because of this, a creditor might have the first priority position in Asset A but only the second or third priority position in Asset B. Thus, it is misleading to think about what priority position a creditor has in all of the collateral. The priority positions of creditors must be evaluated separately for each particular asset.

Other priority rules. Although Article 9 has dozens of different priority rules, it is not the sole repository of such rules. On occasion, other sources of law – whether state or federal, statutory or judicial – must be consulted to determine the relative priorities of various parties. This is particularly true when the priority battle pits the rights of an Article 9 secured party against those of a holder of a statutory lien. Any attempt to resolve that dispute without reviewing the provisions of the statute authorizing that lien would be unwise, if not impossible. Indeed, for some such liens Article 9 expressly defers to whatever priority rules the other statute contains. *See* § 9-333. Moreover, if none of the parties contesting priority is an Article 9 secured party, Article 9 will not provide an answer to who wins. For example, the relative priority of two judicial liens is not determined by any rules in Article 9. The lien creditors would have to look to some other state statute or to the judicial decisions of the relevant state to determine their relative rights. Similarly, Article 9 says nothing about the competing claims of two statutory lien creditors or about those of a statutory lien creditor and a judicial lien creditor.[6]

---

[6] Because the priority rules might be supplied by different statutory or common-law regimes, occasionally a situation called circular priority results. Circular priority refers to any situation where, after applying the applicable priority rules, Creditor A's interest has priority over Creditor B's interest, Creditor B's interest has priority over Creditor C's interest, and Creditor C's interest has priority over Creditor A's interest. The priority rules of Article 9 generally do not result in circular priorities. Article 9 contains no rules or processes for "breaking" the circle if a circular priority does occur. We will not address the various methods that courts have used for resolving circular priorities.

However, the priority rules in Article 9 are statutory rules. While it is often useful to consider the equities of a dispute to which a particular rule applies in order to both understand and interpret that rule, courts are – and should be – quite reluctant to disregard Article 9's priority rules, craft exceptions to them, or permit a junior secured party or unsecured creditor to recover under a common-law principle against a secured party with the prior interest.[7]

Roadmap to the Chapter. As you can see without even digging into the meat of any particular priority rule, learning and applying the priority rules requires a very methodical analysis. Our methodology will be to break up the discussion by the type of competing claimant. Thus in Section 2 we consider the priority of an Article 9 security interest as against a non-consensual lien, such as a judicial lien or a statutory lien (other than an agricultural lien). In Section 3, we consider the priority of security interests as against other security interests. The bulk of Article 9's priority rules apply to such disputes. Many of those rules depend upon the type of collateral at issue or the method of perfection used. Others apply only to proceeds of specified types of collateral.

In Section 4, we consider the priority of a security interest created by a buyer or lessee of goods as against the rights of the seller or lessor. In Section 5 we consider the priority of a security interest created by a seller or lessor of goods as against the rights of the buyer or lessee. Finally in Section 6, we consider the priority of a security interest created by a transferor as against the rights of transferees of non-goods collateral. In the event all this merely whets your appetite for more, Chapter Six discusses several more specialized priority contests.

Subordination. One last note before we start our study of the substance of the priority rules. If parties want to, they may by contract alter the priority of their respective security interests. Parties do this through subordination agreements, in which one party agrees to subordinate its interest in one or more items of collateral to another person's interest that would, but for the agreement, have been subordinate. Such agreements are enforceable under the common-law rules

---

[7] *See, e.g.*, GlobalTranz Enters., Inc. v. PNC Bank, 2020 WL 3469114 (Del. Super. Ct. 2020) (a secured party that allegedly either acquiesced in or encouraged the debtor to use the services of a freight broker without disclosing the debtor's poor financial condition to the broker, and which then realized the benefit of those services when the debtor's assets were sold off, had no unjust enrichment liability to the broker; only in unusual circumstances is a secured party liable in unjust enrichment to an unsecured creditor of the debtor, and mere acquiescence to the transactions is insufficient to upend Article 9's priority rules).

governing contracts generally, and nothing in Article 9 interferes with a subordination agreement. § 9-339. Of course, we cannot rely on contractual subordination to establish the relative priorities in every case. After all, a subordination agreement binds only those persons who are party to the agreement. Creditor A and Creditor B may make an agreement that determines which of their security interests has priority over the other. They cannot, however, make an enforceable agreement that subordinates Creditor C's security interest in the same property. Moreover, there is no effective mechanism for getting all creditors – including potential future creditors – to contractually agree to the priority of their respective liens on a particular piece of property. Consequently, the rather complicated scheme of priority rules we are about to study is probably unavoidable.

SECTION 2. SECURITY INTERESTS AGAINST NON-CONSENSUAL LIENS

A. Security Interests against Judicial Liens

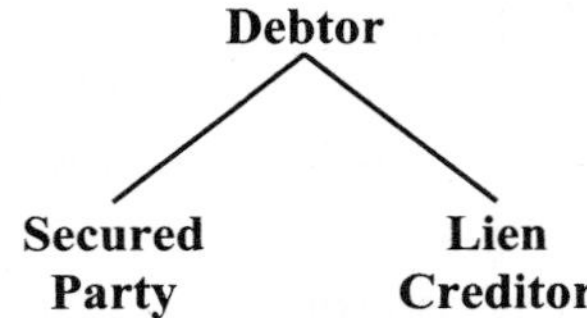

You might expect a book on secured transactions to begin its discussion of priority by dealing with the competing claims of two secured parties. Instead, like most course books on this subject, this one begins with secured parties versus lien creditors. There are three reasons for this.

First, Article 9 has far fewer rules governing secured party vs. lien creditor disputes than it has dealing with the relative rights of two or more secured parties. As a result, secured party vs. lien creditor disputes are less complex, easier to understand, and serve as a better entree into the subject and the methodology of applying priority rules.

Second, in at least one respect, secured party vs. lien creditor disputes are the most fundamental. The whole concept of perfection is about the ability to beat a subsequent lien creditor. In other words, by definition a perfected security interest has priority over a later arising judicial lien. That's what perfection means. *See* § 9-308 cmt. 1.

Third, while many secured parties do wish to make sure their interests will have priority over those of other secured parties, all want to ensure – and many are content to know – that they will have priority over a lien creditor. As we will learn in Chapter Six, a bankruptcy trustee is deemed to have a judicial lien on all of the debtor's assets.[8] So, being perfected allows a secured party – generally – to come ahead of the bankruptcy trustee. In contrast, an unperfected security interest will be avoided (*i.e.*, eliminated) if the debtor seeks bankruptcy protection. Given that default and bankruptcy often go hand-in-hand, a security interest that will be lost in bankruptcy is not worth much.

1. The Basic Rule

As you might remember from the discussion in Chapter One, a lien creditor is a creditor whose lien is created by judicial process. *See* § 9-102(a)(52). In most states, this requires that the creditor first obtain a judgment, then procure a writ of execution, deliver the writ to the sheriff, and then have the sheriff levy upon property of the debtor. The sheriff's levy in that process creates the judicial lien on behalf of the judgment creditor. In other states, the judicial lien might arise upon delivery of the writ to the sheriff or upon recording a notice of the judgment with the Secretary of State. When a secured party has a security interest on the same personal property on which the lien creditor has a judicial lien, § 9-201(a) provides the rule that presumptively determines the relative priority of the judicial lien and the security interest.

Read § 9-201(a). It is the default rule for all priority disputes between a secured party and some other type of creditor. Pursuant to § 9-201(a), the secured party has priority unless some other provision in the UCC provides otherwise. In short, the secured party wins. Why is that the default rule for determining the priority of security interests and judicial liens? Well, a cynical person might say it is because Article 9 was written largely by and for secured parties. Put another way, there is no effective lobby for the future judgment lienors of the world. A more persuasive justification is that, as mentioned above, judicial lien creditors are not reliance parties – they did not rely on the value of the collateral when they became a creditor of the debtor – whereas secured parties are, at least to some extent.

Regardless of the reason, it is vital to understand that § 9-201(a) governs only if there is no statutory exception: some more specific rule that provides a contrary

---

[8] 11 U.S.C. § 544(a)(1). This hypothetical lien arises the moment the bankruptcy petition is filed. *See also* § 9-102(a)(52)(C).

result. This brings us to § 9-317(a)(2), which is merely the first and most basic of the many exceptions to the default rule of § 9-201(a).

A quick read of § 9-317(a)(2) reveals that it is principally a timing rule. A security interest is subordinated (*i.e.*, the lien creditor wins) if the lien creditor's lien arises before the secured party does either of two things: (1) perfects its security interest (review § 9-308(a), (b)); or (2) files a financing statement and satisfies the requirements of § 9-203(b)(3).

What's the difference between these two situations? How can a security interest be unperfected yet still be the subject of a filed financing statement and compliance with § 9-203(b)(3)? Recall that perfection requires attachment plus some other applicable step, usually filing a financing statement. *See* § 9-308(a), (b). Attachment of a security interest, in turn, requires three things: (i) that value be given; (ii) that the debtor have rights in the collateral or power to transfer rights in the collateral; and, in most cases, and (iii) that the debtor has signed a security agreement with an adequate collateral description. § 9-203(b). Section 9-203(b)(3) deals with only the last of these requirements. Thus, a secured party who files and complies with § 9-203(b)(3), typically by getting a signed security agreement, need not yet have fulfilled the first requirement – given value – for its security interest to have priority over a lien creditor.

The importance of this rule is best understood through its impact on the lending process. A cautious, prospective lender will begin by filing a financing statement against the debtor. Then it will search for any financing statements filed by another party, conduct a physical inspection of the property offered as collateral (to verify its existence and condition, confirm the absence of a secured party perfected by possession, and confirm that the property has not been levied upon), and, only if the results of both the search and the inspection reveal no problems, make the loan.

However, until it makes the loan, its security interest does not attach and therefore cannot be perfected. *See* § 9-203(b)(1).[9] The rule of § 9-317(a)(2)(B) allows the prospective lender to use its normal process with assurance that it will have priority

[9] Actually, its security interest could attach prior to making the loan if the lender had committed to making the loan. That is because a binding commitment to lend, possibly even one subject to a condition, constitutes value. *See* § 1-204(1), (4). If the lender follows such a process, § 9-317(a)(2)(B) is unnecessary.

over a lien creditor whose levy occurs after the physical inspection but before the loan is made (in the darkly shaded area in the chart above), as long as it gets a signed security agreement before the levy.[10] Without this rule, any delay between the physical inspection – which proved the absence of a levy at that time – and making the loan would subject the creditor to the risk that it would not have the priority it was counting on.[11]

What about the second requirement for attachment of a security interest, that the debtor have rights in the collateral? § 9-203(b)(2). Remember that a lien creditor generally may obtain a lien only on property that the debtor has an interest in at the time of the levy. In other words, there is normally no "after-acquired property" concept associated with the typical lien creditor's lien.[12] If the debtor has an interest in the collateral at the time of the levy, sufficient for the resulting judicial lien to attach, the debtor will also generally have an interest in the collateral sufficient for the security interest to have attached. Thus, effectively, the only missing requirement for attachment that § 9-317(a)(2)(B) addresses is the lack of value.

Because the lien creditor vs. secured party priority rule depends upon the timing of the relevant events, it is often very useful to draw a timeline of those events before attempting to apply the rule.

---

[10] In fact, § 9-317(a)(2)(B) also allows the prospective lender to have priority over a lien creditor whose levy occurred in the lightly shaded area, but such a priority dispute is unlikely to arise. If the levy occurs before the prospective lender inspects the collateral, the prospective creditor is unlikely to make the loan. After all, the levy itself suggests that the debtor might be experiencing financial problems. More important, the prospective lender is unlikely to be able to ascertain whether the levy occurred before or after the financing statement was filed. Unless it can be sure that the financing statement was filed before the levy occurred, the prospective lender cannot be sure that its security interest will have priority.

[11] As should be evident, this rule makes prefiling the financing statement very important. *See* In re Millivision, Inc., 474 F.3d 4 (1st Cir. 2007) (bankruptcy trustee, who is deemed to have a judicial lien on all of the debtor's assets, could avoid a security interest of lenders who loaned $500,000 to the debtor one day before the debtor's creditors filed an involuntary petition against it because the lenders did not pre-file their financing statement).

[12] This conclusion should be checked for the particular state whose law gave rise to the judicial lien and it might vary with respect to the type of property at issue or the type of writ used to create the judicial lien.

Problem 5-1

Deep Sea Specialists, Inc. is a Nebraska corporation that manufactures and sells scuba gear. On May 1, a few days after Deep Sea applied for a loan, National Bank filed an authorized financing statement against "Deep Sea Specialists, Inc." in the Nebraska Secretary of State's office listing the collateral as "all assets" and National Bank as the secured party. On May 5, Finance Company obtained a judicial lien on Deep Sea's inventory in an Iowa warehouse to enforce a judgment obtained against Deep Sea in Iowa. The judgment was for $20,000 and the goods are estimated to be worth $75,000. On June 1, Deep Sea signed a document in which it granted National Bank a security interest in all its "inventory and equipment now owned or hereafter acquired to secure all obligations that the debtor now owes or hereafter owes to National Bank." On June 3, National Bank loaned Deep Sea $100,000.

A. Does National Bank have a security interest in those goods located in Iowa? If so, when did that security interest attach? Is it perfected?
B. If National Bank has a security interest, what is the priority of National Bank's security interest against Finance Company's judicial lien? *See* § 9-317(a)(2).
C. How, if at all, would the analysis change if the judicial lien was created on June 2 instead of on May 5?
D. How, if at all, would the analysis change if the judicial lien was created on June 4 instead of on May 5?
E. What would the priorities be if the judicial lien was created on June 2 and the debtor's correct name, as shown in the Nebraska corporate records, is "Decompression Specialists, Inc."? *See* § 9-506.
F. Assume the judicial lien was created on May 5 and that Deep Sea acquired some additional items of inventory on June 5. What is the priority of interests in those new items of inventory? Does Finance Company even have a lien on those items?
G. What would be the priorities if the judicial lien was created on June 2 and National Bank's perfection lapsed after that date (because, for example, National Bank's financing statement lapsed and National Bank failed to file a continuation statement)? *See* § 9-515(c) & cmt. 3.

Problem 5-2

Deeply Engrossing Films, Inc. ("DEF"), a Delaware corporation, borrowed $2 million from Lender, signed a promissory note to repay the debt, and granted Lender an effective security interest in all its personal property. Lender promptly filed a sufficient financing statement in the appropriate Delaware office indicating the collateral as "all assets." A few months later, Jilted obtained a judgment in California against DEF and had a writ of garnishment issued against County Bank, where DEF had $400,000 on deposit. County Bank is located in California. Lender intervened in the action claiming priority in DEF's deposit account at County Bank. If the deposit account balance is traceable to the loan from Lender – that is, it is what remains of the funds Lender loaned to DEF – who has priority in the deposit account? *See Full Throttle Films, Inc. v. National Mobile Television, Inc.*, 103 Cal. Rptr. 3d 560 (Cal. Ct. App. 2009).

2. Purchase-money Security Interests against Judicial Liens

Practical concerns also underlie § 9-317(e). Consider the following situation. A buyer decides to buy a new piece of equipment for use in its business. The seller is willing to sell on credit to the buyer but insists on retaining a security interest in the equipment to secure the price. The buyer and seller agree on terms, the buyer signs the sales agreement granting the seller a security interest in the equipment, and the buyer takes physical delivery of the equipment. Moments later, a creditor of the buyer levies on the equipment. The next day, seller perfects its security interest by filing an effective financing statement covering the equipment in the jurisdiction where the buyer is located.

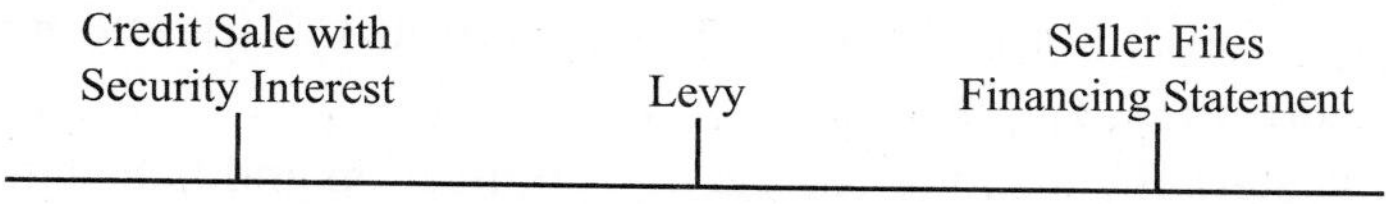

Credit Sale with Security Interest — Levy — Seller Files Financing Statement

Under § 9-317(a)(2), the seller's security interest would be subordinate to the levying creditor's lien because the seller would not have perfected or filed prior to the creation of the judicial lien. The rule of § 9-317(e) is an exception to the rule in § 9-317(a)(2). It allows the secured party – which has a purchase-money security interest – to have priority over the judgment creditor's lien even though the secured party took its perfection step subsequent to the levy, as long as the secured party files an effective financing statement within 20 days after the debtor receives delivery of collateral. If § 9-317(e) did not exist, to be assured of having priority the secured party would need to file before relinquishing possession of the goods, and that would frustrate buyers and needlessly delay many credit sales of goods.

Notice what the last sentence of the prior paragraph just did. It identified the policy – or at least one of the policies – underlying the priority rule of § 9-317(e), and it did so through the perspective of one of the competing claimants in a typical transaction. The discussion of § 9-317(a)(2) a few pages above did the same. Article 9, like most statutes, does not typically explain the policies underlying its rules. But to fully understand any rule, you need to appreciate why it exists and what it is intended to do. Therefore, throughout the remainder of this Chapter, pay close attention to the book's discussion of the policy underlying each priority rule. In addition, try to discern if there are other policies in play. To do so, imagine yourself in the position of each of the competing claimants and consider what that claimant wants to do, what information it needs, and whether or how it can obtain that information.

Problem 5-3

On Saturday, June 1, Driver bought a new car from Dealer. Dealer helped Driver obtain approval of a bank loan from State Bank for the purchase price minus a down payment supplied by Driver to Dealer. Driver signed a document in which it granted State Bank a security interest in the car to secure the loan. Driver drove the car home on Saturday afternoon. On the following Thursday, June 6, Finance Company had the sheriff levy on the car in execution of a judgment entered the previous month against Driver. On Friday, June 7, State Bank submitted the title application with its lien statement to the Department of Motor Vehicles.

A. Between State Bank and Finance Company, whose lien on the car has priority? *See* Uniform Motor Vehicle Certificate of Title and Anti-Theft Act § 20(b); U.C.C. § 9-317(a)(2), (e).
B. What if State Bank submitted the title application and lien statement to the Department of Motor Vehicles on June 15? How does that change your analysis? *See* §§ 9-317(e) & cmt. 8; 9-311(b) & cmts. 5, 6. *See also In re O'Neill*, 344 B.R. 142 (Bankr. D. Colo. 2006), *rev'd*, 370 B.R. 332 (10th Cir. BAP 2007).
C. How, if at all, does the analysis change if the title application and lien statement were delivered to the Department of Motor Vehicles on June 28?
D. What if the levy took place on June 10? Is § 9-317(e) relevant?

Problem 5-4

On August 1, Degas purchased a painting on credit from Art Dealer, who retained an effective security interest in the painting to secure the unpaid portion of the purchase price. Degas proudly displays the painting in the living room of Degas' home. On December 1, Johnson caused the sheriff to levy on the painting in an effort to collect on a judgment against Degas. Between Art Dealer and Johnson, who has priority if Art Dealer never filed a financing statement? *See* §§ 9-309(1), 9-317(a)(2), (e).

e-Exercise 5-B
SP v. Lien Creditor

3. Security Interest Securing Future Advances against Judicial Liens

If a security interest is subordinated to the rights of a lien creditor, say because the secured party had neither filed nor perfected prior to the levy, and the secured party thereafter loans the debtor more money, the security interest securing the future advance will likewise be subordinated. However, the converse is not true, at least not completely. Consider the following example.

> Secured Party loans $20,000 to Debtor secured by Debtor's equipment, which is worth $35,000. Secured Party promptly and properly perfects its security interest by filing a financing statement. The security agreement provides that any future advances will also be secured by the equipment.[13] Six months later, Creditor obtains a judgment against Debtor, and has the sheriff levy on the equipment pursuant to a writ of execution. Assuming the amount of the debt to Secured Party and the value of the collateral are roughly unchanged ($20,000 and $35,000, respectively), Creditor is hoping and expecting to be able to extract some of the $15,000 excess value for itself. Two days after the levy, Secured Party loans Debtor another $15,000.

---

[13] The original security agreement should not need to have a future advances clause as long as the parties in fact agree that the new loan will be secured by the collateral. After all, the "security agreement" is the bargain of the parties. *See* §§ 1-201(b)(3), 9-102(a)(74). It need not be contained in a single writing and may be amended from time to time. A mere oral agreement or amendment providing that the collateral secures the new loan may, however, not be sufficient, given the signature requirement in § 9-203(b)(3).

If Secured Party's security interest has priority over Creditor's judicial lien with respect to the new loan, Creditor will have lost all equity in the equipment. On the other hand, if Creditor's judicial lien has priority over Secured Party's security interest, then lenders will need to conduct a physical inspection of the collateral not merely before the initial advance, but before each subsequent advance as well. Given that some lenders extend credit on a daily and even an intra-day basis, this would be very cumbersome. Moreover, a physical inspection of the collateral might not reveal the judicial lien because in some states a creditor acquires a judicial lien by filing a notice of the judgment in the public record rather than by having an officer levy on (take possession of) the collateral.

Article 9 deals with these conflicting concerns by sometimes giving priority to the security interest securing the future advance and sometimes giving priority to the lien creditor's lien. Read § 9-323(b). If the advance is made within 45 days after the lien creditor's lien arises, or if the advance is made after 45 days and without knowledge of the lien creditor's lien, the lien creditor's lien is subordinate to the security interest securing that advance. If, however, the advance is made after 45 days and with knowledge of the lien creditor's lien, the lien creditor's lien is superior to the security interest securing that advance.

Problem 5-5

One very useful technique for understanding complex statutory text is to rephrase the provision using your own language. The act of doing this often aids comprehension to a significantly greater degree than almost anything else the reader could do. In dealing with Article 9's priority rules, one of the best ways to do this is to "flip" the provision: if the statute as written indicates when the secured party wins, rewrite the provision to explain when the competing secured party does not win; conversely, if the statute as written indicates when the competing creditor wins, redraft the provision to explain when the competing creditor does not win.[14] As your first flipping

---

[14] Note, stating when a specified creditor "does not win" under a specific statutory provision is not the same thing as stating when that creditor loses (or when a competing lienor wins). The statement merely means that the provision does not grant the specified creditor's interest priority (*i.e.*, that the rule does not apply). In some situations, another rule might bestow

exercise, "flip" the priority rule expressed in § 9-323(b) so that it indicates when a security interest securing future advances is not subordinated to the rights of a lien creditor. For simplicity, ignore the reference to subsection (c).

Problem 5-6

Secured Party has a properly perfected security interest in Dentist's equipment valued at $50,000 to secure a loan of $25,000. Lien Creditor levies on the equipment in execution of a $10,000 judgment.

A. The week after the levy and without knowledge of it, Secured Party loaned the debtor an additional $20,000. To what extent does Secured Party's security interest have priority over Lien Creditor's judicial lien? *See* §§ 9-323(b), 9-204.
B. How, if at all, would the analysis of Part A change if Secured Party made the $20,000 loan 60 days after the levy and without knowledge of it?
C. How, if at all, would the analysis of Part A change if Secured Party made the $20,000 loan one week after the levy but with knowledge of it?
D. How, it at all, would the analysis of Part A change if Secured Party made the $20,000 loan 60 days after the levy and with knowledge of it?

One of the reasons for subordinating a secured party's security interest with respect to future advances is that it would be unfair to allow the secured party to purposefully lend more money so as to take equity in the collateral away from a levying creditor. That rationale does not apply, or applies with much less force, when the secured party is not acting voluntarily in lending or deciding to lend additional funds. But not all increases in a secured obligation result from voluntary decisions to lend. On most debts, interest accrues on a daily basis and does so without any voluntary action by the secured party. Similarly, the secured party might incur expenses in trying to collect the secured obligation, expenses for which the debtor has agreed to be liable, even though the secured party would much prefer to avoid such costs. Such increases in the secured obligation – often referred to as "non-advances" – are never subordinated by § 9-323(b). Security interests securing

---

priority on the specified creditor's interest.

such increases are deemed to have the same priority as the security interest securing the debt to which they relate. *See* § 9-323 cmt. 4.[15]

Problem 5-7

Secured Party has a properly perfected security interest in Dentist's equipment valued at $50,000 to secure a loan of $25,000 and all future obligations owed to Secured Party. Lien Creditor levies on the equipment in execution of a $10,000 judgment. Sixty days after the levy and with knowledge of it, Secured Party loans the debtor an additional $20,000. Thereafter, interest accrues on all the obligations, increasing each by 10%. In addition, Secured Party incurs $2,000 in expenses in attempting to collect the debt by foreclosing on the collateral.

A. To what extent does Secured Party's security interest have priority over Lien Creditor's judicial lien?
B. How would the answer to Part A change if, just before foreclosure, Dentist made an $8,000 payment to Secured Party? *See In re McAllister*, 267 B.R. 614 (Bankr. N.D. Iowa 2001).

Notice that neither § 9-317(a)(2) nor § 9-323(b) addresses the priority contest that might arise as to proceeds of collateral that have been levied on. No matter who sells the collateral – the secured party pursuant to Part 6 of Article 9 or the sheriff pursuant to a writ – the secured party's security interest will attach to the proceeds. Conceivably, this security interest would be entitled to priority under § 9-201. However, it is unlikely that, if the lien creditor had priority in the collateral sold, a court would give priority in the proceeds to the secured party.

---

[15] The comment as phrased in 1998 confirmed this rule expressly but that comment was amended by the Permanent Editorial Board in 1999 and it now confirms this point more cryptically. *See also* UNI Imports, Inc. v. Aparacor, Inc., 978 F.2d 984 (7th Cir. 1992); P.E.B. Commentary # 2 (March 10, 1990); Dick Warner Cargo Handling Corp. v. Aetna Business Credit, Inc., 746 F.2d 126 (2d Cir. 1984). *Cf.* Boers v. Payline Sys., Inc., 928 P.2d 1010 (Or. Ct. App. 1996) (law firm's services to client are more properly regarded as advances than as non-advances, but nevertheless had priority because they were made pursuant to a commitment entered into before the judicial lien arose).

B. Security Interests against Possessory Liens Arising by Operation of Law

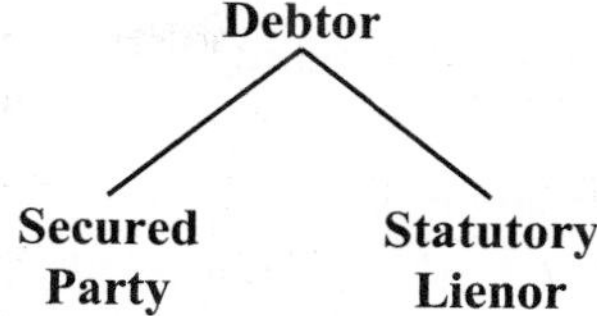

Section 9-333 provides a rule for determining the priority of some statutory and common-law liens as against a security interest. Read it. Note how limited the rule is. It does not apply to all statutory and common-law liens, only to possessory liens on goods that secure payment for services and materials used to repair such goods (a type of mechanic's lien).[16] Nor does it govern all priority disputes involving such possessory liens; it applies merely to those against security interests.

Under § 9-333(b), a possessory lien has priority over a security interest provided: (i) the lienholder has possession of the goods; and (ii) the statute creating the lien does not provide otherwise. This is true even if the security interest attached and was perfected before the possessory lien arises.

Problem 5-8

Consider the equities present in a typical priority dispute between the holder of a possessory, statutory lien and an Article 9 secured party. Given that Article 9 was written largely by and for secured lenders, why does the default rule of § 9-333(b) grant priority to the possessory lien even if the secured party perfected its security interest before the possessory lien arose?

Problem 5-9

Deep Sea Specialists, Inc. is a Nebraska corporation that manufactures and sells scuba gear. On May 1, a few days after Deep Sea applied for a loan, National Bank filed an authorized financing statement against "Deep Sea Specialists, Inc." in the Nebraska Secretary of State's office listing the collateral as "all assets" and National Bank as the secured party. On June 1,

---

[16] Technically, the possessory lien need not be a statutory lien; it could be created by the common law. *See* § 9-333(a)(2). In the vast majority of situations, however, it is likely to be a creature of statute. More to the point, it is referred to here as a statutory lien primarily to distinguish it from judicial liens (which arise through a judicial process) and consensual liens (which are created by contract).

Deep Sea signed a document in which it granted National Bank a security interest in all its "inventory and equipment now owned or hereafter acquired to secure all obligations that the debtor now owes or hereafter owes to National Bank." On June 3, National Bank loaned Deep Sea $100,000. On July 1, Deep Sea delivered several copy machines to Gadgets, Inc. for repair. Gadgets fixed the copy machines and charged $5,000 for the parts and labor. Gadgets still has possession of the copiers and a state statute gives Gadgets a possessory lien on the copy machines to secure the costs of repair.

A. What is the priority of Gadgets' lien as against National Bank's security interest? What do you need to know to answer that question?
B. If Gadgets delivers the copy machines back to Deep Sea without getting paid for the repair work, does Gadgets still have a lien on the copy machines? If so, what is the priority between Gadgets' lien and National Bank's security interest? *See In re Bordon*, 361 B.R. 489 (8th Cir. BAP 2007).

When a statutory lien not covered by § 9-333 comes into conflict with an Article 9 security interest, there is often no clear guidance on which has priority and the answer might well vary from state to state. Occasionally courts rely on the statement in § 9-201(a) that security interests have priority over the debtor's creditors unless the UCC expressly states otherwise. More commonly, courts derive a rule based on first-in-time principles.[17]

---

[17] *See, e.g.*, Watkins v. GMAC Fin. Servs., 785 N.E.2d 40 (Ill. Ct. App. 2003); McGonigle v. Combs, 968 F.2d 810 (9th Cir.); Colorado Nat'l Bank-Boulder v. Zerobnick & Sander, P.C., 768 P.2d 1276 (Colo. Ct. App. 1989). If the priority of such claimants is not established by statute, what arguments should a lawyer make to convince a court to depart from the first-in-time rule? *See* Atascadero Factory Outlets, Inc. v. Augustini & Wheeler LLP, 99 Cal. Rptr. 2d 911 (Cal. Ct. App. 2000). *See also* § 9-324(a), (b).

SECTION 3. SECURITY INTEREST AGAINST SECURITY INTEREST: THE BASICS

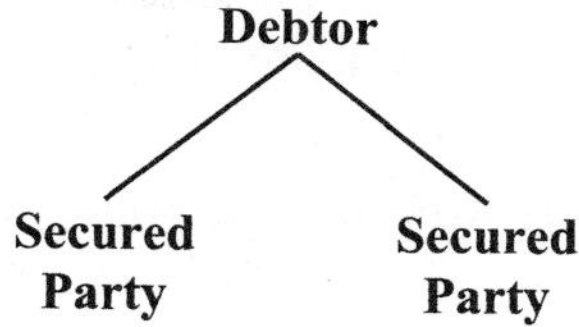

In this section we consider the priority of multiple security interests in the same collateral. We start with the three basic rules found in § 9-322(a). After studying them and their implications for secured parties, we will explore the numerous exceptions to those rules.

A. First to File or Perfect

Read § 9-322(a). That section has three priority rules, which are best explored in reverse order of their presentation in the statute. Subsection (3) provides that if the conflicting security interests are unperfected, priority goes to the first to attach. As you can see, this rule is simply a codification of the "first in time, first in right" principle. The priority rule of subsection (2) is a major deviation from that principle, but not one which should be surprising. It grants priority to a perfected security interest over an unperfected one.

Problem 5-10

Deserving recently became a certified public accountant and wishes to start her own practice. Because she has no credit history, no clients, and no track record of earning money, no commercial lender is willing to lend her the money she needs to rent and furnish office space and advertise her services. However, Deserving does have several relatives who believe in her honesty and diligence and who are willing to lend her the capital she needs.

Grandfather is the first to cough up some dough; he lends Deserving $20,000 on July 1. Although confident in Deserving's abilities, Grandfather is not sanguine that Deserving will be financially successful in the competitive marketplace. So, Deserving grants Grandfather an effective security interest in all her existing and after-acquired office equipment to secure the loan. Since Grandfather is not familiar with Article 9, he files no financing statement.

On July 15, Aunt lends Deserving $30,000. She too gets an effective security interest in all existing and after-acquired office equipment to secure the loan.

A. If Aunt also fails to file a financing statement, who has priority in the collateral?

B What if, two years later, Aunt files a proper financing statement in the appropriate office?

The most important rule in § 9-322(a) is in subsection (1), which governs the priority of two or more perfected security interests. It contains what is known as the "first-to-file-or-perfect" rule, which accords priority to a security interest that was perfected or covered by a filed financing statement before a competing security interest was perfected or covered by a filed financing statement, provided that there is no time thereafter when there is neither a filing covering the collateral nor perfection of the security interest.

Why does subsection (1) not simply give priority to the first to perfect? The answer lies in the mechanics of the filing system. If the rule were first to perfect, there would be no way for a secured lender to be assured of its priority. No matter how early on it filed, its priority would not be established until it made the loan and its security interest attached. Given that there will always be some time lag between searching for prior liens and actually making the loan, there would always be the risk that another creditor could sneak in and perfect during that interval. Under the first-to-file-or-perfect rule, filing preserves a creditor's place in line (sort of like having a friend save you a seat at the movie theater or a place in the supermarket checkout line). A lender may file when the debtor first inquires about a loan, leisurely conduct a search of the filing office to ensure its filing is first in time, and then, whenever it later chooses, make the loan and acquire its security interest.

Because the first-to-file-or-perfect rule sets the priority for security interests that attach after the financing statement is filed, it implicitly also sets the priority for security interests in after-acquired property. Consider the following example.

In late May, Manufacturer approaches Bank for a loan to modernize its main manufacturing facility. On June 1, Bank files a sufficient financing statement against Manufacturer in the correct location, listing equipment as the collateral, which Manufacturer has authorized Bank to do in a signed record (perhaps in the loan application). On June 7, Bank conducts its search of the UCC records. That search reveals Bank's own filing and no others against Manufacturer. On June 9, Bank approves the loan and so notifies

Manufacturer. On June 11, Manufacturer signs a security agreement granting Bank a security interest in all of Manufacturer's existing and after-acquired equipment in return for a $1 million loan, which Bank advances that day. On August 1, Manufacturer acquires some new equipment.

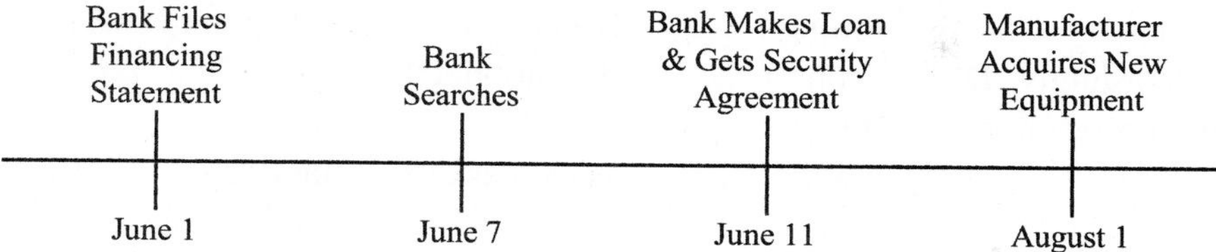

Bank's priority in the equipment Manufacturer acquired before Bank made the loan and Bank's priority in the equipment Manufacturer acquired on August 1 is the same. For all of the equipment, Bank's priority dates from when it first filed its sufficient financing statement: June 1. This is so even though Bank's security interest in the equipment Manufacturer acquired on August 1 did not attach (and was not perfected) until August 1.

Indeed, even if the original security agreement did not have an after-acquired property clause, a filed financing statement can still set the secured party's priority with respect to property the debtor later acquires. As long as the security interest attaches to that new property, either because the parties amend the original security agreement or because they enter into a new one, the original financing statement will fix the priority of the secured party's interest in that new property. *See* § 9-322 cmt. 5.

Of course, an implicit assumption of the first-to-file-or-perfect rule is that the filed financing statement is an effective perfection step for the type of collateral concerned. Also implicit in this rule is that the financing statement is properly filled out and filed in the appropriate place to perfect a security interest. If there was an error that renders the financing statement insufficient to perfect, the financing statement is not a "filing" for purposes of the first-to-file-or-perfect rule. Accordingly, whether a financing statement was completed properly and filed in the appropriate office will often be the key questions in applying the first-to-file-or-perfect priority rule. That is one reason we explored the requirements for financing statements in such depth in Chapter Four.

Problem 5-11

Digital Equipment, Inc. is a Nebraska corporation engaged in manufacturing computer chips. On April 1, as it entered its new fiscal year, it became apparent to Digital's corporate officers that it needed additional financing to make it through what was likely to be a slow summer season. Accordingly, Digital approached both National Bank and State Bank to inquire about possible loans.

On May 1, National Bank filed in the Nebraska Secretary of State's office a financing statement listing "Digital Equipment, Inc." as the debtor, National Bank as the secured party and the collateral as "all assets." Digital's president signed an authorization for the filing.

On May 5, State Bank filed a financing statement in the Nebraska Secretary of State's office naming "Digital Equipment, Inc." as the debtor, the collateral as "inventory and equipment" and State Bank as the secured party. That same day, Digital's president signed a document in which Digital granted State Bank a security interest in "inventory and equipment then owned or thereafter acquired to secure any and all obligations now owed or hereafter owed" to State Bank. On May 6, State Bank disbursed $50,000 to Digital.

On June 1, Digital's president signed a document in which Digital granted National Bank a security interest in "all of debtor's inventory and equipment now owned or hereafter acquired to secure all obligations that the debtor now owes or hereafter owes to National Bank." On June 3, National Bank disbursed $100,000 to Digital.

A. What is the priority of National Bank's and State Bank's security interests in Digital's inventory?
B. In July, Digital manufactured additional computer chips and purchased materials for making more chips from Silicon Supply Co. What is the priority of National Bank's and State Bank's security interests in those new goods?
C. How, if at all, would the analysis change if Digital's president had not signed an authorization for National Bank to file its financing statement? *See* §§ 9-322 cmt. 4, 9-509 cmt. 3.
D. How, if at all, would the analysis change if National Bank's financing statement had been filed in Iowa?
E. How, if at all, would the analysis change if State Bank's financing statement had been filed in Nebraska on April 30?

While the first-to-file-or-perfect rule is designed to make the filing system work and is applied most commonly to security interests perfected by filing, the rule also applies to security interests perfected in a manner other than by filing. For example, if SP-1's security interest were perfected by possession and SP-2's security interest were automatically perfected, § 9-322(a)(1) still applies and their priority will depend upon whose perfection occurred first. Alternatively, if SP-1's security interest were perfected by filing and SP-2's security interest were perfected by possession, the priority between the two security interests would be determined by comparing the time SP-1 first filed or perfected to the time SP-2 perfected by possession.

Problem 5-12

Same facts as in Problem 5-11 but on May 30, Finance Company loaned Digital $20,000 and, pursuant to Digital's oral agreement, took possession of a piece of equipment to secure the loan. Among Finance Company, National Bank, and State Bank, what are the relative priorities of their interests in the piece of equipment?

e-Exercise 5-C
First to File or Perfect

A secured party's priority date for the first-to-file-or-perfect rule is the date when it first either files a financing statement with respect to the relevant collateral or perfects, provided there is no period thereafter when it lacks both perfection and an effective filing against the relevant collateral. If a secured party's perfection lapses at a time when it has no effective filing, then its original priority date will no longer apply and a new date will be created if and when it refiles or re-perfects. Consider the following example:

> Lender A perfects a security interest in Debtor's equipment by filing a financing statement on June 1, 2015 Lender B perfects a security interest in the same equipment by filing a financing statement on July 1, 2016. Lender A files a new financing statement on August 1, 2020. Lender B files a continuation statement on May 1, 2021.

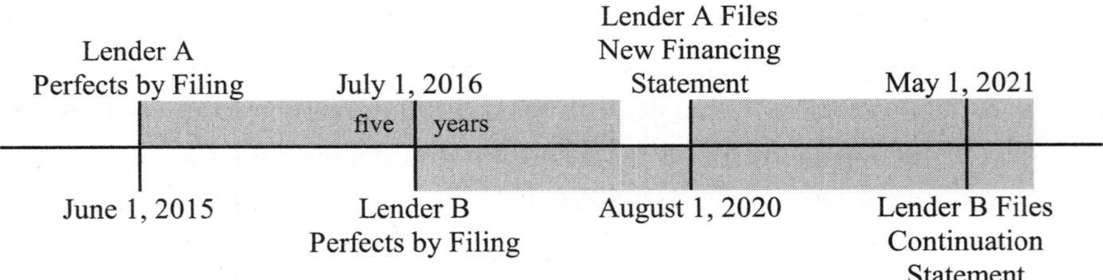

Lender B has maintained perfection continuously because its continuation statement was filed in a timely manner. *See* § 9-515(c), (d). In contrast, Lender A's security interest became unperfected on June 1, 2020, five years after its initial filing, and was re-perfected on August 1, 2020. Because of that gap in perfection, Lender A's priority dates from 2020, not 2015. As a result, Lender B, whose security interest was initially subordinate to Lender A's, now has priority.

Of course, as we saw in Chapter Four, a security interest can be continuously perfected by tacking together two or more contiguous perfection periods arising from different perfection methods. *See* § 9-308(c). Such continuous perfection is critical to the way the first-to-file-or-perfect rule works. Now try your hand at the next two problems, which require that you consider possible lapses in perfection.

Problem 5-13

On May 1, 2021, Dolly borrowed $100,000 from First Bank. To secure the debt, Dolly signed a document in which she granted First Bank a security interest in some expensive jewelry and in a promissory note issued to Dolly by a former business partner. First Bank took possession of the jewelry and the promissory note at the time it made the loan. In 2022, Dolly borrowed $50,000 from Second Bank, and signed a document in which she granted a security interest in all of her existing instruments and jewelry. Second Bank filed an effective financing statement at that time to perfect its security interest.

On June 1, 2023, First Bank returned the promissory note to Dolly so that she could have it copied and the copy attached to a complaint she was filing against the former business partner in connection with an action to collect on the note. On that date, First Bank also let her have the jewelry to wear to a charitable gala. Dolly returned both the promissory note and the jewelry to First Bank three days later.

A. What is the priority of the banks' security interests in the promissory note and the jewelry?
B. How, if at all, would the analysis of Part A change if First Bank had filed a proper financing statement indicating the collateral on May 31, 2023?
C. How, if at all, would the analysis of Part A change if Dolly's security agreement with First Bank was an oral agreement that was not signed?

Problem 5-14

Dan owns and operates a fleet of commercial shrimping boats in Louisiana. In 2021, Dan obtained a $200,000 loan from First Bank and signed a document in which he granted First Bank a security interest in all of his existing and after-acquired inventory and equipment to secure the debt. First Bank perfected its security interest by filing in the appropriate Louisiana office a financing statement that properly described Dan and indicated the collateral as "inventory and equipment" (assume no certificate of title statute applies).

In 2022, Dan decided to borrow more money to finance further expansions. First Bank was willing to lend the funds Dan wanted, but only at an interest rate that Dan thought was unfairly high. So, Dan approached Second Bank, which agreed to make the loan. Second Bank then filed its own authorized financing statement that properly described Dan and indicated the collateral as "all assets." Two days later, Second Bank loaned Dan $300,000 and Dan signed a document in which he granted Second Bank a security interest in all of Dan's existing and after-acquired inventory and equipment to secure the loan.

On February 1, 2023, Dan moved to Florida. Pursuant to a requirement in both security agreements Dan notified both banks in advance of the planned move. Second Bank filed a new and effective financing statement identifying the collateral as "all assets" against Dan in the appropriate office in Florida on March 15 (assume no certificate of title statute applies in Florida either).

A. As of July 30, 2023, what are the relative rights of the banks in the inventory and equipment if First Bank filed a new financing statement listing "inventory and equipment" against Dan in the appropriate office in Florida on July 15, 2020?
B. As of July 30, 2023, what are the relative rights of the banks in the inventory and equipment collateral if First Bank filed a new financing

statement listing "inventory and equipment" against Dan in the appropriate office in Florida on April 15, 2023?

Now try this next problem, which might be more difficult than it first appears.

Problem 5-15

Same facts as in Problem 5-11, but on May 30, Employee, who had successfully sued Digital for wrongful termination, caused the sheriff to levy on some of Digital's manufacturing equipment pursuant to a writ of execution. Among National Bank, State Bank, and Employee, what are the relative priorities of their interests in that equipment? How likely is this scenario? Put another way, what could each of the three creditors have done to have fared better? *See* §§ 9-317(a)(2), 9-322(a)(1).

Lawyers and lenders who use the filing system need to understand how it works in order to fully appreciate what risks to priority exist in a particular transaction. Consider the following problem.

Problem 5-16

On June 1, Deceptive applied to Bank for a $50,000 loan to be secured by certain equipment that Deceptive owns. The application form, which Deceptive signed, authorized Bank to file a financing statement against Deceptive. On June 2, Bank electronically filed a financing statement against Deceptive in the appropriate office. That filing was made by typing the data into fields on the filing office's web site (*i.e.*, not by submitting an electronic copy of a printed filing form). Also on June 2, Bank received an electronic confirmation from the filing office of its filing against Deceptive. On June 3, Bank decided to loan Deceptive the requested $50,000 and submitted a request for an official search of the filing office's records against Deceptive. On June 5, Bank received from the filing office a report that showed only one financing statement filed against Deceptive: the Bank's. Read § 9-523(c). What in the filing office's search report should alert Bank that it might lose priority under the first-to-file-or-perfect rule? What other rules in Article 9 might operate to give effect to filings or perfection methods that are not disclosed in the report?

Problem 5-17

Bank has tentatively agreed to loan $15,000 to Desperate. The loan is to be secured by some of Desperate's equipment. Given the priority rules in § 9-317(a) and § 9-322(a), in what order should Bank do the following four things to best ensure that it will have priority in the equipment?

- File a financing statement;
- Have Desperate sign a security agreement;
- Make the loan; and
- Look for other perfected security interests or liens (by searching for filed financing statements and examining the equipment to see who has possession of it).

Subordination because of problems in the perfection process. Chapter Four discussed § 9-516(b), which authorizes a filing office to reject a financing statement that omits specified information, information in addition to that required by § 9-502. Well, what if a financing statement, instead of omitting that information, contains an error in that information? Assume a financing statement is effective to perfect because it was filed in the right place, §§ 9-501, 9-301, meets the requirements of § 9-502, and was authorized by the debtor, § 9-509. However, it contains an incorrect mailing address for the debtor. The debtor's mailing address is not required for the financing statement to be effective to perfect but is one of the required pieces of information specified in § 9-516(b)(5). The effect of this error is that the security interest to which that filing relates is subordinated to a conflicting perfected security interest if the holder of that conflicting security interest gave value in reasonable reliance on the incorrect information in the filed financing statement. This might occur if the debtor is an individual with a common name and the incorrect address led the second secured party reasonably to conclude that the filing relates to someone else with the same name.[18] Read § 9-338(1). This rule is an exception to the general priority rules in § 9-322(a). *See* § 9-322(f)(1).[19]

---

[18] Review Problem 4-5.

[19] Note, if the financing statement had completely omitted the debtor's mailing address, the filing office should have rejected the financing statement. § 9-520(a). A financing statement that the filing office properly rejects is completely ineffective. § 9-516(b). If, however, the filing office accepted a financing statement that omitted the debtor's address, the financing statement would be sufficient to perfect, *see* § 9-520(c), assuming of course that the filing complied with § 9-502, that it was filed in the right place, and that the filing of the financing

Subordination due to problems in the issuance of a certificate of title. So far we have talked about the filing of a financing statement. If the security interest is perfected through a certificate of title system, compliance with that certificate of title system is the equivalent of the filing of the financing statement. § 9-311. Thus, for the purpose of the first-to-file-or-perfect rule of § 9-322(a), compliance with the applicable certificate of title law is equivalent to the filing of a financing statement.

Read § 9-337(2). Assume a secured party has properly perfected a security interest in titled goods by obtaining notation of the lien on the certificate of title. § 9-311. Subsequently, a new certificate of title for the goods is issued in a second state but the second certificate of title neglects to contain a notation of the already existing security interest. The secured party's security interest remains perfected for up to four months. § 9-316(d), (e). However, § 9-337(2) subordinates the unnoted security interest to a conflicting security interest that is noted on the second certificate as long as the second secured party acquired and perfected its security interest without knowledge of the unnoted security interest.

These two subordination rules protect reliance creditors: those who were misled by the errors in the state of the record.

Problem 5-18

Same facts as in Problem 5-11 but on June 5, National Bank applied to the Minnesota Department of Motor Vehicles to have its lien noted on the Minnesota certificate of title on a delivery van owned by Digital Equipment. On June 30, the Minnesota certificate of title was issued listing National Bank as the first lienholder. On July 15, Digital Equipment applied to the Iowa Department of Motor Vehicles for a new certificate of title on the delivery van by surrendering the Minnesota certificate of title to the Iowa Department of Motor Vehicles. Due to a clerical error at the Iowa Department of Motor Vehicles, the Iowa certificate of title was issued on August 1, without the notation of National Bank as the first lienholder. On September 1, State Bank applied to the Iowa Department of Motor Vehicles to have its security interest noted on the Iowa certificate of title. The Iowa

---

statement is a permissible perfection step for the type of collateral involved. Moreover, such a financing statement would not be subject to the rule of § 9-338. In short, the omission of debtor's mailing address does not affect perfection or priority if the filing office accepts the filing. Financing statements with erroneous information are treated differently from financing statement with missing information because of the different effect they have on the search process. Review Problem 4-5.

certificate of title was reissued on September 15 with State Bank listed as the first lienholder.

A. On August 2, was National Bank's security interest in the delivery van perfected? §§ 9-303(b), 9-316(d).
B. On September 15, which bank's security interest in the delivery van has priority? *See* § 9-337.

Problem 5-19

Six months ago, Deceitful purchased a Porsche on credit from Luxury Cars, LLC, which retained a security interest in the Porsche to secure payment of the purchase price. Luxury Cars promptly perfected its security interest by having the interest noted on the Illinois certificate of title for the car. Two months ago, Deceitful submitted a lien release letter to the Illinois Department of Motor Vehicles. Luxury Cars did not sign or authorize the letter. The Department issued a new certificate of title for the Porsche that showed no liens on the car. Last month, using the new certificate of title, Deceitful borrowed $30,000 from Credit Union, which promptly complied with the Illinois certificate of title statute to perfect its security interest in the Porsche. Which security interest has priority? *See* §§ 9-322(a), 9-337.

Proceeds. We are now ready for our first foray into how Article 9 addresses the priority of a security interest in the proceeds of collateral. As you no doubt remember, a security interest automatically attaches to proceeds. *See* §§ 9-203(f), 9-315(a)(2). Perfection in proceeds is a bit more complicated. Review § 9-315(c), (d) and the material in Chapter Four on perfection in proceeds.

The basic priority rule for proceeds of collateral subject to a security interest is the same as it is for the original collateral: the first to file or perfect wins. For this purpose, the time of filing or perfection in the proceeds relates back to the time of filing or perfection in the original collateral, assuming there was no intermediate period when the security interest was unperfected. *See* § 9-322(b)(1). This rule can be illustrated with the following simple example.

> Bank One perfects a security interest in goods by filing an effective financing statement against the debtor covering the goods. Some time later, Bank Two acquires and perfects a security interest in the same goods by filing an effective financing statement against the debtor covering the goods. While both security interests are perfected, Debtor sells the goods for money:

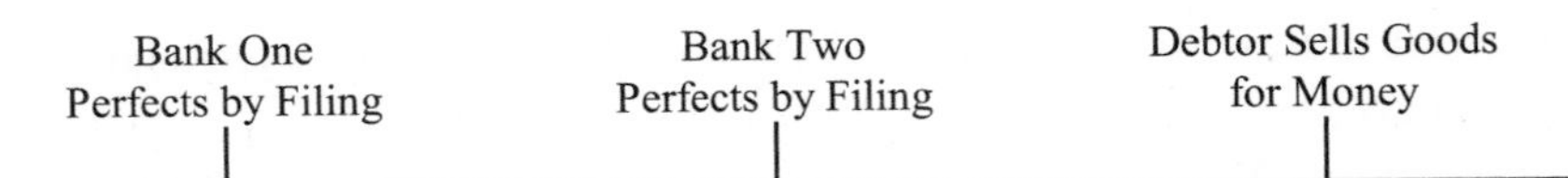

Debtor has possession of the money. Each bank's security interest attaches to the money as identifiable proceeds of the original collateral, goods. § 9-315(a)(2). Each bank's security interest in the money is perfected under § 9-315(c) and (d)(2). Although the banks' security interests in the money attached simultaneously (when Debtor acquired the money), Bank One's security interest in the money has priority over Bank Two's security interest in the money because each bank's priority date for the purposes of the first-to-file-or-perfect rule is the date it perfected its security interest in the goods, § 9-322(b)(1), and there has been no period since then when either bank's perfection lapsed.

Notice the methodology just used – and which you need to follow – to determine the priority of competing security interests. First analyze the perfection and priority of the security interests in the original collateral. Then, for each security interest, determine whether it attached to and is perfected in the proceeds. The answer to this might differ for the various secured creditors. Finally, determine the relative priorities in the proceeds.

Problem 5-20

Defensive Systems, Inc. manufactures and sells bullet-proof vests to police and business executives. On January 1, Defensive Systems signed a document in which it granted First Bank a security interest in all of Defensive Systems' existing and after-acquired inventory to secure a $50,000 loan. On January 5, First Bank filed an effective financing statement against Defensive Systems in the appropriate place indicating the collateral as "inventory." On March 1, Defensive Systems granted a security interest in all its existing and after-acquired inventory and equipment to Second Bank to secure a $75,000 loan. That same day, Second Bank filed an authorized and effective financing statement against Defensive Systems in the proper place indicating the collateral as "all assets."

On June 1, Defensive Systems sold a number of vests to each of four different purchasers. Purchaser 1 signed a document in which it promised to pay Defensive Systems for the vests in full in 30 days. Purchaser 2 signed a promissory note payable to Defensive Systems for the purchase price. Purchaser 3 signed a document in which it promised to pay the purchase price to Defensive Systems and granted Defensive Systems a security interest in the vests sold to secure the payment. Purchaser 4 paid for the vests with a check, which Defensive Systems endorsed over to Computer Company in payment for a new computer which Defensive Systems uses to manage its operations. Defensive Systems still has possession of the note signed by Purchaser 2 and the documents signed by Purchasers 1 and 3.

A. Does First Bank or Second Bank have a security interest in the document signed by Purchaser 1, the note signed by Purchaser 2, the document signed by Purchaser 3, or the computer acquired with the check from Purchaser 4? *See* §§ 9-102(a)(12), (64); 9-315(a)(2).

B. If so, in which property, if any, does each bank have a perfected security interest? *See* § 9-315(c), (d).

C. If so, what is the priority of each bank's security interests in those items? *See* § 9-322(a), (b).

B. Priority of Purchase-money Security Interests

The first-to-file-or-perfect rule presents a considerable obstacle to creditors that want to make loans or credit available to a debtor to acquire additional property. For example, assume a secured party has properly filed an effective financing statement against the debtor covering "equipment." The security agreement provides for a security interest in all equipment then owned or thereafter acquired to secure all the obligations the debtor then owes or thereafter owes to the secured party. The debtor wants to acquire new equipment but lacks the funds to pay up front. The debtor could, for this purpose, borrow more from the secured party, but the seller is willing to offer better financing terms. The seller is willing to sell on credit but only if it retains a security interest in the equipment sold and only if its security interest will be first in priority. Based upon the first-to-file-or-perfect rule however, the secured party's first-filed financing statement will be sufficient to set the priority position of the secured party's security interest in the new equipment even though the secured party's security interest will not attach to the new equipment until the debtor acquires rights in the equipment when it purchases it from the seller.

Section 9-324 addresses this basic problem by creating an exception to the first-to-file-or-perfect priority rule in favor of purchase-money security interests ("PMSIs"). *See* § 9-322(f)(1). A quick review of § 9-324 reveals that there are four main categories of collateral subject to PMSIs that can have priority over a conflicting perfected security interest: inventory, livestock, software, and other goods. The first step in the analysis for dealing with PMSI priority is thus to determine the collateral type. We explored that process in Chapter Two. The second step in the analysis is to determine whether one or more of the secured parties with a security interest in the collateral has a PMSI. *See* § 9-103. We explored what it takes to have PMSI status in Chapter Four.[20] The third step in the analysis is to then determine whether the secured party with the PMSI has done what is required under the applicable rule in § 9-324 to take priority over another security interest in the collateral that would otherwise have priority under the first-to-file-or-perfect rule of § 9-322(a).

Read § 9-324. Note that subsection (a) deals with PMSIs in goods other than inventory or livestock. Subsections (b) and (c) deal with PMSIs in inventory. Subsections (d) and (e) deal with PMSIs in livestock that are farm products. Subsection (f) deals with PMSIs in software. Subsection (g) deals with what happens when there is more than one PMSI in the same item of collateral.

To obtain PMSI priority in goods other than inventory or livestock, subsection (a) requires merely that a secured party perfect its interest either before the debtor receives possession of the collateral or within 20 days thereafter. To obtain PMSI priority in inventory, a secured party must do much more. *See* § 9-324(b). It must perfect by the time the debtor receives possession of the goods and notify specified holders of conflicting security interests[21] that it intends to acquire a PMSI in described inventory of the debtor. The holders of the conflicting security interests must receive that notification before the debtor receives the inventory but not more than five years before.

The reason for these additional requirements for PMSI priority in inventory relates to the way inventory financing actually works. Whereas equipment lenders

---

[20] Two situations not discussed in Chapter Four are as follows. First, a consignor of goods in an Article 9 consignment, § 9-102(a)(20), with a security interest in the consigned goods is deemed to have a purchase-money security interest in inventory. § 9-103(d). Second, under § 9-103(c) a secured party can obtain a purchase-money security interest in software if the software is acquired in the same transaction in which the goods are acquired, the software is for use in those goods, and the secured party has a purchase-money security interest in those goods. In that situation, the security interest in the software is a purchase-money security interest for both the value given to acquire the software and the goods. The security interest in the goods is a purchase-money security interest for both the value given to acquire the software and the goods. § 9-103(b)(3).

[21] Section 9-324(c) sets forth which secured parties must be sent and receive the notification described in subsection (b).

and capital financiers tend to lend on a sporadic basis, inventory financing typically involves frequent transactions between the creditor and debtor. Every time the debtor orders new inventory from its suppliers – something that might occur weekly or even daily – the debtor shows the purchase orders or invoices to the lender, who advances additional funds to cover all or part of the purchase price. The lender does not mind searching for filings against the debtor at the inception of the relationship, but does not wish to have to search before making each advance. That would be very cumbersome. So, if a supplier or other inventory lender wants to gain PMSI priority, it must send the existing inventory lender notification of its plans to do so. The theory is that the existing lender, in receipt of such notification, will then know that it should not expect to have priority in the PMSI inventory and therefore will not advance funds on the strength of that new collateral. This effectively prevents the debtor from being able to use the same inventory as collateral for two new loans.

This explanation might well be true, but does it really explain why lenders with a PMSI in goods other than inventory and livestock are not required to give notice to a previously perfected secured party? After all, the previously perfected secured party is likely to have its security interest in those goods primed by the interest of the PMSI lender under § 9-324(a). Moreover, some equipment lenders and farm products lenders do provide credit on a recurring or rotating basis.

Moreover, most inventory lenders contractually prohibit their debtors from giving a PMSI to any other secured party, and thus receipt of a § 9-324(b) notification functions as evidence that the debtor is in default or is about to default under the security agreement with the original inventory lender. So, while the PMSI priority rules are designed to facilitate PMSI lending against inventory, the reality is that they might not be very effective in that regard.

Problem 5-21

On May 1, National Bank filed in Nebraska an "all assets" financing statement against Dredger Corp., a corporation organized under the laws of Nebraska, sufficiently naming the debtor and the secured party. Dredger's president signed an authorization for the filing. On June 1, Dredger signed a document in which Dredger granted National Bank a security interest in all its "inventory and equipment now owned or hereafter acquired to secure all obligations that Dredger now owes or hereafter owes to National Bank." On June 3, National Bank disbursed $100,000 to Dredger.

A. On May 9, Dredger purchased on credit from Shell Co. a new forklift for use in Dredger's manufacturing plant. The manufacturing plant is located in Iowa. In the purchase agreement between Dredger and Shell, Shell retained title to the forklift until the purchase price was paid in full. Shell delivered the new forklift on May 10 to Dredger's plant in Iowa.

1. Does Shell have a purchase-money security interest in the forklift? *See* § 9-103.
2. Does National Bank have a security interest in the forklift?
3. On June 4, between Shell and National Bank, who has priority in that forklift? *See* § 9-324(a).
4. How, if at all, does the analysis change if Shell filed a properly completed financing statement against Dredger on May 15 in the Iowa Secretary of State's office listing "forklift" as the collateral and itself as the secured party? *See* §§ 9-301(1), 9-307(b).
5. How, if at all, does the analysis change if Shell filed a properly completed financing statement against Dredger on May 15 in the Nebraska Secretary of State's office listing "forklift" as the collateral and itself as the secured party?
6. How, if at all, does the analysis change if Shell filed a properly completed financing statement against Dredger on June 5 in the Nebraska Secretary of State's office listing "forklift" as the collateral and itself as the secured party?

B. On May 9, Dredger purchased on credit from Shell Co. a new forklift for use in Dredger's manufacturing plant. The manufacturing plant is located in Iowa. In the purchase agreement between Dredger and Shell, Shell retained title to the forklift until the purchase price was paid in full. Shell delivered the new forklift on May 10 to Dredger's plant in Iowa. Shell filed a proper financing statement against Dredger on May 15 in the Nebraska Secretary of State's office. The day before, Ben Stone had the sheriff levy on the forklift in execution of a judgment obtained against Dredger in January.

1. What are the relative priorities of the security interests of National Bank, Ben Stone, and Shell in the forklift? *See* §§ 9-317(e), 9-324(a).
2. How, if at all, would the analysis change if the levy had occurred on June 2?

C. On June 2, Dredger contracted to purchase on credit from Shell Co. a new forklift for use in Dredger's manufacturing plant. In the purchase agreement between Dredger and Shell, Shell retained title to the forklift until the purchase price was paid in full. On June 3, when National Bank made its loan to Dredger, it disbursed the funds partly to Dredger directly and partly, at Dredger's request, to Shell as Dredger's down payment on the forklift. Shell delivered the new forklift 4 to Dredger's plant in Iowa. on June 4. Shell then filed a proper financing statement against Dredger on June 15 in the Nebraska Secretary of State's office. What is the relative priority of the security interests of National Bank and Shell in the forklift? *See* § 9-324(g).

Problem 5-22

Consider your answer to Problem 5-21(C). What should the entity that lost priority under § 9-324(g) do to guard against that result?

Problem 5-23

Technically, § 9-324(a) applies to a PMSI in consumer goods and gives it priority over a conflicting security interest in the same goods. However, it is rarely needed in that context. Why is that? *See* §§ 9-204(b), 9-309(1).

Problem 5-24

For the last eight years, State Bank has provided capital and inventory financing to Diversions, Inc., a retailer of toys and games. Throughout this period, State Bank has held a security interest in all of Diversions' existing and after-acquired inventory, equipment, and accounts to secure all existing and future obligations owed to State Bank, and that security interest is perfected by a proper financing statement on file in the appropriate office.

Shortly before the start of the holiday season, Wonder Wizards came out with a new game that quickly became all the rage. Diversions ordered three shipments of the game:

Date Received	Price
October 5	$20,000
October 15	$15,000
November 1	$10,000

As is customary in the toy industry, Diversion did not pay in advance or on delivery. Instead, it promised to pay for each shipment within 45 days after delivery. As part of the sale, Wonder Wizards obtained a security interest in all of Diversions' inventory to secure payment of the purchase price. On

October 10, Wonder Wizards filed a proper financing statement against Diversions in the appropriate office listing the collateral as "inventory." On the same date, Wonder Wizards sent State Bank a letter stating that it was selling games on credit to Diversions and taking a security interest in Diversions' inventory. State Bank received the letter on October 16.

A. To what extent, if any, does Wonder Wizards have a purchase-money security interest in the inventory of Diversions? *See* § 9-103(b).

B. Between Wonder Wizards and State Bank, who has priority in the inventory of Diversions, and to what extent? What should the subordinate party have done differently to assure itself of priority? *See* § 9-324(b).

Proceeds of PMSIs. The special priority rules for PMSIs also extend to proceeds of the goods. In fact, they are one of several exceptions to application of the first-to-file-or-perfect rule to proceeds. *See* § 9-322(f)(1). Notice, though, that PMSI priority in proceeds of inventory is much more limited than PMSI priority in proceeds of other goods. PMSI priority in non-inventory goods, livestock, and software extends to all proceeds of the original collateral. § 9-324(a), (d), (f). PMSI priority in inventory extends only to cash proceeds, and only if such proceeds are received by the debtor prior to delivery of the inventory to the buyer. § 9-324(b).[22]

Problem 5-25

Dynamo is a manufacturer. On January 1, Dynamo signed a document in which it granted State Bank a security interest in all of Dynamo's existing and after-acquired equipment and inventory to secure a $500,000 loan. On January 5, State Bank filed an effective financing statement against Dynamo in the appropriate office indicating the collateral as "equipment and inventory." In early spring, Dynamo decided to modernize its manufacturing plant and, as part of that effort, purchased four solar power generators on

---

22 Section 9-324(b) also purports to give priority to proceeds of inventory in the form of chattel paper and instruments, but it does so only when another provision, § 9-330, grants such priority to the PMSI lender. Such priority, when available, is largely independent of the purchase-money status of the original security interest, *see* § 9-330(a), (b); *but cf.* § 9-330(e), and thus inclusion of this language in § 9-324 should be viewed as little more than a cross-reference. The rules of § 9-330 are covered in this Chapter, Section 6.C and D.

credit from Seller. Dynamo signed a document in which it granted Seller a security interest in the generators to secure payment of the purchase price. Prior to delivery of the generators to Dynamo, Seller filed an effective financing statement against Dynamo in the correct office listing the collateral as "generators."

After using the generators for six months, Dynamo concluded that they were not needed. Dynamo sold one generator to each of four different purchasers. Purchaser 1 signed a sales agreement in which it promised to pay Dynamo for the generator in full in 30 days. Purchaser 2 signed a promissory note payable to Dynamo for the purchase price of the generator. Purchaser 3 signed a sales agreement in which it promised to pay the purchase price to Dynamo and granted Dynamo a security interest in the generator sold to secure the payment. Purchaser 4 paid for the generator with a check. Dynamo still has possession of the note signed by Purchaser 2, the sales agreements signed by Purchasers 1 and 3, and the check issued by Purchaser 4.

A. Do State Bank and Seller have security interests in the amounts due from Purchasers 1 and 3, the note provided by Purchaser 2, and the check from Purchaser 4? *See* §§ 9-102(a)(12), (64); 9-315(a)(2).
B. If so, in which of these items, if any, does each party have a perfected security interest? *See* § 9-315(c), (d).
C. What is the relative priority of any competing security interests of State Bank and Seller in these items? *See* §§ 9-322(b), 9-324(a).
D. Dynamo deposited the check received from Purchaser 4 into a checking account at Local Bank. Assuming that the security interests of both State Bank and Seller attach to the checking account as identifiable proceeds (up to the amount of the check), which security interest has priority? *See* §§ 9-315(c), (d), 9-324(a). *See also* § 9-102 cmt. 13c.

Problem 5-26

Same facts as in Problem 5-25 but Dynamo is a manufacturer of generators. Dynamo purchased the solar power generators from Seller to satisfy obligations to Dynamo's own customers when Dynamo's manufacturing plant was unable to produce goods fast enough to meet demand. In addition, one week prior to delivery of the generators to Dynamo, State Bank received from Seller a letter indicating that Seller was selling generators on credit to Dynamo and retaining a security interest in the generators sold to secure payment of the purchase price.

A. Which secured party had priority in the generators after Dynamo acquired them but before Dynamo sold them to the purchasers? *See* § 9-324(b).
B. Do State Bank and Seller have security interests in the amounts due from Purchasers 1 and 3, the note provided by Purchaser 2, and the check from Purchaser 4? *See* §§ 9-102(a)(12), (64); 9-315(a)(2).
C. If so, in which of these items, if any, does each party have a perfected security interest? *See* § 9-315(c), (d).
D. What is the relative priority of any competing security interests of State Bank and Seller in these items? *See* §§ 9-322(b), 9-324(b).
E. How, if at all, would the analysis of Part D change if Purchaser 4 had paid by debit or credit card, instead of by check?

Problem 5-27

Two years ago, Bank acquired a security interest in Driller's existing and after acquired equipment to secure a loan. Bank perfected the security interest by filing a financing statement in the appropriate office. Nine months ago, Supplier sold a large drill on credit to Driller, retaining a security interest in the drill to secure payment of the purchase price. Supplier perfected the security interest ten days after Supplier delivered the drill to Driller by filing an appropriate financing statement.

A. Three weeks ago, Driller traded the drill and a hydraulic compressor for a derrick. What is the relative priority of Bank's and Supplier's security interest in the derrick?
B. How, if at all, would the analysis of Part A change if, instead of trading the drill and compressor for a derrick, Driller sold them together for a single price of $200,000, which is due in 30 days?

e-Exercise 5-D
Priority on Proceeds

C. The Double-Debtor Problem

The first-to-file-or-perfect rule of § 9-322(a)(1) and the PMSI priority rules of § 9-324(a) and (b) work well when both secured parties claim a security interest from the same debtor (depicted graphically below on the left). However, they do not reach the appropriate result when the secured parties claim through different debtors (as they do in the right side of the graphic below).

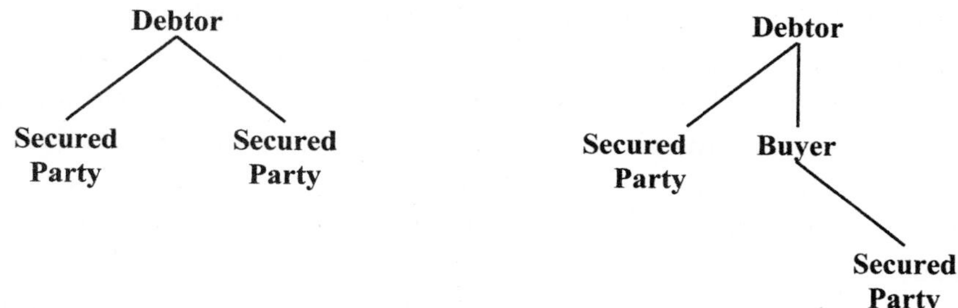

Consider the following scenario.

Bank One has a security interest in an item of equipment in Doctor's possession. Bank One perfected its interest by filing a sufficient financing statement against Doctor in the proper place on May 1. On August 1, Doctor sold that piece of equipment to Buyer, who is located in the same jurisdiction as Doctor. The piece of equipment is still subject to Bank One's properly perfected security interest. Review §§ 9-315(a)(1), 9-507(a). Prior to the sale, Buyer had granted Bank Two a security interest in all of Buyer's equipment then owned or thereafter acquired and Bank Two had filed a sufficient financing statement against Buyer in the proper place on April 1.

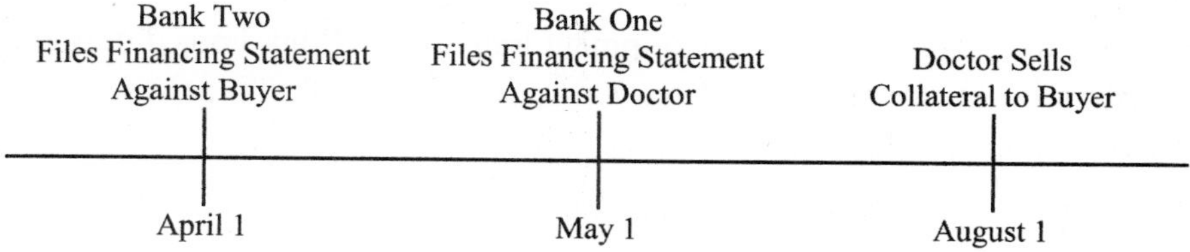

> When Buyer acquired the piece of equipment, Bank Two's security interest attached to it (pursuant to the after-acquired property clause in the security agreement) and was perfected by its financing statement already on file. Even though Bank One had a perfected interest in the item of equipment long before Bank Two did, under the first-to-file-or-perfect rule, Bank Two's security interest would have priority over Bank One's security interest as it was first filed before Bank One either filed or perfected.

Following the first-to-file-or-perfect rule here would violate one of the fundamental property principles discussed at the beginning of this Chapter: that a person may transfer only those rights in property that a person has. What is more, there would be nothing that Bank One – the first secured party to acquire an interest in the collateral – could do to protect itself from getting primed in this way. Even if it carefully searched for filings against Doctor, the original debtor, and conducted a physical inspection of the property to ensure no creditor was perfected first, it could not discover this problem in advance. After all, there is no way for Bank One to know in advance who the buyer will be. Put another way, the problem is not in establishing priority initially, the problem is that such priority, even if established, would be lost.

The same issue arises under the PMSI priority rules. Consider this additional scenario.

> Bank Three has a security interest in an item of equipment in Dentist's possession. Bank Three perfected its interest by filing a sufficient financing statement against Dentist in the proper place on May 1. Months later, Dentist sold that piece of equipment to Buyer, who is located in the same jurisdiction as Dentist. The piece of equipment is still subject to Bank Three's properly perfected security interest. To finance the purchase, Buyer borrowed all or part of the purchase price from Bank Four and granted a security interest in the item sold to secure that loan. Bank Four filed a proper financing statement against Buyer within 20 days of when Buyer received delivery of the equipment from Dentist. Even though Bank Three had a perfected security interest in the item of equipment long before Bank Four did, Bank Four's security interest would have priority over Bank Three's security interest under § 9-324(a).

Again, there is nothing the first secured party – Bank Three in this scenario – could do to protect itself from this. In contrast, Buyer and Bank Four have the ability to protect themselves. They know who their seller is and need merely to conduct a search – before buying the goods – to determine if any financing statements are filed against the seller.

Now read § 9-325. It changes the result in both of the scenarios described above. To see why, let us go through the language of the section, applying it to the facts of the first scenario above, with the understanding that when the section refers to "a debtor," it is referring to the second debtor (*i.e.*, to Buyer).

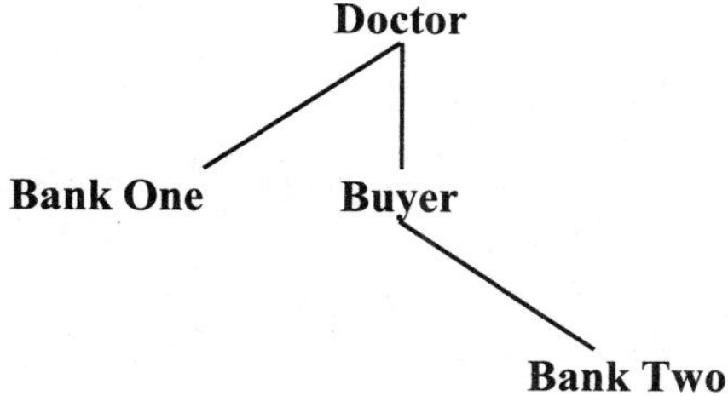

1. Did the debtor (Buyer) acquire the collateral subject to a security interest created by another person? – Yes, the security interest granted to Bank One was created by another person (Doctor), and the debtor acquired the collateral subject to the security interest. *See* § 9-315(a)(1).[23]
2. Was the earlier security interest perfected when Buyer acquired the equipment? – Yes, the facts as presented indicated that Bank One had perfected its security interest by filing a sufficient financing statement against Doctor in the proper place before the sale to Buyer.
3. Did Bank One's security interest remain continuously perfected? – Yes, Bank One's financing statement remains effective with respect to the collateral transferred, as long as the new owner is located in the same state as the original debtor. *See* §§ 9-507(a), 9-316(a)(3).
4. Would Bank Two's security interest have priority under § 9-322(a) or § 9-324, or did it arise solely under § 2-711(3) or § 2A-508(5)? – Yes, Bank Two's security interest would have priority under § 9-322(a)(1) because Bank Two filed (April 1) before Bank Two filed or perfected (May 1).

---

[23] Later in this chapter we will encounter some rules that allow a buyer of collateral to take free of a security interest. For the purposes of this discussion, assume none of those rules applies.

Consequently, the security interest of Bank Two is subordinated to the security interest of Bank One.[24]

Double-debtor priority issues are not particularly difficult to resolve. The key to doing so is simply to identify when such an issue has arisen. The best way to do that is to diagram the facts, something recommended near the beginning of this Chapter, on page 356.

D. Future Advances

How does the first-to-file-or-perfect rule work when the secured party is making advances subsequent to the first advance? The general rule is that the security interest securing the subsequent advance has the same priority as the security interest securing the first advance. If you think about it, this makes perfect sense. After all, the time when an advance is made is not normally relevant to priority among competing secured parties. Recall that the first-to-file-or-perfect rule is designed to give efficacy to a financing statement filed prior to attachment, something expressly authorized by § 9-502(d). Given that the priority of a security interest securing an *initial loan* is determined by an earlier filed financing statement, there is no reason that the priority of a security interest securing *subsequent advances* should not similarly be based on that early filing. *See* § 9-323 cmt. 3.

There is a somewhat narrow exception to this general rule, however. Read § 9-323(a). It applies only when a security interest is automatically perfected under § 9-309 or § 9-312. In such a case, the perfection and priority of the security interest securing the future advance dates from the time the advance is made. Apply § 9-322(a) and § 9-323(a) to the following problem.

Problem 5-28

Dragon Games, Inc. is in the business of selling a variety of board games. Some of the inventory is stored in a warehouse run by Storage Monster. Storage Monster did not issue a warehouse receipt covering the goods. On April 5, Dragon obtained a loan of $10,000 from State Bank. Dragon signed a document in which it granted State Bank a security interest in all its

---

[24] The analysis would be the same under the second scenario, involving Dentist, except that the reason the answer to question 4 is "yes" would be that Bank Four would have priority under § 9-324(a) rather than under § 9-322(a)(1).

existing and after-acquired inventory to secure all obligations then owed or thereafter owed to State Bank. On April 15, State Bank notified Storage of State Bank's security interest and obtained Storage Monster's acknowledgment in a signed writing that Storage Monster was holding Dragon's goods in Storage Monster's possession for the benefit of State Bank.

On May 1, Dragon signed a document in which it granted National Bank a security interest in all its existing and after-acquired inventory to secure all obligations then owed or thereafter owed to National Bank. On May 2, National Bank filed a properly filled out financing statement in the appropriate office against Dragon listing the collateral as "inventory." On May 5, National Bank loaned $20,000 to Dragon.

A. 1. At this point, which bank has priority in the portion of Dragon's inventory stored with Storage Monster? Does it matter when the goods were placed in the warehouse? *See* §§ 9-313(c), 9-322(a).
   2. Which bank has priority in the inventory of Dragon not stored with Storage Monster?

B. On May 15, State Bank notified Storage Monster to let Dragon obtain possession of some of the goods from the warehouse in order for Dragon to sell the goods. Dragon picked up those goods the same day.
   1. On May 16, while Dragon still had possession of the goods released from the warehouse, which bank has priority in those goods? *See* §§ 9-312(f), 9-322(a).
   2. On June 16, which bank has priority in the goods released from Storage Monster's warehouse (assuming Dragon still owns them)?

C. On May 15, State Bank notified Storage Monster to let Dragon obtain possession of some of the goods from the warehouse in order for Dragon to sell the goods. Dragon picked up those goods the same day. Those goods are worth $38,000. On May 20, State Bank made another loan of $5,000 to Dragon. On May 25, National Bank made a loan of $7,000 to Dragon.
   1. On May 26, what are the priorities of the security interests in Dragon's inventory still in Storage Monster's warehouse?
   2. On May 26, what are the priorities of the security interests in the inventory released from Storage Monster's warehouse (assuming Dragon still owns them)?

E. Deposit Accounts

Deposit accounts as original collateral. From our study of perfection in Chapter Four, we know that the only way to perfect a security interest in a deposit account as original collateral[25] (as opposed to a deposit account as proceeds of other collateral) is for the secured party to obtain control of the deposit account. *See* § 9-312(b). It is possible for two or more secured parties to obtain control of a deposit account under the provisions on control in § 9-104.[26] When that occurs, the priority of those security interests is determined under § 9-327. That section contains yet another series of exceptions to the first-to-file-or-perfect priority rule for competing security interests. *See* § 9-322(f).

The rules of § 9-327 create a priority ladder based on the method of control used to perfect the security interest in the deposit account. Unfortunately, the rules are listed in ascending order, rather than descending order – that is, as you read the section from top to bottom, statute, priority goes up rather than down – which might be confusing for some. For that reason, here is a graphical depiction of the priority rules in § 9-327:

Control by becoming the depositary bank's customer
Control by depositary bank
Control via a control agreement
No control

[25] Recall that in a consumer transaction, and only in a consumer transaction, an assignment of rights in a deposit account as original collateral is excluded from the scope of Article 9. § 9-109(d)(13).

[26] Remember, the depositary bank need not enter into a control agreement with another secured party and, even if it does, the depositary bank is obligated to fulfill only those promises it makes in that control agreement. §§ 9-341, 9-342.

As you can see, control acquired by becoming the customer on the deposit account creates the highest priority. [27] Control by virtue of being the depositary bank comes next. Below that is control acquired through a control agreement with the debtor and the depositary bank. If two or more secured parties obtain control through a control agreement, the relative priority of their interests is determined by the time they obtained control. § 9-327(2). On the lowest rung is a security interest for which the secured party does not have control.[28]

Because so few secured parties acquire control by becoming the customer on the deposit account, this effectively means that a security interest held by the depositary bank will have priority over a security interest held by any other secured party.

A depositary bank's setoff and recoupment rights are treated similarly. The depositary bank's setoff and recoupment rights against the debtor have priority over a security interest unless the secured party has obtained control by becoming the customer with respect to the deposit account. *See* § 9-340(a), (c).

Problem 5-29

Docket Services, Inc. maintains a checking account at State Bank. Docket signed a document in which it granted a security interest to Finance Company in all "bank accounts" in which Docket has an interest. Finance Company, State Bank, and Docket all signed a document that provided that State Bank would follow Finance Company's instructions regarding the account without need for further approval from Docket. Docket failed to pay an unsecured debt that it owed State Bank and State Bank set off the amount of that debt from the balance in Docket's checking account. Does Finance Company have grounds for complaint against State Bank? Would it make any difference in your analysis if Docket had signed a document in which it granted a security interest to State Bank in all of Docket's bank accounts? If you conclude that State Bank has priority in the deposit account, what could Finance Company do to obtain priority?

---

[27] Technically, this provide priority only over a security interest of the depositary bank.

[28] If there are multiple security interests in a deposit account in the last rung – that is, for which the secured parties lack control – priority among those secured parties would be determined by some provision other than § 9-327, such as by § 9-322 or § 9-324.

Deposit accounts as proceeds of other collateral. Given that every form of control requires either being the depositary bank or having an agreement with the depositary bank, all parties with a security interest in a deposit account as original collateral are likely to be aware of one another and have a contract with one another. They could therefore readily agree to whatever priority they want. *See* § 9-339 (giving efficacy to subordination agreements). Because of that, the rules in § 9-327 do not matter much in that context. They are little more than default rules from which the parties are free to depart.

In another context, however, the rules of § 9-327 are extremely important: when the deposit account is proceeds of other collateral. In that situation, they apply to secured parties who probably have no relationship with each other and they trump the normal first-to-file-or-perfect rule of § 9-322(a), the PMSI priority rules of § 9-324, and even the double-debtor rules of § 9-325. § 9-327 cmt. 2. Consider the following problem.

Problem 5-30

Dynamo manufactures and sells electric generating equipment. On January 1, Dynamo signed a document in which it granted First Bank a security interest in all of Dynamo's existing and after-acquired inventory to secure a $500,000 loan. On January 5, First Bank filed an effective financing statement against Dynamo in the appropriate place indicating the collateral as "inventory." In early spring, Dynamo experienced some production problems and on March 15, in order to meet its contractual obligations to one of its regular customers, Dynamo purchased three generators with financing provided by Second Bank. Dynamo granted Second Bank a security interest in the generators to secure payment of the purchase price. Prior to delivery of the generators to Dynamo, Second Bank filed an effective financing statement against Dynamo in the correct office listing the collateral as "inventory" and First Bank received from Second Bank written notification of the planned transaction with Dynamo.

A. At this point which bank's security interest has priority in the generators?
B. Dynamo then sold the generators to Purchaser on open account. Which bank's security interest has priority in that account?
C. Thirty days after the sale in Part B, Dynamo received a check from Purchaser in payment of the purchase price. Which bank's security interest has priority in that check?

D. Shortly after receipt of the check in Part C, Dynamo deposited the check into its checking account at Second Bank and the check was not thereafter dishonored. Which bank's security interest has priority in the deposit account? *See* § 9-327(1).

Proceeds of a deposit account. The priority rules in § 9-327 are, because of subsection (3), euphemistically known as "the depositary bank always wins" rule. The depositary bank will always have priority in deposited funds unless it agrees otherwise. That rule is designed to allow depositary banks to rely on any deposits they maintain when deciding to extend credit, without searching for UCC filings. Because of that limited purpose, the priority rules in § 9-327 do not extend to most proceeds of a deposit account.

Now read § 9-322(c)–(e). These priority rules are yet more exceptions to the first-to-file-or-perfect rule, *see* § 9-322(a) ("except as otherwise provided in this section").

Section 9-322(c) applies to security interests in specified types of proceeds if a security interest in the original collateral qualified for priority under one of several specified exceptions to the first-to-file-or-perfect priority rule. To illustrate one situation to which the rule applies, consider the following example:

> SP-1 has a security interest in a deposit account and its security interest is perfected by control. SP-2 has a perfected security interest in the same deposit account as proceeds of other collateral in which it had a security interest perfected by a filed a financing statement. As a result, SP-2's security interest in the deposit account is also perfected. *See* § 9-315(d)(2). Pursuant to § 9-327, SP-1's security interest in the deposit account has priority over SP-2's security interest in the deposit account, regardless of the relative time of filing or perfection as to those interests. The debtor withdraws cash from deposit account and retains possession of that cash. Assume that both security interests attach to the cash as identifiable proceeds of the deposit account. Both security interests in the cash are perfected. *See* § 9-315(c), (d)(2). Under § 9-322(c)(2), SP-1's security interest in the cash has priority over SP-2's security interest in the cash. This is true regardless of the order in which the secured parties perfected their interest in the original collateral, regardless of the order in which they filed, and regardless of whether SP-1 ever filed. In short, § 9-322(c)(2) extends the priority accorded by § 9-327 to identifiable cash proceeds.

When § 9-322(c) does not apply, § 9-322(d) might.[29] It applies to some types of proceeds of collateral if the security interest in the original collateral was perfected other than by filing. To continue the above illustration:

> Assume that instead of withdrawing cash from the deposit account, the debtor wired funds from the deposit account to a seller to pay for a piece of equipment. The equipment is identifiable proceeds of the deposit account. Both SP-1 and SP-2 have attached security interests in the equipment, § 9-315(a)(2), and both security interests in the equipment are, at least temporarily, perfected. § 9-315(c). Section 9-322(d) provides that the priority of those security interests in the equipment is determined by whoever was first to file as to the equipment, which in this case was SP-2. This rule has its real bite if SP-1's perfection in the deposit account predates SP-2's filing. For example, assume SP-1's perfection by control in the original collateral (the deposit account) predates SP-2's filing as to its original collateral (the goods): 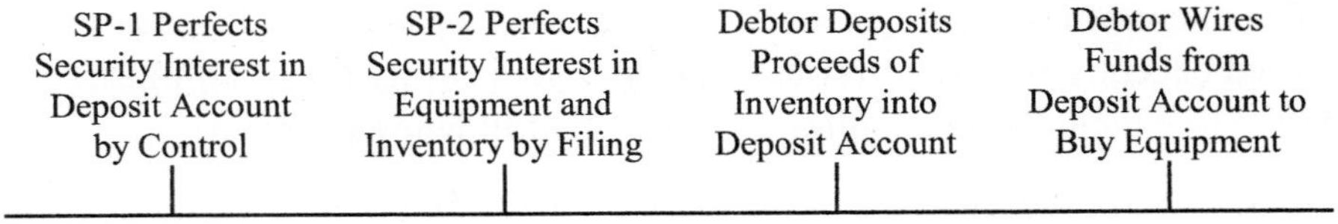
>
> | SP-1 Perfects Security Interest in Deposit Account by Control | SP-2 Perfects Security Interest in Equipment and Inventory by Filing | Debtor Deposits Proceeds of Inventory into Deposit Account | Debtor Wires Funds from Deposit Account to Buy Equipment |
> |---|---|---|---|
>
> If the first-to-file-or-perfect rule applied as to the equipment that is proceeds of the deposit account, SP-1 would have priority over SP-2 because SP1's priority date would be when it first obtained control over the deposit account, which was before SP-2 filed or perfected as to the inventory and equipment. § 9-322(a), (b). However, § 9-322(d) applies and it is an exception to the first-to-file-or-perfect rule. It provides that priority of the security interests in the new equipment will be determined by a first-to-file rule. Because SP-2 has filed and SP-1 has not, SP-2 has priority.
>
> Now try your hand at the following problems.

---

29 Although neither subsection (c) nor (d) contains an ordering principle – that is, neither is expressly subject to the other – a close reading reveals that the circumstances to which each applies do not overlap.

Problem 5-31

Same facts as in Problem 5-30 through Part D. The deposit account agreement between Dynamo and Second Bank gives Second Bank a security interest in all deposit accounts to secure all debts Dynamo owes or comes to owe to Second Bank.

A. Dynamo withdrew money from the checking account for its petty cash stash at the corporate office. Does either First Bank or Second Bank have perfected security interests in the money? If so, what bank's security interest in the money has priority? *See* §§ 9-315(c), (d), 9-322(a), (c)–(e), 9-327.

B. Dynamo wrote a check drawn on the checking account and gave the check to Brokerage Inc. to purchase a securities entitlement in IBM, Inc. Assuming First Bank and Second Bank each has security interest in the securities entitlement, which bank's security interest has priority?

C. Dynamo wrote a check drawn on the checking account and gave the check to Merchandise Manufacturer to purchase a new item of inventory. Assuming First Bank and Second Bank each has a security interest in the new item of inventory, which bank's security interest has priority?

Problem 5-32

Delectables, LLC owns and operates fast food restaurants. Several years ago, Bank One obtained a security interest in Delectables' existing and after-acquired equipment and perfected that security interest by filing a financing statement in the appropriate office. At the same time, Bank One also entered into a control agreement with Delectables and State Bank, at which Delectables maintains its only checking account. Last year, Delectables opened a new restaurant with financing from Bank Two. Bank Two obtained a purchase-money security interest in the new restaurant equipment and perfected that security interest by filing in the appropriate office a financing statement indicating the collateral as "goods." The financing statement was filed before Delectables received delivery of the new equipment. The new restaurant was not successful and one month ago Delectables sold the new restaurant equipment to Buyer, who paid with a check that Delectables deposited into its checking account at State Bank. Delectables then used funds credited to its checking account to buy new computers for its headquarters. Assume that under applicable tracing principles, the computers are identifiable proceeds of the sold restaurant equipment. Which bank's security interest in the computers has priority?

e-Exercise 5-E
Priority in Deposit Accounts

SECTION 4. THE RIGHTS OF SELLERS AND LESSORS OF GOODS AGAINST SECURITY INTERESTS GRANTED BY THE BUYER OR LESSEE

A. The Secured Party against a Seller of Goods

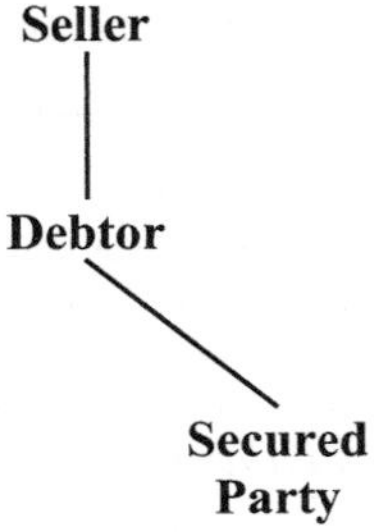

In general, sellers of goods do not fare well against the secured parties of their buyers once the buyers receive the goods. Let us begin with the most basic transaction.

> Seller owns a good and sells it to Debtor. Debtor grants a security interest in that good to Secured Party. Upon sale and delivery of the good to Debtor, Seller has no further property interest in the good. *See* § 2-401. At this point there is and can be *no* priority contest between Seller and Secured Party. This is true even if Debtor purchased the good on credit. Seller simply has no property rights in the good. The only entities with property interests in the good are Debtor and Secured Party. Their rights relative to each other will be determined by the terms of the security agreement.

Admittedly, Article 2 does give a seller the right to get goods back in some circumstances. For example, if shortly after delivery the seller discovers the buyer is insolvent, the seller may reclaim the goods. *See* § 2-702(2). Similarly, if the buyer paid with a check that was later dishonored, the seller may recover the goods.

See § 2-507(2). However, both of these rights are subject to the rights of a good faith purchaser for value. §§ 2-403(1), 2-702(3). Because a secured party is a purchaser and the secured obligation constitutes value, *see* §§ 1-201(b)(29), (30); 1-204, the rights of the buyer's secured party (*i.e.*, a good faith purchaser for value) to the goods are superior to the right of a reclaiming seller to recover the goods.

Now vary the transaction in one respect. Seller sold the good on credit and in the purchase agreement between Seller and Debtor, Seller retained title to the good until full payment. Seller then delivered the good to Debtor. Seller's retention of title is treated as a security interest and that "retention" does not actually prevent title from passing to Debtor. *See* §§ 2-401, 1-201(b)(35).[30] When Secured Party's security interest then attaches pursuant to its security agreement with Debtor, the priority contest between Seller (a secured party with a security interest) and Secured Party is determined by the rules we have already studied. In short, instead of looking like a dispute represented by the diagram above, the law re-characterizes it as the following kind of dispute:

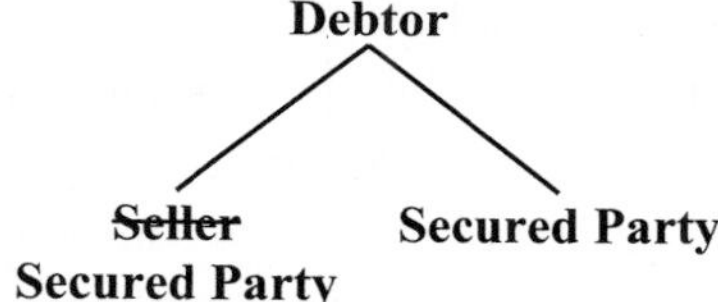

Who wins that battle will depend on whether the parties perfected, when they filed or perfected, and whether Seller, which has a purchase-money security interest in the good, has done what it necessary to have priority under § 9-324.

If Debtor has not yet obtained possession of the good, the results are generally different. First, if the good was not identified when the sales contract was formed and Seller has not yet shipped the good or marked it for shipment, the good is likely not yet identified to the contract. *See* § 2-501. Accordingly, Debtor does not yet have property rights in the good and Secured Party's security interest will not have attached. *See* § 9-203(b)(2).

Second, even if the good is identified, if Debtor breaches the sales contract prior to delivery, Seller generally has a right to withhold or stop delivery. *See* §§ 2-702(1), 2-705. Unlike a seller's reclamation rights, these rights are not subject to the rights of a good faith purchaser for value. Thus, even if Secured Party's

---

[30] The same is true of a shipment under reservation. As we saw in Chapter One, Section 8, Part C, that too is treated merely as retention of a security interest.

security interest attaches to the good, as long as Debtor does not obtain possession of the good, Seller's rights will have priority. *See* § 9-110(4) & cmt. 5.[31]

Finally, if Seller retained title to the good in the purchase agreement with Debtor, then even if identification has occurred and Secured Party's interest has attached, prior to delivery Seller will have priority under § 9-110(4). Even without that rule, Seller would likely have priority. Recall that Seller has a PMSI and Seller's continued possession would be sufficient for perfection. Nevertheless, because of § 9-110(4), Seller need not comply with the notification rule of § 9-324(b) (if the good would be inventory in Debtor's hands). Until the debtor obtains possession of the good, Seller wins.[32]

Problem 5-33

On June 1, Derrick Corp. signed a document in which it granted a security interest in "all inventory and equipment now owned or hereafter acquired to secure any and all obligations now owed or hereafter owed to National Bank." That same day, National Bank perfected its interest by filing a sufficient financing statement in the appropriate office. In July, Derrick contracted to purchase bolts for its manufacturing process from Supplier, which agreed to deliver 10,000 bolts every Wednesday morning for the next 3 months. Thereafter, on each Monday, Supplier manufactures the bolts, packages them, and marks the packages for delivery to Derrick. On Tuesdays, Supplier loads the bolts onto a Carrier Express delivery truck for delivery to Derrick on Wednesday.

A. When does National Bank's security interest attach to the bolts?
B. Supplier delivered 10,000 bolts on the first Wednesday in August and Derrick has not yet paid for the bolts. Can Supplier get that shipment of bolts back from Derrick? Does your answer change if Derrick gave Supplier a check for the bolts and the check was dishonored for insufficient funds?
C. As to the bolts referred to in Part B, will Supplier's claim to the return of the bolts be superior to National Bank's security interest in the bolts?

---

31 In re Kellstrom Indus., Inc., 282 B.R. 787 (Bankr. D. Del. 2002).

32 The same result is obtained if the seller ships the goods under reservation. §§ 2-505, 9-110.

D. In the third week of August, Supplier discovers that Derrick is insolvent after the bolts are loaded on Carrier's truck but before Carrier has arrived at Derrick's location. Advise Supplier as to what it should do regarding those bolts on the truck. If National Bank asserts a superior right to those bolts on the truck, will National Bank win?

E. In the purchase agreement with Derrick, Supplier retained title to the bolts until full payment by Derrick. Several shipments of bolts were delivered to Derrick. Derrick failed to pay. Supplier demands possession from Derrick of the bolts that Derrick has not yet paid for. Does Supplier have a right to possession of those bolts? [Hint: what is the basis for Supplier's demand for possession: Article 2 or Article 9?] If National Bank asserts that it has a superior security interest in those bolts, will it win?

F. What should Supplier do to fully protect itself against National Bank's security interest in the bolts that Supplier is selling to Derrick?

B. The Secured Party against a Lessor of Goods

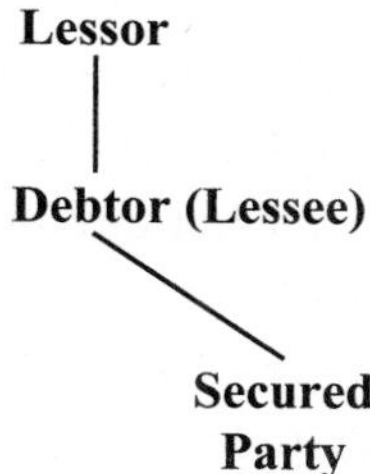

A lessor of goods fares better against secured parties of the lessee than a seller of goods does against secured parties of the buyer. This should not be surprising given the law's general respect for the derivation principle: the debtor's rights in the goods are derived from the lessor, and the debtor can normally transfer no more rights in the goods than the debtor has. Accordingly, creditors of the lessee take subject to the lease contract. *See* §§ 2A-307(1); 9-203 cmt. 6. This means that the lessee's secured party can obtain a security interest in the debtor's leasehold interest in the goods, but not in the remainder interest retained by the lessor.

This is true even in those relatively rare situations when the debtor has the power to transfer more rights than the debtor actually has. For example, if the debtor acquires a voidable leasehold interest – say perhaps by deceiving the lessor as to the debtor's identity or by paying rent with a check that is later dishonored – the debtor can transfer a good leasehold to certain good faith transferees for value. *See*

§ 2A-305(1). However, there is no suggestion that such transferees can or do acquire the lessor's rights to the goods after the lease term ends or in any way undermine the lessor's rights to recover the goods during the lease term if the rent is not paid when due.

SECTION 5. THE RIGHTS OF BUYERS AND LESSEES OF GOODS AGAINST SECURITY INTERESTS GRANTED BY THE SELLER OR LESSOR

A. The Secured Party against a Buyer of Goods

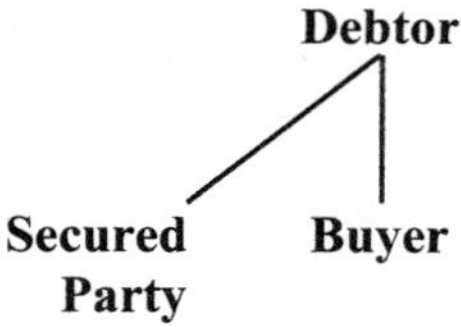

Now we look at a purchase of goods transaction from the buyer's perspective. The basic scenario is this. Debtor has granted a security interest in one or more goods to Secured Party. Debtor then contracts to sell some or all of the goods to Buyer. Under what circumstances does Buyer take the goods subject to the security interest of Secured Party and under what circumstances does Buyer take free of Secured Party's interest in the goods?

As is probably immediately apparent, there are several competing interests and policies at issue in these types of disputes and the law will have to strike a balance among them. Secured parties and buyers are both reliance parties; both give value in reliance on obtaining an interest in the goods involved in the transaction. Both therefore deserve some measure of protection. In addition, sales of goods are such a ubiquitous component of American commerce and American culture that it would be utterly impractical for the law to give buyers – or at least all buyers – a need to search for financing statements before buying. Remember, the UCC is designed to facilitate commerce, not to frustrate or hamper it. *See* § 1-103(a).

Nevertheless, as with priority disputes between secured parties and lien creditors, we start with the basic rule of § 9-201(a): secured party with a security interest wins. *See also* § 9-315(a)(1). Only if some other provision of Article 9 expressly provides otherwise – or the secured party authorizes the sale free and clear of the security interest (*i.e.*, waives its lien) – will the buyer take free of the security interest. This rule should not be surprising; it merely recognizes the underlying reality that the secured party's interest in the goods was necessarily created before the sale to the buyer. In other words, it is a codification of the first-in-time, first-in-right principle.[33]

Problem 5-34

Why is it that, in a priority dispute between a secured party and a buyer of goods, the secured party's interest must have arisen before the sale to the buyer? *See* § 9-203(b).

With this baseline rule in mind, we now consider one clarification and four exceptions. Some of these exceptions are minor but at least one is quite significant and commonly available. In fact, that exception might be so common that many think of it as the general rule and then regard the rule of § 9-201 as an exception to it. Nevertheless, it is useful not to lose sight of Article 9's structure. The secured party's security interest wins unless Article 9 expressly provides otherwise.

Clarification. Section 9-315(a)(1) tells us that a security interest continues in collateral notwithstanding its disposition unless the secured party authorizes the disposition free of its security interest. Such authorization for the debtor to sell collateral free and clear of the secured party's interest might be given expressly, either in the signed security agreement or by a subsequent written or oral statement.[34] Alternatively, such authorization might be implied from the parties' course of dealing or course of performance. This might happen when the secured party knows of the debtor's practice of disposing of collateral and does not protest or put a stop to that practice.[35]

---

[33] Even if the seller of the good does not have a right to get the good back from the buyer, that fact does not determine whether the seller's secured party will have its security interest continue in the good.

[34] *See, e.g.*, Citizens Nat'l Bank of Madelia v. Mankato Implement, Inc., 441 N.W.2d 483 (Minn. 1989) (bank's oral consent to debtor's trade-in of collateral was effective to extinguish its security interest in collateral despite a written provision in security agreement that such consent must be in writing); Peoples Nat'l Bank and Trust v. Excel Corp., 695 P.2d 444 (Kan. 1985) (bank officer's oral instruction to debtor when loan was made that debtor was free to sell the cattle at any time trumped provision of written security agreement prohibiting debtor from selling livestock).

[35] *See, e.g.*, Gretna State Bank v. Cornbelt Livestock Co., 463 N.W.2d 795 (Neb. 1990) (debtor's sale of cattle was impliedly authorized by years of bank's failure to object to such sales as long as debtor retained 60 head); Neu Cheese Co. v. FDIC, 825 F.2d 1270 (8th Cir.

If a secured party authorizes the debtor to sell collateralized goods free of the security interest, there is no priority contest between the secured party and the buyer.[36] The secured party no longer has an interest in the goods after the sale of the goods to the buyer. The security interest has been stripped off the goods ("de-attached") by the secured party's authorization. Thus, from the secured party's perspective, losing to a buyer is very different from losing to a lien creditor. When a lien creditor takes priority over a secured party, the security interest remains. If the collateral is worth more than the debt owed to the lien creditor, the secured party still has valuable rights in the collateral and might well benefit from a foreclosure on it. In contrast, a buyer who takes collateral free of a security interest leaves the secured party with no rights to the property purchased, regardless of how much the buyer paid or the value of the property sold.[37]

Exception 1: Unperfected security interests. Read § 9-317(b). If the secured party's security interest is unperfected, a buyer of goods that gives value and receives delivery of the goods without knowledge of the security interest and before the security interest is perfected will take the goods free of the security interest. To illustrate:

> Assume Lender has a security interest in a piece of Debtor's equipment. Lender has not perfected its security interest in the equipment. Debtor sold and delivered that equipment to Buyer. Lender did not explicitly or implicitly authorize Debtor to sell the equipment to Buyer free of Lender's security interest. Thus the security interest would normally remain attached to the equipment in the hands of Buyer. § 9-315(a)(1). However, if Buyer had no knowledge of the security interest when it took delivery of the

---

1987) (creditor consented to sales of milk free and clear by failing to object to more than 700 prior sales); Farmers State Bank v. Farmland Foods, Inc., 402 N.W.2d 277 (Neb. 1987) (secured party authorized sales of hogs free and clear by failing to object to more than 130 previous sales).

[36] RFC Cap. Corp. v. Earthlink, Inc., 55 U.C.C. Rep. Serv. 2d 617 (Ohio Ct. App. 2004) (buyer did not take free of security interest because secured party authorized the sale on the condition that the loan be paid in full and the loan was not paid, even though the secured creditor agreed to withhold knowledge of the condition from the buyer).

[37] Of course, even if a buyer takes free of a security interest in the property sold, the secured party with a security interest still has a right to any identifiable proceeds. *See* § 9-315(a). *See also* Problem 2-12.

equipment and gave value, Buyer has the equipment free of Lender's security interest under the rule of § 9-317(b).

Note, application of this rule is augmented somewhat by the continuity-of-perfection rules in § 9-316. Recall that a secured party whose security interest is perfected by a financing statement filed in the jurisdiction of the debtor's location has one year to refile in the jurisdiction of the buyer's location – if different from the debtor's location – to remain perfected. § 9-316(a)(3). If the secured party fails to refile within that period, not only does its interest become unperfected, but its unperfected status is retroactive to the time of the sale. *See* § 9-316(b). As a result, a buyer who had no knowledge of the security interest at the time of the sale, and who will have, at the time of the sale, taken subject to the security interest, will later take the property free of the security interest if the secured party does not file a financing statement in the new jurisdiction within one year of the sale.

A somewhat similar rule protects buyers if a secured party has perfected its security interest by notation on a certificate of title and the goods thereafter become covered by a clean certificate of title issued by another state. Even though the security interest might remain perfected and have priority over a lien creditor, *see* § 9-316(d), a buyer that gives value and takes delivery without knowledge of the security interest and before the lien is noted on the new certificate takes free of the security interest if the secured party does not get its lien noted on the new certificate within four months of when the goods become covered by the new certificate. *See* § 9-316(e) & cmt. 5, ex. 8. *Compare* § 9-337(1) (providing a similar protection for a more limited class of buyers even if the secured party does re-perfect within the four-month period).

Also bear in mind that some secured parties that are perfected against a lien creditor are treated as unperfected against a buyer who gives value without knowledge of the security interest. For example, we have already seen that if a secured party files a financing statement that is effective to perfect but which has an incorrect address for the debtor, a purchaser of the goods, other than a secured party, takes free of the security interest if the purchaser gave value and received delivery of the goods in reasonable reliance on the incorrect information. *See* §§ 9-338(2); 9-516(b)(5).

Problem 5-35

First Bank has an unperfected security interest in a piece of Derringer's equipment to secure a $50,000 debt. The piece of equipment is worth

$75,000. Purchaser then acquires an interest in the piece of equipment in exchange for $25,000.

A. If Purchaser is a secured party who properly perfects, what are the parties' relative rights to the piece of equipment? Put another way, assuming the full value of the piece of equipment can be realized, who gets what? *See* § 9-322(a)(2).
B. If Purchaser is a buyer, what are the parties' relative rights to the piece of equipment? Put another way, assuming the full value of the piece of equipment can be realized, who gets what? *See* § 9-317(b).

Problem 5-36

First Bank acquires an enforceable security interest in a piece of Derringer's equipment to secure a $50,000 debt. The piece of equipment is worth $75,000. First Bank promptly perfects its security interest by filing an effective financing statement in State A, where Derringer is located. Purchaser, who is located in State B, then acquires an interest in the piece of equipment in exchange for $25,000. First Bank never files a financing statement in State B.

A. If Purchaser is a secured party who perfects its security interest in the equipment by filing an effective financing statement, what are the parties' relative rights to the piece of equipment? *See* §§ 9-316(a), 9-322(a).
B. If Purchaser is a buyer, what are the parties' relative rights to the piece of equipment? *See* § 9-316(a), (b).

Problem 5-37

Digger is a farmer. On December 1, Digger acquired a new tractor on credit from Seller, who retained a security interest to secure the unpaid portion of the purchase price. On December 10, Congress passed a new farm bill. That legislation dramatically increased the compensation for farmers to take a portion of their arable land out of production. Digger decided to do this, and consequently had little need for the new tractor. On December 12, Digger sold the tractor to Neighbor, who is also a farmer. On December 15, Seller filed in the appropriate office a financing statement identifying Digger as the debtor and indicating the tractor as the collateral. It is now December 29. Assuming no certificate-of-title statute applies to the tractor, who has priority in the tractor? *See* § 9-317(b), (e).

Problem 5-38

Driver granted an enforceable security interest to Bank to secure the purchase price of a delivery van used in Driver's business and Bank obtained notation of its security interest on the van's certificate of title issued by Montana's Department of Motor Vehicles. Driver then moved to Idaho and obtained a new certificate of title from the Idaho Department of Motor Vehicles. The Idaho certificate of title failed to reflect Bank's security interest due to an error at the Idaho Department of Motor Vehicles. Driver sold the van to Buyer, a neighbor, delivering both the signed Idaho certificate of title and the van. Bank finds out that Driver moved without notifying Bank, a default under the terms of the security agreement, and seeks to replevy the van from Buyer.

A. Assume Bank is seeking to replevy the van nine months after Driver obtained the Idaho certificate of title. Will Buyer lose the van to Bank? §§ 9-317(b), 9-316(d), (e).
B. Assume Bank is seeking to replevy the van three months after Driver obtained the Idaho certificate of title. Will Buyer lose the van to Bank? §§ 9-317(b), 9-316(d), (e), 9-337(1).
C. Assume Buyer is a used car dealer and Driver sold the van to Buyer when Driver traded it for another van. Does that change your analysis of either question above?

Just because the secured party loses in a priority contest with the buyer does not mean that the debtor has a license to conduct the sale transaction. We saw in Problem 3-4 that several states have statutes that make criminal any attempt by the debtor to conceal collateral in an effort to prevent repossession. Some of those statutes also make criminal any sale of the collateral without authorization and without promptly remitting the sale proceeds to the secured party.[38]

Exception 2: Buyers in ordinary course of business. So far so good. Unfortunately for most of the buyers in this world, most secured parties perfect their security interests in the debtor's goods before the debtor sells the goods to a buyer. Does this mean that all buyers need to search for filed financing statements or otherwise be on the lookout for perfected security interests before purchasing the

---

38 *See, e.g.*, Tex. Penal Code § 32.33(e); Kan. Stat. § 21-5830; State v. Orcutt, 222 P.3d 564 (Kan. Ct. App. 2010).

food they eat, the clothes they wear, the beds they sleep on, or the equipment and supplies they need to run their businesses? No. Read § 9-320(a). If the buyer qualifies as a special type of buyer – a buyer in ordinary course of business – the buyer will take free of the security interest created by the seller even if the buyer knows of the security interest. Now read § 1-201(b)(9). That section provides that, to qualify as a buyer in ordinary course of business, a buyer must satisfy all six of the following requirements:

(1) Buy goods;
(2) In good faith;
(3) Without knowledge that the sale violates the rights of another person in the goods;
(4) In the ordinary course;
(5) From a person in the business of selling goods of the kind; and
(6) Take possession of the goods or have a right to take possession of the goods from the seller under Article 2.[39]

Notice that the definition gives some guidance on the fourth requirement, buying "in the ordinary course." Such a transaction might be on secured or unsecured credit or for cash. However, a purchase in bulk, or as security for or in total or partial satisfaction of an already existing debt, is not in the ordinary course.

The first and most important thing to draw from these requirements is the type of property to which this rule is implicitly limited. Because a person qualifies as a buyer in ordinary course of business only if the seller is in the business of selling goods of the kind, the rule of § 9-320(a) is effectively limited to buyers of the seller's inventory. It does not apply to buyers of accounts, instruments, or even to buyers of other types of goods.[40] If the goods are not inventory in the debtor's hands, a transferee cannot be a buyer in ordinary course of business.

Because of that, it might be helpful to think of the rule of § 9-320(a) not so much as an exception to the general rule of § 9-201 (secured party wins), but as a corollary to the clarification of § 9-315(a)(1) (security interest survives unless secured party authorizes the sale free and clear of its interest). After all, what does a creditor with a security interest in inventory want the debtor to do with the

---

[39] The buyer not in possession will normally have a right to get possession of the goods only if the buyer has that right under § 2-502 or § 2-716.

[40] Note that even though a debtor might be in the business of selling farm products, the rule of § 9-320(a) does not protect a buyer in the ordinary course of farm products.

inventory? Sell it. In essence, the rule of § 9-320(a) is nothing more than a conclusive presumption that the secured party has authorized the debtor to sell its inventory free and clear of the security interest.[41]

Understanding the rule in this way then helps when considering whether a transfer is a disqualifying transfer in bulk. A bulk sale is not solely or strictly a matter of volume, but a matter of usualness. Thus, if a debtor normally sells inventory in large lots, a buyer of a large lot can still be a buyer in ordinary course. After all, that is what the secured party is probably expecting the debtor to do. If, however, the debtor does not normally sell in large lots, then a buyer of a large lot is doing something unusual, perhaps something not expected or authorized by the secured party and perhaps suggesting that the debtor might be about to liquidate all its inventory and go out of business (without paying the secured party). Such a buyer is not protected by § 9-320(a).[42]

The protection for buyers in ordinary course of business is critical to commerce. Whenever you buy something in a store, it is likely that the store's inventory is subject to a perfected security interest in favor of the store's secured creditor. If § 9-320(a) did not exist, when the store defaulted on its obligations to that secured creditor, the secured creditor could show up on your doorstep and demand a return of the goods you purchased from the store, and do so without returning the amount you paid.[43] Consider the following case on what it takes to be a buyer in ordinary course of business.

---

[41] *See* Valley Bank & Trust Co. v. Holyoke Cmty. Fed. Credit Union, 121 P.3d 358 (Colo. Ct. App. 2005) (buyers of automobiles took free of security interest held by seller's secured lender because lender was deemed to have authorized the sales free and clear and because the buyers qualified as buyers in ordinary course of business).

[42] While neither Article 9 nor the official comments to it indicates how large or unusual a sale must be to be "a transfer in bulk," it seems likely that this is an oblique reference to UCC Article 6, now largely repealed, which defines a "bulk sale" to include only sales of more than half of the seller's inventory, measured by value. *See* § 6-102(1)(c).

[43] This assumes that the secured party did not authorize the sale to you free of the security interest by virtue of its security agreement with the debtor or by its course of conduct concerning the debtor's sale of inventory.

IN RE HAVENS STEEL COMPANY
317 B.R. 75 (Bankr. W.D. Mo. 2004)

Jerry W. Venters, Chief Judge

* * *

I. BACKGROUND

The Debtor is a fully integrated steel construction company providing "design-build" services to contractors and subcontractors. These services include the procurement of raw materials, design, fabrication, and erection of steel structures. On or about March 31, 2003, Defendant Commerce Bank loaned the Debtor $15 million to fund the operation of its business. As of the petition date, March 18, 2004, the Debtor owed Commerce $11,344,579.70 plus interest and fees. This indebtedness was secured by, among other things, the Debtor's inventory, accounts receivable, and all proceeds thereof. The parties have stipulated to the validity of Commerce's security interest.

On February 5, 2003, the Debtor entered into a contract ("Subcontract") with The Austin Company * * * to furnish, fabricate, and erect steel for the construction of the Kansas City Star newspaper's new printing facility (the "Project"). More specifically, under the Subcontract the Debtor was required to: (1) prepare shop drawings and erection drawings for each piece of steel that would be used on the Project; (2) purchase finished components and the structural steel shapes identified in the shop drawings; (3) transform the structural steel shapes into usable steel for the Project; and (4) erect the finished steel. The parties agree that the services portion of the Subcontract predominates over the goods portion.

As of the petition date, the Project was not finished and a large amount of steel was in various stages of the design-build process: 85,611 pounds of steel, with a value of $20,889.72, was in the Debtor's possession and in the process of being fabricated; 376,424 pounds of fabricated steel, with a value of $556,908.72, was located at the Ottawa Plant; and 402,305 pounds of fabricated steel, with a value of $154,485.12, was being stored at the Project site. In total, $732,283.56 worth of steel had been identified for the Project but not erected.

The Debtor agreed to complete the work under the Subcontract for a total price of $7,518,390, but because it would be very difficult, if not impossible, for the Debtor to wait until the Project was completed to receive full payment, the Subcontract provided for a procedure according to which the Debtor could apply for partial "progress" payments before completion of the Project. * * *

Pursuant to this process, as of the petition date Austin had paid for $447,260.08 of the steel located at the Plant and for $107,813.18 of fabricated steel delivered to the Project site but not erected.

In the course of the hearing, the parties argued that two other provisions of the Subcontract are germane to the Court's inquiry. Austin contends that paragraph 8.2.2, which provides that "the Subcontractor (the Debtor) warrants that title to all Work covered by an Application for Payment will pass to the Owner no later than the time of payment," controls the transfer of title for the inventory paid for by Austin. In response, Commerce argues that because Subcontract paragraph 8.2.1.3 provides that "[s]uch [payment] applications shall not include request for payments of amounts on account of materials and equipment not yet incorporated into the Work," Austin wasn't entitled to apply for payment on account of steel not yet incorporated into the project, *i.e.*, erected, and, therefore, title did not pass to Austin for any steel not yet erected.

II. DISCUSSION

The starting point for our answer to the question posed above – When does a lender's security interest in a seller's inventory terminate? – is UCC Revised Article 9, and more particularly, UCC §§ 9-201 and 9-315. Section 9-201 provides that a security agreement is effective against purchasers of collateral and § 9-315 provides that "a security interest . . . continues in collateral notwithstanding sale, lease, license, exchange, or other disposition thereof unless the secured party authorized the disposition free of the security interest." The Official Comments to both §§ 9-201 and 9-315 * * * explain that these code sections contain the general rule that a secured party's interest in collateral continues upon the sale of the collateral unless the secured party consents to the release of its security interest or one of the provisions in Article 9 under which a party takes free and clear of the security interest applies. Both comments list § 9-320, the "buyer in ordinary course" – the code section relied upon by Austin – as an example of such an exception.

However, before moving on to our discussion of whether Commerce consented to the sale of its collateral free of its security interest or whether § 9-320 applies to any of the steel at issue here, it is important to note the effect §§ 9-201 and 9-315 have on Commerce's primary argument that the transfer of title determines when a buyer takes collateral free of a lender's security interest, without regard to the buyer's BIOC status under § 9-320. Under § 9-201 and § 9-315 a buyer (other than a buyer in ordinary course) of goods subject to a security interest takes title to the goods purchased, but that title is subject to the lender's security interest. It seems that Commerce may have lost sight of this fundamental rule of secured transactions in its zeal to fix the point in time when its security interest finally ceded priority to Austin at the last possible moment, *i.e.*, upon the steel's incorporation into the project. It is hard to imagine, though, that Commerce, a major lending institution, does not routinely take the position that a buyer who purchases Commerce's collateral, sold without contractual or statutory authorization, takes title to the collateral *subject to Commerce's continuing security interest.* However, Commerce's argument on this point is directly contrary to that position and the law and, will therefore, be disregarded.

The proper inquiry is whether Commerce consented to the sale of its collateral free of its security interest or whether Austin qualified as a buyer in ordinary course.

A. Commerce's Consent

The parties did not offer any evidence of Commerce's contemporaneous consent (or lack thereof) to the Debtor's sale of Commerce's collateral, but the security agreement between the Debtor and Commerce submitted as a joint exhibit sets forth the conditions upon which the Debtor has authority to sell Commerce's collateral free and clear of Commerce's security interest. Specifically, it provides that, "while Grantor (the Debtor) is not in default under this Agreement, Grantor may sell Inventory, but only in the ordinary course of its business and only to *buyers in the ordinary course of business.*" Thus, under this provision Austin would have to show that the Debtor was not in default on the date the Debtor "sold" the inventory to Austin and that Austin qualifies as a buyer in the ordinary course of business. In light of our ruling below regarding Austin's status as a buyer in the ordinary course of business, we do not need to address how the term "sell" applies here, whether the Debtor was in default on the date of the sale, and ultimately, whether Commerce consented to the sale of its collateral; however, we do note that the security agreement, presumably a Commerce form document, belies Commerce's position at trial that § 9-320 does not apply to the Subcontract.

B. Buyer in Ordinary Course of Business

Section 9-320 provides that "a buyer in ordinary course of business takes free of a security interest created by the buyer's seller, even if the security interest is perfected and the buyer knows of its existence." UCC § 9-320. Official Comment 3 to § 9-320 references § 1-201 for the definition of buyer in ordinary course of business, which, in turn, provides in pertinent part:

> "Buyer in ordinary course of business" means a person that buys goods in good faith, without knowledge that the sale violates the rights of another

> person in the goods, and in the ordinary course from a person . . . in the business of selling goods of that kind. A person buys goods in the ordinary course if the sale to the person comports with the usual or customary practices in the kind of business in which the seller is engaged or with the seller's own usual or customary practices.... Only a buyer that takes possession of the goods or has a right to recover the goods from the seller under Article 2 may be a buyer in ordinary course of business.

Under this definition, we find that Austin qualifies as a BIOC of all of the steel in its possession, and with regard to the steel located at the Ottawa Plant, Austin is a BIOC of the steel for which it had paid.

1. Conduct, Knowledge, and Ordinary Course

Section 1-201's requirement that Austin buys goods "in good faith, without knowledge that the sale violates the rights of another person in the goods, and in the ordinary course from a person . . . in the business of selling goods of that kind," is easily dispatched. Good faith in this context means "honesty in fact in the conduct or transaction concerned," UCC § 1-201, and there has been no allegation or evidence introduced that Austin was dishonest in its conduct in the transactions with the Debtor.[44] The parties stipulated to the existence of the rest of these elements.

2. When Does BIOC Status Attach?

In contrast, because the UCC does not identify the point in a transaction when a buyer attains BIOC status, this element requires considerably more analysis, especially since the Court has not found any dispositive cases * * * on this issue.

There are at least five potential points at which the ascendancy to the honored role of BIOC can be fixed – upon contracting, upon identification of the goods, upon transfer of title, upon delivery, or upon acceptance of the goods – but only transfer of title and identification have received serious consideration. And, not surprisingly, the parties do not agree on which event controls. To the extent that Commerce recognizes that BIOC status is an issue here, it advocates using title as the watershed, and as mentioned above, Commerce contends that title did not pass

---

[44] Although Austin bears the burden of proof to establish that it is entitled to protection as a BIOC under § 9-320, including the element of good faith, good faith is difficult to prove in the affirmative. It is similar to proving the negative--we were not dishonest. Accordingly, in the absence of allegations or evidence to the contrary, the Court will infer Austin's good faith in its conduct with the Debtor.

until the steel was incorporated into the project. (Austin maintains that it took title to the steel when it paid for the steel.) Austin, on the other hand, argues that a buyer attains BIOC status when goods are identified to a contract, and the parties have stipulated that all of the steel at issue had been identified.

Commerce's position – as well as the position of the cases favoring title as the determining factor – is that a sale must have taken place in order for a purchaser to be a BIOC, and "sale" is defined in UCC Article 2 (§ 2-106) as the passing of title from the seller to the buyer for a price. Therefore, Commerce reasons, a purchaser cannot be a BIOC until it obtains title to goods. The Court declines to adopt this position for four reasons.

First, the Court believes that it misconstrues the statute. The statute does not specifically require that a sale has taken place (interposing "contract for sale" would be equally sensible), and to the extent that § 1-201 implicitly requires a sale, the reference to Article 2's definition of sale is unwarranted in light of Article 2's express de-emphasis of the importance of title, and perhaps more importantly, the existence of a specific cross-reference to Article 2 in *another part of the statute.* Rules of statutory construction dictate that the cross-reference to Article 2 in one section militates against a reference to Article 2 where it is not mentioned.

Second, identification makes more sense in the context of the statute. One of the requirements of § 1-201 (discussed in greater detail below) is that a BIOC either has possession of the goods or has "the right to recover the goods from the seller under Article 2." The quoted section of the statute is understood to refer to a buyer's remedy to recover goods from an insolvent seller under § 2-502 or a buyer's right to replevin or specific performance under § 2-716. A review of these provisions reveals that identification, rather than title, is key to the buyer's right to recover goods. *See* UCC §§ 2-502, 2-716.

Third, there is an apparent trend in the case law away from transfer of title as the point at which BIOC status is attained. After *Daniel* [*v. Bank of Hayward*, 425 N.W.2d 416 (Wis. 1998),] the case that overruled *Chrysler* [*Corp. v. Adamatic Inc.*, 208 N.W.2d 97 (Wis. 1973)] (the seminal case advocating the use of title), there are apparently no cases holding that BIOC status is attained upon the transfer of title.

Finally, from a policy standpoint we note that using identification rather than passage of title advances Article 9's policy of protecting innocent buyers and places the risk of loss on the secured party who has the ability to protect itself by requiring various inventory controls and reports and who may be in a better position to absorb the loss.

Therefore, the Court concludes that a buyer attains BIOC status at the time goods are identified to a contract, and in this case, the parties stipulated that all of the steel had been identified to the Subcontract.

3. Possession of, or Right to Recover, the Steel

Having determined that Austin had reached the point in the transaction when it could qualify for BIOC status, whether Austin actually attained BIOC status with regard to particular steel turns on the final test set forth in § 1-201, which limits BIOC status to buyers who "take possession of the goods or [have] a right to recover the goods from the seller under Article 2." Because Austin had physical possession of the 402,305 pounds of steel (worth $154,485.12) located at the Project site, no further discussion is necessary; Austin was a BIOC with regard to that steel. Austin was also a BIOC of most of the steel at the Ottawa Plant as of the petition date, but the application of the statute with regard to that steel is not as straightforward.

At first blush, the statute appears to preclude Austin from being a BIOC of the steel in the Debtor's possession on the petition date because Austin did not have physical possession of that steel and Austin did not have the right to recover it *under Article 2*, inasmuch as the Subcontract was not covered by Article 2.[45] However, upon comparison of the revised § 1-201 to its predecessor statute and a consideration of cases applying the predecessor statute and of the official comment to revised § 1-201, we find that a party that can establish a common law (versus an Article 2-based) "right to recover" may qualify as a BIOC, assuming the other requirements of the statute are met.

The former UCC § 1-201 did not contain the requirement that a BIOC have possession of or the right to recover the good from the seller under Article 2. Nor did the cases applying former § 1-201. Based on a review of the cases applying former § 1-201, the incorporation of the "right to recover" requirement into revised § 1-201 is most likely a function of the fact that BIOC litigation most often arises in the context of a replevin action brought by or against the buyer of goods in which the seller's lender has a security interest, and establishing a right to possession is a fundamental element of a replevin action. In light of the origins of the "right to recover" requirement, the Court does not believe that the embodiment of that

---

[45] As mentioned above, the parties stipulated that the services portion of the Subcontract predominated, so the Subcontract would not be governed by Article 2. *See* Bonebrake v. Cox, 499 F.2d 951, 960 (8th Cir. 1974) (explicating the "predominate purpose test" for determining whether Article 2 applies to a particular transaction).

requirement into § 1-201 was intended to limit recourse under the statute to only Article 2 buyers. Official Comment 9 to Revised § 1-201 further supports this interpretation, stating:

> The penultimate sentence [of § 1-201(b)(9)] prevents a buyer that does not have the right to possession as against the seller from being a buyer in ordinary course of business. Concerning when a buyer obtains possessory rights, see Sections 2-502 and 2-716. However, the penultimate sentence is not intended to affect a buyer's status as a buyer in ordinary course of business in cases (such as a "drop shipment") involving delivery by the seller to a person buying from the buyer or a donee from the buyer. The requirement relates to whether *as against the seller* the buyer or one taking through the buyer has possessory rights.

Official Comment 9, Revised § 1-201 (emphasis in original).

This Comment suggests that the inclusion of the Article 2 "requirement" was for referential value rather than for purposes of restricting the statute to Article 2 contracts. Therefore, the Court believes that a party that establishes its possessory rights over goods *as against the seller*, without reference to Article 2, also qualifies as a BIOC under this portion of the statute. The Court finds that Austin had such a right with respect to the steel located at the Ottawa Plant and which had been identified for the Project.

There are at least two common law causes of action which would give rise to Austin's right to recover. And it is no surprise that these parallel similar rights were granted by Article 2 to purchasers of goods. Under a replevin theory (UCC § 2-716(3)), Austin had a right to recover the goods for which it had paid, and Austin had an equitable right to specific performance (UCC § 2-716(1) and (2)) for delivery of all of the steel in the Debtor's possession, although Austin would have to pay for any steel for which payment was owing.

[The court then discussed why Austin could prevail on both a replevin claim and an action for specific performance under Missouri common law – ed.] * * *

CONCLUSION

In sum, for the reasons stated above, the Court finds that Commerce's security interest in the steel identified to the Austin project as of the petition date terminated to the extent Austin qualifies as a buyer in ordinary course of business under UCC § 9-320. The Court further finds that Austin qualifies as a buyer in ordinary course of business with regard to the $154,485.12 worth of steel in Austin's possession and the $384,017.08 worth of steel for which Austin had paid, and which was located at the Debtor's Ottawa Plant. Thus, in total, Austin has an interest superior to Commerce in $538,502.20 of the $732,283.56 of steel at issue. In light of the Court's March 25, 2004, ruling, as incorporated in the May 10, 2004 Final Order, this finding translates to a requirement that Commerce turn over to Austin $538,502.20 of the money Commerce now holds in the segregated account. * * *

Problem 5-39

Drips, Inc. is a wholesaler of plumbing supplies. For the last several years, Bank has had an enforceable security interest in all of Drips' existing and after-acquired inventory and accounts to secure all obligations owed at any time to Bank, perfected by a sufficient financing statement filed in the appropriate filing office. Four months ago, Supplier sold some plumbing fixtures to Drips on credit, retaining a security interest in the plumbing fixtures sold. Under the terms of the security agreement with Supplier, Drips is permitted to sell the plumbing fixtures for cash and cash equivalents (*e.g.*, checks), but is not permitted to sell them on open account *(i.e.*, on credit). Supplier properly perfected its security interest in the plumbing fixtures through a sufficient filing in the appropriate filing office, and gave sufficient notification to Bank as required under § 9-324(b). Last week, Betty Plumber purchased on open account from Drips several of the plumbing fixtures Drips had acquired from Supplier.

A. Why does the security agreement between Supplier and Drips prohibit Drips from selling on open account? *See* § 9-324(b).
B. In which of the following cases, if any, does Betty take the plumbing fixtures free of Supplier's security interest (assume Betty is located in the same jurisdiction as Drips, Inc.)? *See* §§ 1-201(b)(9), 9-320(a).
   1. At the time of the sale, Betty did not know of Supplier's security interest.
   2. At the time of the sale, Betty knew that Supplier had a security interest in the fixtures she was purchasing from Drips.
   3. At the time of the sale, Betty knew that Supplier had a security interest in the fixtures she was purchasing from Drips and knew that the security agreement prohibited sales on open account.

Despite its importance, the protection for buyers in ordinary course in § 9-320(a) has three limitations. First, the security interest from which the buyer takes free must have been created by the buyer's seller. Consider this illustration.

Illustration

Lender has a perfected security interest in Manufacturer's equipment. Manufacturer sells an item of equipment to Dealer, who is in the business of buying and selling used manufacturing equipment. Under § 9-315(a)(1), Dealer takes the equipment subject to Lender's security interest. Moreover, assuming Lender perfected by filing, Lender need not do anything to its financing statement against Manufacturer to reflect the transfer to Dealer unless Dealer is located in a jurisdiction different than Manufacturer's location. *See* §§ 9-507(a), 9-316(a)(3). Thereafter, Dealer sells the item of equipment to Buyer. Even if Buyer qualifies as a buyer in ordinary course of business from Dealer, Buyer does not take free of Lender's security interest. § 9-320(a) & cmt. 3, ex. 1.

To depict this graphically, the rule of § 9-320(a) applies to transactions diagramed on the left side of the diagram that follows, not to those diagramed on the right.

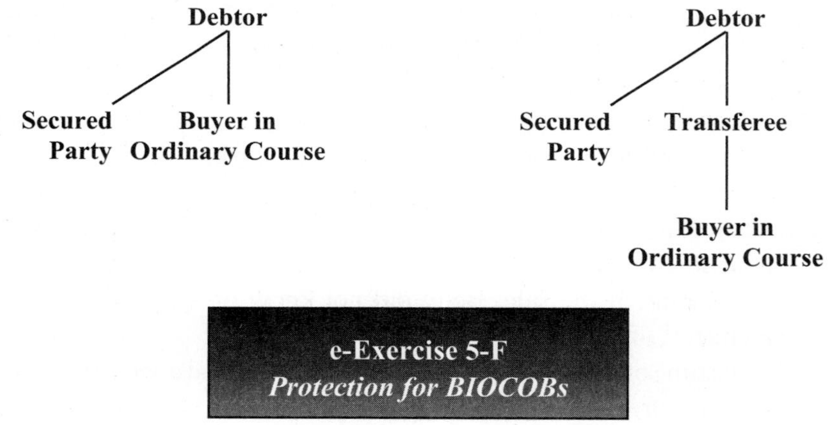

e-Exercise 5-F
Protection for BIOCOBs

Problem 5-40

A. Given that Buyer in the right-hand illustration above does not take free of Lender's security interest under § 9-320(a), what else might come to

Buyer's aid? In other words, under what other provision might Buyer take free? *See* §§ 2-403(2), 9-315(a)(1), 9-320 cmt. 3, ex. 2.

B. Given the reasons already described for protecting buyers in ordinary course of business, why does § 9-320(a) protect such buyers only from security interests created by their sellers?

C. Consumer visits Antique Store, which recently acquired a seventeenth century mahogany desk. Antique Store offers Consumer the desk for $200,000. Consumer thinks the price is fair but wants to be sure that the desk will be completely unencumbered upon completion of the sale. What must Consumer do to be certain that no security interests will remain in the desk?

D. How big a problem does the "created by the buyer's seller" limitation in § 9-320(a) create for retail buyers? Put another way, what types of goods are most likely to remain subject to a security interest upon sale to retail buyers (*i.e.*, to buyers in ordinary course of business)?

The second limitation on the ability of a buyer in ordinary course of business to take free of a security interest is if the secured party has possession of the goods. *See* § 9-320(e). Recall that to qualify as a buyer in ordinary course of business, a buyer must either have possession of the goods or have the right to obtain possession from the seller. *See* § 1-201(b)(9). Accordingly, this limitation applies only when the buyer has the right to possession vis-á-vis the seller, but the secured party or its agent has actual possession. Consider the following illustration.

Illustration

Bank has a security interest in Debtor's inventory. Bailee is in possession of some of the inventory. Pursuant to § 9-313(c), Bank has obtained Bailee's signed agreement to hold the goods on Bank's behalf. Debtor sells the goods to Buyer. Buyer does not yet have physical possession of the goods but, under the circumstances, has a right to compel Debtor to deliver them under § 2-716. Buyer otherwise meets all the requirements of a buyer in ordinary course of business under § 1-201(b)(9). Pursuant to § 9-320(e), Buyer nonetheless would not take the goods free of Bank's security interest unless and until Buyer obtains actual physical possession of the goods.

This rule is a fairly minor limitation on the protections for buyers in ordinary course and can be viewed as creating a different priority rule for perfection by possession.

The final limitation exempts from the rule's protection buyers of farm products from a farmer. It exists because a preemptive federal law, the Food Security Act of 1985, 7 U.S.C. § 1631, governs such situations and protects those buyers, and thus Article 9's drafters thought it unnecessary for the UCC to deal with these transactions.[46]

Under the Food Security Act, a buyer in the ordinary course of business, *see* 7 U.S.C. § 1631(c)(1), of farm products from a farmer takes the farm products free of a security interest created by the farmer unless any of three exceptions applies. 7 U.S.C. § 1631(d), (e).

First, if the secured party has, prior to the sale, notified the buyer in writing of its interest in the farm products, the buyer will take subject to the security interest. 7 U.S.C. § 1631(e)(1). Strict compliance with these rules is necessary for the secured party to maintain its security interest.[47] To facilitate this process, the Act does two things: (i) it provides a system for buyers to register in advance with the state Secretary of State as buyers of farm products; and (ii) it encourages farmers to provide their secured lenders with an accurate list of regular buyers by providing that if a farmer sells farm products to someone not on the list, the farmer will be subject to a civil penalty. 7 U.S.C. § 1631(h)(2), (3).

Second, if the state has set up a central filing system for farm products, the buyer has not registered, and the secured party has filed in that system a notice of its security interest in the farm products, the buyer will take subject to the security interest. 7 U.S.C. § 1631(e)(2).[48]

Third, if the state has set up a central filing system for farm products, the buyer receives notification that indicates the farm products being sold are subject to a central filing, and the buyer does not secure a waiver or release from the secured party, the buyer will take subject to the security interest. 7 U.S.C. § 1631(e)(3).

---

[46] At least one state has omitted this limitation. *See, e.g.*, Cal. Com. Code § 9320(a). At least two others have a non-uniform rule that protects some buyers of farm products. *See, e.g.*, 810 Ill. Comp. Stat 5/9-320; Ind. Code § 26-1-9.1-320.

[47] *See* State Bank of Cherry v. CGB Enters., Inc., 984 N.E.2d 449 (Ill. 2013) (the secured party's failure to identify in the notification the counties in which the farm products were grown or located rendered the notification ineffective even though the notification stated that it covered "farm products wherever located").

[48] *See also* Fin Ag, Inc. v. Hufnagle, Inc., 700 N.W.2d 510 (Minn. Ct. App. 2005), *aff'd*, 720 N.W.2d 579 (Minn. 2006) (buyer of corn took subject to security interest under Food Security Act because it presumptively received notice from the secretary of state of the secured party's interest in the corn and failed to obtain a waiver of that interest).

It is important to understand that the notice that a secured party may file in a state's central filing system – called "an effective financing statement" – is not the same thing as an Article 9 financing statement. The Food Security Act uses some of the same terminology that Article 9 does but contemplates that the statement filed pursuant to the federal law will have different requirements and be filed in a different database system than Article 9 financing statements. *See* 7 U.S.C. § 1631(c)(2), (4). For example, an effective financing statement must identify "each county or parish in which the farm products are produced or located." 7 U.S.C. § 1631(c)(4)(C)(iv).[49] Nineteen states have established a central filing system that the U.S. Department of Agriculture has certified as meeting the requirements of the Food Security Act.[50]

Exception 3: Consumer to consumer sales. This exception, codified in U.C.C. § 9-320(b), is a very limited rule. It applies only when the goods are consumer goods in the hands of the seller and consumer goods in the hands of the buyer. It is therefore euphemistically known as the "garage sale" exception. Under this rule, a consumer buyer takes free of a security interest if the buyer does not have knowledge of the security interest, buys for value, and the secured party has not filed a financing statement.

Because buyers already take free of most unperfected security interests under § 9-317(b), this rule is really relevant only to perfected security interests. Because it protects the buyer only when the secured party has not filed a financing statement, then by implication the rule is relevant to only those situations when the secured party has perfected by some other means. Because complying with a certificate of title law is the equivalent of filing a financing statement, § 9-311(b), the rule does not aid buyers in taking free of a secured party that has noted its interest on a certificate of title. § 9-320 cmt. 5. Because the buyer will almost invariably take

---

[49] *See* In re Moore, 2013 WL 2154383 (Bankr. N.D. Miss. 2013) (bank's financing statement that identified the debtor's farms in two counties was adequate to perfect the bank's security interest in the portion of debtor's sweet potato crop grown in those two counties but not the portion grown in a third; unregistered buyer took free of security interest in potatoes grown in the unlisted county but subject to security interest of potatoes grown in the listed counties).

[50] *See* https://www.gipsa.usda.gov/laws/cleartitle.aspx. The states are Alabama, Colorado, Idaho, Louisiana, Maine, Minnesota, Mississippi, Montana, Nebraska, New Hampshire, New Mexico, North Dakota, Oklahoma, Oregon, South Dakota, Utah, Vermont, West Virginia, and Wyoming.

possession of the goods (and might not even qualify as a "buyer" until it takes possession), the rule has minimal significance to secured parties perfected by possession. As a result of all this, the rule is basically limited to instances when the secured party has perfected automatically. In short, the rule generally has the most effect on creditors with an automatically perfected purchase-money security interest in consumer goods not subject to a certificate of title law. § 9-309(1).

Problem 5-41

Shortly after passing the California bar exam, Delaney went to the local Best Deals store to purchase a wide-screen, high-definition television. Delaney selected a television priced at $2,400 and then applied for and received permission from Best Deals' credit department to purchase the television on credit. The written credit-purchase agreement, which Delaney signed, granted Best Deals a security interest in the television to secure the purchase price. Best Deals did not file a financing statement in connection with the transaction.

Six months later, Delaney was accepted into the FBI Training Academy at Quantico, Virginia. To facilitate the move there, Delaney sold the television to Friend for $1,000.

A. If Delaney fails to pay Best Deals, may Best Deals enforce its security interest in the television?
B. How, if at all, would the analysis of Part A change if one month after the purchase, Best Deals filed a financing statement against Delaney in California (where Delaney lives) listing the collateral as "consumer electronics"?

Problem 5-42

On May 1, Dentist signed a document in which Dentist granted State Bank a security interest in all of Dentist's existing and after-acquired equipment to secure all obligations that Dentist then owed or thereafter owed to State Bank. On May 2, State Bank filed in the appropriate office an effective financing statement against Dentist listing the collateral as "equipment" and the secured party as State Bank. On May 15, State Bank advanced $50,000 to Dentist.

On August 1, Dentist purchased some new office furniture from Comfort Furniture Co. for use in Dentist's office. In the written purchase agreement,

Dentist granted Comfort Furniture a security interest to secure payment of the purchase price. The furniture was delivered on September 1 and on September 15, Comfort Furniture filed a sufficient financing statement against Dentist in the appropriate office listing the collateral as "office furniture" and Comfort Furniture as the secured party.

A. Dentist did not like the furniture and so sold it to one of the hygienists, Employee, for cash. The furniture was delivered to Employee's home on October 15, where Employee uses it for personal use. What is the priority of interests in that furniture? *See* §§ 9-320(a), 9-322(a), 9-324(a).

B. Same facts as in Part A, but on November 1, Employee sold one of the items of furniture, a couch, to Neighbor for $100 cash. What is the priority of interests in the couch? *See* § 9-320(b).

Exception 4: Future advances. In Section 2, Part A(3), we considered whether a lien creditor takes subject to a security interest securing advances made by the secured party after the creation of the judicial lien. Here we consider when and to what extent a buyer of goods is similarly subject to security interests securing future advances made by the secured party.

Logically, this question matters only if the buyer takes the goods subject to the security interest in the first instance under the rules explored above. If the buyer takes the goods free of the security interest under the rules we have explored, the security interest is no longer attached to the goods involved. At that point, it simply makes no sense to inquire what obligations are "secured" by the nonexistent security interest. *See* § 9-323 cmt. 6.

If the buyer does take the goods subject to the security interest, then the question is whether a subsequent advance by the secured party to the debtor after the buyer's purchase is also secured by that security interest, that is, whether it "primes" the buyer's interest in the goods. The answer lies in § 9-323(d) and (e). Unless the secured party makes the advance (or commits to make the advance) within 45 days after the purchase *and* without knowledge of the purchase, the buyer takes the goods free of the security interest securing the future advance.

Problem 5-43

"Flip" the priority rule expressed in § 9-323(d) so that it indicates when a buyer does not take free of a security interest securing future advances. How does this differ from the flipped version of § 9-323(b) that you created in response to Problem 5-6?

Problem 5-44

Secured Party has a properly perfected security interest in Dentist's equipment valued at $50,000 to secure a loan of $25,000 and all obligations then or thereafter owed to Secured Party. Dentist sold the equipment to Buyer.

A. The week after the sale and without knowledge of it, Secured Party loaned the debtor an additional $20,000. To what extent does Secured Party have priority over Buyer?
B. How, if at all, would the analysis of Part A change if Secured Party made the $20,000 loan 60 days after the sale and without knowledge of it?
C. How, if at all, would the analysis of Part A change if Secured Party made the $20,000 loan one week after the sale but with knowledge of it?
D. How, it at all, would the analysis of Part A change if Secured Party made the $20,000 loan 60 days after the sale and with knowledge of it?
E. How do the answers above compare to the answers to Problem 5-6?

Problem 5-45

First Street Café operates an upscale restaurant. For the last several years, Local Bank has had an enforceable security interest in all of First Street's equipment to secure all of First Street's existing and future obligations to Local Bank. That security interest is perfected by a properly filed financing statement, filed on December 1, three years ago. Three months ago, First Street decided to change its decor. It sold its tables and chairs to Second Hand Furniture Store, a dealer in used furniture. Last month, Second Hand sold the tables and chairs to Baker for use in Baker's restaurant. Last week, Local Bank loaned First Street an additional $10,000. Do the tables and chairs sold to Baker secure that new loan? *See* §§ 2-403, 9-320, 9-323(d). *Cf.* PEB Commentary No. 6 (March 10, 1990) (discussing former § 9-301(1), the predecessor to the rules now contained in § 9-317 and § 9-323).

Brief Review. The following problems bring together many of the issues and rules relating to buyers of goods.

Problem 5-46

On May 1, Divine Fixtures, Inc. signed a document in which it granted National Bank a security interest in all of Divine's existing and after-acquired inventory to secure all obligations that Divine then owed or thereafter owed to National Bank. On May 2, National Bank filed an effective financing statement against Divine listing the collateral as "inventory" and itself as the secured party. The financing statement was filed in the Iowa Secretary of State's office. Divine is incorporated in Iowa. On May 15, National Bank advanced $50,000 to Divine. Divine manufactures appliances such as stoves, refrigerators, and microwave ovens.

A. On July 1, Divine sold and delivered a load of microwave ovens that it had manufactured at its plant in Minnesota to a Wisconsin retail outlet operated by Best Deals, Inc. The sale was on credit with payment due in 30 days. Divine retained title to the microwave ovens until the purchase price was paid in full. Best Deals is incorporated in Illinois.
   1. Did Best Deals take the microwave ovens free of National Bank's security interest? *See* § 9-320(a).
   2. On July 5, National Bank advanced an additional $5,000 to Divine. Are the microwave ovens delivered to Best Deals subject to a security interest to secure that advance? *See* §§ 9-320(a), 9-323(d).
   3. Did Best Deals take the microwave ovens free of Divine's security interest?
   4. On July 10, Best Deals sold one of the microwave ovens for $100 to Customer who took the microwave oven home that day. Did Customer take the microwave oven free of National Bank's security interest? Did the customer take the microwave oven free of Divine's security interest?

B. On August 1, Divine entered into a contract with Best Deals to sell it 45 refrigerators. The refrigerators are identified to the contract for sale that day and slated for shipment on the 5th. On August 2, does Best Deals have an interest in the refrigerators that is free of National Bank's security interest? *See* §§ 1-201(b)(9), 2-502, 2-716.

Problem 5-47

On May 1, last year, Deluxe Cabinetry signed a document in which it granted National Bank a security interest in all "goods that Deluxe Cabinetry now owns or hereafter acquires to secure any and all obligations that Deluxe Cabinetry now owes or hereafter owes to National Bank." On May 2, National Bank filed an effective financing statement listing Deluxe as the debtor, the collateral as "goods" and the secured party as National Bank. The financing statement was filed in the Iowa Secretary of State's office. Deluxe Cabinetry is incorporated in Iowa. On May 15, National Bank advanced $50,000 to Deluxe.

On January 2, two years ago, Big Store signed a document in which it granted to State Bank a security interest in Big Store's goods then owned or thereafter acquired to secure any and all obligations then owed or thereafter owed. That same day, State Bank filed an effective financing statement in the correct place to perfect its security interest in the goods.

Deluxe delivered a load of cabinets to Big Store in Wisconsin in exchange for a check for the purchase price. The check was dishonored by Big Store's bank for insufficient funds.

A. Deluxe, National Bank, and State Bank all claim superior interests in the cabinets delivered to Big Store. What is the priority of interests in those cabinets? *See* §§ 1-201(b)(9), 9-315(a), (c), (d), 9-316(a)(3), 9-317(b), 9-320, 9-322(a), 9-325, 9-507(a).

B. How, if at all, would the analysis change if National Bank's financing statement had an incorrect address for Deluxe? *See* § 9-338.

C. How, if at all, would the analysis change if the items sold and delivered to Big Store were several used desks and small appliances that Deluxe had used in its corporate offices?

B. The Secured Party against a Lessee of Goods

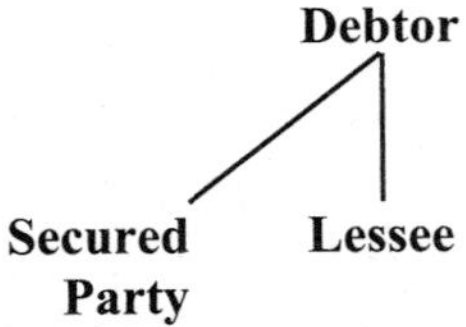

The rules for lessees are closely modeled on those for buyers. If the lessee acquires right to the goods before a security interest in them is perfected, the lessee takes its leasehold interest free of the security interest. *See* § 9-317(c). *Cf.* § 9-317(b) (similarly protecting buyers). This means that, if the debtor/lessor defaults, the secured party may collect the rents from the lessee (such rent is proceeds of the goods), but may not repossess the goods from the lessee. Only if the lessee defaults on its lease obligations – or the lease expires by its own terms – may the debtor or the debtor's secured party recover the goods from the lessee.

If the security interest in the goods is perfected before the lease agreement is entered into, the lessee generally takes subject to the security interest. § 2A-307(2), (3). However, Article 9 protects lessees in ordinary course of business in much the same way that it protects buyers in ordinary course of business. *See* § 9-321(c). It also protects lessees from the same future advances from which it protects buyers. *See* § 9-323(f), (g).

SECTION 6. SECURITY INTERESTS AGAINST THE RIGHTS OF PURCHASERS OF COLLATERAL OTHER THAN GOODS

A. Introduction

Section 5 covered the rights of a transferee of goods – a buyer or lessee – against a security interest created by the transferor. This section deals with the rights of a transferee of assets other than goods. In particular, this section covers accounts (other than controllable accounts), chattel paper, instruments, general intangibles (other than controllable payment intangibles), money, and funds from deposit accounts.[51] For the most part, Article 9 treats each of these types of property differently. This adds greatly to the complexity of Article 9.

Nevertheless, many of these rules are extremely important for two related reasons. First, many of the rules apply not to "buyers," but to "purchasers." As you no doubt remember, a "purchaser" is anyone who receives a voluntary transfer of an interest in property, *see* § 1-201(b)(29), (30), and thus includes a secured party. Consequently, many of these priority rules apply not merely to secured party vs. buyer disputes, but also to secured party vs. secured party disputes. Second, most types of business collateral are routinely converted into one or more of these types of property. For example, inventory is regularly sold to generate accounts, chattel paper, and instruments. Accounts and instruments frequently generate proceeds that find their way into and out of deposit accounts. Consequently, the priority rules discussed in the previous sections of this Chapter are often superseded by the rules discussed here, as the collateral transmutes from one type to another in the ordinary course of the debtor's business, and is then transferred.

If there is any consolation for this complexity, it is that teachers are unlikely to ask you to memorize and master all these rules. It is more important that you know such rules exist, so that you can access them when necessary, and that you

---

[51] Chapter Six discusses the rights of purchasers of documents of title, investment property, controllable accounts, controllable electronic records, and controllable payment intangibles.

understand and are able to follow the same general approach to priority issues that we use throughout Article 9:

(1) Identify and classify the collateral;
(2) Determine which parties' security interests have attached;
(3) For each attached interest, determine whether it was ever perfected;
(4) For each perfected interest, determine whether any later event or circumstance undermined perfection;
(5) As new collateral is created – whether as after-acquired property or proceeds – go back to step one;
(6) Determine who the competing claimant is (*e.g.*, lien creditor, buyer, secured party, or statutory lienor); and then
(7) Isolate and apply the appropriate priority rules, taking PMSI status and future advances into account when necessary.

B. Purchasers of Accounts

We start with the general proposition that Article 9 applies to a sale of accounts, subject to the narrow exceptions in § 9-109(d). *See* § 9-109(a)(3), (d)(4)–(7). Thus, a seller of accounts is a "debtor" and a "secured party" includes not just a lender with a security interest, but also a buyer of accounts. *See* § 9-102(a)(28)(B), (73)(D). In essence, although in form and substance the transaction looks like the left side of the diagram below, if the transaction is governed by Article 9, the transaction is re-characterized as depicted on the right side of the diagram.

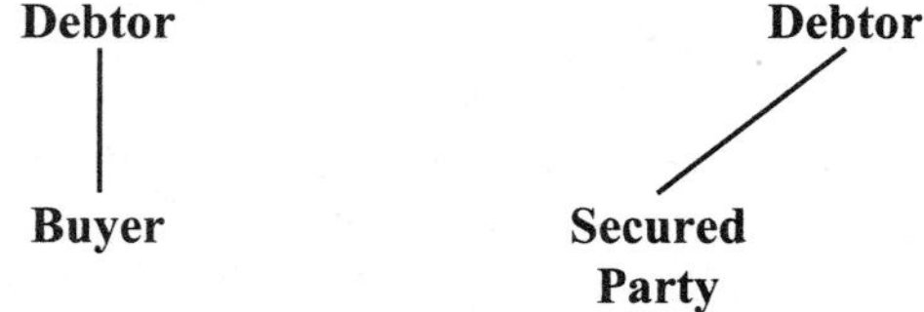

The significance of this can be demonstrated through a relatively simple illustration.

Illustration

Debtor borrows money from Lender and grants Lender a security interest in Debtor's accounts to secure the debt. Thereafter, Debtor sells its accounts to Buyer.

Article 9 applies to both transactions, and treats the resulting priority dispute as one between two secured parties, rather than as one between a secured party and a buyer (*i.e.*, as the right side of the diagram below, rather than the left side).

The parties' priority is then governed not by any special rule, but by the first-to-file-or-perfect rule of § 9-322(a)(1).[52] That generally means that the first to file wins, because there is no way to perfect a security interest in accounts other than by filing, except for a fairly narrow automatic perfection rule. *See* § 9-309(2).[53]

If the transaction with Buyer preceded the transaction with Lender, the result is only marginally different. Normally, we would conclude that following a sale of property, the seller does not have any rights left in the property sold and thus cannot

---

52 If Article 9 does not apply to the sale of accounts, then a buyer of accounts is not a secured party and the priority rule in § 9-317(d) will apply to govern the priority between an unperfected security interest in the accounts (whether created by a sale or not) and the rights of a buyer of accounts that is not a secured party.

As discussed in Chapter Six, the relative priority of multiple security interests in a controllable account is sometimes governed by § 9-326A, which is an exception to the first-to-file-or-perfect rule of § 9-322(a)(1).

53 One of the reasons for Article 9 to bring sales of certain types of receivables into its scope is to facilitate a process called a securitization. In concept, a securitization functions as follows. An obligee is owed receivables in the form of accounts. The obligee sells its interest in its accounts to an entity, usually a trustee of some sort formed specifically to buy the accounts. The trustee/buyer of accounts files a financing statement to perfect its interest in the accounts. Such perfection effectively precludes a subsequent buyer or secured party from obtaining an interest in the accounts sold. § 9-318. The trustee/buyer entity will then sell equity interests in the pool of accounts to investors. The return to the investors is determined by the stream of payments on the accounts made by the persons obligated on the accounts. This financing device not only provides liquidity to an obligee but also helps to insulate the investors from the risk of the obligee's bankruptcy. For an analysis of the legal and economic basis of securitization as a financing device, *see* Steven L. Schwarcz, *The Future of Securitization*, 41 CONN. L. REV. 1313 (2009); Kenneth C. Kettering, *Securitization and its Discontents: The Dynamics of Financial Product Development*, 29 CARDOZO L. REV. 1553 (2008); Thomas E. Plank, *Sense and Sensibility in Securitization: A Prudent Legal Structure and A Fanciful Critique*, 30 CARDOZO L. REV. 617 (2008); Thomas E. Plank, *The Security of Securitization and the Future of Security*, 25 CARDOZO L. REV. 1655 (2004).

grant a security interest in it. *See* §§ 9-203(b)(2), 9-318(a). However, § 9-318(b) creates an exception for sales of accounts if the buyer does not perfect its interest. In such a case, the seller is deemed to have retained sufficient rights for a subsequent security interest to attach. Thus, continuing with our hypothetical, if Debtor sells its accounts to Buyer and then, before Buyer files, Debtor uses the accounts as collateral for a loan from Lender, both Buyer and Lender have rights in the accounts and the first-to-file-or-perfect rule governs priority. If, however, Buyer files before Debtor purports to use the accounts as collateral for a loan from Lender, Debtor has no rights left in the account, Lender's security interest fails to attach, and Buyer is the only entity with an interest in the accounts. In that case, there is therefore no real priority dispute, but the first to file – Buyer – still wins.

Problem 5-48

On August 1, in a sales transaction, Factor purchased from Donnybrook Corp. all of its accounts generated between July 1 and July 30 from sales of inventory. Factor paid approximately 70% of the face value of the accounts but did not file a financing statement. On August 15, Donnybrook borrowed $10,000 from State Bank and signed a document in which it granted a security interest in all of Donnybrook's "presently owned or hereafter acquired accounts" to secure all obligations then owed and thereafter owed to State Bank. That same day State Bank filed in the appropriate office a financing statement identifying itself as the secured party, "Donnybrook Corp." as the debtor, and the collateral as "accounts." Between Factor and State Bank, who has priority in the accounts generated between July 1 and July 30 from sales of Donnybrook's inventory? *See* §§ 9-109(d)(4)–(7), 9-309, 9-318, 9-322(a).

C. Purchasers of Chattel Paper

The rules discussed above for accounts also apply to chattel paper. An outright sale of chattel paper creates a security interest (assuming the transaction is not excluded from Article 9, § 9-109(d)). Thus, the seller of the chattel paper is a "debtor" and the buyer of the chattel paper is a "secured party." And, if the buyer fails to perfect its security interest, the debtor can create subsequent security interests in the chattel paper, either by borrowing against it or selling it to another party. *See* §§ 9-109(a)(3), 9-318. If that happens, the first-to-file-or-perfect rule of

§ 9-322(a) generally[54] determines the relative priority of two competing secured parties with an interest in chattel paper. Thus, consider the following illustration.

Illustration

Debtor leases several items of machinery to Lessee. The leases constitute tangible chattel paper. § 9-102(a)(11), (79). Debtor then grants a security interest in the chattel paper to Bank One to secure a loan. Some time later, Debtor grants a security interest in the same chattel paper to Bank Two, either by using it as collateral for a loan or by selling it outright.

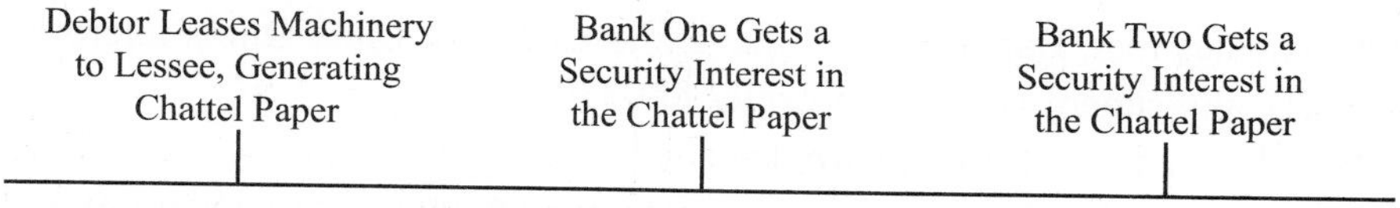

Debtor Leases Machinery to Lessee, Generating Chattel Paper	Bank One Gets a Security Interest in the Chattel Paper	Bank Two Gets a Security Interest in the Chattel Paper

Neither Bank One nor Bank Two takes possession of the chattel paper.

The resulting priority dispute between Bank One and Bank Two is governed by § 9-322(a). If neither party perfected by filing, Bank One would have priority because its interest attached first. § 9-322(a)(3). If one, and only one, of the two banks filed, that filing bank would be perfected and would have priority over the other, unperfected bank under § 9-322(a)(2). Finally, if both banks perfected by filing, priority would go under § 9-322(a)(1) to the first to file.

However, whereas a security interest in accounts can normally be perfected only by filing, a security interest in tangible chattel paper can also be perfected by possession, § 9-313(a), and a security interest in electronic chattel paper can be perfected by control, § 9-314. Moreover, given the nature of chattel paper and the way in which businesses deal with and transfer it, possession (of tangible chattel paper) or control (of electronic chattel paper) is critical. Consequently, possession or control of chattel paper gives the secured party a better priority than filing. Read § 9-330. Notice that it grants priority to a "purchaser" but, as we know, that term

---

[54] If Article 9 does not apply to the sale of chattel paper, then a buyer of chattel paper is not a secured party and the priority rule in § 9-317(b) (if tangible chattel paper) or § 9-317(d) (if electronic chattel paper) will govern the priority between an unperfected security interest in the chattel paper (whether created by a sale or not) and the rights of a buyer of chattel paper that is not a secured party.

includes a secured party. In short, § 9-330 creates yet another exception to the general priority rules of § 9-322.

Returning to the hypothetical used above, if Bank Two took possession of the tangible chattel paper when it acquired its interest in it, Bank Two would have priority over Bank One – even if Bank One had filed first – provided Bank Two gave "new value," *see* § 9-102(a)(57), and took possession of the chattel paper in good faith, in the ordinary course of Bank Two's business, and without knowledge that the purchase violates the rights of Bank One. § 9-330(b).[55] Bank One can prevent this from occurring either by taking possession first or by making sure that the chattel paper itself indicates that it has been assigned to Bank One. If the chattel paper indicates that, Bank Two will have knowledge of Bank One's interest, *see* § 9-330(f), and cannot get priority under § 9-330.[56]

The rules in § 9-330(a), (b) are designed to protect reliance parties. Thus, if Bank Two gave value, but not *new* value, it could not get priority under § 9-330(a) or (b).[57] However, there is an exception to this limitation if Bank Two has a PMSI in the debtor's inventory. Read § 9-330(e). To illustrate how that provision works, consider this additional twist.

> Bank One has a properly perfected security interest in the existing and after-acquired inventory of Debtor to secure all obligations whenever owing to Bank One. Bank One filed its effective financing statement against Debtor covering inventory. Supplier then sold new items of inventory to Debtor and retained a PMSI in the new inventory. Supplier qualified for PMSI priority in the new inventory over the security interest of Bank One. § 9-324(b). One of the items of inventory that is subject to the PMSI is sold to Purchaser, generating tangible chattel paper (Purchaser's promise to pay and grant of a security interest in the item to secure the promise to pay, documented in a

---

[55] The same provision applies if the chattel paper is electronic chattel paper and Bank Two obtains "control," of it under § 9-105, instead of "possession" of it.

[56] Because of § 9-330(f), the substantive difference between § 9-330(a) and (b) is relatively small. *See* PEB Commentary No. 8 (Dec. 10, 1991), as amended to apply to Revised Article 9.

[57] Bank Two's only hope for priority in such a situation would be if Bank One made a mistake in the information required by § 9-516(b)(5) in its filed financing statement and Bank Two reasonably relied on the incorrect information. *See* § 9-338(1). *See also* § 9-338(2) (which will apply only if the transaction in which Bank Two purchased the tangible chattel paper is excluded from the scope of Article 9 by § 9-109(d)).

tangible record). Under § 9-324(b), the PMSI priority as to the inventory item does not extend to the chattel paper absent any further action by Supplier. However, assume that Supplier took possession of the tangible chattel paper in good faith and in the ordinary course of Supplier's business, and the chattel paper did not indicate that it had been assigned to another person. Supplier's rights in the chattel paper are superior to Bank One's security interest in the chattel paper. § 9-330(a), (e).

Problem 5-49

You are in-house counsel to Local Bank, which frequently extends loans to used car dealers to finance their inventory. Before the bank makes such a loan, you always make sure that the bank files a proper financing statement, a UCC search is conducted, and no financing statement other than the bank's is disclosed in the search report. You are confident that the bank will have priority in the dealer's inventory (although a subsequent lender might acquire a PMSI, such a lender would have to notify the bank in advance, § 9-324(b)), but remain concerned that the dealer might sell inventory in exchange for chattel paper and then sell the chattel paper to a buyer that takes possession of the chattel paper and thereby acquired priority in the chattel paper under § 9-330(a) or (b).

A. 1. What language do you put in the financing statement to help protect Local Bank against a loss of priority in chattel paper? *See* § 9-330(a), (b).
   2. Under what circumstances will the language added not protect the bank? *See* § 9-330 cmt. 6.

B. 1. What language do you put in the security agreement to help protect Local Bank against a loss of priority in chattel paper?
   2. Under what circumstances will the language added not protect the bank?

C. What else can you do to protect Local Bank against a loss of priority in chattel paper?

D. Purchasers of Instruments

The priority of security interests in an instrument is much like the priority of security interests in chattel paper, but with three slight differences. First, a purchaser for value – whether a buyer or a secured lender – that takes possession of an instrument gets priority over a previously perfected security interest in it (*i.e.*, one perfected either by filing or automatically) if the purchaser acts in good faith and without knowledge that the purchase violates the rights of the prior secured party. § 9-330(d). Unlike with chattel paper, there is no requirement that the purchaser give "new value" and there is no requirement that the purchaser act in the ordinary course of its own business. The lack of a "new value" requirement is particularly important if the instrument is proceeds of other collateral. Consider the following illustration.

Illustration

Bank One has a security interest in Debtor's existing and after-acquired inventory. That interest is perfected by a properly filed financing statement. Bank Two has a security interest in Debtor's existing and after-acquired accounts, also perfected by a properly filed financing statement. Bank One filed before Bank Two.

Debtor sells some inventory on open account. Bank Two's security interest attaches to the account under its after-acquired property clause and is perfected by the filing. Bank One's security interest also attaches to the account, as proceeds of inventory. § 9-315(a)(2). That security interest is and remains perfected because the place to file against inventory is also the place to file against accounts. § 9-315(c), (d). Although both security interests attached to the account simultaneously, when it was created, Bank One has priority over Bank Two in the account because it filed first. § 9-322(a)(1).

Some time later, the account debtor sends Debtor a check in settlement of the account obligation (or gives Debtor a promissory note to memorialize the payment obligation). Bank Two takes possession of the check (or note). Both secured parties have a security interest in the check (or note) as proceeds of the account. Both security interests are perfected under § 9-315(d)(2) (or under (d)(1) for the note). However, priority is no longer governed by the first-to-file-or-perfect rule of § 9-322(a)(1); it is governed by § 9-330(d). Bank Two wins. If, however, the check (or note) had been marked with notification of Bank One's interest, Bank Two would not be able to use § 9-330(d) to gain priority over Bank One. § 9-330(f).

The second difference for instruments applies if the instrument is negotiable and the purchaser becomes a "holder in due course" as to that instrument. A holder in due course takes free of any security interest in the instrument. §§ 9-331, 3-302,

3-306. What it takes for an instrument to be negotiable, § 3-104, and for a purchaser to qualify as a holder in due course, § 3-302, are issues beyond the scope of these materials. For our purposes, it is enough to understand the basic concept: a transferee of the negotiable instrument who takes possession of the instrument for value, in good faith and without notice of any property claims to the instrument and without notice of any defenses to payment on the instrument, qualifies as a holder in due course. § 3-302. The fact that a filed financing statement purports to cover the instruments is not notice of a defense to payment or a claim to the instrument. § 9-331(c).

The third difference for instruments relates to the fact that Article 9 applies to sales of promissory notes, § 9-109(a)(3), and that a security interest created by the sale of promissory notes is automatically perfected. § 9-309. So, whereas the security interest of a buyer of accounts or chattel paper might or might not be perfected, a buyer of a promissory note will always have a perfected security interest if the sale to the buyer was a transaction covered by Article 9.[58] To the extent the resulting priority dispute between the buyer of a promissory note (who is deemed a secured party if the sale of the promissory note is within the scope of Article 9, §§ 9-102(a)(73), 9-109(a), (d)) and a secured party who is not a buyer is determined by the first-to-file-or-perfect rule of § 9-322(a), the automatic perfection rule might be very relevant. Of course, the automatic perfection rule applicable to sales of promissory notes will not protect the buyer from the operation of the priority rules in § 9-330(d) or § 9-331 which protect purchasers that take possession of tangible chattel paper, control of electronic chattel paper, or possession of an instrument.

Problem 5-50

Dynamo manufactures and sells electric generating equipment. On January 1, Dynamo signed a document in which it granted First Bank a

---

[58] Article 9 does not apply to sales of other types of instruments, such as checks. A buyer of a promissory note might not be a secured party as defined in § 9-102(a)(73) if the sale of the promissory note is a transaction excluded from Article 9 under § 9-109(d). A buyer of instruments that is not an Article 9 secured party might be able to utilize the priority rule of § 9-317(b) to take the instrument free of an unperfected security interest. Similarly, a buyer of an instrument that is not a secured party might be able to utilize the priority rule of § 9-338(2) if the secured party that has filed its financing statement to perfect as to instruments has included in the financing statement § 9-516(b)(5) information that is incorrect.

security interest in all of Dynamo's existing and after-acquired inventory to secure a $500,000 loan. First Bank neglected to file a financing statement. On June 1, Dynamo sold generators to three different purchasers. Purchaser 1 signed a sales agreement in which it promised to pay Dynamo for the generator in full in 30 days. Purchaser 2 signed a promissory note payable to Dynamo for the purchase price. Purchaser 3 signed a sales agreement in which it promised to pay the purchase price to Dynamo and granted Dynamo a security interest in the generator sold to secure the payment. On July 1, Dynamo sold its rights against all three purchasers to Second Bank. Second Bank took possession of the note signed by Purchaser 2 and the sales agreements signed by Purchasers 1 and 3.

A. What is are the relative priorities of First Bank and Second Bank in the note signed by Purchaser 2, and the amounts due from Purchasers 1 and 3? *See* §§ 9-322(a), (b); 9-330, 9-331.

B. How, if at all, would the analysis of Part A change if in January First Bank had filed in the appropriate office a financing statement identifying Dynamo as the debtor and the collateral as inventory?

C. How, if at all, would the analysis of Part B change if, instead of taking possession of the note signed by Purchaser 2 and the sales agreements signed by Purchasers 1 and 3, Second Bank had filed a financing statement against Dynamo in the appropriate office indicating the collateral as accounts, chattel paper, and instruments?

Problem 5-51

Dynamo manufactures and sells electric generating equipment. On January 1, Dynamo signed a document in which it granted First Bank a security interest in all of Dynamo's existing and after-acquired inventory to secure a $50,000 loan. On January 5, First Bank filed an effective financing statement against Dynamo in the appropriate place indicating the collateral as "inventory."

In early March, Dynamo experienced some production problems. On March 15, in order to meet its contractual obligations to three of its regular customers, Dynamo purchased three generators on credit from Industrial Supplier, which retained a security interest in the generators to secure payment of the purchase price. Prior to delivery of the generators to Dynamo, Industrial Supplier filed an effective financing statement against Dynamo in the correct office listing the collateral as "inventory" and First

Bank received from Industrial Supplier sent written notification of its planned transaction with Dynamo.

Dynamo then sold the generators to three different purchasers. Purchaser 1 signed a sales agreement in which it promised to pay Dynamo for the generator in full in 30 days. Purchaser 2 signed a promissory note payable to Dynamo for the purchase price. Purchaser 3 signed a sales agreement in which it promised to pay the purchase price to Dynamo and granted Dynamo a security interest in the generator sold to secure the payment. Industrial Supplier took possession of the note signed by Purchaser 2 and the sales agreements signed by Purchasers 1 and 3.

A. What are the relative priorities of First Bank and Industrial Supplier in the note signed by Purchaser 2 and the documents signed by Purchasers 1 and 3? *See* §§ 9-322(a), 9-324(b), 9-330, 9-331.

B. What, if anything, could the party without priority have done to ensure that it had priority?

C. Now assume that, instead of First Bank having a perfected security interest in inventory, First Bank had a perfected security interest in equipment and that the generators that Dynamo purchased were used by Dynamo for a time in its business. Dynamo then sold the generators to the three Purchasers. How, if at all, does this change in the classification of the collateral affect the analysis of the priority of the interests of First Bank and Industrial Supplier in the rights against the Purchasers?

D. Assume that Third Bank purchased from Dynamo all of the rights against Purchasers and that Third Bank (instead of Industrial Supplier) took possession of the note signed by Purchaser 2 and the documents signed by Purchaser 1 and 3. What are the relative priorities of First Bank, Industrial Supplier, and Third Bank in the rights against the Purchasers?

E. Transferees of Money or of Funds From a Deposit Account

Now consider the rights of a transferee of money. Money, as defined in § 1-201(b)(24), consists of coins and paper currency. It is the most negotiable and freely transferable kind of asset and, not surprisingly, the drafters of Article 9 did not want to do anything to undermine that.

A security interest can attach to money as original collateral in the normal manner, that is, by listing "money" as the collateral in a signed security agreement, giving value, and the debtor having rights in the money. § 9-203. More commonly, it arises when the money is proceeds of other collateral. To perfect a security interest in tangible money as original collateral, a secured party must take possession of the money. § 9-312(b)(3). If the money is proceeds of other collateral, the security interest in it is automatically perfected if the security interest in the original collateral was perfected. § 9-315(c), (d)(2). However, failure to take possession leaves the secured party in a very vulnerable position. A transferee of money – "transferee" is an undefined term but presumably refers to someone who acquires possession – takes the money free of the security interest unless the transferee is somehow acting in collusion with the debtor to violate the rights of the secured party. § 9-332. As one court put it:

> the drafters of Article 9 recognized that it is necessary to balance the interests of the secured creditor against the interests of an innocent transferee[ ] of cash proceeds, and despite valid concerns for the secured creditor, an interest in ensuring the free flow of funds and in ensuring the finality of a completed transaction, trumps the interests of a secured creditor.[59]

A transferee of funds from a deposit account has similar protection. A secured party might acquire a security interest in a deposit account as original collateral. Such a security interest may be perfected only by control of the deposit account. §§ 9-312(b)(1), 9-314, 9-104. However, control of the deposit account need not prevent the debtor from transferring funds from the deposit account. § 9-104(b). More commonly, security interests attach to deposit accounts as proceeds of other collateral. If so, those security interests are generally perfected automatically. § 9-315(c), (d)(2). Even if the security interest in the deposit account is perfected – either by control or automatically as cash proceeds of other collateral in which the secured party had a perfected security interest – a transferee of funds from the deposit account takes the funds free of the security interest as long as the transferee does not act in collusion with the debtor in violating the rights of the secured party. § 9-332(b).

Of course, the protections given to transferees of money and transferees of funds from a deposit account have no bearing on whether any security interest will attach to or be perfected in whatever the transferee provided to the debtor in return for the money or funds. Remember to separate the analysis of the original collateral (the money or funds being transferred to the transferee) from the analysis of proceeds (what the transferee provides in return).

---

59 Keybank v. Ruiz Food Products, Inc., 2005 WL 2218441 (D. Idaho 2005).

Problem 5-52

Downtown Office Supply is in the business of selling office furniture to commercial entities. To finance its operations, Downtown obtained a loan from State Bank of $500,000 and signed a document in which it granted State Bank a security interest in all of its "equipment, inventory, accounts, chattel paper, instruments, general intangibles, documents of title, deposit accounts, and investment property now owned or hereafter acquired to secure all obligations now owed or hereafter owed to State Bank." State Bank filed an authorized and sufficient financing statement against Downtown in the appropriate office listing the collateral as "all assets."

Downtown sold several tables and chairs to Constellation, Inc. for cash. Downtown deposited the cash into its bank account at State Bank and then initiated a wire transfer from its bank account to Merchandise Manufacturer to pay for inventory that Downtown had purchased. Those funds were credited to Merchandise Manufacturer's deposit account. Between State Bank and Merchandise Manufacturer, what is the priority of their interests in those funds? *See* § 9-332(b).

Problem 5-53

Construct a factual scenario in which a transferee of money would not take free of a perfected security interest in the money. In other words, provide an example of when a transferee of money would be acting "in collusion with the debtor to violate the rights of the secured party."

Problem 5-54

Six months ago, to secure a loan, Bank obtained and perfected a security interest in the existing and after-acquired accounts of Delicious Foods, Inc., a store that imports exotic goods from around the world.

A. Advise Bank how to preserve its priority in the accounts – and their proceeds – in the event another creditor subsequently obtains and perfects a security interest in the debtor's accounts. *See* § 9-607 cmt. 5. *See also* §§ 3-302(a), 3-306, 9-327, 9-330(d), 9-331 & 9-332.
B. Delicious Foods is now experiencing cash-flow problems and approached Shifty Finance Co. for emergency financing. Shifty suggests a transaction by which Shifty will buy $100,000 of Delicious Foods' accounts for $75,000. How should Shifty arrange to receive payment so that Shifty

will be most likely to have the right to retain the payments made by the account debtors?

F. Purchasers of General Intangibles

The priority rules applicable most general intangibles – those other than controllable electronic records and controllable payment intangibles[60] – are, thankfully, fairly simple. This is probably attributable to the fact that possession and control are not methods for perfecting an interest in such general intangibles. Article 9 has special priority rules for purchasers of chattel paper and instruments because the drafters wanted to prefer one perfection method over another in order to account for the way such property is customarily transferred. In other words, the drafters did not want Article 9's priority rules to interfere with normal commercial transactions and practices. Such concerns do not exist with respect to most general intangibles. Consequently, the general first-to-file-or-perfect rule of § 9-322(a) controls, unless other law intervenes.

We start the analysis by noting that Article 9 covers most sales of payment intangibles. *See* § 9-109(a)(3), (d)(4)–(7). This means, as discussed before, that a buyer of payment intangibles is deemed a secured party, § 9-102(a)(73), and the first-to-file-or-perfect rule of § 9-322(a) applies to disputes between the buyer and a prior secured party. The one twist is that the security interest of a buyer of payment intangibles is automatically perfected in a sale of a payment tangible that is not excluded from Article 9. § 9-109(d)(4)–(7), 9-309(3). Therefore, the only relevant fact needed to resolve the priority dispute is whether the competing secured party perfected or filed prior to the sale. If, so, the secured party wins. If not, the buyer has priority.[61]

---

[60] The priority rules applicable to controllable electronic records and controllable payment intangibles are discussed in Chapter Six.

[61] However, if the secured party that filed the financing statement had an error in the information required by § 9-516(b)(5) and the buyer of the payment intangible gave value in reasonable reliance on that incorrect information, even though the filed secured party is perfected, the buyer of the payment intangible will prevail. § 9-338(1).

Note, it is not possible for a priority dispute to exist if the first secured party bought the payment intangible in a transaction governed by Article 9. *See* § 9-109(d)(4)–(7). Because of the automatic perfection rule for sales of payment intangibles governed by Article 9, the buyer in such a sale will always have a perfected interest and therefore the debtor (the seller) will not retain any rights in the payment intangible sufficient to allow a later security interest

Now consider the rights of buyers of other types of general intangibles. Recall that a sale of a general intangible that is not a payment intangible is not within the scope of Article 9. § 9-109(a). Similarly, some sales of payment intangible are excluded from Article 9 under § 9-109(d). These transactions – that is, a sale of a general intangible that is not a payment intangible or a sale of a payment intangible excluded from Article 9 – do not create a security interest and the buyer in such a transaction is not a secured party. Thus we again return to the general rule of § 9-201 and § 9-315(a)(1). Absent an express or implied authorization to sell the general intangible free of the security interest, the buyer takes subject to a previously created security interest. The one exception in Article is § 9-317(d). The buyer takes free of the security interest if the buyer purchased the general intangible for value, without knowledge of the security interest, and before it was perfected.

This analysis is preempted by federal law when the general intangible is a federally registered copyright. Specifically, § 205 of the Copyright Act governs the priority of competing "transfer[s] of copyright ownership."[62] For this purpose, a "transfer of copyright ownership" is defined broadly and apparently includes the grant of a security interest.[63] Section § 205(d) accords priority to the first executed transfer, rather than to the first recorded transfer, provided the transfer is recorded in the Copyright Office within one month after execution.[64] If the first transfer is not so recorded within that one-month period, the subsequent transfer has priority if it was: (i) recorded first; and (ii) taken in good faith, for valuable consideration and without notice of the earlier transfer.[65]

This priority rule – which essentially grants a one-month grace period to file – presents a challenge for lenders who wish to ensure that they will have a first-priority security interest in a registered copyright. A search of the Copyright Office might not reveal a recently executed but presently unrecorded transfer, even though

---

to attach. *See* § 9-318.

[62] 17 U.S.C. § 205(d).

[63] *See* 17 U.S.C. § 101.

[64] The grace period to record is two months if the transfer is executed outside the United States.

[65] Section 205 is not a well-drafted rule because it is possible for neither sentence to apply. For example, if: (i) the first transfer is recorded more than one month after it was made and after the second transfer was recorded, but (ii) the purchaser in the second transfer knew of the first transfer, then § 205 would seem not to provide a governing rule.

the transfer, if later recorded, will have priority. Moreover, because the transfer documents are what is recorded, rather than a notice of the transfer, and the Copyright Office requires that document submitted for recording be complete,[66] there is effectively no way for the searcher to pre-file to preserve its own priority.[67]

Whether federal law preempts Article 9's priority rules with respect to patents and trademarks is less clear. Although the Patent Act contains no express reference to a security interest, § 261 does provide that "an assignment, grant, or conveyance" is void as against any subsequent purchaser or mortgagee for a valuable consideration, without notice, unless the assignment grant or conveyance is recorded in the Patent and Trademark Office (PTO) within three months from its date or before the subsequent purchase or mortgage.[68] If a security interest arises from an "assignment, grant, or conveyance" within the meaning of this provision, then the Act would seem to govern the relative priority of the secured party and a subsequent buyer. If the phrase "purchaser or mortgagee" also includes secured parties, then the Act would seem to govern the relative priorities of multiple security interests in the same patent.

However, in in *In re Cybernetic Services, Inc.*,[69] the Ninth Circuit indicated that a security interest does not arise from an "assignment, grant, or conveyance" within the meaning of § 261. In so doing, the court relied on some very old Supreme Court cases and its analysis is not compelling. As a result, many secured parties record in the PTO to protect themselves against a subsequent purchaser.

There are no known cases dealing with the priority of a security interest in a trademark. The Lanham Act contains language almost identical to the portion the Patent Act discussed above.[70] Thus, the priority of a security interest in a trademark is subject to the same uncertainty as is the priority of a security interest in a patent.

Licensees of general intangibles – such as those who receive a nonexclusive license of a patent or copyright – are treated much like buyers and lessees of goods are. Section 9-321 allows a licensee in ordinary course of business to take free of

---

[66] *See* 37 C.F.R. § 201.4(c)(2).

[67] This problem can be exacerbated by the logistical problems that can arise if the copyright was registered concurrently or only shortly before the time that a transfer document pertaining to the copyright was recorded, in which case the registration number might not be known or available when the transfer document is submitted.

[68] 35 U.S.C. § 261.

[69] 252 F.3d 1039 (9th Cir. 2001).

[70] *See* 15 U.S.C. § 1060(a)(4).

a security interest created by the licensor, even if the security interest is perfected and the licensee knows of its existence. That section defines who qualifies as a licensee in ordinary course of business in a manner similar to how the terms "buyer in ordinary course of business" and "lessee in ordinary course of business" are defined. To illustrate this provision, consider the following hypothetical.

> Licensor granted a security interest in all of its general intangibles to Bank. Bank perfected that security interest. Licensor is in the business of creating and licensing software. Software is a subcategory of "general intangibles." § 9-102(a)(42). Licensor enters into a nonexclusive license for software with Licensee. Licensee qualifies as a licensee in ordinary course of business. § 9-321(a). Licensee's rights under the software license are free of the security interest of Bank. § 9-321(b).[71]

Problem 5-55

Downtown Office Supply is in the business of selling office furniture to commercial entities. To finance its operations, Downtown obtained a loan from State Bank of $500,000 and granted State Bank an effective security interest in all of its "equipment, inventory, accounts, chattel paper, instruments, general intangibles, documents of title, deposit accounts, and investment property now owned or hereafter acquired to secure all obligations now owed or hereafter owed to State Bank." State Bank filed an effective and authorized financing statement against Downtown in the appropriate office listing the collateral as "all assets."

A Downtown licensed 20 copies of some accounting software it owned to Local Retailer in return for Local Retailer's promise to pay a monthly license fee. Does State Bank have a security interest in the accounting software? If so, is that security interest subject to the terms of the

---

[71] If Bank were not perfected and the licensee were not a licensee in ordinary course of business, § 9-317(d) would be available to allow the licensee to take its rights under the license free of the security interest.

If the copyright in the software was registered with the Copyright Office – something few software developers do – then § 205(e) would potentially apply. It allows a nonexclusive license to prevail over any subsequent transfer and over any prior unrecorded transfer of which the licensee was without notice. 17 U.S.C. § 205(e). Nothing in that rule permits a licensee – even a licensee in ordinary course of business – to take free of a previously recorded transfer. Whether this rule preempts § 9-321(b) is unclear.

licenses? *See* §§ 9-317(d), 9-408. Does State Bank have a security interest in the licenses granted to Local Retailer? *See* § 9-315(a)(2).

B. How, if at all, would the analysis change if Downtown were in the business of writing and licensing accounting software? *See* § 9-321(a), (b).

This next problem requires you to deal with the proceeds priority rules as they apply to a variety of types of collateral and proceeds of proceeds. Review § 9-322 and the various special priority rules that we have studied in this Chapter (§§ 9-324, 9-325, 9-327, 9-330, 9-331, 9-332) and then try an analysis of the following fact scenario.

Problem 5-56

On January 1, Drilling Equipment Company signed a document in which it granted a security interest to First Bank in "equipment and inventory now owned or hereafter acquired to secure all obligations now owed or hereafter owed to First Bank." On January 5, First Bank filed an effective financing statement against Drilling in the proper place indicating the collateral as "equipment and inventory." On January 10, First Bank loaned Drilling $50,000.

On February 1, Drilling sold industrial drills for oil rigs to three different purchasers. Purchaser 1 signed a document in which it promised to pay Drilling for the drill in full in 30 days. Purchaser 2 signed an installment promissory note payable to Drilling for the purchase price, with equal monthly payments for one year. Purchaser 3 signed a document in which it promised to pay the purchase price to Drilling and granted a security interest in the drill to Drilling to secure the payment. The drills were delivered to the purchasers the next day.

On February 15, Drilling sold its rights in the documents and the note to Great Finance Company. Great Finance took possession of both the note and the documents and then notified the purchasers to make payments to Great Finance. Each of the purchasers made one payment to Great Finance.

A. Which party, First Bank or Great Finance, has priority in the payments the purchasers made to Great Finance. *See* §§ 9-315(a), (c), (d), 9-322(a), 9-330, 9-331, 9-332.

B. Each of the purchasers decided that the drills did not conform to the promises that Drilling made about the quality of the drills. Drilling agreed and took the drills back. Between First Bank and Great Finance, what is the priority of their interests in the three returned drills? *See* §§ 9-102(a)(64), 9-315(a), (c), (d), 9-330(c).

C. Purchaser 2 was having trouble making the payments to Great Finance on the promissory note and so offered to supply Great Finance with several computer servers in satisfaction of its obligation under the note. Great Finance agreed and took delivery of the computer servers. Does First Bank have a security interest in those computer servers? If so, what is the priority of interests in the servers between Great Finance and First Bank?

D. How, if at all, would the analysis of Parts A through C change if the transaction between Great Finance and Drilling were not a sale of Drilling's rights in the documents and note but a transaction in which Drilling granted a security interest in those rights to Great Finance to secure a loan that Great Finance made to Drilling?

SECTION 7. CONCLUSION

Now that you have worked your way through the bulk of Article 9's provisions and concepts, reconsider the questions posed at the end of Chapter One. How well does Article 9 balance the relative interests of creditors and debtors? Does Article 9 have a unifying theme in balancing the interests of creditors as against each other? If you were appointed to a drafting committee to revise Article 9, would you advocate a wholesale re-conceptualization of the law or would you merely seek to "tweak" various provisions? If the former, how would you re-conceptualize it? If the latter, which provisions would you like to revise and how?

Test Your Knowledge
Exam Seven – Priority

CHAPTER SIX
ISSUES AND PROBLEMS ASSOCIATED WITH SPECIALIZED COLLATERAL AND TRANSACTIONS

This Chapter is designed for those teachers and students who wish to explore how Article 9 applies to some specialized collateral and transactions. Placement of these matters here is not intended to imply that they are unimportant in the world of commercial finance. It merely reflects either the judgment that the matter is not essential for students to understand the basic structure and scheme of Article 9 or the reality that few teachers are likely to have the time or inclination to cover these subjects in an introductory course.

For the most part, each of the sections within this Chapter stands alone. Any one section can be studied without having to devote time to any of the others. Moreover, the material in each of these sections can either be treated as a discreet subject and tackled as a whole – in which case it can serve as a review of the main concepts of scope, attachment, enforcement, perfection, and priority, applied in new setting – or divided into parts and integrated into the portions of Chapters Two through Five to which they most naturally relate.

SECTION 1. SPECIALIZED COLLATERAL

A. Real-Estate-Related Collateral

1. Scope and Attachment

As we learned back in Chapter Two, Article 9 applies to security interests in personal property, not to interests in real property. *See* § 9-109(a), (d)(11). Several types of collateral, however, might start as real property and become personal property, or conversely, start as personal property and then become real property. In addition, some property might be treated as both real property and personal property at the same time.

Real property that becomes personal property. Article 9 deals explicitly with two types of property that start as real property and become personal property: (i) "timber to be cut"; and (ii) "as-extracted collateral." "Timber to be cut" is not specifically defined in Article 9, but is referenced in the definition of goods in

§ 9-102(a)(44), which in turn refers obliquely to the Article 2 section that divides "goods" from real property. § 2-107(2) (timber to be cut under a contract for sale of the timber is treated as goods).[1] "As-extracted collateral" is defined in § 9-102(a)(6) to include oil, gas, and other minerals that the debtor has an interest in before extraction and to which a security interest attaches upon extraction.[2] In an abundance of caution, the drafters expressly excluded from the definition of "goods" oil, gas, and other minerals before extraction. *See* § 9-102(a)(44). Thus, prior to extraction, oil, gas, and other minerals are part of the real property in which they are located and are not goods.

Personal property that becomes real property. There are two paradigm examples of property that starts as personal property and then becomes real property. The first is goods that become incorporated into a structure in connection with a building project. For example, a builder might buy lumber (goods) and then use that lumber to frame a house (real property). At some point the lumber loses its characterization as "goods" and becomes part of the house, and thus real property. This point is recognized in § 9-334(a) (second sentence). Another

---

1 The definition of farm products (a subcategory of goods) in § 9-102(a)(34) expressly excludes "standing timber." It is not entirely clear what the purpose of this statement is. In the parlance of Article 2, "standing timber" is distinguished from "timber to be cut," with the latter constituting goods and the former considered real property. If the drafters of Article 9 intended "standing timber" to refer to something that is not goods, then the express reference to it in § 9-102(a)(34) was unnecessary. It is also arguably misplaced: it would have made more sense to incorporate the exclusionary language in the definition of "goods" in § 9-102(a)(44), which includes timber to be cut. Nevertheless, the reference to standing timber might simply have been drafted out of an abundance of caution, to make it clear that trees growing on a tree farm – prior to becoming timber to be cut – are not to be treated the same as more traditional agricultural crops, such as wheat or corn. Alternatively, the drafters might merely have wanted to make it clear that timber can never be farm products, even if the trees qualified as timber to be cut. If that is what was intended, however, the exclusion should have referred to "timber to be cut" rather than "standing timber." This interpretative problem can be relevant; it affects the classification of collateral that consists of timber to be cut. Under the first interpretation of the exclusionary language, the exclusion refers only to non-goods, and thus timber to be cut – which is goods – can qualify as farm products. Under the second interpretation of the exclusionary language, timber to be cut cannot be a farm product even though it is a good.

2 "As-extracted collateral" also includes accounts stemming from the sale of oil, gas, or minerals at the wellhead. This is an example of one definition using two different classifications: goods (oil, gas or minerals once extracted) and accounts. The discussion here is concerned with the "goods" aspect of the "as-extracted collateral" definition.

example is a manufactured home (which starts as goods) that becomes significantly attached to real property, or through other state law process, is deemed to become part of the real property and loses its "goods" characterization.

Property that is both real and personal. "Fixtures" are goods that retain their characterization as goods even though for some purposes they are treated as real property, often because they have been affixed[3] to real property in a permanent or quasi-permanent manner. *See* §§ 9-102(a)(41) (definition of fixtures); 9-102(a)(44) (definition of goods). This means that fixtures are goods that straddle the line between personal and real property. It also means that fixtures are therefore governed simultaneously by two different legal regimes: a consensual lien in a fixture might arise either under personal property law (through Article 9) or under real property law (through the law of mortgages).[4] *See* § 9-334(b). Accordingly, a creditor may use Article 9 or real property law to create a security interest in fixtures.[5] If the creditor uses Article 9, all of the normal attachment rules studied

---

[3] Do not be misled by this word. Affixing the good to real estate is not essential to the definition of fixtures. Instead, the focus in each state is on how the law treats a good associated with real estate, and whether an interest in that good can be created under that state's real estate law.

[4] As noted in Chapter Two, *see supra* page 149, although Article 9 does not apply to a security interest in a real property lessor's right to rent, *see* § 9-109(d)(11), Article 9 does apply to a security interest in a right to payment arising from the sale of real property. Such a right to payment would likely be an account, unless evidenced by an instrument. *See* § 9-102(a)(2) (defining "account" to include a right to payment for property sold). However, in some jurisdictions, real property law might also apply to a security interest in a seller's right to payment, with the result that perfection might be attainable through recording in the real property records. *See* In re Blanchard, 819 F.3d 981 (7th Cir. 2016) (even though a vendor's interest in a land contract constitutes an account under Article 9, and filing a financing statement might be an effective way to perfect a consensual lien on that interest, because the vendor still has legal title to the real property, recording a mortgage is effective method to perfect the lien). If so, a diligent searcher should examine both the applicable real property records and the applicable UCC records.

[5] The official text of § 9-334(a) states that an Article 9 security interest "may be created in goods that are fixtures or may continue on goods that become fixtures." This language implies that whether the security agreement is entered into before or after the goods become fixtures is irrelevant. Louisiana, however, has a non-uniform version of § 9-334(a) that is substantially narrower. It provides that an Article 9 security interest can be created in *goods that are to become fixtures*, but not in goods *after they become fixtures*, *see* La. Rev. Stat. §§ 10:9-334(a), 10:9-502(a)(4), thus indicating that sequence does matter. To create and

in Chapter Two will govern the attachment of the security interest to the fixtures. Review § 9-203.

When some item of property – other than a fixture – is part of realty, real property law governs attachment of a consensual lien to that item. Thus for oil, gas, or other minerals, the law of real property must be consulted to determine whether or how a lien has or can be attached to those items before extraction.[6] Moreover, such a real property lien *might* survive extraction from the real property. In other words, a lien on real property that encumbers oil and gas before extraction might continue to encumber oil and gas after it is extracted.[7] Creation of a consensual lien on such property after extraction from the real property, however, is governed solely by Article 9.

There is one other real-property-related point to consider. Assume that a landowner has executed a note and mortgage in favor of lender. The lender sells and delivers the note to a third party. That sale of the note will typically be an Article 9 transaction and, if so, the purchaser will have a security interest in the note. *See* §§ 9-109(a)(3), 9-109(d)(4)–(7). Review Chapter Two, Section 8. If Article 9 applies, the special attachment rule in § 9-203(g) – collateral follows the note – also applies. Review Chapter Two, Section 7. Consider what this special attachment rule means. The secured party with a security interest in the note (including both an outright buyer of the note and a creditor who took a consensual security interest in the note to secure an obligation) is also deemed to have a security interest in the mortgage. Comment 9 to § 9-203 goes further and implies that the purchaser would become the mortgagee. Regardless of whether one follows or does not follow that rather expansive comment, Article 9 does not create any new rights in the real property.

---

perfect a security interest in goods that already are fixtures, a creditor must apparently comply with real property law. The statute further provides that "a security interest in goods that become fixtures continues in the fixtures if the security interest was perfected by a fixture filing when the goods become fixtures," La. Rev. Stat. § 10:9-334(a), thereby conditioning continued attachment on perfection, and indeed on perfection through a fixture filing.

6 The same might be true for standing timber. *But cf.* § 9-501 cmt. 3 ("Unlike as-extracted collateral, standing timber may be goods before it is cut."). It is also worth noting that by giving a secured party with a perfected security interest in crops priority over the rights of an encumbrancer of the real property, § 9-334(i) seems to imply that a security interest in crops might arise under real property law.

7 *See* Fullop v. Salem Nat'l Bank, 6 F.3d 442 (7th Cir. 1993) (decided prior to adoption of revised Article 9).

2. Enforcement

To enforce its security interest in fixtures, as-extracted collateral, or timber to be cut, a secured party may use the processes in Part 6 of Article 9, which we studied in Chapter Three. Alternatively, if the security for the obligation also includes real property, the secured party may use real property law to enforce its interest in both the personal property collateral and the real property. § 9-601, § 9-604(a), (b).

If the collateral is fixtures and the secured party has taken its interest in the fixtures under Article 9, the secured party may enforce its security interest in the fixtures by removing them from the real property and disposing of or retaining them only if the secured party has priority in those fixtures over all persons that assert an interest in the fixtures pursuant to real property law. § 9-604(c).[8] The secured party is liable to the real property claimants for any physical damage to the real property that results from removing the fixture, but is not liable for any diminution in value of the real property attributable to removal of the fixture itself. § 9-604(d).[9]

---

[8] Technically, the statute is phrased as granting permission to remove the fixtures if the security interest has priority. The negative inference is that, if the security interest does not have priority, then the secured party is not permitted remove the fixtures, but this is merely an inference. Moreover, it is an inference that is somewhat at odds with the general authority to repossess granted in § 9-609. However, this inference is undoubtedly what the drafters intended.

[9] Several respected commentators have asserted that a secured party with priority over a mortgagee in fixtures would be entitled to share in the proceeds of the mortgagee's foreclosure on the real property. *See* 4 JAMES J. WHITE & ROBERT S. SUMMERS, UNIFORM COMMERCIAL CODE § 33-5.c (6th ed. 2010); 2 BARKLEY CLARK & BARBARA CLARK, THE LAW OF SECURED TRANSACTIONS UNDER THE UNIFORM COMMERCIAL CODE ¶ 9.03[5] (3d ed. 2012). This conclusion is questionable, however. Section 9-604(b)(2) was undoubtedly intended to overrule cases such as Maplewood Bank & Trust v. Sears, Roebuck & Co., 625 A.2d 537 (N.J. Super. Ct. 1993), *aff'd*, 638 A.2d 140 (N.J. 1994), which held that the secured party's only remedy under former Article 9 was to remove the fixtures and sell them separately. *See* § 9-604 cmt. 3. But that does not mean that the secured party is entitled to share in the proceeds of a mortgagee's foreclosure. The right to share in the proceeds of the mortgagee's foreclosure is governed by real estate foreclosure law. If the secured party's security interest in the fixtures has priority, its lien might survive the mortgagee's foreclosure but it will not likely be entitled to any of the proceeds. Both of these questions (survival of the security interest and right to proceeds of sale) are governed by real estate law. *Cf.* §§ 9-615(a), 9-617(a) (both inapplicable to mortgage foreclosures but likely similar to the law that does apply).

These two special rules regarding enforcement against fixtures do not apply to "timber to be cut" or "as-extracted collateral." Indeed, nothing in Article 9 deals with enforcement of a security interest in such collateral as against a real property claimant who had an interest in standing timber, before it became subject to a sales contract and thus became "timber to be cut," or who had an interest in oil, gas or other minerals before extraction. Perhaps that is because a real property claimant will not have an interest in "timber to be cut" or "as-extracted collateral" because those items constitute personal property, not real property. In other words, perhaps execution of a sales contract regarding timber or the extraction of the oil, gas, or other minerals – and the concomitant transmutation of the property concerned into goods – will cause the real property claimant's interest to evaporate. However, Article 9 is silent on this point and the issue of whether a lien on real property encumbers timber to be cut and as-extracted collateral might be a matter of real property law.[10]

If the secured party's collateral is a note secured by a mortgage on real property, the secured party may seek to enforce the mortgage when its debtor defaults. Section 9-607(a)(3) expressly gives the secured party the right to enforce the mortgage, and that should be all the secured party needs if it wishes to foreclose the mortgage judicially. If local real property law permits nonjudicial foreclosure of the mortgage and the secured party wishes to proceed in that manner, the secured party might have a problem. Generally, as a matter of real property law, the mortgagee is the only person authorized to foreclose a mortgage nonjudicially. However, Article 9 provides that if the secured party is collecting on the right to payment secured by the mortgage, the secured party may record in the appropriate real property office a copy of the security agreement and a sworn affidavit that a default has occurred under that agreement and that the secured party is entitled to enforce the mortgage under the state law nonjudicial process for foreclosing mortgages. § 9-607(b). If the secured party uses this process, it should be able to enforce the mortgage nonjudicially. Of course, a prudent secured party will routinely obtain an assignment of the mortgage at the same time it obtains a security interest in the note the mortgage secures. *See* § 9-607, cmt. 8.[11] That assignment

---

[10] Query whether a mortgage that creates a lien on the real property could be interpreted to operate as a security agreement concerning timber to be cut and as-extracted collateral. *See* § 9-502(c).

[11] Because mortgage loans are often transferred through complex securitization transactions, it is common for an agent to be named as the nominal mortgagee. Then, if the note and

is not necessary in order to attach the secured party's rights to the mortgage but rather is a step that will smooth the way for enforcement of the mortgage, in the event that becomes necessary.

3. Perfection

"Perfecting" a consensual lien in oil, gas, or other minerals before extraction or in standing timber is governed by applicable real property law.[12] A security interest in as-extracted collateral or timber to be cut is generally perfected by the filing of a financing statement. The financing statement must be filed in the real property recording office where the real property is located. §§ 9-301(3)(B), (4), 9-501(a)(1)(A). That financing statement must also comply with the general requirements of § 9-502(a) for sufficiency to perfect as well as the more specialized requirements in § 9-502(b) and (c).[13]

Problem 6-1

Deep Down Mining, LLC ("DDM"), a Delaware entity, owns gold and silver mines in Idaho, Montana, and South Dakota. After it mines gold and silver on its property, it smelts the metals on site, turning them into ingots. DDM wants to borrow funds to expand operations and has approached Silver State Bank for a $25 million loan, to be secured by DDM's inventory of gold and silver.

---

mortgage are sold, and the agent continues to function in that capacity, no assignment of the mortgage should be necessary, although there has been significant litigation on this issue since the collapse of the residential housing market in 2007.

12 The word "perfecting" is placed in quotations in this sentence because the term might not apply outside Article 9.

13 It is unclear when, if ever, the debtor's use of as-extracted collateral can cause it to cease qualifying as as-extracted collateral. For example, if oil taken from a well is as-extracted collateral, a security interest in the oil is perfected by filing in the location of the wellhead, *see* § 9-301(4), and the debtor refines the oil into gasoline, will the gasoline also constitute as-extracted collateral? If not, will the gasoline be: (i) proceeds of the oil, with perfection governed by § 9-315(c), (d); (ii) a product or mass resulting from commingling, with perfection governed by § 9-336(d); or (iii) neither, with perfection now governed by the general rules of Article 9 as enacted in the jurisdiction where the debtor is located? There are no simple answers to these questions.

A. If Silver State Bank makes the loan and obtains a security interest in all gold and silver ore that DDM has or thereafter acquires, in what office or offices must the bank file to perfect its security interest?
B. How, if at all, would the analysis of Part A change if the bank instead acquires a security interest in all of DDM's existing and after-acquired ingots of gold or silver?
C. In both Parts A and B, in what office or offices should the bank search for prior perfected interests?

Because fixtures are "goods," a security interest in them may be perfected in all the ways normally available for perfecting an interest in goods: by the filing of an effective financing statement covering the goods (either centrally, in the jurisdiction where the debtor is located, or as a fixture filing where the goods are located); by taking possession of the goods; or even automatically if they are consumer goods encumbered by a purchase-money security interest. *See* §§ 9-309(1), 9-310, 9-313. In rare circumstances, perfection might require notation on a certificate of title, such as if a mobile home covered by a certificate of title is attached to real property.[14] *See* § 9-311(a)(2). Regardless of how perfection can be achieved under Article 9, a consensual lien on fixtures can also be created and perfected under real property law. *See* § 9-334(b). Note, perfection pursuant to Article 9 is permissible only if the fixture constitutes personal property (*i.e.*, goods). If a fixture, such as a mobile home, has become real property and not goods, then compliance with real property law would be the only way to obtain a consensual lien on the fixture. Article 9 does not control the determination of whether a good qualifies as a fixture or whether a good attached to real property has ceased to be a good and become real property.

If the secured party wants to have the best chance of having priority for its security interest in fixtures over an interest in the fixtures arising under real property law (such as a mortgage or the rights of an owner of the real property), the secured party must file a fixture financing statement, commonly referred to as a "fixture filing." A fixture filing must meet the same requirements for sufficiency to perfect as a non-fixture financing statement, § 9-502(a), as well as some additional requirements related to the fact that the fixture filing will be filed and

---

[14] *See* In re Renaud, 308 B.R. 347 (8th Cir. BAP 2004). Moreover, perfection obtained through compliance with a certificate-of-title statute before the home is affixed to real property might continue afterwards. *See* Ark Real Estate Servs., Inc. v. 21st Mortg. Corp., 2020 WL 4342722 (Fla. Ct. App. 2020); In re Riffe, 2018 WL 3788973 (Bankr. S.D.W. Va. 2018).

indexed in the real property recording office for the county where the real property is located. *See* §§ 9-301(3)(A), 9-501(a)(1)(B). Read § 9-502(b) and (c). Note, however, that while a fixture filing is a permissible method to perfect and is desirable as a way of obtaining priority, it is not the only way to perfect a security interest in fixtures. A secured party may perfect its security interest in the fixtures by filing an effective financing statement against the debtor in the central filing office in the jurisdiction where the debtor is located because, after all, fixtures are goods. §§ 9-301, 9-501 & cmt. 4.[15]

Problem 6-2

Deneb, Inc. is a Delaware corporation that owns and operates equipment for generating and transmitting electricity. The equipment constitutes fixtures and is located in several counties across Arkansas, Kentucky, and Tennessee. Bank, which is making a large loan to Deneb secured by the fixtures, will be making fixture filings in each of those three states. Why, if at all, should Bank also file a financing statement against Deneb in Delaware? *See* § 9-315(d).

States that have enacted Alternative A to § 9-503, the "only if" approach to the individual debtor's name issue (see discussion in Chapter Four, Section 2), also adopted § 9-502(c)(3)(B), to allow for an individual debtor's name on a mortgage filed as a financing statement to be sufficient if it is the debtor's individual name or the debtor's surname and first personal name, even if those names are not the names listed on the individual's driver's license.

4. Priority

The Article 9 priority rules we studied in Chapter Five govern the priority of two or more competing security interests in fixtures, timber to be cut, and as-extracted collateral if each of those interests was created under Article 9, that is, the personal property system. This is true even if one security interest is perfected by a central filing where the debtor is located and the other is perfected by a fixture filing.

---

[15] If the debtor is a transmitting utility, the place to file a fixture filing is the central filing office of the state where the fixture is located, rather than the real property recording office in that state. *See* §§ 9-301(3)(A), 9-501(b). This facilitates filing against transmitting utilities, which often own fixtures in many counties.

Similarly, the Article 9 rules applicable to purchasers of collateral determine whether a purchaser takes free of an Article 9 security interest in fixtures, timber to be cut, and as-extracted collateral.

Article 9 does not have a priority rule that mediates between an interest created in timber while it was real property and another created later under Article 9 after it became timber to be cut (under a contract for sale). Nor does it have a rule that determines the relative priority of an interest taken under real property law in oil, gas or minerals that were part of the real property in which they were contained and an interest taken in such property under Article 9 after it came out of the ground (as-extracted collateral). Presumably either some priority rule from real property law or a common-law, first-in-time priority rule would apply to such disputes.

Article 9 does have a rule that mediates between an Article 9 security interest in fixtures and an interest in fixtures arising under real property law. Read § 9-334. The baseline rule is that the security interest in the fixture is subordinate to the conflicting interest of a real property claimant (other than the debtor). § 9-334(c). However, that general rule is subject to several exceptions.

The most important exception is if the security interest is perfected by an effective "fixture filing" in the real property records before the interest of the real property claimant is recorded there. *See* § 9-334(e)(1). This is nothing more than an ordinary first-to-file rule. It also gives the secured party an incentive to make a fixture filing, even though only a centralized filing is necessary to perfect its security interest.

The second-most important exception concerns fixtures that are the subject of a purchase-money security interest. If the PMSI arises before the goods become fixtures and the secured party records a fixture filing before or within 20 days after the goods become fixtures, the secured party's PMSI has priority over a real property claimant. § 9-334(d). This rule is limited somewhat if the mortgage is a construction mortgage. *See* § 9-334(h). *See also* § 9-334(a) & cmt. 3 (indicating that ordinary construction materials might lose their status as goods upon incorporation into a structure or foundation).

The remaining exceptions are probably of lesser importance. First, any Article 9 security interest in the goods that was properly perfected before the goods became fixtures – regardless of whether the secured party recorded a fixture filing – has priority over a real property claimant's interest if the goods are among the specific types listed in § 9-334(e)(2). Second, an interest arising under real property law is subordinated if it was obtained by legal or equitable proceedings (such as a judgment lien on real property or an execution lien) after the Article 9 security interest was perfected by any method permitted under Article 9. § 9-334(e)(3). Third, a PMSI in a manufactured home will have priority over a real property claimant if the home was not inventory of the debtor and the security interest is perfected by notation on the certificate of title for the home. § 9-334(e)(4). Finally, priority goes to an Article 9 secured party if the real property claimant has consented to the security interest in the fixture or disclaimed its interest in the fixture or the debtor has a right to remove the fixture as against the real property claimant. § 9-334(f). In this last circumstance, it does not matter whether the security interest in the fixture is perfected.

Test your understanding of the rules by trying the following problems.

Problem 6-3

In January, Distributor Corp. purchased a warehouse in Cerro Guerdo County, Iowa. Distributor financed the purchase with a loan from Local Bank and secured the loan by granting Local Bank a mortgage on the warehouse. Local Bank recorded the mortgage in the Cerro Guerdo County real property records in January. Under Iowa real property law, a mortgage is an encumbrance on fixtures located on the encumbered real property. On May 1, Distributor signed a document in which it granted a security interest in "all goods now owned or hereafter acquired to secure all obligations now owed or hereafter owed to National Bank." That same day, National Bank filed a financing statement against Distributor Corp. in the secretary of state's office in Minnesota, the state in which Distributor was incorporated, listing National Bank as the secured party and the collateral as "equipment, inventory, and fixtures." On May 3, National Bank loaned Distributor $100,000.

A. What is the priority of interests in any items in the warehouse that are fixtures under Iowa law? *See* § 9-334(c)–(e).

B. In July, Renovator and Distributor entered into a written agreement in which Renovator agreed to provide and install shelving in the warehouse, Distributor promised to pay for the shelving and its installation within six months, and Distributor granted Renovator a security interest in the shelving to secure the purchase price and the installation costs. Prior to installation, Renovator filed a financing statement against Distributor Corp. in the Minnesota secretary of state's office, listing Renovator as the secured party and the collateral as "shelving." Upon installation, the shelving became a fixture under Iowa law. What is the priority of interests in the installed shelving? *See* § 9-324(a). *Cf. Yeadon Fabric Domes, Inc. v. Maine Sports Complex, LLC*, 901 A.2d 200 (Me. 2006).

C. How, if at all, does the analysis of Part B change if, prior to installation, Renovator filed a financing statement against Distributor Corp. in the real property records of Cerro Guerdo County, listing Renovator as the secured party, the collateral as "shelving," describing the real property parcel on which the warehouse is located, and indicating that it covered fixtures and was to be filed in the real property records?

D. How, it at all, does the analysis of Part C change if the shelves were delivered on July 5, Distributor installed the shelving on July 10, and Renovator filed the financing statement in the real property records on July 28?

E. How, if at all, would the analysis of Part C change if the following facts were true? Renovator sold the shelving to Distributor for use in a remodeling project for the warehouse. The entire remodeling project was funded by a loan from State Bank that was secured by a second mortgage entered into by Distributor. State Bank recorded the mortgage in the Cerro Guerdo real property records prior to Renovator's filing of its financing statement in those real property records. *See* § 9-334(h).

F. How, if at all, would the analysis of Part B change if, after Renovator filed its financing statement against Distributor, Lois Carlson recorded a judgment against Distributor in Cerro Guerdo County? Under Iowa law, that recording creates a judgment lien on the debtor's real property in that county, including fixtures. *See* §§ 9-317(a)(2), 9-334(e)(3).

G. Same facts as Part B. In October, Distributor removed the shelving and sold it to Purchaser in return for a check for the purchase price. Who has an interest in the shelving? That is, does Purchaser take the shelving free of any or all of the security interests or other liens? *See* §§ 9-317, 9-320. Who has an interest in the check and what are their relative priorities? *See* §§ 9-315, 9-322, 9-324.

Problem 6-4

Duplex Industries, Inc. is a Pennsylvania corporation with its chief executive office in Virginia. Three years ago, Bank One acquired an enforceable security interest in Duplex's existing and after-acquired inventory and equipment to secure a sizeable loan. At that time, Bank One perfected its security interest by filing a financing statement in Pennsylvania.

In February of this year, Duplex borrowed from Bank Two to purchase a new furnace for its office in Virginia and granted Bank Two a security interest in the furnace. The furnace was installed in February. Bank Two perfected its security interest by making a fixture filing in the appropriate office in Virginia in May. In July, Duplex granted Bank Three a mortgage on its real property in Virginia to secure a new loan. Under Virginia real property law, the mortgage is an encumbrance on fixtures located on the encumbered real property. Bank Three recorded the mortgage in July. What are the relative priorities of the banks' security interests in the furnace? *See Sturtz Machinery, Inc. v. Dove's Industries, Inc.*, 2014 WL 1383403 (N.D. Ohio 2014).

Problem 6-5

Landlord owns an apartment building. First Fleet has a properly recorded mortgage on the apartment building. Under real property law, the mortgage covers fixtures on the real property, including fixtures installed after the mortgage was granted. Tenant, living in an apartment in the building, decides to replace the dishwasher in the apartment. Tenant buys the new dishwasher on credit from Seller and grants Seller an enforceable security interest in the dishwasher to secure the purchase price. Seller does not file a financing statement covering the dishwasher. The dishwasher is installed in the apartment. Under real property law, the dishwasher is considered a fixture.

A. What is the priority of interests in the dishwasher? *See* § 9-334(d), (e)(2).
B. What result if Landlord purchased the new dishwasher from Seller and Seller filed a proper financing statement in the central UCC filing office where the Landlord was located before delivering the dishwasher?

Problem 6-6

Several years ago, Ma and Pa Kettle purchased a mobile home and affixed it to realty that they owned. Recently, they obtained a home improvement loan from Back Road Bank and granted the bank an enforceable security interest in the mobile home to secure that loan. What must the bank do to perfect its security interest? *See In re Hoggard*, 330 B.R. 595 (Bankr. W.D. Mich. 2005); *In re Renaud*, 308 B.R. 347 (8th Cir. BAP 2004); UMVCTA §§ 1, 2.

B. Commingled Goods

1. Scope and Attachment

Review Chapter Two, Section 3.D, in which we considered attachment of a security interest to commingled goods. As you might recall, commingled goods are those that are physically united in such a way that their separate identity is lost in a product or mass. § 9-336(a). Because commingled goods are goods, a security interest in them is within the scope of Article 9, *see* § 9-109, and the basic rules in § 9-203 on attachment govern, subject to the two special rules in § 9-336. Pursuant to those special rules, once goods are commingled, a security interest cannot be created in the separate goods that have become commingled and any existing security interest in those separate goods disappears. § 9-336(b). However, a security interest attached to goods before commingling automatically attaches to the resulting product or mass. § 9-336(c). Of course, a debtor can also can grant a security interest directly in the product or mass that results from the commingling. A security interest that a debtor does grant in the product or mass is not governed by § 9-336(c), but by the normal attachment rules in § 9-203.

2. Enforcement

The rules in Part 6 of Article 9 apply to a secured party's efforts to enforce its security interest in the product or mass resulting from a commingling of goods.

3. Perfection

The basic rules on perfection of a security interest in goods studied in Chapter Four apply to the product or mass resulting from the commingling of goods. The main exception is that if a security interest in commingled goods is attached and perfected prior to commingling, the resulting security interest in the product or mass is also perfected. § 9-336(d).

4. Priority

The rules on priority of security interests in commingled goods include a partial exception to the first-to-file-or-perfect rule of § 9-322(a). If two or more secured parties have perfected security interests in goods that are later commingled, § 9-336(f) provides that the secured parties share priority in proportion to the value of their respective commingled goods. Beware, though, this rule does not apply to any secured party who claims a security interest in the product or mass other than by virtue of commingling (*e.g.*, one whose security agreement describes the collateral as whatever the product or mass is), nor does it apply to multiple secured parties who each had a security interest in the same goods prior to commingling. In both of those situations, the normal priority rules of § 9-322(a) and § 9-324 apply. Consider the following illustration.

Illustration

SP-1 has a security interest in wheat produced by Debtor at Farm 1. SP-2 has a security interest in wheat produced by Debtor at Farm 2. SP-3 has a security interest in all of Debtor's farm products then owned or thereafter acquired. Each creditor has properly perfected its security interest by filing a financing statement. Thereafter, Debtor commingles the goods by mixing the wheat from Farm 1 and Farm 2 in a central storage bin.

SP-1's attached and perfected security interest in the wheat from Farm 1 attaches to the entire mass of mixed wheat in the storage bin and is perfected. SP-2's security interest in the wheat from Farm 2 is similarly now a perfected security interest in the entire mass of wheat in the bin. SP-3's security interest attached to the wheat from Farm 1 and Farm 2 – and to the intermixed wheat – but not because of the rule of § 9-336(c), but because of the broader manner in which its security agreement described the collateral.

The relative priority of the security interests of SP-1 and SP-2 in the commingled wheat from both farms is determined by § 9-336(f). They are equal in rank, but share in proportion to the relative value of the wheat from each farm. The priority of both SP-1 and SP-2 against SP-3 in the entire mass of wheat in the bin is determined by the Article 9 rules other than § 9-336.

Problem 6-7

On April 1, Delicious Mills signed a document in which it granted Bank One a security interest in its existing and after-acquired inventory to secure a $6,000 loan. That same day, Bank One filed in the appropriate office a financing statement identifying Delicious Mills as the debtor and indicating the collateral as "inventory." On May 1, Delicious Mills, a maker of breakfast cereals, signed a document in which it granted a security interest in all its existing and after-acquired corn to secure a $20,000 loan from Bank Two. That same day, Bank Two filed in the appropriate office a financing statement identifying Delicious Mills as the debtor and indicating the collateral as "corn." On June 1, Delicious Mills signed a document in which it granted a security interest to Bank Three in all its existing and after-acquired rice to secure a $40,000 loan. That same day Bank Three filed in the appropriate office a proper financing statement identifying Delicious Mills as the debtor and indicating the collateral as "rice." Delicious Mills processed some of its rice and corn into a cereal for sale to consumers. The cereal is worth $30,000 and contains approximately $4,000 worth of corn and $2,000 worth of rice.

A. Which party or parties have a security interest in the cereal? If more than one security interest exists, what are their relative priorities?
B. How, if at all, would the analysis of Part A change if Bank Three's security interest in the rice were a PMSI?
C. How, if at all, would the analysis change if Bank Two had filed its financing statement in March?

Section 9-336 does not say anything about priority in the proceeds of commingled goods. Presumably, therefore, such priority is generally governed by the first-to-file-or-perfect rule of § 9-322(a)(1) or the other special priority rules that we studied in Chapter Five. Query if this makes sense.

C. Accessions

1. Scope and Attachment

As we learned in Chapter Two, Section 3.D, accessions are goods that are physically united in such a way that their separate identity is not lost. § 9-102(a)(1). The attachment rules applicable to accessions – and to the goods with which they are united – are the same as the normal rules for attachment. A secured party who has a security interest in a good that becomes an accession when united with some other good does not lose its security interest merely because the goods have become an accession. § 9-335(a).[16] However, the secured party does not necessarily acquire

[16] The security agreement could, of course, alter this rule by providing that the security interest de-attaches from goods that become an accession. For example, a lender financing an airline's inventory of spare parts might be willing to allow its security interest in any

a security interest in the other good. The language of the security agreement will determine whether the security interest extends to that other good or to the "whole." *See* § 9-335, cmts. 3, 5.

2. Enforcement

The rules in Part 6 of Article 9 apply to a secured party's efforts to enforce its security interest in accessions, subject to one qualification similar to the limitation on enforcement of a security interest in a fixture. Read § 9-335(e) and (f). Just as with a fixture, in order to remove an accession from the whole, the secured party seeking to do so must have priority in the accession over all persons that have an interest in the whole.[17] If the secured party is entitled to remove the accession and conduct a disposition or acceptance pursuant to the rules in Part 6 of Article 9, the secured party must compensate the parties (other than the debtor) with an interest in the whole for any physical harm to the whole, but not the diminution in value, resulting from the accession's removal.

3. Perfection

The basic rules on perfection of a security interest in goods studied in Chapter Four apply to accessions. If a secured party has perfected its security interest in a good prior to it becoming an accession to another good, the security interest remains perfected in the accession after the accession is affixed to the other good. § 9-335(b). Whether the security interest is perfected in the other good to which the accession is attached or to the whole depends on whether the security interest attached to the other good or to the whole and whether the secured party has taken the necessary perfection step as to the other good or to the whole. Just as there is no automatic attachment rule that extends the security interest to the other good or

---

particular part to expire once the part is installed in an aircraft.

[17] The secured party's lack of permission to sever an accession if the secured party does not have priority in the whole is merely a negative inference from the limited permission granted by § 9-335(e), but it is undoubtedly what the drafters meant. *See supra* note 8. *See also* In re Brady, 508 B.R. 736 (Bankr. E.D. Wash. 2014) (because a tire seller's security interest in tires sold was subordinate to another lender's perfected security interest in the debtor's car, the tire seller did not have a right to repossess the tires).

the whole, there is no automatic perfection of a security interest in the other good or the whole.

4. Priority

The priority of security interests in an accession and in the whole are determined by the normal priority rules of § 9-322(a) and § 9-324 (PMSI) except in one situation. *See* § 9-335(c). To illustrate the basic rules and the exception consider the following example.

> SP-E took a PMSI security interest in an engine and perfected that security interest within 20 days of delivery of the engine to the debtor by filing a financing statement covering the "engine and machines in which it is installed." The engine is installed in a bulldozer in which SP-B has a security interest perfected by filing.

After the engine is installed in the bulldozer, SP-E retains its perfected security interest in the engine. *See* § 9-335(b). Whether SP-E's security interest attaches to the bulldozer is fundamentally one of contract interpretation and depends on the description of the collateral in the security agreement between SP-E and the debtor. Assuming the collateral description in SP-E's security agreement was the same as the indication of collateral in the financing statement (quoted above), SP-E would have a security interest in the engine and in the bulldozer into which the engine was installed. Even though the purchase-money obligation (the purchase price of the engine) would now be secured by non-purchase-money collateral (the bulldozer), SP-E would still have a PMSI in the engine. *See* § 9-103(f).

Similarly, whether SP-B's security interest in the bulldozer extends to the new engine is a matter of interpretation of the security agreement between SP-B and the debtor. If SP-B has a security interest in the engine, whether that security interest is perfected depends on whether SP-B had taken an appropriate perfection step as to the engine. If SP-B's security agreement described the collateral as the "bulldozer and all goods installed in or on the bulldozer," and the financing statement indicated the collateral in the same manner, there should be no question that SP-B has a perfected security interest in the new engine.

How would the resulting priority conflict between SP-E and SP-B be resolved as to both the engine and the bulldozer? Section 9-335(c) tells us that, as long as the goods are not subject to a certificate of title statute, priority is determined by the rules we have already studied. Thus as to the engine itself, § 9-324(a) would give priority to SP-E's security interest (recall that SP-E perfected before expiration of the applicable 20-day period). As to the bulldozer, the priority conflict would be resolved by the first-to-file-or-perfect rule of § 9-322(a), which would leave SP-B's security interest with priority assuming that it filed first as to the bulldozer.

Now for the exception. Read § 9-335(d). If the whole is covered by a certificate of title, the security interest in the accession is subordinated to any security interest in the whole perfected under the certificate of title system. So let us change the hypothetical above in one respect. The bulldozer is covered by a certificate of title statute and SP-B perfected its security interest in the bulldozer and all accessions to the bulldozer through compliance with that system. The PMSI of SP-E, the engine seller, in the engine would be subordinate to the security interest of SP-B in the bulldozer and engine. § 9-335(d).[18]

Just as with commingled goods, Article 9 does not address the question of priority in proceeds of accessions. Presumably, therefore, such priority is generally governed by the first-to-file-or-perfect rule of § 9-322(a)(1) or the other priority rules that we studied in Chapter Five.

Problem 6-8

A. Designer granted an enforceable and properly perfected security interest to National Bank in all of its existing and after-acquired equipment. Thereafter, Designer bought from Seller new graphics cards for the computers in Designer's offices and granted an enforceable security interest in the graphics cards to Seller to secure the obligation to pay the purchase price. Seller filed an effective financing statement against Designer in the appropriate office indicating the collateral as "graphics cards" 10 days after Seller delivered the graphics cards to Designer.
   1. Between National Bank and Seller, which security interest has priority in the computers? In the graphics cards?
   2. How, if at all, would the analysis change if Seller described the collateral in both the security agreement and the financing statement as "computer equipment"?

B. National Bank properly perfected a security interest in Designer's delivery truck by obtaining notation of its security interest on the truck's certificate of title. The description of collateral in the written security

---

[18] Indeed, SP-E's security interest in the bulldozer would be unperfected unless SP-E has complied with the certificate of title law.

agreement stated all "motor vehicles now owned or hereafter acquired." Designer purchased four new tires on credit from Tires, Inc., which retained title to the new tires until the purchase price was paid in full. Tires, Inc. filed an effective financing statement indicating the collateral as "tires" against Designer the correct place five days after it installed the tires on the truck. Between Tires, Inc. and National Bank, who has priority in the truck? In the tires?

Problem 6-9

Designer makes expensive custom jewelry for the super rich, and is well known for using a proprietary alloy of two-thirds platinum and one-third gold, which Designer calls "elysium." Buyer commissioned Designer to make and sell a large emerald-elysium necklace. To make the necklace, Designer purchased on credit: (i) fifty carats of emeralds from Emerald Supplier for $30,000; (ii) five troy ounces of gold from Gold Supplier for $12,000; and (iii) ten troy ounces of platinum from Platinum Supplier for $8,000. Each supplier retained a security interest in the goods it sold to Designer to secure payment of the purchase price. Each supplier perfected its security interest by filing a financing statement indicating the collateral as the goods sold; Emerald Supplier filed first, then Gold Supplier, then Platinum Supplier. Designer then made the necklace using the goods acquired from the three suppliers.

A. Prior to Designer's sale of the necklace to Buyer, in what property does each supplier have a security interest and what are the priorities of the suppliers' security interests? *See* §§ 9-322(a), 9-335(c), 9-336(f).
B. How, if at all, would the analysis of Part A change if Emerald Supplier's security agreement covered all existing and after-acquired inventory? *See* §§ 9-324(b), 9-336(e) & cmt.7.
C. Same facts as in Part A except that Designer sold the necklace for $300,000 to Buyer on open account. To what extend does each supplier have a security interest in that account and what are the priorities of those security interests?

D. Documents of Title

As we learned in Chapter Two when discussing classification of collateral, a document of title is a specialized commercial record that describes goods, is issued by or to a bailee that has or purports to have possession of the described goods, and is accepted as evidence that the person that has possession or control of the document of title has the right to possession of the goods covered by the document. The document of title must be in a "record" and might be either in a tangible medium or an electronic medium. Review the definition in § 1-201(b)(16). UCC Article 7 provides rules that govern documents of title and the relationship between the bailee and the bailor.

While a full study of Article 7 is beyond the scope of these materials, some understanding of the basic concept of bailment is important. Typically a bailee is an entity that is engaged in either the commercial storage of goods or the commercial shipment of goods. Entities engaged in storage are called warehouses and entities engaged in shipment are referred to as carriers. A warehouse might issue a type of document of title called a warehouse receipt. § 1-201(b)(42). A carrier might issue a type of document of title called a bill of lading. § 1-201(b)(6). While there are other documents of title, these are the main types and the ones discussed in this section.

As we saw in Chapter Four, documents of title might be either negotiable or nonnegotiable. This designation has to do with the form of the document of title. A negotiable document of title is one that, "by its terms," provides that the goods "are to be delivered to bearer or to the order of a named person." § 7-104(a). Thus a negotiable document of title will state the goods are to be "delivered to bearer" or will state that the goods are to be "delivered to the order of [a named person]." Without those "magic words," the document of title is nonnegotiable.

Also, as we learned in Chapter Four, the basic consequence of having a negotiable document of title is that a holder that takes the document by due negotiation will be deemed to have not only title to the document but title to the goods covered by the document. §§ 7-501, 7-502. A person that has a nonnegotiable document of title is not deemed to have title to the goods; rather, the document of title functions more as a receipt for the goods. A person that has possession of a tangible, nonnegotiable document of title or control of an electronic, nonnegotiable document of title merely has the rights its transferor had in the goods. § 7-504.

The bailee of the goods has an obligation to deliver the goods to the person that has the document of title and might be liable for failure to do so. § 7-403. The bailee has the obligation to take reasonable care of goods in its possession.

§§ 7-204, 7-309. Finally, Article 7 does not require a bailee to issue a document of title covering the goods, but if the bailee does so, Article 7 will govern the rights arising out of that document of title.

One last point. Carriers and some types of warehouses are subject to extensive federal regulation. Thus, in an actual case concerning a bailee and rights arising out of a document of title, one must always check to see if the rules we will discuss are altered in any way due to federal preemption.

1. Scope and Attachment

As already noted in Chapter Two, a document of title (whether negotiable or nonnegotiable, tangible or electronic) is a type of personal property and thus Article 9 governs the ability of a creditor to take a security interest in the document of title. § 9-109. All of the rules regarding attachment of the security interest that we studied in Chapter Two therefore apply to documents of title with one huge caveat. That caveat concerns whether a security interest in the document of title carries with it a security interest in the goods the document covers. Nothing in the text of Article 9 expressly covers this. However, subsections (c) and (d) of § 9-312 discuss how to *perfect* an interest in the goods by perfecting an interest in the document, and thus implicitly refer to *attachment* as well. *See also* § 9-312 cmt. 7.

The rules can be summarized as follows. For goods covered by a *negotiable* document of title, there are three main rules: (i) a security interest in the goods that predates issuance of the negotiable document remains attached; (ii) a security interest that attaches to the negotiable document gives the secured party a security interest in the goods covered by the document; and (iii) a security interest in the goods directly can still be created after issuance of the negotiable document, but remains very vulnerable. For goods covered by a *nonnegotiable* document of title, the rules are similar but not identical: (i) a security interest in the goods that predates issuance of the nonnegotiable document remains attached; (ii) a security interest that attaches to the nonnegotiable document might not give the secured party a security interest in the goods covered by the document (Article 9 is very unclear on this point), but issuance of the document in the name of the secured party does; and (iii) a security interest in the goods can be created after issuance of the nonnegotiable document using the normal rules applicable to attachment of security interests in goods.

Finally as to goods covered by a document or title, whether negotiable or nonnegotiable, if a creditor acquires a security interest in the document of title only, then even if that results in attachment of the security interest in the goods covered by the document, the security interest in the goods will be lost as to any goods released from the bailee's possession and which thereby are no longer covered by the document of title. Thus, regardless of the type of document of title, a secured party should make sure that the security agreement describes the collateral as "goods" in addition to describing any documents of title covering the goods.

2. Enforcement

The basic enforcement rules in Part 6 of Article 9 apply to documents of title with the caveat that what actually has value are the goods covered by the document of title. Consequently, § 9-601(a)(2) provides that when the collateral is documents of title, the secured party may proceed either against the documents or the goods covered by the documents.[19]

3. Perfection

In Chapter Four, we learned that a secured party may perfect its security interest in documents of title (of all types, electronic, tangible, negotiable, or nonnegotiable) by filing a financing statement covering the document. We also learned that the secured party may perfect its security interest in the covered goods by filing a financing statement as to the goods. The secured party may also perfect its security interest in tangible negotiable documents of title by possession, § 9-313(a), in electronic documents of title by control, § 9-314, and in some circumstances, will have a temporary period of perfection, § 9-312(e), (f).

We also learned that if the document of title is negotiable, the secured party should perfect its interest in the goods by perfecting its interest in the negotiable

---

[19] This authorization ignores the practical issue of to whom the bailee must or may deliver the goods. Consider a situation in which a business in the United States is buying goods from a seller in Asia. The seller ships the goods via a carrier that issues a bill of lading for the goods. While the goods are in transit, a creditor of the buyer acquires a security interest in the bill of lading. If the bill of lading is nonnegotiable, the carrier is permitted to follow the instructions of the consignor (*i.e.*, the seller) even over the objection of the named consignee (*i.e.*, the buyer / debtor). §§ 7-303(a)(2), 7-403(a)(5). Consequently, the goods might be redirected to the seller in Asia, making it difficult or impossible for the buyer or its secured party to reach the goods.

document of title.[20] § 9-312(c). If the document of title is nonnegotiable, the secured party should perfect its interest in the goods by complying with § 9-312(d), which means filing as to the goods, giving notification to the bailee of the secured party's security interest, or having the document issued in the secured party's name. The bailee acknowledgment rule stated in § 9-313(c) only applies if there is no document of title issued by a bailee that covers goods that are in the possession of a bailee.

Note that if the secured party has a security interest in a document of title perfected by possession or control, the secured party has the obligation to deal with the collateral in accordance with § 9-207. A former secured party that maintains control over a document of title in which that person no longer has a security interest has an obligation to relinquish control. § 9-208(b)(6).

4. Priority

A purchaser (which, as you no doubt remember, includes a secured party, § 1-201(b)(29), (30)) of a document of title obtains rights to the goods covered by a document of title because of the purchase of the document of title. The strength of the purchaser's rights to the goods depends on whether the document of title is negotiable or nonnegotiable.

a. Nonnegotiable Documents of Title

The rights of a transferee of a nonnegotiable document of title are covered in § 7-504. The basic rule is that the transferee obtains the rights of the transferor, a derivative rights rule. Thus if the transferor has granted a security interest in the goods covered by the nonnegotiable document of title, the transferee will take the nonnegotiable document of title and the goods subject to that security interest, absent explicit or implicit authorization to transfer the goods or the nonnegotiable document of title free of the security interest, § 9-315(a)(1), or application of one of the "take free" rules applicable to buyers of goods. §§ 9-317(b), (d); 9-320.

---

[20] In addition, the secured party should probably also take a perfection step directly as to the goods to avoid losing perfection if the goods should become uncovered by the negotiable document of title, even if the secured party's security interest remains attached to the goods by virtue of the secured party's obtaining a security agreement describing the collateral as goods.

While a secured party may perfect its security interest in the nonnegotiable document of title itself (such as by filing a financing statement covering the nonnegotiable document of title, § 9-310), because the nonnegotiable document of title does not represent title to the goods, the secured party's perfection of a security interest in a nonnegotiable document of title does not effect a perfection of a security interest in the goods. § 9-312 cmt. 7. To perfect its security interest in goods covered by the nonnegotiable document of title, the secured party must comply with § 9-312(d).

If the secured party has not perfected its security interest in the goods covered by the nonnegotiable document of title, the transferee might be able to obtain the nonnegotiable document of title and the goods covered by that document free of the security interest under § 9-317(b) and (d). To take the goods covered by the nonnegotiable document free of the unperfected security interest in the goods, the transferee of the goods must give value and take delivery of the goods while the security interest in the goods is unperfected and without knowledge of the security interest.

b. Negotiable Documents of Title

If the document of title is negotiable, a purchaser of the document of title that takes the document through a "due negotiation" obtains title to the document and the goods covered by the document. § 7-502. A "due negotiation" is a negotiation of the document to a purchaser that purchases in good faith, for value, without notice of any claim or defense to the document and in the ordinary course of business or financing. § 7-501(a)(5), (b)(3). A negotiation of a tangible negotiable document of title where the goods are deliverable to bearer is through delivery of the document of title to another person. § 7-501(a)(2). Delivery is a voluntary transfer of possession of a tangible document of title. § 1-201(b)(15). If the tangible negotiable document of title states that the goods are deliverable "to the order of" a named person, negotiation requires the indorsement of that named person on the document and delivery of the document to another person. § 7-501(a)(1). An electronic negotiable document of title is negotiated by voluntary transfer of control of the document to another person. §§ 7-501(b)(1), 1-201(b)(15), 7-106.

Remember that a secured party perfects its security interest in goods covered by a negotiable document of title by perfecting its security interest in the negotiable document of title. § 9-312(c). Such perfection can be achieved by filing a financing statement covering the negotiable document of title, by taking possession of a tangible negotiable document of title, or by taking control of an electronic negotiable document of title. § 9-312(a), 9-313(a), 9-314(a). In limited circumstances, the secured party may enjoy temporary, automatic perfection of its security interest in a negotiable document of title. § 9-312(e), (f).

If the security interest in a negotiable document of title is unperfected, a buyer of that document will take free of the security interest in the document and, by implication, free of the security interest in the goods covered by the document, if the conditions of § 9-317(b) or (d) are fulfilled. If the security interest in a negotiable document of title is perfected, then a purchaser of the document will take free of the security interest only if the document is "duly negotiated" to the purchaser. § 9-331(a). If the security interest in a negotiable document of title is perfected and the document is not duly negotiated to the purchaser, then the purchaser will take the document and the goods covered by that document subject to the perfected security interest. §§ 9-315(a)(1), 7-504.

The purchaser of a negotiable document of title has one last chance to take the goods free of the perfected security interest: if the secured party's financing statement contains an incorrect address for the debtor and the purchaser reasonably relies on that incorrect information. *See* §§ 9-338(2), 9-516(b)(5).

One last wrinkle. Assume the debtor has granted a security interest in goods to a secured party and that secured party has duly perfected its security interest by filing an effective financing statement covering the goods. The debtor then stores the goods with a bailee and the bailee issues a negotiable document of title covering the goods. The debtor then duly negotiates that negotiable document of title to a purchaser. Between the purchaser's rights to the goods and the secured party's perfected security interest in the goods, which should have priority? In answering this, it is important to first note that neither storage of the goods nor issuance of the negotiable document of title "unperfects" the previously attached and perfected security interest in the goods. Second, the rights of a purchaser that has taken the negotiable document of title by due negotiation are subject to the rule stated in § 7-503, which addresses this hypothetical. § 7-502. Resolution of the priority dispute between the secured party and the purchaser of the document of title turns on a factual question: whether the secured party "entrusted" the goods to the debtor with the authority to store or sell them or with power to do so under other law, or whether the secured party "acquiesced" in the debtor's procurement of the document of title. If the secured party did so, then the purchaser's rights will be paramount. If the secured party did not do so, then the secured party's rights will be paramount. Unfortunately, the cases are in disarray regarding what conduct of the secured party counts as "entrustment" or "acquiescence."

Problem 6-10

Downtown Office Supply Inc. is in the business of selling office furniture to commercial entities. To finance its operations, Downtown obtained a loan from State Bank of $500,000 and signed a document in which it granted State Bank a security interest in all of its "equipment, inventory, accounts, chattel paper, instruments, general intangibles, documents of title, deposit accounts, and investment property now owned or hereafter acquired to secure all obligations now owed or hereafter owed to State Bank." At that time, Downtown had stored inventory with Storage Monster, Inc., which had issued a negotiable warehouse receipt covering the goods. State Bank filed an authorized and effective financing statement against Downtown in the appropriate office listing the collateral as "all assets."

Downtown transferred possession of the warehouse receipt to Great Finance Co. to secure a loan from Great Finance. Great Finance took possession of the warehouse receipt.

A. Between State Bank and Great Finance, whose interest has priority in the goods stored with Storage Monster?
B. How, if at all, would the analysis change if the warehouse receipt were nonnegotiable?
C. How, if at all, would the analysis change if Great Finance did not take possession of the negotiable warehouse receipt but Downtown signed an agreement granting a security interest to Great Finance in "documents of title" and Great Finance filed an effective financing statement against Downtown in the appropriate office indicating the collateral as "documents of title"?
D. How, if at all, would the analysis change if State Bank had a security interest in the inventory before it was stored with Storage Monster and before Storage Monster's issuance of the negotiable warehouse receipt?

E. Investment Property

1. Scope and Attachment

As we learned in Chapter Two when we discussed collateral classification, investment property is a big category that contains several subcategories. Review Chapter 2, Section 3.B and the definitions of the various types of investment property. §§ 9-102(a)(14), (15), (49), 8-102(a)(4), (15), (16), (17), 8-501(a). Also reread the prefatory note to UCC Article 8. Investment property is an important type of collateral because it can be very valuable and highly liquid. Security interests in investment property are covered by Article 9.

To consider the rights of parties in investment property, one must separate the analysis into four different types of investment property:

(1) Securities, whether certificated or uncertificated;
(2) Securities entitlements;
(3) Commodities contracts; and
(4) Commodity accounts.

Securities are stocks, bonds, and other similar property for which the owner's interest is noted on the issuer's books. § 8-102(a)(15). Securities entitlements are, in contrast, securities held indirectly, through a securities intermediary, such as a broker. That is, they are the rights of a broker's customer to securities owned by the broker and credited to the customer's account on the broker's books. §§ 8-102, 8-501. Commodities contracts and commodity accounts are defined somewhat analogously in § 9-102(a)(15) and (a)(14), respectively. A commodity contract is a futures or option contract to buy or sell a commodity. A commodity account is the right of a customer of a commodity intermediary to the commodity contracts credited to the customer's account.

To illustrate these mechanisms for holding rights in securities, consider the following example.

> Corporation issued 10,000 shares of stock. Assume for each 100 shares of stock, Corporation A issued a written certificate that represented the shares. That is an example of a certificated security.[21] Now assume that instead of issuing certificates, Corporation A simply

---

[21] There is no such thing as an electronic certificated security. If a certificate is issued only in electronic form, such as a pdf file, the security is not a certificated security and the certificate is not a security certificate. *See* § 8-102 cmts. 16 & 18.

registers the names of the holder of each share on its books. This is an example of an uncertificated security. Assume further that Broker A is the registered holder of 1,000 shares of Corporation stock, in either certificated or uncertificated form. Broker A in turn sells a $^{4}/_{10}$ position in those shares to Customer 1, sells a $^{6}/_{10}$ position in those shares to Broker B, and notes those interests in Broker A's books. Broker B, in its books, credits those shares to Customer 2. The parties' relationships can be diagramed as follows:

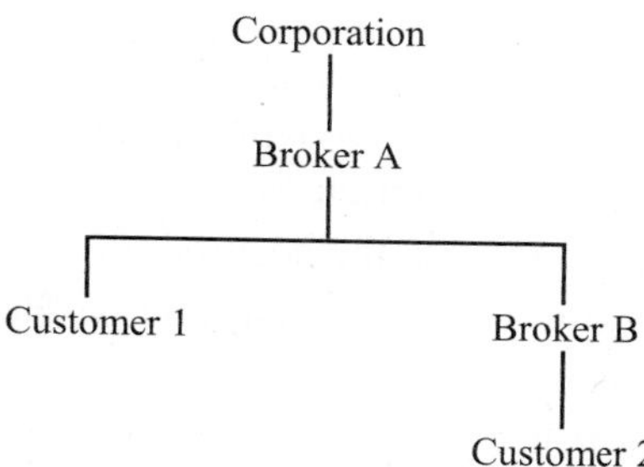

Broker A is a "securities intermediary" that owns a security. § 8-102(a)(14). Customer 1 and Customer 2 are "entitlement holders," each of which owns a "securities account" and a "security entitlement." §§ 8-102(a)(7), (17), 8-501. Broker B is both an entitlement holder and a securities intermediary.

The usual rules in § 9-203 for attaching a security interest apply to investment property. However, in a consumer transaction, the security agreement must describe with greater specificity the debtor's securities entitlements, securities accounts, or commodity accounts. § 9-108(e)(2). As an alternative to obtaining a signed security agreement with a collateral description, the secured party may possess a certificated security or take control of investment property with the debtor's oral agreement that the certificated security or investment property is security for an obligation. §§ 9-203(b)(3)(C), (D), 9-313(a), 9-314, 8-106. Also, as you might recall, there are some automatic attachment rules for investment property: a security interest in a securities account automatically encumbers the security entitlements credited to the account; and a security interest in a commodities account automatically covers the commodity contracts in the account. § 9-203(h), (i).

Several additional types of automatic attachment are described in § 9-206. If a securities intermediary sells a financial asset, § 8-102(a)(9) (which includes investment property), to a customer for credit to the customer's securities account, the securities intermediary has an attached security interest in that financial asset to secure the customer's obligation to pay the price. § 9-206(a), (b). If a certificated security or a financial asset that is represented by a writing is sold and delivered in the ordinary course of business to a person in the business of dealing with those types of assets and the purchase price is not paid, the person to whom the certificated security or financial asset is delivered has a security interest in the item to secure the obligation to pay the purchase price. § 9-206(c), (d).

2. Enforcement

The enforcement of a security interest in investment property is governed by the rules we studied in Chapter Three. Article 9 does not provide the debtor or obligor with any special rights or impose on the secured party any special duties merely because the collateral constitutes investment property. However, because the sales of certain types of investment property are regulated by a variety of state or federal legislation, a secured party needs to be sure that its disposition of investment property complies with those rules.

3. Perfection

As we learned in Chapter Four, security interests in investment property may be perfected by filing a financing statement or by control. §§ 9-310, 9-314. Review Chapter Four, Section 2 (perfection by filing a financing statement) and Section 3.C (perfection by control).

With respect to perfection by filing, the normal rules governing the content of financing statements apply with one small caveat. If the transaction is a consumer transaction and the collateral is a security entitlement, a securities account, or a commodity account, describing the collateral as "investment property" or "security entitlements" is insufficient. *See* § 9-108(e)(2).[22] However, a financing statement indicating the collateral as "all assets" or "all personal property" is, apparently, sufficient in such a transaction. *See* § 9-504(2).

To perfect a security interest in investment property by control requires a determination of what type of investment property is involved. §§ 9-314, 9-106, 8-106.

---

[22] As discussed in Chapter Two, describing the collateral in reference to the holding in a specific brokerage account is adequate. *See* § 9-108 cmt. 5.

Control of a certificated security. Control of a certificated security depends upon whether it is in bearer or registered form. A certificated security in bearer form is one in which the security is payable to bearer. § 8-102(a)(2). A certificated security in registered form is one in which a named person is entitled to rights under the security. § 8-102(a)(13).

Control of a certificated security in bearer form requires that the secured party take delivery of the certificate. § 8-106(a). Delivery of the certificate requires either that the secured party take possession of the certificate or that a third person other than a securities intermediary acknowledge that it holds the certificate on behalf of the secured party. § 8-301(a). This also qualifies as perfection by possession. *See* § 9-313(a).

Control of a certificated security in registered form may be accomplished by a number of different methods. One method is that the secured party have possession of the certificate and that the certificate be either: (i) indorsed in blank or to the secured party; or (ii) re-registered in the name of the secured party. §§ 8-106(b), 8-301(a). Another method is that the certificate be in the possession of a third party, other than a securities intermediary, who has acknowledged the secured party's security interest in the certificate and the certificate is either: (i) indorsed in blank or to the secured party; or (ii) re-registered in the name of the secured party. §§ 8-106(b), 8-301(a). Finally, if a certificate in registered form is in the possession of the securities intermediary and registered in the name of the secured party, indorsed to the secured party, or payable in the name of the secured party, and not indorsed in blank or to the securities intermediary, the secured party also has control. §§ 8-106(b), 8-301(a). Generally, compliance with § 8-301(a) in taking delivery of the certificated security effects perfection of a security interest by possession. § 9-313(a).

Control of an uncertificated security. A secured party has control of an uncertificated security if the secured party becomes the registered owner of the security or another person, other than a securities intermediary, becomes the registered owner and acknowledges that it holds the uncertificated security on behalf of the secured party. §§ 8-106(c), 8-301(b). A secured party might also have control of an uncertificated security if the issuer of the security agrees that it will comply with the instructions of the secured party regarding the security without further consent of the debtor. § 8-106(c).

Control of a securities entitlement. A secured party has control of a security entitlement if it becomes the entitlement holder, that is, a person noted on the records of the securities intermediary as entitled to give orders concerning the security entitlement. §§ 8-106(d)(1), 8-102(a)(7). A secured party might also have control of a security entitlement if the securities intermediary agrees that it will comply with the secured party's instructions concerning the entitlement without further consent of the entitlement holder. § 8-106(d)(2). Finally, a secured party might have control of a security entitlement when a person with control of the security entitlement other than the debtor (as described above) acknowledges that it holds the entitlement on behalf of the secured party. § 8-106(d)(3).

If the secured party is the securities intermediary holding the securities entitlement, the securities intermediary automatically has control of the securities entitlement. § 8-106(e). Note how this is similar to one of the rules applicable to deposit accounts: if the person with a security interest in a deposit account is the depositary bank, the depositary bank is deemed to have control. § 9-104(a)(1).

If a secured party has control over all securities entitlements in a securities account, the secured party is deemed to have control of the securities account.[23] § 9-106(c). This rule helps bridge the gap between the terminology applicable to attachment and the terminology applicable to control. For example, a creditor seeking to obtain a security interest in investment property may include "securities accounts" in the collateral description of the security agreement. In contrast, control is typically obtained in the securities entitlements in the securities account. By virtue of the rule of § 9-106(c), the security interest in the securities account is perfected by control over all the securities entitlements held in that account.

Commodity contracts. The rules on control of commodity contracts parallel the rules on control of securities entitlements. § 9-106(b). *Compare* §§ 9-203(h), (i), 9-308(f), (g).

Automatic perfection. In limited circumstances, a security interest in certain types of investment property might be automatically perfected. Review Chapter 4, Section 3.D.3, discussing § 9-312(e), (f), (g) as they apply to instruments and documents of title. Notice that subsections (e) and (g) – but not subsection (f) – also apply to certificated securities (whether in registered or bearer form).

In addition, as we saw in Chapter 4, Section 3.D.2, perfection in one type of collateral might serve to perfect a security interest in another type of collateral. Similarly, § 9-308(f) and (g) provide that perfection of a security interest in a

---

23 Similarly, control of all commodity contracts in a commodity account is deemed control of the commodities account.

securities account automatically perfects a security interest in securities entitlements held in that account and perfection of a security interest in a commodity account automatically perfects a security interest in the commodity contracts carried in that account. *Compare* § 9-203(h) and (i) (automatic attachment).

Finally there are automatic perfection rules stated in § 9-309(9), (10) and (11). Subsection (9) deals with automatic perfection of a security interest created under § 9-206(c). The other two provisions govern when the securities intermediary or the commodity intermediary are debtors giving security interests in the investment property they hold to a secured party. The secured party's security interest in that investment property is automatically perfected. Read § 9-309 cmt. 6.

Choice of law. In Chapter Four, Section 4 we considered Article 9's choice-of-law rules for perfecting security interests. As you no doubt remember, for most security interests, the law of the jurisdiction in which the debtor is located governs perfection. *See* § 9-301(1). This is also the rule for a security interest in investment property perfected by filing a financing statement. § 9-305(c)(1). However, different rules apply for security interests in investment property perfected in other ways. These rules are designed to help ensure the free flow of assets in commercial markets by making the law of the jurisdiction of the issuer or financial intermediary govern, thereby restricting the number of states' laws such parties have to be concerned about. The following chart summarizes the choice-of-law rules for perfecting a security interest by a non-filing method.

Type of Investment Property	Method of Perfection	Governing Law Perfection
Certificated Security	Control, possession, or automatically under § 9-312(e) or (g).	Jurisdiction where the certificate is located. § 9-305(a)(1).
Uncertificated Security	Control	Issuer's jurisdiction. § 9-305(a)(2).
Securities Entitlement or Securities Account	Control	Securities intermediary's jurisdiction. § 9-305(a)(3).
Commodity Contract or Commodity Account	Control	Commodity intermediary's jurisdiction. § 9-305(a)(4).

Type of Investment Property	Method of Perfection	Governing Law Perfection
Any	Automatic perfection under § 9-309(10), (11).	Debtor's location. § 9-305(c).

The jurisdiction of an issuer or a securities intermediary is determined under § 8-110. A commodity intermediary's jurisdiction is determined under § 9-305(b).

One note of caution is in order. For transactions in intermediated securities that involve a choice between the laws of different nations, the UCC's choice-of-law rules are augmented and partially preempted by the Hague Convention on The Law Applicable to Certain Rights in Respect of Securities Held with an Intermediary. The Hague Convention's rules can be triggered if, among other things, any of the parties to a securities account, the issuer of any of the securities credited to the account, or an adverse claimant to the securities is located in a different nation. They can also be triggered if the terms of the account agreement select as governing law the law of a nation other than the U.S. Consequently, a cautious lawyer must always proceed on the assumption that the Convention might apply, if not at the inception of a planned transaction, at least sometime thereafter.

For the most part, the Convention's rules are designed to work well with Article 9 and to point to the same state's or nation's law as Article 9 does. However, in some situations and for some transactions, the Convention might point to a different state's or nation's law. When it does, the Convention supersedes Article 9's choice-of-law rules pursuant to the Supremacy Clause in the U.S. Constitution. Although further discussion of the Convention is beyond the scope of this book, lawyers seeking to perfect a security interest in investment property should familiarize themselves with it.[24]

Once a secured party perfects a security interest in investment property, it might need to take action to maintain perfection. For the most part, all the post-closing events that might undermine or affect perfection of security interests in other types of assets also apply to security interests in investment property. Review Chapter Four, Section 5.

Finally, note that if the secured party has a security interest in a certificated security perfected by possession or a security interest in any investment property

---

[24] For a brief discussion of the Convention, see Carl S. Bjerre and Sandra M. Rocks, *Say Hello to the Hague Securities Convention*, 7 THE TRANSACTIONAL LAW. 1 (Feb. 2017).

perfected by control, the secured party has the obligation to deal with the collateral in accordance with § 9-207. A secured party that maintains control over investment property in which the secured party no longer has a security interest has an obligation to relinquish control. § 9-208(b)(4).

4. Priority

To account for the different ways in which security interests in investment property are perfected, and to ensure that Article 9 does not interfere with the ways in which investment property is used and traded in commerce, § 9-328 creates yet another exception to the first-to-file-or-perfect rule of § 9-322(a). *See* § 9-322(f).

The dominant priority rule for investment property is that a security interest perfected by control has priority over a security interest perfected by some other method. § 9-328(1). Thus, a secured party that perfects its security interest in investment property by filing a financing statement will have a lower priority than a secured party that perfects its security interest by taking control of the investment property, even if such control were obtained after the other secured party filed. If a securities intermediary has a security interest in the securities account or security entitlement, or a if commodity intermediary has a security interest in a commodity contract or commodities account, the security interest is perfected by control. §§ 9-106, 8-106. That security interest has priority over any other security interest in that type of collateral. § 9-328(3), (4). If two persons (other than a securities or commodity intermediary holding a securities or commodity account) obtain control of the investment property, then priority is determined by the time control was obtained. *See* § 9-328(2).

If a security interest in a certificated security in registered form is perfected by taking delivery, that is, by possession under § 9-313(a), but that delivery does not result in the transferee having control of the certificated security under § 8-106, the security interest perfected by that taking of delivery will have priority over security interests perfected by a method other than control of the certificated security, that is, by filing a financing statement or by automatic perfection. § 9-328(5).

Finally, if the debtor is a securities intermediary or commodity intermediary and has granted competing security interests in investment property it holds to two or more lenders, and if those lenders rely on automatic perfection under § 9-309(10) or (11), those lenders' priority in the investment property will be a co-equal priority. § 9-328(6). If one of those lenders perfects by control, the general rule of § 9-328(1) will apply so that the lender that perfects by control will have priority for its security interest over a secured party that relies on automatic perfection for its security interest. If none of those priority rules apply, then the baseline rule in § 9-322(a) will apply. § 9-328(7).

Study the examples in the comments to § 9-328, then try your hand at the following problem.

Problem 6-11

A. Deluxe Retailers, Inc. has a securities account at Pippin Brokerage. As part of the agreement when the account was opened, Deluxe signed a document in which it granted a security interest in all securities entitlements held in the account now or in the future to secure any obligations that Deluxe owed or thereafter owed to Pippin. Two months after the account was opened, Deluxe borrowed $20,000 from State Bank and signed a document in which it granted State Bank a security interest in "all securities accounts" in which Deluxe then or thereafter had an interest to secure all obligations that Deluxe then owed or thereafter owed to State Bank. State Bank filed a financing statement against Deluxe in the correct place listing the collateral as "securities accounts."

1. Between Pippin Brokerage and State Bank, whose security interest has priority in the securities entitlements held in Deluxe's securities accounts held at Pippin Brokerage?
2. How, if at all, would the analysis change if Pippin agreed in a signed record to comply with the directions of State Bank as to disposition of the securities entitlements held in the securities account without further consent of Deluxe?
3. How, if at all, would the analysis of Part A(1) change if the debtor were not Deluxe Retailers, Inc. but an individual who held the securities account for personal investment purposes? *See* § 9-108.

B. Diamond Enterprises has a securities account at Pippin Brokerage, Inc. Two months after the account was opened, Diamond borrowed $20,000 from State Bank and signed a document in which it granted State Bank a security interest in "all securities accounts" in which Diamond then or thereafter had an interest to secure all obligations that Diamond then owed or thereafter owed to State Bank. State Bank obtained an agreement with Pippin Brokerage that Pippin will obey the directions of State Bank as to disposition of the securities entitlements held in the securities account without further consent of Diamond. Diamond then signed a document in which it granted National Bank a security interest in the securities account at Pippin Brokerage to secure a $10,000 loan that National Bank made to Diamond. Diamond agreed that National Bank would be listed on the securities account as a customer and executed the documentation with Pippin to place National Bank on the securities account as a customer. Between State Bank and National Bank, which security interest has priority in the securities entitlements held in the securities account?

Purchasers. Selling a certificated security requires a transfer of the certificate to the purchaser. § 8-301(a). To sell an uncertificated security, the seller must simply cause the issuer to reflect on its books the transfer of the share to the purchaser. § 8-301(b). To sell a securities entitlement, the securities intermediary's customer issues an entitlement order to the intermediary to note on the intermediary's books that the purchaser is now the entitlement holder. § 8-501(b).

Now suppose that the holder of the certificated security, uncertificated security, or securities entitlement has granted a security interest in the security or securities entitlement to a secured party. The holder then sells its security or securities entitlement to a buyer. Does the buyer take the security or securities entitlement free of the secured party's security interest? If the security interest is unperfected, the rules in § 9-317(b) and (d) apply. If the buyer fulfills the requirements of that section, the buyer will take the security or securities entitlement free of the unperfected security interest.[25]

What if the security interest is perfected when a purchaser either buys the security or securities entitlement or obtains a competing security interest in it? Section 9-331 creates an exception to the first-to-file-or perfect rule for priority among competing security interests if the secured party qualifies as a "purchaser" of the investment property protected by the rules of Article 8. That section also protects purchasers of investment property that are not secured parties. The application of § 9-331 depends on how the secured party perfected. Remember that the secured party may perfect a security interest in investment property either by filing an effective financing statement or by taking control. In addition, if the investment property is a certificated security, the secured party may perfect by possession. §§ 9-310, 9-313(a), 9-314.

---

[25] Note that § 9-317(d) also applies to commodity contracts and commodity accounts.

First consider a purchaser of a certificated or uncertificated security in which there is a perfected security interest. Under §§ 8-303 and 9-331, a protected purchaser that gives value, does not have notice of any adverse claim to the security – which would include the existing security interest, *see* § 8-102(a)(1) – and obtains control of the certificated or uncertificated security will take the security free of the perfected security interest. Because it is generally not possible for two entities both to have control over a certificated security, *see* § 8-106 (defining "control"), a secured party with an interest in a certificated security perfected by control cannot lose to a subsequent purchaser under this rule. It is also extremely unlikely that a secured party perfected through control of an uncertificated security would ever lose under this rule. However, a secured party perfected by filing has a very vulnerable position because a purchaser that qualifies as a protected purchaser will take the security certificate or uncertificated security free of the perfected security interest. This is true in part because the secured party's filed financing statement does not provide notice of an adverse claim. §§ 8-105(e), 9-331(c). Note how similar these rules are to those applicable to instruments and chattel paper.

The purchaser of a certificated security that does not qualify as a "protected" purchaser may, in relatively rare situations, nevertheless take free of a perfected security interest in the security if the secured party perfected its security interest by filing but the information required by § 9-516(b)(5) is incorrect. Read § 9-338(2).

The rules applicable to a purchaser of a securities entitlement are substantially similar to the protected purchaser rules for certificated and uncertificated securities. If the purchaser gives value, does not have notice of an adverse claim to the security entitlement, and obtains control of the security entitlement, the purchaser takes the security entitlement free of a previously perfected security interest, unless the secured party has and retains control. §§ 8-510(a), (c), 9-331.

Here's one last wrinkle. Assume that the securities intermediary, not the entitlement holder, has granted a security interest in the financial assets it holds. That security interest is automatically perfected. § 9-309(10). The securities intermediary sells a position in that financial asset to a purchaser. The purchaser has a securities entitlement in that financial asset. § 8-501. As long as the secured party does not obtain control over the financial asset but relies on its automatic perfection, the secured party will lose to the entitlement holder in a priority contest. §§ 8-511, 9-331. However, if the secured party obtains control of the financial asset, § 8-106, the secured party will have priority over the rights of the purchaser (the entitlement holder) unless the secured party acts in collusion with the securities intermediary in violating the rights of the entitlement holder. §§ 8-511(b), 8-503(e).

Problem 6-12

Downtown Office Supply, Inc. is in the business of selling office furniture to commercial entities. To finance its operations, Downtown obtained a loan from State Bank of $500,000 and signed a document in which it granted State Bank a security interest in all "equipment, inventory, accounts, chattel paper, instruments, general intangibles, documents of title, deposit accounts, and investment property now owned or hereafter acquired to secure all obligations now owed or hereafter owed to State Bank." State Bank filed an effective financing statement against Downtown in the appropriate office listing the collateral as "all assets."

Downtown sold its 10 shares of stock in Excellent Computing, Inc. to Future Investors, Inc. Between State Bank and Future Investors, Inc., who has priority in the 10 shares of stock? What do you need to know to answer this question?

One final point about securities is in order. The term "securities" in the UCC is broader than the term is for the purposes of federal securities laws. All or almost all shares in a corporation are securities for the purpose of Articles 8 and 9, even if those shares are privately held. What matters is that the shares be "of a type" dealt in or traded on securities exchanges or securities markets, not that they actually are publicly traded. *See* § 8-102(a)(15)(iii)(A).

A member's interest in a limited liability company, however, is less likely satisfy this standard and therefore less likely to fall within the definition of a security. Nevertheless, a lender acquiring a security interest in the debtor's interest in a limited liability company – a common practice for reasons discussed in Chapter Three[26] – needs to reliably determine whether that interest is a security. If the interest is a security, the discussion above about perfection and priority applies. This means that, to be assured of priority, the lender will want to obtain control of the security. If the interest is not a security, the interest is a general intangible. In such a case, the only way to perfect is by filing a financing statement. Moreover, because control is not an option for general intangibles,[27] priority cannot be lost to

---

[26] *See supra* pages 255-258.

[27] Control would be a permissible method to perfect if the general intangible were evidenced by a controllable electronic record and the relevant property rights run with record, in the sense that they are automatically transferred to a transferee of that record.

someone who later acquires control as long as the interest remains a general intangible.

To remove the uncertainty about whether a member's interest in a limited liability company is a security or a general intangible,[28] there is a sort of opt-in to Article 8. If the organizational documents for the company (*i.e.*, the operating agreement) expressly provide that interests in the entity are securities, then that statement will be given effect provided the other elements of the definition of security are satisfied. *See* § 8-102(a)(15)(iii)(B). The following language suffices:

> Each interest in [name of issuer] constitutes a "security" within the meaning of Section 8-102(a)(15) of the Uniform Commercial Code as enacted by [state of organization of issuer].

If the company chooses to issue certificates for membership interests, the certificates will often, but not always, contain similar language noting that the company has elected to opt in under Article 8. But the absence of a statement on the certificates will not affect the efficacy of an election made in the company's organizational documents. Moreover, including the opt-in language only on the certificate, not in the operating agreement, is ineffective. The opt-in language must be in the entity's organizational documents for the opt-in to be effective.

Unfortunately, while the opt-in procedure can provide certainty that the interests are securities, lenders need to understand that opt-in status can change. A company that had not opted in when the loan was made and the security interest was granted could opt in later. Alternatively, a company that had opted in before the loan was made and the security interest was granted could later rescind that election.

Illustrations

1. To secure a loan, Borrower A grants Lender a security interest in Borrower A's membership interest in LLC. Lender perfects its security interest in the membership interest by filing a financing statement. LLC has opted into Article 8, and thus the membership interest is a security. Lender is at risk of losing priority under § 9-328 to a purchaser that later acquires possession or control of the security.

2. To secure a loan, Borrower B grants Lender a security interest in Borrower B's membership interest in LLC. Lender perfects its security

---

28 *See* § 8-103 cmt. 4.

interest in the membership rights by filing a financing statement. LLC has not opted into Article 8. If LLC later opts into Article 8, Borrower B's membership interest will immediately become a security, rather than a general intangible. Lender's security interest will remain perfected even if the financing statement indicated the collateral as "general intangibles." § 9-507(b).[29] Nevertheless, Lender is at risk of losing priority under § 9-328 to a purchaser that later acquires possession or control of the security.

3. To secure a loan, Borrower C grants Lender a security interest in Borrower C's membership interest in LLC. LLC has opted into Article 8, and thus the membership interest is a security. Lender perfects its security interest in the membership interest by obtaining control of the membership interest. If LLC later rescinds the opt-in Article 8, and the membership interest does not otherwise constitute a security, Borrower B's membership interest will immediately become a general intangible, rather than a security. Lender's security interest will remain perfected only if Lender filed an effective financing statement covering the membership interest.[30]

To avoid these problems, some lenders insist that the company's operating agreement require the lender's consent to any amendment (or to any amendment relating to opting into Article 8). The law in several states authorizes an operating agreement to require the consent of a non-member to an amendment, and provides that any amendment without that consent is ineffective.[31] This practice prevents the lender's collateral from transmuting from a security to a general intangible, or from a general intangible to a security, without the lender's knowledge and consent.

---

29 This assumes that the change in classification does not undermine attachment under the terms of the security agreement.

30 Again, this assumes that the change in classification does not undermine attachment under the terms of the security agreement.

31 *See, e.g.*, Cal. Corp. Code § 17701.12(a); Del. Code tit. 6, § 18-302(e); D.C. Code § 29-801.09(a); Fla. Stat. § 605.0107(1); Idaho Code § 30-25-107(a); Iowa Code § 489.112(1); Minn. Stat. § 322C.0112(1); Neb. Rev. St. § 21-112(a); N.J. Stat. § 42:2C-13(a); N.D. Cent. Code § 10-32.1-15(1); Utah Code § 48-3a-114(1); Vt. Stat. tit. 11, § 4003(k); Wyo. Stat. § 17-29-112(a). *See also* Uniform LLC Act § 107(a).

F. Letters of Credit

1. Scope and Attachment

Article 9 applies to security interests in letter-of-credit rights. § 9-109(a). A letter of credit is generally issued by a financial institution at the request of an applicant for payment of money to a beneficiary upon a presentation by the beneficiary of whatever documents comply with the terms of the letter of credit. § 5-102(a)(10).

A letter-of-credit right is defined as the right to payment or performance of the letter of credit but does not include the right to demand payment or performance of the letter of credit. § 9-102(a)(51). The only party entitled to demand payment or performance of the letter of credit is the party named as the beneficiary in the letter of credit. *See* §§ 5-102(a)(3), 5-108. What does this rather perplexing distinction mean? Well, an analogy might be useful. You might recall from Chapter Three, Section 4.C that Article 9 invalidates many contractual and legal anti-assignment rules. Thus, if a contract or law would otherwise prevent the owner of a valuable right from granting a security interest in that right, Article 9 overrides that rule and allows the owner to transfer an enforceable security interest. *See, e.g.*, §§ 9-401(b), 9-406(d), (f), 9-408(a), (c). However, in some of those situations, the secured party is left with little or no way to enforce that right against the person obligated. *See* § 9-408(d). In those instances, the security interest is valuable primarily as an interest in the proceeds of the right, rather than in the right itself. Such is the case with letters of credit. A secured party may acquire a security interest in a letter-of-credit right, but will often not be able to compel the issuer to pay. Nevertheless, the security interest can be an important way to ensure that the secured party has an interest in whatever payment the issuer of the letter of credit does make. Restrictions on the ability to grant a security interest in letter-of-credit rights are generally not enforceable. § 9-409(a).

To attach a security interest to a letter-of-credit right requires that the secured party meet the requirements for attachment in § 9-203 that we studied in Chapter Two. As an alternative to the signed security agreement with a collateral description, the secured party may take control of the letter-of-credit right pursuant to the debtor's agreement that the right will be security for an obligation. § 9-203(b)(3)(D). If the letter-of-credit right is a supporting obligation for a right to payment, and the secured party attaches its security interest to the right to payment, the security interest automatically attaches to the letter-of-credit right. § 9-203(f). Chapter Two, Section 7.

Article 9 also recognizes that the issuer of a letter of credit has an automatically attached security interest in documents presented under a letter of credit to the extent the issuer honors or gives value for the presentation. §§ 9-109(a)(6), 5-118(a). There is no need for the issuer to have a security agreement to attach this security interest to the documents presented pursuant to the letter of credit. § 5-118(b)(1).

2. Enforcement

Article 9 does not contain any special enforcement rules for enforcing the security interest against a letter-of-credit right except for the limitation on enforcement stated in § 9-409(b). Thus, all of the normal rules regarding enforcement of security interests that we learned in Chapter Three apply to a security interest in a letter-of-credit right. Of primary importance to the secured party, however, is the limitation from letter-of-credit law that only the beneficiary has the right to demand payment from the issuer of the letter of credit. Thus, a secured party with only a security interest in the letter-of-credit right does not have the right to demand payment under the letter of credit. Rather, as indicated above, the secured party's security interest is really in the proceeds of the letter of credit once they are paid. On the other hand, if the secured party becomes the transferee beneficiary of the letter of credit, the secured party will have the right to make the documentary presentation and demand payment from the issuer. A secured party cannot become the transferee beneficiary unless the issuer of the letter of credit agrees. *See* §§ 5-112, 5-113, 5-114. To protect the rights of a transferee beneficiary to demand payment under Article 5, § 9-109(c)(4) provides that Article 9 does not apply to the rights of a transferee beneficiary to the extent that those rights are "independent and superior under Section 5-114."

The enforcement rules in Part 6 of Article 9 also apply to the issuer's enforcement of the security interest in the documents presented to the issuer. § 5-118(b).

3. Perfection

To perfect a security interest in a letter-of-credit right as original collateral, the usual rule is that the secured party must have control of the letter-of-credit right.

See § 9-312(b).[32] To acquire control, the issuer of the letter of credit must consent to an assignment to the secured party of the right to the proceeds of the letter of credit. §§ 9-107, 5-114(c). The issuer of the letter of credit normally has no duty to grant such consent. *See* § 5-112. A secured party need not obtain control of the letter-of-credit right, however, if the letter-of-credit right is a supporting obligation to a right to payment. In such a case, a security interest in a letter-of-credit right is automatically perfected if the security interest in the right to payment is perfected. *See* §§ 9-102(a)(78), 9-203(f), 9-308(d), 9-312(b).

A secured party may also obtain rights under a letter of credit by becoming the transferee beneficiary of the letter of credit, an act which would give the secured party the right to draw on the letter of credit. The issuer of the letter of credit does not have any obligation to agree to a transfer of rights as a beneficiary to the secured party unless it has previously agreed to do so. § 5-112. The rights of a transferee beneficiary are superior to and independent from an interest in the letter-of-credit right. § 5-114.

The issuer's security interest in the documents presented under the letter of credit is automatically perfected if the documents presented are not in a tangible or written medium (i.e. electronic). §§ 9-309(8), 5-118(b)(2). If the documents presented are in a tangible or written medium, then the issuer's security interest in those documents is automatically perfected if the document is *not* of a certain type and the debtor does not have possession of the document. The types of tangible documents to which this automatic perfection does not apply are certificated securities, tangible chattel paper, tangible documents of title, instruments, and the letter of credit itself. §§ 9-309(8), 5-118(b)(3). As to these types of tangible documents, the usual rules of perfection as set forth in Article 9 apply. § 5-118, cmt. 2.

---

[32] The choice of law provision for purposes of perfecting a security interest in a letter-of-credit right is the law of the issuing bank's jurisdiction if the bank is located in a state of the United States and if perfection in the letter-of-credit right is not automatic. § 9-306. The issuing bank's jurisdiction is determined under § 5-116. If perfection of the security interest in the letter of credit right is automatic, that is by perfecting a security interest in a right to payment supported by the letter of credit right, the choice of law rule is the location of the debtor. § 9-301(1). However, unlike choice of law with respect to perfection by filing – which affects in which state to file a financing statement – unless the developing law on what constitutes control varies from state to state, the choice of law for perfection in a letter-of-credit right should not matter too much.

4. Priority

If a secured party becomes the transferee beneficiary of the letter of credit, its rights are superior to the rights of a person that has control of the letter-of-credit right through an assignment of the right to proceeds consented to by the issuer. §§ 5-114(e), 9-109(c)(4). A secured party that has control of the letter-of-credit right through a consented-to assignment has priority over a person that has a security interest in the letter-of-credit right that is perfected by a method other than control (*i.e.*, automatically perfected because the letter-of-credit right is a supporting obligation). § 9-329(1).[33] If more than one security interest is perfected by control, the security interests rank in priority according to the order in which control was obtained. § 9-329(2).

In the event the secured party has control of the letter-of-credit right, the secured party has the obligations stated in § 9-207 and § 9-208(b)(5).

If the letter-of-credit right is proceeds of other collateral, the special priority rules of § 9-329 trump the application of the baseline priority rule in § 9-322(a). *See* § 9-322(f). If a security interest has priority in the letter-of-credit right because of § 9-329, then the security interest might also have priority in the proceeds of the letter-of-credit right under § 9-322(c) through (e).

The issuer's security interest in documents is subject to the usual priority rules in Article 9 for those types of documents except that if the security interest is in tangible documents *other than* a certificated security, tangible chattel paper, tangible documents of title, instruments, or the letter of credit itself, the issuer's security interest will have priority over a conflicting security interest in those tangible documents as long as the debtor is not in possession of the document. § 5-118(b)(3).

Try to apply these rules in the following problem.

Problem 6-13

To secure an operating loan from State Bank, Best Retailer, Inc. signed a document in which it granted a security interest in all its "accounts now owned or hereafter acquired to secure all obligations now owed or hereafter

---

[33] This is analogous to the rules of § 9-327(1) and § 9-328(1), which give a person with a security interest in a deposit account or investment property perfected by control priority over a person with a conflicting security interest perfected by some other method.

owed" to State Bank. State Bank filed an effective financing statement against Best Retailer in the proper place listing the collateral as "accounts."

Best Retailer sold several items of inventory on credit to Grace Enterprises. Pursuant to the agreement between Best Retailer and Grace Enterprises governing that sale of inventory, Grace Enterprises had to provide a letter of credit. On the application of Grace Enterprises, Nations Bank, located in the United States, issued a letter of credit for the benefit of Best Retailer that enabled Best Retailer to draw on the letter of credit in the event Grace Enterprises failed to pay the amounts owed to Best Retailer for its purchases of inventory from Best Retailer.

Best Retailer granted an effective security interest in the proceeds of the letter of credit to First Bank to secure a loan. First Bank obtained Nations Bank's consent to the assignment of the proceeds of the letter of credit.

A. What is the priority of security interests in the letter-of-credit right as between State Bank and First Bank? *See* § 9-329.

B. Nations Bank honored Best Retailer's draw on the letter of credit and issued a certified check to Best Retailer in the amount payable under the letter of credit. What is the priority of interests in that certified check between State Bank and First Bank? *See* §§ 9-329, 9-322(c).

C. What should the bank with the lower priority in the proceeds of the letter of credit have done to obtain the higher priority in those proceeds?

D. When Nations Bank honored the draw on the letter of credit, it retained the documents that Best Retailer presented. Grace Enterprises wants those documents from Nations Bank.

   1. What is Nations Bank's authority to keep those documents? *See* § 5-118(a).

   2. Prior to the presentation of documents to Nations Bank, Grace Enterprises had granted a valid security interest to State Bank in all of Grace's tangible and intangible personal property then owned or thereafter acquired and State Bank has filed an effective and authorized financing statement against Grace Enterprises in the correct place as against "all assets." Does State Bank have a security interest in the documents that Nations Bank has in its possession? If so, what is the priority of the interests in those documents between Nations Bank and State Bank? What do you need to know to answer this question? *See* § 5-118(b). [Hint: What type of documents does Nations Bank have possession of?]

G. Controllable Electronic Records

1. Scope and Attachment

As noted in Chapter Two, a core aspect of the 2022 UCC Amendments was the creation of three new classifications of property: "controllable electronic record" ("CER"), "controllable account," and "controllable payment intangible." A CER is defined as a record in electronic form that is susceptible to a specified method of control. *See* § 12-102(a)(1). A controllable account is defined as an account, evidenced by a CER, that provides that the account debtor undertakes to pay the person having control of the CER. § 9-102(a)(27A). A controllable payment intangible is defined similarly: as a payment intangible, evidenced by a CER, that provides that the account debtor undertakes to pay the person having control of the CER. § 9-102(a)(27B). These definitions are not, by themselves, very illuminating. The meaning comes from the further definition of "control." To have control of a CER, a person must have:

- The power to avail itself of substantially all the benefit from the record;
- The exclusive power to prevent others from availing themselves of substantially all the benefit from the record;
- The exclusive power to transfer control of the record; and
- The ability readily to identify itself (by name, number, cryptographic key, account number, or otherwise) as the person having these powers.

§ 12-105(a).

Before proceeding with this discussion further, it is vital to understand that the amendments generally do not alter or dictate what rights come with ownership of a CER. In other words, it is essential to differentiate between the *record* and the *rights* evidenced by the record.

Some CERs have intrinsic value, in the sense that people are willing to pay for the CER itself. Bitcoin and other so-called crypto currencies are examples of CERs with intrinsic value. So too are many non-fungible tokens ("NFTs"). Note, there is no account debtor or other person obligated on such CERs; it is the CER itself that has value (although that value might fluctuate significantly).

Other CERs evidence ownership of some tangible or intangible asset or right. In most cases, whether an assignment of the CER effects an assignment of that underlying asset is left to law outside the UCC. Consider the following scenarios:

Illustration 1

Customer buys a lithograph, one of a limited edition, from Art Dealer. In connection with the transaction, Art Dealer provides Customer with a written Certificate of Authenticity attesting to the genuineness of the lithograph and the total number of lithographs comprising the limited edition. If Customer sells the Certificate to Purchaser, Purchaser might or might not acquire ownership of or rights in the lithograph. Resolution of that question will depend on whether applicable law treats the sale of the Certificate as either an assignment of property rights in the lithograph or as a contract to sell the lithograph. Purchaser might become the owner of the Certificate but acquire no property rights in the lithograph, and the Certificate itself may be of little or no value.

If the Certificate were instead issued as a CER, the same analysis would apply. Whether Purchaser acquires any rights in or to the lithograph by acquiring the CER is left to law outside the UCC.

Illustration 2

Seller and Buyer enter into a contract for the sale of specified property. The contract provides that, on a specified date, Seller is to deliver the property (or otherwise transfer title thereto) and Buyer is to pay the designated price. Assume that the contract is in writing. If Buyer sells to Purchaser the writing on which the contract is printed, Purchaser might or might not acquire the right to receive the specified property. Resolution of that question will depend on whether applicable law treats the sale of the writing as an assignment of the contract rights. Purchaser would become the owner of the writing, but the writing itself may be of little or no value.[34]

---

[34] This would almost certainly be the case if the time for Seller's performance had long passed and Seller had performed.

One notable example of a sale of a written contract on which performance remained due, but which did not transfer any rights to that performance, was the sale at auction of Bobby Bonilla's somewhat notorious deferred-compensation contract with the New York Mets. The Mets released Bonilla in 2000 (he retired the following year) while still owing him $5.9 million. Instead of paying at the time, Mets ownership thought it better financially to defer payments across a 25-year period, with 8% interest. Under the contract, Bonilla is entitled to receive just under $1.2 million on each July 1 from 2011 through 2035. This has prompted some in the sports world to refer to July 1 as "Bobby Bonilla Day." Obviously, if the sale – which occurred in August, 2022 for $180,000 – entitled the buyer to receive the

If, instead, the contract between Seller and Buyer was evidenced by a CER, the same analysis would apply. The right evidenced by CER (*i.e.*, Buyer's right to receive the property from Seller) would be the valuable asset, not the record itself. But whether that right travels with the record, so that Purchaser becomes the owner of the right by becoming the owner of the record, is left to law outside the UCC.

However, the amendments treat accounts and payment intangibles evidenced by a CER (*i.e.*, "controllable accounts" and "controllable payment intangibles") differently. Because the account debtor on a controllable account or controllable payment intangible undertakes to pay the person in control, a transfer of a controllable account or controllable payment intangible transfers with it the underlying right to payment to a transferee that obtains control. *See* § 12-104.

Illustration 3

Seller and Buyer enter into a contract for the sale of specified property. The contract provides that, on a specified date, Seller is to deliver the property (or otherwise transfer title thereto) and Buyer is to pay the designated price. Assume that the contract is evidenced by a CER and that the right to payment is a controllable account because Buyer has promised to pay the person in control of the CER. Seller sells the CER to Purchaser. Purchaser acquired the right to payment from Buyer.

Illustration 4

Lender makes a loan to Borrower and in return Borrower provides Lender with a promissory note. If the promissory note is in a writing, it would almost assuredly be an "instrument" under Article 9 and might also qualify as a negotiable instrument under Article 3.

If, instead, the promissory note was issued in electronic form, then the promissory note could not be an instrument under Article 9 or a negotiable instrument under Article 3 because the promissory note is not in a writing.

---

more than $15 million remaining due, the sales price would have been much higher. The buyer did, however, become entitled to receive two 30-minute Zoom calls, one with Bonilla and one with Dennis Gilbert, the agent who negotiated Bonilla's contract, a game-used bat from Bonilla's personal collection, a signed baseball, a letter of provenance from Gilbert, a letter of authenticity, and a 1-of-1 NFT of Bonilla's contract.

Consequently, Lender's right to payment from Borrower is a payment intangible. If the promissory note is a CER, and Borrower promised to pay the person in control of the CER, then the note would be a controllable payment intangible. A transferee of the promissory note from Lender who obtains control of the CER would acquire the right to payment from Borrower.

2. Enforcement

Enforcement of a security interest in a CER is governed by the rules studied in Chapter Three, with two minor exceptions.

First, a new subsection (b) to § 9-605 and a new subsection (f) to § 9-628 deal with a secured party who does not know the identity of a debtor or how to communicate with the debtor. Collectively, the new rules provide that a secured party is not absolved of Part 6 duties or liability to that person if, at the time the secured party obtains control of the CER, the secured party knows that such information is not provided by the collateral, a record attached to or logically associated with the collateral, or the system in which the collateral is recorded. This provision is grounded in: (i) the observation that practices are developing under which lenders extend secured credit without knowing, or having the ability to discover, the identity of their borrowers; and (ii) the policy determination that a secured party should not be free to avoid statutory duties when the secured party knows that the collateral, records associated with the collateral, and the system in which the collateral is recorded do not provide the secured party with the information necessary to fulfill normal statutory duties. The secured party in such situations may protect itself by choosing not to enter into a transaction in which it might be unable to comply with its statutory duties or by conditioning its participation on disclosure of the debtor's identity and contact information.

Second, if the CER evidences a controllable account or controllable payment intangible, § 12-107, rather than § 9-406, governs when the account debtor is obligated to pay the secured party[35] and when the account debtor's obligation is discharged. *See* § 9-406(*l*) (making subsections (a)–(c) and (g) inapplicable to controllable accounts and controllable payment intangibles). The rules in § 12-106 are modeled on those in § 9-406, but differ slightly to deal with the electronic nature of the receivable and the concept of control. Specifically:

---

35 Remember, a buyer of accounts or payment intangibles is normally a secured party.

The account debtor may generally discharge its obligation by paying either the person currently in control of the CER (typically, the secured party) or a person that previously had control (typically, the debtor). § 12-106(a).

However, the account debtor may not discharge its obligation by paying a person previously in control of the CER, and may discharge its obligation only by paying the person currently in control, after the account debtor has received a signed instruction to pay the person currently in control. § 12-106(b), (c). That instruction must be preceded by a signed agreement between the account debtor and a person then in control of the CER on how a person must prove that control has been transferred, § 12-106(d)(1), and if the account debtor requests such proof, then until such proof is provided the account debtor may discharge its obligation by paying a person previously in control of the CER. § 12-106(e).

The remaining Article 9 rules regarding collection of accounts and payment intangibles, §§ 9-607 and 9-608, apply to accounts and payment intangibles evidenced by a CER.

3. Perfection

A security interest in a CER, controllable account, or controllable payment intangible may be perfected by filing a financing statement. For this purpose, the law governing perfection by filing (and determining the appropriate place to file) is the law of the jurisdiction where the debtor is located, § 9-306B(b)(1), which is the law that generally governs perfection by filing.

The general rules on how to indicate the collateral in the financing statement also apply. Hence, an indication by collateral type (*e.g.*, "controllable electronic records") or an indication such as "all assets" is sufficient. *See* §§ 9-108(b), 9-504.[36] Moreover, because CERs are a subset of general intangibles, a financing statement that indicates the collateral as "general intangibles" is effective with respect to CERs. Similarly, because controllable accounts are a subset of accounts, a financing statement indicating the collateral as "accounts" is effective with respect to controllable accounts. And for much the same reason, an indication of collateral in a financing statement as "general intangibles" or as "payment intangibles" is effective to cover controllable payment intangibles.

---

[36] Presumably, a more specific description, such as "Bitcoin" or "crypto currency" would also suffice.

If the secured transaction is a sale of a controllable payment intangible, perfection is automatic. *See* § 9-309(3). *See also* § 9-306B(b)(2) (the law of the jurisdiction where the debtor is located governs automatic perfection).

A security interest in a CER may also be perfected by control. For reasons discussed below in connection with the discussion of priority, perfection by control is preferable to both perfection by filing and automatic perfection. Section 12-105, discussed above at the beginning of Section G, specifies what constitutes "control" of a CER, and was discussed above.

Problem 6-14

On June 1, Bank makes a loan to Debtor and obtains a security interest in all of Debtor's Bitcoin. At the time, Debtor provides Bank the public and private keys to the Bitcoin but retains a copy of each. Is Bank's security interest in the Bitcoin perfected?

4. Priority

As they do with investment property and deposit accounts, the UCC's priority rules regarding CERs, controllable accounts, and controllable payment intangibles place a premium on control. In fact, the perceived need for such rules was arguably the primary impetus for the creation of the committee that studied the issues relating to emerging technologies and ultimately drafted the amendments. To understand why, consider this following illustration based on the law prior to the 2022 UCC Amendments.

Illustration 5

Debtor, the owner of a Bitcoin, borrowed funds from Lender and granted Lender a security interest in the Bitcoin to secure the loan. Because the Bitcoin was a general intangible, the only way for Lender to perfect the security interest was by filing a financing statement in the jurisdiction where Debtor was then located, which Lender did. But the blockchain on which Bitcoin transactions are recorded is not organized by the names of Bitcoin owners, and provides no way to identify the names of former owners. Moreover, there was no rule that permitted a transferee of general intangibles to take free of a perfected security interest. Consequently, if Debtor used the Bitcoin to purchase property or services, the transferee would take subject to

Lender's security interest, as would every subsequent transferee of the Bitcoin.[37] And even if the initial transferee knew of Debtor's name and could conduct a search for financing statements filed against Debtor, subsequent transferees would have no practical ability to do that. On the other hand, if Lender sought to enforce the security interest in the Bitcoin, Lender would face considerable challenges identifying and locating transferees. The only way Lender could prevent this problem was to have Debtor transfer the Bitcoin to Lender or to an intermediary until the secured obligation was satisfied. In short, Bitcoin, like other crypto currencies, was designed to be a store of value and a payment method that was both anonymous and non-intermediated. But to function as collateral, Bitcoin could not be both of those things.

The amendments address priority in CERs, controllable accounts, and controllable payment intangibles in both Article 9 and Article 12. New § 9-326A provides a simple rule that a security interest in a CER, controllable account, or controllable payment intangible perfected by control has priority over a conflicting security interest not perfected by control.

Article 12 does something far more significant. It bestows on each of those types of property something like the negotiability accorded to money. Specifically, § 12-104(e) provides that a "qualifying purchaser" of a CER acquires its rights free of other property rights CER. "Qualifying purchaser" is defined as a purchaser that "obtains control of" a CER "for value, in good faith, and without notice of a claim of a property right" in the CER. § 12-102(a)(2). The filing of a financing statement does not provide notice of a claim of a property right in a CER. § 12-104(h). Consequently, a purchaser of Bitcoin that obtains control of the Bitcoin will generally take free of any security interest in the Bitcoin.

But a qualifying purchaser takes free not only of security interests, but of all claims to the CER. This includes claims of ownership by a person from whom the CER was stolen. This is an attribute accorded to few types of property. Absent expiration of the applicable statute of limitations, a theft victim normally has the right to recover stolen property not merely from the thief, but from anyone who acquired the property directly or indirectly from the thief, no matter how pure of heart and no matter how many transfers took place after the theft. Prior to the 2022

---

[37] They would until perfection was lost under § 9-316(a)(3) – generally, a year after a transfer of the Bitcoin to a debtor located in a different jurisdiction – at which point a buyer without knowledge of the security interest could take free under § 9-317(d).

UCC Amendments, the only exceptions to this rule were money,[38] certificated and uncertificated securities transferred to a protected purchaser,[39] and negotiable instruments payable to bearer and negotiated to a holder in due course.[40] Section § 12-104(e) extends this special status to CERs.

Section 12-104(a) provides that the rights of a qualifying purchaser of a controllable account or controllable payment intangible are the same as a qualifying purchaser of the CER evidencing the account or payment intangible.

Problem 6-15

A. Given that § 12-104(e) provides that a qualifying purchaser of a CER takes free of a claim of a property right in a CER, why is § 9-326A necessary?
B. Why does § 9-326A omit a rule stating that multiple security interests in a CER perfected by control rank according to the time when control was obtained? *Cf.* § 9-327(2), § 9-328(2) (dealing, respectively, with deposit accounts and investment property).

---

38 *See, e.g.*, City of Portland v. Berry 739 P.2d 1041 (Or. Ct. App. 1987) (a person who acquires stolen money in good faith and for valuable consideration obtains good title and prevails over the victim of the theft).

39 *See* § 8-303(b) (protected purchaser takes free of adverse claims to a security). *See also* §§ 8-102(a)(1); 8-303(a) (defining, respectively, "adverse claim" and "protected purchaser").

40 *See* § 3-306 (a holder in due course takes free of claims to an instrument). This rule applies if the note is originally issued in bearer form or is indorsed in blank so that it becomes payable to bearer. *See* § 3-205(b) (when indorsed in blank, an instrument becomes payable to bearer). If, instead, an instrument were issued to the order of a specified person, stolen from that person, and then that person's signature was forged, the result would be different. The thief/forger would not be a person entitled to enforce the instrument. If the thief/forger sold the instrument to an unsuspecting buyer, the buyer would also not a person entitled to enforce because the original payee did not indorse the note. The thief's forgery of the payee's name is not the payee's indorsement. *See* § 3-403. Instead, the thief has converted the note under the first sentence of § 3-420(a) and the buyer has converted the note under the second sentence of § 3-420(a).

Problem 6-16

On June 1, First Bank makes a loan to Debtor, obtains a security interest in all of Debtor's personal property, and perfects the security interest by filing a proper financing statement in the appropriate office. At the time, Debtor owns several Bitcoin, which Debtor has stored with Exchange. Assume that under the storage arrangement, Exchange has control of the Bitcoin but Debtor remains the owner of the Bitcoin. On July 1, Second Bank, which knows of First Bank's relationship with Debtor, makes a loan to Debtor secured by Debtor's Bitcoin and obtains an acknowledgment from Exchange that Exchange has control on Second Bank's behalf.

A. What is the relative priority of the banks' security interests in Debtor's Bitcoin?

B. How, if at all, would the analysis of Part A change if on August 1, Exchange acknowledges that it has control also on First Bank's behalf?

C. How, if at all, would the analysis of Part B change if Second Bank had not known of First Bank's relationship with Debtor when Second Bank made the loan and acquired its security interest in the Bitcoin?

D. How, if at all, would the analysis of Parts A and B change if, upon storing the Bitcoin with Exchange, the Exchange became the owner of the Bitcoin and Debtor acquired a right to receive on demand an equal number of Bitcoin from Exchange?

5. Governing Law

It is worth noting that the rules on what law governs perfection and priority of a security interest in a CER, controllable account, or controllable payment intangible. Perfection by filing and automatic perfection[41] are governed by the law of the jurisdiction where the debtor is located. *See* § 9-306B(b). Thus, the place to file a financing statement with respect to a security interest in such property is where the debtor is located, which is the place to file as to most types of personal property collateral.

However, perfection by control and priority are governed by the CER's jurisdiction. *See* § 306B(a). A waterfall of rules – that is, a series of options listed

[41] Recall, a sale of a payment intangible is automatically perfected. *See* § 9-309(3).

in descending order of preference – determines what a CER's jurisdiction is. Under that waterfall, a CER's jurisdiction is:

(1) The jurisdiction expressly designated as the CER's jurisdiction in the CER;
(2) The jurisdiction expressly designated as the CER's jurisdiction in the rules of system in which the CER is recorded;
(3) The jurisdiction whose law is selected to govern in the CER;
(4) The jurisdiction whose law is selected to govern in the rules of the system in which the CER is recorded; and
(5) The District of Columbia.[42]

§ 12-107(c). As you can see, these rules prefer a declaration about the CER's jurisdiction over a statement about governing law, although those two statements might not seem all that different. They also prefer a statement in the CER itself over a statement in the rules of the system in which the CER is recorded.

But at present, few CERs expressly state their jurisdiction or governing law, and few system rules do that either. Consequently, the law of the District of Columbia is likely to govern perfection by control and priority of interests in most CERs, (and possibly in many controllable accounts and controllable payment intangibles). This should work well once all or most states enact the 2022 UCC Amendments. Whether it will work well before widespread enactment is an open question.

SECTION 2. SPECIALIZED TRANSACTIONS

A. Consignments

1. Scope and Attachment

As we learned in Chapter Two, Article 9 applies to consignments that are, in reality, disguised security transactions. We also learned that Article 9 applies to consignments that are not disguised security transactions but that fall within the definition of consignment in § 9-102(a)(20). § 9-109(a). Review Chapter Two, Section 8.A.2. For a consignment that is really a disguised security transaction, there are no special rules. Article 9's provisions regarding security interests in goods apply with full force. Thus, in this segment we are really dealing not with

---

42 If the District of Columbia has not enacted Article 12, governing law is stated to be the law of the District of Columbia as if it had enacted Article 12. *See* § 12-107(d).

consignments that are disguised security transactions but with those that are true consignments yet nevertheless fall within the scope of Article 9 solely because § 9-109(a)(4) brings that type of transaction within Article 9.

In such true consignments, the consignor is a secured party and the consignee is the debtor. § 9-102(a)(28), (73). The consigned goods are the collateral and the consignor's ownership interest in the goods is deemed to be a security interest for purposes of Article 9. §§ 1-201(b)(35), 9-102(a)(12). The consignment agreement satisfies the requirement of a signed security agreement with collateral description, assuming that it is in fact signed and adequately describes the collateral. § 9-203. We explored these concepts in Chapter Two, Section 8A.2.

Note one implication of this. If a transaction falls within the Article 9 definition of "consignment" but the consignment agreement is oral, the consignor will have no attached security interest in the consigned goods. As a result, by entering into the transaction, the consignor will have subjected the goods to the rights and claims of the consignee's creditors but the consignor will not have retained an enforceable security interest. In a dispute merely between themselves, the consignor will be entitled to get the goods back from the consignee, but the consignor is likely to lose priority to secured party of the consignee and even to a lien creditor of consignee.

2. Enforcement

A consignor in a true consignment is in a very real sense the actual owner of the consigned goods. Because of that, the Article 9 drafters thought that it was not necessary for the consignor to go through the processes in Part 6 of Article 9 to retrieve and dispose of the goods. Thus, the consignor is relieved of any obligation to comply with the rules in Part 6 when dealing with the goods and the consignee. § 9-601(g).

When a secured party of a consignee, other than the consignor, is enforcing its security interest in the consigned goods, however, that secured party will have an obligation to disburse the proceeds derived from a disposition of the goods in the manner set forth in § 9-615(a)(3), (4). Review Chapter Three, Section 3.B.3.

3. Perfection

Because the consignor is deemed to be a secured party with a security interest in goods, the usual rules on perfecting a security interest in goods apply. The consignor may either file a financing statement against the consignee that covers the goods or take possession of the goods. Review Chapter Four on those perfection methods. Of course, possession is extremely unlikely because it would no doubt defeat the underlying purpose of the consignment: to enable the consignee to sell the goods.

4. Priority

Even though the consignor has an ownership interest in the consigned goods and the consignee has the rights of a bailee with permission to sell the goods, Article 9 allows the consignee to give a security interest in the goods to the consignee's creditors if the consignee is in possession of the goods. § 9-319(a). In effect, § 9-319(a) gives power to the consignee to transfer more rights than it actually has for purposes of Article 9. Thus, the usual priority dispute is between the consignor (who is deemed to have a security interest) and a secured party of the consignee. The secured party of the consignee has typically taken and perfected a security interest in all of the consignee's inventory.

In many ways, the consignor is like a typical supplier of inventory and Article 9 treats the consignor as such by classifying the consignor's security interest as a PMSI in inventory. § 9-103(d). Thus, the consignor may take advantage of the priority rule for PMSIs in inventory and obtain priority over a perfected security interest in the consigned goods granted by the consignee. § 9-324(b). If PMSI priority is not obtained (because, for example, the consignor did not give timely notice to the competing secured party), then the usual first-to-file-or-perfect rule will apply. § 9-322(a). In short, the usual priority rules of Article 9 as they apply to security interests in goods and proceeds of goods will apply to determine the rights of a consignor in the goods and their proceeds against competing secured parties. Review Chapter Five, Section 3.

If the consignor has perfected its security interest and that interest has priority over the security interest of a competing secured party of the consignee, then the property interest of the consignee in the consigned goods is determined under other law, § 9-319(b), because § 9-319(a) no longer applies to give the consignee power to transfer more rights than the consignee has. The effect of this rule will usually be that the consignee has limited property rights in the goods (such as having merely the rights of a bailee) and thus could not grant better rights than it had to its creditor.[43]

---

43 For an analogous rule, *see* § 9-318(b), which effectively allows a seller of accounts to

As to the rights of people who buy the consigned goods from the consignee, generally the consignor has empowered the consignee to sell the goods to buyers, in effect giving the consignee the right to transfer the consignor's rights to those buyers. In addition, the consignee is deemed to have the ability to transfer the consignor's title and rights to the goods. § 9-319(a). Thus, buyers can potentially take free of the consignor's rights under the buyer in ordinary course of business rule of § 9-320, the protection for reliance purchasers in § 9-338(2), or, if the consignor's interest is unperfected, under the rule of § 9-317(b). Review Chapter Five, Section 5.

Problem 6-17

Dealer, located in California, is in the business of selling expensive works of art. Dealer owns most of the art Dealer sells but Dealer also sells some items owned by others, retaining a commission of 15% of the sales price (*i.e.*, sells on consignment).

Last year, State Bank acquired and perfected a security interest in "all of Dealer's presently owned and after-acquired inventory" to secure a loan of $1 million. Three months ago, Artist, who is also located in California, delivered to Dealer a sculpture Artist had recently completed. Pursuant to the parties' written agreement, Dealer is to attempt to sell the sculpture for no less than $7,500 and is entitled to retain 15% of the sales proceeds. Any time prior to sale, Dealer must return the sculpture to Artist upon Artists's demand therefor. Artist did not file a financing statement or provide notification of the transaction to State Bank.

Last month, Dealer returned the sculpture to Artist, pursuant to Artist's demand. Artist then sold the sculpture to Buyer at a private sale for $60,000. Artist provided no advance notification of the sale to either State Bank or Dealer. What rights, if any, does each party have to the sculpture and what claims, if any, does each party have against the other parties?

---

transfer the accounts again, but only if the buyer – who by definition qualifies as a secured party, *see* § 9-102(a)(73)(D) – fails to perfect.

B. New Debtors

1. Scope, Attachment, and Enforcement

Article 9 addresses the issues involved when a "new debtor," § 9-102(a)(56), becomes bound to a security agreement entered into by the "original debtor," § 9-102(a)(60). Typically, this occurs during a corporate merger or other type of business reorganization. Let us pause for a moment to consider the potential significance of this. A purchaser of collateral who takes subject to the security interest thereby becomes the "debtor," *see* § 9-102(a)(28)(A), and can therefore be said to be subject to the *security interest* in the collateral. But that is different from being bound by the terms of the *security agreement*. In particular, the security agreement might purport to cover after-acquired property. A purchaser of collateral is not normally subject to such a clause (*i.e.*, property the purchaser acquires after the purchase is not normally encumbered by the security interest). In contrast, a "new debtor" is bound by an after-acquired property clause in the security agreement entered into by the original debtor.

Now read § 9-203(d) and (e). Subsection (d) describes two ways in which a person can become bound to a security agreement entered into by another person. The first method is when, by other law (*i.e.*, law outside Article 9) or by agreement, the new debtor is bound to the original debtor's security agreement. § 9-203(d)(1). The second method is stated in Article 9 and derives from corporate succession law. If the new debtor becomes obligated for the original debtor's debts and acquires substantially all of the original debtor's assets, the new debtor is bound to the security agreements entered into by the original debtor. § 9-203(d)(2).

In either circumstance stated in subsection (d), subsection (e) treats the new debtor becoming bound to the original debtor's security agreement as the equivalent of the new debtor signing a security agreement with a collateral description. The subsection also expressly states that after-acquired property – that is, property acquired by the new debtor after it became a new debtor – is encumbered by the security interest (to the extent that the property is described in the security agreement). Noticeably absent from both Article 9 and the comments is any statement that future advances to the new debtor are also secured by the collateral. However, it seems likely that is implicit in the concept that the new debtor is bound not merely by the *security interest*, but by the *security agreement* entered into by the original debtor. Thus, if the security agreement with the original debtor purports to make the collateral secure future advances, that should be sufficient to cover advances the secured party makes to the new debtor.

Once the new debtor is bound by the original debtor's security agreement, all of the enforcement rules in Part 6 of Article 9 apply to enforcement attempts against the new debtor. No special rules apply.

2. Perfection

Now for the perfection rules as they apply to this situation. To determine whether a secured party of the original debtor has a perfected security interest in the assets of the new debtor, three different collateral categories must be considered:

(1) Collateral the original debtor transferred to the new debtor (and in which the secured party had a security interest prior to the transfer);
(2) Collateral that the new debtor owned at the time it became bound by the security agreement entered into by the original debtor; and
(3) Collateral that the new debtor acquires after it became bound by the original debtor's security agreement.

As to the first category of assets, § 9-315(a)(1) provides that the security interest of the secured party of the original debtor remains attached to the collateral transferred to the new debtor even after the transfer to the new debtor. Section 9-507(a) then provides that the original financing statement filed against the original debtor remains effective to maintain perfection of the security interest in those assets. *See* § 9-508(c). If, however, the new debtor is located in a different jurisdiction than the original debtor, then § 9-316(a)(3) gives the secured party one year after the transfer to file against the new debtor in the new jurisdiction in order to maintain continuous perfection in those assets.

As to the second and third categories of assets, § 9-203(d) and (e) operate to bind the new debtor to the security agreement entered into by the original debtor as to those assets described in the security agreement. Section 9-508(a) then provides that the financing statement against the original debtor is sufficient to perfect the security interest in the assets held by the new debtor or acquired by the new debtor thereafter. However, if the difference between the name of the original debtor and the name of the new debtor renders the financing statement filed against the original debtor seriously misleading as to the new debtor, the financing statement will be effective only as to collateral acquired by the new debtor before or within four months after the new debtor became bound to the original security agreement. To be perfected in assets acquired by the new debtor more than four months after the new debtor became bound, the secured party must file an initial financing statement with the name of the new debtor before the end of the four-month period. *See* § 9-508(b).[44]

If the new debtor is located in a different jurisdiction than the original debtor, a financing statement filed in the jurisdiction in which the original debtor was located, and which has not lapsed, will be effective to perfect a security interest in collateral the new debtor owned before or acquires within four months after the new debtor becomes bound by the security agreement. However, such perfection lasts only for four months (or less time if the original filing expires before then). To remain continuously perfected in the collateral that the new debtor has or acquires within the four-month period, the secured party will need to file in the new state before the four-month period expires. § 9-316(i).

What about a secured party that did not have a security interest that was effective against the original debtor, but is merely lending to the new debtor? All of the normal attachment and perfection rules apply. The new debtor is the debtor. The secured party must attach and perfect its security interest by obtaining a security agreement with the new debtor, and taking the appropriate perfection step as to the collateral. If that perfection step is filing a financing statement, the secured party would generally file a financing statement against the new debtor in the jurisdiction where the new debtor is located.

PERFECTION IN COLLATERAL OF NEW DEBTOR

	Transferred Assets	**Assets Owned by New Debtor Before It Became New Debtor**	**Assets Acquired by New Debtor After It Became New Debtor**
Attachment	Yes, generally. § 9-315(a)(1).	Determined by contract and other law. § 9-203(d), (e).	
Perfection, if new debtor is located in same jurisdiction as original debtor	Yes. § 9-507(a).	Yes. § 9-508.	Yes, if the filing against the original debtor is not seriously misleading. If the filing is seriously misleading, it is effective only as to collateral acquired within four months. § 9-508(b).

44 For an example, see In re Summit Staffing Polk County, Inc., 305 B.R. 347 (Bankr. M.D. Fla. 2003).

	Transferred Assets	Assets Owned by New Debtor Before It Became New Debtor	Assets Acquired by New Debtor After It Became New Debtor
Perfection, if new debtor is located in different jurisdiction than original debtor	Yes, for one year. § 9-316(a)(3).	Yes. § 9-508. However, becomes unperfected – retroactively – unless perfected under the law of the new jurisdiction within four months. § 9-316(i).	Yes, if the filing against the original debtor is not seriously misleading. If the filing is seriously misleading, it is effective only as to collateral acquired within four months. § 9-508(b). Moreover, the security interest becomes unperfected – retroactively – unless perfected under the law of the new jurisdiction within four months. § 9-316(i).

Problem 6-18

On March 1, National Bank filed an authorized and sufficient financing statement against Acme Corp. in the secretary of state's office in Minnesota, the state in which Acme Corp. is incorporated. The financing statement listed the collateral as "inventory." On March 10, Acme Corp. signed a document in which it granted National Bank a security interest in "all inventory now owned or hereafter acquired" to secure "all obligations now owed or hereafter owed to National Bank." On March 11, National Bank loaned Acme Corp. $500,000 and Acme Corp. signed a promissory note promising to repay that amount on demand of National Bank. Acme Corp. manufactures and sells microwave ovens.

A. On December 1, Acme Corp. dissolved and reincorporated in Minnesota under the name, Ovenlast, Inc. It is now May 1 of the following year. Does National Bank have a perfected security interest in the microwave ovens in which Ovenlast has an interest?

B. On December 1, Acme Corp. dissolved and reincorporated in Delaware under the name Acme East Corp. It is now May 1 of the following year. Does National Bank have a perfected security interest in the microwave ovens in which Acme East has an interest?

3. Priority

When a new debtor becomes bound by a security agreement entered into by an original debtor, § 9-326 provides another exception to the general priority rule of § 9-322(a). *See* § 9-322(f). It is easier to understand these rules if we first consider a situation in which the original debtor(s) and the new debtor are all located in the same jurisdiction.

Consider the three categories of assets discussed above:

(1) Collateral the original debtor transferred to the new debtor (and in which the secured party had a security interest prior to the transfer);
(2) Collateral that the new debtor owned at the time it became bound by the security agreement entered into by the original debtor; and
(3) Collateral that the new debtor acquires after it became bound by the original debtor's security agreement.

As to the first category of collateral, the priority is governed by the general rule of § 9-322, as modified by the other priority rules in Part 3 of Article 9 other than § 9-326 (*i.e.*, as modified by all the other rules discussed above in this Chapter and Chapter Five). So for example, if the priority contest is between two secured parties of the original debtor, the first-to-file-or-perfect rule would normally apply unless one of the security interests qualified for protection under another rule in Article 9, such as the PMSI priority rules in § 9-324 or priority in deposit accounts under § 9-327. If the priority contest were between a secured party of the original debtor (whose interest survived the transfer to the new debtor) and a secured party of the new debtor that took a security interest in the transferred assets after the transfer, the double-debtor rule of § 9-325 might apply to prevent the secured party of the new debtor from having priority for its security interest in the transferred assets pursuant to the first-to-file-or-perfect rule of § 9-322(a)(3).[45]

As to the second and third categories of collateral, the priority rule of § 9-326 applies. Under it, a secured party who, pursuant to § 9-508, relies on its filing against the original debtor to perfect its security interest in the second and third categories of collateral described above will be subordinate to a security interest that is perfected by an effective filing against the new debtor. § 9-326(a). Thus

---

[45] If the old debtor and the new debtor are located in different jurisdictions, the rule of § 9-316(a)(3) will apply and the secured party will need to refile against the new debtor merely to maintain perfection in the collateral that was transferred from the original debtor to the new debtor.

when a new debtor becomes bound by a security agreement entered into by an original debtor, the secured party has every incentive to file a financing statement against the new debtor as quickly as possible. Bear in mind, though, that a financing statement filed against the original debtor will generally be effective to perfect a security interest in the third category of assets only if those the assets were acquired within four months after the new debtor became bound by the security agreement. § 9-508. As to assets acquired after the four-month period (assuming the name on the original financing statement has become seriously misleading), the filing against the original debtor is totally ineffective. This is an even bigger reason for the secured party to file quickly against the new debtor, particularly if the collateral is of the type that turns over quickly, such as inventory and accounts.

If two secured parties of the original debtor fail to file a financing statement against the new debtor, the priority of their security interests is determined by the rules in Part 3 of Article 9 other than § 9-326. *See* § 9-326(b), first sentence. In most cases, this means application of one of the rules in § 9-322(a) or a PMSI rule from § 9-324.

In the unlikely event that two competing secured parties have a security interest in the assets of two different original debtors, a new debtor becomes bound to both of those security agreements, and neither secured party files an effective financing statement against the new debtor, the priority of their security interests in the second and third categories of assets will be determined by the order in which the new debtor became bound to the security agreements of the original debtors. § 9-326(b), second sentence.

Problem 6-19

On January 1, Corporation A signed a document in which it granted a security interest in all of its existing and after-acquired equipment to Alpha Bank to secure all obligations then owed or thereafter owed to Alpha Bank. That same day, Alpha Bank filed an effective financing statement against Corporation A in the correct office. On February 1, Corporation B signed a document in which it granted a security interest in all its equipment then owned or thereafter acquired to Beta Bank to secure all obligations then owed or thereafter owed to Beta Bank. That same day, Beta Bank filed an effective financing statement against Corporation B in the correct office. On March 1, Corporation A and Corporation B merged to form Corporation AB. All of the corporations are located in Delaware.

A. What is the priority of the security interests in the following assets?

1. Equipment that Corporation A owned prior to the merger.
2. Equipment that Corporation B owned prior to the merger.
3. Equipment that Corporation AB acquired two weeks after the merger.
4. Equipment that Corporation AB acquired eight months after the merger.

B. How, if at all, does the analysis change if Beta Bank filed a financing statement covering equipment against Corporation AB in the correct place on April 1?

C. How, if at all, would the analysis of Parts A and B change if both Corporation A and Corporation B were located in New Jersey but Corporation AB was located in Delaware?

C. Agricultural Liens

1. Scope and Attachment

As you might recall from Chapter Two, Article 9 applies to agricultural liens, which are liens on farm products created by statute to secure payment or performance of an obligation for goods or services furnished in connection with the debtor's farming operation or for rent of farm land. *See* §§ 9-102(a)(5), 9-109(a)(2).

An agricultural lien is not a "security interest," as that term is defined in § 1-201(b)(35).[46] However, the lienholder is a "secured party," § 9-102(a)(73)(B), the property subject to the lien is "collateral," § 9-102(a)(12), and the person whose property is subject to the lien is a "debtor," § 9-102(a)(28). One major implication of this definitional dichotomy is that each Article 9 rule granting a right or imposing a duty on either the secured party or the debtor, and reach rule referring to the collateral, presumptively applies to agricultural liens, whereas the Article 9 rules relating to a security interest do not.

For example, the requirements in § 9-203 for attachment of a security interest do not apply to agricultural liens. This makes sense because an agricultural lien is created by statute, not by contract. However, it also means that the rules in § 9-203(f) and (g), which provide that a security interest automatically attaches to identifiable proceeds, supporting obligations, and supporting liens, do not apply to

---

46 In contrast, recall that the interest of a consignor or of a buyer of accounts, chattel paper, promissory notes, or payment intangibles is a "security interest."

agricultural liens.[47] Consequently, one must consult the statute creating the agricultural lien, and perhaps the case law interpreting it, to determine whether the lien attaches to such things.[48]

2. Enforcement

Because agricultural liens are a type of nonconsensual lien, the parties are unlikely to have an agreement that defines default. Therefore, default is defined for such liens in § 9-606 as the time when the statute creating the lien allows the lien to be enforced. Aside from that, agricultural liens are enforced the same way that security interests are, unless the statute creating the agricultural lien provides otherwise. Thus, an agricultural lienholder seeking to enforce its rights has the same basic option to conduct a disposition or acceptance of the collateral, subject to the right of redemption. Moreover, an agricultural lienholder has the duties under Part 6 of Article 9 unless the agricultural lien statute provides otherwise.

3. Perfection

Filing a financing statement is the only way to perfect an agricultural lien. *See* § 9-310(a). The law of the jurisdiction where the farm products are located governs perfection. § 9-302. Because this might not be where the debtor is located, a searcher investigating whether farm products are encumbered needs to check for perfected security interests by looking for financing statements filed where the debtor is located and needs to check for perfected agricultural liens by looking for financing statements filed where the farm products are located.

An agricultural lienholder has authority to file a financing statement that covers the collateral subject to the agricultural lien, but that authority does not arise until

---

47 *See* §§ 9-302 cmt. 2 ("no agricultural lien on proceeds arises under this Article"); 9-315 cmt. 9 ("This Article does not determine whether a lien extends to proceeds of farm products encumbered by an agricultural lien.").

48 *See, e.g.*, Neb. Rev. Stat. § 52-1406(1)(c), (d) (indicating that an agricultural lien on crops attaches to proceeds of the crops and an agricultural lien on feed attaches to livestock that consume the feed and to products and proceeds of that livestock); In re Schley, 509 B.R. 901, 907-13 (Bankr. N.D. Iowa 2014) (concluding that an agricultural lien on livestock under Iowa law does extend to proceeds of the livestock); Great W. Bank v. Willmar Poultry Co., 780 N.W.2d 437 (N.D. 2010) (assuming without discussion that cash proceeds of the livestock subject to a North Dakota agricultural lien were also encumbered by the lien).

the agricultural lien has already attached to the collateral. *See* § 9-509(a)(2). Therefore, without express authorization from the debtor, which is unlikely, an agricultural lienholder cannot pre-file. Agricultural lienholders also need to be aware that, in some states, the information needed on a financing statement to perfect an agricultural lien is more extensive than what is needed to perfect a security interest.[49]

Maintaining perfection of an agricultural lien is much like maintaining perfection of a security interest. There are, however, two things worth noting. First, recall from Chapter Four that a change in the debtor's name jeopardizes perfection only as to collateral acquired by the debtor more than four months after the change. *See* § 9-507(c). Thus, unless the agricultural lien attaches to after-acquired property, a change in the debtor's name will not affect the perfection of an agricultural lien. Whether the agricultural lien does extend to after-acquired property is an issue left to the statute creating the lien. Second, a change in location of collateral can affect perfection. Consider the following problem.

Problem 6-20

Feed Supply delivered feed to an individual farmer's cattle ranch in northern Iowa. The farmer gave Feed Supply a security interest in the farmer's cattle to secure payment of the purchase price for the seed. The farmer lives in southern Minnesota. Under Iowa state law, Feed Supply also has a statutory lien on the farmer's livestock to secure the price of feed delivered to the farmer.

A. 1. In what state must Feed Supply file a financing statement to perfect its security interest?
   2. In what state must Feed Supply file a financing statement to perfect its agricultural lien?

B. What, if anything, will happen to Feed Supply's security interest and agricultural lien if, after Feed Supply perfects them, the farmer moves the cattle to Minnesota.

---

[49] *See, e.g.*, Neb. Rev. Stat. §§ 52-1402(2), 52-1407(1); In re Hill, 2018 WL 1916172 (Bankr. D. Neb. 2018) (because the financing statement filed by the party with an agricultural lien on crops lacked the dates of the transactions giving rise to the lien, a signature of the person to whom the pesticides and fertilizer were furnished, and the lienholder's tax identification number, the agricultural lien was unperfected).

4. Priority

a. Agricultural Lien vs. Security Interest or Other Agricultural Lien

The first-to-file-or-perfect rule of § 9-322(a) generally governs the priority of an agricultural lien as against either another agricultural lien or a security interest. However, there are two points worth noting about the rule with respect to agricultural liens. First, agricultural liens are perfected only by filing. So while a security interest in farm products could be perfected in another manner, such as through possession, an agricultural lien cannot be. Second, there is an exception in § 9-322(g). If the statute creating the agricultural lien gives the agricultural lien priority over an earlier perfected security interest, the priority rule of that statute will control.

It is also worth noting that the priority rules in § 9-322(b) through (e) apply only to proceeds of a security interest, and thus do not apply to proceeds of an agricultural lien. Thus, if an agricultural lien does extend to proceeds and is perfected as to the proceeds – issues to which Article 9 does not provide an answer – the priority of the agricultural lien will likely be a matter of some doubt.

Problem 6-21

Seed Supplier sold seed to Farmer on credit. The seed was delivered on April 1. Farmer used the seeds to plant crops on May 1. Under applicable state law, Seed Supplier has a lien on Farmer's crops grown from the seed to secure the purchase price for the seed. On May 15, Farmer borrowed $50,000 from National Bank to use in operating Farmer's farm. Farmer signed a document in which it granted a security interest in all of Farmer's "goods now owned or hereafter acquired to secure all obligations that Farmer now owes or hereafter owes to National Bank." On May 20, National Bank filed a financing statement against Farmer in the state where Farmer lived using Farmer's proper name, listing National Bank as the secured party and indicating the collateral as "all goods." On October 1, Seed Supplier filed a properly filled out financing statement against Farmer in the state where the crops were located. Between National Bank and Seed Supplier, what is the priority of their interests in the crops?

b. Agricultural Lien vs. Other Interests

Recall from Chapter Five that the basic priority rule for security interests is in § 9-201(a). Because that rule refers to a "security agreement," and an agricultural lienholder typically has no security agreement, it is unclear whether § 9-201(a) provides the basis rule for the priority of an agricultural lien. That is somewhat problematic when it comes to a priority dispute between an agricultural lien and a judicial lien. As you might remember, § 9-317(a) occasionally subordinates a security interest to a judicial lien. When it does not, the basic rule of § 9-201(a) applies and the security interest has priority. Well, § 9-317(a) also occasionally subordinates an agricultural lien to a judicial lien.[50] When § 9-317(a) does not do so, the implication is that the agricultural lien has priority, but neither § 9-201(a) nor anything else in Article 9 expressly so states.

The same problem can apply to a dispute between an agricultural lien and a buyer. Section 9-320 does not apply to agricultural liens. Therefore, if an agricultural lien is perfected, and thus the priority rule of § 9-317(b) does not apply, and assuming the agricultural lienholder did not authorize the sale free and clear of its interest, *see* § 9-315(a)(1), the buyer presumably takes the farm products subject to the perfected agricultural lien (unless a priority rule outside of Article 9 provides otherwise), but technically Article 9 does not so provide.

Several other priority rules in Article 9 do not apply to agricultural liens. For example, the priority rules in § 9-323 regarding future advances do not apply to an agricultural lien, perhaps because an agricultural lien is, in most states, unlikely to secure future advances. Similarly, § 9-333 does not deal with the relative priority of a possessory lien and an agricultural lien.

Problem 6-22

Seed Supplier sold seed to Farmer on credit. The seed was delivered on April 1. Farmer used the seed to plant crops on May 1. Under applicable state law, Seed Supplier has a lien on Farmer's crops grown from the seed to secure the purchase price for the seed. On October 1, Seed Supplier filed a properly filled out financing statement against Farmer in the state where the crops were located. On October 5, Juarez, a creditor with a judgment against Farmer levied on the crops as Farmer harvested the crops.

---

50 Note that only paragraph (A) of § 9-317(a)(2) applies to an agricultural lien, because paragraph (B) refers to § 9-203(b)(3), which deals only with security interests.

A. Between Seed Supplier and Juarez, who has first priority in the crops?
B. How, if at all, would the analysis change if the levy took place on September 30?
C. Assume that Seed Supplier filed its financing statement on October 1 in the state where Farmer lived, which is different from the state where the crops were planted. The levy took place on October 5. Between Seed Supplier and Juarez, who has priority in the crops?

Problem 6-23

Seed Supplier sold seed to Farmer on credit. The seed was delivered on April 1. Farmer used the seeds to plant crops on May 1. Under applicable state law, Seed Supplier has a lien on Farmer's crops grown from the seed to secure the purchase price for the seed. On October 1, Seed Supplier filed a properly filled out financing statement against Farmer in the state where the crops were located. When the crops were harvested and stored with Harvester Storage Inc. in late October, the crops were infested with a fungus. Harvester treated the stored crop with chemicals to kill the fungus. The treatment cost $2,000. State law gives Harvester a lien on the crop in its possession to secure the cost of the antifungal treatment. What is the priority between Harvester's lien and Seed Supplier's lien?

Problem 6-24

Feed Supplier sold feed to Farmer for use in feeding Farmer's hogs. A statute in the state where the hogs are located gives Feed Supplier a lien on the hogs to secure the price of feed. Two years before, Farmer granted an enforceable security interest on all farm products then owned or thereafter acquired to secure any and all obligations that Farmer then owed or thereafter owed to National Bank. At that time, National Bank filed an effective financing statement against Farmer in the state where Farmer is located listing the collateral as "farm products." Currently Farmer owes $100,000 to National Bank.

A. Farmer gives a few of the hogs to Bill in payment of a debt that Farmer owes Bill. Does Bill take the hogs free of Feed Supplier's lien? Does Bill take the hogs free of National Bank's security interest? If Bill takes the hogs subject to both the lien and the security interest, what is the priority of interests in the hogs?

B. Feed Supplier filed a financing statement properly naming Farmer in the state where the hogs are located, listing the collateral as "hogs" and Feed Supplier as secured party. A few weeks after the filing, Farmer sold the hogs to Betty for cash. Does Betty take the hogs free of Feed Supplier's lien? Does Betty take the hogs free of National Bank's security interest? What else do you need to know to answer these questions?

C. How, if at all, would the analysis to Part B change if the financing statement filed by Feed Supplier contained an incorrect mailing address for Farmer?

D. Federal Tax Liens

1. Attachment and Enforcement of the Tax Lien

The federal tax lien is one of the principal weapons in the federal government's arsenal when it seeks to collect a taxpayer's tax liability. Although state governments often impose tax liens as well, we focus on the federal tax lien scheme, in part because the rules do not vary from state to state and in part because federal tax liability tends to greatly exceed state tax liability.

Enforcing federal tax liability begins with " assessment," a somewhat automatic administrative action of the Internal Revenue Service.[51] Notice to the taxpayer of the assessment is not required but if payment is not forthcoming, assessment is usually followed by a demand on the taxpayer to pay the liability.[52] If the taxpayer fails to pay after such a demand for payment, the tax lien arises and relates back to the time of the assessment.[53]

The federal tax lien attaches to all real and personal property of the taxpayer, and in this case "all" means everything. The tax lien attaches to property which is otherwise exempt under state law from the reach of creditors: the taxpayer's home, tools of trade, and the entire amount of the taxpayer's wages.[54] As the Supreme Court stated:

---

[51] 26 U.S.C. § 6201.

[52] 26 U.S.C. §§ 6303, 7524.

[53] 26 U.S.C. § 6321, 6322.

[54] 26 U.S.C. § 6321. *See* American Trust v. American Cmty. Mut. Ins. Co., 142 F.3d 920 (6th Cir. 1998) (although the property might be exempt from a tax levy under 26 U.S.C. § 6334, the asset is not exempt from the tax lien or enforcement of the tax lien).

> The federal tax lien statute itself "creates no property rights but merely attaches consequences, federally defined, to rights created under state law." . . . Accordingly, "[w]e look initially to state law to determine what rights the taxpayer has in the property the Government seeks to reach, then to federal law to determine whether the taxpayer's state-delineated rights qualify as 'property' or 'rights to property' within the compass of the federal tax legislation."[55]

Any property acquired by the taxpayer after the assessment is also subject to the lien. Moreover, funds in a joint bank account, which might not be subject to garnishment for the debt of only one account holder, are subject to levy for the unpaid taxes of one of the joint depositors.[56]

The lien continues until the tax liability is paid or the statute of limitations runs.[57] If, within the limitations period, the taxpayer does not pay the assessed tax or negotiate with the IRS for a settlement or extension, the government will levy on liquid assets or even padlock the debtor's business to induce payment.[58]

2. Priority

The federal tax lien is very powerful; it takes priority over many other encumbrances. Pursuant to 26 U.S.C. § 6323(a), however, that priority does not kick in unless and until the IRS files a notice of federal tax lien in accordance with 26 U.S.C. § 6323(f). This notice, which is analogous to a financing statement, "must identify the taxpayer." Treas. Reg. § 301.6323(f)-1(d)(2).

Most courts construing this requirement have adopted a "constructive notice" approach as the general rule. Under this approach, a notice is effective if the name of the taxpayer on it is sufficient for a third party searcher to find the notice and understand that it might relate to the taxpayer.[59] This approach is somewhat similar to Article 9's "seriously misleading" standard. *See* § 9-506(a). However, it lacks the clear rules in § 9-506(b)–(d) that require a filing to either have the proper name

---

[55] United States v. Craft, 535 U.S. 274, 278 (2002).

[56] United States v. National Bank of Commerce, 472 U.S. 713 (1985).

[57] 26 U.S.C. § 6322.

[58] 26 U.S.C. §§ 6331–6343.

[59] *See* In re Hudgins, 967 F.2d 973 (4th Cir. 1992).

of the debtor or be retrieved pursuant to a search under the "correct" name. As a result, several courts have been fairly lenient toward the IRS with respect to errors in the taxpayer's name.[60]

There are some significant implications that flow from this. In most states, notices of a federal tax lien are filed in the same office as the UCC records and are indexed with them. A searcher, relying on revised § 9-506(b)–(d), who searches only under the debtor's exact legal name might not discover a filed notice of tax lien that has a slight misspelling of the debtor/taxpayer's name. However, because the validity of a notice of federal tax lien is governed by federal law, not the UCC, such a notice might still be effective. Over time, courts may: (i) move towards adopting a bright-line rule, such as in § 9-506(b)–(d), that requires the IRS to get the debtor's name right;[61] (ii) maintain the constructive notice approach but find that the IRS failed to meet its burden if a search under the right name does not disclose the notice; or (iii) maintain the constructive notice approach, with its attendant uncertainties, and thereby require searchers to guess at and search for various misspellings or abbreviations that a court would be likely to overlook. In the interim, searchers need to be very careful. A Sixth Circuit decision appears to continue the last approach and reject the approach used in Article 9, at least with respect to common abbreviations. In its analysis, the court stated:

---

[60] *See, e.g., id.* (notice recorded against "Hudgins Masonry, Inc.," a corporation whose existence had been terminated for failure to pay certain fees, effective as to the business assets of Michael Hudgins, who continued to do business under the corporate name); Richter's Loan Co. v. United States, 235 F.2d 753 (5th Cir. 1956) ("Joseph Freidlander" instead of "Joseph Friedlander" was adequate); United States v. Feinstein, 717 F. Supp. 1552 (S.D. Fla. 1989) (notice against "Taragon" instead of "Tarragon" was effective). *But cf.* Haye v. United States, 461 F. Supp. 1168 (D. Cal. 1978) (notice listing the taxpayer as "Manual de Castello" instead of "Manuel de Castillo" was inadequate); Continental Inv. v. United States, 142 F. Supp. 542 (W.D. Tenn. 1953) (notice filed in the name of "W.B. Clark, Sr." instead of "W.R. Clark, Sr." was not sufficient); United States v. Ruby Luggage Corp., 142 F. Supp. 701 (S.D.N.Y. 1954) (notice filed against "Ruby Luggage Corporation" instead of "S. Ruby Luggage Corporation" was not effective); In re Reid, 182 B.R. 443 (Bankr. E.D. Va. 1995) (notice in the name of "Gary A. Reid, Jr." instead of "Cary A. Reid, Jr." was not effective).

[61] *See* In re Spearing Tool and Mfg. Co., 302 B.R. 351 (E.D. Mich. 2003), *rev'd*, 412 F.3d 653, 654 (6th Cir. 2005) ("Each lien identified Spearing as 'SPEARING TOOL & MFG. COMPANY INC.,' which varied from Spearing's precise Michigan-registered name, because it used an ampersand in place of 'and,' abbreviated 'Manufacturing' as 'Mfg.,' and spelled out 'Company' rather than use the abbreviation 'Co.' ").

The critical issue in determining whether an abbreviated or erroneous name sufficiently identifies a taxpayer is whether a "reasonable and diligent search would have revealed the existence of the notices of the federal tax liens under these names." * * *

Crestmark should have searched here for "Spearing Tool & Mfg." as well as "Spearing Tool and Manufacturing." "Mfg." and the ampersand are, of course, most common abbreviations – so common that, for example, we use them as a rule in our case citations. Crestmark had notice that Spearing sometimes used these abbreviations, and the Michigan Secretary of State's office *recommended* a search using the abbreviations. Combined, these factors indicate that a reasonable, diligent search by Crestmark of the Michigan lien filings for this business would have disclosed Spearing's IRS tax liens. * * *

A requirement that tax liens identify a taxpayer with absolute precision would be unduly burdensome to the government's tax-collection efforts. Indeed, such a requirement might burden the government at least as much as Crestmark claims it would be burdened by having to perform multiple lien searches. "The overriding purpose of the tax lien statute obviously is to ensure prompt revenue collection." *United States v. Kimbell Foods, Inc.*, 440 U.S. 715, 734-35 (1979). "[T]o attribute to Congress a purpose so to weaken the tax liens it has created would require very clear language," which we lack here. *Union Central*, 368 U.S. at 294. Further, to subject the federal government to different identification requirements – varying with each state's electronic-search technology – "would run counter to the principle of uniformity which has long been the accepted practice in the field of federal taxation."[62]

---

[62] In re Spearing Tool and Mfg., Co., 412 F.3d 653, 656-57 (6th Cir. 2005). The court did distinguish a few earlier decisions that also gave the IRS wide latitude in its tax lien notices. Those decisions involved searches using a paper index, on which entries with misspellings could nevertheless readily be discovered. The court seemed to recognize that such decisions are inapposite to electronic searches of a computer database. This suggests that while the Sixth Circuit was willing to impose on creditors the burden of searching under the finite number of possible *abbreviations* of the debtor's name, it would not compel them to search against the infinite number of possible *misspellings*. *Id.* at 656. *Cf.* In re Crystal Cascades Civil, LLC, 415 B.R. 403 (9th Cir. BAP 2009) (a notice of federal tax lien that omitted a word in the taxpayer's name and identified the taxpayer as a corporation instead of limited liability company was ineffective). *But cf.* Lake Las Vegas Master Trust v. United States, 2016 WL 1248699 (D. Nev. 2016) (a notice of federal tax lien identifying the corporate

Beyond this, searchers must be careful about where they search for notices of tax liens. Tax lien notices are to be filed in the state in which the taxpayer's property is located. Personal property is then deemed located at the residence of the taxpayer.[63] While the combination of these rules makes the place to file and search for notices of tax liens appear similar to that for most Article 9 financing statements, in fact the office might be different for any or all of the following three reasons: (i) a taxpayer's residence is not necessarily in the same jurisdiction as a debtor's location under § 9-307; (ii) the relevant office within the state of the taxpayer's residence might be different from the office in which UCC records are filed; and (iii) notices of tax liens might be kept in a database or indexing system separate from UCC records even if filed within the same office.

For example, for purposes of filing a notice of tax lien, a corporate or partnership taxpayer is deemed to reside where its principal executive office is located.[64] This is not necessarily the state where that entity is deemed located for Article 9 purposes. *Cf.* § 9-307. Within a particular state, the state might have designated an office other than the secretary of state's office to file notices of tax liens or the state might have failed to designate the office, in which case the designated office is the United States District Court clerk's office for the judicial district where the property is located.[65] Even if the same office is designated by the state, such as the secretary of state's office, the secretary of state might maintain two different databases, with separate types of search logic, for tax liens and financing statements.

---

taxpayer as "ZS," instead of "Z's" was effective); In re Green Pastures Christian Ministries, Inc., 437 B.R. 465 (N.D. Ga. 2010) (notices of federal tax lien that misspelled the debtor's name as "Green Pastures Christain Ministries, Inc." – transposing the "i" and "a" in "Christian" – were effective); The Trane Co. v. CGI Mechanical, Inc., 2010 WL 2998516 (D.S.C. 2010) (a notice of federal tax lien listing the debtor by its former name, "Clontz-Garrison Mechanical Contractors, Inc.," instead of its current name, "CGI Mechanical, Inc.," was effective).

[63] 26 U.S.C. § 6323(f).

[64] *See* 26 U.S.C. § 6323(f)(2).

[65] *See* 26 U.S.C. § 6323(f)(1)(B). Massachusetts is apparently the only state that has not designated a state office in which to file notices of federal tax liens. *Cf.* Mass. Gen. Laws ch. 36, § 24 (apparently dealing only with real property). As a result, such notices are to be filed with the Clerk of U.S. District Court. *See* SSG, Inc. v. Omni Medical Health & Welfare Trust, 71 A.F.T.R.2d ¶ 93-2022, 93-1 U.S.T.C. ¶ 50,353 (D. Mass. 1993); In re Tourville, 216 B.R. 457 (Bankr. D. Mass.1997); Rev. Rul. 85-89, 1985-2 I.R.B. 18, 1985-2 C.B. 326.

Based on the latest available information, in the following sixteen states, a notice of federal tax lien is filed in an office other than the office in which UCC financing statements are filed:

Alaska	Ohio
Indiana	Pennsylvania
Kentucky	Rhode Island
Maryland	South Carolina
Massachusetts	Tennessee
Missouri	Utah
New Jersey	Vermont
New Mexico	West Virginia

In the following three additional states, notices of federal tax lien and UCC financing statements are filed in the same office but are, apparently, not indexed together, so that a separate search of each database is necessary:

Florida
Georgia
Illinois

In addition to this, the federal statutes that preempt the UCC filing system in favor of a federal filing, such as those for copyrights and aircraft, do not apply to notices of tax liens.[66] A notice of tax lien filed locally, in the applicable state office, will be effective as to the types of property otherwise covered by a central, federal filing system for all types of assignments, including security interests. Finally, 26 U.S.C. § 6323(f) does not require the IRS to take any action to file a new notice if the debtor moves or changes its name and the cases are not consistent in deciding whether the IRS has to do anything to maintain the effectiveness of its filing. For our purposes, we assume the IRS has no such duty and thus we consider a notice of tax lien to be effective once it is filed in the correct place.

If the IRS has properly filed a notice of tax lien, 26 U.S.C. § 6323(a) establishes a sort of first-in-time rule for determining the tax lien's priority over the interest of a purchaser, holder of a security interest, mechanic's lienor, or judgment lien creditors. The tax lien has priority if the notice of it is filed before the competing interest arises.[67]

---

[66] *See* 26 U.S.C. § 6323(f)(5).

[67] Technically, § 6323(a) does not say that. It says that the tax lien is not valid against such claimants "until" the notice is filed. Arguably that means that the tax lien gains priority –

What is tricky about this priority rule is that the determination of when the competing interest arises for this purpose is based upon a different set of rules than what we are used to under the priority rules in Article 9. To determine whether the tax lien filing or the competing interest is first in time for the purpose of applying the priority rule in 26 U.S.C. § 6323(a), we need to read the definitions in 26 U.S.C. § 6323(h) of "security interest" and "purchaser." "Judgment lien creditor" is not defined but the U.S. Supreme Court has held that, for purposes of the tax lien statute, the judgment lien creditor's interest in property arises when the identity of the lienor, the property subject to the lien, and the amount of the lien are established.[68]

Now try your hand at this simple problem.

Problem 6-25

A. The IRS assessed tax liability against Debtor. Creditor then made an unsecured loan to Debtor. The IRS then filed a notice of tax lien against Debtor in the proper place. Debtor has real and personal property but not enough value in it to pay both the IRS and Creditor. What is the relative priority of the interests of the IRS and Creditor in Debtor's property?

B. The IRS assessed tax liability against Debtor. Secured Party then made a loan to Debtor and Debtor granted an effective security interest in a piece of equipment to Secured Party to secure the loan. The same day Secured Party filed an effective financing statement against Debtor in the correct place listing the collateral as "equipment." The IRS then filed a notice of tax lien against Debtor in the correct place. What is the relative priority of interests in the piece of equipment?

C. The IRS assessed tax liability against Debtor. Secured Party then made a loan to Debtor and Debtor granted an effective security interest in a piece of equipment to Secured Party to secure the loan. The IRS then filed a notice of tax lien against Debtor in the correct place. The next day, Secured Party filed an effective financing statement against Debtor in the correct place listing the collateral as "equipment." What is the relative priority of the interests in the piece of equipment?

---

even over previously existing interests – once the notice is filed. That is not the way in which the rule is interpreted, however.

68 IRS v. McDermott, 507 U.S. 447, 449-50 (1992).

D. The IRS assessed tax liability against Debtor. Debtor then signed a document in which it granted a security interest in equipment to Secured Party to secure all obligations that Debtor then owes or thereafter incurs to Secured Party. The same day Secured Party filed an effective financing statement against Debtor in the correct place listing the collateral as "equipment." The IRS then filed a notice of tax lien against Debtor in the correct place. Secured Party then loaned money to Debtor. What is the relative priority of the interests in the piece of equipment under 26 U.S.C. § 6323(a)?

E. The IRS assessed tax liability against Debtor. Debtor then signed a document in which it granted a security interest in equipment to Secured Party to secure all obligations that Debtor then owes or thereafter incurs to Secured Party. The same day Secured Party filed an effective financing statement against Debtor in the correct place listing the collateral as "equipment." The next day, Judgment Creditor levied on the equipment. The IRS then filed a notice of tax lien against Debtor in the correct place. Secured Party then loaned money to Debtor. What are the relative priorities of the interests in the piece of equipment under 26 U.S.C. § 6323(a) and UCC Article 9?

The general, first-in-time rule of 26 U.S.C. § 6323(a) is subject to several exceptions. Read 26 U.S.C. § 6323(b)–(d). Section 6323(b) covers casual purchases of household goods for small amounts of money, retail sales of goods, purchases of securities and motor vehicles, and transactions which tend to increase the value of the taxpayer's property. These priorities exist because searching for federal tax liens in such cases is not feasible. Thus, people who buy stocks, securities, motor vehicles, or certain household goods take free of the tax lien, provided they did not actually know of its existence.

Of perhaps greater relevance is 26 U.S.C. § 6323(c), which protects a secured creditor's security interest in after-acquired property so long as the debtor acquires the property within 45 days following the date the tax lien was filed.[69] Similarly, under U.S.C. § 6323(d), a secured creditor can make protected future advances for

---

[69] If accounts are acquired more than 45 days after notice of the lien is filed, the creditor with a security interest in the accounts will still prevail if the accounts are proceeds of other collateral in which the creditor has a perfected interest. In re National Fin. Alternatives, Inc., 96 B.R. 844 (Bankr. N.D. Ill. 1989).

45 days following the filing of the tax lien notice, so long as the creditor had no actual knowledge of the tax lien. *Cf.* U.C.C. § 9-323(b). To the extent these provisions do not apply, however, a federal tax lien for which the IRS has filed a notice of lien will have priority over a previously perfected security interest in after-acquired property or that secures future advances. This puts an important burden on secured parties – particularly those with floating liens – to monitor their debtors.

Finally, although the Internal Revenue Code facially provides to the contrary, the IRS concedes that its lien is subordinate to a purchase-money mortgage or purchase-money security interest acquired after notice of the tax lien is filed,[70] although presumably only if the security interest is perfected within the grace period provided by §§ 9-317(e) and 9-324(a). The IRS concession is based on some cryptic legislative history and the general belief that the IRS loses nothing by this rule, since without it the lender would not make the loan at all and the taxpayer would therefore not acquire a new asset to which the tax lien could attach. However, because priority for a PMSI is not expressed in the statute, it might be that numerous potential lenders are reluctant to rely on the revenue ruling and thus refrain from extending new credit once notice of a tax lien is filed. If nothing else, the lien indicates that the debtor is probably having serious financial difficulties.

Now try the following problems.

Problem 6-26

A. How, if at all, does 26 U.S.C. § 6323(d) change the answer to Problem 6-25, Parts D and E?

B. The IRS assessed tax liability of $20,000 against Debtor. Secured Party made a loan of $10,000 to Debtor and Debtor signed a document in which it granted Secured Party a security interest in all equipment now owned or hereafter acquired to secure all obligations now owed or hereafter owed to Secured Party. Secured Party then filed an effective financing statement covering equipment against Debtor in the correct place. The IRS then filed against Debtor a notice of tax lien in the proper place.

   1. Secured Party then loaned an additional $5,000 to Debtor 30 days after the tax lien filing. What is the priority of interests in the equipment?

---

70 Rev. Rul. 68-57, 1968-1 C.B. 553. *See also* Slodov v. United States, 436 U.S. 238, 258 (1978); First Interstate Bank of Utah v. IRS, 930 F.2d 1521 (10th Cir. 1991); First Nat'l Bank of Marlton v. Coxson, 1976 WL 1034 (D.N.J. 1976).

2. Would your answer to (1) change if the Secured Party knew about the tax lien filing when it loaned the additional $5,000 to Debtor?
3. Secured Party then loaned an additional $5,000 to Debtor 50 days after the tax lien filing. What is the priority of interests in the equipment?

C. The IRS assessed tax liability of $20,000 against Debtor. Secured Party made a loan of $10,000 to Debtor and Debtor signed a document in which it granted Secured Party a security interest in all equipment now owned or hereafter acquired to secure all obligations now owed or hereafter owed to Secured Party. Secured Party then filed an effective financing statement covering equipment against Debtor in the correct place. The IRS then filed against Debtor a notice of tax lien in the proper place. After the tax lien filing, Debtor acquired a new piece of equipment.
1. What is the priority of interests in that new piece of equipment?
2. Secured Party then loaned an additional $5,000 to Debtor 30 days after the tax lien filing. What is the priority of interests in the new piece of equipment?

Problem 6-27

The IRS assessed tax liability of $20,000 against Debtor. Secured Party made a loan of $10,000 to Debtor and Debtor signed a document in which it granted Secured Party a security interest in all inventory now owned or hereafter acquired to secure all obligations now owed or hereafter owed to Secured Party. Secured Party then filed an effective financing statement covering inventory against Debtor in the correct place. The IRS then filed against Debtor a notice of tax lien in the proper place. After the tax lien filing, Debtor acquired a new item of inventory.

A. Secured Party then loaned an additional $5,000 to Debtor 30 days after the tax lien filing. What is the priority of interests in the inventory in which Debtor had an interest prior to the tax lien notice filing? What is the priority of interests in the new item of inventory that was acquired after the tax lien filing? *See* 26 U.S.C. § 6323(c).

B. How, if at all, would the answer to Part A change if Secured Party knew about the tax lien filing when it loaned the additional $5,000 to Debtor?

C. Secured Party loaned an additional $5,000 to Debtor 50 days after the tax lien filing. What is the priority of interests in the inventory that Debtor had an interest in prior to the filing and the inventory that Debtor acquired after the tax lien filing?

D. How, if at all, would the answer to Part A change if, after the notice of tax lien was filed, Debtor sold an item of inventory and received cash in return? Between the IRS and Secured Party, whose interest would have priority in the cash? *See* 26 U.S.C. § 6323(b)(1), (h)(4).

E. Effect of Debtor's Bankruptcy Filing

We saw in Chapter Two, Section 9 how the debtor's bankruptcy affects attachment. Basically, 11 U.S.C. § 552 cuts off the efficacy of an after-acquired property clause in the security agreement (although it does not prevent the security interest from attaching to proceeds). In Chapter Three, Section 6.D, we saw how bankruptcy affects the enforcement process. More specifically, we examined the impact of the automatic stay and what generally happens to a secured claim in bankruptcy. We saw that secured parties normally retain their *in rem* rights in the collateral even if the debtor's *in personam* liability is discharged, and thus eventually can extract the value from the collateral to satisfy all or part of the secured obligation, although the manner and timing of doing so will depend on the type of bankruptcy proceeding and whether the secured party is oversecured, fully secured, or undersecured. Beyond that, it is worth noting that *over*secured creditors are entitled to charge the collateral for both postpetition interest on their claims as well as for any attorney's fees or other costs of collection to the extent the security agreement so provides. 11 U.S.C. § 506(b). For this reason, creditors should make sure that the attorney's fee provision in the security agreement is sufficiently broad to cover fees arising from defense of actions in bankruptcy.[71]

In Chapter Four, Section 5.C.5, we briefly noted that the automatic stay does not generally prevent a perfected secured party from doing whatever is necessary to maintain its perfected status, although in most instances it prevents an unperfected secured party from trying to perfect.

All of those previous discussions about secured claims were premised on the assumption that the secured party's lien would not be avoided – that is, invalidated – in bankruptcy. However, several different provisions of the Bankruptcy Code allow the trustee or debtor to avoid a creditor's lien. These provisions serve a

---

71 *Compare* In re Connolly, 238 B.R. 475 (9th Cir. BAP 1999), and In re LCO Enters., Inc., 180 B.R. 567 (9th Cir. BAP 1995), *aff'd*, 105 F.3d 665 (9th Cir. 1997), *with* Pitney Bowes, Inc. v. Manufacturers Bank, 1997 WL 289680 (D. Conn. 1997) and In re Moran, 188 B.R. 492 (Bankr. E.D.N.Y. 1995), all of which are discussed *infra* in Section 2.D.3.

variety of different policies, yet each is important. If some provision of the Bankruptcy Code allows the trustee or the debtor to avoid the lien, then to the extent the lien is avoided, the creditor is left with an unsecured claim.[72] In this context, recall that secured claims are generally paid in full whereas unsecured claims rarely fare so well. Thus, lien avoidance is one of the most critical moves that the players might make in the game of bankruptcy. The stakes are often very high.

1. The Bankruptcy Trustee as a Lien Creditor

Read U.C.C. § 9-102(a)(52)(C) and 11 U.S.C. § 544(a)(1). Each of those provisions grants to the bankruptcy trustee the status of a hypothetical lien creditor. The trustee is deemed to have a judicial lien that arises upon the filing of the bankruptcy petition on all of the debtor's property. By itself, these provisions have no effect. However, combined with what we learned in Chapter Five, Section 2, this status is critically important. Review U.C.C. §§ 9-317(a), (e) and 9-201. These latter provisions give lien creditors priority over most unperfected security interests. Thus, the bankruptcy trustee's status as a lien creditor, and its Article 9 rights as such a lien creditor, generally allow the trustee to take priority over unperfected security interests.

To apply these rules in a bankruptcy context, start by ascertaining when the bankruptcy petition was filed. That is the date the bankruptcy trustee's hypothetical judicial lien arose. Then determine whether the security interest was perfected before or after that time (remember perfection means both attachment of the security interest and the accomplishment of the required perfection step). If the security interest was perfected under the rules of Article 9 before the filing of the bankruptcy petition, then the trustee's status as a lien creditor will not enable the trustee to avoid – gain priority over – the security interest.

If a security interest is unperfected at the time of the bankruptcy filing, then determine if the secured party has fulfilled the two requirements of U.C.C. § 9-317(a)(2)(B) prior to the bankruptcy filing. If the secured party has taken those steps prior to the filing of the bankruptcy petition, the security interest is not avoidable by the bankruptcy trustee under 11 U.S.C. § 544.[73]

---

[72] In addition, the avoided lien is preserved for the benefit of the estate. 11 U.S.C. § 551. This can be important if there is a junior lienor. In such a case, the bankruptcy trustee effectively steps into the shoes of the senior lienor.

[73] If an agricultural lien was unperfected when the bankruptcy petition was filed, the

If the security interest is not protected by U.C.C. § 9-317(a)(2), the secured party has one last gasp at preventing avoidance of its security interest. If the secured party has a PMSI, and therefore has a 20-day grace period in which to perfect under U.C.C. § 9-317(e), the trustee cannot avoid the security interest if the debtor files bankruptcy during that period and the secured party files a proper financing statement before that grace period expires. 11 U.S.C. § 546(b)(1)(A).[74]

As you can see by the above discussion, the holder of a security interest risks much by not perfecting its interest in the debtor's property prior to the bankruptcy filing. A secured party needs to ascertain what the appropriate perfection step is, take that step, and do it properly, all before the debtor seeks bankruptcy protection. If, for example, a secured party files a financing statement but a financing statement is not an appropriate way to perfect,[75] fails to adequately describe the debtor or indicate the collateral,[76] or is filed in the wrong place,[77] or if, after the financing statement is properly filed, subsequent events undermine the statement's effectiveness to perfect,[78] the secured party will have an unpleasant surprise when the debtor files bankruptcy.

Problem 6-28

On February 1, Diner gave an effective security interest in certain ovens used as equipment to Bank One for a loan. Bank One never filed a financing statement. On July 1, Diner gave an effective security interest in the same equipment to Bank Two in return for a loan. Bank Two filed an effective financing statement against Diner in the correct place on the day it advanced the funds. In December, Diner filed for Chapter 7 bankruptcy protection.

---

agricultural lien is avoidable. What this means is that the agricultural lienholder will not be able to assert a secured claim in the bankruptcy proceeding but will have only an unsecured claim in the bankruptcy proceeding. In short, unperfected agricultural liens are wiped out in bankruptcy.

[74] *See also* 11 U.S.C. § 362(b)(3) (allowing the secured party to file a financing statement despite the automatic stay).

[75] *See* U.C.C. §§ 9-311, 9-312(b).

[76] *See* U.C.C. §§ 9-502, 9-506.

[77] *See* U.C.C. §§ 9-301 through 9-307, 9-501.

[78] *See* Chapter Four, Section 5.

Can the bankruptcy trustee avoid the security interests under 11 U.S.C. § 544, and what is the priority of all the interests in the equipment? *See* 11 U.S.C. §§ 544, 551. *See also* U.C.C. §§ 9-317(a), 9-322(a).

2. Preference Avoidance

Outside the bankruptcy process, debt collection from an insolvent debtor is a cross between a wedding banquet and a feeding frenzy. On the one hand, creditors whom the debtor favors – whether through familial affection or commercial need – are apt to receive a disproportionate share of the debtor's available assets. On the other hand, creditors who seek to compel payment through legal process or other means operate in a first-come-first-served world, where only those who diligently fight for a share of the debtor's wealth will get anything. In short, the ones who are fed from the debtor's wealth are those whom the debtor invites to the table and those pesky few who grab an uninvited chair. The patient creditors, those who try to accommodate the debtor but who do not become one of the debtor's favorites, are left hungry and angry.

One of the principal tenets of bankruptcy is that the process should be fair to creditors. This normally means that, absent some policy that warrants favored treatment for some claimants, creditors should share ratably in the debtor's available assets. Clearly, there is a tension between this tenet and pre-bankruptcy practice. If, shortly before bankruptcy, a debtor were permitted to pay a favored creditor or a shark-like creditor were able to extract payment, then the principle of creditor equality inside bankruptcy would become meaningless. The bankruptcy estate would often contain only the crumbs left after selected creditors had their fill.

Preference law is an attempt to deal with this problem. It is designed to undo certain pre-bankruptcy transactions that frustrate the bankruptcy distribution scheme. Thus, if the bankruptcy estate has only enough assets to pay creditors ten cents on the dollar, and shortly before bankruptcy the debtor paid one creditor in full, preference law would "avoid" the "transfer" and compel the creditor to return the money received and then stand in line with the other creditors. In short, preference law is an effort to deal with the fact that bankruptcy process occupies just a small part of the time line of the debtor's financial affairs, and it allows the bankruptcy court to go back in time, before the filing of the bankruptcy petition, and unwind certain transactions that frustrate bankruptcy policy. In effect, the law puts the debtor and the creditor back in the relative positions they occupied before the avoidable transfer was made. Assets transferred by the debtor are recovered, and the debt that was paid is revived. In a few bankruptcy cases, the only significant assets in the estate are preference claims against certain creditors.

What has been written so far makes preference law seem perfectly reasonable and appropriate, perhaps even innocuous. That is because it was written from the bankruptcy lawyer's perspective (or perhaps from the unpaid creditor's perspective). From the preferred creditor's perspective, preferences are monstrous. The very idea that, after a lawfully created debt has been properly paid, the creditor might have to disgorge the money seems to them preposterous. Why, they ask, should a diligent creditor who compelled payment have to return it so that slothful creditors may share in those assets?

A traditional response to this question notes that preference law encourages creditor restraint, which helps debtors with cash flow problems get through difficult times, and thereby helps save businesses and jobs. You should question that response, however, for two reasons. First, it is far from clear that the economy truly benefits from creditor restraint. Perhaps the economy would benefit more if creditors diligently pursued their debtors and got money out of doomed enterprises and into more productive uses. Unless and until empirical research can tell us which approach produces the most social utility, we should not jump to any conclusions. Second, it is not at all clear that preference law really promotes creditor restraint. A diligent creditor who extracts a preferential payment might have to return the money, but otherwise suffers no penalty. In short, creditors have everything to gain by seeking payment (perhaps they will get it and get to keep it, either because the debtor never files for bankruptcy protection or does so after enough time has passed to insulate the payment from preference avoidance) and nothing to lose except the costs of enforcement, which might be fairly minimal. Nevertheless, despite creditor criticism, preference law does further the bankruptcy policy of fair and equal treatment of creditors once the debtor files bankruptcy.

There are two main intersections of preference law and secured claims. The first involves whether a prepetition *payment* to a secured creditor is an avoidable preference. The second, and by far more important, is whether the *creation of the lien* itself is a preferential transfer of property rights. Before examining either of them, it is useful to note what the essential elements of an avoidable preference are. They are listed in 11 U.S.C. § 547(b). Read it. Most bankruptcy treatises suggest that there are five elements to an avoidable preference, one in each of the five paragraphs of § 547(b). However, the flush language of § 547(b) also has an important element, so it is more useful to think of there being six elements. They are:

(1) A transfer of an interest in the debtor's property – § 547(b)
(2) To or for the benefit of a creditor – § 547(b)(1)
(3) Made on account of an antecedent debt – § 547(b)(2)
(4) Made while the debtor was insolvent – § 547(b)(3)
(5) Made within the 90 days preceding the bankruptcy petition, or within one year if made to or for the benefit of an insider – § 547(b)(4)
(6) That enables the creditor to receive more than if the transfer had not been made and the debtor's assets liquidated in Chapter 7 – § 547(b)(5).

The first thing to notice about these elements is the trustee has to prove all of them in order to avoid a transfer. 11 U.S.C. § 547(g). The trustee is aided in this endeavor by a rebuttable presumption that the debtor was insolvent during the 90-day period prior to the filing of the bankruptcy petition. 11 U.S.C. § 547(f). The second is that no particular state of mind is required for either the debtor or the creditor. In other words, there need be no intent to prefer or to be preferred. Because of this, there is no blame associated with making or receiving a transfer that later proves to be preferential. While that might seem strange, it is countered by numerous affirmative defenses that insulate many ordinary transfers from avoidance. The third thing to notice is a timing issue. Preference analysis applies only to transfers that occur before the bankruptcy petition is filed, not to transfers made after the bankruptcy petition is filed. Postpetition transfers of interests in the estate property are potentially avoidable under 11 U.S.C. § 549.

a. Avoiding Pre-petition Payments to a Secured Party as a Preference

The main focus of preference law is the last element: an avoidable preference is a transfer that enables the creditor to receive more than such creditor would have received had the transfer not been made and the debtor's estate liquidated under Chapter 7. 11 U.S.C. § 547(b)(5). If a creditor is fully secured – in other words, if the creditor's interest in the collateral is worth more than the amount of the debt it secures – then the creditor would receive full payment upon liquidation of the debtor's assets.[79] Accordingly, any prepetition payment to such a creditor could not

---

[79] This payment might not occur in the bankruptcy proceeding itself, since distributions are rarely made on secured claims, *see* 11 U.S.C. § 726. It normally occurs outside bankruptcy when the creditor forecloses on the collateral, either after getting relief from the automatic stay or after the automatic stay ends. 11 U.S.C. § 362.

have increased such creditor's recovery. In short, such payment generally is not preferential and thus cannot be avoided. Looking at it from the trustee's perspective, the estate was not depleted by the transfer. Although the estate lost cash equal to the amount of the payment, it gained an equal amount because the payment, by decreasing the secured obligation, increased the debtor's equity in the collateral. Case law on this point is surprisingly sparse, perhaps because the issue is so basic, but it all supports this analysis.[80]

If, however, the creditor were undersecured, the result would be very different. For example, consider a creditor who is owed $1,000 and has a valid and unavoidable security interest on property worth $800. If the debtor were to pay the entire debt within the preference period and while insolvent, the creditor would be preferred and the transfer would be prima facie avoidable. In essence, the creditor would get the $1,000 payment instead of $800 on the secured claim and something less than $200 on the unsecured claim. A pre-petition payment of only part of the debt would also be preferential. Because the partial payment does not by itself affect the value of the collateral or the secured party's rights in it, such a partial payment necessarily reduces first the unsecured portion of the creditor's claim. If the debtor is truly insolvent and cannot pay creditors in full, the pre-petition payment will be preferential and prima facie avoidable.

So, in sum, pre-petition payments to undersecured creditors have preferential effect, and will be avoidable unless some preference defense exists. Pre-petition payments to fully secured creditors generally have no preferential effect[81] and thus cannot be avoided under 11 U.S.C. § 547. However, if the creditor's lien is itself avoidable, either as a preference or for some other reason, then any prepetition payment to such a creditor is essentially a payment to an unsecured creditor.

If a pre-petition payment to the secured party is prima facie avoidable under 11 U.S.C. § 547(b), it might nevertheless be insulated from actual avoidance by any of several affirmative preference defenses in 11 U.S.C. § 547(c). The most likely of these to apply is § 547(c)(2), which protects transfers made in the ordinary course

---

80 *See* In re Powerine Oil Co., 59 F.3d 969, 972 (9th Cir. 1995) (dicta quoting 4 COLLIER ON BANKRUPTCY ¶ 547.08, at 547-47 (Lawrence P. King ed., 15th ed. 1995)); Hashimoto v. Clark, 264 B.R. 585, 608 (D. Ariz. 2001).

81 A senior secured party who is fully secured and who received a payment could potentially be liable for a preference if the effect of that payment was to allow a junior secured creditor to receive more than it would otherwise. *See* 11 U.S.C. §§ 547, 550. Exploration of such "indirect" preferences is beyond the scope of this book but is likely in a bankruptcy course.

of business. Read it. This "ordinary course" exception to preference avoidance is based upon two factual questions posed by the language of the subsection. If: (i) the debt on which payment was made was incurred in the ordinary course of business of both the debtor and the creditor; and (ii) the payment was made either according to ordinary business terms or in the ordinary course of the parties' businesses, then the transfer is not avoidable.[82] As might be evident, this is a very broad exception that protects a great many pre-petition transfers.

Another exception that might apply to help an undersecured secured party defend against avoiding a payment to the secured party as a preference is 11 U.S.C. §547(c)(4), the so called "new value" exception. This example illustrates how the exception works:

> Secured Party has a security interest in collateral worth $50,000 to secure a debt of $70,000. Secured Party is therefore undersecured by $20,000. Within the 90-day preference period, the debtor makes a payment of $5,000 to Secured Party. That payment would have preferential effect under 11 U.S.C. § 547(b)(5) because, in essence, the payment is credited against the unsecured portion of the debt, thus allowing the secured party to obtain more by keeping the transfer than it would otherwise get in a Chapter 7. Assume that the payment does not qualify for protection under the very broad "ordinary course of business" exception discussed above. Subsequent to the debtor's payment, Secured Party makes an additional loan to the debtor of $2,000. Applying the elements of 11 U.S.C. § 547(c)(4), that additional loan is "new value" extended after the preferential payment to Secured Party, the new value is not secured (because Secured Party is already undersecured), and the debtor did not make any further transfers of an interest in property to Secured Party on account of the new value. The $5,000 payment is avoidable but § 547(c)(4) provides a partial defense and limits avoidance to $3,000.

---

[82] Prior to enactment of the 2005 Bankruptcy Act, the § 547(c)(2) defense required that both halves of the second question be proved, not merely either one of them. *See* Pub. L. No. 109-8, § 409(1), 119 Stat. at 106. The Act therefore greatly expanded this already broad preference defense.

Problem 6-29

Desperate Homemakers, Inc. provides home cleaning services to professionals who are too busy to attend to such matters. Three years ago, when it was just beginning operations, Desperate borrowed $75,000 from Bank to buy cleaning equipment and advertise its services. At that time, Bank took a security interest in all of Desperate's equipment and properly perfected that interest. Under the terms of the loan agreement, Desperate is supposed to make payments of $2,500 to Bank on the first of each month. In fact, Desperate has usually been late in paying, occasionally by as much as 45 days and on average by about 25 days.

Desperate filed for bankruptcy protection on June 1. On that date, it still owed Bank $37,000 and the collateral for that debt, all of which was now rather old, was worth only $12,000. In the three months before filing the bankruptcy petition, Desperate made the following payments to Bank: (i) $2,100 on March 23; (ii) $2,900 on April 15; (iii) $2,500 on May 21; and (iv) $2,500 on May 29 (in payment of the amount due June 1).

A. Which, if any, of these payments is avoidable? *See* 11 U.S.C. § 547(b), (c)(2). In analyzing this problem, first determine whether the payments meet all of the criteria for a prima facie case of an avoidable preference in subsection (b). Then, and only if they do, consider whether Bank has a defense to the trustee's action to recover those payments.

B. How, if at all, would the analysis change if the May 21st payment were made by certified check a few hours after Bank's loan officer called Desperate and threatened to declare the loan in default and replevy the collateral if payment were not made immediately?

C. How, if at all, would the analysis change if the collateral were worth $40,000 on June 1?

D. How, if at all, would the analysis in Part B change if the Bank made a loan of $5,000 to Desperate on April 30? On March 20?

b. Avoiding the Creation of a Security Interest as a Preference

Generally speaking, if an insolvent debtor pays an unsecured, nonpriority creditor within the preference period, that payment will be an avoidable preference. 11 U.S.C. § 547(b). The same is true with respect to transfers of property other than cash: § 547(b) applies to transfers of any "interest of the debtor in property" and payments in kind deplete the bankruptcy estate just as much as payments in cash do. *See also* 11 U.S.C. § 101(54) (defining "transfer").

Well, if the debtor transfers a limited property right, such as a lien, rather than complete ownership of a piece of property, the same principle applies. If value was transferred, then the creditor was preferred. Before you jump to the conclusion that all security interests obtained in the preference period are avoidable, remember that an avoidable preference must be a transfer on account of an antecedent debt. 11 U.S.C. § 547(b)(2). Some – perhaps most – security interests attach at the same time the secured party gives value to the debtor. In such situations, the transfer of the security interest would not be on account of an antecedent debt, and thus cannot be avoided.

Still, many security interests are created to secure a pre-existing obligation. This occurs most commonly when the security agreement contains an after-acquired property clause and the debtor acquires new collateral some time after the secured party initially extended credit. *See* 11 U.S.C. § 547(e)(3). It also occurs when there is a delay between attachment and perfection. Read 11 U.S.C. § 547(e)(2). Under the rules of 11 U.S.C. § 547(e)(2), if a security interest is perfected within 30 days of when it attached, it is deemed to have been transferred when it attached. If the date of attachment is also the date when the secured party gave value, the transfer of the security interest will not be made on account of an antecedent debt. If, however, more than 30 days pass after a security interest attaches before it is perfected, the security interest is deemed to have been transferred when it was perfected.[83] This rule almost invariably makes the creation of a security interest under an after-acquired property clause a transfer on account of an antecedent debt.

Even when a security interest is transferred on account of an antecedent debt, any one of several preference defenses might protect the transfer from avoidance. Read 11 U.S.C. § 547(c). Their collective reach probably protects the vast majority of security interests from preference attack. We will consider three of them now.[84]

The first defense is in paragraph (c)(1) and protects "contemporaneous exchanges" for new value. If the secured party perfects its security interest more than 30 days after the security interest attached, the secured party might

---

[83] The 2005 Bankruptcy Act changed the time period to 30 days. Previously it was 10 days. *See* Pub. L. No. 109-8 § 403, 119 Stat. at 104.

[84] A fourth defense, in paragraph (c)(6) and 11 U.S.C. § 545, provides protection against the avoidance of statutory liens. For this purpose, an agricultural lien is a "statutory lien." *See* 11 U.S.C. § 101(53).

nevertheless argue that the "contemporaneous exchange" exception should apply. That is, that the transfer of the security interest was in fact substantially contemporaneous with the new value (*i.e.*, the loan) that the secured party provided to the debtor. This argument is not likely to prevail. Prior to the 2005 amendment of § 547(e)(2), several courts rejected the argument that perfection more than *10 days* after attachment could be "substantially contemporaneous."[85] While some others were a bit more forgiving,[86] few are likely to treat a discrepancy of 30 days as substantially contemporaneous.

The second defense is in paragraph (c)(3). It protects purchase-money security interests and is rather straightforward.[87] Note, however, that unlike the PMSI rules of Article 9, this rule is not restricted to goods and software; it can apply to any type of collateral. *Cf.* U.C.C. § 9-103(b), (c).

The third defense is in paragraph (c)(5) and is anything but straightforward. It protects security interests in inventory and receivables, such as accounts, that have attached during the preference period. As you no doubt recall, inventory and accounts receivable normally turn over within a short period of time. Thus it is highly likely that some of the inventory and receivables owned by the debtor when the bankruptcy petition is filed will have been acquired by the debtor within the 90-day preference period. Because a security interest in such collateral is, by virtue of 11 U.S.C. § 547(e)(3), deemed to have been transferred to the secured party when the debtor acquired rights in the new item, that transfer (*i.e.*, creation of the security interest) could be an avoidable preference under 11 U.S.C. § 547(b) if the debtor were insolvent at the time. Consider the following example.

> Debtor signed document in which it granted Bank a security interest in all Debtor's existing and after-acquired inventory to secure all obligations now or hereafter owed to Bank. Bank filed a sufficient financing statement in the

---

[85] *E.g.*, In re Arnett, 731 F.2d 358 (6th Cir. 1984).

[86] *See* In re Dorholt, Inc., 224 F.3d 871 (8th Cir. 2000); Pine Top Ins. Co. v. Bank of Am. Nat'l Trust & Sav. Ass'n, 969 F.2d 321 (7th Cir. 1992); In re Marino, 193 B.R. 907 (9th Cir. BAP 1996), *aff'd without opinion*, 117 F.3d 1425 (9th Cir. 1997); In re Stephens, 242 B.R. 508 (D. Kan. 1999).

[87] The 2005 amendment to 11 U.S.C. § 547(e)(2), *see supra* note 83, probably renders the PMSI defense in § 547(c)(3) almost totally unnecessary. The only time it would seem to be relevant is if perfection occurred more than 30 days after attachment but less than 20 days after delivery of the property to the debtor. That could only occur if there were a substantial interval between attachment and delivery.

appropriate office. During the 90 days prior to Debtor's bankruptcy, Debtor continued to sell and buy inventory. Those sales of inventory do not constitute preferential transfers to the Bank. In fact, Bank's security interest is likely being stripped off each item of inventory sold by virtue of the protection for buyers in ordinary course of business. U.C.C. § 9-320(a). However, also during the 90-day period, Debtor used the proceeds of the inventory sales to buy new pieces of inventory. Bank's security interest automatically attached to those new items because of the after-acquired property clause in the security agreement (and possibly also because they might be identifiable proceeds). Although Bank's priority position in the old and new inventory as against any other secured parties is based on the time it filed the financing statement, *see* U.C.C. § 9-322(a), for bankruptcy purposes the transfer of its security interest in the new inventory does not relate back in time. 11 U.S.C. § 547(e)(3). The security interest in each item of new inventory is deemed to have been transferred to Bank when Debtor acquired it, during the 90-day preference period. The transfer is therefore on account of an antecedent debt because it secures the loan that Bank made to Debtor earlier in time.

If security interests such as Bank's were avoidable as preferences, inventory lenders would frequently find themselves completely unsecured once their debtors sought bankruptcy protection. Inventory and receivables typically turn over faster than once every 90 days. Section 547(c)(5) therefore provides a limited defense to preference avoidance through use of what is known as the "improvement in position test." Avoidance is limited to the extent that the secured party became less undersecured during the 90 days prior to bankruptcy. Consider the following illustration of how this works.

Illustration 1

Lender has a perfected security interest in Debtor's inventory. On the 90th day before bankruptcy, the inventory was worth $150,000 and Debtor owed Lender $200,000. Thus Lender was undersecured by $50,000. During the 90 days before bankruptcy, Debtor sold $45,000 worth of inventory and purchased $35,000 worth of new inventory. Thus on the date of the bankruptcy petition, the debt was still $200,000 and the value of the inventory was $140,000. Lender is undersecured by $60,000. Thus, Lender is actually $10,000 worse off on the petition date than Lender was 90 days before:

	90 Days Before Bankruptcy	Bankruptcy Petition Date
Amount of Debt	$200,000	$200,000
Value of Inventory	$150,000	$140,000
Amount of Unsecured Debt	$50,000	$60,000

Despite that, under § 547(b), the potential preference is $35,000, because Lender's security interest attached to new inventory with that value during the 90-day preference period. However, because Lender's position did not improve, § 547(c)(5) provides Lender with a complete defense and no part of the transfer (of the security interest in the new inventory) is avoidable.

With a slight change in the facts, we can see § 547(c)(5) operate to provide only a partial defense:

Illustration 2

Same facts except that Debtor sold $35,000 of inventory and acquired $45,000 worth of inventory during the preference period. Thus, the total value of the collateral increased by $10,000 and Lender became less undersecured by that amount:

	90 Days Before Bankruptcy	Bankruptcy Petition Date
Amount of Debt	$200,000	$200,000
Value of Inventory	$150,000	$160,000
Amount of Unsecured Debt	$50,000	$40,000

The potential preference is $45,000 because Lender's security interest attached to new inventory with that value during the preference period. However, because Lender's position has improved only by $10,000, avoidance of the preferential transfer (of the security interest) is limited to $10,000.

The computation in § 547(c)(5), by focusing on the amount the creditor is undersecured, implicitly also takes into account any increases in the amount of the secured obligation. Consider this variation of the scenario:

Illustration 3

Lender loaned an additional $30,000 during the preference period. Debtor sold $35,000 of inventory and acquired $45,000 worth of inventory during the preference period. The potential preference is still $45,000 because the security interest attached to new inventory with that value during the preference period, but none of it is avoidable as Lender did not improve its position due to the new loan. In fact, it is $20,000 more undersecured on the petition date than it was 90 days before:

	90 Days Before Bankruptcy	Bankruptcy Petition Date
Amount of Debt	$200,000	$230,000
Value of Inventory	$150,000	$160,000
Amount of Unsecured Debt	$50,000	$70,000

There are two more, rather complicated and complicating, things to note about the § 547(c)(5) defense. First, the defense applies only to a transfer of an interest in the debtor's inventory and receivables. It does not apply to a prepetition payment of a portion of the secured obligation. Consider the following permutation:

Illustration 4

Debtor sold $35,000 worth of inventory and purchased $45,000 worth of inventory during the preference period. Debtor also made a $20,000 payment to Lender during the preference period. There are now two potential preferences: (i) attachment of the security interest to the $45,000 in inventory purchased during the preference period; and (ii) the $20,000 payment. Subsection (c)(5) applies only to former, not the latter. It limits avoidance of the transfer of the security interest to $30,000, the amount by which Lender's position has improved:

	90 Days Before Bankruptcy	Bankruptcy Petition Date
Amount of Debt	$200,000	$180,000
Value of Inventory	$150,000	$160,000
Amount of Unsecured Debt	$50,000	$20,000

It provides no defense to avoidance of the $20,000 payment. To protect that transfer, Lender will have to seek refuge in some other preference defense, perhaps the § 547(c)(2) defense for payments made in the ordinary course of business.[88]

Second, sometimes the change in the value of the collateral, which in turn affects whether or to what extent the secured party's position was improved, results from both appreciation of old collateral and the acquisition of new collateral. Because § 547(c)(5) does not purport to deal with the former but certainly covers the latter, indeed, preference law as a whole does not cover the former because mere appreciation does not involve a "transfer of the debtor's interest in property," *see* § 547(b), sorting through the details can be quite problematic. Similarly, sometimes an increase in the value of inventory is partly the result of an investment of labor or materials, such as when the debtor transforms unfinished goods into finished goods during the preference period. Figuring out how to apply § 547(c)(5) to such situations is extraordinarily difficult.

Problem 6-30

A. Finance Company made an unsecured demand loan to Discovered on the morning of April 1. Finance Company believed that Discovered was financially sound. Later that day Finance Company received a credit report indicating that Discovered was in financial difficulty and might be insolvent. Finance Company immediately talked to Discovered, who acknowledged the truth of the credit report. When Finance Company demanded immediate payment of the loan, Discovered offered instead to secure the loan with a security interest in Discovered's existing equipment, which was worth more than the amount of the loan. Finance Company agreed and Discovered signed a document in which it granted Finance Company a security interest in equipment on the evening of April 1. Finance Company perfected its security interest by filing a financing statement. If Discovered was insolvent on April 1 and filed a petition in bankruptcy on June 1, can the security interest in equipment be avoided as a preference? *See* 11 U.S.C. § 547(b), (c)(1), (e)(2).

---

[88] Note, by the way, how the pre-petition payment has the potential to doubly hurt Lender. But for the payment, the transfer of the security interest in $45,000 of new inventory would be avoidable only to the extent of $10,000 because Lender's position would have been improved only to that extent (as in the second version of this scenario). The payment, however, both further improves Lender's position and is potentially avoidable in itself.

B. On April 1, Bank loaned $10,000 to Doctor by crediting that amount to Doctor's checking account. The loan agreement signed on that day provided that the $10,000 would be used to buy certain described equipment and that Doctor granted a security interest in that equipment to Bank to secure the loan. Bank filed in the appropriate office an otherwise sufficient financing statement covering the equipment on April 1. On April 7, Doctor bought the equipment described in the loan agreement. On June 20, Doctor filed a petition in bankruptcy.

1. Under 11 U.S.C. § 547(e), when did a transfer of property to Bank occur?
2. If Doctor was insolvent on April 1 and at all times thereafter, can Bank's security interest be avoided? *See* 11 U.S.C. § 547(b), (c)(1), (c)(3)?
3. How, if at all, would the analysis change if Doctor had acquired the equipment on April 30?

C. On July 1, Deluxe Builders granted Security Bank an enforceable security interest in some construction equipment Deluxe already owned in return for a $50,000 loan. On the same day Security Bank mailed a properly executed financing statement covering the collateral to the appropriate filing office, accompanied by the applicable filing fee. On July 5, Judgment Creditor obtained a judicial lien on the construction equipment by having the sheriff seize it pursuant to a writ of execution. The filing office received the financing statement on July 6. Deluxe Builders filed a Chapter 7 bankruptcy petition on July 7. The value of the equipment is $75,000, the Judgment Creditor is owed $40,000, and Security Bank is owed $50,000. Among Security Bank, Judgment Creditor, and the bankruptcy trustee, what is the priority of their interests in the construction equipment? *See* 11 U.S.C. §§ 547, 551. *See also* U.C.C. § 9-317(a)(2).

3. Drafting Issues Relating to Preferences

Even in bankruptcy, secured creditors are entitled to charge the collateral for the postpetition interest on their claims as well as for any attorney's fees or other costs of collection to the extent the security agreement so provides. *See* 11 U.S.C. § 506(b). They cannot generally seek to collect these amounts from the debtor, but they can add them to the secured obligation and eventually collect them from the collateral. The one major qualification to this is that the security agreement must expressly permit this. That is rarely an issue with respect to collection costs; virtually all security agreements include them in the secured obligation. Occasionally, though, the attorney's fees provision in the security agreement is not sufficiently broad to cover a preference defense. For example, in *In re Connolly*,[89] the agreement provided:

> In any action or proceeding brought to enforce or interpret the terms of this agreement, the prevailing party shall be entitled to reasonable costs and expenses thereof, including attorneys' fees, as may be determined by the court.

The court denied attorney's fees in a successful preference defense because it concluded that such an action was not one to enforce or interpret the agreement. In contrast, in *Pitney Bowes, Inc. v. Manufacturers Bank*,[90] an indemnity clause broadly covered:

> any and all liabilities, obligations, . . . claims, actions, suits, costs, expenses, and disbursements (including, without limitation, reasonable legal fees and expenses) of any kind and nature whatsoever . . . in any way relating to or arising out of this Lease or any document contemplated hereby.

The court ruled that this covered a preference action to recover lease payments.

SECTION 3. A BRIEF REVIEW

Now try your hand at a problem that incorporates many issues covered in this Chapter.

---

[89] 238 B.R. 475 (9th Cir. BAP 1999). *See also* In re LCO Enters, Inc., 180 B.R. 567 (9th Cir. BAP 1995), *aff'd,* 105 F.3d 665 (9th Cir. 1997) (landlord not entitled to attorneys' fees in successful preference defense because action was not one to enforce or based on the lease).

[90] 1997 WL 289680 (D. Conn. 1997). *See also* In re Moran, 188 B.R. 492 (Bankr. E.D.N.Y. 1995) (provision of mortgage providing that mortgagee would be entitled to reasonable attorneys' fees for "any litigation to prosecute or defend the rights and lien created by this mortgage," was broad enough to permit recovery of legal fees incurred by mortgagee in defending trustee's action to avoid mortgage as preferential transfer).

Problem 6-31

On July 1, the IRS assessed Hardware Store, Inc. with a $50,000 income tax liability.

On September 1, National Bank filed a financing statement against "Hardware Store" in the Iowa Secretary of State's office. The financing statement identified the collateral as "inventory and equipment." On September 2, Hardware Store signed a document in which it granted National Bank a security interest in "all inventory and equipment now owned or hereafter acquired" to secure "all obligations that debtor now owes or hereafter owes to National Bank." On September 5, National Bank loaned Hardware Store $200,000. Hardware Store has one retail outlet in Ramsey County, Minnesota and another in Washington County, Iowa. It is incorporated in Iowa.

On October 1, Mortgage Lender took a mortgage on the Hardware Store's outlet in Ramsey County, Minnesota and recorded that mortgage in the Ramsey County real property records. The mortgage secured a loan of $100,000.

On November 1, Hammer Supply sold tools to Hardware Store for $100,000. The purchase agreement stated that Hammer Supply retained title to the tools until Hardware Store paid for them. That same day, prior to delivery of the tools to Hardware Store's outlet in Ramsey County, Hammer Supply filed a financing statement against Hardware Store in the Minnesota Secretary of State's office identifying the collateral as "tools."

On November 5, the IRS filed proper notices of the tax lien against Hardware Store in the proper places in both Iowa and Minnesota.

On November 10, Hardware sold $30,000 worth of the tools that Hammer Supply had delivered to the Ramsey store location to Best Construction Company on credit and required that Best Construction sign a promissory note promising to pay $30,000 plus interest to Hardware Store by January 30, of the next year. Hardware Store took possession of the promissory note.

On November 30, Hardware Store filed a Chapter 11 bankruptcy petition. You represent the trustee in bankruptcy and have been asked to do the following:

A. Evaluate the relative claims and priority of claims in the following assets, including whether the trustee has any ability to avoid any liens or security interests in the debtor's property as a hypothetical lien creditor:

1. The retail outlet in Ramsey County, Minnesota and the retail outlet in Washington County, Iowa;
2. The counters, cabinets, shelving, desks, computers, and cash registers located in both retail outlet locations;
3. The items held for sale at both retail outlet locations;
4. The tools sold to Best Construction; and
5. The promissory note that Best Construction issued to Hardware Store.

B. Evaluate whether the trustee has a viable claim to recover a preference against anyone based upon the above set of facts. If you need more facts, what do you need to know?

Test Your Knowledge
Exam Eight – Cumulative